Folksinger's Wordbook

Folksinger's Wordbook

Compiled and Edited by
Irwin and Fred Silber

© 1973
Oak Publications ● New York
Music Sales Limited ● London

Book design by Carol Freeman
Cover photograph by Jan Fleetwood

©1973 Oak Publications
A Division of Embassy Music Corporation
33 West 60th Street
New York 10023

Music Sales Limited
78 Newman Street
London, W1E 4JZ.

Music Sales Australia (Pty.) Limited
27 Clarendon Street
Artarmon, Sydney NSW, Australia

Library of Congress Catalogue Card Number 73-75905
International Standard Book Number 0-8256-0140-1 (soft)
0-8256-0146-0 (hard)

CONTENTS

ALL OVER THIS LAND

Songs of green places, big cities, mountain ranges, waterways and prairies. . . .

I BEEN DOING SOME HARD TRAVELIN'

Songs of roving, rambling and plain hard luck. . . .

BEEN IN THE PEN SO LONG

Songs of chain gangs, jails and prisoners. . . .

THE BLUES AIN'T NOTHIN'

BLOW THE MAN DOWN

*Songs of sailing ships and fishermen,
and sailors on the deep blue sea....*

*Come all ye rounders and jokey-boys if
you want to hear some songs of . . .*

RAILROADERS AND LUMBERJACKS

GIT ALONG, LITTLE DOGGIES

*Songs of cowboys, trail-herders, saddle
tramps, and tenderfoots just from town....*

THE FARMER IS THE MAN

*Songs of renters, hayseeds,
sharecroppers and workers on the land....*

*Songs of coal miners, textile weavers, long-line
skinners, track-liners, field hands and other*

HARD-WORKING PEOPLE

SOLIDARITY FOREVER

Songs of picket-lines, strikes and union struggles....

I KNOW MY LOVE

Songs of true love . . . and not-so-true.

ROLL IN MY SWEET BABY'S ARMS

THEY'LL LOVE YOU AND LEAVE YOU

Songs of those who loved not wisely but all too well. . . .

DON'T MARRY A MAN BEFORE YOU TRY HIM

Songs of marriage, courtship and the vicissitudes of matrimony....

DIED FOR LOVE

Songs of broken hearts, untimely deaths and lonesome graves....

HARD IS THE FORTUNE OF ALL WOMANKIND

Housewives, betrayed lovers and hard-working women....

I KNOW WHERE I'M GOING

Songs of women who know what they want....

HEROES AND HELL-RAISERS

DOWN, DERRY, DERRY DOWN

Traditional ballads from England, Scotland and the U.S. . . .

MURDER MOST CRUEL

Songs of cruel mothers, jealous lovers, quarreling brothers and other bloody ballads. . . .

JUG OF PUNCH

Songs of the joys and perils of drink. . . .

THERE AIN'T NO BUGS ON ME!

Fun and games and fancy nonsense....

IN THE EVENING BY THE MOONLIGHT

*Old Favorites ... of home, hearth
and living room piano*

PICTURES FROM LIFE'S OTHER SIDE

Tear-jerkers, tragedies and sentimental songs

WITH YOUR GUNS AND DRUMS

Songs of soldiers, war and peace....

YANKEE DOODLES

Songs from American history....

WE SHALL OVERCOME

Songs of struggle and liberation....

DING DONG DOLLAR, EVERYBODY HOLLER!

A handful of topical songs of yesterday and today....

ERIN GO BRAUGH!

Songs of croppy boys and bold Fenian men, of Easter rebels and the Shan Van Vogt....

ALL OVER THIS WORLD

FOLK DIALOGUES

*concerning marriage, murder, money
and most anything else*

GIVE ME THAT OLD TIME RELIGION

THE SEASON OF THE YEAR

Songs of Christmas, Chanuke and the New Year....

HA, HA, THIS A-WAY

Playparties, singing games and children's songs....

HUSH LITTLE BABY

Lullabies . . . work songs for mothers, fathers and baby-sitters

ANIMAL FAIR

Songs of birds, beasts, bugs, big and little fishes. . . .

ROUNDS

FOREWORD

A book—and most particularly, a book of song lyrics—is something of an anomaly.

Like chess, the reading of a book can be the most passive and the most active of pursuits simultaneously. To see someone reading a book, calmly sitting before a roaring fire (if we are to abuse an image it may as well be the traditional one) or huddled into some forsaken corner provides no clue—except our own experience—that we are observing a magical process whereby the individual has been transported into some ecstasy of the mind oblivious of more mundane surroundings.

Such a book—it may be a novel, a history, a story of travel or a work of philosophy or politics—is, in a certain sense, a completed process. One may—but need not—engage in some other activity as the result of the experience.

The present volume is something else again. It is not intended as a book one sits down to read of a long winter's night—or even a short summer's eve for that matter.

It is, quite simply, a tool, a resource book. Here are the lyrics to more than 1,000 songs—mostly folk and traditional songs. It is an encyclopedia of sorts, designed to provide a ready reference for a vast repertoire, most of which have become a part of the popular literature of the English-speaking world. While guitar chords are indicated so that simple accompaniments may be fashioned on the spot, there is no musical notation.

For the most part, guitar players learn their tunes from records and from other singers. It is felt, therefore, that a collection such as this one which presumes either the familiarity of the tunes—or, at least, their accessibility—will be most useful to those who want one handy storehouse of folk, traditional and topical song.

Of course, certain limitations imposed themselves mercilessly. That backbone of the private property system—copyright—made it impossible to include in this collection a truly representative sampling of the topical-political songs of the past decade, although a few such do appear here. The selection of one or another set of lyrics is of course an arbitrary matter. We have been guided by considerations of familiarity, typicality and personal taste.

It is assumed that the melodies to the songs included will be reasonably familiar to those using this book. However for those who may want further guides to the musical notation a brief bibliography of song collections containing a large percentage of the melodies to the lyrics in this book is appended. Guitar players are referred to the back of the book for guitar chord fingerings should any of the symbols used in this collection prove unfamiliar.

Certain biases inevitably shape any song collection, but we have tried to be true to the concept of completeness insofar as traditional songs are concerned. If the more recent songs reflect a left-liberal tendency, that political bent is certainly reflective of the general framework within which the song movement of this country has grown and matured.

The great interest in folk heritage which, in its own terms, was something of a counter-cultural upheaval of the 1940s, was rooted in a concern for the very real problems of survival and emotional fulfillment confronting the masses of people of the planet. There were many, then, who felt that the spoon-fed mass culture of the era was an artfully-contrived diversion, a popular placebo designed to create an oasis of the mind in the midst of an oppressive reality.

Folk song, and a new kind of pertinent expression created in the folk tradition, seemed to offer a meaningful alternative to the automated mass-produced music. In time, the commodity machine learned how to absorb such materials into its insatiable maw providing some with the illusion that a revolution in consciousness was under way from within the heart of an exploitative society. That this seeming shift in direction in mass culture took place simultaneously with an acceleration of U.S. military aggression and intervention throughout the world did not seem to occur to those who felt that real changes were being made because the Top 40 music charts now featured songs like Tom Dooley or "Blowing in the Wind" instead of "Tea for Two" or "Chatanooga Choo Choo."

No, a light industry of books, records, musical instruments and other paraphernalia reflecting a degree of alienation from contemporary reality and a yearning for some other seemingly more balanced era has not presaged any significant change in the material conditions of society. But it is hoped that a book of this kind, in addition to performing a pleasantly useful function of making readily available in concise, handy form a vast body of song, will also provide materials for those particular consciousness-changers who will be able to fashion and hone tools that may be used in the process of fundamental social change.

It is for them—the doers, the carers, the militants, the singers of conscience and motion—that we have compiled this collection.

—Irwin Silber

PUTTING ON THE STYLE

Comic glees and cameos....

Abdul, The Bulbul Amir

G7   C
The sons of the prophet are hardy and bold
F   C
And quite unaccustomed to fear,
G7   C
But the bravest of all was a man I am told
      G7 C
Named Abdul, the Bulbul Amir.

When they needed a man to encourage the van,
Or to harass a foe from the rear,
Storm fort or redoubt, they had only to shout
For Abdul, the Bulbul Amir.

This son of the desert in battle aroused,
Could split twenty men on his spear.
A terrible creature, sober or soused,
Was Abdul, the Bulbul Amir.

Now the heroes were plenty and well known to fame
Who fought in the ranks of the Czar;
But the bravest of these was a man by the name
Of Ivan Skavinsky Skivar.

He could imitate Irving, play poker and pool,
And strum on the Spanish guitar;
In fact, quite the cream of the Muscovite team
Was Ivan Skavinsky Skivar.

The ladies all loved him, his rivals were few;
He could drink them all under the bar.
As gallant or tank, there was no one to rank
With Ivan Skavinsky Skivar.

One day this bold Russian had shouldered his gun,
And donned his most truculent sneer;
Downtown he did go, where he trod on the toe
Of Abdul, the Bulbul Amir.

"Young man," said Bulbul, "has your life grown so dull
That you're anxious to end your career?
Vile infidel, know you have trod on the toe
Of Abdul, the Bulbul Amir."

"So take your last look at sunshine and brook,
And send your regrets to the Czar,
By which I imply, you are going to die,
Mr. Ivan Skavinsky Skivar."

Said Ivan, "My friend, your remarks in the end
Will avail you but little, I fear;
For you ne'er will survive to repeat them alive,
Mr. Abdul, the Bulbul Amir."

Then that bold Mameluke drew his trusty skibouk,
With a cry of "Allah Akbar."
And with murderous intent, he ferociously went
For Ivan Skavinsky Skivar.

They parried and thrust, they sidestepped and cussed,
Of blood they spilled a great part;
The philologist blokes, who seldom crack jokes,
Say that hash was first made on that spot.

They fought all that night, 'neath the pale yellow moon
The din, it was heard from afar,
And huge multitudes came, so great was the fame,
Of Abdul and Ivan Skivar.

As Abdul's long knife was extracting the life,
In fact he had shouted "Huzzah"
He felt himself struck by that wily Calmuck
Count Ivan Skavinsky Skivar.

The sultan drove by in his red-breasted fly,
Expecting the victor to cheer,
But he only drew nigh just to hear the last sigh
Of Abdul, the Bulbul Amir.

Czar Petrovich, too, in his spectacles blue,
Rode up in his new crested car;
He arrived just in time to exchange a last line
With Ivan Skavinsky Skivar.

There's a tomb rises up where the Blue Danube rolls,
And 'graved there in characters clear
Are, "Stranger, when passing, oh pray for the soul
Of Abdul, the Bulbul Amir."

A Muscovite maiden her lone vigil keeps
'Neath the light of the pale polar star,
And the name that she murmurs so oft as she weeps,
Is Ivan Skavinsky Skivar.

Mama Don't 'Low

A
Mama don't 'low no banjo playin' round here.
                 E7
I say that mama don't 'low no banjo playin' round here.
A   A7
Well, I don't care what mama don't 'low,
  D   Dm
Gonna play my banjo anyhow,
A   E7   A
Mama don't 'low no banjo playin' round here.

Mama don't 'low no guitar playin' round here, etc.

Mama don't 'low no bass playin' round here, etc.

Mama don't 'low no talkin' round here, etc.,
Gonna shoot my mouth off anyhow, etc.

Mama don't 'low no singin' round here, etc.,
Gonna sing my head off anyhow, etc.

Ain't Gonna Grieve My Lord No More

               F
Oh, the Deacon went down, (Oh, the Deacon went down)

To the cellar to pray (To the cellar to pray)
          C7
He found a jug (He found a jug)
             F
And he stayed all day (And he stayed all day).
F7   **B♭**
Oh the deacon went down to the cellar to pray
     F
He found a jug and he stayed all day,

Chorus:

     C7   **F**
I won't grieve my Lord no more (my Lord no more)
F7   **B♭**
I ain't gonna grieve my Lord no more
        F
Ain't a-gonna grieve my Lord no more
      C7   **F**
Ain't a-gonna grieve my Lord no more.

You can't get to Heaven
On roller skates,
'Cause you'll roll right by
Them pearly gates.

Oh, the devil is mad
And I am glad,
He lost a soul
He thought he had.

You can't get to Heaven
In a rocking chair,
'Cause the Lord don't want
No lazybones there.

You can't get to Heaven,
In an old Ford car,
'Cause the damned old car
Won't go that far.

You can't get to Heaven
On a pair of skis;
You'll shuss right through
Saint Peter's knees.

You can't get to Heaven
In a limousine,
'Cause the Lord don't sell
No gasoline.

If you get to Heaven
Before I do,
Just drill a hole
And pull me through.

If I get to Heaven
Before you do,
I'll plug that hole
With shavings and glue.

You can't get to Heaven
With powder and paint,
It makes you look
Like what you ain't.

You can't chew tobaccy
On that golden shore
The Lord don't have
No cuspidor.

That's all there is
There ain't no more,
Saint Peter said
As he closed the door.

There's one thing more
I forgot to tell,
If you don't go to Heaven,
You'll go to Hell.

I'll put my grief
Up on the shelf,
If you want some more
Make 'em up yourself.

Ain't It A Shame

E
Ain't it a shame to go fishing on a Sunday?
A   **E**
Ain't it a shame?

Ain't it a shame to go fishing on a Sunday?
       B7
Ain't it a shame?
E
Ain't it a shame to go fishing on a Sunday—
A
When you got Monday, Tuesday, Wednesday,
E
Oh, Thursday, Friday, Saturday—
A   **E**
Ain't it a shame?

Ain't it a shame to kiss the girls on Sunday,
    ain't it a shame?
Ain't it a shame to kiss the girls on Sunday,
    ain't it a shame?
Ain't it a shame to kiss the girls on Sunday,
When you got Monday, Tuesday, Wednesday,—
    Thursday, Friday, Saturday;
Ain't it a shame!

Ain't it a shame to take a drink on Sunday, etc.

The Devil and The Farmer's Wife

Child Ballad 278

E
There was an old man lived over the hill,
            A   B7
If he ain't moved away he's living there still,
        E
Singing fah-de-ing, ding

Dah-de-ing-ding

Di-di-um da-de ing ding

Didium da de ing ding
B7   E
Di-di-um day.

Well, the devil came up to him one day,
Said one of your family I'm gonna take away.
Singing etc.

Oh please don't take my eldest son,
There's work on the farm that's gotta be done.
Singing etc.

It's all I want, that wife of yours,
Well you can take her with all of my heart.
Singing etc.

Well, he picks the wife up upon his back,
And off to hell he goes clickitty-clack.
Singing etc.

He carries her on about a mile down the road,
He said old woman you're a devil of a load.
Singing etc.

He carries her down to the gates of hell,
He says poke up the fire we'll scorch her well.
Singing etc.

There were two little devils with ball and with chain,
She ups with her foot and she kicks out their brains.
Singing etc.

And nine little devils went climbing up the wall,
Saying take her back daddy, she'll murder us all.
Singing etc.

Well, I got up next morning, I spied through a crack
I seen the old devil come a dragging her back.
Singing etc.

He said here is your wife, both sound and well,
If I'd a kept her there longer she'd a torn up hell.
Singing etc.

He said I've been a devil most all of my life,
But I'd never been in hell till I met with your wife.
Singing etc.

Now, this only goes to show, what a woman can do,
She can whup out the devil and her husband too.
Singing etc.

This shows that the women are better than men,
They can go down to hell and come back again.
Singing etc.

Crawdad

E
You get a line and I'll get a pole, honey,
                                    B7
You get a line and I'll get a pole, babe.
E   E7
You get a line and I'll get a pole,
    A7
And we'll go down to the Crawdad hole,
E   B7   E
Honey, sugar baby, mine,

Get up old man, you slept too late, honey, (twice)
Get up old man, you slept too late,
Last piece of crawdad's on your plate,
Honey, sugar baby mine.

Get up old woman, you slept too late, honey, (twice)
Get up old woman, you slept too late,
Crawdad man done passed your gate,
Honey, sugar baby mine.

Along come a man with a sack on his back, honey, (twice)
Along come a man with a sack on his back,
Packin' all the crawdads he can pack,
Honey, sugar baby mine.

What you gonna do when the lake goes dry, (twice)
What you gonna do when the lake goes dry,
Sit on the bank and watch the crawdads die,
Honey, sugar baby mine.

What you gonna do when the crawdads die, honey?
    (twice)
What you gonna do when the crawdads die,
Sit on the bank until I cry,
Honey, sugar baby mine.

I heard the duck say to the drake, honey, (twice)
I heard the duck say to the drake,
There ain't no crawdads in this lake,
Honey, sugar baby mine.

Putting On The Style

D   A7
Young man in a carriage, driving like he's mad,
                                   D
With a pair of horses he borrowed from his dad.
                                     A7
He cracks his whip so lively just to see his lady smile,
                             D
But she knows he's only putting on the style.

Chorus:

D   A7
Putting on the agony, putting on the style,
                                   D
That's what all the young folks are doing all the while.
                             A7
And as I look around me, I'm very apt to smile,
                           D
To see so many people putting on the style.

Sweet sixteen goes to Church just to see the boys;
Laughs and giggles at every little noise.
She turns this way a little, then turns that way a while,
But everybody knows she's only putting on the style.

Young man in a restaurant smokes a dirty pipe;
Looking like a pumpkin that's only half-way ripe.
Smoking, drinking, chewing—and thinking all the while
That there is nothing equal to putting on the style.

Young man just from college makes a big display
With a great big jawbreak which he can hardly say;
It can't be found in Webster's and won't be for a while,
But everybody knows he's only putting on the style.

Preacher in the pulpit shouting with all his might,
Glory Hallelujah — puts the people in a fright.
You might think that Satan's coming up and down the
     aisle,
But it's only the preacher putting on the style.

See the young executive in his charcoal gray,
Talking with some union men who've come to have
     their say.
Sitting at his office desk and wearing a toothpaste smile,
That's the executive putting on the style.

Congressman from Washington looking mighty slick,
Wants to get elected and go back there right quick.
Beats his breast and hollers and waves the flag a while,
But we know he's only putting on the style.

Adam In The Garden Pinning Leaves

Chorus:

E
Oh, Eve, where's Adam?
B7   E
Oh, Eve, where's Adam?
               A
Oh, Eve, where's Adam?
B7   E
Adam in the garden pinning leaves.

Verses:

Well, I know my God is a man of war,
B7   E
Adam in the garden pinning leaves,

He fought the battle at the Jericho wall,
B7   E
Adam in the garden pinning leaves.

Well, the first time God called, Adam refused to answer,
Adam in the garden pinning leaves,
The first time God called, Adam refused to answer,
Adam in the garden pinning leaves.

The next time God called, God hollered louder,
Adam in the garden pinning leaves,
The next time God called, God hollered louder,
Adam in the garden pinning leaves.

The Dodger Song

      D
Oh, the candidate's a dodger,

Yes a well-known dodger,

Oh, the candidate's a dodger,
      A7   D
Yes, and I'm a dodger, too.

He'll meet you and treat you and ask you for your vote,
    G   A7   D
But look out, boys, he's a dodging for your note!

Chorus:

    D
Oh, we're all dodging,

A-dodging, dodging, dodging,

Yes, we're all dodging
      A7   D
On our way through the world.

Oh, the lawyer he's a dodger,
Yes, a well-known dodger,
Oh, the lawyer he's a dodger,
Yes, and I'm a dodger, too.
He'll plead your case and claim you for a friend,
But look out, boys, he's easy for to bend!

Oh, the merchant he's a dodger,
Yes, a well-known dodger,
Oh, the merchant he's a dodger,
Yes, and I'm a dodger, too.
He'll sell you the goods at double the price,
But when you go to pay him, you'll have to pay him twice!

Oh, the farmer he's a dodger,
Yes, a well-known dodger,
Oh, the farmer he's a dodger,
Yes, and I'm a dodger, too.
He'll plow his cotton, he'll plow his corn,
But he won't make a living just as sure as you're born!

Oh, the sheriff he's a dodger,
Yes, a well-known dodger,
Oh, the sheriff he's a dodger,
Yes, and I'm a dodger, too.
He'll act like a friend and a mighty fine man,
But, look out, boys, he'll put you in the can.

Oh, the lover he's a dodger,
Yes, a well-known dodger,
Oh, the lover he's a dodger,
Yes, and I'm a dodger, too.
He'll hug you and kiss you and call you his bride,
But, look out, girls, he's telling you a lie!

The Rich Man And The Poor Man

```
      G      Am7      D    G
There was a rich man and he lived in Jerusalem,
           C  D7  G
Glory Hallelujah, Hi ro je-rum.
      G      Am7      Bm        G7
He wore a silk hat and his coat was very sprucium,
Em   G        C  D7  G
Glory Hallelujah, Hi ro je-rum.
```

Chorus:

```
   G
Hi ro je-rum, (Hey),
   C
Hi ro je-rum, (Hey),
G                      D7
Skinna malinky doodlyum, skinna malinky doodlyum,
G          D7    G
Glory Hallelujah, Hi ro je-rum.
```

And at his gate there sat a human wreckium, Glory, etc.
He wore a bowler hat
   and the rim was round his neckium, Glory, etc.

The poor man asked for a piece of bread and cheesium,
The rich man replied, "I'll call for a policium,"

The poor man died and his soul went to Heavium,
He danced with the angels 'til a quarter past elevium,

The rich man died, but he didn't fare so wellium,
He couldn't get to Heaven, so he had to go to Hellium,

The devil said, "This is no hotelium,"
"It's just a very common, very ordinary Hellium."

The moral of this story is: Riches are no jokium,
We'll all go to heaven, 'cause we're all stony-brokium.

Ta-Ra-Ra- Boom-Der-E
Henry J. Sayers

```
   C    Cdim7  C
A sweet Tuxedo girl you see,
       Cdim7 C
   queen of swell society
           G7
Fond of fun as fond can be,
       C
   when it's on the strict Q.T.
       Cdim7     C
I'm not too young, I'm not too old,
       Cdim7 C
   not too timid, not too bold,
              G
Just the kind you'd like to hold,
   G7          C
   just the kind for sport, I'm told.
```

Chorus:

```
C Cdim7 C          Cdim7 C
Ta-ra-ra Boom-der-é, Ta-ra-ra Boom-der-é,
      G7          C
Ta-ra-ra Boom-der-é, Ta-ra-ra Boom-der-é,
   Cdim7 C        C Cdim7 C
Ta-ra-ra Boom-der-é, Ta-ra-ra Boom-der-é,
      G7          C
Ta-ra-ra Boom-der-é, Ta-ra-ra Boom-der-é.
```

I'm a blushing bud of innocence,
   Papa says at big expense,
Old maids say I have no sense,
   boys declare I'm just immense;
Before my song I do conclude,
   I want it strictly understood,
Tho' fond of fun, I'm never rude,
   tho' not too bad, I'm not too good.

The Fireship

<pre>
  F   C7
As I strolled out one evening upon a night's career,
  F   C7
I spied a lofty fireship and after her I steered;
                                            F
I hoisted up my sig-a-nals which she did quickly view,
  C7   F   D7   G7
And when I had my bunting up, she immediately hove
  C7
   to . . . o . . . o . . .
</pre>

Chorus:

<pre>
        F
She had a dark and a roving eye,
     G7   C7
And her hair hung down in ring-a-lets,
     F   Bb
She was a nice girl, a decent girl,
     F   C7   F
But one of the rakish kind.
</pre>

Oh, sir, you must excuse me for being out so late,
For if my parents knew of it, then sad would be my fate,
My father he's a minister, a true and honest man,
My mother is a Methodist, and I do the best I can.

I took her to a tavern and I treated her to wine,
Little did I think that she was of the rakish kind;
I handled her, I dandled her, and found to my surprise,
She was nothing but a fireship rigged up in a disguise.

I Was Born About Ten Thousand Years Ago

<pre>
     F   C7
I was born about ten thousand years ago,
                                      F
And there's nothing in this world that I don't know,
     Bb
I saw Peter, Paul, and Moses
        F
   playing ring around the roses,
     C7   F
And I'll lick the guy who says it isn't so.
</pre>

I saw Satan when he looked the garden o'er.
I saw Eve and Adam driven from the door,
When the apple they were eating
   I was 'round the corner peeking,
I can prove that I'm the guy that ate the core.

I saw Jonah when he shoved off in the whale,
And I thought he'd never live to tell the tale,
But old Jonah'd eaten garlic,
   so he gave the whale a colic
And he coughed him up and let him out of jail.

I saw Absalom a-hanging by the hair;
When they built the wall of China I was there.
I saved King Solomon's life and he offered me a wife.
I said, "Now you're talking business, have a chair."

I saw Israel in the battle of the Nile;
The arrows were flying thick and fast and wild.
I saw David with his sling pop Goliath on the wing;
I was doing forty seconds to the mile.

I saw Samson when he laid the village cold,
I saw Daniel tame the lions in their hold;
I helped build the tower of Babel
   up as high as they were able,
And there's lots of other things I haven't told.

The queen of Sheba fell in love with me.
We were married in Milwaukee secretly.
In Washington I shook her,
   just to join with General Hooker
Chasing skeeters out of sunny Tennessee.

Ilkley Moor Baht 'At

<pre>
C   G7   C
Where hast thou been since I saw thee
     F   Dm   G
On Ilkley Moor baht 'at.
G7   G   C
Where hast thou been since I saw thee?
D   G   D7 G G7
Where hast thou been since I saw thee?
     C   G C
On Ilkley Moor baht 'at,
G C   G C
On Ilkley Moor baht 'at,
     Dm C F   G C
On Ilkley Moor baht 'at.
</pre>

I've been a-courting Mary Jane,
On Ilkley Moor baht 'at.
I've been a-courting Mary Jane
I've been a-courting Mary Jane
On Ilkley Moor baht 'at,
On Ilkley Moor baht 'at,
On Ilkley Moor baht 'at.

Thou'll 't surely catch thy death of cold; etc.
Then we shall have to bury thee;
Then worms will come and et thee oop;
Then dooks will come and et oop worms;
Then we will come and et oop dooks;
Then we will have our loved ones back.

Note:
Ilkley Moor baht 'at – Ilkley Moor without a hat
et – eaten
oop – up
dooks – ducks

Eddystone Light

C
Me father was the keeper of the Eddystone light
       F   G7   C
And he slept with a mermaid one fine night.

From this union there came three,
     F   G7   C
A porpoise and a porgy and the other was me!

Chorus:

G7   D7   G7
Yo ho ho, the wind blows free,
               C
Oh for a life on the rolling sea!

One night, as I was a-trimming of the glim,
Singing a verse from the evening hymn,
A voice on the starboard shouted "Ahoy!"
And there was my mother, a-sitting on a buoy.

"Oh, where are the rest of my children three?"
My mother then she asked of me.
"One was exhibited as a talking fish,
The other was served from a chafing dish."

Then the phosphorous flashed in her seaweed hair:
I looked again, and my mother wasn't there.
But her voice came echoing back from the night,
"To Hell with the keeper of the Eddystone Light!"

It's The Syme The Whole World Over

      F   Bb
She was just a parson's daughter,
           C7   F
Pure, unstyned was her fyme,
  Bb
Till a country squire came courtin',
      C7   F
And the poor girl lorst 'er nyme.

It's the syme the whole world over,
It's the poor what gets the blyme,
While the rich 'as all the plysures,
Now ain't that a blinkin' shyme.

So she went aw'y to Lunnon,
Just to 'ide 'er guilty shyme.
There she met another squire,
Once ag'yn she lorst 'er nyme.

Look at 'im with all 'is 'orses,
Drinking champygne in 'is club,
While the wictim of 'is passions
Drinks 'er Guiness in a pub.

Now 'e's in 'is ridin' britches,
'Untin' foxes in the chyse,
While the wictim of 'is folly
Mykes 'er livin' by 'er wice.

When she tried to go from Lunnon,
Once ag'yn to 'ide 'er shyme,
She was 'syved' by an army chaplain,
Once ag'yn she lorst 'er nyme.

'Ear 'im as 'e jaws the Tommies,
Warnin' o' the flymes o' 'ell.
With 'er 'ole 'eart she 'ad trusted,
But ag'yn she lorst 'er nyme.

So she settled down in Lunnon,
Sinkin' deeper in 'er shyme,
Till she met a lybor leader,
And ag'yn she lorst 'er nyme.

Now 'e's in the 'ouse of Commons
Mykin' laws to put down crime,
W'ile the wictim o' 'is plysure
Walks the street each night in shyme.

Then there cyme a bloated bishop.
Marriage was the tyle 'e told.
There was no one else to tyke 'er,
So she sold 'er soul for gold.

See 'er in 'er 'orse and carriage,
Drivin' d'yly through the park.
Though she myde a wealthy marriage,
Still she 'ides a breakin' 'eart.

In a cottage down in Sussex
Lives 'er payrents old and lyme,
And they drink the wine she sends 'em,
But they never speaks 'er nyme.

In their poor and 'umble dwelling,
There 'er grievin' payrents live.
Drinkin' champygne as she sends 'em
But they never can forgive.

My Sweetheart's The Mule In The Mines

    C   G7   C
My sweetheart's the mule in the mines.
  F   C
I drive her without any lines.
        F   C
On the bumper I sit, and I chew and I spit.
  G7   C
All over my sweetheart's behind.

Willy The Weeper

Dm   A7 Dm
Did you ever hear the story 'bout Willy the Weeper?
Gm
He had a job as a chimney sweeper.
Dm
He had the habit and he had it bad.
                             A7 Dm
Listen while I tell you 'bout the dream he had.

Chorus:

Dm
Tee dee dee dee dee,

Too too doo doo doo,
        A7
Ya da da dee da, dee da,
   Dm
Dee dee doo.

He went to a hop joint the other night,
Where he knew the lights were always shining bright,
And, calling for someone to bring some hop,
He started in smoking like he wasn't gonna stop.

After he'd smoked about a dozen pills,
He said, "This ought to cure all my aches and ills."
And turning on his side he fell asleep,
And dreamt he was a sailor on the ocean deep.

He played draw poker as they left the land,
And won a million dollars on the very first hand.
He played and he played till the crew went broke.
Then he turned around and took another smoke.

The Queen of Sheba was the first he met.
She called him lovey-dovey, and honey pet.
She gave him a great big automobile,
With a diamond headlight, and golden wheel.

He landed with a splash in the river Nile,
A-ridin' a sea-goin' crocodile.
He winked at Cleopatra; she said, "Ain't he a sight,
How about a date for next Saturday night?"

He went to Monte Carlo where he played roulette,
And couldn't lose a penny but won every bet—
Played and he played till the bank went broke.
Then he turned around and took another smoke.

He went to Turkey by special request;
Stayed seven years as the Sultan's guest.
But when he got in with that harem crew,
What was a poor fellow like Willy to do?

He had a million cattle, and he had a million sheep;
He had a million vessels on the ocean deep;
He had a million dollars all in nickels and dimes;
Well—he knew it cause he'd counted it a thousand times.

He landed in New York one evening late.
He asked his sugar for an after date;
He started to kiss her, and she started to pout
When—Bingity! Bang! and the dope gave out.

Now this is the story of Willie the Weeper;
Willie the Weeper was a chimney sweeper.
Someday a pill too many he'll take,
And dreaming he's dead, he'll forget to awake.

The Desperado

        C
There was a desperado from the wild and woolly West,
                              G7
He came into Chicago just to give the West a rest.
        C
He wore a big sombrero and a gun beneath his vest,
      F   C   G7 C
And ev'rywhere he went he gave his war whoop.

Chorus:

        C
Oh, a big brave man was this desperado,
                            G7
From Cripple Creek way down in Colorado,
        C
And he walked around like a big tornado,
      F   C   G7 C
And ev'rywhere he went he gave his war whoop.

He went to Coney Island just to take in all the sights,
He saw the hootchie-kootchie and the girls dressed
    up in tights,
He got so darned excited that he shot out all the lights,
And everywhere he went he gave his war whoop.

A great big fat policeman was a-walking down his beat,
He saw the desperado come a-walking down the street.
He grabbed him by the whiskers, and he grabbed him
    by the seat,
And threw him where he couldn't give his war whoop.

Take A Whiff On Me

Chorus:

G
Take a whiff, take a whiff, take a whiff on me,
C
Ev'rybody take a whiff on me,
D7   G
Hey, hey, baby take a whiff on me.

Take a whiff, take a whiff, take a whiff on me,
C
Ev'rybody take a whiff on me,
D7   G
Hey, hey, baby take a whiff on me.

Verses:

G
I got a woman six feet tall,
C
Sleepin' in the kitchen with her feet in the hall,
D7   G
Hey, hey, baby take a whiff on me.

Two old maids a-fishin' in the creek,
They ain't caught a man since a-way last week,
Hey, hey, baby take a whiff on me.

Want to get a woman let me tell you a word,
Grease your hair down as slick as lard,
Hey, hey, baby take a whiff on me.

I'm a-walkin' down the road with my hat in my hand,
Lookin' for a woman who needs a worried man,
Hey, hey, baby take a whiff on me.

Walkin' down the road, the road is mighty muddy,
Slippin' and slidin' and I can't stand steady,
Hey, hey, baby take a whiff on me.

I know my woman ain't a-treatin' me right,
She don't get home till the day gets light
Hey, hey, baby take a whiff on me.

Meet a lot of women out a-ramblin' around,
But the Boston women are the best that I found,
Hey, hey, baby take a whiff on me.

Sing your song all night long,
Sing to my woman from midnight on,
Hey, hey, baby take a whiff on me.

The Man That Waters The Workers' Beer

Paddy Ryan / Tune: *Ramblin' Wreck from Georgia Tech*

Chorus:

D
I'm the man, the very fat man,
   A7   D
That waters the workers' beer.
                        D #dim7
Yes, I'm the man, the very fat man,
   A   E7   A
That waters the workers' beer,
   G
And what do I care if it makes them ill,
   D   A7   D
If it makes them terribly queer,
A7   D
I've got a car and a yacht and an aeroplane,
       G   A   D
And I waters the workers' beer.

Now when I makes the workers' beer,
I puts in strychinine,
Some methylated spirits
And a drop of paraffin;
But since a brew so terribly strong
Might make them terribly queer,
I reaches my hand for the water tap,
And I waters the workers' beer.

Now ladies fair beyond compare,
And be ye maid or wife,
O, sometimes lend a thought for one
Who leads a sorry life;
The water rates are shockingly high,
And malt is shockingly dear,
And there isn't the profit there used to be
In wat'ring the workers' beer.

Now a drop of good beer is good for a man
Who's thirsty and tired and hot,
And I sometimes has a drop for myself
From a very special lot;
But a fat and healthy working class
Is the thing that I most fear,
So I reaches my hand for the water tap,
And I waters the workers' beer.

The Frozen Logger
James Stephens

    D   A7
As I sat down one evening
           D
within a small cafe,
G   A7
A forty-year-old waitress to me
         D
these words did say:

"I see that you are a logger and not
    just a common bum.
'Cause nobody but a logger stirs his
    coffee with his thumb.

My lover, he was a logger, there's
    none like him today,
Well, if you'd pour whiskey on him,
    well he'd eat a bale of hay.

Well, he never used a razor to
    shave his horny hide,
He'd just drive them in with a hammer,
    then he bit them off inside.

My lover he came to see me, 'twas
    on a freezing day,
He held me in a fond embrace that
    broke three vertebrae,

Well, he kissed me when we parted
    so hard that he broke my jaw,
And I could not speak to tell him
    he forgot his mackinaw.

I saw my lover leaving, a-sauntering
    through the snow,
While going grimly homeward at
    forty-eight below.

Well, the weather it tried to freeze him,
    it tried its level best,
At a hundred degrees below zero,
    why he buttoned up his vest.

It froze clean through to China;
    and it froze to the stars above,
And at a thousand degrees below zero,
    it froze my logger love.

And so I lost my lover, and to this
    cafe I come,
And here I wait till someone stirs
    his coffee with his thumb."

Goodbye 'Liza Jane

C
There's a house in Baltimore,

Sixteen stories high,

And every story in that house
    G7   C
Was full of chicken pie.

Chorus:

C
Oh Liza, poor girl,

Oh Liza Jane.

Oh Liza, poor girl,
G7   C
She died on the train.

I went up on the mountain
To give my horn a blow,
And every girl in the countryside
Said, "Yonder comes my beau."

When I was a little boy,
I liked to go in swimmin',
Now I am a bigger boy,
I like to go with women.

I wish I had a candy box
To put my sweetheart in,
I'd take her out and kiss her twice,
And put her back again.

One day I set a-courting
A girl as dear as life,
When a woman she said to me,
"Mr. Jones, how is your wife?"

The Lavender Cowboy

        E   A
He was only a lavender cowboy,
      E   B7
The hairs on his chest were two,
    E   A
But he wished to follow the heroes
    B7   E
And fight like the he-men do.

But he was inwardly troubled
By a dream that gave him no rest,
That he'd go with heroes in action
With only two hairs on his chest.

First he tried many a hair tonic,
'Twar rubbed in on him each night,
But still when he looked in the mirror
Those two hairs were ever in sight.

But with a spirit undaunted
He wandered out to fight,
Just like an old-time knight errant
To win combat for the right.

He battled for Red Nellie's honor
And cleaned out a holdup's nest,
He died with his six guns a-smoking
With only two hairs on his chest.

The Blue-Tail Fly

        A
When I was young I used to wait
  E   B7
On master and serve him his plate,
    A
And pass the bottle when he got dry,
  B7   E
And brush away the blue-tail fly.

Chorus:

                    B7
Jimmy crack corn and I don't care.
                 E
Jimmy crack corn and I don't care.
                 A
Jimmy crack corn and I don't care,
  B7   E
My master's gone away.

And when he'd ride in the afternoon
I'd follow with a hickory broom,
The pony being rather shy
When bitten by the blue-tail fly.

One day he rode around the farm
The flys so numerous they did swarm,
One chanced to bite him on the thigh
The devil take a blue-tail fly.

The pony jump, he toss, he pitch
He threw my master in the ditch,
He died and the jury wondered why
The verdict was the blue-tail fly.

He lies beneath a 'simmon tree
His epitaph is there to see,
Beneath this stone I'm forced to lie
The victim of a blue-tail fly.

Cosher Bailey's Engine

D
Cosher Bailey had an engine,
  Em   A7
It was always wanting and mending
  Bm
And according to the power,
   A7
She could do four miles an hour.

Chorus:

  D G
Did you ever see,
  A7
Did you ever see,
  D G
Did you ever see
  D A7 D
Such a funny thing before?

On the night run up from Gower,
She did twenty mile an hour,
As she whistled through the station
Man, she frightened half the nation.

Cosher bought her second-hand,
And he painted her so grand,
When the driver went to oil her
Man, she nearly burst her boiler.

Cosher Bailey's sister Lena,
She was living up in Blaina,
She could knit and darn our stockings
But her cooking, it was shocking.

Cosher Bailey's brother Rupert,
He played stand-off-half for Newport,
When they played against Llanelly,
Someone kicked him in the belly.

Cosher Bailey had a daughter,
Who did things she didn't aughta
She was quite beyond the pale,
But over that we'll draw a veil.

Cosher Bailey went to Exford,
For to pass matriculation,
But he saw a pretty barmaid
And he never left the station.

Oh, the sight it was heart-rending,
Cosher drove his little engine,
And he got stuck in the tunnel,
And went up the blooming funnel.

Yes, Cosher Bailey he did die,
And they put him in a coffin,
But, alas, they heard a knocking,
Cosher Bailey, only joking.

Well the devil wouldn't have him,
But he gave him sticks and matches,
For to set up on his own,
On the top of Barford Hatches.

Oh, How He Lied

  C
There was an old villain

Who smoked a cigar,
B♭7
Smoked a cigar,
C
Smoked a cigar,

There was an old villain

Who smoked a cigar,
G7 C
Smoked a cigar.

There was a young maiden
Who played a guitar,
Played a guitar,
Played a guitar,
There was a young maiden
Who played a guitar,
Played a guitar.

He told her he loved her
But, Oh, how he lied, etc.

She told him she loved him
But she didn't lie, etc.

They were to be married
But she up and died, etc.

He went to her funeral
But she didn't lie, etc.

He sat on her tombstone
And boo-hoo he cried, etc.

She went up to heaven
And flip flop, she flied, etc.

He went down to Hades
And sizzle, he fried, etc.

Let this be a lesson
To lovers that lie, etc.

My God, How The Money Rolls In
Tune: *My Bonnie*

  G   C   G
My mother makes beer in the bathtub,
       A7   D7
My father makes synthetic gin.
  G   C   G
My sister makes fudge for a quarter,
  C   D7   G
My God, how the money rolls in.

Chorus:

G   C
Rolls in, rolls in,
 D7   G
My God, how the money rolls in.

My mother she drowned in the bathtub,
My father he died of his gin,
My sister she choked on her chocolate—
My God, what a jam I am in.

I tried making beer in the bathtub,
I tried making synthetic gin,
I tried making fudge for a living,
Now look at the shape I am in.

My uncle's a poor veterinary,
He'll save any mutt for a fin,
He'll save you a blonde for five dollars,
My God, how the money rolls in.

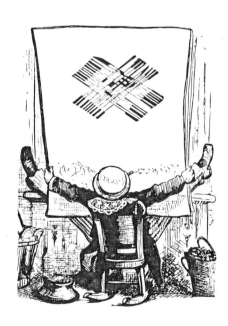

BILE THEM CABBAGE DOWN

Hoedowns, jigs and reels....

The Arkansas Traveler

```
        D        E        D
Oh, once upon a time in Arkansas,
     G       D      G       A7
An old man sat in his little cabin door,
     D           G          A7    D
And fiddled at a tune that he liked to hear,
          G        A7      D
A jolly old tune that he played by ear.
             Em       D      A7
It was raining hard, but the fiddler didn't care,
     D      A    D     A
He sawed away at the popular air,
            D    Em      D  A7
Though his rooftop leaked like a waterfall,
     D       G      D    A7 D
That didn't seem to bother the old man at all.
```

A traveler was riding by that day,
And stopped to hear him a-fiddling away;
The cabin was afloat and his feet were wet,
But the old man still didn't seem to fret.
So the stranger said, "Now, the way it seems to me,
You'd better mend your roof," said he,
But the old man said as he played away:
"I couldn't mend it now, it's a rainy day."

The traveler replied, "That's all quite true,
But this, I think, is the thing for you to do;
Get busy on a day that is fair and bright,
Then patch the old roof till it's good and tight."
But the old man kept on a-playing at his reel,
And tapped the ground with his leathery heel:
"Get along," said he, "for you give me a pain;
My cabin never leaks when it doesn't rain!"

Uncle Joe

```
        C
Did you ever go to meetin', Uncle Joe, Uncle Joe?
                                   G7
Did you ever go to meetin', Uncle Joe?
        C
Did you ever go to meetin', Uncle Joe, Uncle Joe?
     F               G7        C
Don't mind the weather when the wind don't blow.
```

Chorus:

```
C
Hop up, my ladies, three in a row,
            G7
Hop up my ladies, three in a row,
C
Hop up, my ladies, three in a row,
     F               G7        C
Don't mind the weather when the wind don't blow.
```

Will your horse carry double, Uncle Joe, etc.

Is your horse a single-footer, Uncle Joe, etc.

Would you rather ride a pacer, Uncle Joe, etc.

Sally Goodin

```
E
Had a piece of pie an' I had a piece of puddin',
                                      C#m
An' I gave it all away just to see my Sally Goodin.
E
Had a piece of pie an' I had a piece of puddin',
                                    C   m
An' I gave it all away just to see my Sally Goodin.
     E                              C#m
Well, I looked down the road an' I see my Sally comin',
     E                   B7       E
An' I thought to my soul that I'd kill myself a-runnin'.
     E                              C#m
Well, I looked down the road an' I see my Sally comin',
     E                   B7       E
An' I thought to my soul that I'd kill myself a-runnin'.
```

Love a 'tater pie an' I love an apple puddin',
An' I love a little gal that they call Sally Goodin.
Love a 'tater pie an' I love an apple puddin',
An' I love a little gal that they call Sally Goodin.
An' I dropped the 'tater pie an' I left the apple puddin',
But I went across the mountain to see my Sally Goodin.
An' I dropped the 'tater pie an' I left the apple puddin',
But I went across the mountain to see my Sally Goodin.

Sally is my dooxy an' Sally is my daisy,
When Sally says she hates me I think I'm goin' crazy.
Sally is my dooxy an' Sally is my daisy,
When Sally says she hates me I think I'm goin' crazy.
Little dog'll bark an' the big dog'll bite you,
Little gal'll court you an' big gal'll fight you.
Little dog'll bark an' the big dog'll bite you,
Little gal'll court you an' big gal'll fight you.

Rainin' an' a-pourin' an' the creek's runnin' muddy,
An' I'm so drunk, Lord, I can't stand studdy,
Rainin' an' a-pourin' an' the creek's runnin' muddy,
An' I'm so drunk, Lord, I can't stand studdy,
I'm goin' up the mountain an' marry little Sally,
Raise corn on the hillside an' the devil in the valley.
I'm goin' up the mountain an' marry little Sally,
Raise corn on the hillside an' the devil in the valley.

Camptown Races

Stephen Foster

C
Oh, the Camptown ladies sing this song,
G7
Doo-da, doo-da,
    C
The Camptown race track's two miles long,
G7   C
Oh, de doo-da day.

Chorus:

C
Goin' to run all night,
F   C
Goin' to run all day,

I bet my money on a bob-tailed nag,
G7   C
Somebody bet on the bay.

Oh, the long tailed filly and the big black horse,
Doo-da, doo-da,
Come to a mud hole and they all cut across,
Oh, de doo-da day.

I went down South with my hat caved in,
Doo-da, doo-da,
I come back North with a pocket full of tin,
Oh, de doo-da day.

Pop Goes The Weasel

C G   C
All around the cobbler's bench,
     G   C
The monkey chased the weasel.
         G   C Am7
The monkey thought 'twas all in fun,
Dm7 G7   C
Pop goes the weasel!
Am   Em
I've no time to wait and sigh,
   Am   Em
No patience to wait till by 'n by,
    Dm
So kiss me quick, I'm off, goodbye,
Dm7 G7   C
Pop goes the weasel!

A nickel for a spool of thread,
A penny for a needle,
That's the way the money goes,
Pop goes the weasel!
You may try to sew and sew,
And never make something regal,
So roll it up and let it go,
Pop goes the weasel!

I went to a lawyer today,
For something very legal,
He asked how much I'm willing to pay—
Pop goes the weasel!
I will bargain all my days,
But never again so feeble,
I paid for ev'ry legal phrase,
Pop goes the weasel!

A painter would his lover to paint,
He stood before the easel,
A monkey jumped all over the paint,
Pop goes the weasel!
When his lover she did laugh,
His temper got very lethal,
He tore the painting up in half,
Pop goes the weasel!

I went hunting up in the woods,
It wasn't very legal,
The dog and I were caught with the goods,
Pop goes the weasel!
I said I didn't hunt or sport,
The warden looked at my beagle,
He said to tell it to the court,
Pop goes the weasel!

My son and I we went to the fair,
And there were lots of people,
We spent a lot of money, I swear,
Pop goes the weasel!
I got sick from all the sun,
My sonny boy got the measles,
But still we had a lot of fun,
Pop goes the weasel!

I went up and down on the coast,
To find a golden eagle,
I climbed the rocks and thought I was close,
Pop goes the weasel!
But, alas! I lost my way,
Saw nothing but just a sea gull,
I tore my pants and killed the day,
Pop goes the weasel!

I went to a grocery store,
I thought a little cheese'll
Be good to catch a mouse in the floor,
Pop goes the weasel!
But the mouse was very bright,
He wasn't a mouse to wheedle,
He took the cheese and said "goodnight,"
Pop goes the weasel!

Cotton-Eyed Joe

A   D
Do you remember a long time ago,
A   E7
There was a man called Cotton-Eyed Joe,
        E   A E A
There was a man called Cotton-Eyed Joe.

I could have been married a long time ago,
If it hadn't a-been for Cotton-Eyed Joe, (twice)

Old bull fiddle and a shoe-string bow,
Wouldn't play nothin' but Cotton-Eyed Joe, (twice)

Play it fast or play it slow,
Didn't play nothin' but Cotton-Eyed Joe, (twice)

Don't you remember a long time ago,
Daddy worked a man called Cotton-Eyed Joe, (twice)

Where you you come from? where do you go?
Where do you come from Cotton-Eyed Joe? (twice)

Come for to see you, come for to sing,
Come for to show you my diamond ring. (twice)

Sourwood Mountain

D
Chickens a-crowin' on Sourwood Mountain,
        A7   D
Hey, ho, diddle-um day.
              G
So many pretty girls I can't count 'em,
D   A7   D
Hey ho, diddle-um day.

My true love's a blue-eyed daisy,
She won't come and I'm too lazy.

Big dog bark and little one bite you,
Big girl court and little one spite you.

My true love's a blue-eyed daisy,
If I don't get her, I'll go crazy.

My true love lives at the head of the holler,
She won't come and I won't foller.

My true love lives over the river,
A few more jumps and I'll be with her.

Ducks in the pond, geese in the ocean,
Devil's in the women if they take a notion.

Cindy

        G
You ought to see my Cindy,

She lives way down south;

She's so sweet the honey bees
D7   G
Swarm around her mouth.

Chorus:

         C
Get along home, Cindy, Cindy,
        G
Get along home, Cindy, Cindy,
         C
Get along home, Cindy, Cindy,
   D7   G
I'll marry you some day.

The first I seen my Cindy
She was standing in the door,
Her shoes and stockings in her hand,
Her feet all over the floor.

She took me to her parlor,
She cooled me with her fan;
She said I was the prettiest thing
In the shape of mortal man.

She kissed me and she hugged me,
She called me sugar plum;
She throwed her arms around me,
I thought my time had come.

Oh, Cindy is a pretty girl,
Cindy is a peach.
She threw her arms around my neck,
And hung on like a leech.

And if I was a sugar tree
Standing in the town,
Every time my Cindy passed
I'd shake some sugar down.

And if I had a thread and needle
Fine as I could sew,
I'd sew that gal to my coat tails
And down the road I'd go.

I wish I was an apple
A-hanging on a tree,
Every time that Cindy passed,
She'd take a bite of me.

Weevily Wheat

Em
I don't want none of your weevily wheat
    Bm
An' I don't want none o' your barley,
G   Bm
Take some flour in half an hour
   Em Bm   Em
An' bake a cake for Charley.

Chorus:

Em
O Charley, he's a nice young man,
  Bm
An' Charley he's a dandy,
G   Bm
Every time he goes to town
   Em Bm , Em
He brings the girls some candy.

The higher up the cherry tree
The riper grows the cherry,
The sooner that you court a gal,
The sooner she will marry.

Take her by her lilywhite hand
And lead her like a pigeon,
Make her dance the weevily wheat
And scatter her religion.

Charley here and Charley there
And Charley over the ocean,
Charley, he'll come back some day
If he don't change his notion.

Ida Red

G
Ida Red, Ida Green,
        D7 G
Purtiest gal I ever seen.

Ida Red lives in town,
Weighs three hundred and forty pounds.

Ida Red, Ida Red,
I'm just crazy 'bout Ida Red.

Ida Red, Ida Blue,
Ida bit a hoecake half in two.

Ida Red, Ida Red,
Everybody's crazy 'bout Ida Red.

If I'd a-listened to what Ida said,
I'd a-been sleeping in Ida's bed.

Buffalo Gals

  C
As I was walking down the street,
G7   C
Down the street, down the street,

A pretty girl I chanced to meet,
      G   C
And we danced by the light of the moon.

Chorus:

F   C
Buffalo gal won't you come out tonight,
G7   C
Come out tonight, come out tonight?
F   C
Buffalo gal won't you come out tonight,
   G7   C
And dance by the light of the moon?

Old Joe Clark, the preacher's son,
Preached all over the plain,
The only text he ever knew
Was "High, low jack and the game."

Old Joe Clark had a mule,
His name was Morgan Brown,
And every tooth in that mule's head
Was sixteen inches around.

Old Joe Clark had a yellow cat,
She would neither sing or pray,
She stuck her head in the buttermilk jar
And washed her sins away.

Old Joe Clark had a house
Fifteen stories high,
And every story in that house
Was filled with chicken pie.

I went down to old Joe's house,
He invited me to supper,
I stumped my toe on the table leg
And stuck my nose in the butter.

Now I wouldn't marry a widder,
Tell you the reason why,
She'd have so many children
They'd make those biscuits fly.

Sixteen horses in my team,
The leaders they are blind,
And every time the sun goes down
There's a pretty girl on my mind.

Eighteen miles of mountain road
And fifteen miles of sand,
If I ever travel this road again,
I'll be a married man.

Turkey In The Straw

```
D7      G
Well, I had an old hen and she had a wooden leg,
                              D7
Just the best old hen that ever laid an egg;
              G
Well, she laid more eggs than any hen on the farm,
                              D7        G
But another little drink wouldn't do her any harm.
```

Chorus:

```
G
Turkey in the hay, in the hay, hay, hay!
C
Turkey in the straw, in the straw, straw, straw!
G                          D7
Pick 'em up, shake 'em up, any way at all,
      G              D7        G
And hit up a tune called 'Turkey in the Straw.'
```

Well, I hitched up the wagon and I drove down the road,
With a two horse wagon and a four horse load;
Well I cracked my whip and the lead horse sprung,
And I said, "Goodbye" to the wagon tongue.

Well, if frogs had wings and snakes had hair
And automobiles went a-flying thro' the air;
Well if watermelons grew on a huckleberry vine,
We'd have winter in the summer time.

Oh, I went out to milk and I didn't know how,
I milked a goat instead of a cow.
A monkey sitting on a pile of straw,
A-winkin' his eyes at his mother-in-law.

Well, I come to the river and I couldn't get across,
So I paid five dollars for an old blind horse,
Well, he wouldn't go ahead and he wouldn't stand still,
So he went up and down like an old saw mill.

Cripple Creek

```
D           G       D
I got a gal and she loves me,
              A7          D
She's as sweet as sweet can be.
                    G     D
She's got eyes of baby blue,
                        A7      D
Makes my gun shoot straight and true.
```

Chorus:

```
D        G6
Goin' down Cripple Creek,
D
Goin' in a run,
              G6
Goin' down Cripple Creek
D     Em  D
To 'ave some fun.
```

I got a beau and he loves me,
He's as sweet as sweet can be.
He's got eyes of darkest brown,
Makes my heart jump all around!

L'il Liza Jane

```
C
I've got a gal who loves me so,
F  C
L'il Liza Jane,

Way down South in Baltimore,
  G7  C
L'il Liza Jane.
```

Chorus:

```
C      FC F  C
Oh, E–liza, L'il Liza Jane,
        F  C    G7  C
Oh, E–liza, L'il Liza Jane.
```

Liza Jane looks good to me,
Sweetest gal I ever see.

I fell in love when I first saw,
Now I've got me a mother-in-law.

House and lot in Baltimore,
Lots of children 'round the door.

I don't care how far I roam,
The very best place is home sweet home.

Captain Jinks

G
I'm Captain Jinks of the Horse Marines,
  C   D7   G
I feed my horse on corn and beans,

And sport young ladies in their teens,
           C   G
Though a Captain in the Army.
  C   G
I teach the ladies how to dance,
A7   D7   G
How to dance, how to dance;
  C   Cm G
I teach the ladies how to dance
   A7   D D7
For I'm the pet of the Army.

Chorus:

   G   D7   G
I'm Captain Jinks of the Horse Marines,
  C   D7   G
I feed my horse on corn and beans,

And often live beyond my means,
      C   D7   G
For that's the style in the Army.

I joined my corps when twenty-one,
Of course I thought it capital fun;
When the enemy comes of course I run,
For I'm not cut out for the Army.
When I left home, mamma she cried,
Mamma she cried, mamma she cried,
When I left home, mamma she cried,
"He's not cut out for the Army."

The first time I went out for drill
The bugler sounding made me ill,
Of the battlefield I'd had my fill
For I'm not cut out for the Army.
The officers they all did shout,
They all did shout, they all did shout,
The officers they all did shout,
"Why, kick him out of the Army!"

Green Corn

G
Wake, shake, day's a-breakin'
D7
Peas in the pot and hoe-cakes a-bakin'.
G
Early in the morning, almost day;
     D7
If you don't come soon gonna throw it away.

Chorus:

G
Green corn, come along, Cholly,
D7
Green corn, don't-cha tell Polly.
G
Green corn, come along Cholly.
D7
Green corn, don't-cha tell Polly.
G
Green corn.

All I need in this creation,
Three months work and nine vacation.
Tell my boss any old time,
Daytime's his but nighttime's mine.

All I need to make me happy,
Two little kids to call me pappy.
One named Bill, the other named Davy,
They like their biscuits slopped in gravy.

Uncle Reuben

Chorus:

     C
Uncle Reuben caught a coon, done gone,

Chick-a-chick, done gone,

Chick-a-chick, done gone, chick-a-chick,

Uncle Reuben caught a coon, done gone,
             G7   C
Chick-a-chick, and left me here behind.

Verses:

C
Rabbit runnin' through the grass,
          G7
Foxes close behind,
C
Trees and weeds and cockleburrs
  G7   C
Is all the foxes find.

Possum up a 'simmon tree,
Raccoon on the ground,
Raccoon say, "Mr. Possum,
Won't you shake one 'simmon down?"

If you don't love me, Liza Jane,
Put your hand in mine,
You won't lack for no corn-bread
As long as the sun do shine.

Fly Around My Blue-Eyed Gal

Chorus:

G
Fly around my blue-eyed gal,
Fly around my daisy,
Fly around my blue-eyed gal,
You almost drove me crazy.

Verses:
Once I had a fortune,
I laid it in a trunk,
Lost it all a-gambling
One night when I got drunk.

Wished I was in the West country
Sittin' in a big armchair,
One arm 'round my whiskey barrel,
The other 'round my dear.

If I had a scolding wife
Tell you what I'd do,
Trade her off for a Barlow knife,
Paddle my own canoe.

It's every day and Sunday too,
It seems so dark and hazy,
I'm thinking about my blue-eyed gal,
She's done run me crazy.

If I had no horse at all,
I'd be found a-crawlin',
Up and down this rocky road
A-lookin' for my darling.

Went up on the mountain top
To give my horn a blow,
Thought I heard somebody say,
"Yonder comes my beau."

Black-Eyed Susie

G   D7
All I want in this creation
G   C
Pretty little wife and a big plantation.

Chorus:

G   C   D7
Hey, little black-eyed Susie,
G   C_   D7
Hey, little black-eyed Susie,
G   C   D7   G
Hey, little black-eyed Susie, hey!

All I need to keep me happy,
Two little boys to call me pappy.

Up Red Oak and down salt water,
Some old man gonna lose his daughter.

Black-eyed Susie went huckleberry pickin',
The boys got drunk and Susie took a lickin'.

Some got drunk and some got boozy,
I went home with black-eyed Susie.

Black-eyed Susie about half-grown,
Jumps on the boys like a dog on a bone.

I asked her to be my wife,
She come at me with a barlow knife.

Love my wife, love my baby,
Love my biscuits sopped in gravy.

Boatman's Dance
Dan Emmett

D
Boatman dance, boatman sing,
           F♯7   Bm
Boatman do most anything.
E7   A7   D
Dance, boatman, dance,
E7   A7   D
Dance, boatman, dance.
E7   A7   D7   G
Dance all night till broad daylight,
          D   A7   D
And go home with the gals in the morning.
D7   G
Heigh-ho, boatman row,
D   A7 D
Sailing down the river on the O-hi-O,
D7   G
Heigh-ho, boatman row,
D   A7 D
Sailing down the river on the O-Hi-O.

And when the boatman gets on shore,
He spends his money and he works for more.
Dance boatman dance, etc.

I never saw a pretty girl in my life,
But that she was a boatman's wife.
Dance boatman dance, etc.

When the boatman blows his horn,
Look out, old man, your daughter is gone.
Dance boatman dance, etc.

Sky blue jacket and tarpulin' hat,
Look out my boys, for the nine tail cat.
Dance boatman dance, etc.

Bile Them Cabbage Down

A
Went up on the mountain
                 E7
Just to give my horn a blow,
A   D
Thought I heard my true love say,
A   E7   A
"Yonder comes my beau!"

Chorus:

A   D
Bile them cabbage down, down,
A   E7
Turn them hoecakes round,
     A   D
The only song that I can sing
   A   E7   A
Is bile them cabbage down.

Took my gal to the blacksmith shop
To have her mouth made small
She turned around a time or two
And swallowed shop and all.

Possum in a 'simmon tree,
Raccoon on the ground,
Raccoon says, "You son-of-a-gun,
Shake some 'simmons down!"

Someone stole my old 'coon dog,
Wish they'd bring him back,
He chased the big hogs through the fence
And the little ones through the crack.

Met a possum in the road,
Blind as he could be,
Jumped the fence and whipped my dog
And bristled up at me.

Once I had an old gray mule,
His name was Simon Slick,
He'd roll his eyes and back his ears,
And how that mule would kick.

How that mule would kick!
He kicked with his dying breath;
He shoved his hind feet down his throat
And kicked himself to death.

Jubilee

E
It's all out on the old railroad,

It's all out on the sea,

All out on the old railroad,
A   E
Far as I can see.

Chorus:

A
Swing and turn, Jubilee,
B7   E
Live and learn, Jubilee.

Hardest work I ever done,
Workin' on the farm,
Easiest work I ever done,
Swingin' my true love's arm.

If I had a needle and thread,
As fine as I could sew,
I'd sew my true love to my side
And down this creek I'd go.

If I had no horse to ride,
I'd be found a-crawlin'
Up and down this rocky road
Lookin' for my darlin'.

Some will come on Saturday night,
Some will come on Sunday,
If you give 'em half a chance,
They'll be back on Monday.

I won't have no widder man,
Neither will my cousin,
You can get such stuff as that
For fifteen cents a dozen.

Coffee grows on a white oak tree,
Sugar runs in brandy,
Girls are sweet as a lump of gold,
Boys as sweet as candy.

ALL OVER THIS LAND

Songs of green places, big cities, mountain ranges, waterways and prairies. . . .

Sail Away Ladies

E
Ain't no use to sit and cry,

Sail away, ladies, sail away.

You'll be an angel by an' by,

Sail away, ladies, sail away,

Chorus:
          A
Don't you rock 'im die-dy-o,
          E
Don't you rock 'im die-dy-o,
          B7
Don't you rock 'im die-dy-o,
          E
Don't you rock 'im die-dy-o.

I've got a home in Tennessee, Sail, etc.
That's the place I wanna be, Sail, etc.

If ever I get my new house done,
I'll give the old one to my son,

Come along, boys, and go with me,
We'll go down to Tennessee,

Ever I get my new house done,
Love you, pretty girls, one by one.

Hush, little baby, don't you cry,
You'll be an angel by and by.

My Home's Across The Smokey Mountains

      D
My home's across the Smokey Mountains,
  A7   D
My home's across the Smokey Mountains,

My home's across the Smokey Mountains,
      A7   D
And I'll never get to see you any more, more, more,
      A7   D
I'll never get to see you any more.

Goodbye honey, sugar darlin', (3 times)
And I'll never get to see you any more, more, more,
I'll never get to see you any more.

Rock my baby, feed her candy, (3 times)
And I'll never get to see you any more, more, more,
I'll never get to see you any more.

Elanoy

        Dm   Am   Dm
Way down upon the Wabash, such land was never known;
        E7   F   A7   Dm
If Adam had passed over it, the soil he'd surely own;
        Bb   F   Dm
He'd think it was the garden he'd played in as a boy,
C   Dm   C   Dm
And straight pronounce it Eden in the state of El-a-noy.

Chorus:
        Bb
Then move your fam'ly westward,
        F   Dm
  good health you will enjoy,
C   Dm   C   Dm   Gm Dm
And rise to wealth and honor in the state of El-a-noy.

'Twas here the Queen of Sheba came, with Solomon of old.
With an ass load of spices, pomegranates and fine gold;
And when she saw this lovely land,
    her heart was filled with joy,
Straightway she said: "I'd like to be a queen in El-a-noy."

She's bounded by the Wabash, the Ohio and the Lakes,
She's crawfish in the swampy lands,
    the milk-sick and the shakes;
But these are slight diversions and take not from the joy,
Of living in this garden land, the state of El-a-noy.

Away up in the northward, right on the borderline,
A great commercial city, Chicago, you will find.
Her men are all like Abelard, her women like Heloise;
All honest virtuous people, for they live in El-a-noy.

Last Chorus:
Then move your family westward,
    bring all your girls and boys,
And cross at Shawnee ferry to the State of El-a-noy.

The Eyes Of Texas
Tune: *I've Been Working On The Railroad*

G
The eyes of Texas are upon you
C   G
All the livelong day.

The eyes of Texas are upon you.
    A7   D7
You cannot get away.
                        G
Do not think you can escape them
      C   B7
From night till early in the morn.
      C   G
The eyes of Texas are upon you
    D7   G
Till Gabriel blows his horn.

In Kansas

Tune: *The Praties*

D
All who want to roam in Kansas,
         G   D
All who want to roam in Kansas,
                    C
All who want to roam, go and get yourself a home,
  A7   D
Be contented with your doom in Kansas.

Oh, the girls they do grow tall in Kansas (twice)
The girls they do grow tall and the boys they love them all,
And they marry 'em in the fall, in Kansas.

Oh, they chew tobacco thin in Kansas (twice)
Oh, they chew tobacco thin and it dribbles in their chin,
And they lick it back again, in Kansas.

The roosters they lay eggs in Kansas (twice)
The roosters they lay eggs as big as whiskey kegs,
And there's whiskers on their legs in Kansas.

The people never wed in Kansas (twice)
The people never wed, or so I've heard it said,
They just tumble into bed, in Kansas.

Bowling Green

A
                                 F♯m
Wish I was in Bowling Green sittin' in a chair
A
One arm 'round my pretty little miss

    the other 'round my dear
                     F♯m
The other 'round my dear, Bowling Green
A   F♯m   A
Hey, good old Bowling Green.

If you see that man of mine, tell him once for me
If he loves another girl, yes I'll set him free . . .
Yes I'll set him free, Bowling Green
Hey, good old Bowling Green.

Wish I was a bumblebee sailing through the air
Sail right down to my feller's side, touch him if you dare.
Touch him if you dare, Bowling Green
Hey, good old Bowling Green.

Goin' through this whole wide world,
   I'm goin' through alone
Goin' through this whole wide world,
   I ain't got no home
I ain't got no home, Bowling Green
Hey, good old Bowling Green.

E-ri-e

             A
We were forty miles from Albany
         E7   A
Forget it, I never shall.
            E7   A   D
What a terrible storm we had one night,
    A E7   A
On the E-ri-e Canal.

Chorus:

E7   A E7   A
Oh the E-ri-e was a-rising,
                E7   A
And the gin was a-getting low.
 ·   E7   A   D
And I scarcely think we'll get a drink,
    A   E7   A
Till we get to Buffalo,
    D   E7   A
Till we get to Buffalo.

We were loaded down with barley,
We were chock-up full on rye;
The captain he looked down on me
With his gol-durn wicked eye.

Two days out from Syracuse,
The vessel struck a shoal,
We like to all be foundered
On a chunk o' Lackawanna coal.

We hollered to the captain
On the towpath, treadin' dirt,
He jumped on board and stopped the leak
With his old red flannel shirt.

The cook she was a grand old gal,
She wore a ragged dress,
We heisted her upon the pole
As a signal of distress.

The wind begins to whistle,
The waves begin to roll,
We had to reef our royals
On that raging Canal.

When we got to Syracuse,
Off-mule he was dead,
The nigh mule he got blind staggers
We cracked him on the head.

The captain, he got married,
The cook, she went to jail,
And I'm the only sea-cook son
That's left to tell the tale.

The Rackets Around The Blue Mountain Lake

```
     Am                    E(G)
Come all you good fellows wherever you be,
     Am        Dm      E
Come sit down awhile and listen to me,
     Am              E
The truth I will tell you without a mistake,
          Am                    E        Am
'Bout the rackets we had 'round the Blue Mountain Lake.
```

Refrain:

```
Am              E       Am
Derry, down, down, down derry down.
```

There's the Sullivan brothers and big Jimmy Lue,
And ole Morse Gillet and Dandy Pat too,
A good lot of fellows as ever was seen,
And they all worked for Griffin on Township nineteen.

Bill Mitchel, you know, he kept our shanty,
And as mean a damn man as you ever did see,
He lay round the shanty from morning to night,
And if a man said a word, he was ready to fight.

One morning 'fore daylight, Jim Lue, he got mad,
Knocked hell out of Mitchel, and the boys was all glad,
And his wife she stood there, and the truth I must tell,
She was tickled to death to see Mitchel catch hell.

Old Griffin stood there, the crabby old drake,
A hand in the racket we thought he would take,
When some of the boys came and led him away,
"Be cripes," said old Griffin, "I have nothing to say."

You can talk of your fashion and your styles to be seen,
But none can compare with the cook of Nineteen,
She's short, thick and fat without a mistake,
And the boys call her Nelly, the belle of Long Lake.

And now you good fellows, adieu to you all,
Christmas is coming and I'm going to Glen Falls,
And when I get there, I'll go out on a spree,
For you know when I have money the devil's in me.

East Virginia

```
C
I was born and raised in East Virginia
C7        F      C
North Carolina I did go
C7        F        C
And there I met the fairest maiden
          G7
Her name and age I do not know.
```

Well, her hair was dark in color
And her cheeks were rosy red;
On her breast she wore white lilies
Where I longed to lay my head.

I'd rather be in some dark holler,
Where the sun refuses to shine,
Than for you to be another man's darling,
And to know you'll never be mine.

Columbia The Gem of The Ocean
Thomas a' Becket

```
        G        D7        G
Oh, Columbia, the gem of the ocean,
        C        Am        G D7
The home of the brave and the free,
        D              A7        D
The shrine of each patriot's devotion,
     A7                      D
A world offers homage to thee;
        D7                    G
Thy mandates make heroes assemble
                              D7
When Liberty's form stands in view;
        G              C
Thy banners make tyranny tremble
        Am        D7          G
When borne by the red, white and blue.
```

Chorus:

```
        D7                       G
When borne by the red, white and blue,
        D7                       G
When borne by the red, white and blue,
                              C
Thy banners make tyranny tremble,
        Am        D7          G
When borne by the red, white and blue.
```

When war winged its wide desolation,
And threatened the land to deform,
The ark, then, of freedom's foundation,
Columbia rode safe through the storm:
With her garlands of victory around her,
When so proudly she bore her brave crew;
With her flag floating proudly before her,
The boast of the red, white and blue.

The boast of the red, white and blue, etc.

The star-spangled banner bring hither,
O'er Columbia's true sons let it wave;
May the wreaths they have won never wither,
Nor its stars cease to shine on the brave:
May thy service, united, ne'er sever,
But hold to their colors so true,
The army and navy forever,
Three cheers for the red, white and blue.

Three cheers for the red, white and blue, etc.

On The Banks Of The Wabash

Paul Dresser

```
         G           C              G  D7
'Round my Indiana homestead wave the cornfields,
G            G7          A7       D7        G
In the distance loom the woodlands clear and cool.
                           C            G  D7
Oftentimes my thoughts revert to scenes of childhood,
G             G7         A7      D7      G
Where I first received my lessons, nature's school,
      B7                           Em
But one thing there is missing in the picture,
      A7                     D7
Without her face it seems so incomplete.
   G          C           G  D7
I long to see my mother in the doorway,
G              G7    A7   D7     G
As she stood there years ago, her boy to greet.
```

Chorus:

```
       G              B7            C
Oh, the moonlight's fair tonight along the Wabash,
E7       Am                  A7          D7
From the fields there comes the breath of new-mown hay.
       G             B7            C
Through the sycamores, the candle lights are gleaming,
C#dim   G       A7     D7 G
On the banks of the Wabash, far away.
```

Many years have passed since I strolled by the river,
Arm in arm with Sweetheart Mary by my side.
It was there I tried to tell her that I loved her,
It was there I begged of her to be my bride,
Long years have passed
    since I strolled through the church-yard,
She's sleeping there, my angel Mary dear.
I loved her but she thought I didn't mean it,
Still I'd give my future were she only there.

The Colorado Trail

```
D
Eyes like the morning star,
A        D
Cheeks like a rose,

Annie was a pretty girl,
Bm          A7
God almighty knows.
D
Weep all you little rains,
A7        D
Wail winds wail,
Bm
All along, along, along
     G      D
The Colorado Trail.
```

Dixie

Daniel D. Emmett

```
   C
I wish I was in the land of cotton,
F
Old times there are not forgotten,
         C                G7           C
Look away, look away, look away, Dixie Land!

In Dixie Land where I was born in
F
Early on one frosty mornin',
         C                G7           C
Look away, look away, look away, Dixie Land!
```

Chorus:

```
                      F      D7    G7
Then I wish I was in Dixie, hooray! hooray!
      C           F
In Dixie Land I'll take my stand
      C    D7  G7    C   G7
To live and die in Dixie, away, away,
      C                      Dm
Away down south in Dixie, away, away,
   A7       D7     G7 C
Away down south in Dixie.
```

Old Mrs. marry Will the Weaver,
William was a gay deceiver,
Look away, etc.
But when he put his arm around her,
He smiled as fierce as a forty-pounder,
Look away, etc.

His face was sharp as a butcher's cleaver,
But that did not seem to grieve her,
Look away, etc.
Old Mrs. acted the foolish part,
And died for a man that broke her heart,
Look away, etc.

Swannanoa Tunnel

```
B7      E       A         E
Ashville Junction, Swannanoa tunnel
            B       B7     E
All caved in babe, all caved in.
```

I'm goin' back to Swannanoa Tunnel,
That's my home, honey, that's my home.

When you hear that hoot-owl squallin'
Somebody's dyin', honey, somebody's dyin'.

And when you hear that pistol groan, baby,
Another man's gone, another man's gone.

If I could gamble like Tom Dooley,
I'd leave my home, honey, I'd leave my home.

The State Of Arkansas

Tune: *Joe Bowars*

```
    Dm          F      Dm
My name is Stamford Barnes, I come from Nobleville

    town,
                        Bb
I've travelled this wide world over,
        F
    I've travelled this wide world round;
    Dm              Bb
I've met with ups and downs in life,
        F           Bb
        and better days I've saw;
    Dm              F           Dm
But I never knew what mis'ry were, till I came to Arkansas.
```

I landed in St. Louis with ten dollars and no more,
I read the daily papers until both my eyes were sore,
I read them evening papers until at last I saw,—
Ten thousand men were wanted in the state of Arkansas.

I wiped my eyes with great surprise
    when I read this grateful news,
And straightway off I started to see the agent,
    Billy Hughes;
He said, "Pitch me down five dollars
    and ticket you shall draw
To ride upon the railroad to the state of Arkansas."

I started off one morning at a quarter after five,
I started from St. Louis, half dead and half alive,
I bought me a quart of whiskey, my misery to thaw,
I got drunk as a biled own when I left for Old Arkansas.

'Twas in the year of '82 in the merry month of June,
I landed in Ft. Smith one sultry afternoon;
Up stepped a walking skeleton and gave to me his paw
Invited me to his hotel, "The best in Arkansas."

I followed my conductor into his dwelling place,
Poverty were depictured in his melancholy face;
His bread it was corn dodger, his beef I could not chaw;
He charged me fifty cents for this in the state of Arkansas.

I started off next morning to catch the morning train,
He says to me, "You'd better work,
    I have some land to drain.
I'll pay you fifty cents a day, your board and wash and all,
You'll find yourself a different man
    when you leave old Arkansas."

I worked six weeks for this son-of-a-gun,
    Jessie Herring was his name,
He was six foot seven in his stocking feet
    and taller than any crane,
His hair hung down like rat tails
    on his long and lantern jaw,
He was the photygraph of all the gents
    who lived in Arkansas.

He fed me on corn dodgers, as hard as any rock,
Till my teeth began to loosen and my knees
    began to knock,
I got so thin on sassafras tea, I could hide behind a straw
And, indeed I was a different man,
    when I left old Arkansas.

Farewell to swamp-angels, canebrakes and chills,
Farewell to sage and sassafras and corn dodger pills,
If I ever see this land again, I'll give to you my paw,
It will be through a telescope—*from here to Arkansas.*

America The Beautiful

Katherine Lee Bates and Samuel A. Ward

```
        C           G7
Oh beautiful for spacious skies,
                    C
For amber waves of grain,
G7 C            G
For purple mountain majesties
            D7      G
Above the fruited plain.
G7C         G7
America! America!
                        C
God shed His grace on thee,
C7  F                   C
And crown thy good with brotherhood
    F       G7      C
From sea to shining sea.
```

Oh beautiful for pilgrim feet
Whose stern impassioned stress
A thoroughfare for freedom beat
Across the wilderness.
America! America!
God mend thine every flaw,
Confirm thy soul in self-control,
Thy liberty in law.

Oh beautiful for heroes proved
In liberating strife,
Who more than self their country loved
And mercy more than life.
America! America!
May God thy gold refine
Till all success be nobleness,
And every gain divine.

Oh beautiful for patriot dream
That sees beyond the years,
Thine alabaster cities gleam,
Undimmed by human tears.
America! America!
God shed His grace on thee,
And crown thy good with brotherhood
From sea to shining sea.

Alabama Bound

Chorus:

C
I'm Alabama bound,

I'm Alabama bound,
F
I'm Alabama bound,

I'm Alabama bound,
          C   G7
And if this train don't stop and turn around,
          C
I'm Alabama bound,

I'm Alabama bound.

Oh, don't you leave me here, (4 times)
But if you must go anyhow,
Leave me a dime for beer. (twice)

Oh, don't you be like me, (4 times)
You can drink your good Sherry wine
And let the whiskey be. (twice)

Way Out In Idaho

Tune: *Wait For The Wagon*

       C
Remember what I promised you
 G7   C
As we set side by side,

Beneath that old persimmon tree,
 F   G7   C
I said I'd be your bride.

Chorus:

C
Way out in Idaho,
       E7   F
We're coming, Idaho;
C
With a four-horse team, we'll soon be seen
      F G7 C
Way out in Idaho.

We're bound to cross the plains,
And up the mountains go,
We're bound to seek our fortunes there,
Way out in Idaho.

Farewell, it's mother and child,
I'm off to stay for a while,
So won't you kiss me before I go,
And call me your darling child.

Oleanna

Satirical song about Norwegian immigration
to the United States

E
Oh, to be in Oleanna!
A   E
That's where I'd like to be,
B7   E
Than be bound in Norway,
    B7   E
And drag the chains of slavery.

Chorus:

E   A   E
Ole, Ole, anna, Ole, Ole, anna.
B7   E   B7   E
Ole, Ole, Ole, Ole, Ole, Ole anna.

In Oleanna land is free;
The wheat and corn just plant themselves.
Then grow a good four feet a day,
While on your bed you rest yourself.

Beer as sweet as Munchener
Springs from the ground and flows away.
The cows all like to milk themselves
And hens lay eggs ten times a day.

Little roasted piggies
Rush about the city streets,
Inquiring so politely
If a slice of ham you'd like to eat.

Say, if you'd begin to live,
To Oleanna you must go;
Than be bound in Norway
Becomes a Duke in a year or so.

Oh, to be in Oleanna,
That's where I'd like to be;
Than be bound in Norway
And drag the chains of slavery.

Sidewalks of New York

James W. Blake and Charles B. Lawlor

```
F       C    F      Bb              F
Down in front of Casey's old brown wooden stoop,
Bb          F    Dm7   G7         C7
On a summer's evening we formed a merry group;
F       C    F      Bb            F
Boys and girls together we would sing and waltz
        Bb               D7+D7 G7       C7
While Tony played the organ on  the sidewalks of
        F
        New York.
```

Chorus:

```
F               Bb            F
East side, west side, all around the town
        Bb            F
The tots sang "ring—a—rosie,"
     D7+D7  G7              C7
     "London   Bridge is falling down."
F       C    F      Bb              F
Boys and girls together, me and Mamie O'Rourke
Bb              F
Tripped the light fantastic
     D7+   D7 G7         C7        F
     on     the  sidewalks of New York.
```

That's where Johnny Casey, little Jimmy Crowe
Jakey Krause, the baker who always had the dough
Pretty Nellie Shannon (with a) dude as light as cork
She first picked up the waltz step
        on the sidewalks of New York.

Things have changed since those times, some are up in "G"
Others they are wand'rers but they all feel just like me
They'd part with all they've got,
        could they once more walk
With their best girl and have a twirl
        on the sidewalks of New York.

Acres Of Clams

```
        C
I've traveled all over this country,
                              Am
Prospecting and digging for gold.
        C
I've tunneled, hydraulicked and cradled,
F       C      G7        C
And, I have been frequently sold.
```

First Chorus:
```
C
And I have been frequently sold,
                              Am
And I have been frequently sold,
        C
I've tunneled, hydraulicked and cradled,
F       C       G7       C
And, I have been frequently sold.
```

For one who gets riches by mining
Perceiving that hundreds grow poor,
I made up my mind to try farming,
The only pursuit that is sure.

Second Chorus:
The only pursuit that is sure, (twice)
I made up mind to try farming
The only pursuit that is sure.

So, rolling my grub in my blanket,
I left all my tools on the ground,
And started one morning to shank it
For a country they call Puget Sound.

Third Chorus:
For a country they call Puget Sound, (twice)
And started one morning to shank it
For a country they call Puget Sound.

No longer the slave of ambition,
I laugh at the world and its shams,
And I think of my happy condition
Surrounded by acres of clams.

Fourth Chorus:
Surrounded by acres of clams, (twice)
And think of my happy condition
Surrounded by acres of clams.

Abilene

```
E       E7
Abilene, Abilene,
     A7              E       B7
Prettiest town you ever seen,

Folks there don't treat you mean,
        E       A7    E  B7
In Abilene, my   Abilene.
```

I sit alone most every night,
Watch them trains roll out of sight,
Wish that they were carrying me,
To Abilene, my Abilene.

Crowded city, there ain't nothin' free,
Ain't nothin' in this town for me,
Wish to God that I could be,
In Abilene, my Abilene.

Home On The Range

```
    E                        A
Oh! Give me a home where the buffalo roam,
         E          F♯    B7
Where the deer and the antelope play;
       E    E7        A       Am
Where seldom is heard a discouraging word,
       E       B7      E
And the sky is not clouded all day.
```

Chorus:

```
E    B7      E
Home, home on the range!
                  F♯    B7
Where the deer and the antelope play
       E    E7        A       Am
Where seldom is heard a discouraging word,
       E       B7      E
And the sky is not clouded all day.
```

Oh! give me the land where the bright diamond sand
Throws its light from the glittering streams,
Where glideth along the graceful white swan,
Like the maid to her heavenly dreams.

Oh! give me a gale of the Solomon vale
Where the lifestreams with buoyancy flow;
On the banks of the Beaver, where seldom if ever,
Any poisonous herbage doth grow.

How often at night, when the heavens were bright,
With the light of the twinkling stars,
Have I stood here amazed and asked as I gazed
If their glory exceeds that of ours.

I love the wild flowers in this bright land of ours,
I love the wild curlew's shrill scream;
The bluffs and white rocks and antelope flocks,
That graze on the mountain so green.

The air is so pure and the breezes so free,
The zephyrs so balmy and light,
That I would not exchange my home here to range
Forever in azures so bright.

Far Above Cayuga's Waters

```
G         C      D7
Far above Cayuga's waters, with its waves of blue,
G           C        D7       G
Stands our noble Alma Mater, glorious to view
G         C          D7
Far above the busy humming of the bustling town
G            C            D7           G
Reared against the arch of Heaven looks she proudly down.
```

Chorus:

```
G    D7  G
Raise the chorus, speed it onward,
C    G   D7
Loud her praises tell
G            C
Hail to thee our Alma Mater
D7          G
Hail! all hail! Cornell!
```

Firm upon the rugged hilltops stand her granite walls,
Firmer may her sons press onward,
    onward through her halls,
When with moments swiftly flying, ages roll between
Sons as yet unborn shall hail thee Alma Mater, Queen.

Hear the rippling of the waters as they glide along;
Listen to the evening breezes with their whispered song,
Heed the thrilling notes of gladness
    of the wakening morn,
All with joyful echoes murmur, that Cornell is born.

Cumberland Gap

```
F                      Dm
Lay down boys, take a little nap,
            F
We're all goin' down to Cumberland Gap.
                         Dm
Cumberland Gap, Cumberland Gap.
        F              G7    F
We're all goin' down to Cumberland Gap.
```

Me and my wife, and my wife's pap
We all live down to Cumberland Gap.
Cumberland Gap, Cumberland Gap
We all live down to Cumberland Gap.

I got a gal in Cumberland Gap,
She's got a baby calls me pap.
Cumberland Gap, Cumberland Gap
We're all going down to Cumberland Gap.

Cumberland Gap it ain't very fur,
It's just three miles from Middlesboro, etc.

The Great American Bum

     C   G7
Come all you jolly jokers, if you want to have some fun,

And listen while I relate the tale
                   C
  of the great American bum;

From east and west and north and south
               G7
Like a swarm of bees they come,

They sleep in the dirt and wear a shirt
             C
That's lousy and full of crumbs.

Chorus:

C
I am a bum, a jolly old bum,
           G7
And I live like a royal Turk;

And I have good luck,

And I bum all my chuck,
                        C
And the heck with the man that works.

It's early in the morning when the dew is on the ground,
A bum arises from his nest and gazes all around.
While going east they're loaded,
And going west sealed tight,
"I reckon we'll have to ride aboard
  the fast express tonight."

Well, I met a man the other day that I never met before,
And he asked me if I wanted a job a-shovelin' iron ore;
I asked him what the wages was
And he said: "Ten cents a ton."
I said: "Old fellow scratch your . . . neck,
  I'd rather be on the bum."

Oh, lady would you be kind enough
  to give me somethin' to eat,
A piece of bread and butter and a tender slice of meat;
Some apple pie and custard
Just to tickle me appetite,
For really I'm so hungry,
  don't know where I'll sleep tonight.

I BEEN DOING SOME HARD TRAVELIN'

Songs of roving, rambling and plain hard luck....

The Tramp
Joe Hill

     E
If you all will shut your trap,
   A   E
I will tell you 'bout a chap

                                  B7
That was broke and up against it too, for fair;
    E
He was not the kind that shirk,
  A   E
He was looking hard for work,
  A   B7   E
But he heard the same old story ev'rywhere:

Chorus:

                     A   E
Tramp, tramp, tramp and keep on tramping,
B7   E   B7
Nothing doing here for you;
    E
If I catch you round again,
    A   E
You will wear the ball and chain,
    A   B7   E
Keep on tramping, that's the best thing you can do.

He walked up and down the street
'Til the shoes fell from his feet,
In a house he spied a lady cooking stew,
And he said, "How do you do,
May I chop some wood for you?"
What the lady told him made him feel so blue.

'Cross the street a sign he read,
"Work for Jesus," so it said,
And he said, "Here is my chance, I'll surely try,"
So he kneeled upon the floor
'Til his knees got rather sore,
But at eating time he heard the preacher cry:

Down the street he met a cop
And the copper made him stop,
And he asked him, "When did you blow into town?"
"Come with me and see the judge,"
But the judge he said, "Oh, fudge,
Bums that have no money needn't come around."

Finally came that happy day
When his life did pass away,
He was sure he'd go to heaven when he died.
When he reached the Pearly Gate,
Saint Peter, mean old skate,
Slammed the gate right in his face and loudly cried:

In despair he went to hell,
With the Devil for to dwell,
For the reason he'd no other place to go.
And he said, "I'm full of sin,
So for Christ's sake let me in,"
But the Devil said, "Oh, beat it, you're a 'bo."

I Can't Help But Wonder Where I'm Bound
Tom Paxton

        C
It's a long and dusty road,
   F   Am Dm
It's a hot and heavy load,
       G7   C
And the folks I meet ain't always kind.

Some are bad and some are good,
             F   Am   Dm
Some have done the best they could,
       G7   C
Some have tried to ease my troublin' mind.

Chorus:

         Dm   G7   C
And I can't help but wonder where I'm bound,
   Em   Am
where I'm bound,
     Dm   G7   C
And I can't help but wonder where I'm bound.

I have been around this land
Just a-doin' the best I can,
Tryin' to find what I was meant to do.
And the faces that I see
Are as worried as can be
And it looks like they are wonderin', too.

I had a little gal one time,
She had lips like sherry wine,
And she loved me 'til my head went plumb insane.
But I was too blind to see
She was driftin' away from me
And one day she left on the morning train.

I've got a buddy from home,
But he started out to roam
And I hear he's out by 'Frisco Bay.
And sometimes when I've had a few,
His voice comes singin' through
And I'm goin' out to see him some old day.

If you see me passin' by
And you sit and wonder why
And you wish that you were a rambler, too;
Nail your shoes to the kitchen floor,
Lace 'em up and bar the door,
Thank your stars for the roof that's over you.

Hand Me Down My Walking Cane

G
Hand me down my walkin' cane
  D7   G
Hand me down my walkin' cane
C
Hand me down my walkin' cane,
G
I'm gonna catch the midnight train,
  D7   G
'Cause all my sins are taken away.

Oh, hand me down my bottle of corn,
I'll get drunk as sure's you're born.

Oh, I got drunk and I landed in jail,
And there wasn't no one to go my bail.

Come on, Mom, won't you go my bail,
And get me out of this Goddamn jail?

The meat is tough, and the beans are bad,
Oh, my God, I can't eat that.

If I had listened to what you said,
I'd be at home in my feather bed.

If I should die in Tennessee,
Just send my bones home C.O.D.

But if I die in New York State,
Just ship my body back by freight.

The devil chased me 'round a stump,
I thought he'd catch me at every jump.

Oh, hell is deep, and hell is wide,
Ain't got no bottom, ain't got no side.

Now some folks say, it ain't no fun,
When a song like this goes on and on.

Yes, on and on and on and on,
On and on and on and on.

900 Miles

  Am
I'm a walking down the track,

I've got tears in my eyes,

I'm tryin' to read a letter from my home;

If that train runs me right,

I'll be home Saturday night,

'Cause I'm nine hundred miles from my home.
 E7   Am
And I hate to hear that lonesome whistle blow,

 E7   Am
That long lonesome train whistlin' down.

Well this train I ride on,
Is a hundred coaches long,
You can hear her whistle blow a hundred miles;
And if this train runs me right,
I'll see my woman Saturday night,
'Cause I'm nine hundred miles from my home.
And I hate to hear that lonesome whistle blow,
That long lonesome train whistling down.

I will pawn you my wagon,
I will pawn you my team,
I will pawn you my watch and my chain;
And if this train runs me right,
I'll be home Saturday night,
'Cause I'm nine hundred miles from my home.
And I hate to hear that lonesome whistle blow,
That long lonesome train whistling down.

Mighty Day

  Dm   A7
I remember one September,
Dm   A7
Storm winds swept the town;
Dm   Gm
Women and children were dyin',
  A7
God! Death was all around.

Chorus:

Dm   Dm7
Wasn't it a mighty day!
     G   Bb7
Wasn't it a mighty day!
     Dm
Wasn't it a mighty day, Great God.
         A7   Dm
That morning when the storm winds swept the town.

There was a seawall there in Galveston,
To keep the waters down;
But the high tide from the ocean, God,
Put water into the town.

The waters, like some river,
Came rushing to and fro;
Seen my father drowning, God,
I watched my mother go.

Well, the trumpets gave them warning,
You'd better leave this place;
But they never meant to leave their homes
Till death was in their face.

The sea began to rollin',
The ships they could not land,
Heard a captain crying, "God,
Please save this drowning man!"

Rambling, Gambling Man

    D
Well, I am a rambling, gambling man,

I gamble down in town,

Whenever I meet with a deck of cards
  G   D
I lay my money down, boys,
  A7   D
I lay my money down.

Chorus:

      G   D
I'm a rambler I'm a gambler
      G   D
I'm a ramblin' gamblin' man
      G   D
I'm a rambler I'm a gambler
         A7   D
And I gamble when I can.

Now, if you want to gamble,
Your luck you want to try,
Just pass the queens, and check the kings,
And bet your aces high, boys,
And bet those aces high.

Well, I've gambled around in Vegas town,
With money in my jeans,
But I lost my money where I won my honey,
Way down in New Orleans, boys,
Way down in New Orleans.

She took me in her parlor,
And she cooled me with her fan,
And she swore I was the prettiest thing
In the shape of mortal man, boys,
In the shape of mortal man.

My daughter, my dear daughter,
How can you treat me so,
And leave your dear old mama,
And with this gambler go, boys,
And with this gambler go.

Well, deal around the cards, boys,
Give me just five cards,
I'll show you rambling, gambling men,
A lover's hand at hearts, well,
A lover's hand at hearts.

Well, I hear the train a-coming,
She's blowing down the line,
You can bet your stack, when we come back,
We'll beat three of a kind, boys,
We'll beat three of a kind.

Baby Mine

G
Oh, I'm goin' round the world, baby mine,
I'm goin' round the world, baby mine,
I'm goin' round the world,
I'm a banjo-pickin' girl,
Oh, I'm goin' round the world, baby mine.

Oh, I'm going to Arkansas, baby mine, etc.
You can tell ma and paw, etc.

Oh, I'm goin' to Chattanooga, etc.
And from there on to Cuba, etc.

Oh, I'm goin' to North Carolina, etc.
And from there on to China, etc.

Oh, I'm goin' cross the ocean, etc.
If I don't change my notion, etc.

Oh, if you ain't got no money, baby mine, etc.
Get yourself another honey,
'Cause I'm goin' round the world, baby mine.

Danville Girl

     E
My pocket book was empty,
  A   E
My heart was full of pain,
  A   E
Ten thousand miles away from home
B7   E
Bumming the railroad train.

I was standing on the platform
Smoking a cheap cigar
Listening for that next freight train
To carry an empty car.

Well I got off at Danville
Got stuck on the Danville girl
You bet your life she's out of sight
She wore those Danville curls.

She took me in her kitchen
She treated me nice and kind
She got me in the notion
Of bumming all the time.

She wore her hair on the back of her head
Like high-toned people do
But the very next train come down the line
I bid that girl adieu.

I pulled my cap down over my eyes
Walked down to the track
Then I caught a westbound freight;
Never did look back.

The Blind Fiddler

Dm
I lost my eyes in the blacksmith shop
             Gm Dm
  in the year of 'Fifty-Six,
   Bb   F   C   Am
While dusting out a T-planch, which was out of fix.
   Bb   F   C   Am
It bounded from the tongs and there concealed my doom.
  Dm   A7   Gm   Dm
I am a blind fiddler and far from my home.

I've been to San Francisco, I've been to Doctor Lane,
He operated on one of my eyes, but nothing could he gain.
He told me that I'd never see, and it's no use to mourn:
I am a blind fiddler and far from my home.

I have a wife and three little ones, depending now on me;
To share all my troubles, whatever they may be.
I hope that they'll be careful while I'm compelled to roam.
I am a blind fiddler and far from my home.

The Other Side Of Jordan

New Lost City Ramblers

C
I'm going to sing you a brand new song,
              G7
It's all the truth for certain,
  C   F
If we can't live high, we can still get by,
  G7   C
And get on the other side of Jordan.

Chorus:

C   F
Oh, pull off your overcoat and roll up your sleeves,
C   G7
Jordan is a hard road to travel,
  C   F
Oh, pull off your overcoat and roll up your sleeves,
  C   G7   C
Oh, Jordan is a hard road to travel, I believe.

The public schools and the highways
Are raising quite an alarm,
Get a country man educated just a little
And he ain't going to work on the farm.

I don't know, but I believe I'm right
The auto's ruined the country,
Let's go back to the horse and buggy
And try to save some money.

I know a man that's an evangelist,
Tabernacle's always full,
People come for miles around
Just to hear him shoot the bull.

You can talk about your evangelists,
You can talk about Mister Ford, too,
But Henry is a-shaking more hell out of folks
Than all the evangelists do.

It rained forty days, and it rained forty nights,
And it rained in the Allegheny mountains,
It rained forty horses and a Dominicker mule,
And they landed on the other side of Jordan.

The Titanic

      D   G   D
Oh they built the ship Titanic to sail the ocean blue,

And they thought they had a ship
          E7   A7
  that the water would never go thru,
      D
But the Lord's Almighty hand
          G   D
  knew that ship would never land,
          A7   D
It was sad when that great ship went down.

Chorus:

       G   D
It was sad—It was sad.
                       A7
It was sad when the great ship went down.
  (To the bottom of the)
D   D7   G
Husbands and wives, little children lost their lives—
     D   A7   D
It was sad when that great ship went down.

Oh, they sailed from England,
  and were almost to the shore,
When the rich refused to associate with the poor,
So they put them down below,
  where they were the first to go,
It was sad when the great ship went down.

The boat was full of sin, and the sides about to burst,
When the captain shouted, "A-women and children first!"
Oh, the captain tried to wire, but the lines were all on fire,
It was sad when the great ship went down.

Oh, they swung the lifeboats out
  o'er the deep and ragin' sea,
When the band struck up with,
  "A-nearer My God to Thee."
Little children wept and cried,
  as the waves swept o'er the side,
It was sad when the great ship went down.

Prospecting Dream

Tune: *Oh, Susannah*

       C
Well, I dreamed a dream the other night
              G7
  when ev'rything was still,
C   G7   C
I dreamed that I was carryin' my long-tom down a hill,

My feet slipped out and I fell down,
              G7
  oh how I jarred my liver,
C   G7
I watched my long-tom 'til I saw it fetched up
      C
  in the river.

Chorus:

F   C   G7
Oh, what a miner, what a miner was I,
  C   G7   C
All swelled up with scurvy so I really thought I'd die.

My matches, flour, and Chili beans,
  lay scattered all around,
I felt so bad that I wished to die, as I lay on the ground;
My coffee rolled down by a rock,
  my pepper I could not find,
'Twas then I thought of Angeline, the girl I left behind.

Well, I took my shovel, pick and pan,
  to try a piece of ground,
I dreamed I struck the richest lead
  that ever had been found;
Then I wrote home that I had found a solid lead of gold,
And I'd be home in just a month, but what a lie I told!

Well, I went to town and I got drunk,
  in the morning to my surprise,
I found that I had got a pair of roaring big black eyes,
And I was strapped, had not a cent,
  not even pick or shovel,
My hair snarled up and my breeches torn,
  looked like the very devil.

Next thing I did, I hired out to be a hardware clerk,
I got kicked out cause I couldn't write,
  so again I went to work;
But when they caught me stealing grub,
  a few went in to boot him,
And others round were singing out,
    "Hang him, hang him, shoot him!"

There's A Man Goin' 'Round Takin' Names

         C   G7   C
There's a man goin' 'round takin' names,
                             G7
There's a man goin' 'round takin' names,
            C
He has taken my father's name,
            F   C
  and he's left my soul in vain.
                G7   C
There's a man goin' 'round takin' names.

There's a man goin' 'round takin' names,
There's a man goin' 'round takin' names,
He has taken my mother's name
  and has left me here in vain;
There's a man goin' 'round takin' names.

He has taken my sister's name, etc.

He has taken my brother's name, etc.

This Train

E
This train is bound for glory, this train,
                               B7
This train is bound for glory, this train,
E   E7
This train is bound for glory,
A   E
Don't ride nothin' but the righteous and the holy,
       B7   E
This train is bound for glory, this train.

This train don't carry no gamblers, this train,
This train don't carry no gamblers, this train.
This train don't carry no gamblers,
No hypocrites, no midnight ramblers,
This train is bound for glory, this train.

This train is built for speed now, etc.
Fastest train you ever did see,
This train is bound for glory, this train.

This train don't carry no liars, etc.
No hypocrites and no high flyers,
This train is bound for glory, this train.

This train you don't pay no transportation, etc.
No Jim Crow and no discrimination,
This train is bound for glory, this train.

This train don't carry no rustlers, etc.
Sidestreet walkers, two-bit hustlers,
This train is bound for glory, this train.

Wild Rover

<pre>
    D   A7   D
I've been a wild rover for a number of years,
                             G   A7
I've spent all my money on whisky and beer,

Now I'll save up my wages, keep money in store,
       D   G   D
And I never will play the wild rover no more.
</pre>

Chorus:

<pre>
     A7   D   G   A7
Wild rover, wild rover, wild rover no more
     D   A7   D
And I never will play the wild rover no more.
</pre>

I went to a pub where I used to resort,
I told the landlady my money was short;
I asked her to trust me, her answer was, Nay,
Such custom as yours we can get any day.

So save up your wages, keep your money in store,
Don't you never play the wild rover no more.

Put my hand in my pocket, so manly and bold,
And down on the table threw a handful of gold;
Here's beer and here's whisky, saying,
   Bob, you're a good bloke,
And it's, Don't you take no notice, I was having a joke.

Never mind about your wages, nor your money in store,
And you can be a wild rover evermore.

You can keep all your whisky and your beer likewise too,
For not another penny am I spending with you;
For the money I've got, mum, I'm taking good care,
And I never will play the wild rover no more.

Wild rover, wild rover, wild rover no more,
And it's never will I play the wild rover no more.

I'll go home to my parents and I'll tell what I've done,
And ask em to pardon their prodigal son;
And if they'll forgive me, as they've done before,
Oh, it's never will I play the wild rover no more.

Wild rover, wild rover, wild rover no more,
No never will I play the wild rover no more.

Root, Hog, Or Die

<pre>
     C   G7
Oh, I went to California in the spring of seventy-six,
                                   C
And when I landed there, I was in a terrible fix.
                              F
I didn't have no money, my victuals for to buy,
     G7   C
And the only thing for me to do was root, hog, or die.
</pre>

I went out in the country, commenced to making hay,
The wages that I got was a dollar and a half a day.
You get no supper after night, and there's no use to cry,
There's no use of whining, it was root, hog, or die.

Oh, I went from there down to Bellew,
I met with a stranger, who helped to put me through.
It was in a game of poker and he gave the cards a sly,
And he soon got my money and it's root, hog, or die.

Oh, I got mad and I began to swear,
I forced down the corn juice till I got on a tear.
The marshall of the city who was standing nearby,
He took me to the calaboose to root, hog, or die.

Oh, he took me out to court next morning just at ten,
There set the judge and a dozen other men;
They fined me twenty dollars and I found it rather high,
But there's no use of whining, it was root, hog, or die.

Oh, along about then I begun to repent,
They fined me twenty dollars and I didn't have a cent.
As good luck would have it, a friend was standing by,
And he paid off my fine, saying root, hog, or die.

Come all you young men and take my advice,
To never play poker or to throwing at dice,
For if you do, you'll get too much of rye,
And you'll land in the calaboose to root, hog, or die.

Man Of Constant Sorrow

<pre>
G   C   F
I am a man of constant sorrow,
       G   C
I've seen trouble all my days;
G   C   F
I bid farewell to old Kentucky,
            G   C
The place where I was born and raised.
</pre>

For six long years I've been in trouble,
No pleasure here on earth I found,
For in this world I'm bound to ramble,
I have no friends to help me now.

It's fare you well, my own true lover,
I never expect to see you again;
For I'm bound to ride that northern railroad,
Perhaps I'll die upon this train.

You may bury me in some deep valley
For many years where I may lay,
Then you may learn to love another
While I am sleeping in my grave.

Maybe your friends think I'm just a stranger,
My face you never will see no more,
But there is one promise that is given,
I'll meet you on God's golden shore.

Deep Blue Sea

```
G     C   G
Deep blue sea,
      C        G
Baby, deep blue sea,
      C   G
Deep blue sea,
         Am       D7
Baby, deep blue sea,
G
Deep blue sea,
         C        G
Baby, deep blue sea,

It was Willie what got drowned
C     G   D7  G
In the deep blue sea.
```

Lower him down with a golden chain (3 times)
It was Willie what got drownded in the deep blue sea.

Dig his grave with a silver spade. (3 times)
It was Willie what got drownded in the deep blue sea.

Wrap him up in a silken shroud. (3 times)
It was Willie what got drownded in the deep blue sea.

Golden sun bring him back to me. (3 times)
It was Willie what got drownded in the deep blue sea.

Motherless Children

```
E                        A7
Motherless children have a hard time when
    E
    mother is dead,
E7
Motherless children have a hard time when
    E
    mother is dead,
E7
Wandrin' round from door to door
    A7
    they don't have no place to go.

Motherless children have a hard time when
    E
    mother is dead,
```

Some people say "Sister will do when your
   Mother is dead", (twice)
Some people say "Your sister will do"-
   soon as she marries, turn her back on you.
Motherless children. . .

Your wife or your husband may be good to you
   when your Mother is dead, (twice)
Wife or your husband may be good to you -
   nobody treat you like your Mother do.

Some people say "Your auntie will do
   when your Mother is dead," (twice)
Some people say "Your auntie will do"
   make a start then prove untrue,
Nobody else can take your Mother's place
   when Mother is dead.

Jesus will be a Father to you when
   your Mother is dead. (twice)
Jesus will be a Father to you -
   through pains and sorrow lead you through.

Run Come See

```
              C
It was in nineteen-hundred and twenty-nine
                            G7
My God I remember that day pretty well,
                 G7
Run come see, run come see,
              C                    F
It was in nineteen hundred and twenty-nine,
         C   G7 C
Run come see Jerusalem.
```

They were talkin' 'bout the stormin' in the island
My God, what a beautiful morning
Run come see, run come see,
They were talkin' 'bout the stormin' in the island,
Run come see Jerusalem.

There was three sails leavin' out the harbor,
My God, they was bound for Andros
Run come see, run come see,
Three sails leavin' out the harbor,
Run come see Jerusalem.

They was the Ethel and the Myrtle and Praetoria
With the women and the children on board,
Run come see, etc.

Now a big sea built up in the northwest,
And the children come a-running to their mothers, etc.

An' the big sea hit the Praetoria,
An' the mothers come a-runnin' for the children, etc.

An' it sent her head downward to the bottom,
An' the cap'n come a-runnin' for the tiller, etc.

There was thirty-three souls upon the water,
Swimmin' and a-prayin' to the Daniel God, etc.

Now George Brown he was the cap'n
And he shouted, "My children, come pray," etc.

He said, "Come now witness your judgment,"
He shouted, "My children come pray," etc.

Hard Traveling

Woody Guthrie

© 1947 by People's Songs Inc.

D
I've been doing some hard traveling,

I thought you knowed.

I've been doing some hard rambling,
A7
Way down the road.
D
I've been doing some hard rambling,
G
Hard drinking, hard gambling,
A7   D
I've been doing some hard traveling, Lord.

I've been doing some hardrock mining,
I thought you knowed,
I've been leaning on a pressure drill,
Way down the road.
Well, the hammer flying and the air hose sucking,
And six feet of mud and I sure been a-mucking,
And I've been doing some hard traveling, Lord.

I've been laying in a hard rock jail,
I thought you knowed, boys,
I've been laying out ninety days,
Way down the road,
Well, the darned old judge he said to me,
It's ninety days for vagrancy,
And I've been doing some hard traveling, Lord.

I've been riding them fast passengers,
I though you knowed, boys,
I've been hitting them flat wheelers,
Way down the road,
I've been riding them blind passengers,
Dead enders, kicking up cinders,
I've been doing some hard traveling, Lord.

I've been doing some hard harvesting,
I thought you knowed,
From North Dakota to Kansas City,
Way down the road,
Been a-cutting that wheat and a-stacking that hay,
Just trying to make about a dollar a day,
And I've been doing some hard harvesting, Lord.

I've been walking that Lincoln Highway,
I thought you knowed,
I've been hitting that 66,
Way down the road,
Got a heavy load, I got a worried mind,
I'm looking for a woman that's hard to find,
And I've been doing some hard traveling, Lord.

The Dreary Black Hills

E
Kind friends, won't you listen to my pitiful tale,
                              B7
I'm an object of pity and looking quite stale,
A   E   B7   E
I gave up my job selling Aire's Patent Pills
  A   E   B7   E
To prospect for gold in the Dreary Black Hills.

Chorus:

E
Don't travel away, stay at home if you can,
                              B7
Stay away from that city, they call it Cheyenne,
A   E   B7   E
Where the blue waters roll and Comanche Bill
     A   E   B7   E
Will lift up your hair in the Dreary Black Hills.

The round house in Cheyenne is filled every night
With loafers and bummers of most every plight;
On their backs there's no clothes, in their pockets no bills,
Each night they keep leaving for the Dreary Black Hills.

I got to Cheyenne, no gold could I find,
And I thought of the maiden I'd left far behind;
The rain, hail and snow froze plumb to the gills,
They call me the orphan of the dreary Black Hills.

Kind friends, to conclude my advice I'll unfold,
Don't go to the Black Hills and search there for gold;
Railroad speculators their pockets you'll fill
By taking a trip to the Dreary Black Hills.

Wandering

D   G7
I've been a wandering early and late,

New York City to the Golden Gate,
        A7
And it looks like
    G7   Bb   D
I'm never gonna cease my wandering.

Been working in the army, working on a farm,
All I got to show for it's just this muscle in my arm,
And it looks like
I'm never gonna cease my wandering.

There's snakes on the mountain, there's eels in the sea,
Red-headed woman made a fool out of me,
And it looks like
I'm never gonna cease my wandering.

My daddy is an engineer, my brother drives a hack,
Sister takes in washing and the baby balls the jack,
And it looks like
I'm never gonna cease my wandering.

Roving Gambler Blues

F   F7
I am a roving gambler, I've gambled all around,
Bb   F
Wherever I meet with a deck of cards,
                               C7
   well, I lay my money down,
      Bb7   F
I am a roving gambler; rambling, gambling man.

I've gambled down in Washington,
   I've gambled over in Spain;
I'm on my way to Georgia to knock down my last game.
I am a roving gambler; rambling, gambling man.

When I was down in Washington
   many more weeks than three,
I fell in love with a pretty little girl
   and she fell in love with me.
I am a roving gambler; rambling, gambling man.

She took me in her parlor, she cooled me with her fan,
She whispered low to her mother,
   "Oh, I know I love this gambling man."
I am a roving gambler; rambling, gambling man.

"Oh, daughter, oh, dear daughter,
   how could you treat me so,
To leave your dear old mother here alone
   and with a gambler go?"
I am a roving gambler; rambling, gambling man.

"Oh, mother, Oh, dear mother, you know I love you well,
But the love I feel is really real,
   so real no human tongue can tell."
I am a roving gambler; rambling, gambling man.

"Wouldn't marry with a farmer, he's always in the rain;
But I'll be a slave for the man I crave
   who wears a great big golden chain."
I am a roving gambler; rambling, gambling man.

"Wouldn't marry with a blacksmith,
   he's always in the dirt;
I want a man, this gambling man,
   who always wears a ruffled shirt."
I am a roving gambler; rambling, gambling man.

"Wouldn't marry with a doctor,
   he's always gone from home;
That gambler, that rambler,
   I know he can't leave me alone."
I am a roving gambler; rambling, gambling man.

"Wouldn't marry with a railroad man,
   this is the reason why:
I never saw a railroad man
   that wouldn't tell his wife a lie."
I am a roving gambler; rambling, gambling man.

I hear the train a-coming, she's coming 'round the curve,
She's a whistling and a-blowing and straining every nerve,
I am a roving gambler; rambling, gambling man.

"Oh, mother, oh, dear mother, I'll tell you if I can;
If you ever see me coming back again
   I'll be with the gambling man."
I am a roving gambler; rambling, gambling man.

I'm Going Down This Road Feeling Bad

          E   E7
I'm going down this road feeling bad,
     A   E
I'm going down this road feeling bad,
     A   E
I'm going down this road feeling bad, Lord Lord,
   B7   E
And I ain't gonna be treated this a-way.

I'm down in that jail on my knees, (twice)
I'm down in that jail on my knees, Lord, Lord,
I ain't gonna be treated this-a-way.

They fed me on cornbread and beans, etc.
Takes a ten dollar shoe to fit my feet, etc.
'Cause your two dollar shoes hurt my feet, etc.
I'm going where the weather suits my clothes, etc.
That's why I'm going down this road feeling bad, etc.

He Was A Friend Of Mine

G7   C
He was a friend of mine
G7   C
He was a friend of mine.
F   C   E7   F
Never had no money to pay his fine
G7   C
He was a friend of mine.

He died on the road, (twice)
Never had no money (to) pay for his board,
He was a friend of mine.

He never done no wrong, (twice)
He was just a poor boy, a long way from home,
He was a friend of mine.

I stole away and cried, (twice)
Never had no money and I can't be satisfied,
He was a friend of mine.

He was a friend of mine, (twice)
When I hear his name
You know I just can't keep from crying,
He was a friend of mine.

The Big Rock Candy Mountain

Introduction:

```
     D    A7   D      A7
One evening as the sun went down
     D    A7        D
And the jungle fires were burning,
                     A7      D
Down the track came a hobo hiking.
           A7        D
He said "Boys I'm not turning;
       G      D      G D
 I'm heading for a land that's far away
       G         A7
Beside that crystal fountain.
     D    A7   D    A7
I'll see you all this coming fall
         D    A7   D
In the Big Rock Candy Mountain."
```

```
        D
In the Big Rock Candy Mountains,
      G        D
It's a land that's fair and bright,
      G         D
The handouts grow on bushes
        Em7        A7
And you sleep out ev'ry night;
      D
The box-cars are all empty
         G        D
And the sun shines ev'ry day
      G    D      G  D
I'm bound to go where there ain't no snow
         G       D
Where the sleet don't fall
         G      D
And the wind don't blow,
       A7       D
In the Big Rock Candy Mountain
```

Chorus:

```
        D
Oh the buzzing of the bees in the cigarettes trees,
      G     D
By the soda water fountains,
        A7                      D
By the lemonade springs where the bluebird sings,
        A7      D
In the Big Rock Candy Mountain.
```

In the Big Rock Candy Mountains
You never change your socks,
Little streams of alky-hol
Comes trickling down the rocks.
Oh the shacks all have to tip their hats,
And the railroad bulls are blind,
There's a lake of stew and gingerale too,
And you can paddle all around it
In a big Canoe,
In the Big Rock Candy Mountain.

In the Big Rock Candy Mountains
The cops have wooden legs,
The bull-dogs all have rubber teeth
And the hens lay soft-boiled eggs.
The Box-cars all are empty
And the sun shines every day.
I'm bound to go where there ain't no snow,
Where the sleet don't fall,
And the wind don't blow,
In the Big Rock Candy Mountain.

In the Big Rock Candy Mountains
The jails are made of tin,
You can slip right out again
As soon as they put you in.
There ain't no short handled shovels,
No axes, saws nor picks.
I'm bound to stay where you sleep all day,
Where they hung the jerk
That invented work,
In the Big Rock Candy Mountain.

My Ramblin' Boy
Tom Paxton

```
        G7              C
He was a man and a friend always,
            G7            C
He stuck with me in the hard old days;
        F           C
He never cared if I had no dough,
            G7              C
We rambled 'round in the rain and snow.
```

Chorus:

```
                F          C
And here's to you, my ramblin' boy,
              G7            C
May all your ramblin' bring you joy.
            F          C
Here's to you, my ramblin' boy,
              G7            C
May all your ramblin' bring you joy.
```

In Tulsa town we chanced to stray,
We thought we'd try to work one day;
The boss said he had room for one,
Said my old pal, we'd rather bum.

Late one night in a jungle camp,
The weather it was cold and damp;
He got the chills and he got 'em bad,
They took the only friend I had.

He left me here to ramble on,
My ramblin' pal is dead and gone;
If when we die we go somewhere,
I bet you a dollar he's a ramblin' there.

The Oak And The Ash

```
  Em                        D
A North Country maid up to London had strayed,
  C                      B
Although with her nature it did not agree,
    G                    D
Which made her repent, and so bitterly lament,
   Em      B7        Em      B7
Oh I wish once again for the North Country.
```

Chorus:

```
   G      Em      Am7    D
Oh the oak and the ash and the bonnie ivy tree,
   Em      B7        Em  D  Em
They flourish at home in my own country.
```

O fain would I be in the North Country,
Where the lads and lasses are making of hay;
There should I see what is pleasant to me,
A mischief light on them entic'd me away!

I like not the court, nor the city resort,
Since there is no fancy for such maids as me;
Their pomp and their pride I can never abide,
Because with my humor it does not agree.

How oft have I been in the Westmoreland green,
Where the young men and maidens resort for to play,
Where we with delight, from morning till night,
Could feast it and frolic on each holiday.

The ewes and their lambs, with the kids and their dams,
To see in the country how finely they play;
The bells they do ring, and the birds they do sing,
And the fields and the gardens are pleasant and gay.

At wakes and at fairs, being freed of all cares,
We there with our lovers did use for to dance;
Then hard hap had I, my ill fortune to try,
And so up to London, my steps to advance.

But still I perceive, I a husband might have,
If I to the city my mind could but frame;
But I'll have a lad that is North Country bred,
Or else I'll not marry, in the mind that I am.

A maiden I am, and a maid I'll remain,
Until my own country again do I see,
For here in this place I shall ne'er see the face
Of him that's allotted my love for to be.

Then farewell my daddy, and farewell my mammy,
Until I do see you, I nothing but mourn;
Rememb'ring my brothers, my sisters, and others,
In less than a year I hope to return.

Sometimes I Feel Like A Motherless Child

```
     Em
Sometimes I feel like a motherless child,
  Am                  Em
Sometimes I feel like a motherless child,

Sometimes I feel like a motherless child,
  Am  Em        B7
A long way from home—
Em  C  B7       Em
A long way from home.
```

Sometimes I feel like I'm almost gone (3 times)
A long ways from home. (twice)

Sometimes I feel like a feather in the air (3 times)
A long ways from home. (twice)

The Gambler

```
     C
Good morning Mister Railroad man.
     F              C
"What time do your trains roll by?"
     F
"At nine-sixteen and two forty-four
     G7              C
"And twenty-five minutes till five."
```

"It's nine-sixteen and two-forty-four,
"Twenty-five minutes till five,
"Thank you Mr. Railroad man,
"I want to watch your trains roll by."

Standing on a platform,
Smoking a cheap cigar
Waiting for an old freight-train
That carries an empty car.

Well, I pulled my hat down over my eyes,
And I walked across the track,
And I caught me the end of an old freight-train,
And I never did come back.

I sat down in a gamblin' game,
And I could not play my hand,
Just thinkin' about that woman I love
Run away with another man.

Run away with another man, Poor Boy,
Run away with another man,
I was thinking about that woman that I love,
Run away with another man.

Poor Howard

G
Poor Howard's dead and gone,
D7   G
Left me here to sing this song.

Poor Howard's dead and gone,
D7   G
Left me here to sing this song.
C   G
Poor Howard's dead and gone,
D   D6   G
Poor Howard's dead and gone,
C   G
Poor Howard's dead and gone,
D7
Left me here to sing this song.

Who's been here since I've been gone?
Pretty little girl with a red dress on. } (twice)

Pretty little girl with a red dress on, etc.

Who's been here since I've been gone?
Great big man with a derby on, etc.

Freight Train

C   G   G7
Freight train, freight train, run so fast,
                             C
Freight train, freight train, run so fast,
E7   F
Please don't tell what train I'm on,
                 C   F   G7 C
So they won't know what route I've gone.

When I am dead and in my grave,
No more good times here I'll crave,
Place the stones at my head and feet
And tell them all that I'm gone to sleep.

When I die, Lord, bury me deep,
Way down on old Chestnut Street,
So I can hear old Number Nine
As she comes rolling by.

When I die, Lord, bury me deep,
Way down on old Chestnut Street,
Place the stones at my head and feet
And tell them all that I'm gone to sleep.

BEEN IN THE PEN SO LONG

Songs of chain gangs, jails and prisoners....

Ain't No More Cane On This Brazos

```
G              D7      G
There ain't no more cane on this Brazos
    D7   Bm
Oh, o-oh, oh,
               C        D7      G  Em
They done ground it all to molasses,
C  D7   G
Oh, o-oh, oh.
```

Well I been on this Brazos since nineteen oh four,
Oh, o-oh, oh,
You seen a dead man lyin' in almost every door,
Oh, o-oh, oh.

Well, I come to this Brazos with a number for a name,
They started us right in a-cuttin' the cane.

Should a-been on this Brazos in nineteen ten,
They drove the women like they drove the men.

Should a-been on this Brazos when the storm winds came,
Man lyin' dead, we cut him out of the chain,

Captain, don't you do me like ya done do Shine,
Done drove that bully till he come plum blind.

Well if I had a sentence like ninty-nine and nine,
Wouldn't be no captain keep me out on this line.

Columbus Stockade Blues

```
       E
Way down in Columbus, Georgia,
B7                        E
Want to go back to Tennessee.
```

Way down in Columbus Stockade,
   B7
My friends all turned their backs on me.

Chorus:
```
            A                E
Well, you can go and leave if you want to.
A              B7
Never let it cross your mind,
            E
For in your heart you love another,
B7                      E
Leave, little darlin', I don't mind.
```

Last night as I lay sleeping,
I dreamed I held you in my arms,
When I woke, I was mistaken,
I was peeping through the bars.

Many hours with you I've rambled,
Many nights with you I've spent alone,
Now you've gone, you've gone and left me,
And broken up our happy home.

Baby, Please Don't Go

```
C
Baby, please don't go.
                     F
Baby, please don't go.
C
Baby, please don't go back to New Orleans
               G7      C
You know it hurts me so.
```

Babe, I'm way down here,
You know I'm way down here.
Babe, I'm way down here in a rollin' fog,
Baby, please don't go.

Babe, I'm way down here,
You know I'm way down here.
Babe, I'm way down here on old Parchman Farm*,
Baby, please don't go.

Baby, please don't go, (twice)
Baby, please don't go and leave me here,
You know it's cold down here.

You know it's cold down here.
Babe, it's cold down here.
You know it's cold down here on old Parchman Farm,
Baby, please don't go.

I'm half dead down here. (twice)
I'm half dead down here on old Parchman Farm,
Baby, please don't go.

_____
* A prison farm in Parchman, Mississippi.

Been In The Pen So Long

```
A               D7
Been in the pen so long,
A         D7      Dm
Honey, I'll be long gone.
A       F#m   D7
Been in the pen and I gotta go back again,
          G7  C7     F7
Baby, where you been so long?
B7        E7         A
Baby, where you been so long?
```

Awful lonesome, all alone and blue, (twice)
All alone and blue,
No one to tell my troubles to,
Baby where you been so long? (twice)

Some folks crave for Memphis, Tennessee. (3 times)
But New Orleans is good enough for me,
New Orleans is good enough for me.

Foggy Mountain Top

Chorus:

```
E           A          E
If I was on some foggy mountain top,
                   B7
I'd sail away to the West;
   E        A          E
I'd sail all around this whole wide world
             B7     E
To the girl I love the best.
```

Verses:

```
             A   E
Now if you see that girl of mine,
                            B7
There's something I want you to tell her.
E           A          E
Tell her not to be wasting her time
                 B7        E
Running around with some other feller.
```

Oh she's caused me to weep and she's caused me to moan,
She caused me to leave my home,
The lonesome pines and the good old times,
I'm on my way back home.

Oh if I'd only listened to what my mama said,
I would not have been here today,
Lying around this old jail cell,
Just a-weeping my poor life away.

Old Reilly

Chorus:

```
  E
Old Reilly walked the water
                        A E
Well, old Reilly walked the water
         A    E
On them long hot summer days.
E
Here, Rattler, Here, Rattler; Here, Rattler, here
                     B7        E
Here, Rattler, Here, Rattler, Here Rattler, Here.
```

Old Reilly, he's a long-gone (twice)
On them long, hot, summer days.

Well, Old Reilly left here walking (twice)
On them long, hot, summer days.

Well, Old Reilly he's a long-gone (twice)
On them long, hot, summer days.

Alternate Chorus:
Old Reilly gone like a turkey through the corn,
  here Rattler, here, (twice)

Well, Old Reilly walked the water (twice)
On them long, hot summer days.

Second Alternate Chorus:
Old Reilly gone with his long clothes on,
  here Rattler, here. (twice)

Tramp! Tramp! Tramp!
George F. Root

```
        G
In the prison cell I sit,
            C            G
Thinking, mother, dear, of you,
                        A7       D7
And our bright and happy home so far away,
        G
And the tears they fill my eyes
        C        G
'Spite of all that I can do,
        C         D7          G
Though I try to cheer my comrades and be gay.
```

Chorus:

```
G
Tramp, tramp, tramp, the boys are marching,
D7
Cheer up, comrades, they will come,
        G                     C        G
And beneath the starry flag we shall breathe the air again
B7   Em    A7   D7        G
Of the free land in our own beloved home.
```

In the battle front we stood,
When their fiercest charge they made,
And they swept us off a hundred men or more,
But before we reached their lines,
They were beaten back dismayed,
And we heard the cry of vict'ry o'er and o'er.

So within the prison cell
We are waiting for the day
That shall come to open wide the iron door,
And the hollow eye grows bright,
And the poor heart almost gay,
As we think of seeing home and friends once more.

The Boston Burglar

<pre>
       D   Am   D
Oh I was born in Boston, a city you all know well,
                              Am   D
Brought up by honest parents, the truth to you I'll tell.
                              Am   D
Brought up by honest parents, and raised most tenderly,
                  G   A7   D
'Till I became a sportin' man at the age of twenty-three.
</pre>

My character was taken, and I was sent to jail,
My friends found out it was in vain, to try and set my bail:
The jury found me guilty, the clerk he wrote it down,
The judge then passed the sentence,
   I was sentenced to Charlestown.

See my aged father, standing at the bar,
Likewise my poor old mother, tearing out her hair,
Yes tearing out those old grey locks,
   while tears come pouring down,
Crying "Son, oh son, what have you done,
   to be sentenced to Charlestown?"

I was put on board an eastern train,
   one cold December day.
And every station that we passed,
   I could hear the people say;
"There goes the Boston burglar,
   in strong chains he is bound,
For some crime or another, he is going to Charlestown."

Now there's a girl in Boston, a girl that I love well,
And when I gain my freedom, along with her I will dwell,
Yes when I gain my freedom, bad company I will shun,
Likewise night-walking, rambling, and also drinking rum.

All you that have your freedom, pray keep it if you can,
And don't go 'round the streets at night
   breaking laws of God and man,
For if you do, you'll surely rue,
   and find yourself like me,
Serving up full twenty years in the penitentiary.

Another Man Done Gone

<pre>
Am
Another man done gone (3 times)
</pre>

A-from the country farm
<pre>
D   Am
Another man done gone.
</pre>

He had a long chain on, etc.

I didn't know his name, etc.

He killed another man, etc.

Another man done gone, etc.

Botany Bay

<pre>
       C   G7   C
Farewell to old England the beautiful!
       C   F   C
Farewell to my old pals as well!
                  F   G   Am
Farewell to the famous Old Baily   (whistle)
Dm   C   G7   C
Where I used to cut such a swell.
</pre>

Chorus:

<pre>
G   C   G7   C
My too-ral li Roo-lal li Laity
C   F   C
Too-ral lo Roo-lal lo Lay
Am   F   EmAm
Too-ral li Roo-lal li Laity
C   G7   C
Too-ral li Roo-lal li Lay!
</pre>

It's seven long years I been serving,
It's seven I got for to stay,
For beatin' a cop down our alley
An' takin' his truncheon away.

There's the captain what is our commandier,
The bos'n an' all the ship's crew,
The married and also the single ones
Knows what us poor convicts goes through.

It ain't that they don't give us grub enough,
It ain't that they don't give us clothes;
It's all 'cause we light-fingered gentry
Goes about with a chain on our toes.

O had I the wings of a turtle dove,
I'd spread out my pinions and fly
Into the arms of my Polly love
And on her soft bosom I'd lie.

Now all you young viscounts and duchesses
Take warning by what I do say
And mind it's all yours what you touches-es
Or you'll land down in Botany Bay.

Darlin'

```
Em                              B7 Em  B7 Em
If I'd a-known my captain was blind, Darlin', Darlin',
G                                          B7
If I'd a-known my captain was blind, Darlin', Darlin',
Em
If I'd a-known my captain was blind,
C7                        B7        Em
Wouldna gone to work 'til half past nine,
        B7 Em
    Darlin', Darlin'.
```

I asked my captain for the time of day, darlin', darlin',
    (twice)
I asked my captain for the time of day,
He got so mad he threw his watch away, darlin', darlin.'

Fight my captain and I'll land in jail, darlin', darlin',
    (twice)
Fight my captain and I'll land in jail,
Nobody 'round to go my bail, darlin', darlin'.

Told my captain he don't know my mind, darlin', darlin',
    (twice)
Told my captain he don't know my mind,
I'm a-laughin' just to keep from cryin', darlin', darlin.'

If I'd done like mama said, darlin', darlin', (twice)
If I'd done like mama said,
I'd be home in mama's bed, darlin', darlin'.

It's Almost Done

```
      C           G7
On a Monday I was arrested,
                    C
On a Tuesday locked in jail,
                            G7
On a Wednesday my trial was attested,
                        C
On a Thursday nobody to go my bail.
```

Chorus:

```
            F      C
Well it's all, almost done,
            F      G7
Well, it's all, almost done,
      .  C  F    C
Well, it's all, almost done,
      F              G7          C
And I ain't gonna see those pretty gals no more.
```

Take these stripes, stripes from off of my shoulder,
Take these chains, chains from around my leg,
Lord, these stripes, stripes they sure don't worry me —
But these chains, chains gonna kill me dead.

Long John

```
    G
One day, one day, (one day, one day)

I was walking along, (I was walking along)

I heard a little gal, (I heard a little gal)
            C7        G        C7        G
She was singing this song (she was singing this song)
        G
About Long John, (about Long John)
            C7
With his long clothes on, (with his long clothes on).
```

Chorus:

```
C7
He's Long John (he's Long John),

He's long gone (he's long gone),

Like a turkey through the corn

    (like a turkey through the corn),

With his long clothes on (with his long clothes on),

He's Long John (He's Long John),
    D7          G
He's long gone, He's long gone John.
```

Now if I had listened to what my mama said,
I'd have been sleeping in a feather bed,
But I didn't listen, I just wandered about.
Well, now I'm in jail, but I'm gettin' out.

Well hurry up gal and shut the door,
The sheriff's on my trail and I got to go.
Give me two or three minutes for to catch my wind,
Give me two or three minutes and I'm gone again.

Now Long John had a pair of shoes,
Strangest pair of shoes that you ever did see,
Had a heel in front and a heel behind,
And you couldn't quite tell if he's a-comin' or gwine.

Now Long John's gone to heaven I know,
And I'm sure he'll get thru the golden door,
With a heel in front and a heel behind,
The devil can't tell if he's comin' or going.

Portland County Jail

D   A7
I'm a stranger to your city and my name is Patty Flynn,
                                           D
I got drunk the other night and the coppers run me in,
                                         G
I had no money to pay my fine, no one to go my bail,
   A7   D
So I'm stuck for ninety days in the Portland County Jail.

Now the only true friend I had was happy sailor Jack,
He told me all the lies he know
    and all the safes he'd cracked,
He'd cracked 'em in Seattle
    and he'd robbed the Western Mail,
T'would freeze the blood of an honest man
    in the Portland County Jail.

Oh, what a crowd of devils no one ever saw,
Robbers, thieves, and highwaymen, breakers of the law,
They sang a song the whole night long,
    the curses fell like hail,
I'll bless the day that takes me 'way
    from the Portland County Jail.

The only true friend I had was officer McGurk,
He called me a lazy loafer, a no-good, shiftless shirk,
Then I got tight one Saturday night,
    he turn me in the can,
And now you see he's made of me a honest working man.

Take This Hammer

        C   G7
Take this hammer, carry it to the captain
                              C
Take this hammer, carry it to the captain,
                              F
Take this hammer, carry it to the captain
        C   G7   C
Tell him I'm a-gone, tell him I'm gone.

If he asks you, was I running (3 times)
Tell him I was flying.

If he asks you, was I laughing (3 times)
Tell him I was crying.

I don't want no cornbread and 'lasses (3 times)
It hurts my pride.

Sam Hall

         Am   Dm   Am
Oh, my name it is Sam Hall, it is Sam Hall,
                      Dm   Am . . . E7
Oh, my name it is Sam Hall, it is Sam Hall,
        Am Dm Am   E7   Am
Oh, my name it is Sam Hall, and I hate you one and all,
                  E7
You're a bunch of muckers all,
       Am
Damn your eyes, damn your eyes,
                        E7   Am
You're a bunch of muckers all, God damn your eyes.

Oh, I killed a man 'tis said, so 'tis said, etc.
Oh, I killed a man 'tis said, and I bashed his bloody head,
And I left him there for dead,
    (And I kicked him where he bled).

Oh, they took me to the quad, to the quad,
Oh, they took me to the quad,
    and they left me there, by God,
With a ball and chain and rod,

Now the preacher he did come, he did come,
Now the preacher he did come,
    and he looked so God-damn glum,
As he talked of Kingdom Come,
    (He can kiss my ruddy bum).

Oh, the sheriff he come too, he come too,
Oh, the sheriff he come too, with his little boys in blue,
Sayin', "Sam, we'll see you through,"

Oh, it's up the rope I go, up I go,
Oh, it's up the rope I go, with those bastards down below,
Sayin', "Sam, we told you so,"

I saw Nellie in the crowd, in the crowd,
I saw Nellie in the crowd,
    and she looked so stooped and bowed,
That I hollered right out loud,
    ("Hey Nellie! Ain't you proud!")
(Like to see her in her shroud.)

Let this be my parting nell, parting nell,
Let this be my parting nell, hope to see you all in Hell,
Hope to hell you sizzle well,

It's in Heaven now I dwell, now I dwell,
It's in Heaven now I dwell, and it is a bloody cell,
All the whores are down in Hell,
Damn their eyes, damn their eyes,
All the whores are down in Hell, God damn their eyes.

Poor Boy

G   D7   G   G7
When I went down to the river, poor boy,
    C   G
To see the ships go by;

My sweetheart stood on the deck of one,
            D7 G
Where she waved to me goodbye.

Chorus:
Bow down your head and cry, poor boy,
Bow down your head and cry;
Stop thinking about that woman you love,
Bow down your head and cry.

I followed her for months and months,
She offered me her hand;
We were about to be married, when
She ran off with a gamblin' man.

He came at me with a big jack-knife,
I went for him with lead,
And when the fight was over, poor boy,
He lay on the ground cold and dead.

They took me to the big jail-house,
The months and months rolled by;
The jury found me guilty, poor boy,
And the judge said, "You must die."

"Oh, do you bring me silver, poor boy,
Or do you bring me gold?"
"I bring you neither," said the man,
"I bring you a hangman't fold."

"Oh, do you bring me pardon, poor boy,
To turn me a-loose?"
"I bring you nothing," said the man,
"Except a hangman's noose."

And yet they call this justice, poor boy,
Then justice let it be!
I only killed a man who was
A-fixin' to kill me.

The Popular Wobbly

T-Bone Slim

      G   D7
I'm as mild-mannered man as can be,
                         G
And I've never done no harm as I can see.

Still on me they put a ban,
      C
And they threw me in the can,
  A7   D7   G
They go wild, simply wild over me.

They accuse me of rascality,
But I can't see why they always pick on me,
I'm as gentle as a lamb
But they take me for a ram,
They go wild, simply wild over me.

Oh the "bull" he went wild over me,
And he held his gun where everyone could see,
He was breathing rather hard
When he saw my union card —
He went wild, simply wild over me.

Then the judge he went wild over me,
And I plainly saw we never could agree,
So I let "his Nibs" obey
What his conscience had to say,
He went wild, simply wild over me.

Oh the jailer he went wild over me,
And he locked me up and threw away the key —
It seems to be the rage
So they keep me in a cage,
They go wild, simply wild over me.

They go wild, simply wild over me,
I'm referring to the bedbug and the flea,
They disturb my slumber deep
And I murmur in my sleep,
They go wild, simply wild over me.

Will the roses grow wild over me,
When I'm gone into the land that is to be?
When my soul and body part
In the stillness of my heart,
Will the roses grow wild over me?

Old Hannah

G
Won't you go down, old Hannah?
C   G
Well, well, well.
C   G
Won't you rise no more!
C   G
Won't you rise no more!
                C7
Won't you go down, old Hannah?
        G
Won't you rise no more!

Well, if you rise in the morning,
Well, well, well.
Bring Judgement Day. (twice)
If you rise in the morning,
Bring Judgement Day.

Well, I looked at my partner, etc.
He was almost dead. (twice)
Well, I looked at my partner,
He was almost dead.

Well, I said, wake up old dead man, etc.
Help me carry my row, (twice)
Won't you wake up old dead man,
Help me carry my row.

Well, my partner looked around, etc.
This is what he said; (twice)
Well, my partner looked around,
This is what he said.

Well, you oughta been in this prison, etc.
Nineteen and ten. (twice)
They was drivin' the women
Like they do the men.

Well, now it seems like everything, etc.
Everything I do; (twice)
Well, it seems like everything
That I do is wrong.

When First Unto This Country

        C   F
When first unto this country
     G7   C
A stranger I came,
  F   Em   F
I courted a fair maid
        G7
And Nancy was her name.

I courted her for love,
Her love I didn't obtain,
Do you think I've any reason
Or right to complain?

I rode to see my Nancy,
I rode both day and night,
I courted dearest Nancy,
My own heart's true delight.

I rode to see my Nancy,
I rode both night and day,
Till I noticed a stallion
Both white-looking and gray.

The sheriff's men had followed
And overtaken me.
They carted me away
To the penitentiary.

They opened up the door
And then they shoved me in;
They shaved off my hair
And they cleared off my chin.

They beat me and they banged me,
They fed me on dry beans,
Till I wished to my own heart
I'd never been a thief.

With my hands in my pockets,
My cap set on so bold,
And my coat of all colors
Like Jacob's coat of old.

Midnight Special

G   C
Well you wake up in the morning,
            G
Hear the ding dong ring,
                D7
You go a-marching to the table,
           G
See the same damn thing;
            C
Well, it's on a one table,
            G
Knife, a fork and a pan,
                D7
And if you say anything about it,
           G
You're in trouble with the man.

Chorus:

            C
Let the midnight special
            G
Shine her light on me;
            D7
Let the midnight special
C   D7   G
Shine her ever loving light on me.

If you ever go to Houston,
You better walk right;
You better not stagger,
You better not fight;
Sheriff Benson will arrest you,
He'll carry you down,
And if the jury finds you guilty,
Penitentiary bound.

Yonder come little Rosie,
How in the world do you know,
I can tell her by her apron,
And the dress she wore.
Umbrella on her shoulder,
Piece of paper in her hand,
She goes a-marching to the captain,
Says I want my man.

THE BLUES AIN'T NOTHIN'

Back Water Blues

      D
Well it rained five days and the sky was dark as night,
      G   D
Yes, it rained five days and the sky was dark as night.
      A7   G7   D
There's trouble in the lowlands tonight.

I got up one morning,
    I couldn't even get out of my door (twice)
That was enough trouble to make a poor boy
    wonder where to go.

I went and stood up on a high old lonesome hill (twice)
I did all I could to look down on the house
    where I used to live.

It thundered and lightninged,
    and the wind began to blow (twice)
There were thousands of poor people
    didn't have no place to go.

Betty And Dupree

D   A7   G7   D
Betty told Dupree, "I want a diamond ring,"
G7   D
Betty told Dupree, "I want a diamond ring."
A7   D
Dupree told Betty, "I'll give you most anything."

He said, "Lie down, little Betty,
    see what tomorrow brings," (twice)
"It may bring sunshine, may bring you
    that diamond ring."

Then he got his pistol, went to the jewelry store, (twice)
Killed a policeman and he wounded four or five more.

Then he went to the post office
    to get his evening mail, oh, babe.
Went to the post office to get his evening mail.
Sheriff caught poor Dupree
    and put him in that old Atlanta jail.

Dupree's mother said to Betty,
    "Looka here what you done done."
She said to Betty, "See what you done done," oh, babe.
"Made my boy rob and steal, now he is gonna be hung."

"Give my daddy my clothes—poor Betty,
    give her my shoes," oh, babe.
"Give my daddy my clothes, give my baby, Betty, my shoes.
If anybody asks you, say I died
    with the heart-breaking blues."

Sail on, sail on, sail on, Dupree, sail on. (twice)
You don't mind sailing, you'll be gone so doggone long.

Bottle Up And Go

      C
She may be old, ninety years,
                       C7
But she ain't too old to shift them gears.

Chorus:

           F7   C
You got to bottle up and go, got to bottle up and go,
       G7   F7   C
All you high power women, all got to bottle up and go.

Well, a nickel is a nickel and a dime is a dime,
You shake yours and I'll shake mine.

I'm so glad the world's round like a ball,
There's enough pretty women here for us all.

When God made a woman, well he made her
    mighty funny,
Made the stuff around her lips taste just like honey.

Brown's Ferry Blues

E   E7
Hard luck poppa, a-countin' his toes,
        A7
You can smell his feet wherever he goes,
E   B7
Lord, Lord, and he's got those Brown's Ferry Blues.
E   E7
Hard luck poppa done lost his stuff,
        A7
The trouble with him he's played too rough.
E   B7 E
Lord, Lord, and he's got those Brown's Ferry Blues.

Two old maids a-sitting in the sand,
Each one wishing that the other was a man.
Lord, Lord, got those Brown's Ferry Blues
Two old maids done lost their style,
If you want to be lucky you got to smile.
Lord, Lord, got those Brown's Ferry Blues.

Early to bed and early to rise,
And your girl goes out with other guys.
Lord, Lord, got those Brown's Ferry Blues
If you don't believe me try it yourself,
Well I tried it and I got left.
Lord, Lord, got those Brown's Ferry Blues.

Hardluck poppa standing in the rain,
If the world was corn he couldn't buy grain.
Lord, Lord, got those Brown's Ferry Blues
Hardluck poppa standing in the snow,
His knees knock together but he's raring to go.
Lord, Lord, got those Brown's Ferry Blues.

Alberta

```
    Am          F7        Am
Alberta, let your hair hang low
    C           G7        C
Alberta, let your hair hang low.
C7  F           Em  E7        Am  C7 F7
I'll give you more gold than your apron can hold,
Fm    C    A7  D7 G7   C
If you just let your hair hang low.
```

Alberta, what's on your mind?
Alberta, what's on your mind?
You keep me worried, you keep me bothered all the time.
Alberta, what's on your mind?

Alberta, don't you treat me unkind,
Alberta, don't you treat me unkind.
Oh, my heart is sad 'cause I want you so bad.
Alberta, don't you treat me unkind.

All Night Long

Chorus:

```
C      F         C
All night long, all night long,
       G           C
All night long, from midnight on.
```

Verses:

```
C7          F
Down in the depot (down in the depot),
            C
Ready to go (ready to go),
              G7
If the train don't come (if the train don't come),
                      C
Something's wrong down the road
```

(something's wrong down the road).

If I live
And don't get killed,
I'll make my home
In Louisville.
In Louisville, in Louisville,
If I live and don't get killed.

I'd rather be dead
And in my grave,
Than in this old town
Treated this way.

If anyone asks you
Who wrote this song,
Tell 'em it was me
And I'll sing it all night long.

Worried Man Blues

```
  G
It takes a worried man to sing a worried song.
  C                                    G
It takes a worried man to sing a worried song.
```

It takes a worried man to sing a worried song.
```
          D7                      G
I'm worried now but I won't be worried long.
```

I went across the river, and I lay down to sleep (3 times)
When I woke up, had shackles on my feet.

Twenty nine links of chain around my leg (3 times)
And on each link, an initial of my name.

I asked that judge, tell me, what's gonna be my fine
   (3 times)
Twenty-one years on the Rocky Mountain line.

The train arrived, sixteen coaches long (3 times)
The girl I love, she's on that train and gone.

I looked down the track, as far as I could see (3 times)
A little bitty hand, was waving after me.

If anyone should ask you, who made up this song
   (3 times)
Tell 'em it was me, and I sing it all day long.

Sporting Life Blues

```
        E          E7
I got a letter from my home,
          A7              Am
Most of my friends are dead and gone.
                 E      B7          E
That old night life, that sporting life is killing me.
```

My mother used to say to me,
"So young and foolish that I can't see."
Ain't got no mother, my sister and brother
   won't talk to me.

I've been a liar and a cheater too,
Spent all my money on booze and you.
That old night life, that sportin' life is killin' me.

I've been a gambler and a cheater too,
But now it's come my turn to lose,
That old sportin' life has got the best hand,
   what can I do?

There ain't but one thing that I've done wrong,
Lived this sportin' life, my friend, too long;
I say it's no good, please believe me, please
   leave it alone.

I'm gettin' tired of runnin' 'round,
Think I will marry and settle down;
That old night life, that sportin' life is killing me.

Cocaine Bill And Morphine Sue

G
Cocaine Bill and Morphine Sue
A7
Strolling down the avenue two by two.

Refrain:

D7   G
Oh, honey, won't you have a little *sniff* on me,
     D7 G
Have a *sniff* on me.

Said Sue to Bill, "It'll do no harm,
If we both just have a little shot in the arm."

Said Bill to Sue, "I can't refuse,
'Cause there's no more kick in this darned ol' booze."

So they walked down First and they turned up Main,
Looking for a place they could buy cocaine.

They came to a drugstore full of smoke,
Where they saw a little sign sayin', "No more coke."

Now in the graveyard on the hill,
Lies the body of Cocaine Bill.

And in a grave right by his side,
Lies the body of his cocaine bride.

All o' you cokies is a-gonna be dead
If you don't stop a-*sniff*ing that stuff in your head.

Now where they went, no one can tell
It might have been Heaven or it might have been *sniff*.

Easy Rider

A   A7
Easy rider, just see what you have done; oh, Lord,
D7   A
Easy rider, just see what you have done;
A7 D7   A
Well, you made me love you, now your gal has come.
     B7 F7 E7 A
Well, it's hey, hey, hey, hey, hey.

If I was a catfish, swimmin' in the deep blue sea,
If I was a catfish, swimmin' in the deep blue sea,
I would swim across the ocean, bring by baby back to me.
Well, it's hey, hey, hey, hey, hey.

I'm goin' away, rider, and I won't be back till fall,
I'm goin' away, rider, and I won't be back till fall,
And if I find me a good man, I won't be back at all.
Well, it's hey, etc.

Good Morning Blues

   C
Good morning, blues,
         C7
Blues how do you do?
   F7
Good morning, blues,
         C
Blues how do you do?
    D7
Well I'm doing all right,
   F7   C
Good morning, how are you?

I lay down last night,
Turning from side to side,
Yes, I was turning
From side to side.
I was not sick,
I was just dissatisfied.

I got up this morning,
Blues walkin' 'round my bed,
Up this morning,
Blues walkin' 'round my bed.
Went to eat my breakfast,
Blues was all in my bread.

I sent for you yesterday,
Here you come a-walkin' today,
Sent for you yesterday,
Here you come a-rackin' today.
You got your mouth wide open—
You don't know what to say.

Hesitation Blues

    G   F#   G   F#
Well, standing on the corner with a dollar in my hand,
G   F#   G   F# F
Lookin' for a woman who's looking for a man,

Refrain:

    C C7 G G+Bb
Tell me how long, do I have to wait,
   D7   g— e#— d—c—bb—g G
Can I get you now, or must I hesitate?

Well, the eagle on the dollar say, "In God we trust,"
Woman wants a man, she wants to see a dollar first,

Well, pussy ain't nothin' but meat on the bone,
You can ——— it you can ——— it you can leave it alone,

Well, you hesitate by one, and you hesitate by two,
Angels up in heaven singing hesitatin' blues,

St. James Infirmary

    Am   E7   Am
It was down in old Joe's barroom.
    Dm   G7   C   E7
On the corner by the square,
    Am   E7   Am
The drinks were served as usual
         E7   Am
And the usual crowd was there.

Now on my left stood big Joe McKennedy,
And his eyes were bloodshot red,
And he looked at the gang around him,
And these were the very words he said.

I went down to the St. James Infirmary,
I saw my baby there,
She was stretched out on a long, white table,
So cold, so pale, and fair.

Let her go, let her go, God bless her,
Wherever she may be.
She can ramble this wide world over,
And never find another man like me.

Now when I die please bury me,
In my hightop Stetson hat,
Just put a twenty dollar gold piece on my watch chain,
So the gang will know I'm standing pat.

I want six crap shooters for my pall bearers,
And a chorus girl to sing me a song,
Put a jazz band on my hearse wagon,
Just to raise hell as we roll along.

And now that you have heard my story,
I'll take another shot of booze,
If anyone should happen to ask you,
Well, I've got the gambler's blues.

Corinna

E   A7
Corinna, Corinna
            E
Where you been so long?
        B7
Corinna, Corinna
            E
Where you been so long?

Corinna, Corinna, why'd you leave me alone?
Corinna, Corinna, got no place to call my own.

Corinna, Corinna, bye-bye, so long,
Bye-bye, Corinna, bye-bye, so long.

Corinna, Corinna, bye-bye, so long,
I'll have the blues, Corinna, long as you stay gone.

Things About Comin' My Way

         E
Ain't got no money,

Can't buy no grub,
        A7
Back-bone and navel
        E
Doing the belly rub.

Refrain:

E
Now after all my hard trav'ling,
        B7   E
Things about comin' my way.

The pot was empty,
The cupboard bare
I said, "Mama,
What's going on here?"

The rent was due,
The light was out
I said, "Mama,
What's it all about?"

Sister was sick,
The doctor couldn't come
'Cause we couldn't pay him
The proper sum.

Cocaine Blues

C   C7
Yonder comes my baby all dressed in blue.
F   F7
Hey baby, what you gonna do?
C   G7   C
Cocaine all around my brain.

Chorus:

E7
Hey, baby, won't you come here quick
F   F7
This old cocaine is makin' me sick
C   G7   C
Cocaine all around my brain.

Yonder comes my baby all dressed in white,
Hey, baby, gonna stay all night?

Rocks And Gravel

```
A7                          E      E7
Rocks and gravel makes a solid road,
A7                          E
Rocks and gravel makes a solid road,
    B7          A7          E  A7  E
Takes a do right woman satisfy my soul.
```

Well I'm going out West just to see my pony run, (twice)
If I win any money I'm gonna send my gal some.

Here's a dollar Momma, made it in the rain, (twice)
It's a hard old dollar—made it just the same.

That's your tone Daddy, every time you come, (twice)
I ain't got no money but I'll soon have some.

A man in the army wants a furlough home, (twice)
He said, "About face rookie, you ain't been here long."

A man in the army eatin' out of a trough, (twice)
Just waiting for Uncle Sam soon to pay him off.

I got a girl in the country and she won't come to town,
    (twice)
Got one in Louisiana and she's waterbound.

I can't see how can you treat your Daddy mean, (twice)
When you lays all night and your Daddy's on benzedrine.

Evil-Hearted Man

```
E
Well, I woke up this morning,
                      E7
I was feeling mighty bad,
                 E
Well, my baby said, "Good morning,"
      A7
Hell, it made me so mad,
```

Chorus:

```
      E
Because I'm evil, well, evil-hearted me,
    B7                       E
I am so doggone evil, evil as a man can be.
```

Yeh, she made my breakfast,
And she brought it to my bed,
Well, I took a sip of coffee,
Threw the cup at her head,

Now I don't even care,
If my baby leaves me flat,
'Cause I got forty-leven others,
If it comes to that,

I Know You Rider

```
C                Bb    F     G
I know you rider, gonna miss me when I'm gone,
C                Bb    F     G
I know you rider, gonna miss me when I'm gone,
                      F
Gonna miss your little momma
       G7          C
from a-rolling in your arms.
```

I'm goin' down the road
    where I can get more decent care, (twice)
Goin' back to my used-to-be rider
    'cause I don't feel welcome here.

I know my baby sure is bound to love me some, (twice)
'Cause he throws his arms around me
    like a circle 'round the sun.

I laid down last night tryin' to take a rest, (twice)
But my mind kept rambling
    like the wild geese in the West.

I'm goin' down to the river,
    set in my rocking chair, (twice)
And if the blues don't find me,
    gonna rock away from here.

Lovin' you baby, just as easy as rollin' off a log, (twice)
But if I can't be your woman,
    I sure ain't gonna be your dog.

I will cut your wood, baby, I will make your fire, (twice)
And I will tote your water, baby, from that Fresno Bar.

Sun gonna shine in my back yard some day, (twice)
And the wind gonna rise up, baby, blow my blues away.

Kansas City Blues

```
G
River is deep and the river is wide,
                      G7
Gal I love is on the other side.
```

Chorus:

```
        C7
I'm gonna move to Kansas City,
G
Move to Kansas City, I'm gonna
D7        C7                      G
Move, honey baby, where they don't 'low you.
```

If I was a catfish swimmin' in the sea,
All them pretty gals would come swimmin' after me.

If you don't like my peaches, don't you shake my tree,
I like my woman, sure, and she likes me.

When Things Go Wrong With You

From the singing of Big Bill Broonzy

        E
I love you, baby, I ain't gonna lie,
        A7   E
Without you, honey, I just can't be satisfied,

Refrain:

E   B7
'Cause when things go wrong, so wrong with you,
          E A7 E
Well, it hurts me too.

So, run here, baby, put your hand in mine,
Got something to tell you that will change your mind,

I want you, baby, just to understand,
Don't want to be your boss, just want to be your man,

When you go home, you don't get along,
Come back to me, baby, where I live, that's your home.

I love you, baby, you know it's true,
I wouldn't mistreat you, baby,
    nothing in this world like you,

Tell Old Bill

A   Bm   A   E   A   Bm
Tell old Bill, when he comes home this morning,
A   Bm   A   Bm   A C♯m
Tell old Bill, when he comes home this evening,
A   Bm   A   E
Tell old Bill, when he comes home,
                A   Bm   A E
he better leave them downtown gals alone,
     A   Bm   A E   A
This morning, this evening, so soon.

Bill left by the alley gate this morning,
Bill left by the alley gate this evening,
Bill left by the alley gate,
    and old Sal says, "Now don't be late."
This morning, this evening, so soon.

Bill's wife was a-baking bread this morning,
Bill's wife was a-baking bread this evening,
Bill's wife was a-baking bread,
    when she found out that her Bill was dead,
This morning, this evening, so soon.

Oh no, that cannot be this morning,
Oh no, that cannot be this evening,
Oh no, that cannot be,
    they killed my Bill in the first degree,
This morning, this evening, so soon.

They brought Bill home in a hurry-up wagon this morning,
They brought Bill home in a hurry-up wagon this evening,
They brought Bill home in a hurry-up wagon,
    poor dead Bill how his toes were a-dragging,
This morning, this evening, so soon.

Oh no, that cannot be this morning,
Oh no, that cannot be this evening,
Oh no, that cannot be,
    they shot my Bill in the third degree,
This morning, this evening, so soon.

Tell old Bill when he comes home this morning,
Tell old Bill when he comes home this evening,
Tell old Bill when he comes home,
    to leave them downtown gals alone,
This morning, this evening, so soon.

Salty Dog Blues

Chorus:

F   D7
Let me be your salty dog,
   G7
Or I won't be your man at all,
C7   F
Honey, let me be your salty dog.

Verses:

F   D7
Standing on the corner with the low-down blues,
   G7
A great big hole in the bottom of my shoes,
C7   F
Honey, let me be your salty dog.

Look here, Sal, I know you,
With a low-down slipper and a brogan shoe,
Honey, let me be your salty dog.

We pulled the trigger and the gun said go,
The shot rung over in Mexico,
Honey, let me be your salty dog.

Shorty George

        C   C7
Well-a, Shorty George, he ain't no friend of mine,
        F   C
Well-a, Shorty George, he ain't no friend of mine,
        G   G7   C
He's taken all the women and left the men behind.

Well, my papa died when I was just a lad,
My papa died when I was just a lad,
And ever since that day, I been to the bad.

Got a letter from my baby, couldn't read from crying,
   (twice)
She said my mama weren't dead yet,
     but she was slowly dying.

Well, I took my mama to the burying ground, (twice)
I never knowed I loved her till the coffin sound.

Yes, I went down to the graveyard,
     peeped in my mama's face, (twice)
"Ain't it hard to see you in this lonesome place?"

Stealin', Stealin'

Chorus:

G   G7   C
Stealin', stealin', pretty mama don't you tell on me,
Cm G   D7   G
I'm stealin' back to my same old used to be.

Verses:

      G
Now put your arms around me like a circle 'round the sun,
  C
I want you to love me, mama, like my easy rider done,
                   G   C   G
If you don't believe I love you, look what a fool I've been,
                    C   G   D7   G
If you don't believe I'm sinkin', look what a hole I'm in.

The woman I'm a-lovin', she's just my height and size,
She's a married woman, come to see me sometime;
If you don't believe, etc.

Step It Up And Go

G
Used to have a gal, she was little and low,
                      G7
She used to love me, but she don't no more.

Chorus:

      C7
She had to step it up and go,
   D7   C7
She couldn't stay there, I declare,
             G
She had to step it up and go!

Out with a woman, havin' some fun,
In come a man with a great big gun,
I had to step it up and go, etc.

Jumped in the river, tried to get across,
Jumped on an alligator, thought it was a horse,
I had to step it up and go, etc.

Two old maids, sittin' in the sand,
Each one wishin' the other was a man,
So step it up and go, etc.

Take Your Fingers Off It

Chorus:

C
Take your fingers off it, and don't you dare touch it,
   D7   G7   C
You know it don't belong to you.
                                  A7
Take your fingers off it, and don't you dare touch it,
   D7
You know it don't belong to you.

Verses:

G7   C   G7
You know it's sad to see a woman, an extra good 'n',
F7   F♯dim
Holdin' back on her sugar puddin',
C   A7
Take your fingers off it, and don't you dare touch it,
   D7   G   C
You know it don't belong to you.

Two old maids a-laying in bed,
One turned over toward the other and said,
Take your fingers off it, don't you dare touch it,
You know it don't belong to you.

A nickel is a nickel, a dime is a dime,
A house full of children, none of them's mine.
Take your fingers off it, etc.

I may be little and I may be thin,
But I'm an awful good daddy for the shape I'm in.
Take your fingers off it, etc.

I never been to heaven but I been told
St. Peter taught the angels how to jelly roll.
Take your fingers off it, etc.

Big fish, little fish swimming in the water,
Come back here, man, and marry my daughter.
Take your fingers off it, etc.

There's just one thing that I could never understand,
Why a bow-legged woman likes a knock-kneed man.
Take your fingers off it, etc.

Talking Blues

       G   C
If you want to get to heaven, let me tell you what to do,
       D7   G
You gotta grease your feet in a little mutton stew.
G7   C
Slide right out of the devil's hand,
   D7   G
And ease over to the Promised Land.
     C   D7 G C D7 G
Take it easy!   Go greasy!

I was down in the holler just a-settin' on a log,
My finger on the trigger and my eye on a hog;
I pulled that trigger and the gun went "zip",
And I grabbed that hog with all of my grip.
'Course I can't eat hog eyes, but I love chitlins.

Down in the hen house on my knees,
I thought I heard a chicken sneeze,
But it was only the rooster sayin' his prayers,
Thankin' the Lord for the hens upstairs.
Rooster prayin', hens a-layin'.
Little pullets just pluggin' away best they know how.

Mama's in the kitchen fixin' the yeast,
Poppa's in the bedroom greasin' his feet,
Sister's in the cellar squeezin' up the hops,
Brother's at the window just a-watchin' for the cops.
Drinkin' home brew—makes you happy.

Now, I'm just a city dude a-livin' out of town,
Everybody knows me as Moonshine Brown;
I make the beer, and I drink the slop,
Got nine little orphans that call me Pop.
I'm patriotic—raisin' soldiers, Red Cross nurses.

Ain't no use me workin' so hard,
I got a gal in the rich folks' yard.
They kill a chicken, she sends me the head.
She thinks I'm workin', I'm a-layin' up in bed.
Just dreamin' about her. Havin' a good time. . .
   two other women. . .

Number Twelve Train

       E
Number Twelve train took my baby.
  A7   E
  I could not keep from cryin'.
E7   A
Number Twelve took my baby,
            E
  I could not help from cryin'.
          B7   A7   E
Sometimes I'm not myself; sometimes I think I'm dyin'.

She left me all night long, I could not help myself. (twice)
I thought she was loving me;
  I found she had somebody else.

I may be wrong, but I'll be right some day. (twice)
'Cause the next gal I get will have to do what poppa say.

Poor Man Blues

   C   Am   Dm7
I never had a barrel of money,
G7   C
I never had a ruby red ring.
       C7   F
I'm gonna die and go to heaven, Lord,
Fmaj7   F7
There I'll set and sing.

Refrain:

Gm6 A7 D7
Lord, this song ain't nothin',
A7   D7♭5   C
No, this song ain't nothin'
      D7   Fmaj7 F7   C(6)
But a poor man singin' the blues.

I don't need a barrel of money,
I can't use a ruby red ring.
All I want is you, my honey,
To set and listen to me sing.

I'm goin' on down to the station,
Gonna catch me a fast-moving train.
I'm goin' back to East Virginia,
Never leavin' home again.

The first time I seen the boll weevil
He was a settin' on the square.
The next time I seen the boll weevil,
He had his whole damn family there.

The climate 'round here doesn't suit my clothing,
And the water 'round here tastes like turpentine.
I'm goin' home to East Virginia
Where the water tastes like ever-lovin' wine.

I'm A Stranger Here

C
Ain't it hard to stumble
                   C7
When you got no place to fall?
       F7
Ain't it hard to stumble,
                C
When you got no place to fall?
         G7
In this whole wide world
         C
I got no place at all.

Chorus:

  Gdim   G7
I'm a stranger here,
C
A stranger ev'rywhere.
               G7
I would go home, but honey
        C
I'm a stranger there.

Hitch up my pony,
Saddle up my black mare, } (twice)
I'm gonna find me a fair shake
In this world somewhere.

Baby took the Katy,
Left me a mule to ride, } (twice)
When the train pulled out
That mule laid down and died.

BLOW THE MAN DOWN

Songs of sailing ships and fishermen, and sailors on the deep blue sea....

Pay Me My Money Down

Chorus:

D
Pay me, oh pay me,
      A7
Pay me my money down,

Pay me or go to jail!
          D
Pay me my money down.

Verses:

D
I thought I heard the captain say,
      A7
Pay me my money down,

"Tomorrow is our sailing day,"
          D
Pay me my money down.

The very next day we cleared the bar,
Pay me my money down,
He knocked me down with the end of a spar,
Pay me my money down.

I wish I was Mr. Howard's son, etc.
Sit in the house and drink good rum, etc.

I wish I was Mr. Steven's son, etc.
Sit on the bank and watch the work done, etc.

Fire Down Below

Chorus:

      C   F
There is fire in the lower hold,
      C   G7
There's fire down below,
C   F
Fire in the main well,
     C   G7 C
The captain didn't know.

There is fire in the forepeek,
Fire in the main,
Fire in the windlass,
Fire in the chain.

There is fire in the foretop,
Fire down below,
Fire in the chain-plates,
The boats'ain didn't know.

There is fire up aloft,
There is fire down below,
Fire in the galley,
The cook he didn't know

Reuben Ranzo

      G   D G
Oh, pity Reuben Ranzo!
D
Ranzo, boys, Ranzo!
      G   D G
Oh, poor old Reuben Ranzo!
     D   G
Ranzo, boys, Ranzo!

Now Ranzo was no sailor,
Ranzo, boys, Ranzo!
But he shipped on board a whaler.
Ranzo, boys, Ranzo!

And he could not do his duty, Ranzo, etc.
So they took him to the gangway. Ranzo, etc.

For Ranzo was a tailor,
But Ranzo was no sailor.

They gave him nine-and-thirty,
Yes, lashes nine-and-thirty.

The captain being a good man,
Took him into his cabin.

He gave him wine and water,
Rube kissed the captain's daughter.

To fit him for his station,
They taught him navigation.

Though Ranzo was no sailor,
He's first mate of that whaler.

Round The Bay Of Mexico

       E
Then 'round the Bay of Mexico,
       A   E
Way, oh Susianna;
A G$\sharp$m F$\sharp$m   B7
Mexico is the place that I belong in,
E   B7 E
'Round the Bay of Mexico.

Those Nassau girls they love me so,
Way, Oh Susianna,
'Cause I don't say everything that I know,
'Round the Bay of Mexico.

When I was a young man in my prime,
I loved those young gals two at a time.

Nassau gals ain't got no comb,
Comb their hair with a whipper backbone.

Goodbye girls of Nassau town,
I'm bound away for the fishing ground.

Hullabaloo Belay

Dm
Me mother kept a boarding house,

Hullabaloo belay, Hullabaloo bela belay.

And all the boarders were out to sea,
A7   Dm
Hullabaloo belay.

A fresh young fellow named Shallo Brown,
Hullabaloo, etc.
Followed me mother all 'round the town,
Hullabaloo, etc.

Me father said, "Look her, me boy,"
To which he quickly made reply,

One day when father was in the "Crown,"
Me mother ran off with Shallo Brown,

Me father slowly pined away,
Because me mother come back the very next day,

Jack Is Every Inch A Sailor

Chorus:

C   G7
Jack is every inch a sailor;
                    C
He'll see a pretty girl and hail 'er.
                    G7
He'll vow his love will never fail 'er,
                              C
Then go sailing with his heart still free.

Verses:

        C
When Jack steps down the gang-plank
                              G7
    there's a quiver through the town,

And all the girls past seventeen
                    C
    come gaily running down.

They know that night that one of them
                    G7
    has happiness in store,

And each believes that if it's her,
                    C
    he'll never leave the shore!

He's got a prize from ev'ry port to win a woman's heart;
Brocade and silk and lace and pearls and oriental art.
Somewhere he'll meet a girl whose kiss
    can keep him on the shore;
But while he looks for her,
    he'll kiss at least a thousand more!

Jack Was Every Inch A Sailor

            D
Now, 'twas twenty-five or thirty years
                              A7
Since Jack first saw the light;

He came into this world of woe
                    D
One dark and stormy night.

He was born on board his father's ship
                    A7
As she was lying to,

'Bout twenty-five or thirty miles
                    D
Southeast of Bacalhao.

Chorus:

        A7
Jack was every inch a sailor,
        D
Five and twenty years a whaler,
        A7
Jack was every inch a sailor,
                              D
He was born upon the deep blue sea.

When Jack grew up to be a man,
He went to Labrador.
He fished in India'n Harbour
Where his father fished before.
On his returning in the fog,
He met a heavy gale,
And Jack was swept into the sea
And swallowed by a whale.

The whale went straight for Baffin's Bay
'Bout ninety knots an hour,
And ev'ry time he'd blow a spray,
He'd send it in a shower.
"Oh, now," says Jack unto himself
"I must see what he's about."
He caught the whale all by the tail
And turned him inside out.

Shenandoah

```
      D              G       D
Oh, Shenandoah, I long to see you,
   G   A7         D
Away, you rolling river.
   G           F♯m    Bm
Oh, Shenandoah, I long to see you,
   D
Away, I'm bound away, 'cross
   G      D
The wide Missouri.
```

O, Shenandoah, I love your daughter,
Away, etc.
O, Shenandoah, I love your daughter,
Away, we're bound, etc.

O, Shenandoah, I long to see you,
O, Shenandoah, I'll not deceive you,

O, seven years, I've been a rover,
For seven years I've been a rover,

South Australia

```
     C              F  C
In South Australia, I was born,
F     C   F   C
Heave away, haul away,
                  G        Am
In South Australia 'round Cape Horn,
      C             G7 C
We're bound for South Australia.
```

Chorus:
```
               F   C
Haul away your rolling king,
F     C   F   C
Heave away, haul away,
                    Am
Haul away, oh hear me sing,
      C             G7 C
We're bound for South Australia.
```

As I walked out one morning fair, etc.
'Twas there I met Miss Nancy Blair, etc.

I shook her up, I shook her down
I shook her round and round the town.

There ain't but one thing grieves my mind,
To leave Miss Nancy Blair behind.

And as we wallop around Cape Horn,
You'll wish to God you'd never been born.

Blow Ye Winds In The Morning

```
      F          C
Tis advertised in Boston,
      F
New York and Buffalo,
      B♭    C7     F
Five hundred brave Americans,
   G7          C7
A whaling for to go.
```

Chorus:

```
             F
Singing Blow ye winds in the morning,
```

And blow ye winds, high-o!
```
B♭              F
Clear away your running gear,
   C7              F
And blow, ye winds, high-o!
```

They send you to New Bedford,
That famous whaling port,
And give you to some land-sharks -
To board and fit you out.

They send you to a boarding-house,
There for a time to dwell;
The thieves there they are thicker
Than the other side of hell!

They tell you of the clipper-ships,
A-going in and out,
And say you'll take five hundred sperm,
Before you're six months out.

It's now we're out to sea my boys,
The wind begins to blow,
One half of the watch is sick on deck
And the other half below.

The skipper's on the quarter-deck
A-squinting at the sails,
When up aloft the look-out
Sights a school of whales.

Now clear away the boats, my boys,
And after him we'll travel,
But if you get too near his fluke,
He'll kick you to the devil!

Now we've got him turned up,
We tow him alongside,
We over with our blubber hooks
And rob him of his hide.

Ten Thousand Miles Away

Bb
Sing ho! for a brave and a gallant ship,
Eb
And a stiff and fav'ring breeze,
Bb
With a bully crew and a captain true
C7m
To carry me over the seas.
F7 Bb
To carry me over the seas, my boys,
Eb
To my true love far away,
Bb
Who took a trip on a Government ship
C7   F7   Bb
Ten thousand miles away!

Chorus:

Bb
Then blow, ye winds, heigh ho!
Eb
A-roving I will go,
Bb
I'll stay no more on England's shore,
C7m
To hear the music play;
F   Bb
I'm off on the morning train
Eb
To cross the raging main,
Bb
I'm taking a trip on a Government ship
F7   Bb
Ten thousand miles away.

My true love she was beautiful,
My true love she was young,
Her eyes were like the diamonds bright,
And silvery was her tongue.
And silvery was her tongue, my boys,
Though now she's far away,
She's taken a trip on a Government ship
Ten thousand miles away.

Oh, dark and dismal was the day
When last I seen my Meg,
She'd a Government band around each hand,
And another one round her leg;
And another one round her leg, my boys,
As the big ship left the bay—
"Adieu," said she, "remember me,
Ten thousand miles away!"

Little Sally Racket

F
Little Sally Racket,
Haul 'em away,
Shipped aboard a packet,
Haul 'em away,
And she never did regret it,
Haul 'em away,
With a haul-ey-hi-o
Haul 'em away.

Little Kitty Carson
Haul 'em away
Slept with a parson
Haul 'em away
Now she's got a little barson
Haul 'em away
With a haul-ey-hi-ho
Haul 'em away.

Little Nancy Riddle, etc.
Broke her brand new fiddle, etc.
Got a hole right up the middle, etc.

Little Nancy Tucket, etc.
Washes in a bucket, etc.
She's a whore, but doesn't look it, etc.

Little Polly Skinner, etc.
Says she's a beginner, etc.
She prefers it to her dinner, etc.
So up, boys, and win her, etc.

Little Nancy Taylor, etc.
Would never touch a sailor, etc.
Till she was harpooned by a whaler, etc.
Oh, we'll go and make her, etc.

Up me fighting cocks now, etc.
Up and split her blocks now, etc.
And we'll stretch her luff, boys, etc.

Johnny Boker

Bb
Do my Johnny Boker,
Gm   Eb
Come rock and roll me over;
Bb   Eb F Bb
Do my Johnny Boker, do!

Oh do, my Johnny Boker,
Come roll me down to Dover.
Do my Johnny Boker, do!

Do, my Johnny Boker,
The skipper is a rover, etc.

Do, my Johnny Boker,
The mate he's never sober,

Do, my Johnny Boker,
The Old Man he's a soaker,

Do, my Johnny Boker,
In London lives your lover,

Do, my Johnny Boker,
Come haul away the bowline,

Do, my Johnny Boker,
Come roll me in the clover,

Rock 'N' Row Me Over

D7
Oh, row me cross the river,
G   D
I heard a young gal say,
D7
Oh, row me to my lover,
G D7 G
One more day.

Chorus:

D7
Only one more day for Johnny,
G   D
One more day,
D7
Oh, rock 'n' row me over,
G D7 G
One more day!

Oh, row me to my lover,
Tell him I won't delay,
Soon we will be in clover,
One more day.

Oh, Johnny he's a rover,
He says he'll sail away,
He wants to leave the river,
One more day.

But stay, my John, and tarry
For just another day;
'Tis you I want to marry,
One more day.

Haul Away Joe

Am   Em
When I was a little lad,
    Dm   Em
And so my mother told me
Am   Em   Dm Em Am
Way, haul away, we'll haul away, Joe.
Am   Em
That if I did not kiss the girls
  Dm   Em
My lips would grow all mouldy.
Am   Em   Dm Em Am
Way, haul away, we'll haul away, Joe.

King Louis was the King of France
Before the revolution.
Way, haul away, etc.
But then he got his head cut off
Which spoiled his constitution.
Way, haul, etc.

Oh, once I had a German girl
And she was fat and lazy,
Then I got a Brooklyn gal,
She damn near drove me crazy.

So I got a Chinese girl
And she was kind and tender,
And she left me for a Portugee,
So young and rich and slender,

Way, haul away,
I'll sing to you of Nancy.
Way, haul away,
She's just my cut and fancy.

Oh, once I was in Ireland,
A-digging turf and praties,
But now I'm in a Yankee ship
A-hauling on sheets and braces.

The cook is in the galley,
Making duff so handy,
And the captain's in his cabin
Drinkin' wine and brandy.

Way, haul away,
The good ship is a-bowling
Way, haul away,
The sheet is now a-blowing.

Way, haul away,
We'll haul away together.
Way, haul away,
We'll haul for better weather.

Haul On The Bowline

G   D
Haul on the bowline
    Em
Our bully ship's a rollin'.
G   D
Haul on the bowline
  D7   G
The bowline haul
G   D
Haul on the bowline
               Em
The top and the main-sail bowline,
G   D
Haul on the bowline
  D7   G
The bowline haul.

Haul on the bowline,
Kitty is my darling,
Haul on the bowline,
Kitty lives at Liverpool,
Haul on the bowline,
The old man is a growlin'.
Haul on the bowline,
It's a far cry to payday.
Haul on the bowline,
So early in the morning.

Hanging Johnny

      D
Oh, they call me Hanging Johnny,
  G D
Hooray, boys, hooray,
        G D   Bm
And they say I hang for money,
  D A7 D
So hang, boys, hang.

They say I hang for money,
Hooray, boys, hooray,
But hanging is so funny,
So hang, boys, hang.

At first I hanged me daddy, etc.
And then I hanged me mommy, etc.

Oh, yes I hanged me mother, etc.
Me sister and me brother, etc.

I hanged me sister Sally, etc.
I hanged the whole damn family, etc.

A rope, a beam, a ladder, etc.
I'd hang you all together, etc.

We'll hang and haul together, etc.
We'll hang for better weather, etc.

Can't You Dance The Polka?

C   F
As I walked down on Broadway,
  G   C
One evening in July,
               F
I met a maid who asked my trade,
  G   C
"A sailor John," says I.

Chorus:

            F
Then away, you Santy,
G   C
My dear Annie,
      F
Oh, you New York gals,
G7   C
Can't you dance the polka?

To Tiffany's I took her,
I did not mind expense,
I bought her two gold earrings,
They cost me fifty cents.

Says she, "You limejuice sailor,
Now see me home you may."
But when we reached her cottage door
She unto me did say:

"My flashman, he's a Yankee,
With his hair cut short behind,
He wears a tarry jumper
And he sails the Black Ball Line."

Boney Was A Warrior

D
Boney was a warrior,
      A7
Away ay-yah!

A warrior and a terrior,
     D
John Franswah!

Boney beat the Prooshians,
Away, ay-yah!
Boney beat the Rooshians,
John Franswah!

Boney went to Moscow, etc.
Moscow was a-blazing, etc.

Boney went to Elbow,
Boney he came back,

Boney went to Waterloo,
There he got his overthrow,

They took Boney off again,
'Board the *Billy Ruffian*,

Boney he was sent away,
Way to St. Helena,

Boney broke his heart and died,
Boney broke his heart and died.

Sacramento

  D
A bully ship and a bully crew,
A7
Hoo-dah, to me hoo-dah,
  D
A bully mate and a captain, too
G   A7   D
Hoo-dah, hoo-dah day.

Chorus:

D
Then blow, boys, blow
  G   D
For Californi-o,
     Bm
There's plenty of gold
   D
So I've been told
     F#   A7   D
On the banks of the Sacramento.

Round Cape Horn in the months of snows,
Hoo-dah, to me hoo-dah,
If we get there nobody knows,
Hoo-dah, hoo-dah day.

Oh around the Horn with a mainsail set,
Around Cape Horn and we're all wringing wet.

Oh, around Cape Horn in the month of May,
Oh, around Cape Horn is a very long way.

To the Sacramento we're bound away,
To the Sacramento's a hell of a way.

Oh, a bully ship with a bully crew,
But the mate is a bastard through and through.

Ninety days to 'Frisco Bay,
Ninety days is damn good pay.

Sing and heave and heave and sing,
Heave and make them handspikes ring.

I wish to God I'd never been born,
To go a-rambling around Cape Horn.

Across The Western Ocean

     D
Oh the times are hard and the wages low,
  A   D
Amelia, where you bound to?
    G   D
The Rocky Mountains is my home,
     A   D
Across the Western Ocean.

That land of promise there you'll see,
Amelia, where you bound to?
I'm bound across that Western Sea,
It's time for us to leave her.

To Liverpool I'll take my way,
Leave her, bullies, leave her,
To Liverpool, that Yankee school,
It's time for us to leave her.

There's Liverpool Pat with his tarpaulin hat,
Amelia, where you bound to?
And Yankee John, the packet rat,
It's time for us to leave her.

Beware these packet ships, I pray,
Amelia, where you bound to?
They steal your stores and clothes away,
Across the Western Ocean.

A-Roving

D
In Amsterdam there lived a maid,

Mark well what I do say,
G   D
In Amsterdam there lived a maid
  E7   A7
And she was mistress of her trade,
  D   G   D A7 D
I'll go no more a-roving with you fair maid.

Chorus:

  G   D
A-roving, a-roving,
    E7   A7
Since roving's been my ru-i-in,
  D   G
I'll go no more a-roving
  D A7 D
With you fair maid.

Her eyes are like two stars so bright,
Mark well . . . etc.
Her eyes are like two stars so bright,
Her face is fair, her step is light;
I'll go no more a-roving . . . etc.

Her cheeks are like the rosebuds red, etc.
Her cheeks are like the rosebuds red,
There's wealth of hair upon her head; etc.

I love this fair maid as my life, etc.
I love this fair maid as my life,
And soon she'll be my little wife; etc.

And if you'd know this maiden's name, etc.
And if you'd know this maiden's name,
Why soon like mine, 'twill be the same; etc.

Lowlands

  G7   C
I dreamed a dream the other night,

Lowlands, Lowlands, away, my John,
  G   C
I dreamed a dream the other night,
  G   C
My lowlands away!

I dreamed I saw my own true love, Lowlands, etc.
I dreamed I saw my own true love, My Lowlands, etc.

She came to me all in my sleep, (twice)

And then I knew my love was dead, (twice)

Sailing Sailing

Godfrey Marks

         G
Y'heave ho! my lads, the wind blows free;
  D7
A pleasant gale is on our lee,
    G
And soon across the ocean clear,
    D   A7   D
Our gallant bark shall bravely steer.
    D7   G
But ere we part from England's shores tonight,
    D7   G
A song we'll sing for home and beauty bright.

Chorus:

Em   B7   C   G
Then here's to the sailor, and here's to the hearts so true,
                    B7
Who will think of him upon the waters blue?
G   C   G
Sailing, sailing, over the bounding main,
    D7   G   Em
For many a stormy wind shall blow
      D   A7   D7
  ere Jack comes home again;
G   C   G
Sailing, sailing, over the bounding main,
    C   B7   Em   A7
For many a stormy wind shall blow
       G   D7   G
  ere Jack comes home again.

The sailor's life is bold and free;
His home is on the rolling sea,
And never heart more true or brave,
Than he who launches on the wave.
Afar he speeds in distant climes to roam;
With jocund song he rides the sparkling foam.

The tide is flowing with the gale;
Y'heave ho! my lads, set every sail.
The harbor bar we soon shall clear,
Farewell once more to home so dear;
For when the tempest rages loud and long,
That home shall be our guiding star among.

Blood Red Roses

      C
Our boots and clothes are all in pawn,
F   Am F
Go down, you blood red roses, go down.
         C
And it's mighty drafty around Cape Horn.
F   Am F
Go down, you blood red roses, go down.
C
Oh, you pinks and posies.
F   Am F
Go down you blood red roses, go down.

You've had your advance and to sea you must go,
A-chasin' whales through the frost and the snow.

Oh my old mother, she wrote to me,
My dearest son come home from sea.

But 'round Cape Horn you've got to go,
For that is where them whalefish blow.

Just one more and that'll do,
For we're the gang to kick her through.

Blow The Man Down

Chorus:

    D   D6   D   D6
Oh blow the man down bullies, Blow the man down,
     D   D6 Em   A7
To me way! hey! Blow the man down,
    Em   A7   Em
Oh, Blow the man down bullies, Blow him away,
A7   D
Give me some time to blow the man down.

As I was a-walkin' down Paradise Street,
To me way! hey!—Blow the man down!
A pretty young damsel I chanced for to meet,
Give me some time to blow the man down.

She hailed me with her flipper, I took her in tow,
To me way! hey!—Blow the man down!
Yard-arm to yard-arm away we did go
Give me some time to blow the man down.

As soon as that Packet was clear of the bar,
To me way! hey!—Blow the man down!
The mate knocked me down with the end of a spar,
Give me some time to blow the man down.

Its yard-arm to yard-arm away you will sprawl,
Way! hey!—Blow the man down!
For kicking Jack Rogers commands the Black Ball
Give me some time to blow the man down.

Next comes the stowing down, my boys,
'Twill take both night and day,
And you'll all have fifty cents apiece
On the 190th lay.

Now we are bound into Tuckoona,
Full more in their power,
Where the skippers can buy the Consul up
For half a barrel of flour.

When we get home, our ship made fast,
And we get through our sailing,
A winding glass around we'll pass
And damn this blubber-whaling.

Blow Ye Winds Westerly

     F   Bb   F
Come all you bold fishermen, listen to me,
                    G7   C7
I'll sing you a song of the fish in the sea.

Chorus:

     F   Bb   F
So blow ye winds westerly, westerly blow,
                   Bb   C7
We're bound to the southward, so steady we go.

First comes the bluefish a-wagging his tail,
He comes up on deck and yells, "All hands make sail!"

Next come the herrings with their little tails,
They manned sheets and halyards and set all the sails.

Next comes the porpoise with his short snout,
He jumps on the bridge and yells, "Ready about!"

Next comes the swordfish, the scourge of the sea,
The order he gives is, "Helm's a-lee!"

Then comes the mackerel with his striped back,
He flops on the bridge and yells, "Board the main tack!"

Next comes the flounder quite fresh from the ground,
Crying, "Damn your eyes, chucklehead,
   mind where you sound!"

Along comes the shark with his three rows of teeth,
He flops on the foreyard and takes a snug reef.

Next comes the whale, the largest of all,
Singing out from the bridge, "Haul taut, mainsail, haul!"

Then comes the catfish with his chucklehead,
Out in the main chains for a heave of the lead.

Up jumps the fisherman, stalwart and grim,
And with his big net he scoops them all in.

Home, Boys, Home

```
      F                    Gm   C7  F
Oh, Boston's a fine town with ships in the bay,
                                    C
And I wish in my heart it was there I was today;
  Bb                F
I wish in my heart I was far away from here,
                          C7          F
Sitting in my parlor and talking to my dear.
```

Chorus:

```
F                    Gm   C7  F
Home, boys, home, it's home we ought to be,
                         C
Home, boys, home, in God's country!
  Bb                       F
The apple and the oak and the weeping willow tree!
                   C7          F
Green grows the grass in North Amerikee!
```

In Baltimore a-walking, a lady I did meet,
With her baby on her arm as she walked down the street,
And I thought how I sailed and the cradle standing ready,
And the pretty little babe that has never seen its daddy.

And if it's a girl, oh, she shall live with me,
And it it's a boy, he shall sail the rolling sea;
With his tarpaulin hat and his little jacket blue,
He shall walk the quarterdeck as his daddy used to do.

Coast Of Peru

```
Dm           C                      Dm
Come all ye young sailormen who've rounded the horn,
        Am           G       Am
Come all ye bold whalers who follow the storm,
                            G         Am
The captain has told us and we hope that it's true,
        Dm       C                  Dm
There's plenty of sperm whale on the coast of Peru.
```

It was early in the morning just as the sun rose,
The man on the foremast sang out, "Thar she blows,"
"Where away," said the captain and "where does she lay?"
"Three points to the eastward, not a mile away."

Then lower away your boats, my boys,
    and after him we'll travel,
Steer clear of his flukes or he'll flip you to the devil,
And lay on your oars, my boys, and let your boats fly,
But one thing we've heard of, keep clear of his eye.

The waist boat got down and we made a good start,
"Lay on," says the harpooner, "I'm held fore and aft,"
Well the harpoon struck and the whale straight away,
But whatever he did, my lads, he gave us fair play.

He raced and he sounded, he twist and he spin,
But we hauled along side him and got our lance in,
Which caused him to vomit and bleed from the spout,
But in ten minutes' time, my boys, he rolled them pins out.

We got him turned over and laid along side,
Then over with our blubberhooks and rob him of his hide,
We commenced cutting in boys, and then prying out,
And the mate in the main chains, how loud he did shout.

Now we're bound for old Tumbes in our manly power,
Where a man buys a whorehouse for a barrel of flour,
We'll spend all our money on them pretty girls ashore,
And when it's all gone, me lads,
    we'll go whalin' for more.

High Barbaree

```
        Em                    D         Em
There were two lofty ships from old England came,
                    B7     Em        B7
Blow high, blow low, and so sailed we,
       Em                D
One was the Prince of Luther
              C              B7
    and the other Prince of Wales,
              Em                      D  Em
Cruising down along the coast of High Barbaree.
```

"Aloft there, aloft," our jolly Boats-wain cried,
Blow high, etc.
"Look ahead, Look astern, Look the weather in the lee,"
Cruising down, etc.

There's nought upon the stern,
    and there's nought upon the lee, etc.
But there's a lofty ship to windward
    and she's sailing fast and free. etc.

"O hail her, O hail her," our gallant captain cries, etc.
"O, are you a man of war, or merchant ship," says he, etc.

"I am not a man of war or merchant ship," says he, etc.
"But I'm a salt-sea pirate, a-looking for my fee." etc.

For broadside, for broadside, a long time we lay, etc.
Until at last the frigate shot the pirate mast away. etc.

"For quarter, for quarter!" the saucy pirate cried, etc.
But the quarter that we gave them
    was to sink them in the tide,
Cruising down along the coast of High Barbaree. (twice)

Tommy's Gone To Hilo

```
      F              Gm   Dm
Oh, Tommy's gone, what shall I do?
  Bb F  C
Away, Hilo!
  Gm                Dm
My Tommy's gone, and I'll go too,
F            C7 F
Tommy's gone to Hilo!
```

He's gone away to Hilo Bay,
Away, Hilo!
To Hilo Bay I heard him say,
Tommy's gone to Hilo!

Tommy's gone to Hilo town,
Where all them gals they do come down.

Hilo town is in Peru,
It's just the place for me and you.

Tommy's gone to Baltimore,
To dance upon a sandy floor.

Tommy's gone to Mobile Bay,
A-screwin' cotton all the day.

Tommy's gone to far Quebec,
A-stowin' timber on the deck.

Tommy's gone to Singapore,
Oh, Tommy's gone for evermore.

Oh, I love Tommy and he loves me,
He thinks of me when out at sea.

What Shall We Do With A Drunken Sailor?

```
Em
What shall we do with a drunken sailor?
D
What shall we do with a drunken sailor?
Em
What shall we do with a drunken sailor?
Em  D  Em
Early in the morning.
```

Chorus:

Way, hey, and up she rises, (3 times)
Early in the morning.

Put him in the longboat till he's sober, etc.

Pull out the plug and wet him all over, etc.

Put him in the scuppers with a hose pipe on him, etc.

Heave him by the leg in a running bowline, etc.

Shave his belly with a rusty razor, etc.

Rock About My Saro Jane

```
Em             G
I've got a wife and five little children,
                             Em
Believe I'll make a trip on the big MacMillan,

O Saro Jane!
```

Chorus:

```
G7      C      G            Em
O there's nothing to do but to set down and sing,
D7  G            C D7 G
And  rock  about,  my  Saro Jane.
```

```
O rock about my Saro Jane.
           C          G
O rock about my Saro Jane.
           C      G         Em
O there's nothing to do but to set down and sing,
D7  G            C D7 G
And  rock  about,  my  Saro Jane.
```

Boiler busted and the whistle done blowed,
The head captain done fell overboard.
O Saro Jane!

Engine gave a crack and the whistle gave a squall,
The engineer gone to the hole in the wall.
O Saro Jane!

Yankees built boats for to shoot them rebels,
My musket's loaded and I'm gonna hold her level.
  Saro Jane!

Sally Brown

```
C                 F      C
Sally Brown was a Creole lady,
      G7  C   G7  C
Way,  ay,  roll  and  go!
            F            C
O, Sally Brown was a Creole lady,
G7                        C
Spend my money on Sally Brown.
```

She had a farm on the isle of Jamaica,
Way, ay, roll and go!
Where she drinks rum and chews terbacker,
Spend my money on Sally Brown.

Sally Brown of New York City,
Sally Brown is very pretty.

Sally Brown had a fine young daughter,
That's the one that I was after.

For seven long years I courted Sally,
Seven long years, but she wouldn't marry.

The Mermaid

```
         G              C     G
Twas Friday morn when we set sail
         C       D7        G
And we were not far from the land,
                         C          G
When the captain spied a lovely mermaid
         C         D7      G
With a comb and a glass in her hand.
```

Chorus:

```
G
Oh the ocean waves may roll,
                      D7
And the stormy seas may blow,
         G            C             G
But we poor sailors go skipping to the top
         C       D7          G
And the land lubbers lie down below, below, below,
         C       D7          G
And the land lubbers lie down below.
```

Then up spoke the captain of our gallant ship
And a well-spoken man was he,
"I married me a wife in Salem town,
And tonight she a widow will be."

Then up spoke the cook of our gallant ship,
And a red hot cook was he,
"I care much more for my kettles and my pots,
Than I do for the bottom of the sea."

Then up spoke the cabin-boy of our gallant ship,
And a dirty little rat was he,
"There's nary a soul in Salem town,
Who gives a darn about me."

Then three times around went our gallant ship,
And three times around went she;
Then three times around went our gallant ship,
And she sank to the bottom of the sea.

Rio Grande

```
      C              G7    C
Oh, say were you ever in Rio Grande?
```

Oh, Rio
```
      F          C G7            C
It's there that the river flows down golden sand.
                      G7 C
And we're bound for the Rio Grande.
```

Chorus:
```
      C  G7   C
Then-a-way, love-a-way. Way down Rio,
      F    C     G7         C
So fare ye well, my pretty young girl,
                      G7 C
For we're bound for the Rio Grande.
```

And goodbye, fare you well, all you ladies of town,
Oh, Rio.
We've left you enough for to buy a silk gown.

So it's pack up your donkey and get under way,
Oh, Rio.
The girls we are leaving can take our half-pay.

Now you Bowery ladies, we'd have you to know,
Oh, Rio.
We're bound to the Southward, O Lord, let us go.

John B. Sails

```
    D
We come on the sloop John B.
```

My grandfather and me.
```
                             A7
'Round Nassau town we did roam
         D
Drinking all night,
         G
We got into a fight,
         D
I feel so break-up
A7            D
I want to go home.
```

Chorus:
So hoist up the John B.'s sails,
See how the main sail sets,
Send for the captain ashore, let me go home;
Let me go home, I want to go home,
I feel so break-up, I want to go home.

Well the first mate, he got drunk,
And destroyed the people's trunk,
And constable come aboard, take him away,
Sheriff Johnstone, please let me alone,
I feel so break-up, I want to go home.

Well the poor cook he got fits,
Throw'way all the grits,
Then he took and eat up all of my corn,
Let me go home, I want to go home,
Oh, this is the worst trip since I been born.

The Bonnie Ship The Diamond

```
Dm            Am
The Diamond is a ship my lads,
     Dm            Am
For the Davis Straits she's bound,
      Dm            Am
And the key edge is all garnished up,
    Dm  Am  Dm
With forty lashes round.
```

Captain Thompson gives the orders,
To sail the ocean wide,
Where the sun it never sets my lads,
Nor darkness dims the sky.

Chorus:

```
Dm        Am    Dm
So it's cheer up my lads,
          Am  Dm
Let your 'arts never fail,
                    Am
For the bonnie ship the Diamond,
      Dm  Am   Dm
Goes a-fishing for the whale.
```

Along the keys of Peterhead,
The lassies stand around,
Their shawls all put around their men,
And the sword tails hanging down.

Now don't you weep my bonnie lass,
Though you be left behind,
For the rose will bloom on Greenland's ice.
Before we change our minds.

Here's a health to the Resolution,
Likewise the Eliza Swan,
Here's a health to the Battle of Old Montrose,
And the Diamond ship will pay.

We wear our trousers o'er the white,
Till the jig is o'er the blue,
When we return to Peterhead,
We'll hasten sweethearts to you.

Oh, it'll be brack both day and night,
When the Greenland lads come home,
We've a ship that's full o' oil, my boys,
And money to our names.

We'll make those cradles for to rock,
And the blankets for to tear,
And every lass in Peterhead,
Will sing hush-a-bye my dear.

Greenland Fisheries

```
          G                    C
'Twas in eighteen hundred and fifty three,
D       G        Am      D7
And of June the thirteenth day;
           C      Am    D7
That our gallant ship her anchor weighed,
         G         Am   D
And for Greenland bore away, brave boys,
         G         C    D7G
And for Greenland bore away.
```

The lookout in the crosstrees stood
Spyglass in his hand;
There's a whale, there's a whale,
   there's a whale fish he cried,
And she blows at every span, brave boys,
And she blows at every span.

The captain stood on the quarter-deck,
And a fine little man was he;
"Overhaul! Overhaul! let your davit-tackles fall,
And launch your boats for sea, brave boys,
And launch your boats for sea."

Now the boats were launched and the men aboard,
And the whale was full in view;
Resolv-ed was each seaman bold
To steer where the whalefish blew, etc.

We struck the whale, the line paid out,
But she gave a flourish with her tail;
The boat capsized and four men were drowned,
And we never caught that whale, etc.

"To lose the whale," our captain said,
"It grieves my heart full sore;
But oh! to lose four gallant men,
It grieves me ten times more," etc.

"The winter star doth now appear,
So, boys, we'll anchor weigh;
It's time to leave this cold country,
And homeward bear away," etc.

Oh, Greenland is a dreadful place,
A land that's never green,
Where there's ice and snow, and the whalefishes blow,
And the daylight's seldom seen, etc.

Santy Anno

```
        Em                 Bm7 Em  C6
We're sailing down the river from Liverpool,
        Em        Am7
Heave away, Santy Anno,
    D              F#m  G
Around Cape Horn to Frisco Bay,
    C     Bm7    Em
All on the plains of Mexico.
```

Chorus:

```
                              C6
So heave her up and away we'll go,
D      G    Em   Am
Heave away, Santy Anno;
D       F#m    G      D
Heave her up and away we'll go,
    C     Bm7    Em
All on the plains of Mexico.
```

She's a fast clipper ship and a bully good crew,
Heave away, Santy Anno,
A down-East Yankee for her captain, too
All on the plains of Mexico.

There's plenty of gold so I've been told,
Heave away, Santy Anno,
There's plenty of gold so I've been told
Way out West to California-o.

Back in the days of Forty-nine,
Heave away, Santy Anno,
Those are the days of the good old times,
All on the plains of Mexico.

When Zachary Taylor gained the day,
Heave away, Santy Anno,
He made poor Santy run away,
All on the plains of Mexico.

General Scott and Taylor, too,
Heave away, Santy Anno,
Made poor Santy meet his Waterloo,
All on the plains of Mexico.

When I leave the ship, I will settle down,
Heave away, Santy Anno,
And marry a girl named Sally Brown,
All on the plains of Mexico.

Santy Anno was a good old man,
Heave away, Santy Anno,
Till he got into war with your Uncle Sam,
All on the plains of Mexico.

Red Iron Ore

```
Am                      E       G
Come all ye bold sailors that follow the lakes,
    C     Dm     Am    E
On an iron ore vessel your living to make,
  Am      Dm     C      E
I shipped in Chicago, bid adieu to the shore
        Am            E      Am
Bound away to Escanaba for that red iron ore.
```

Chorus:

```
Am     D9   E       Am
Derry down, down, down derry down.
```

In the month of September on the seventeenth day,
Two dollars and a quarter was all they would pay,
And on Monday morning a trip we did take,
On a ship named the Roberts sailing out in the lake.

The packet she howled across the mouth of Green Bay,
And before her cut water she threw the white spray,
She rounded out San Point and her anchor let go,
We furled in the canvas and the watch went below.

Next morning we hove alongside the Exile,
We soon made her fast to that iron ore pile,
They lowered the shutes which soon started to roar,
They're fillin' the ship with that red iron ore.

Some sailors took shovels and others took spades,
And some took to sluicing, each man to his trade,
We looked like red devils, our backs they got sore,
We cursed Escanaba and that red iron ore.

The dust got so thick you could scarce see your nose,
It got in your eyes and it got in your clothes,
We loaded the Roberts till she couldn't hold more,
Right up to the gunnels with that red iron ore.

We sailed her to Cleveland, made fast stem and stern,
And with our companions we'll spin a big yarn,
Here's a health to the Roberts, she's strong and she's true,
Here's a health to the bold boys who make up her crew.

Cape Cod Girls

F
Cape Cod girls they have no combs,

Heave away! Heave away!

They comb their hair with codfish bones,
          C7 F
We are bound for California!

Chorus:

Bb   F
Heave away, my bully, bully boys,

Heave away! Heave away!
Bb   F
Heave away and don't you make a noise,
          C7 F
We are bound for California!

Cape Cod boys they have no sleds,
They slide down dunes on codfish heads.

Cape Cod doctors they have no pills,
They give their patients codfish gills.

Cape Cod cats they have no tails,
They lost them all in sou'east gales.

Hieland Laddie

Dm
Was you ever in Quebec?
Gm   Am
Bonnie Laddie, Hieland Laddie
Dm
Stowing timber on the deck,
   Gm Am Dm
My Bonnie Hieland Laddie.

Chorus:

Bb F   C7   F
Hey ho, and away we go.
Gm   Am
Bonnie Laddie, Hieland Laddie.
Bb F C7   F
Hey ho, away we go,
   Gm Am Dm
My Bonnie Hieland Laddie.

Was you ever in Callao,
Bonnie Laddie, Hieland Laddie,
Where the girls are never slow,
My Bonnie Hieland Laddie.

Was you ever in Baltimore, etc.
Dancing on that sanded floor, etc.

Was you ever in Mobile Bay,
Loading cotton by the day,

Was you on the Brummallow,
Where Yankee boys are all the go,

Was you ever in Dundee,
There some pretty ships you'll see,

Was you ever in Merrimashee,
Where you make fast to a tree,

Was you ever in Aberdeen,
Prettiest girls you've ever seen,

Rolling Home
Charles Mackay

D
Up aloft amid the rigging
      G
Swiftly blows the fav'ring gale,
A7   D   G
Strong as springtime in its blossom,
B7   Em   A7   D
Filling out each bending sail.
          D
And the waves we leave behind us,
    G
Seem to murmur as they rise,
A7   D   G
We have tarried here to bear you
Bb   Em   A7   D
To the land you dearly prize.

Chorus:

      D
Rolling home, rolling home,
     G
Rolling home across the sea;
A7   D   G
Rolling home to our dear homeland,
C#   D   A7   D
Rolling home, dear land, to thee!

Full ten thousand miles behind us,
And a thousand miles before,
Ancient ocean waves to waft us
To the well-remembered shore.
Newborn breezes swell to send us
To our childhood's welcome skies,
To the glow of friendly faces
And the glance of loving eyes.

Michael, Row The Boat Ashore

Chorus:

D   G D
Michael, row the boat ashore, Allaluya.
      F#m   Em   A7 D
Michael, row the boat ashore, Allaluya.

Verses:
Michael's boat is a music boat, Allaluya, (twice)

Sister help to trim the sail, Allaluya, (twice)

Jordan's River is deep and wide, Allaluya,
Meet my mother on the other side, Allaluya.

Jordan's River is chilly and cold, Allaluya,
Kills the body but not the soul, Allaluya.

Leave Her, Johnny

  G   D   G   D
I thought I heard the old man say,
G   D
Leave her, Johnny, leave her!
    G   D   G
You can go ashore and draw your pay,
         D7 G
It's time for us to leave her!

You may make her fast and pack your gear,
Leave her, Johnny, leave her!
And leave her moored to the West Street pier,
It's time for us to leave her!

The winds were foul, the work was hard, Leave her, etc.
From Liverpool docks to the Brooklyn yard. It's time, etc.

She would neither steer nor wear nor stay,
She shipped it green both night and day.

She shipped it green and she shade us curse,—
The mate is a devil and the old man worse.

The winds were foul, the ship was slow,
The grub was bad, the wages low.

The winds were foul, the trip was long,
But before we go, we'll sing this song.

We'll sing, oh, may we never be
On a hungry bitch the like of she.

The Leaving Of Liverpool

      A   D   A
Farewell to you, my own true love,
         E7
I am going far away.
    A   D   A
I am bound for Cal - i - for - ni - a,
           E7   A
But I know that I'll return some day.

Chorus:

     E   D   A
So fare you well my own true love,
                   E
And when I return, united we will be.
       A   D   A
It's not the leaving of Liverpool that grieves me,
      E7   A
But my darling, it's when I think of thee.

I'm off to California
By way of the stormy Cape Horn,
And I will send you a letter, love,
When I am homeward bound.

I've shipped on a Yankee clipper ship,
Davy Crockett is her name;
And Burgess is the captain of her
And they say she is a floating hell.

I'm bound away to leave you,
Goodbye, my love, goodbye.
There ain't but one thing that grieves me,
That's leaving you behind.

Oh the sun is on the harbor, love,
And I wish I could remain,
For I know it will be some long time
Before I see you again.

Come all ye rounders and jokey-boys if
you want to hear some songs of ...

RAILROADERS AND LUMBERJACKS.

The Raftsmen
(Les Raftsmen)
Quebec

```
A          E      A
The gay raftsmen, oh where are they?
       A   E   A       E7
The gay raftsmen, oh where are they?
      A        D       A
To winter camps they're on their way.
```

Chorus:

```
D      A     D      A
Bing on the ring! Bang on the ring!
            D     F#m
Hear the raftsmen loudly sing!
D      E7       A
Bing on the ring! Bing, bang! (Hey)
```

Across Bytown they went today, (twice)
They've packed their grub, they cannot stay.

In bark canoes they make their way; (twice)
They reach the camp and shout, "Hurray!"

When meal time comes the men all say, (twice)
"It's pork and beans again today."

Their axes sharp, with no delay, (twice)
They swing and strike, the tall trees sway.

The logs they trim and drag away. (twice)
To drive down when the ice gives way.

In spring they draw their winter's pay, (twice)
And go back home on holiday.

To greet them come their ladies gay, (twice)
Who help them spend their hard-earned pay.

Singable French:

```
A          E    A
La ousqu'y sont, tous les raftsmen?
       A   E   A       E7
La ousqu'y sont, tous les raftsmen?
       A          D        A
Dans les chanquiers i sont montés.
D      A     D       A
Bing sur la ring! Bang sur la ring!
             D     F#m
Laissez passer les raftsmen.
D      E7        A
Bing sur la ring! Bing, bang! (Hey)
```

Et par Bytown y sont passés, (twice)
Avec leurs provisions achetées.

En canots d'ecorc' sont montés, (twice)
Et du plaisir y s'sont donné.

Des "porc and beans" ils ont mangé (twice)
Pour les estomacs restaurer.

Dans les chanquiers sont arrivés, (twice)
Des manch's de hache ont fabriqué.

Que l'Outaouais fut étonné, (twice)
Tant faissait d'bruit leur hach' trempée.

Quand le chanquier fut terminé (twice)
Chacun chez eux sont retourné.

Leurs femm's ou blond's ont embrassé, (twice)
Tous tres contents de se r'trouver.

Railroad Bill

Chorus:

```
D
Railroad Bill, Railroad Bill,
                       G
He never worked and he never will
        D     A7       D
I'm gonna ride old Railroad Bill.
```

Verses:

```
D
Railroad Bill he was a mighty mean man
                                    G
He shot the midnight lantern out the brakeman's hand
        D     A7       D
I'm going to ride old Railroad Bill.
```

Railroad Bill took my wife,
Said if I didn't like it, he would take my life,
I'm going to ride old Railroad Bill.

Going up on a mountain, going out west,
Thirty-eight special sticking out of my vest,
I'm going to ride old Railroad Bill.

Buy me a pistol just as long as my arm,
Kill everybody ever done me harm,
I'm going to ride old Railroad Bill.

I've got a thirty-eight special on a forty-five frame,
How in the world can I miss him when I got dead aim,
I'm going to ride old Railroad Bill.

Buy me a pistol just as long as my arm,
Kill everybody ever done me harm,
I'm going to ride old Railroad Bill.

Honey, honey, think I'm a fool,
Think I would quit you while the weather is cool,
I'm going to ride old Railroad Bill.

The Wabash Cannonball

G
I stood on the Atlantic ocean,
C
On the wide Pacific shore,
D7
Heard the Queen of flowing mountains
G
To the South Belle by the door,

She's long, tall and handsome,
C
She's loved by one and all.
D7
She's a modern combination,
G
Called the Wabash Cannonball

Chorus:

G
Listen to the jingle,
C
The rumble and the roar.
D7
Riding thru the woodlands,
G
To the hill and by the shore.

Hear the mighty rush of engines,
C
Hear the lonesome hobo squall,
D7
Riding thru the jungles,
G
On the Wabash Cannonball.

Now the eastern states are dandies,
So the western people say
From New York to St. Louis
And Chicago by the way,
Thru the hills of Minnesota
Where the rippling waters fall
No chances can be taken
On the Wabash Cannonball.

Here's to Daddy Claxton,
May his name forever stand
Will he be remembered
Through parts of all our land,
When his earthly race is over
And the curtain round him falls
We'll carry him on to victory
On the Wabash Cannonball.

Engine 143

G
Along came the F. F. V.,
C   G
The swiftest on the line

Running o'er the C. 'n O. Road
A7   D7
Just twenty minutes behind.
G
Running into Souville,
C   G
Headquarters on the line
C   G
Receiving their strict orders
D7   G
From a station just behind.

Georgie's mother came to him,
A bucket on her arm.
Saying to her darling son,
"Be careful how you run;
"Many a man has lost his life
"Trying to make lost time,
"And if you run your engine right,
"You'll get there just on time."

Up the road she darted,
Against the rock she crushed,
Upside down the engine turned
And Georgie's breast did smash.
His head against the fire-box door,
The flames were rolling high.
"I'm glad I was born for an engineer
To die on the C & O Road."

The doctor said to Georgie,
"My darling boy, be still,
"Your life may yet be saved
"If it is God's blessed Will."
"Oh, no," said George,
"That will not do,
"I want to die so free,
"I want to die for the engine I love,
"One Hundred and Forty-Three."

The doctor said to Georgie,
"Your life cannot be saved,
"Murdered upon a railroad
"And laid in a lonesome grave."
His face was covered up with blood,
His eyes you could not see,
And the very last words poor Georgie said
Was "Nearer my God to Thee."

Jam On Gerry's Rocks

     D   G   D
Come all you true born shanty boys,
    A7   D
Wherever you may be,
    G
Come sit here on the deacon seat
    A7   D
And listen unto me.

                    G
'Tis of six young Canadian boys,
    A7   D
And a hero you should know,
                  G   D
And how they broke the jam on Gerry's Rocks,
    A7   D
With their foreman, young Monroe.

'Twas on a Sunday morning
Ere daylight did appear;
Our logs were piled up mountain high
We could not keep them clear.
Till six of our brave shanty boys
They did agree to go
And break the jam on Gerry's Rocks
With foreman, young Monroe.

We had not picked up many a log
Till Monroe he did say:
I'd have you boys be on your guard
This jam will soon give way.
He had no more than spoke the words
When the jam did break and go,
And with it went those six brave men,
And foreman, young Monroe.

When the rest of all the shanty boys
The sad news came to hear;
They gathered at the river
And downward they did steer.
And there they found to their surprise
And sorrow, grief and woe,
All cut and mangled on the beach,
Lay the form of young Monroe.

They buried him most tenderly,
'Twas on the 4th of May,
Now, come all you bold shanty boys,
And for your comrade pray.
And engraved upon a hemlock tree
Which on the beach did grow
Was the day and date of the drowning
Of foreman, young Monroe.

Pat Works On The Railway

  Dm
In eighteen hundred and forty-one,
 F
I put my corduroy breeches on,
  Dm
I put my corduroy breeches on
          C   Dm
To work upon the railway.

Chorus:

Dm
Fil-li-me-oo-ri-i-ri-aye.
F
Fil-li-me-oo-ri-i-ri-aye.
Dm
Fil-li-me-oo-ri-i-ri-aye.
          C   Dm
To work upon the railway.

In eighteen hundred and forty-two,
I left the old world for the new,
Bad cess to the luck that brought me through
To work upon the railway.

In eighteen hundred and forty-three
'Twas then I met sweet Biddy McGee
An elegant wife she's been to me
While working on the railway.

In eighteen hundred and forty-five,
I thought myself more dead than alive,
I thought myself more dead than alive
While working on the railway.

It's "Pat do this" and "Pat do that,"
Without a stocking or cravat,
Nothing but an old straw hat
While Pat worked on the railway.

In eighteen hundred and forty-seven,
Sweet Biddy McGee she went to heaven,
If she left one kid, she left eleven,
To work upon the railway.

In eighteen hundred and forty-eight,
I learned to drink me whiskey straight,
It's an elegant drink that can't be beat
For working on the railway.

Rock Island Line

Chorus:

G
I say the Rock Island Line is a mighty good road,
                                 A7   D7
I say the Rock Island Line is the road to ride
        G
Oh, the Rock Island Line is a mighty good road,
               C   C7
If you want to ride it, got to ride it like you find it,
      G   D7   G
Buy your ticket at the station on the Rock Island Line.

Verses:

G
Jesus died to save our sins,
D   D7   G
Glory be to God, gonna need him again.

A-B-C, Double X-Y-Z,
Cat's in the cupboard but he can't see me.

I may be right and I may be wrong,
I know you're gonna miss me when I'm gone.

She'll Be Coming 'Round The Mountain

          F
She'll be comin' 'round the mountain when she comes,
                                          C7
She'll be comin' 'round the mountain when she comes,
        F   F7
She'll be comin' 'round the mountain,
          Bb
She'll be comin' 'round the mountain,
        F   C7   F
She'll be comin' 'round the mountain when she comes.

She'll be drivin' six white horses when she comes, etc.

She'll be shinin' just like silver when she comes, etc.

Oh, we'll all go out to meet her when she comes, etc.

She'll be breathin' smoke an' fire when she comes, etc.

We'll be singin' "hallelujah" when she comes, etc.

We will kill the old red rooster when she comes, etc.

We'll all have chicken an' some dumplin's
     when she comes, etc.

Casey Jones (Union)
Joe Hill

       C   Dm   C   Dm
The workers on the S.P. Line to strike sent out a call,
       C   D7   G7
But Casey Jones, the engineer, he wouldn't strike at all;
       C   Dm   C   Dm
His boiler it was leaking and its drivers on the bum,
       C   G7   C
And his engine and its bearings they were all out of plumb.
                                  F
Casey Jones, kept his junk-pile running,
C   G7
Casey Jones, was working double time;
C   F
Casey Jones, got a wooden medal
     Gdim   G7   C
For being good and faithful on the S.P. Line.

The workers said to Casey: "Won't you help us
     win this strike?"
But Casey said: "Let me alone, you'd better take a hike."
Then Casey's wheezy engine ran right off
     the worn out track,
And Casey hit the river with an awful crack.

Casey Jones, hit the river bottom,
Casey Jones broke his blooming spine,
Casey Jones became an angeleno,
He took a trip to heaven on the S. P. Line.

When Casey Jones got up to heaven to the Pearly Gate,
He said: "I'm Casey Jones, the guy that pulled
     the S. P. freight."
"You're just the man," said Peter,
     "our musicians are on strike;
"You can get a job a-scabbing anytime you like."

Casey Jones got a job in heaven;
Casey Jones was doing mighty fine;
Casey Jones went scabbing on the angels,
Just like he did to workers on the S. P. Line.

The angels got together, and they said it wasn't fair,
For Casey Jones to go around a-scabbing everywhere.
The Angels Union No. 23, they sure were there,
And they promptly fired Casey down the Golden Stair.

Casey Jones went to Hell a-flying.
"Casey Jones," the Devil said, "Oh fine;
"Casey Jones, get busy shoveling sulphur
"That's what you get for scabbing on the S. P. Line."

Jay Gould's Daughter

A
Jay Gould's daughter said before she died,
E7
Papa, fix the blinds so the bums can't ride.
A
If ride they must, they got to ride the rod.
E7   A
Let 'em put their trust in the hands of God.
D
In the hands of God.
A
In the hands of God.
E7   A
Let them put their trust in the hands of God.

Jay Gould's daughter said, before she died,
There's two more trains I'd like to ride.
Jay Gould said, "Daughter, what can they be?"
The Southern Pacific and the Santa Fe.
The Santa Fe, etc.

Jay Gould's daughter said, before she died,
There's two more drinks I'd like to try.
Jay Gould said, "Daughter what can they be?
They's a glass o' water and a cup o' tea.
A cup o' tea, etc.

On a Monday morning it begin to rain.
'Round the curve come a passenger train.
On the blinds was Hobo John.
He's a good old hobo, but he's dead and gone.
Dead and gone, etc.

Charlie Snyder was a good engineer
Told his fireman not to fear
Pour on your water, boys, and shovel on your coal
Stick your head out the window, see the drivers roll
See the drivers roll, etc.

In The Pines

Em   Am Em
True love, true love, don't lie to me,
B7   Em
Tell me where did you sleep last night?

In the pines, in the pines,
        Am   Em
Where the sun never shines,
B7   Em
I shivered the whole night through.

True love, true love, where did you go?
I went where the cold wind blows,
In the pines, in the pines,
Where the sun never shines,
And I shivered the whole night through.

My husband was a railroad man,
Killed a mile and a half from town,
His head was found
In a driver's wheel,
And his body has never been found.

True love, true love, don't lie to me,
Tell me, where'd you sleep last night?
In the pines, in the pines,
Where the sun never shines,
And I shivered the whole night through.

I've Been Workin' On The Railroad

G   C   G
I've been workin' on the railroad, all the live-long day;

I've been workin' on the railroad,
        A7   D7
    just to pass the time away.
                        G
Don't you hear the whistle blowin,
        C   B7
    rise up so early in the morn,
C   G
Don't you hear the captain shoutin':
    D7   G
    "Dinah, blow your horn."
G   C
Dinah, won't you blow, Dinah won't you blow,
    D7   G
    Dinah won't you blow your horn.
G   C
Dinah, won't you blow, Dinah won't you blow,
    D7   G
    Dinah won't you blow your horn.

Someone's in the kitchen with Dinah;
                        D7
    someone's in the kitchen I know
G   C
Someone's in the kitchen with Dinah,
    D7   G
    strummin' on the old banjo.

Fee, fie, fiddle-i-o, fee, fie fiddle-i-o-o,
Fee, fie, fiddle-i-o, strummin' on the old banjo.

Someone's makin' love to Dinah,
    someone's makin' love I know,
Someone's makin' love to Dinah,
    'cause I can't hear the old banjo.

No one's in the kitchen with Dinah,
    no one's in the kitchen I know,
No one's in the kitchen with Dinah,
    'cause Dinah's got B.O.

The Wreck Of The Old 97

Tune: *The Ship That Never Returned*

```
         A                    D
Well, they gave him his orders at Monroe, Virginia.
         A                    E7
Sayin' "Steve you are way behind time.
         A                    D
"This is not thirty-eight, but it's old ninety-seven,
         A                    E7 A
"You must put her into Danville on time."
```

He turned and said to his black greasy fireman,
"Just shovel on a little more coal,
"And when we cross the White Oak Mountain
"You can watch old 'ninety-seven' roll."

It's a mighty rough road from
    Lynchburg to Danville,
On a line on a three mile grade,
It was on this grade that he lost his average,
You can see what a jump he made.

He was going down the grade makin' ninety miles an hour,
When his whistle broke into a scream . . .
They found him in the wreck with his hand on the throttle,
He was scalded to death by the steam.

Now ladies, you must take warning,
From this time now on learn,
Never speak harsh words to your true loving husband,
He may leave you and never return.

Canada-I-O

Tune: *Buffalo Skinners*

```
C              F        G7        C
Come all ye jolly lumbermen and listen to my song,
    F                    C         Am
But do not get discouraged, the length it is not long,
    F                    C         F
Concerning of some lumbermen who did agree to go,
    C              Dm   G7    C
To spend one pleasant winter up in Canada-i-o.
```

It happened late one season in the fall of 'fifty-three,
A preacher of the gospel one morning came to me,
Said he, "My jolly fellow, how would you like to go,
"To spend one pleasant winter up in Canada-i-o?"

To him I quickly made reply and unto him did say,
"This going out to Canada depends upon the pay.
"If you will pay good wages, my passage to and fro,
"I think I'll go along with you to Canada-i-o."

"Yes, we will pay good wages and will pay
    your passage out,
"Provided you sign papers that you will stay the route.
"But if you do get homesick and swear
    that home you'll go,
"We never can your passage pay from Canada-i-o."

It was by his gift of flattery he enlisted quite a train,
Some twenty-five or thirty, both well and able men.
We had a pleasant journey, o'er the road we had to go,
Till we landed at Three Rivers up in Canada-i-o.

After we had suffered there some eight or ten long weeks,
We arrived at headquarters up among the lakes,
We thought we'd found a paradise, at least they told us so,
God grant there may be no worse hell than Canada-i-o.

To describe what we have suffered is past the art of man,
But to give a fair description, I will do the best I can.
Our food, the dogs would snarl at it,
    our beds were on the snow,
We suffered worse than murderers up in Canada-i-o.

Our hearts were made of iron and our souls
    were cased in steel,
The hardships of that winter could never make us yield,
Field, Philips and Norcross,
    they found their match, I know,
Among the boys that went from Maine to Canada-i-o.

But now our lumbering is over and we are returning home,
To greet our wives and sweethearts
    and never more to roam,
To greet our wives and sweethearts and never more to go
Unto the God-forsaken place called Canada-i-o.

GIT ALONG, LITTLE DOGGIES

Songs of cowboys, trail-herders, saddle
tramps, and tenderfoots just from town. . . .

Blood On The Saddle

      D
There was blood on the saddle
  G   D
And blood on the ground,

And a great big puddle
  A7   D
Of blood all around.

The cowboy lay in it,
All covered with gore,
And he won't go riding
No broncos no more.

Oh, pity the cowboy,
All bloody and red,
For his bronco fell on him
And mashed in his head.

Doney Gal

Chorus:

    G   C   G
We're alone, Doney Gal, in the rain and hail;
             C   G   D7
Got to drive these dogies down the trail.

Verses:

    G   G7 G
We ride the range from sun to sun
    C   D
For a cowboy's work is never done;
    G   Bm   G
He's up and gone by the break of day
C   D
Drivin' the dogies on their weary way.

It's rain or shine, sleet or snow,
Me and my Doney Gal on the go;
Yes, rain or shine, sleet or snow,
Me and my Doney Gal are bound to go.

A cowboy's life is a dreary thing,
For it's rope and brand and ride and sing;
Yes, day or night in the rain or hail,
He'll stay with his dogies out on the trail.

Rain or shine, sleet or snow,
Me and my Doney Gal are on the go;
We travel down that lonesome trail
Where a man and his horse seldom ever fail.

We whoop at the sun and yell through the hail,
But we drive the poor dogies on down the trail;
And we'll laugh at the storms, the sleet and snow,
When we reach the little town of San Antonio.

I Ride An Old Paint

    G
I ride an old paint and I lead an old Dan,
  D7   G
I'm goin' to Montana to throw the Hoolian,
  D7   G
They feed 'em in the coulees, they water in the draw,
  D7   G
Their tails are all matted, their backs are all raw.

Chorus:

    D7
Ride around little doggies,
      G
Ride around them slow,
    D7
For the fiery and snuffy
      G
Are raring to go.

Old Bill Jones had a daughter and a son,
Son went to college and the daughter went wrong,
His wife got killed in a pool-room fight,
Still he keeps singing from morning till night.

When I die take my saddle from the wall,
Put it on to my pony, lead him out of his stall,
Tie my bones to his back, turn our faces to the west,
And we'll ride the prairie that we love the best.

Goodbye Old Paint

Chorus:

    A
Goodbye, old Paint, I'm a-leavin' Cheyenne,
                    E7   A
Goodbye, old Paint, I'm a-leavin' Cheyenne,

Verse:

        A   D   A   F♯m
I'm a-leavin' Cheyenne, I'm off to Montana,
      A   E7   A
Goodbye, old Paint, I'm a-leavin' Cheyenne.

My foot in the stirrup, my pony won't stand,
Goodbye, old Paint, I'm a-leavin' Cheyenne.

Old Paint's a good pony, he paces when he can,
Goodbye, little Annie, I'm off to Cheyenne.

Oh, hitch up your horses and feed 'em some hay,
And seat yourself by me so long as you stay.

My horses ain't hungry, they'll not eat your hay,
My wagon is loaded and rolling away.

My foot in the stirrup, the reins in my hands,
Good morning, young lady, my horses won't stand.

The Zebra Dun

```
        C                      G7            C
We were camped on the bend at the head of the Cimarron,

When along came a stranger,

   and he stopped to argue some,

Well, he looked so very foolish we began to look around,
                                            G7           C
We thought he was a greenhorn, just escaped from town.
```

He said he'd lost his job upon the Santa Fe,
And was going cross the prairie to strike the 7D,
He didn't say how come it, some trouble with the boss,
And asked if he could borrow, a fat, saddle horse.

This tickled all the boys to death,
   they laughed right up their sleeves,
Oh, we will lend you a fine horse,
   as fresh and fast as you please,
Then Shorty grabbed the lariat,
   and he roped the Zebra Dun,
And he gave him to the stranger, and waited for the fun.

Now old Dunny was an outlaw, he had grown so very wild,
But he could paw the moon down,
   boys he could jump a mile,
Old Dunny stood right still, as if he didn't know,
Until he was saddled, and ready for to go.

When the stranger hit the saddle,
   well old Dunny quit the earth,
He travelled right straight upwards
   for all that he was worth,
A-bucking and a-squealing, and a-having wall-eyed fits,
His hind feet perpendicular, his front feet in the bits.

We could see the tops of the mountains
   under Dunny's every jump,
The stranger he was glued there, like the camel's hump,
The stranger sat upon him,
   and he curled his black mustache,
Just like a summer boarder who was waiting for his hash.

Well, he thrumped him in the shoulders,
   and he spurred him when he whirled,
He hollered to the punchers, I'm the wolf of the world,
And when he had dismounted once more upon the ground,
We knew he was a thoroughbred,
   and not a gent from town.

Now the boss who was a-standing round,
   a-watching of the show,
He walked up to the stranger, and he said he needn't go,
If you can handle a lariat, like you rode the Zebra Dun,
You're the man that I've been been looking for,
   since the year of one.

Well, there's one thing, and a sure thing,
   I've learned since I've been born,
That every educated feller, ain't a plumb greenhorn.

Rag Time Cowboy Joe

by Grant Clarke, Lewis F. Muir and Maurice Abrahms
Copyright MCMXII F. A. Mills
Copyright Assigned MCMXL Fred Fisher Music Co., Inc.,
   New York
All Rights Reserved Including the Right of Public Performance
   for Profit
Used by Permission

```
C         F        C      F
Out in Arizona where the bad men are,
        C             A7        D    G7
And the only friend to guide you is an evening star;
        C           F        C
The roughest, toughest man by far
Am  D7    G7       C
Is Ragtime  Cowboy Joe.
G                  C        G       C
Got his name from singing to the cows and sheep,
G               E              A7  D7 G7
Every night they say he sings the herd to sleep,
C     F     C        F
In a basso rich and deep,
G7       B7      E
Crooning soft and low
```

Chorus:

```
G7          C
He always sings raggy music to the cattle,
        D7
As he swings back and forward in the saddle
        G7
On a horse that is syncopated gaited.
             C          Am
And there's such a funny meter
          D7        G7
   to the roar of his repeater,
             C
How they run when they hear that fellow's gun,
          D7
Because the western folks all know,
          F
He's a high-faluting, scooting,
                              F
   shooting son-of-a-gun from Arizona,
D7          G7
Ragtime Cowboy Joe.
```

Dressed up every Sunday in his Sunday clothes,
He beats it for the village where he always goes.
And every girl in town is Joe's
'Cause he's a ragtime bear.
When he starts a spieling on the dance hall floor,
No one but a lunatic would start a war.
Wise men know his forty-four
Makes men dance for fair.

The Old Chisholm Trail

E
Well, come along boys and listen to my tale,
                                     A   E
I'll tell you of my troubles on the Old Chisholm Trail.

Chorus:

       B7   E
Come a ti-yi yippee, yippee yeah, yippee yeah,
       B7   E
Come a ti-yi yippee, yippee yeah!

Now, a ten-dollar horse and a forty-dollar saddle,
I'm a-going to punching Texas cattle.

My horse throwed me off, just like I was a bird,
He throwed me off near the 2-U herd.

Last time I saw him he was goin' on the level,
A-kickin' up his heels and running like the devil!

As soon as I recovered from the damned hard jolt,
I got a job a-punchin' for old man Bolt.

Old Ben Bolt was a fine old man,
And you knowed there was whiskey wherever he'd land.

Old Ben Bolt was a fine old boss,
But he'd go to see the gals on a sore-backed horse.

'Twas early in the morning of October twenty-third,
When we started up the trail with the 2-U herd.

I woke up one morning on the Old Chisholm Trail,
A rope in my hand and a cow by the tail.

I'm in my saddle before daylight,
And afore I sleeps, the moon shines bright.

A-roping and a-tying and a-branding all day,
I'm working mighty hard for mighty little pay.

Well, it's bacon and beans most every day,
I'd as soon be eatin' prairie hay.

It's cloudy in the west and a-lookin' like rain,
And my damned old slicker's in the wagon again.

The wind begin to blow and the rain begin to fall,
And it looked, by grab, like we was goin' to lose 'em all.

Well, I jumped in the saddle and grabbed hold the horn,
Best god-damned cowboy ever was born.

My feet are in the stirrups and my rope is on the side,
Show me a horse that I can't ride.

We didn't give a damn if they never did stop,
We'd ride along like an eight-day clock.

A heifer went loco and the boss said, "Kill it!"
Shot him in the arse with a long-handed skillet.

I'll drive my herd to the top of the hill,
And I'll kiss my gal, by grab, I will.

I got a gal, prettiest gal you ever saw,
And she lives on the banks of the Deep Cedar Draw.

Well, I met a little gal and I offered her a quarter,
She says, "Young man, I'm a gentleman's daughter."

We all hit town, and we hit her on the fly,
We bedded down the cattle on a hill nearby.

Then we rounded 'em up and we put 'em in the cars,
And that was the end of the Two Old Bars.

I've herded and I've hollered and I done very well,
Till the boss said, "Boys, just let 'em go to hell!"

Goin' back to town to draw my money,
Goin' back to town to see my honey.

I went to the boss to draw my roll,
He figgered me out nine dollars in the hole.

So I went to the boss and we had a little chat,
I hit him in the face with my big slouch hat.

The boss says to me, "Why, I'll fire you;
Not only you, but the whole damn crew!"

I'll sell my horse and I'll sell my saddle;
You can go to hell with your longhorn cattle.

I'll sell my outfit just as soon as I can,
I won't punch cattle for no damned man.

I'll sell my saddle and I'll buy me a plow,
And I swear, by God, I'll never rope another cow.

I'm goin' to Oklahoma to get me a squaw,
And raise papooses for my paw-in-law.

Now I've punched cattle from Texas to Maine,
And I've known some cowboys by their right name.

With my feet in the stirrup and my seat in the sky,
I'll quit punchin' cows in the sweet bye-and-bye.

Wake Up, Jacob
Cowboy's Gettin' Up Holler

```
C              Am
```
Wake up, Jacob, day's a-breakin',
```
C              G7     C
```
Peas in the pot and hoe-cake's bakin'.

Bacon's in the pan and coffee's in the pot,
Come on round and get it while it's hot.

Early in the morning, almost day,
If you don't come soon, gonna throw it all away.

Trail To Mexico

```
G          C        D7
```
I made up my mind in the early morn,
```
G              Em
```
To leave the home where I was born,
```
G              Em
```
To leave my native home for a while,
```
Am D7      G
```
And travel west for many a mile.

'Twas in the year of '83,
That A. J. Stinson he hired me,
He said, "Young man, I want you to go,
And follow my herd to Mexico."

'Twas in the springtime of the year,
I volunteered to drive the steers,
I'll tell you boys, 'twas a long hard go,
As the trail rolled on into Mexico.

When I arrived in Mexico,
I wanted my girl, but I could not go,
So I wrote a letter to my dear,
But not a word from her did I hear.

So I returned to my one time home,
Inquired for the girl whom I adore,
She said, "Young man, I've wed a richer life,
Therefore young fellow, go and get another wife."

"Oh curse your gold and your silver too,
Oh curse the girl who won't prove true,
I'll go right back to the Rio Grande,
And get me a job with a cowboy band."

"Oh Buddy, oh Buddy, oh please don't go,
Oh please don't go to Mexico,
If you've no girl more true than I,
Oh please don't go where the bullets fly."

"If I've no girl more true than you,
If I've no girl who will prove true,
I'll go right back where the bullets fly,
And follow the cow trail till I die."

Git Along, Little Dogies

```
      F           G        C
```
As I was a-walking one morning for pleasure,
```
          F       G      C
```
I spied a cowpuncher a-riding along;
```
                     Dm7    Em        Am
```
His hat was thrown back and his spurs were a-jinglin',
```
      C    F        G7       C
```
As he approached me singin' this song:

Chorus:

```
        Gm7      C        F
```
Whoopee ti yi yo, git along, little dogies,
```
        C      Am    Dm7     G
```
It's your misfortune and none of my own;
```
              C        Em       Am
```
Whoopee ti yi yo, git along, little dogies,
```
          C     F      Em       C
```
For you know Wyoming will be your new home.

Early in the springtime we'll round up the dogies,
Slap on their brands and bob off their tails;
Round up our horses, load up the chuck wagon,
Then throw those dogies upon the trail.

It's whooping and yelling and driving the dogies,
Oh, how I wish you would go on,
It's whooping and punching and go on, little dogies,
For you know Wyoming will be your new home.

Some of the boys goes up the trail for pleasure,
But that's where they git it most awfully wrong;
For you haven't any idea the trouble they give us,
When we go driving them dogies along.

When the night comes on
    and we hold them on the bed-ground,
These little dogies that roll on so slow;
Roll up the herd and cut out the strays,
And roll the little dogies that never rolled before.

Your mother she was raised way down in Texas,
Where the jimson weed and sandburs grow;
Now we'll fill you up on prickly pear and cholla,
Till you are ready for the trail to Idaho.

Oh, you'll be soup for Uncle Sam's Injuns,
"It's beef, heap beef," I hear them cry.
Git along, git along, git along, little dogies,
You're going to be beef steers by and by.

Buffalo Skinners

Dm
Come all you old time cowboys
And listen to my song.
Please do not grow weary,
I'll not detain you long;
Concerning some wild cowboys
Who did agree to go
And spend the summer pleasant
On the trail of the buffalo.

I found myself in Griffin
In the spring of '83,
When a well-known, famous drover
Come a-walking up to me,
Saying, "How do you do, young feller,
And how would you like to go,
And spend a summer pleasant
On the trail of the buffalo?"

Well, me being out of work right then,
To the drover I did say,
"This going out on the buffalo range
Depends upon your pay.
But if you will pay good wages —
Transportation to and fro,
I think I might go with you
To the trail of the buffalo."

"Of course I'll pay good wages —
Give transportation too,
If you'll agree to work for me
Until the season's through.
But if you do grow weary,
And you try to run away,
You'll starve to death along the trail,
And also lose your pay."

Well with all his flattering talking,
He signed up quite a train,
Some ten or twelve in number —
Some able-bodied men.
Our trip it was a pleasant one
As we hit the westward road,
And crossed old Boggy Creek
In old New Mexico.

There our pleasures ended
And our troubles all begun.
A lightning storm did hit us,
And made our cattle run.
Got all full of stickers
From the cactus that did grow,
And outlaws waiting to pick us off
In the hills of Mexico.

Well, the working season ended
And the drover would not pay.
"You all have drunk too much," he said,
"And you're all in debt to me."
But the cowboys never had heard of
Such a thing as a bankrupt law,
So we left that drover's bones to bleach
On the trail of the buffalo.

Bury Me Not On The Lone Prairie

Em   G
"Oh, bury me not on the lone prairie,"
Em   G
Those words came low and mournfully
Bm   Em
From the pallid lips of a youth who lay
G   A   C   D
On his dying bed at the close of day.

Chorus:

G   D7 G
"Oh, bury me not on the lone prairie,
                    D7   Em
Where the wild coyotes will howl o'er me,
G   D7 Bm
In a narrow grave just six by three.
C   D6 D7 G
Oh bury me not on the lone prairie.

"It matters not, I've oft been told,
Where the body lies when the heart grows cold.
Yet grant, oh grant, this wish to me:
Oh, bury me not on the lone prairie.

"I've always wished to be laid when I died
In the little churchyard on the green hillside;
By my father's grave there let mine be,
And bury me not on the lone prairie.

"Let my death-slumber be where my mother's prayer
And a sister's tear will mingle there;
Where my friends can come and weep o'er me.
Oh bury me not on the lone prairie."

"Oh, bury me not"—and his voice failed there,
But we took no heed of his dying prayer.
In a narrow grave just six by three
We buried him on the lone prairie.

And the cowboys now as they roam the plain,
For they marked the spot where his bones were lain,
Fling a handful of roses o'er the grave
With a prayer to Him who his soul will save.

"Oh, bury me not on the lone prairie,
Where the wolves can howl and growl o'er me.
Fling a handful of roses o'er my grave
With a prayer to Him who my soul will save."

The Strawberry Roan

     C   G7
I was hangin' round town just a spendin' my time,
                   C
Out of a job and not makin' a dime,
                        F
When a feller steps up and says, "I suppose
G7   C
You're a bronc rider, by the looks of your clothes."
                        G7
"You got me right, and a good one," I claim,
                      C
"Do you happen to have any bad ones to tame?"
                     F
He says: "I've got one and a bad one to buck,
      G7   C
And at throwin' good riders he's had lots of luck."

Chorus:

        G7   C
Well, it's Oh, that Strawberry Roan;
F   C
Oh, that Strawberry Roan.
     F   C
They say he's a cayuse that's never been rode,
     F   C
The man that gets on him is bound to be throwed,
    G7   C
Get off that Strawberry Roan.

I gets all excited and I ask what he pays
To ride this old goat for a couple of days.
He offers a ten spot. I says, "I'm your man,
For the bronc never lived that I couldn't fan;
No, the bronc never lived, nor he never drew breath
That I couldn't ride till he starved plumb to death."
He says, "Get your saddle, I'll give you a chance."
We got in the buckboard and rode to the ranch.

Chorus:
Well, it's Oh, that strawberry roan,
Oh, that strawberry roan!
We stayed until morning, and right after chuck
We goes out to see how this outlaw can buck,
Oh, that strawberry roan!

Down in the horse corral standing alone
Is this old caballo, a strawberry roan.
His legs is all spavined, he has pigeon toes,
Two little pig eyes and a big Roman nose.
Little pin ears that touched at the tips,
And a big 44 run on his left hip.
He's ewe-necked and old, with a long lower jaw,
I could see with one eye he was a reg'lar outlaw.

Chorus:
Well, it's Oh, that strawberry roan,
Oh, that strawberry roan!
He's ewe-necked and old, with a long lower jaw,
You can see with one eye he's a reg'lar outlaw,
Oh, that strawberry roan.

I buckle on my spurs, I'm sure feelin' fine,
I picks up my hat, an' curls up my twine.
I piles my rope on him, and well I know then,
That afore I get rode, I've sure earned my ten.
I gets the blinds on him, it sure is a fight,
Next comes my old saddle, an' I screws her on tight,
Then I steps onto him and raises the blinds,
I'm right in his middle to see him unwind.

Chorus:
Well, it's Oh, that strawberry roan,
Oh, that strawberry roan!
He lowered his neck, and I think he unwound,
He seemed to quit living down there on the ground,
Oh, that strawberry roan.

He went up towards the east and came down towards
    the west;
To stay in the middle I'm doin' my best.
He's about the worst bucker I've seen on the range:
He can turn on a nickel and give you some change,
He turns his old belly right up to the sun,
He sure is one sun-fishin' son of a gun!
I'll tell you, no foolin', this pony can step,
But I'm still in his middle and buildin' a rep.

Chorus:
Well, it's Oh, that strawberry roan,
Oh, that strawberry roan!
He goes up on all fours and comes down on his side,
I don't see what keeps him from losing his hide,
Oh, that strawberry roan!

I loses my stirrup and also my hat,
I starts pulling leather, I'm blind as a bat;
With a big forward jump, he goes up on high,
Leaves me sittin' on nothing way up in the sky;
I turns over twice, and I comes back to earth,
I lights in a-cussin' the day of his birth.
I know there is ponies I'm unable to ride;
Some are still living, they haven't all died.

Chorus:
Well, it's Oh, that strawberry roan,
Oh, that strawberry roan!
I'll bet all my money the man ain't alive
That can stay with old strawberry
    when he makes his high dive,
Oh, that strawberry roan!

Tyin' A Knot In The Devil's Tail

Gail Gardner

D
Way high up in the Syree peaks,
               A7
   where the yellow pines grow tall,
                                    D
Sandy Bob and Buster Jiggs had a round-up camp last fall.

They took along their runnin' irons,
   and maybe a dog or two,
And they 'lowed they'd brand every long-eared calf
   that came within their view.

Well, many a long-eared dogie that didn't hush up by day,
Had his long ears whittled
   and his old hide scorched in a most artistic way.

Then one fine day said Buster Jiggs,
   as he throwed his cigo down:
"I'm tired of cowpiography and I 'lows I'm goin' to town."

They saddles up and they hits them a lope,
   fer it weren't no sight of a ride,
An' them was the days when an old cowhand
   could oil up his insides.

They starts her out at Kentucky bar
   at the head of Whisky Row,
And they winds her up at the Depot House,
   some forty drinks below.

They sets her up and turns her around
   and goes her the other way,
And to tell you the God-forsaken truth,
   them boys got drunk that day.

Well, as they was a-headin' back to camp
   and packin' a pretty good load,
Who should they meet but the Devil himself,
   come prancin' down the road.

Now the Devil he said:
   "You cowboy skunks, you better go hunt your hole,
'Cause I come up from the hell's rim-rock
   to gather in your souls."

Said Buster Jiggs: "Now we're just from town
   an' feelin' kind o' tight,
And you ain't gonna get no cowboy souls
   without some kind of a fight."

So he punched a hole in his old throw-rope
   and he slings her straight and true,
And he roped the Devil right around the horn,
   he takes his dallies true.

Old Sandy Bob was a reata-man
   with his rope all coiled up neat,
But he shakes her out and builds him a loop
   and he roped the Devil's hind feet.

They threw him down on the desert ground
   while the irons was a-gettin' hot,
They cropped and swallow-forked his ears
   and branded him up a lot.

And they pruned him up with a dehorning saw
   and knotted his tail for a joke,
Rode off and left him bellowing there,
   tied up to a little pin-oak.

Well, if you ever travel in the Syree peaks
   and you hear one helluva wail,
You'll know it's nothin' but the Devil himself,
   raisin' hell about the knots in his tail.

The Cowboy's Dream

Tune: *My Bonnie*

     G   C   G
Last night I lay on the prairie,
                        A7   D7
And looked up at the stars in the sky,
     G   C   G
I wondered if ever a cowboy,
           C   D7   G
Would drift to that sweet by and by.

Chorus:

G   C A7 D7   G
Roll on, roll on; roll on, little dogies, roll on, roll on.
       C A7   D7   G
Roll on, roll on, roll on little dogies, roll on.

The road to that bright happy region,
Is a dim narrow trail, so they say;
But the broad one that leads to perdition,
Is posted and blazed all the way.

They say there will be a great round-up,
And cowboys, like dogies, will stand,
To be mavericked by the Riders of Judgement,
Who are posted and know every brand.

Oh, they tell of another great owner
Who is ne'er overstocked, so they say,
But who always makes room for the sinner
Who departs from the straight narrow way.

Utah Carroll

G
Oh, kind friend you may ask me
     C   G
   what makes me sad and still,
                       Em   A7   D
And why my brow is darkened like clouds upon a hill,
     G   C   G
Run in your pony closer and I'll tell you a tale,
  Em   G   C   D7   G
Of Utah Carroll, my partner, and his last ride on the trail.

In a grave without a headstone, without a date or name,
Quietly lies my partner in the land from which I came,
Long, long we rode together, had ridden side by side,
I loved him like a brother, I wept when Utah died.

While rounding up one morning,
    our work was almost done,
The cattle quickly started on a wild and maddening run,
The boss's little daughter who was riding on that side,
Rushed in to stop the stampede,
    'twas there poor Utah died.

Lenore upon her pony tried to turn the cattle right,
Her blanket slipped beneath her,
    but she caught and held on tight.
But when we saw that blanket each cowboy held his breath,
For should her pony fail her,
    none could save the girl from death.

When the cattle saw the blanket
    almost dragging on the ground,
They were maddened in a moment
    and charged with deafening sound,
The girl soon saw her danger; she turned her pony's face,
And bending in her saddle, tried the blanket to replace.

Just then she lost her balance in front of that wild tide.
Carroll's voice controlled the round up,
    "Lie still, little girl," he cried.
And then close up beside her came Utah riding fast,
But little did the poor boy know
    that ride would be his last.

Full often from the saddle had he caught the trailing rope,
To pick her up at full speed was now his only hope.
He swung low from his saddle to take her to his arm,
We thought that he'd succeeded,
    that the girl was safe from harm.

Such a strain upon his saddle had never been put before,
The cinches gave beneath him and he fell beside Lenore.
When the girl fell from her pony,
    she had dragged the blanket down,
It lay there close beside her where she lay upon the ground.

Utah took it up again and to Lenore he said,
"Lie still," and quickly running
    waved the red thing o'er his head.
He turned the maddened cattle from Lenore,
    his little friend,
As the mighty herd rushed toward him,
    he turned to meet his end.

And as the herd came on him his weapon quickly drew,
He was bound to die defended as all brave cowboys do.
The weapon flashed like lightning,
    it sounded loud and clear,
As the cattle rushed and killed him,
    he dropped the leading steer.

When I broke through that wide circle
    to where poor Utah lay,
With a thousand wounds and bruises
    his life blood ebbed away,
I knelt down close beside him
    and I knew that all was o'er,
As I heard him faintly whisper,
    "Good-bye, my sweet Lenore."

Next morning at the churchyard I heard the preacher say,
"Don't think our kind friend Utah
    was lost on that great day,
He was a much-loved cowboy, and not afraid to die,
And we'll meet him at the round up
    on the plains beyond the sky."

The Railroad Corral

Tune: *The Irish Washerwoman*

            F
Oh, we're up in the morning ere breaking of day,
    C7
The chuck-wagon's busy, the flapjack's in play;
    F
The herd is astir over hillside and vale,
    C7   F
With the night-riders rounding them into the trail.

So come take up your cinches, come shake out your reins,
Come wake your old bronco and break for the plains,
Come roust out your steers from the long chapparal,
For the outfit is off to the railroad corral.

The sun circles upward; the steers as they plod,
Are pounding to powder the hot prairie sod,
And it seems when the dust makes you dizzy and sick,
That we'll never reach noon and the cool, shady crick.

But tie up your handkerchief, play up your nag,
Come dry up your rumbles and try not to lag,
Drive up your steers from the long chapparal,
For we're well on the road to the railroad corral.

The Tenderfoot

C
I thought one spring, just for fun,
  F   C
I'd see how cow-punching was done;
   F   C
And when the round-ups had begun,
  G   C
I tackled the cattle-king.

Says he, "My foreman is in town,
     F   C
He's at the plaza, his name is Brown;
  F   C
If you see him he'll take you down."
  G   C
Says I, "That's just the thing."

We started for the ranch next day;
Brown augured me most all the way.
He said that cow-punching was child play,
That it was no work at all,
That all you had to do was ride,
'Twas only drifting with the tide;
Oh, how that old cow-puncher lied —
He certainly had his gall.

He put me in charge of a cavyard,
And told me not too work too hard,
That all I had to do was guard
The horses from getting away;
I had one hundred and sixty head,
I sometimes wished that I was dead;
When one got away, Brown's head turned red,
And there was hell to pay.

Straight to the bushes they would take,
As if they were running for a stake,
I've often wished their neck they'd break,
But they would never fall.
Sometimes I could not head them at all,
Sometimes my horse would catch a fall,
And I'd shoot on like a cannon ball.
Till the earth came in my way.

They saddled me up an old gray hack
With two set-fasts on his back;
They padded him down with a gunny sack
And used my bedding all.
When I got on he quit the ground,
Went up in the air and turned around,
And I came down and hit the ground,
It was an awful fall.

They picked me up and carried me in
And rubbed me down with an old stake-pin.
"That's the way they all begin;
You're doing well," says Brown.
"And in the morning, if you don't die,
I'll give you another horse to try."
"Oh, say, can't I walk?" says I.
Says he, "Yes—back to town."

I've traveled up and I've traveled down,
I've traveled this country round and round,
I've lived in city and I've lived in town,
But I've got this much to say:
Before you try cow-punching, kiss your wife,
Take a heavy insurance on your life,
Then cut your throat with a barlow knife,
For it's easier done that way.

The Gal I Left Behind Me

  D   G
I struck the trail in seventy-nine,
    D   F♯m
The herd strung out behind me;
    Bm   G
As I jogged along my mind went back
     A7   D
To the girl I left behind me.

Chorus:

D
That sweet little gal, that true little gal,
          Bm F♯
That gal I left behind me,
  G   E7
That sweet little gal, that true little gal,

That gal I left behind me.

If I ever get off the trail
And the Indians they don't find me,
I'll make my way straight back again
To the gal I left behind me.

The wind did blow, the rain did flow,
The hail did fall and blind me;
I thought of that gal, that sweet little gal,
That gal I'd left behind me.

She wrote ahead to the place I said,
I was always glad to find it;
She says, "I'm true, when you get through,
Ride back and you will find me."

When we sold out, I took the train,
I knew when I would find her;
When I got back, we had a smack,
And that was no gol-darned liar.

Red River Valley

```
E              B7        E
From this valley they say you are going,
                              B7
We will miss your bright eyes and sweet smile;
         E        E7       A
For they say you are taking the sunshine
         E         B7        E
That has brightened our pathways awhile.
```

Chorus:

```
E                 B7        E
Come and sit by my side, if you love me,
                  B7
Do not hasten to bid me adieu,
         E        E7       A
Just remember the Red River Valley
         E         B7        E
And the cowboy who loved you so true.
```

I've been thinking a long time, my darling,
Of the sweet words you never would say,
Now, alas, must my fond hopes all vanish?
For they say you are going away.

Do you think of the valley you're leaving?
O how lonely and how dreary it will be.
Do you think of the kind hearts you're breaking?
And the pain you are causing to me?

They will bury me where you have wandered,
Near the hills where the daffodils grow,
When you're gone from the Red River Valley,
For I can't live without you I know.

The Streets Of Laredo

```
    D       A7      D      A7
As I walked out in the streets of Laredo,
    D       A7      D      A7
As I walked out in Laredo one day,
    D          A7          D        A7
I spied a poor cowboy wrapped up in white linen,
    D            G       A7       D
All wrapped in white linen and cold as the clay.
```

"I see by your outfit that you are a cowboy,"
These words he did say as I proudly stepped by,
"Come sit down beside me and hear my sad story,
Got shot in the breast and I know I must die.

" 'Twas once in the saddle I used to go dashing,
'Twas once in the saddle I used to go gay;
'Twas first to drinkin', and then to card-playing,
Got shot in the breast and I'm dying today.

"Let six jolly cowboys come carry my coffin,
Let six pretty gals come carry my pall;
Throw bunches of roses all over my coffin,
Throw roses to deaden the clods as they fall.

"Oh, beat the drum slowly, and play the fife lowly,
And play the dead march as you carry me along,
Take me to the green valley and lay the earth o'er me,
For I'm a poor cowboy and I know I've done wrong."

Oh we beat the drum slowly and we played the fife lowly,
And bitterly wept as we carried him along,
For we all loved our comrade,
    so brave, young and handsome,
We all loved our comrade although he done wrong.

THE FARMER IS THE MAN

Songs of renters, hayseeds,
sharecroppers and workers on the land....

Times Are Getting Hard

F   Gm7
Times are gettin' hard, boys,
C7   F
Money's gettin' scarce,
                    G7
If times don't get no better, boys,
    C7   F
I'm bound to leave this place.
           Gm7
Take my true love by the hand,
C7   F
Lead her through the town,
F   Gm7
Say goodbye to everyone,
    C7   F
Goodbye to everyone.

Take my Bible from the bed,
Shotgun from the wall,
Take old Sal and hitch her up,
The wagon for to haul.
Pile the chairs and beds up high,
Let nothing drag the ground,
Sal can pull and we can push,
We're bound to leave this town.

Made a crop a year ago,
It withered to the ground,
Tried to get some credit
But the banker turned me down.
Goin' to Californi-ay,
Where everything is green,
Goin' to have the best old farm
That you have ever seen.

The Hayseed

Arthur L. Kellog/Tune: *Rosin The Beau*
Populist Song

    E   A
I once was a tool of oppression,
    E   C♯m B7
As green as a sucker could be,
      E
And monopolies banded together
A E   B7   E
To beat a poor hayseed like me.

Refrain:

    E   A
To beat a poor hayseed like me,
    E   C♯m
To beat a poor hayseed like me,
B7 E
The monopolies banded together
A E   B7   E
To beat a poor hayseed like me.

The railroads and old party bosses,
Together did sweetly agree,
They thought there would be little trouble
In working a hayseed like me.

In working a hayseed like me, etc.

But now I've roused up a little,
And their fraud and corruption I see,
And the ticket we vote next November
Will be made up of hayseeds like me.

Will be made up of hayseeds like me, etc.

Seven Cent Cotton And Forty Cent Meat

A
Seven cent cotton and forty cent meat,
                         E7
How in the world can a poor man eat?
A
Flour up high and cotton down low,
                    E7
How in the world can we raise the dough?
D   A
Clothes worn out, shoes run down,
B7   E7
Old slouch hat with a hole in the crown:
A
Back nearly broken and fingers all sore,
                E7   A
Cotton gone down to rise no more.

Seven cent cotton and forty cent meat,
How in the world can a poor man eat?
Mules in the barn, no crops laid by,
Corn crib empty and the cow's gone dry.
Well water low, nearly out of sight,
Can't take a bath on Saturday night.
No use talking, any man is beat,
With seven cent cotton and forty cent meat.

Seven cent cotton and eight dollar pants,
Who in the world has got a chance?
We can't buy clothes and we can't buy meat,
Too much cotton and not enough to eat.
Can't help each other, what shall we do?
I can't explain it so it's up to you.
Seven cent cotton and two dollar hose,
Guess we'll have to do without any clothes.

Seven cent cotton and forty cent meat,
How in the world can a poor man eat?
Poor getting poorer all around here,
Kids coming regular every year.
Fatten our hogs, take 'em to town,
All we get is six cents a pound.
Very next day we have to buy it back,
Forty cents a pound in a paper sack.

The Farmer Is The Man

      G
When the farmer comes to town

With his wagon broken down,
   Em   D   G
Oh the farmer is the man who feeds them all.

If you'll only look and see,
 Em
I think you will agree
       C   D7   G
That the farmer is the man who feeds them all.

First Chorus:

   G
The farmer is the man,
   Bm
The farmer is the man,
C   D
Lives on credit till the fall;
       G
Then they take him by the hand
      Em   G
And they lead him from the land,
       C   D   G
And the middleman's the man who gets it all.

Oh the lawyer hangs around
While the butcher cuts a pound,
But the farmer is the man who feeds them all;
And the preacher and the cook
Go a-strolling by the brook,
But the farmer is the man who feeds them all.

Second Chorus:
The farmer is the man, (twice)
Lives on credit till the fall;
With the interest rate so high,
It's a wonder he don't die,
For the mortgage man's the man who gets it all.

When the banker says he broke
And the merchant's up in smoke,
They forget that it's the farmer feeds them all.
It would put them to the test
If the farmer took a rest,
Then they'd know that it's the farmer feeds them all.

Third Chorus:
The farmer is the man, (twice)
Lives on credit till the fall;
His pants are wearing thin,
His condition, it's a sin,
He's forgot that he's the man who feeds them all.

Ballad Of The Boll Weevil

D7   G
Oh, the boll weevil is a little black bug

Come from Mexico, they say,
                Em
Come all the way from Texas,
  A7   G
Just a-lookin' for a place to stay,
           D7
Just a-lookin' for a home,
           G
Just a-lookin' for a home.

Now, the first time I seen the boll weevil,
He was settin' on the square,
The next time I seen the boll weevil,
Had his whole family there,
Just a-lookin' for a home, (twice)

The farmer took the boll weevil,
He put him in the hot sand,
The weevil say, "This is mighty hot,
But I'll stand it like a man,"
This'll be my home, (twice)

Then the farmer took the boll weevil
And put him in a cake of ice,
The weevil say to the farmer,
"This is mighty cool and nice,"
This'll be my home, (twice)

Then the boll weevil say to the doctor,
"You can throw out all them pills,
'Cause when I get through with the farmer,
Cain't pay no doctor bills,"
Won't have no home, (twice)

Well the merchant got half the cotton,
The boll weevil got the rest,
Didn't leave that farmer's wife
But one old cotton dress,
And it's full of holes, (twice)

Well the farmer say to the merchant,
"We ain't made but only one bale;
And before we give you that one
We'll fight and go to jail,"
We'll have a home, (twice)

And if anybody should ask you
Who it was that made this song,
Just tell him it was a poor farmer,
With a pair of blue overalls on,
Ain't got no home, (twice)

The Praties

(B7)   Em   C
Oh, the praties they grow small,
     Am   Em
Over here, over here,

Oh the praties they grow small,
       Am   B7
And we dig them in the Fall,
      C   Em
And we eat them coats and all,
     Am   C   Em
Over here, over here.

Oh I wish that we were geese,
Night and morn, night and morn,
Oh I wish that we were geese,
For they fly and take their ease,
And they live and die in peace,
Eatin' corn, eatin' corn.

Oh we're trampled in the dust,
Over here, over here,
Oh we're trampled in the dust,
But the Lord in whom we trust
Will give us crumb for crust,
Over here, over here.

Dakota Land

Tune: *Beulah Land*

     F
I've reached the land of desert sweet,
   C7   F
Where nothing grows for man to eat;

The wind that blows this awful heat,
  C7   F
In all this world is hard to beat.

Chorus:

    F   C7
O Dakota land, sweet Dakota land,
          F
As on the burning soil I stand,

And look away across the plains
    C7   F
And wonder why it never rains;

Till Gabriel blows the trumpet sound,
   C7   F
And says the rain has gone around.

The farmer goes out in his corn,
And there he stands and looks forlorn;
He stands and looks and is most shocked
To see the corn has missed the stock.

We have no wheat, we have no oats,
We have no corn to feed our shoats;
Our chickens are too poor to eat,
Our hogs go squealing down the street.

Our fuel is of the cheapest kind,
Our women are all of one mind;
With bag in hand and upturned nose,
They pick the chips of buffaloes.

Our horses are of bronco race,
Starvation stares them in the face;
We do not live, we only stay,
We are too poor to get away.

Robert's Farm

D
Come ladies and gentlemen, listen to my song,
I'll sing it to you now, but you might think it wrong;
It might make you mad, but I mean no harm;
Just about the renters on Roberts' farm.

Refrain:

D   A7   D
It's hard times in the country, out on Roberts' farm.

You move out to Mr. Roberts' farm,
Plant a big crop of cotton and a little crop of corn,
He'll come round to plan and to plot,
Till he gets a chattel mortgage on everything you got.
It's hard . . . etc.

Yonder comes Paul Roberts with a flattering mouth;
He moves you to the country in a little log house.
You got no windows but the cracks in the wall;
He'll work you all summer and rob you in the fall.

You go to the field and you work all day,
Till way after dark and you get no pay;
Just a little piece of meat and a little turn of corn,
It's hell to be a renter on Roberts' farm.

Roberts' renters, they'll go down town,
With their hands in their pockets,
   and their heads hung down.
We'll go in the store and the merchant will say,
"Your mortgage is due and I'm a-lookin' for my pay."

I went down to my pocket with a trembling hand,
"I can't pay you all but I'll do what I can."
The merchant jumped to the telephone call:
"I'm going to put you in jail if you don't pay it all."

Mr. Paul Roberts with a big Overland!
He's a little tough luck but you don't give a damn.
He'll run you in the mud like a train on the track;
He'll haul you to the mountains
   but he won't bring you back.

When I First Came To This Land

```
D           G    D
When I first came to this land,
G     D     A7   D
I was not a wealthy man.
              G    D
So I got myself a shack,
Em  A7     D
I did what I could.
        G    D    A7      D
And I called my shack "Break my back,"
              G    D
But the land was sweet and good,
        Em A7  D
And I did what I could.
```

When I first came to this land, etc.
So I got myself a cow, etc.
Called my cow "No milk now,"
And I called my shack "Break my back,"
But the land was sweet and good,
And I did what I could.

Duck . . . out of luck.

Wife . . . run for your life.

Son . . . my work's done.

The Miller

```
D
There was an old miller and he lived all alone,
    G            D
He had three sons all fully grown.
```

And when he came to make his will,

All he had left was a little grist mill,
```
                         A7      D
Singing fol diggy dido, fol diggy day.
```

He called to him his eldest son,
Said, "Son, oh son, my race is run.
And if a miller of you I make,
Pray tell me what toll you'd take."
Singing fol diggy di-do, etc.

"Father, oh father, my name is Bill,
Out of each bushel I'd take a jill."
"You fool, you fool!" the old man cries,
"Out of such a little you'd never make a rise."
Singing fol, etc.

He called to him his second son,
"Son, oh son, my race is run;
And if a miller of you I make,
Pray tell me what toll you'd take."

"Father, oh, father, my name is Alf,
Out of each bushel, I'd take half."
"You fool, you fool!" the old man cries,
"Out of such a little you'd never make a rise."

He called to him his youngest son,
"Son, oh son, my race is run;
And if a miller of you I make,
Pray tell me what toll you'd take."

"Father, oh father, my name is Jack,
I'd steal all the corn and swear to the sack."
"Hallelujah!" the miller cries,
And the old man turns up his toes and dies.

They buried him in a little box grave,
Some do think his soul was saved;
Where he went no one can say,
But I rather think he went the other way.

Young Man Who Wouldn't Hoe Corn

```
    G
I'll sing you a song and it's not very long,
                                          Em
It's about a young man who wouldn't hoe corn.
    Bm         F  m Em
The reason why I cannot tell,
             D        Em
For this young man was always well.
```

He planted his corn in the month of June,
And by July it was knee high;
First of September come a big frost,
And all this young man's corn was lost.

He went to the fence and there peeked in,
The weeds and the grass come up to his chin;
The weeds and the grass they grew so high,
It caused this young man for to sigh.

He went down to his neighbor's door,
Where he had often been before;
Saying, "Pretty little miss, will you marry me,
Pretty little miss what do you say?"

"Here you are a-wanting for to wed,
And cannot make your own cornbread;
Single I am, single I'll remain,
A lazy man I'll not maintain."

Well, he went down to the pretty little widder,
And I hope by heck that he don't git her;
She gave him the mitten sure as you're born,
All because he wouldn't hoe corn.

The Little Old Sod Shanty On My Claim

Tune: *Little Old Log Cabin In The Lane*

    F
I am looking rather seedy now
       Bb   F
  while holding down my claim,
                    Dm7   G7
And my victuals are not always served the best;
C7   F   Bb   F
And the mice play shyly round me as I nestle down to rest
     Am   Bb   C7   F
In the little old sod shanty on my claim.

Chorus:

    Bb   F
The hinges are of leather and the windows have no glass,
       Dm   G7   C7
While the board roof lets the howling blizzard in,
     F   F7
And I hear the hungry coyote
     Bb   F
  as he slinks up through the grass
     Dm7   G7   C7   F
Round the little old sod shanty on my claim.

Yet, I rather like the novelty of living in this way,
Though my bill of fare is always rather tame;
But I'm happy as a clam on the land of Uncle Sam
In the little old sod shanty on my claim.

But when I left my Eastern home, a bachelor so gay,
To try and win my way to wealth and fame,
I little thought I'd come down to burning twisted hay
In the little old sod shanty on my claim.

My clothes are plastered o'er with dough,
  I'm looking like a fright,
And everything is scattered round the room;
But I wouldn't give the freedom that I have
  out in the West
For the table of the Eastern man's old home.

Still, I wish that some kind-hearted girl
  would pity on me take,
And relieve me from the mess that I am in;
The angel, how I'd bless her if this her home she'd make
In the little old sod shanty on my claim!

And if fate should bless us with now and then an heir
To cheer our hearts with honest pride of fame,
Oh, then we'd be contented for the toil that we had spent
In the little old sod shanty on our claim.

When time enough had lapsed and all those little brats
To noble man and womanhood had grown,
It wouldn't seem half so lonely as round us we should look
And we'd see the old sod shanty on our claim.

Starving To Death On A Government Claim

F
My name is Tom Hight, an old bach'lor I am,
     C7
You'll find me out west in the country of fame,
     F
You'll find me out west on an elegant plain,
  C7   F
A-starving to death on my government claim.

Chorus:

F
Hurrah for Greer County! the land of the free,
   C7
The land of the bedbug, grasshopper and flea;
   F
I'll sing of its praises, I'll tell of its fame,
   C7   F
While starving to death on my government claim.

My house, it is built of national soil,
Its walls are erected according to Hoyle,
Its roof has no pitch, but is level and plain,
I always get wet if it happens to rain.

My clothes are all ragged, as my language is rough,
My bread is corndodgers, both solid and tough;
But yet I am happy and live at my ease
On sorghum, molasses, bacon and cheese.

How happy am I when I crawl into bed,
A rattlesnake hisses a tune at my head,
A gay little centipede, all without fear,
Crawls over my pillow and into my ear.

Now all you claim holders, I hope you will stay
And chew your hardtack till you're toothless and grey,
But for myself I'll no longer remain
To starve like a dog on my government claim.

Last Chorus:
Goodbye to Greer County where blizzards arise,
Where the sun never sinks and the flea never dies,
And the wind never ceases but always remains
Till it starves us all out on our government claims.

Farewell to Greer County, farewell to the west,
I'll travel back east to the girl I love best,
I'll travel to Texas and marry me a wife
And quit corn dodgers the rest of my life.

Songs of coal miners, textile weavers, long-line skinners, track-liners, field hands and other

HARD-WORKING PEOPLE

John Henry

E
When John Henry was a little baby,
B7
Sitting on his papa's knee,
E   A7
Well he picked up a hammer and little piece of steel,
E   A7
Said "Hammer's gonna be the death of me, Lord, Lord;
E   B7   E
"Hammer's gonna be the death of me."

The captain said to John Henry,
"I'm gonna bring that steam drill around,
"I'm gonna bring that steam drill out on the job,
"I'm gonna whup that steel on down."
   (Lord, Lord!)

John Henry told his captain,
"Lord a man ain't nothing but a man,
But before I'd let your steam drill beat me down,
I'd die with a hammer in my hand!"
   (Lord, Lord)

John Henry said to his shaker,
"Shaker why don't you sing?
Because I'm swinging thirty pounds
   from my hips on down;
Just listen to that cold steel ring."
   (Lord, Lord)

Now the captain said to John Henry,
"I believe that mountain's caving in."
John Henry said right back to the captain,
"Ain't nothing but my hammer sucking wind."
   (Lord, Lord)

Now the man that invented the steam drill,
He thought he was mighty fine;
But John Henry drove fifteen feet,
The steam drill only made nine.
   (Lord, Lord)

John Henry hammered in the mountains,
His hammer was striking fire,
But he worked so hard, it broke his poor heart
And he laid down his hammer and he died.
   (Lord, Lord)

Now John Henry had a little woman,
Her name was Polly Anne,
John Henry took sick and had to go to bed,
Polly Anne drove steel like a man.
   (Lord, Lord)

John Henry had a little baby,
You could hold him in the palm of your hand;
And the last words I heard that poor boy say,
"My daddy was a steel driving man."
   (Lord, Lord)

So every Monday morning
When the blue birds begin to sing,
You can hear John Henry a mile or more;
You can hear John Henry's hammer ring.
   (Lord, Lord)

Pick A Bale Of Cotton

Chorus:

E   A   E
Oh, Lordy, pick a bale of cotton.
              B7   E
Oh, Lordy, pick a bale a day.
E   A   E
Oh, Lordy, pick a bale of cotton.
              B7   E
Oh, Lordy, pick a bale a day.

Verses:

           E
Gonna jump down turn around,
   A   E
   pick a bale of cotton,

Gonna jump down turn around,
   B7   E
   pick a bale a day.

Gonna jump down turn around,
   A   E
   pick a bale of cotton,

Gonna jump down turn around,
   B7   E
   pick a bale a day.

Gonna get on my knees,
   pick a bale of cotton,
Gonna get on my knees,
   pick a bale a day.
Gonna get on my knees,
   pick a bale of cotton,
Gonna get on my knees,
   pick a bale a day.

Gonna jump, jump, jump down, etc.

Me and my gal gonna, etc.

Me and my buddy gonna, etc.

Gonna pick-a, pick-a, pick-a, pick-a, etc.

Ballad Of Springhill
The Springhill Mine Disaster

Ewan MacColl and Peggy Seeger

Copyright © 1960 by Stormking Music Inc.
All Rights Reserved. Used by Permission.

```
    Dm    C      Dm   C
In the town of Springhill, Nova Scotia,
Dm            G        Dm
Down in the dark of the Cumberland Mine,
              G      C    A7
There's blood on the coal and the miners lie
     Dm    C   Dm     C
In the roads that never saw sun nor sky,
     Dm    C   Dm      A
In the roads that never saw sun nor sky.
```

In the town of Springhill, you don't sleep easy,
Often the earth will tremble and roll,
When the earth is restless, miners die,
Bone and blood is the price of coal, (twice)

In the town of Springhill, Nova Scotia,
Late in the year of fifty-eight,
Day still comes and the sun still shines,
But it's dark as the grave in the Cumberland Mine,
Dark as the grave in the Cumberland Mine.

Down at the coal face, miners working,
Rattle of the belt and the cutter's blade,
Rumble of rock and the walls close round
The living and the dead men two miles down,
Living and the dead men two miles down.

Twelve men lay two miles from the pitshaft,
Twelve men lay in the dark and sang,
Long, hot days in the miner's tomb,
It was three feet high and a hundred long,
Three feet high and a hundred long.

Three days passed and the lamps gave out,
And Caleb Rushton he up and said:
"There's no more water nor light nor bread
So we'll live on songs and hope instead.
Live on songs and hope instead."

Listen for the shouts of the bareface miners,
Listen through the rubble for a rescue team,
Six-hundred feet of coal and slag,
Hope imprisoned in a three-foot seam. (twice)

Eight days passed and some were rescued,
Leaving the dead to lie alone,
Through all their lives they dug a grave,
Two miles of earth for a marking stone. (twice)

Molly Malone

```
   C        Am          Dm      G7
In Dublin's fair city where the girls are so pretty,
     C       Am        Dm     G7
'Twas there that I first met sweet Molly Malone.
      C            Am
She wheeled her wheelbarrow
           Dm          G7
   through the streets broad and narrow,
      C        Am     G7      C
Cryin' "Cockles and Mussels alive, alive-o!"
```

Chorus:

```
   C      Am  Dm   G7
Alive, alive-o,    alive, alive-o,
            C       Am   G7      C
Crying "Cockles and Mussels alive, alive-o!"
```

She was a fishmonger, but sure 'twas no wonder,
For so were her father and mother before,
And they each pushed their wheelbarrow
   through streets broad and narrow
Crying cockles and mussels alive, alive, oh!

She died of a "faver," and no one could save her,
And that was the end of sweet Molly Malone;
Her ghost wheels her barrow
   through streets broad and narrow
Crying cockles and mussels alive, alive, oh!

Nine Pound Hammer

```
G                              C
This nine-pound hammer is a little too heavy,
          D7              G
Buddy, for my size, buddy for my size.
```

Chorus:

```
                              C
So roll on, buddy, don't you roll so slow.
          D7              G
How can I roll, when the wheels won't go?
```

Ain't nobody's hammer in this mountain
That rings like mine, that rings like mine.

Well I went up on the mountain just to see my baby
And I ain't a-coming back, Lord,
   I ain't a-coming back.

It's a long way to Hazard, it's a long way to Harlan
Just to get a little booze, just to get a little booze.

The Ox-Driver

Dm
Pop my whip and I bring the blood,
  Gm
I make my leaders take the mud,
    Dm
We grab the wheels and we turn them around,
    Am   Dm
One long, long pull and we're on hard ground.

Chorus:

    Dm
To me rol, to me rol, to my ride-o,
    C
To me rol, to me rol, to my ride-o
    Dm
To my ride-o, to my rudie-o,
    C   Dm
To me rol, to me rol, to me ride-o.

On the fourteenth day of October-o,
I hitched my team in order-o
To drive the hills of Saludi-o,
To me roll, to me roll, to my ride-o.

When I got there, the hills were steep,
'Twould make any tender-hearted person weep,
To hear me cuss and pop my whip
And see my oxen pull and slip.

When I get home I'll have revenge,
I'll land my family among my friends,
I'll bid adieu to the whip and line
And drive no more in the wintertime.

Weave Room Blues

D   A7
Working in a weave-room, fighting for my life,
                         D
Trying to make a living for my kiddies and my wife,
                         G
Some are needing clothing and some are needing shoes,
D   A7   D
But I'm getting nothing but them weave-room blues.

Chorus:

D   F
I got the blues, I got the blues,
         D   A7   D
I got them awful weave-room blues;
              A7   D
I got the blues, the weave-room blues.

With your looms a-slamming, shuttles bouncing
   on the floor,
And when you flag your fixer, you can see that he is sore,
I'm trying to make a living but I'm thinking I will lose,
'Cause I'm a-getting nothing but them weave-room blues.

The harness eyes are breaking and the doubles
   coming through;
The devil's in your alley and he's coming after you;
Our hearts are aching, let us take a little snooze,
For we're simply dying with them weave-room blues.

Slam outs, break outs, knot ups by the score,
Cloth all rolled back and piled up in the floor,
The bats are running ends, the strings are hanging
   to your shoes,
We're simply dying with them weave-room blues.

Weaver's Life

Tune: *Life Is Like A Mountain Railway*

D
Weaver's life is like an engine,
              G   D
   coming 'round a mountain steep,

We have our ups-and-downs a-plenty,
         E7   A7
   and at night we cannot sleep,
         D   G   D
Very often flag your fixer when his head is bending low,

You may think that he is loafing,
         A7   D
   but he's doing all he knows.

Chorus:

              G   D
Soon we'll end this life of weaving,
              A7
Soon we'll reach a better shore,
                         G
Where we'll rest from filling batteries,
         D   A7   D
We will have to weave no more.

Very often meet a partner
   who would like to learn to weave,
And we feel it is our duty, we are bound to believe,
Show him all about those breakouts,
   for he will have them by the score,
When the conversation's over,
   he will want to weave no more.

Very often have a breakout
   that will surely make you sweat,
If you're feeling blue and drowsy,
   they will almost make you quit,
Very often have a headache
   when our looms are running bad,
When we've ground and snagged the lever,
   you can bet your life we're mad.

The Erie Canal

```
        Dm          Gm      Dm
I've got a mule and her name is Sal,
                  Bb 7  A7 Dm
Fifteen  miles  on  the  Erie  Canal.
                            Gm     Dm
She's a good old worker and a good old pal,
                  Bb 7  A7 Dm
Fifteen  miles  on  the  Erie  Canal.
           F      C    F     C7
We've hauled some barges in our day,
Dm            Gm7   A7
Filled with lumber, coal and hay,
     Dm       Gm      Dm
And we know every inch of the way
             Bb 7 A7 Dm C7
From Albany to Buffalo.
```

Chorus:

```
F                 C7
Low bridge, everybody down,
F                       C7      F
Low bridge, for we're going through a town,
                        C7
And you'll always know your neighbor,
      F          Bb
You'll always know your pal,
          Dm   Bb       C7      F
If you've ever navigated on the Erie Canal.
```

We'd better look around for a job, old gal,
Fifteen miles on the Erie Canal.
'Cause you bet your life I'd never part with Sal,
Fifteen miles on the Erie Canal.
    Get up there mule, here comes a lock,
    We'll make Rome 'bout six o'clock,
    One more trip and back we'll go,
    Right back home to Buffalo.

Oh, where would I be if I lost my pal?
Fifteen miles on the Erie Canal.
Oh, I'd like to see a mule as good as Sal
Fifteen miles on the Erie Canal.
    A friend of mine once got her sore,
    Now he's got a broken jaw,
    'Cause she let fly with her iron toe
    And kicked him in to Buffalo.

You'll soon hear them sing all about my gal,
Fifteen miles on the Erie Canal.
It's a darn fine ditty 'bout my darn mule Sal,
Fifteen miles on the Erie Canal.
    Oh, any band will play it soon,
    Darn fool words and darn'd fool tune,
    You'll hear it sung before you go
    From Mexico to Buffalo.

Winnsboro Cotton Mill Blues

```
D
Old man Sargent, sittin' at the desk,
                       E7        A7
The damned old fool won't give us no rest
Em
He'd take the nickels off a dead man's eyes
   A7
To buy a Coca Cola and an Eskimo Pie.
```

Chorus:

```
         D
I got the blues, I got the blues,
                              D7
I got the Winnsboro Cotton Mill Blues.
G        Gm
Lordy, Lordy spoolin's hard,
D
You know and I know, I don't have to tell,
                    Bm       E7      A7
You work for Tom Watson, got to work like hell.
        D
I got the blues. I got the blues.
       B7   E7  A7              D
I got the Winnsboro Cotton Mill Blues.
```

When I die, don't bury me at all,
Just hang me up on the spool room wall,
Place a knotter in my hand,
So I can spool in the promised land.

When I die, don't bury me deep,
Bury me down on 600 Street,
Place a bobbin in each hand,
So I can dolph in the promised land.

Pay Day At Coal Creek

```
G
Pay day, pay day, oh, pay day,
C              G
Pay day at Coal Creek no more.
D7             G
Pay day at Coal Creek no more.
```

Bye-bye, bye-bye, oh, bye-bye,
Bye-bye, my woman, I'm gone, (twice)

You'll miss me, you'll miss me, you'll miss me,
You'll miss me when I'm gone, (twice)

I'm a poor boy, I'm a poor boy, I'm a poor boy,
I'm a poor boy and a long ways from home, (twice)

He's a rider, he's a rider, he's a rider,
Oh, he's a rider, but he'll leave that rail some time.
He's a rider but he'll leave that rail some time.

The Work Of The Weavers

G   C G
We're all met together here, to sit and to crack.

               D7
With our glasses in our hands and our work upon our back.

      G
And there's not a trade among them all

   C   G
can neither mend nor mak'

          D7 G
If it wasna' for the work of the weavers.

Chorus:

   G   D7 Em   Bm
If it wasna' for the weavers, what would they do?

C   G   Am   D7
We wouldna' have cloth made of our wool.

G   C   G
We wouldna' have a coat, neither black nor blue,

          D7 G
If it wasna' for the work of the weavers.

The hireman chiels (mill-owners), they mock us
  and crack aye aboot's,
They say that we are thin-faced,
  bleached like cloots (cloths);
But yet for a' their mockery they canna do wi'oots,
No! They canna want the work of the weavers.

There's our wrights and our slaters and glaziers and a',
Our doctors and our ministers and them that live by law;
And our friends in South America,
  though them we never saw,
But we know they wear the work of the weavers.

There's our sailors and our soldiers,
  we know they're a' bald,
But if they hadna clothes, faith,
  they couldna live for cauld;
The high and low, the rich and poor,
  a'body young and auld—
They winna want the work of the weavers.

There's folk that's independent of other tradesman's work,
The women need no barbers and dykers need no clerk;
But none o' them can do without a coat or a shirt,
No! They canna want the work of the weavers.

The weaving is a trade that never can fail,
As long's we need a cloth to keep another hale;
So let us aye be merry over a bicker of good ale,
And drink to the health of the weavers.

The Squid-Jiggin' Ground

A7 D   Bm   A   D
Oh, this is the place where fishermen gather,

 A7   D   A   G
With oilsikns and boots and Cape Anns battened down;

   D   G   A7   D
All sizes of figures with squid lines and jiggers,

   Bm   A7   D
They congregate here on the squid-jiggin' ground.

Some are workin' their jiggers while others are yarnin',
There's some standin' up and there's more lyin' down;
While all kinds of fun, jokes and tricks are begun
As they wait for the squid on the squid-jiggin' ground.

There's men of all ages and boys in the bargain;
There's old Billy Cave and there's young Raymond Brown;
There's a red rantin' Tory out here in a dory,
A-running down Squires on the squid-jiggin' ground.

There's men from the Harbour and men from the Tickle,
In all kinds of motorboats, green, grey and brown;
Right yonder is Bobby and with him is Nobby,
He's chawin' hard tack on the squid-jiggin' ground.

God bless my sou'wester, there's Skipper John Chaffey;
He's the best at squid-jiggin' here, I'll be bound.
Hello! What's the row? Why, he's jiggin' one now,
The very first squid on the squid-jiggin' ground.

The man with the whiskers is old Jacob Steele;
He's gettin' well up but he's still pretty sound;
While Uncle Bob Hawkins wears six pairs of stockin's
Whenever he's out on the squid-jiggin' ground.

Holy smoke! What a scuffle! All hands are excited.
'Tis a wonder to me that there's nobody drowned.
There's a bustle, confusion, a wonderful hustle,
They're all jiggin' squids on the squid-jiggin' ground.

Says Bobby, "The squids are on top of the water,
I just got me jigger 'bout one fathom down"—
When a squid in the boat squirted right down his throat,
And he's swearin' like mad on the squid-jiggin' ground.

There's poor Uncle Billy, his whiskers are spattered
With spots of the squid juice that's flying around;
One poor little b'y got it right in the eye,
But they don't give a darn on the squid-jiggin' ground.

Now if ever you feel inclined to go squiddin',
Leave your white shirts and collars behind in the town,
And if you get cranky without yer silk hanky,
You'd better steer clear of the squid-jiggin' ground.

Long-Line Skinner

B7   E
I've got a bellyful of whisky

And a head full of gin,

The doctor says it'll kill me,
    E7
But he don't say when.

Chorus:

    A
I'm a long-line skinner
        E
And my home's out West,
    B7
Lookin' for the woman
A7   E
Lord, that'll love me the best.

See, pretty mama, pretty mama,
See what you done done,
You made your daddy love you,
Now your man done come.

I'm down in the bottom
Skinning mules for Johnny Ryan,
A-putting my initials
On a mule's behind.

When the weather it gets chilly
Gonna pack up my line,
'Cause I ain't skinning mules
In the winter time.

Girl Of Constant Sorrow

New Words by Sara Ogan Gunning
© 1965 by Folk Legacy Records

G   D   G   C
I am a girl of constant sorrow,
     D   C   G
I've seen trouble all my days;
G   D   G   C
I bid farewell to old Kentucky,
        D   C   G
The place where I was born and raised.

My mother how I hated to leave her,
Mother dear, now she is dead.
But I had to go and leave her,
So my children could have bread.

Perhaps, dear friends, you're a-wondering,
What the miners eat and wear.
This question I will try and answer
For I think that it is fair.

For breakfast we have bulldog gravy,
For dinner we have beans and bread;
For the miners don't have any supper,
Just a tick of straw that they call a bed.

For our clothes are always ragged,
And our feet are always bare;
And I am sure if there's a heaven
That the miners will be there.

The Factory Girl

     C   Am
No more shall I work in the factory,
C   Em
Greasy up my clothes;
     C   Am
No more shall I work in the factory
    G7   C
With splinters in my toes.

Chorus:

C   Em
Pity me my darling, pity me I say;
C   Am   G7   C
Pity me my darling, and carry me away.

No more shall I hear the bosses say,
"Boys, you'd better daulf,"
No more shall I hear those bosses say,
"Spinners, you'd better clean off."

No more shall I hear the drummer wheels
A-rolling over my head,
When factories are hard at work,
I'll be in my bed.

No more shall I hear the whistle blow,
To call me up so soon;
No more shall I hear the whistle blow,
To call me from my home.

No more shall I see the super come,
All dressed up so proud;
For I know I'll marry a country boy
Before the year is out.

No more shall I wear the old black dress,
Greasy all around;
No more shall I wear the old black bonnet
With holes all in the crown.

Bring Me A Little Water, Sylvie

A
Bring me a little water, Sylvie,

Bring me a little water now.
            D
Bring me a little water, Sylvie,
    E7   A
Ev'ry little once in a while.

Don't you see me comin'?
Don't you see me now?
Don't you see me comin'?
Ev'ry little once in a while.

Bring me a little water, Sylvie,
Bring me a little water, now.
Bring me a little water, Sylvie,
Ev'ry little once in a while.

Don't you hear me comin'?
Don't you hear me now?
Don't you hear me comin'?
Ev'ry little once in a while.

Bring me a little water, Sylvie,
Bring me a little water, now.
Bring me a little water, Sylvie,
Ev'ry little once in a while.

Mule Skinner Blues

    G
Good morning captain,

Good morning son
G7   C
Good morning captain,
       G
Good morning son
   D7
Do you need another mule skinner
         G
Out on your new road line?

Well, I like to work
I'm rolling all the time.
Lord, I like to work
Boy, I'm rolling all the time.
I can pop my initials
Right on a mule's behind.

Well, it's hey little water boy,
Bring your water 'round,
Lord, it's hey little water boy,
Bring your water 'round.
And if you don't like your job
Just set that water bucket down.

I work out on the new road
For a dollar and a dime a day.
Lord, I work out on the new road,
I make a dollar and a dime a day.
I've got three women on Saturday night
Waiting to draw my pay.

Well, I'm going to town honey,
What can I bring you back?
Well, I'm going to town, baby,
What can I bring you back?
Just bring a pint of good rye
And a John B. Stetson hat.

Lord, it's raining here and it's
Storming on the deep blue sea.
Lord, it's raining here and it's
Storming on the deep blue sea.
Cain't no blonde-headed woman
Make a monkey out of me.

If your house catches fire
And there ain't no water 'round.
If your house catches fire
And there ain't no water 'round.
Just throw your good gal out the window
Let your house just burn on down.

Well, I'm leaving here and I
Ain't gonna take no clothes,
I'm leaving here and I
Ain't gonna take no clothes,
There may be good times in this old town
But it's better on down the road.

Banks Of Marble

Les Rice

Copyright © 1950 by Stormking Music Inc.
All Rights Reserved. Used by Permission.

    C   G7   C
I've traveled 'round this country,
    F   C
From shore to shining shore;
  G7   C
It really made me wonder,
  G7   C
The things I heard and saw.

I saw the weary farmer,
Plowing sod and loam;
I heard the auction hammer
A-knocking down his home.

Chorus:

       C
But the banks are made of marble,
  G7   C
With a guard at every door,

And the vaults are stuffed with silver
       G7   C
That the farmer sweated for.

I saw the seaman standing
Idly by the shore,
I heard the bosses saying,
"Got no work for you no more."

I saw the weary miner
Scrubbing coal dust from his back,
I heard his children crying,
"Got no coal to heat the shack."

I've seen my brothers working
Throughout this mighty land,
I prayed we'd get together
And together make a stand.

Final Chorus:
Then we'd own those banks of marble,
With a guard at every door,
And we'd share those vaults of silver
That we have sweated for!

I'se The B'y

G   D
I'se the b'y that builds the boat,
   G   D7
And I'se the b'y that sails her!
G   D
I'se the b'y that catches the fish
  D7   G
And takes 'em home to Liza.

Refrain:

G   D
Hip your partner, Sally Tibbo!
G   D7
Hip your partner, Sally Brown!
G   D
Fogo, Twillingate, Morton's Harbor,
D7   G
All around the circle!

Sods and rinds to cover yer flake,
Cake and tea for supper,
Codfish in the spring o' the year
Fried in maggoty butter.

I don't want your maggoty fish,
That's no good for winter;
I could buy as good as that
Down in Bonavista.

I took Liza to a dance,
And faith, but she could travel!
And every step that she did take
Was up to her knees in gravel.

Susan White, she's out of sight,
Her petticoat wants a border;
Old Sam Oliver, in the dark
He kissed her in the corner.

Drill Ye Tarriers, Drill

Thomas F. Casey

Am
Early in the morning at seven o'clock
      E7
There are twenty tarriers a drilling at the rock,
      Am
And the boss comes around and he says "Keep still!
      E7
And come down heavy on your cast iron drill."

Chorus:

    Am   E7   Am
And drill ye tarriers, drill.
       G   Am
Drill ye tarriers drill.

Well you work all day for the sugar in your tay

Down behind the railway
    Am   E7   Am
And drill ye tarriers drill,

And blast and fire.

Now our new foreman was Jim McGann,
By golly, he was, a blame mean man
Last week a premature blast went off,
And a mile in the sky went Big Jim Goff.

Now when next payday comes around,
Jim Goff a dollar short was found,
When asked the reason, came this reply,
"You were docked for the time you were up in the sky."

Now the boss was a fine man down to the ground,
And he married a lady, six feet round,
She baked good bread, and she baked it well,
But she baked it as hard as the holes in hell.

Four Pence A Day

    C   G7   C
The ore is waiting in the tubs; the snow's upon the fell.
    Am   G   D7   G
Canny folk are sleeping yet, but lead is reet to sell.
F   C   G
Come, me little washer lad, come let's away,
    C   G7   C
We're bound down to slavery for four pence a day.

It's early in the morning, we rise at five o'clock,
And the little slaves come to the door
    to knock, knock, knock.
Come, me little washer lad, come let's away,
It's very hard to work for four-pence a day.

My father was a miner and lived down in the town;
'Twas hard work and poverty that always kept him down.
He aimed for me to go to school but brass he couldn't pay,
So I had to go to the washing rake for four-pence a day.

My mother rises out of bed with tears on her cheeks,
Puts my wallet on my shoulders which has to serve a week.
It often fills her great big heart when she unto me does say,
"I never thought you would have worked
    for four-pence a day."

Fourpence a day, me lad, and very hard to work,
And never a pleasant look from a gruffy looking Turk.
His conscience it may fall and his heart it may give way,
Then he'll raise our wages to ninepence a day.

Timber

Jerry The Mule

Am   C   Am   C   Am
Got to pull this timber 'fore the sun goes down,
             C   Am   C   Am
Get it cross the river 'fore the boss comes 'round,
        C   Em
Drag it down that old dusty road,

Come on, Jerry, let's dump this load,

Refrain:

         Am   C   Em   Am
Hollerin' TIMBER! Lord, this timber's gotta roll.

My old Jerry was an Arkansas mule,
Been everywhere and he ain't no fool,
Weighed nine hundred and twenty-two,
Done everything a poor mule can do . . .

Jerry's old shoulder was six feet tall,
Pulled more timber than a freight can haul,
Work got heavy, ol' Jerry got sore,
Pulled so much he wouldn't pull no more . . .

Boss hit Jerry and made him jump,
Jerry reared up and kicked that boss in the rump,
Now my old Jerry was a good old mule,
If it had-a been me I'd-a killed that fool . . .

The boss he tried to shoot my Jerry in the head,
Jerry ducked the bullet and stomped him dead,
Stomped that boss till I wanted to scream,
Should have killed him myself, he was so damn mean . . .

SOLIDARITY FOREVER

Songs of picket-lines, strikes and union struggles....

Union Maid

Woody Guthrie/Tune: *Redwing*

    C
There once was a Union maid,
  F   C
Who never was afraid
  G7   C
Of goons and ginks and company finks
   D7   G7
And deputy sheriffs who made the raids;
  C
She went to the Union hall,
   F   C
When a meeting it was called,
  G7   C
And when the Legion boys came round,
  G7   C
She always stood her ground.

Chorus:

      F   C
Oh you can't scare me I'm sticking to the Union,
           G7
I'm sticking to the Union,
           C
I'm sticking to the Union,
      F   C
Oh you can't scare me I'm sticking to the Union,
           G7   C
I'm sticking to the Union till the day I die.

This union maid was wise
To the tricks of company spies;
She couldn't be fooled by a company stool,
She'd always organize the guys.
She'd always get her way
When she struck for better pay;
She'd show her card to the national guard,
And this is what she'd say:

You gals who want to be free,
Just take a little tip from me;
Get you a man who's a union man,
And fight together for liberty;
Married life ain't hard
When you got a union card,
A union man has a happy life
When he's got a union wife.

Union Train

Lee Hays, Millard Lampell, Pete Seeger

E
Oh, what is that I see yonder coming,
                B7   E
Oh what is that I see yonder coming,
                 A   E
Oh what is that I see yonder coming,

Won't you get on board.
B7   E
Oh, get on board.

It's that union train a-coming, (3 times)
Won't you get on board.
Oh, get on board.

It has saved a many a thousand, etc.

It will save a many more thousand, etc.

It will carry us to freedom, etc.

We're fighting for our freedom, etc.

Black and white together, etc.

We Are Building A Strong Union

Tune: *Jacob's Ladder*

D   Bm   D
We are building a strong union,
   A7   G   D
We are building a strong union,
D   Bm   G   D
We are building a strong union,
D7   A7   D
Workers in the mill.

We have toiled in dark and danger, (3 times)
Workers of the south.

We are black and white together, (3 times)
Workers in the mill.

Every member makes us stronger, (3 times)
Workers in the mill.

We shall rise and gain our freedom, (3 times)
Workers in the mill.

We are building a strong union, (3 times)
Workers of the south.

Roll The Union On

Claude Williams and Lee Hays

Chorus:

      G
We're gonna roll, we're gonna roll,
                D7
We're gonna roll the union on.

We're gonna roll, we're gonna roll,
                G
We're gonna roll the union on.

Verses:

      G
If the boss is in the way,

We're gonna roll it over him,
        C   D7
We're gonna roll it over him,
        G
We're gonna roll it over him,

If the boss is in the way,

We're gonna roll it over him,
C   D7   G
Roll the union on.

If the scabs are in the way
We're gonna roll it over them, etc.

If Jim Crow is in the way
We're gonna roll it over him, etc.

No matter who is in the way
We're gonna roll it over them, etc.

You Gotta Go Down (And Join The Union)

G   C   G
You gotta go down and join the union,
        D7   G
You gotta join it for yourself.
           C   G
There ain't nobody can join it for you,
                     D7   G
You gotta go down and join the union by yourself.

Sister's got to go down and join the union
She's got to join it for herself.
Ain't nobody here gonna join it for her,
She's got to go down and join the union for herself.

Mama's got to go down and join the union, etc.

Solidarity Forever

Ralph Chaplin/Tune: *Battle Hymn Of The Republic*

       G
When the union's inspiration

    through the workers' blood shall run,
         C   G
There can be no power greater anywhere beneath the sun;

Yet what force on earth is weaker
         G   B7   Em
than the feeble strength of one,
        Am   G   D7 G
For the union makes us strong.

Chorus:

G   C   G
Solidarity Forever, Solidarity Forever,
             G Em
Solidarity Forever,
        Am   G   D7 G
For the union makes us strong.

It is we who ploughed the prairies,
    built the cities where they trade,
Dug the mines and built the workshops,
    endless miles of railroad laid;
Now we stand outcast and starving
    'mid the wonders we have made,
But the union makes us strong.

They have taken untold millions
    that they never toiled to earn,
But without our brain and muscle
    not a single wheel can turn;
We can break their haughty power,
    gain our freedom when we learn
That the union makes us strong.

In our hands is placed a power
    greater than their hoarded gold,
Greater than the might of atoms
    magnified a thousandfold;
We can bring to birth a new world
    from the ashes of the old,
For the union makes us strong.

The Ludlow Massacre

Woody Guthrie

C
It was early springtime that the strike was on,
          F   C
They drove us miners out of doors,

Out from the houses that the company owned,
          G7   C
We moved into tents up at old Ludlow.

I was worried bad about my children,
Soldiers guarding the railroad bridge;
Every once in a while a bullet would fly,
Kick up gravel under my feet.

We were so afraid you would kill our children,
We dug us a cave that was seven foot deep;
Carried our young ones and a pregnant woman
Down inside the cave to sleep.

That very night you soldiers waited
Until us miners was asleep;
You snuck around our little tent town,
Soaked our tents with your kerosene.

You struck a match and the blaze it started;
You pulled the triggers of your gatling guns;
I made a run for the children but the fire wall stopped me,
Thirteen children died from your guns.

I carried my blanket to a wire fence corner,
Watched the fire till the blaze died down;
I helped some people grab their belongings
While your bullets killed us all around.

I never will forget the look on the faces
Of the men and women that awful day
When we stood around to preach their funerals
And lay the corpses of the dead away.

We told the Colorado governor to phone the President,
Tell him to call off his National Guard;
But the National Guard belonged to the governor,
So he didn't try so very hard.

Our women from Trinidad they hauled some potatoes
Up to Walsenburg in a little cart;
They sold their potatoes and brought some guns back
And put a gun in every hand.

The state soldiers jumped us in the wire fence corner;
They did not know that we had these guns;
And the red-neck miners mowed down them troopers,
You should have seen them poor boys run!

We took some cement and walled the cave up,
Where you killed these thirteen children inside;
I said "God bless the Mine Workers' Union,"
And then I hung my head and cried.

Which Side Are You On?

Florence Reese

Bm
Come all of you good workers,
     Em   F♯m Bm
Good news to you I'll tell,
     Em   F♯m Bm
Of how that good old union
  F♯7   Bm
Has come in here to dwell.

Chorus:

Bm   A   Bm
Which side are you on?
      F♯7 D
Which side are you on?
Bm   A   Bm
Which side are you on?
      F♯7 D
Which side are you on?

My daddy was a miner,
And I'm a miner's son,
And I'll stick with the union,
Till every battle's won.

They say in Harlan County,
There are no neutrals there.
You'll either be a union man,
Or a thug for J.H. Blair.

Oh, workers can you stand it?
Oh, tell me how you can.
Will you be a lousy scab,
Or will you be a man?

Don't scab for the bosses,
Don't listen to their lies.
Us poor folks haven't got a chance,
Unless we organize.

We Pity Our Bosses Five

Tune: *Farmer In The Dell*

    G C   G
We pity our bosses five
        C   G
We pity our bosses five
                         Em
A thousand a week is all they get
G   D7   G
How can they stay alive?

We pity the boss's son
We pity the boss's son
He rides around in a Cadillac
The lousy son of a gun!

There Is Power

Joe Hill/Tune: *Power in The Blood Of The Lamb*

G   C
Would you have freedom from wage slavery?
   D7   G
Then join in the grand industrial band;
                        C
Would you from mis'ry and hunger be free,
   D7   G
Then come do your share like a man.

Chorus:

G
There is power, there is pow'r in a band of working men,
            D7   G
When they stand hand in hand.

There's a pow'r, there's a pow'r
             C   G
   that must rule in ev'ry land,
    D7   G
One industrial union grand.

Would you have mansions of gold in the sky,
And live in a shack, way in the back?
Would you have wings up in Heaven to fly
And starve here with rags on your back?

If you've had enough of the blood of the lamb,
Then join in the grand industrial band;
If, for a change, you would have eggs and ham,
Then come do your share like a man.

If you like sluggers to beat off your head,
Then don't organize, all unions despise.
If you want nothing before you are dead,
Shake hands with your boss and look wise.

Come, all ye workers, from every land,
Come join the grand industrial band,
Then we our share of this earth shall demand.
Come on! Do your share, like a man!

We Shall Not Be Moved

G   D
We shall not, we shall not be moved,
D7   G
We shall not, we shall not be moved,
         C   G
Just like a tree that's standing by the water,
        D7   G
We shall not be moved.

The union is behind us, we shall not be moved (twice)
Just like a tree that's standing by the water
We shall not be moved.

We'll stand and fight together, etc.

We're black and white together, etc.

We'll fight for higher wages, etc.

We're not afraid of tear-gas, etc.

We're moving on to victory, etc.

The Commonwealth Of Toil

Ralph Chaplin / Tune: *Darling Nelly Gray*

        C
In the gloom of mighty cities,
           F
'Mid the roar of whirling wheels,
Dm7 C   D G
We are toiling on like chattel slaves of old,
G   C   C7
And our masters hope to keep us
         F
Ever thus beneath their heels,
Dm7 Em   G7   C
And to coin our very lifeblood into gold.

Chorus:

     Dm7   G7
But we have a glowing dream
     C
Of how fair the world will seem
           Em   Am   D G
When each man can live his life secure and free;
        C   C7
When the earth is owned by Labor
        F
And there's joy and peace for all,
Dm7 C   G7   C
In the Commonwealth of Toil that is to be.

They would keep us cowed and beaten
Cringing meekly at their feet,
They would stand between each worker and his bread.
Shall we yield our lives up to them
For the bitter crust we eat?
Shall we only hope for heaven when we're dead?

They have laid our lives out for us
To the utter end of time,
Shall we stagger on beneath their heavy load?
Shall we let them live forever
In their gilded halls of crime
With our children doomed to toil beneath their goad?

When our cause is all triumphant
And we claim our Mother Earth,
And the nightmare of the present fades away,
We shall live with Love and Laughter,
We, who now are little worth,
And we'll not regret the price we have to pay.

Its A Good Thing To Join A Union

Tune: *Tipperary*

```
      C
It's a good thing to join a union,
      F          C
It's a good thing to do,

It's a good thing to join a union,
         D7        G7
It's the finest thing to do.
C            C7
Goodbye, unfair wages,
F            E7   G7
Farewell, long hours, too,
   C                    F C
It's a fine, fine thing to join a union,
   D7   G7  C
For it will help you.
```

Get Thee Behind Me, Satan

Lee Hays, Millard Lampell, and Pete Seeger

```
G7 C
The boss comes up to me with a five dollar bill,
                                    C7
Says: "Get you some whiskey, boy, and drink your fill."
```

Chorus:

```
        F
Get thee behind me, Satan,
      G7    C
Travel on down the line.
   G7
I am a Union man,
F        G7
Gonna leave you behind.
```

A red-headed woman took me out to dine, says:
"Love me, baby, leave your union behind."

On the Fourth of July the politicians say:
"Vote for us, and we'll raise your pay."

Company union sent out a call, said:
"Join us in the summer, we'll forget you in the fall."

Now if anyone should ask you your union to sell, just
Tell him where to go and send him back to Hell.

He's A Fool

```
Gm                     Cm       Adim
One day while walking down Thirty Fifth Street,
D      D7              Gm
We ran into a guy who looked dead on his feet.
   Gm                   Cm      Adim
He had no green button nor smile on his face,
D      D7              Gm
Kept pushing a truck 'round, and getting no place.
```

1st Chorus:

```
Gm               D7
He's a fool, he's a fool,
                            Gm
He's a fool for not joining the union;
                    D7
He's a fool, he's a fool,
                            Gm
He's a fool for not joining the union.
```

He took twenty minutes for lunch every day;
The boss always asked him why the delay.
He worked overtime without any pay,
He worked overtime without pay.

He worked every night till eighty-thirty,
And then asked if he could leave.
The boss gave a look that was dirty,
Or else he just laughed up his sleeve.
Spoken: His sleeve, yeah.

His salary was very meager,
It's a wonder he got paid at all,
I guess the boss wasn't so eager,
For when asked for a raise, he would stall.
Spoken: Stall, stall, yeah.

He cried like a baby, a union he craved,
He wanted a minimum from which he could save.
He joined with the union, boy, did the boss rave.
That's what I get for being so good to my slave.

He's no fool, he's no fool,
For he upped and he joined with the union.
(twice)

So don't trust your boss, he's just good on the surface;
Join 65, for a life with a purpose.
We'll give you happiness, gayness galore;
So brothers and sisters, give out with a roar:

Be no fool, be no fool,
Come on and join with the union.
(twice)

Raggedy

F
Hungry, hungry are we,
                    C7
Just as hungry as hungry can be.
  F   B
We don't get nothing for our labor,
 F   C7
So hungry, hungry are we.

Raggedy, raggedy are we, etc.

Homeless, homeless are we, etc.

Landless, landless are we, etc.

Angry, angry are we, etc.

Union members are we,
Just as union as union can be,
We're going to get something for our labor,
So union members are we.

Talking Union

Lee Hays, Millard Lampell, Pete Seeger

      G   C
If you want higher wages let me tell you what to do;
       D7
You got to talk to the workers in the shop with you;
      G   C
You got to build you a union, got to make it strong,
     D7
But if you all stick together, boys, it won't be long.
     G   C
You get shorter hours, better working conditions.
  D7   G
Vacations with pay, take the kids to the seashore.

It ain't quite this simple, so I better explain
Just why you got to ride on the union train;
'Cause if you wait for the boss to raise your pay,
We'll all be waiting till judgment day;
We'll all be buried—gone to Heaven—
Saint Peter'll be the straw boss then, boys.

Now, you know you're underpaid,
   but the boss says you ain't;
He speeds up the work till you're about to faint.
You may be down and out, but you ain't beaten,
You can pass out a leaflet and call a meetin'—
Talk it over—speak your mind—
Decide to do something about it.

Course, the boss may persuade some poor damn fool
To go to your meeting and act like a stool;
But you can always tell a stool, though, that's a fact,
He's got a rotten streak a-running down his back;
He doesn't have to stool—he'll make a good living—
On what he takes out of blind men's cups.

You got a union, now, and you're sitting pretty;
Put some of the boys on the steering committee.
The boss won't listen when one guy squawks,
But he's got to listen when the union talks—
He'd better—be mighty lonely—
Everybody decided to walk out on him.

Suppose they're working you so hard it's just outrageous,
And they're paying you all starvation wages,
You go to the boss, and the boss will yell,
"Before I raise your pay I'd see you all in hell."
Well, he's puffing a big cigar and feeling mighty slick,
'Cause he thinks he's got your union licked.
He looks out the window, and what does he see
But a thousand pickets, and they all agree
He's a bastard—unfair—slavedriver—
Bet he beats his wife.

Now, boys, you've come to the hardest time;
The boss will try to bust your picket line;
He'll call out the police and the national guard,
They'll tell you it's a crime to have a union card.
They'll raid your meeting, and hit you on the head,
They'll call every one of you a doggone red.—
Unpatriotic—Moscow agents—
   bomb throwers, even the kids.

But out in Detroit here's what they found,
And out in Frisco here's what they found,
And out in Pittsburgh here's what they found,
And down at Bethlehem here's what they found,
That if you don't let redbaiting break you up,
If you don't let stool pigeons break you up,
If you don't let vigilantes break you up,
And if you don't let race hatred break you up—
You'll win—what I mean take it easy—but take it.

Hold The Fort

```
C                      F
We meet today in Freedom's cause
    C               G
And raise our voices high;
      C                  F
We'll join our hands in union strong
    D7      G7
To battle or die.
```

Chorus:

```
C
Hold the fort, for we are coming
F           G7
Union men be strong;
C                   F
Side by side we battle onward,
G7              C
Victory will come.
```

Look my comrades, see the union,
Banners waving high;
Reinforcements now appearing
Victory is nigh —

See our numbers still increasing,
Hear the bugles blow;
By our union we will triumph
Over every foe —

The Picket Line Song
Tune: *Polly Wolly Doodle*

```
   F
To win our fight and our demands,
                 B♭  F  C7
Come and picket on the picket line,
```

```
In one strong union we'll join hands,
         F          C7   F
Come and picket on the picket line.
```

Chorus:

```
F
On the line, on the line,
                B♭  F  C7
Come and picket on the picket line;
```

```
We'll shout and yell and fight like hell,
                             F
Come and picket on the picket line.
```

```
If you've never spent a night in jail,
Come and picket on the picket line,
You will be invited without fail,
Come and picket on the picket line.
```

Miner's Lifeguard
Tune: *Life Is Like a Mountain Railway*

```
           G
Miner's life is like a sailor's,
G7    C           G
'Board a ship to cross the waves.
```

```
Ev'ry day his life's in danger,
       A7            D7
Still he ventures being brave.
             G
Watch the rocks, they're falling daily,
G7    C           G
Careless miners always fail.
```

```
Keep your hand up on the dollar
             D7     G
And your eye upon the scale.
```

Chorus:

```
G   C            G
Union miners stand together,
                  D7
Heed no operator's tale,
    G               C
Keep your hand upon the dollar,
    G  AmD7  G
And your eye upon the scale.
```

You've been docked and docked, my boys,
You've been loading two to one;
What have you to show for working
Since this mining has begun?
Overalls and cans for rockers,
In your shanties, sleep on rails,
Keep your hand upon the dollar
And your eye upon the scale.

In conclusion, bear in memory,
Keep the password in your mind,
God provides for every nation
When in union they combine.
Stand like men and link together,
Victory for you'll prevail,
Keep your hand upon the dollar
And your eye upon the scale.

I KNOW MY LOVE

Songs of true love . . . and not-so-true.

Greensleeves

Em   D
A-las my love, you do me wrong,
C   B7
To cast me off discourteously;
Em   D
And I have lovéd you so long,
C   B7   Em
Delighting in your company.
G   D
Greensleeves was all my joy
Em   B7
Greensleeves was my delight,
G   D
Greensleeves was my heart of gold,
Em B7 Em
And who but my lady Greensleeves.

I have been ready at your hand,
To grant whatever you would crave;
I have both wagered life and land,
Your love and good-will for to have.
If you intend thus to disdain,
It does the more enrapture me,
And even so, I still remain
A lover in captivity.

My men were clothed all in green,
And they did ever wait on thee;
All this was gallant to be seen;
And yet thou wouldst not love me.
Thou couldst desire no earthly thing
But still thou hadst it readily.
Thy music still to play and sing;
And yet thou wouldst not love me.

Well, I will pray to God on high,
That thou my constancy mayst see,
And that yet once before I die,
Thou wilt vouchsafe to love me.
Ah, Greensleeves, now farewell, adieu,
To God I pray to prosper thee,
For I am still thy lover true,
Come once again and love me.

Charlie Is My Darling

Chorus:

Am
Oh, Charlie, he's my darling,
Dm Am
My darling, my darling,

Charlie, he's my darling,
    E7 Am
The young Chevalier.

Verses:

  E7   Am
'Twas on a Monday morning,
  E7   Am
Right early in the year,
  F   C
That Charlie came to our town,
 Dm Am E7
The young Chevalier.

As he was walking up the street,
The city for to view,
O there he spied a bonnie lass,
The window looking through.

Saw light's he jumped up the stair,
And tirled at the pin;
And wha sae ready as hersel
To let the laddie in.

He set his Jenny on his knee,
All in his Highland dress:
For brawly weel he kend the way
To please a bonnie lass.

It's up yon heathery mountain,
And down yon scraggy glen,
 We daurna gang a-milking
For Charlie and his men.

Comin' Through The Rye

G   D7
Gin a body meet a body,
G D7   G
Comin' through the rye,
    D7
Gin a body kiss a body,
G D7 G
Need a body cry?
    D7
Ilka lassie has her laddie,
G7   C
Nane, they say, hae I,
 G D7 G   D
Yet a' the lads they smile at me,
  G D7   G
When comin' through the rye.

Gin a body meet a body,
Comin' frae the toon,
Gin a body greet a body,
Need a body froon?
Among the train there is a swain,
I dearly love mysel',
But what's his name or what's his hame,
I donna care to tell.

My Love Is Like A Red, Red Rose
Robert Burns

   A   D
Oh, my love is like a red, red rose,
A   D   E7
That's newly sprung in June.
   A   D
Oh, my love is like a melody
A Bm7 E7 A
That's sweetly played in tune.
   A   D A
As fair art thou, my bonnie lass,
 E7
So deep in love am I,
   A   D A
And I will love thee still, my dear,
 E7   A
Till all the seas gang dry.
     D
Till all the seas gang dry, my dear,
A D   E7
Till all the seas gang dry,
   A   D
And I will love thee still my dear,
A Bm7 E7 A
Till all the seas gang dry.

Till all the seas gang dry, my dear,
And the rocks melt with the sun,
And I will love thee still, my dear,
While the sands of life shall run.
But fare thee well, my only love,
Oh fare thee well a while,
And I will come again, my love,
Though it were ten thousand mile.
Though it were ten thousand mile, my love,
Though it were ten thousand mile,
And I will come again, my love,
Though it were ten thousand mile.

Love Somebody, Yes I Do

Chorus:

```
C              G7
Love somebody, yes I do;
C              G7
Love somebody, yes I do;
C              Dm
Love somebody, yes I do;
C       G7       C
Love somebody, but I won't tell who.
```

Verses:

```
C
Love somebody, yes I do;
         G
Love somebody, yes I do;
C
Love somebody, yes I do;
F    C    G7   C
And I hope somebody loves me too.
```

Love somebody, yes I do; (3 times)
'Tween sixteen and twenty-two.

Will You Go, Lassie, Go?

```
D
Oh, the summer time is coming,
      G           D
And the trees are sweetly blooming,
        G         D
And the wild mountain thyme,
      G
Blooms around the bloomin' heather.
```

Chorus:

```
      D G   D
Will you go, lassie, go?
       G      D
And we'll all go together,
        G           D
To pull wild mountain thyme,
      G
All around the bloomin' heather,
      D G   D
Will you go, lassie, go?
```

I will build my love a bower,
By yon clear and crystal fountain,
And on it I will pile,
All the flowers of the mountain.

If my true love, she won't go,
I will surely find another,
To pull mountain thyme,
All around the bloomin' heather.

Spanish Is The Loving Tongue

```
C              Am
Spanish is the loving tongue,
C              Dm
Soft as music, light as spray:
C                   Am
'T'was a girl I learned it from,
C           G7  C
Living down Sonora way.
        Cmaj7    Dm  Em
I don't look much like a lover,
C           Fmaj7    G
Yet I say her love words over,
C                  Am
Often when I'm all alone—
Em           G7  C
"Mi amor, mi corazón."
```

Nights when she knew where I'd ride
She would listen for my spurs,
Fling the big door open wide,
Raise them laughin' eyes of hers;
And my heart would nigh stop beating
When I heard her tender greeting,
Whispered soft for me alone—
"Mi amor, mi corazón."

Moonlight in the pation,
Old Señora nodding near,
Me and Juana talking low
So the Madre couldn't hear;
How those hours would go a-flyin'!
And too soon I'd hear her sighin'
In her little sorry tone—
"Adios, mi corazón!"

But one time I had to fly
For a foolish gamblin' fight,
And we said a swift goodbye
In that black unlucky night.
When I'd loosed her arms from clingin'
With her words the hoofs kept ringin'
As I galloped north alone—
"Adios, mi corazón!"

Never seen her since that night—
I can't cross the line, you know.
She was "Mex" and I was white;
Like as not it's better so.
Yet I've always sort of missed her
Since that last wild night I kissed her;
Left her heart and lost my own—
"Adios, mi corazón!"

John Anderson, My Jo (I)

```
     Em
John Anderson, my Jo, John,
         Am
When Nature first began
     Em         Am
To try her canny hand, John,
     G             Em
Her masterwork was man;
     G
And you among them all, John,
     Am
So grand from top to toe,
     Em    Am  Em    Am
She proved to be nae journey-work,
     Em  Bm   Em
John Anderson, my Jo.
```

John Anderson, my Jo, John,
You were my first conceit,
I think no shame to own, John,
I loved you ear' and late.
They say you're turning old, John,
And what though it be so,
Ye're still the same kind man to me,
John Anderson, my Jo.

John Anderson, my Jo, John,
When we were first acquaint,
Your locks were like the raven,
Your bonny brow was brent;
But now your brow is bald, John,
Your locks are like the snow,
Yet blessings on your frosty pow,
John Anderson, my Jo.

John Anderson, my Jo, John,
We climbed the hill together,
And many a canty day, John,
We've had with one another;
Now we must totter down, John,
But hand in hand we'll go,
And sleep together at the foot,
John Anderson, my Jo.

Jackson

A   G   A
Jackson is on sea, Jackson is on shore,
           G   A
Jackson's gone to Mexico to fight the battles o'er.
                    D
"Welcome home, my Jackson, oh welcome home," said she,
     E7   A
"Last night my daughter Mary, lay dreaming of thee."

"What news, Jackson?" "Very poor," says he.
"I lost all my money while crossing the sea.
Go bring your daughter Mary and get her down by me,
We'll drown our melancholy and married we will be."

"Oh Mary's not at home, Jack, nor has not been today;
And if she were at home, Jack, she would not let you stay.
For Mary's very, very rich and you are very poor,
And if she was at home, Jack, she'd show you the door."

Jackson bein' drowsy hung down his head,
He called for a candle to light him off to bed.
The beds are full of strangers,
  and have been so this week—
And now for your lodging, poor Jack, you'll have to seek.

Jack looked upon the strangers, upon them one and all,
He looked upon the landlady and in reckoning he did call.
Twenty shillings of the new and twenty of the old.
With this Jack pulled out his two hands full of gold.

The sight of the money made the old woman rue:
"Mary is at home, Jack, and she'll return to you.
I hope you're not in earnest, for I only spoke in jest.
Without any exception she loves you the best."

Mary came downstairs with a smiling face,
First a sweet kiss, then a fond embrace:
"Oh, welcome home, my Jackson,
  oh welcome home, my dear.
The big beds are empty and you shall lie there."

"Before I'd lie within your beds I'd lie within the street,
For when I had no money, my lodging I must seek.
But now I've plenty money I'll make the tavern hurl,
A bottle of good brandy and on each arm a girl."

The Storms Are On The Ocean

 D G   D
I'm going away for to leave you, love,
  A7   D
I'm going away for a while.
     G   D
But I'll return to you some time,
   A7   D
If I go ten thousand miles.

Chorus:
  G   D
The storms are on the ocean,
         A7   D
The heavens may cease to be.
  G   D
This world may lose its motion, love
  A7   D
If I prove false to thee.

Now, who will shoe your pretty little feet?
And who will glove your hands?
Who will kiss your red rosy cheek
Till I come back again?

Poppa will shoe my pretty little feet,
Momma will glove my hands,
And you can kiss my red rosy cheeks
When you return again.

See that lonesome turtle dove
As he flies from pine to pine;
He's mourning for his own true love
Just the way I mourn for mine.

I'll never go back on the ocean, love,
I'll never go back on the sea,
I'll never go back on the blue-eyed girl
Till she goes back on me.

Goodbye, Little Bonnie, Goodbye

Chorus:

    C   G   C
Goodbye, Little Bonnie, goodbye,
  F   C
Goodbye, Little Bonnie, goodbye.
                 F
I'll see you again, but the Lord knows when,
  C   G   C
Goodbye, Little Bonnie, goodbye.

Verses:
I asked your mother for you,
I asked your papa too,
They both said, "No, little Bonnie can't go."
I'm sorry that's all I can do.

My trunk is packed and gone,
My trunk is packed and gone,
My trunk is gone and I'm alone,
Goodbye, little Bonnie, goodbye.

There's more pretty girls than one,
There's more pretty girls than one,
With all this world I've travelled 'round,
There's more pretty girls than one.

New River Train

Chorus:

    D
I'm riding on that new river train,
                  A7
I'm riding on that new river train,
    D   G
It's the same old train that brought me here,
  A7   D
It's soon gonna carry me away.

Verse:

D
Oh, darling you can't love but one,
                      A7
Oh, darling you can't love but one,
        D   D7   G
Oh, you can't love but love but one and have any fun
  A7   D
Oh, darling you can't love but one.

Darling, you can't love two (twice)
You can't love two, and still to me be true, etc.

Darling you can't love three (twice)
You can't love three, and still be true to me.

Darling, you can't love four, (twice)
You can't love four, and love me any more.

Darling, you can't love five (twice)
You can't love five, get your honey from my bee hive.

Darling, you can't love six (twice)
You can't love six, and do any tricks.

Oh, darling you can't love seven (twice)
You can't love seven and expect to get to heaven.

Darling, you can't love eight (twice)
You can't love eight, and get through the Pearly Gates.

Oh, darling you can't love nine, (twice)
You can't love nine, and still be mine.

My Bonnie Lies Over The Ocean

    G   C   G
My Bonnie lies over the ocean,
               A7   D7
My Bonnie lies over the sea,
    G   C   G
My Bonnie lies over the ocean,
    C   D7   G
Oh, bring back my Bonnie to me.

Chorus:

G   C   D7   G
Bring back, bring back, bring back my Bonnie to me, to me,
               C   D7   G
Bring back, bring back, Oh, bring back my Bonnie to me.

Oh, blow, ye winds, over the ocean,
And blow, ye winds, over the sea,
Oh, blow, ye winds, over the ocean,
And bring back my Bonnie to me.

Last night as I lay on my pillow,
Last night as I lay on my bed,
Last night as I lay on my pillow,
I dreamed my poor Bonnie was dead.

The winds have blown over the ocean,
The winds have blown over the sea,
The winds have blown over the ocean,
And brought back my Bonnie to me.

I Know My Love

D   A7   D
"I know my love by his way o' walkin',
     A7   D
And I know my love by his way o' talkin',
     A7   D
And I know my love in a suit o' blue,
          A7   D
And if my love leaves me what will I do-o-o?"

Chorus:

    A7   D
And still she cried, "I love him the best,
            A7   D
And a troubled mind, sure, can know no rest."
    A7   D
And still she cried, "Bonny boys are few,
          A7   D
And if my love leaves me what will I do?"

"There is a dancehouse in Maradyke,
And there my true love goes ev'ry night.
He takes a strange one upon his knee,
And don't you think now that vexes me-e-e?"

"If my love knew I could wash and wring,
If my love knew I could weave and spin,
I'd make a coat all of the finest kind,
But the want of money, sure, leaves me behind."

Don't Let Your Deal Go Down

D   G
I've been all around this whole wide world
C   F
Way down in Memphis Tennessee.
D   G
Any old place I hang my hat
C   F
Seems like home to me.

Chorus:

D   G
Don't let your deal go down.
C   F
Don't let your deal go down.
D   G
Don't let your deal go down sweet mama
    C   F
For my last old dollar's gone.

When I left my love behind,
She's standin' in the door,
She threw her little arms around my neck and said,
"Sweet daddy please don't go."

Now it's who's gonna shoe your pretty little feet?
Who's gonna glove your hand?
And who's gonna kiss your ruby lips
Honey, who's gonna be your man?

She says, papa will shoe my pretty little feet,
Mama will glove my hand,
You can kiss my rosy lips
When you get back again.

Where did you get them high-heel shoes
And that dress you wear so fine?
Got my shoes from a railroad man
Dress from a driver in the mine.

Nelly Bly

Stephen Foster

C   G7
Nelly Bly! Nelly Bly! Bring the broom along,
   C   F
We'll sweep the kitchen clean, my dear,
 G7   C
And have a little song.

Poke the wood, my lady love,
      G7
And make the fire burn,
  C   F
And while I take the banjo down,
 G7   C
Just give the mush a turn.

Chorus:

C   F
Heigh, Nelly! Ho, Nelly!
C   G7
Listen, love, to me,
  C   F
I'll sing for you and play for you
 G7   C
A dulcet melody.

Nelly Bly has a voice like a turtle dove,
I hear it in the meadow and I hear it in the grove.
Nelly Bly has a heart warm as a cup of tea,
And bigger than the sweet potatoes down in Tennessee.

Nelly Bly shuts her eye when she goes to sleep.
When she wakens up again her eyeballs start to peep.
The way she walks, she lifts her foot,
  and then she bumps it down,
And when it lights, there's music there
  in that part of the town.

Nelly Bly! Nelly Bly! Never, never sigh;
Never bring the tear drop to the corner of your eye.
For the pie is made of pumpkins
  and the mush is made of corn,
And there's corn and pumpkins plenty, love,
  a-lyin' in the barn.

Banks Of The Roses

E   A   E
By the banks of the roses my love and I sat down,
          A   B7
And I took up my violin to play my love a tune,
    E   A   B7
In the middle of the tune, ah, she sighed and she cried,
  E   A   B7 E
"Oh-o, Johnny, lovely Johnny, would you leave me?"

When I was a young man I heard my father say,
I'd rather see you dead and a-buried in the clay,
Sooner than to see you with any run-away,
By the lovely, sweet banks of the roses.

Well, then I am to run away and soon I'll let them know,
That I can take a good glass or leave it well alone,
And the man that does not like me,
  he can keep his girl at home,
And young Johnny will go roamin' with another.

And if ever I get married, 'twill be the month of May,
When all the trees are budding
  and the meadows bright and gay,
And me and my true love can run and sport and play,
By the lovely, sweet banks of the roses.

Round Her Neck She Wore A Yellow Ribbon

C
Round her neck she wore a yellow ribbon,
    Am   C   D7   G7
She wore it fall and winter and in the month of May.
C
And if you asked her why the heck she wore it,
              Em   Am Fm6 C G7 C
She'd say it's for her lover who is far, far away.
   F   C
Far away, far away,
              Em   Am Fm6 C G7 C
She'd say it's for her lover who is far, far away.
   F   C
Far away, far away,
              Em Am Fm6 C G7 C
She wore it for her lover who is far, far away.

Round her neck she wore a golden locket,
She wore it in the night time and wore it ev'ry day.
And if you asked her why the heck she wore it,
She'd say it's for her lover who is far, far away.
Far away, far away,
She'd say it's for her lover who is far, far away.
Far away, far away
She wore it for her lover who is far, far away.

In her home she kept a fire burning,
She kept it fall and winter and in the month of May.
And if you asked her why the heck she kept it,
She'd say it's for her lover who is far, far away, etc.
She kept it for her lover who is far, far away.

Saved her heart and saved her sweetest kisses,
She saved them fall and winter and in the month of May.
And if you asked her why the heck she saved them,
She'd say it's for her lover who is far, far away, etc.
She'd saved them for her lover who is far, far away.

Waillie

      D   F♯m   Bm
When cockle shells turn silver bells,
G Em   A7   D
Then will my love return to me.
A7   D   A7   F♯m
Waillie, Oh Waillie, but love it is bonnie
G Em   A7 D
A little while when it is new.

When roses grow 'neath winter snow,
Then will my love return to me.
Waillie, Waillie, but love it is bonnie
A little while when it is new.

But when love's old, it groweth cold,
And fades away like morning dew.
Waillie, Oh Waillie, but love it is bonnie
A little while when it is new.

Locks And Bolts

D   G   D
I dreamed of my true love last night,
                Am
All in my arms I held her,
           D   Am   D
But when I woke it was a dream,
     G   A7   D
I was forced to lie without her.

Her yellow hair, like strands of gold,
Come rollin' down my pillow,
Her yellow hair, like strands of gold,
Come rollin' down my pillow.

I went unto her uncle's house,
Inquiring for my darling,
The answer was, "She is not here,
I've no such in my keeping."

Her voice came from the roof above,
Came straightway from the window,
"Oh, love, oh love, it's I'd be yours,
But locks and bolts doth hinder."

Oh, passion flew, my sword I drew,
All in that room I entered,
Oh, passion flew, my sword I drew,
All in that room I entered.

I took my sword in my right hand,
My love all in the other,
Come all young men that love like me,
Fight on and take another.

Black Is The Color

D   Am   D
Black is the color of my true love's hair,
   Am   D   Am D
Her lips are like some rosy fair;
   Am   D   Am   D Am D
The purest eyes and the neatest hands,
              Am   D
I love the ground where-on she stands.

I go to the Clyde for to mourn and weep,
But satisfied I never can sleep,
I'll write to you in a few short lines,
I'll suffer death ten thousand times.

I know my love and well she knows
I love the grass whereon she goes,
If she on earth no more I see,
My life will quickly fade away.

A winter's past and the leaves are green,
The time has passed that we have seen,
But still I hope the time will come
When you and I will be as one.

Lady Of Carlisle

F
Down in Carlisle there lived a lady,
      Bb   F
Being most beautiful and gay;

She was determined to live a lady,
      G   C7   F
No man on earth could her betray.

Unless it were a man of honor,
A man of honor and high degree;
And then approached two loving soldiers,
This fair lady for to see.

One being a brave lieutenant,
A brave lieutenant and a man of war;
The other being a brave sea captain,
Captain of the ship that come from far.

Then up spoke this fair young lady,
Saying "I can't be but one man's bride;
But if you'll come back tomorrow morning,
On this case we will decide."

She ordered her a span of horses,
A span of horses at her command;
And down the road these three did travel
Till they come to the lions' den.

There she stopped and there she halted,
These two soldiers stood gazing around;
And for the space of half an hour,
This young lady lies speechless on the ground.

And when she did recover,
Threw her fan down in the lions' den;
Saying, "Which of you to gain a lady
Will return her fan again?"

Then up spoke the brave lieutenant,
Raised his voice both loud and clear,
Saying "You know I am a dear lover of women,
But I will not give my life for love."

Then up spoke this brave sea captain,
He raised his voice both loud and high,
Saying, "You know I am a dear lover of women,
I will return her fan or die."

Down in the lions' den, he boldly entered,
The lions being both wild and fierce;
He marched around and in among them,
Safely returned her fan again.

And when she saw her true lover coming,
Seeing no harm had been done to him,
She threw herself against his bosom,
Saying, "Here is the prize that you have won."

A Rich Irish Lady

    Dm   F   C
A rich Irish lady from Ireland came,
    Dm   F   Dm   Gm
A beautiful lady called Saro by name.
      Dm   F   Gm   Am
Her riches was more than a king could possess,
      Dm   Gm   Dm
Her beauty was more than her wealth at its best.

A lofty young gentleman courtin' her came,
Courtin' this lady called Saro by name.
"O, Saro! O, Saro! O, Saro!" said he,
"I'm afraid that my ruin forever you'll be.

"I'm afraid that my ruin forever you'll prove,
Unless you turn all of your hatred to love."
"No hatred to you nor to no other man,
But this, for to love you, is more than I can.

"So, end all your sorrows, and drop your discourse,
I never shall have you unless I am forced."
Six months appeared and five years had passed,
When I heard of this lady's misfortune at last.

She lay wounded by love, and she knew not for why;
She sent for this young man whom she had denied.
And by her bedside these words they were said:
"There's a pain in your side, love,
      there's a pain in your head."

"Oh no, kind sir, the right you've not guessed;
The pain that you speak of lies here in my breast."
"Then am I your doctor, and am I your cure?
Am I your protector that you sent for me here?"

"You are my doctor, and you are my cure;
Without your protection I'll die I am sure."
"O, Saro! O, Saro! O, Saro!" said he,
"Don't you remember when I first courted thee?

"I asked you in kindness, you answered in scorn,
I'll never forgive you for times past and gone."
"Times past and gone I hope you'll forgive,
And grant me some longer in comfort to live."

"I'll never forgive you as long as I live,
I'll dance on your grave, love,
      when you're laid in the ground."
Then off of her fingers gold rings she pulled three,
Saying, "Take them and wear them
      when you're dancing on me.

"Adieu, kind friends, adieu all around;
Adieu to my true love—God make him a crown;
I freely forgive him, although he won't me,
My follies ten thousand times over I see."

Mary Ann

    A
It's fare thee well, my own true love,
        E
It's fare thee well for a while,
    A   D   A
For the ship is a-waiting and the wind blows free,
         D   E   A
And I am bound away for the sea, Mary Ann.

Ten thousand miles away from home,
Ten thousand miles or more,
The sea may freeze and the earth may burn,
If I never more return to you, Mary Ann.

Do you see that crow thet flies on high?
She will surely turn to white,
If I ever prove false to you, my love,
Bright morn will turn to night, my dear, Mary Ann.

Your company, my dearest dear,
So pleasant it is to me,
It makes me think when I'm away,
That every day is three, my dear, Mary Ann.

I wish my breast were made of glass,
Wherein you might behold,
The secrets of my love are writ,
In letters made of gold, my dear, Mary Ann.

Do you see the grass that under your feet,
Arise and grow again,
But love it is a killing thing,
Did you ever feel the pain, my dear, Mary Ann.

The Foggy Dew

Bm   Em   A   Bm Em Bm
Over the hills I went one day, a lovely maid I spied.
                    Em   A
With her coal black hair and her mantle so green,
  Bm Em Bm
   an image to perceive.
  D   G   D   A
Says I, "Dear girl, will you be my bride
        Bm   Em F m Bm
  and she lifted her eyes of   blue;
                 Em   A
She smiled and said, "Young man I'm to wed,
   Bm   Em Bm
  I'm to meet him in the foggy dew."

Over the hills I went one morn, a-singing I did go.
Met this lovely maid with her coal-black hair,
   and she answered soft and low:
Said she, "Young man, I'll be your bride,
   if I know that you'll be true."
Oh, in my arms, all her charms
   were casted in the foggy dew.

The Dark-Eyed Sailor

G   Em
It was of a comely young lady fair,
        G   C   G
Who was walking out to take the air,
           G7   C
She met a sailor upon her way,
         G   C G
So I paid attention, I paid attention,
        D7   G
To hear what she might say.

Says he, "Fair maid, why walk alone,
When night is coming and day is gone?"
Says she, while tears from her eyes did fall,
"My dark-eyed sailor, my dark-eyed sailor
Is proving my downfall.

"Tis two long years since he left this land,
A ring he took from off his hand.
He broke the token here's half with me,
The other lies rolling, the other lies rolling
At the bottom of the sea."

Says William, "Cast him off your mind,
There's better sailors than him you'll find.
Love turns aside and cold does grow,
Like a winter's morning, a winter's morning
When the hills are clad in snow."

These words did Phoebe's heart inflame.
She cries, "On me you'll play no game.
I will be true to my own dear love,
And my dark-eyed sailor, my dark-eyed sailor
Still claims this heart of mine.

"But a dark-eyed sailor I would never disdain,
And I would always treat the same.
To drink his health here's a piece of coin,
But my dark-eyed sailor, my dark-eyed sailor
Still claims this heart of mine."

Well, when William did the ring unfold,
She seemed distracted midst joy and woe,
Saying, "You're welcome William, I've lands and gold,
For my dark-eyed sailor, my dark-eyed sailor
So manly, true, and bold."

Well, in a cottage down by the riverside,
In happiness and peace they now reside.
So girls be true while your lover is away,
For a cloudy morning, a cloudy morning
Oft brings a pleasant day.

Little Mohee

D   A7   D
As I went out walking upon a fine day,
D   A7   D
I got awful lonesome as the day passed away.
          G   D
I sat down a-musing alone on the grass,
                A7   D
When who should sit by me but a sweet Indian lass.

She sat down beside me upon a fine day,
I got awful lonesome as the day passed away.
She asked me to marry, and gave me her hand,
Said, "My pappy's a chieftain all over this land."

"My pappy's a chieftain and ruler be he,
I'm his only daughter and my name is Mohee."
I answered and told her that it never could be,
'Cause I had my own sweetheart in my own country.

I had my own sweetheart and I knew she loved me.
Her heart was as true as any Mohee.
So I said, "I must leave you and goodbye my dear,
There's a wind in my canvas and home I must steer."

At home with relations I tried for to see,
But there wasn't one there like my little Mohee;
And the girl I had trusted proved untrue to me,
So I sailed o'er the ocean to my little Mohee.

The First Time Ever I Saw Your Face

Ewan MacColl

     E   B7   E
The first time ever I saw your face,
                G#m A
I thought the sun rose in your eyes,
      E   F#m B7   E
And the moon and stars   were the gift you gave
     D   A   E
To the dark and empty skies, my love,
     D   B7   E
To the dark and empty skies.

The first time ever I kissed your mouth,
I felt the earth move in my hand,
Like the trembling heart of a captive bird
That was there at my command, my love,
That was there at my command.

The first time ever I lay with you
And felt your heart beat close to mine,
I thought our joy would fill the earth
And last till the end of time, my love,
And last till the end of time.

Handsome Molly

G
Wish I was in London,
               D7
Or some other seaport town;

I'd set my foot in a steamboat,
  G
I'd sail the ocean 'round.

While sailing a round the ocean,
While sailing a round the sea,
I'd think of handsome Molly
Wherever she might be.
('Course, I would!)

She rode to church a-Sunday,
She passed me on by;
I saw her mind was changing
By the roving of her eye.
(Handsome Molly! Oh, you little Molly!)

Don't you remember, Molly,
When you gave me your right hand?
You said if you ever marry
That I'd be the man.

Now you've broke your promise,
Go home with who you please,
While my poor heart is aching
You're lying at your ease.

Hair was black as a raven,
Her eyes was black as coal,
Her cheeks was like lilies
Out in the morning grown.
(Prettiest woman in the world!
Handsome Molly! Little Molly darling!)

Pretty Saro

      G
Down in some lone valley, in some lonesome place
Where the birds do whistle and their notes do increase,
Farewell pretty Saro, I bid you adieu
And I'll dream of pretty Saro wherever I go.

My love she won't have me so I understand,
She wants a freeholder and I have no land.
I cannot maintain her with silver and gold,
Nor buy all the fine things a big house can hold.

If I were a merchant and could write a fine hand,
I'd write my love a letter that she'd understand.
So I'll wander by the river, where the waters o'er flow,
And I'll dream of pretty Saro wherever I go.

Katy Cline

       A
Well now, who does not know Katy Cline,
           E7
She lives at the foot of the hill,
    A   D
By the shady nook of some old babbling brook,
    E7   A
That runs by her dear old father's mill.

Chorus:
Tell me that you love me, Katy Cline,
Tell me that your love's as true as mine.
Tell me that you love your own turtle dove,
Tell me that you love me, Katy Cline.

It's way from my little cabin door,
Oh, it's way from my little cabin home.
There's no one to weep and there's no one to mourn
And there's no one to see Katy Cline.

If I was a little bird,
I'd never build my nest on the ground.
I'd build my nest in some high yonder tree
Where them wild boys couldn't tear it down.

Wheel Of Fortune

     C   Am
As I went out in Dublin City,
C   Am
'Round the hour of twelve at night,
             Dm
There I spied a fair young maiden,
E7   Am
Washing her feet by candle-light.

First she washed them, then she dried them,
'Round her shoulder wore a towel,
And in all my life I ne'er did see
Such a fine young girl, upon my soul.

Chorus:
She had twenty, eighteen, sixteen, fourteen,
Twelve, ten, eight, six, four, two, none;
She had nineteen, seventeen, fifteen, thirteen,
Eleven, nine, seven, five, three and one.

'Round and 'round the wheel of fortune,
Where she stops it wearies me,
Fair young girls are all deceiving,
Sad experience teaches me.

John Riley

C   Bb   C
As I went out one morning early,
             Bb   C
To breathe the sweet and pleasant air,
               F
Who should I spy but a fair young maiden;
 G7   C
She seemed to me like a lily fair.

I stepped to her and kindly asked her,
"Would you like to be a bold sailor's wife?"
"Oh no kind sir," she quickly answered,
"I choose to lead a sweet single life."

"What makes you different from other women?
What makes you different from other kind?
For you are young, sweet, beautiful and handsome,
And for to marry you, I might incline."

"It's now kind sir that I must tell you.
I might have been married three years ago
To one John Riley who left this country.
He's been the cause of my overthrow."

"He courted me both late and early.
He courted me both night and day.
And when he had once my affections gained,
He left me here and he went away."

"Oh never mind for this Johnny Riley,
Oh come with me to the distant shore.
Why, we'll sail o'er to Pennsylvany,
And bid adieu to Riley for ever more."

"I shan't go with you to Pennsylvany,
Or go with you to the distant shore.
My heart is with Riley, my long lost lover
Although I'll never see him no more."

Oh, when he saw that her love was loyal,
He gave her kisses one, two, and three,
Saying, "I'm the man you once called Johnny Riley,
Saying "I'm the cause of your misery.

"I've sailed the ocean, gained great promotion,
I've laid my money on the English shore,
And now we'll marry, no longer tarry,
And I shall never deceive you any more."

Annie Laurie

William Douglas and Lady John Scott

   Bb   Eb
Maxwelton's braes are bonnie,
    Bb C7   F
Where early fa's the dew,
F7   Bb   Eb
And it's there that Annie Laurie
    Bb   F7   Bb
Gave me her promise true.
      F7   Bb
Gave me her promise true,
        F7   Bb
Which ne'er forgot will be;
    Gm   Eb   Bb
And for bonnie Annie Laurie
      F7   Bb
I'd lay me doon an' dee.

Her brow is like the snawdrift,
Her neck is like the swan,
Her face it is the fairest
That e'er the sun shone on,
That e'er the sun shone on,
An' dark blue is her ee,
And for bonnie Annie Laurie
I'd lay me doon an' dee.

Like dew on the gowan lying
Is the fa' o' her fairy feet;
An' like winds in summer sighing,
Her voice is low an' sweet,
Her voice is low an' sweet,
An' she's a' the world to me,
And for bonnie Annie Laurie
I'd lay me doon an' dee.

She's Like The Swallow

    Bm   F#7   Bm
She's like the swallow that flies so high;
     E   G   Bm   F#m
She's like the river that never runs dry.
   G   Bm   F#m   Bm
She's like the sunshine on the lee shore.
         E   F#Bm
I love my love and love is no more

Down to the garden this fair maid did go,
To pluck the beautiful prim-a-rose.
The more she plucked, the more she pulled,
Until she got her apron full.

Then out of these roses she made
A stony pillow for her head;
She laid her down, no word did say,
And then this poor maid's heart did break.

Down In The Valley

D   A7
Down in the valley, valley so low.
                    D
Hang your head over, hear the wind blow.
D   A7
Hear the wind blow, dear, hear the wind blow.
                  D
Hang your head over, hear the wind blow.

Roses love sunshine, violets love dew
Angels in heaven, know I love you.
Know I love you dear, know I love you
Angels in heaven, know I love you.

If you don't love me, love whom you please
Throw your arms round me, give my heart ease.
Give my heart ease love, give my heart ease
Throw your arms round me, give my heart ease.

Build me a castle forty feet high
So I can see him as he rides by.
As he rides by love, as he rides by
So I can see him as he rides by.

Write me a letter, send it by mail
Send it in care of Birmingham jail.
Birmingham jail love, Birmingham jail
Send it in care of Birmingham jail.

Oh, Dear! What Can The Matter Be?

Chorus:

C
Oh, dear! What can the matter be?
G7
Dear, dear! What can the matter be?
C
Oh, dear! What can the matter be?
Dm   G7   C
Johnny's so long at the fair.

Verse:

      C   G7   C
He promised he'd buy me a gift that would please me,
    Dm   G7
And then for a kiss, oh, he vowed he would tease me;
    C   G7   C
He promised he'd buy me a bunch of blue ribbons,
   Dm   C   G7   C
To tie up my bonnie brown hair.

He promised he'd bring me a basket of posies,
A garland of lilies, a garland of roses,
A little straw hat to set off the blue ribbons,
That tie up my bonnie brown hair.

George Collins

     D   G   D
George Collins drove home one cold winter night;
                A7
George Collins drove home so fine;
     D   G   D
George Collins drove home one cold winter night,
    A7   D
Was taken sick and died.

His little sweet Nell in yonders room
Sat sewing her silk so fine,
But when she heard that George was dead,
She laid her silks aside.

Set down the coffin, take off the lid,
Lay back the linen so fine,
And let me kiss his cold pale cheeks
For I know he'll never kiss mine.

Oh daughter, oh daughter, why do you weep,
There's more young men than one;
Oh mother, oh mother, George has my heart,
His stay on earth is done.

Look up and down that lonesome road,
Hang down your head and cry,
The best of friends is bound to part,
And why not you and I.

Oh don't you see that lonesome dove
That's flying from vine to vine,
He's mourning for his own true love
Just like I mourn for mine.

He's Gone Away

    G   C   G   D7 G
I'm goin' away for to stay a little while
         Bm   Em   Cm
But I'm coming back, if I go ten thousand miles;
         D7   G
Oh, who will tie your shoes?

And who will glove your hand?
          C   G   Cm G
And who will kiss those ruby lips when I am gone?
D7   G
Look away, look away over Yandro.

He's gone away for to stay a little while,
But he's coming back if he goes ten thousand miles.
Oh it's daddy'll tie my shoes,
And mommy'll glove my hands,
And you will kiss my ruby lips when you come back!
Look away, look away over Yandro.

Scarborough Fair

Derived From Child Ballad 2

Dm   Dm7   Em   Dm6
Are you going to Scarborough Fair?
Am   Dm   G   Dm
Parsley, sage, rosemary and thyme;
  Bb   Dm A7   Dm
Remember me to one that lives there,
           G   C   Dm
For once she was a true love of mine.

Tell her to make me a cambric shirt,
Parsley, sage, rosemary and thyme;
Without any seam or fine needlework,
And then she'll be a true love of mine.

Tell her to wash it in yonder dry well,
Parsley, sage, rosemary and thyme;
Where water ne'er sprung, nor drop of rain fell,
And then she'll be a true love of mine.

Tell her to dry it on yonder thorn,
Parsley, sage, rosemary and thyme;
Which never bore blossom since Adam was born,
And then she'll be a true love of mine.

Oh, will you find me an acre of land,
Parsley, sage, rosemary and thyme;
Between the sea foam and the sea sand
Or never be a true lover of mine.

Oh, will you plough it with a lamb's horn,
Parsley, sage, rosemary and thyme;
And sow it all over with one peppercorn,
Or never be a true lover of mine.

Oh, will you reap it with a sickle of leather,
Parsley, sage, rosemary and thyme;
And tie it all up with a peacock's feather,
Or never be a true lover of mine.

And when you have done and finished your work,
Parsley, sage, rosemary and thyme;
Then come to me for your cambric shirt,
And you shall be a true love of mine.

Goodbye, My Lover, Goodbye

   F
The ship goes sailing down the bay,
           C7
Goodbye, my lover, goodbye,

We may not meet for many a day,
           F
Goodbye, my lover, goodbye.

My heart will evermore be true,
           C7
Goodbye, my lover, goodbye,

Though now we sadly say adieu,
           F
Goodbye, my lover, goodbye.

Chorus:
      F   Bb F
Singing by-low, my baby,
C7   F
By-low, my bouncing baby boy;
       Bb F
Singing by-low, my baby,
   C7
Goodbye, my lover, goodbye, goodbye;
           F
Goodbye, my lover, goodbye.

I'll miss you on the stormy deep,
Goodbye, my lover, etc.
What can I do but ever weep?, etc.
My heart is broken with regret!, etc.
But never dream that I'll forget, etc.

Then cheer up till we meet again, etc.
I'll try to bear my weary pain, etc.
Though far I roam across the sea, etc.
My every thought of you shall be, etc.

The Cambric Shirt
From Child Ballad 2

    C   G   C
Go tell her to make me a cambric shirt,
              F   G7
Parsley, sage, rosemary, and thyme,
     C   G
Without a stitch of a seamster's work,
     C   G   C
And then she will be a true lover of mine.

Go tell her to wash it in yonders well,
Parsley, sage, rosemary, and thyme,
Where never was water, and rain never fell,
And then she will be a true lover of mine.

Go tell her to hang it on yonders thorn, etc.
Where leaf never budded since Adam was born, etc.

Go tell him to clear me an acre of land,
Between the sea and the fine sea sand.

Go tell him to plow it all with a thorn,
And plant it all over with one grain of corn.

Go tell him to reap it with an old stirrup-leather,
And bind it all up with a pea-fowl's feather.

Go tell him to thrash it against the wall,
And not one grain on the floor shall fall.

Go tell him to shock it in yonder sea,
And return it back all dry to me.

Go tell him to take it to the mill,
And every grain its bushel shall fill.

Go tell him to wrap it all up in a sack,
And send it to market all on a rat's back.

Go tell this young man when he gets his work done,
To come to my house and his shirt'll be done.

Shady Grove

Em   D
Cheeks as red as the blooming rose,
Em   D   Em
Eyes of the deepest brown,
            D
You are the darling of my heart,
Em   D   Em
Stay till the sun goes down.

Shady Grove, my little love,
Shady Grove, my dear,
Shady Grove, my little love,
I'm goin' to leave you here.

Shady Grove my little love,
Standin' in the door,
Shoes and stockin's in her hand
And her little bare feet on the floor.

Wisht I had a big, fine horse,
Corn to feed him on,
Pretty little girl stay at home,
Feed him when I'm gone.

Shady Grove, my little love,
Shady Grove, I say,
Shady Grove, my little love,
Don't wait till Judgment Day.

The Queen Of Hearts

Am   Dm   Am   E7   Am
To the Queen of Hearts goes the Ace of Sorrow,
     Dm   Am
He is here today, he is gone tomorrow,
     Dm   Am Em E7   Am
Young men are plenty but sweethearts few,
   D7   Am   Em A . . . Am
If my love leaves me, what shall I do?

I have a store on yonder mountain,
Where gold and silver are had for countin',
I cannot count for thought of thee,
My eyes so full I cannot see.

I love my father, I love my mother,
I love my sister, I love my brother,
I love my friends and relations too,
But I'd leave them all to go with you.

My father left me both house and lands,
And servants many at my command,
At my command they ne'er shall be,
I'll leave them all to go with thee.

I Know Where I'm Going

G   D7   G
I know where I'm going,
             D7
And I know who's going with me.
G   G7   Em
I know who I love,
     Am   D
But the dear knows who I'll marry.

I'll wear stockings of silk,
And shoes of bright green leather,
Combs to buckle my hair
And a ring for every finger.

Feather beds are soft,
And painted rooms are bonnie;
But I would trade them all
For my handsome, winsome Johnny.

Some say he's bad,
But I say he's bonnie,
Fairest of them all
Is my handsome, winsome Johnny.

Turtle Dove

     Am   Dm   Am
Now don't you see a little turtle dove
     Dm   Em   Am
Sitting under a mulberry tree?
       Dm   Am
See how that she doth mourn her true love,
   Dm Am   G   Dm
As I my love shall mourn for thee,
   Am   E7   Am
As I shall mourn for thee.

Now fare thee well, my little turtle dove,
Oh fare thee well for a while,
For 'tho I go I will surely come again,
If I go ten thousand miles, my dear,
If I go ten thousand miles.

Ten thousand miles is very far away,
For you to go from me,
You leave me to lament and well-a-day,
My tears you shall not see, my dear,
My tears you shall not see.

The crow that's black, my little turtle dove,
Doth change its color white,
E'er I prove false to the maiden that I love,
The noon day shall be night, my dear,
The noon day shall be night.

The hills shall fly, my little turtle dove,
The roaring billows burn,
E'er I prove false to the maiden that I love,
Or I a traitor turn, my dear,
Or I a traitor turn.

ROLL IN MY SWEET BABY'S ARMS

John Anderson, My Jo (II)

Robert Burns

```
         Em                Am            Bm
John Anderson, my Jo, John, I wonder what you mean,
         Em           Am        G      Em
To rise so soon at morning and sit so late at e'en?
    G                        Am
You'll weary out your eyes, John, and why do you do so?
     Em   Am   Em  Am
Come sooner to your bed at night,
     Em   Bm   Em
John Anderson, my Jo.
```

John Anderson, my friend John,
    when you first in life began,
You had as good a tail tree as any other man,
But now 'tis waxing old, John, and waggles to and fro,
I've still twa oops to your one gae doon,
John Anderson, my jo.

John Anderson, my jo, John,
    you can love where e'er you please,
Either in our warm bed, or else aboon the clothes,
Or you shall have the horns, John, upon your head to grow,
For that was always the cuckold's curse,
John Anderson, my jo.

So when you want to have me, John,
    see that you do your best,
And when you begin to kiss me see that you hold me fast,
See that you grip me fast, John, until that I cry "Oh!"
Your back shall crack, ere I cry, "Slack!"
John Anderson, my jo.

Oh, but it is a fine thing to peek out o'er the fence,
But 'tis a far, far finer thing to see your back commence;
To see your back commence, John, to wriggle to and fro,
'Tis then I like your changer pipe,
John Anderson, my jo.

I'm backit like a salmon, I'm breasted like a swan,
My belly is a down sack, my middle you may span,
From my crown until my toe, John,
    I'm like the new fallen snow,
And 'tis all for your conveniency,
John Anderson, my jo.

It Was A Lover And His Lass

```
    C       Dm   G7
It was a lover and his lass,
                    C   F   C
With a hey and a ho and a hey nonnino,
         G7       C
With a hey nonni nonnino.
                    Dm     G7
That o'er the green cornfield did pass.
```

Chorus:

```
    C
In spring time in spring time,
    F         Dm  G7   C
In spring time, the only pretty ring time,
         F      G7      C
When the birds do sing, Hey ding a ding a ding,
     F                Dm
Hey ding a ding a ding, Hey ding a ding a ding,
    G7  C   G7    C
    sweet lovers love the Spring.
```

Between the acres of the rye,
With a hey, and a ho and a hey nonnino,
And a hey nonni nonnino,
These pretty country folks would lie,

And therefore take the present time,
With a hey, and a ho and a hey nonnino,
And a hey nonni nonnino,
For love is crowned with the prime,

Little Ball Of Yarn

```
             C                                   F
In the merry month of June, when the roses were in bloom,
    G7                        C
The birds were singing gaily on the farm;
                                           F
When I spied a pretty miss and politely asked her this:
         G7                   C
"Will you let me spin your little ball of yarn?
```

Refrain:

```
       F        C
Ball of yarn, ball of yarn,
         G7                        C
Will you let me spin your little ball of yarn?
C7   F        C
Ball of yarn, ball of yarn,
         G7                    C
It was then I spun her little ball of yarn.
```

Well then she gave her consent
    and behind the fence we went;
I promised her I would do no harm.
Then I gently laid her down and I ruffled up her gown;
It was then I spun her little ball of yarn.

It was nine months after that, in a pool room where I sat,
Never thinking I had done her any harm.
When a gentleman in blue said,
    "Young man we're after you,
You're the father of a little ball of yarn."

Maids When You're Young, Never Wed An Old Man

     E
An old man came a-courting me,
       B7
Hay-ding doo-rum-down,
     E
An old man came a-courting me,
       B7
Hay doo-rum down;
     E   A   B7
An old man came a-courting me,
E   B7
Fain would he marry me.
E   A   B7   E
Maids, when you're young, never wed an old man.

Chorus:

                          B7
For they've got no fal-loo-rum, fal-lid-dle fal-loo-rum,
     E   B7
They've got no fal-loo-rum, fal-lid-dle all day;
     E   A
They've got no fal-loo-rum,
B7   E   B7
They've lost their ding doo-rum,
     E   A   B7   E
So, maids when you're young, never wed an old man.

Now when we went to church,
Hay ding doorum down,
When we went to church,
Hay doo-rum down;
When we went to church,
He left me in the lurch.
Maids, when you're young, never wed an old man.

Now when we went to bed,
Hay ding doo-rum down,
When we went to bed,
Hay doo-rum down;
When we went to bed,
He neither done nor said.
Maids, when you're young, never wed an old man.

Now when he went to sleep,
Hay ding doo-rum down,
When he went to sleep,
Hay doo-rum down;
When he went to sleep,
Out of bed I did creep,
Into the arms of a jolly young man.

Last Chorus:
And I found his fal-looral fal-liddle fal-looral,
I found his fal-looral, fal-liddle all day,
I found his fal-loorum and he got my ding doo-rum,
So maids, when you're young, never wed an old man.

Blow The Candles Out

     Dm   C   DmC
When I was apprenticed in London,
     Dm   C   Dm Am
I went to see my dear.
     Dm   C   Dm C
The candles were all burning,
       Dm   C   Dm
the moon shone bright and clear.
C7 F   C7   F C7   Em   Am   Dm
I   knocked upon her window to ease her of her pain.
Am Dm C   Dm C   Dm   C   Dm
She rose to let me in,   then she barred the door again.

I like your well behaviour and thus I often say,
I cannot rest contented whilst you are far away.
The roads they are so muddy, we cannot gang about,
So roll me in your arms, love, and blow the candles out.

Your father and your mother in yonder room do lie,
A-huggin' one another, so why not you and I?
A-huggin' one another without a fear or doubt,
So roll me in your arms, love, and blow the candles out.

And if you prove successful, love, pray name it after me,
Keep it neat and kiss it sweet, and daff it on your knee.
When my three years are ended, my time it will be out,
Then I will double my indebtedness
    by blowing the candles out.

Sal Got A Meatskin

C
Sal got a meatskin hid away,
Sal got a meatskin hid away,
Sal got a meatskin hid away,
Gonna get a meatskin some day.

Chorus:

               G7
Sal got a meatskin don't you know.
               C
Sal got a meatskin don't you know.
               G7
Sal got a meatskin don't you know,
          C
Old Liza told me so.

Sal a-sailing on the sea, (3 times)
Sal got a meatskin a-waiting for me.

Went to see my Sally Gray, (3 times)
Found out Sal is gone away.

Love my Sally more and more, (3 times)
Sal's got a meatskin don't you know.

Reckon I love my Sally Gray, (3 times)
Reckon my Sal is gone away.

The Chandler's Wife

G   D7   G
I went into the chandler's shop some candles for to buy,
                                  A7   D
I looked around the chandler's shop but no one did I spy.
G   A7   D7
I was disappointed and some angry words I said,
              G
Then I heard the sound of a (knock, knock, knock)
        D7   G
   up above my head.
D7   G
Oh, I heard the sound of a (knock, knock, knock)
        D7   G
   up above my head.

Well I was slick and I was quick, and up the stairs I sped,
And much to my surprise I found
   the chandler's wife in bed;
And with her was another man of most gigantic size,
And they were having a (knock, knock, knock)
   right before my eyes. (twice)

When the fun was over and done
   and the lady raised her head,
She was quite surprised to find me standing by the bed.
"If you will be discreet, my lad, if you would be so kind,
I'll let you come up for some (knock, knock, knock)
   whenever you feel inclined." (twice)

So, many a day and many a night
   when the chandler wasn't home,
To get myself some candles
   to the chandler's shop I'd roam.
But nary a one she gave to me, but gave to me instead,
A little bit more of the (knock, knock, knock)
   to light my way to bed. (twice)

So, all you married men take heed,
   if ever you come to town,
If you must leave your woman alone,
   be sure to tie her down.
Or, if you would be kind to her, just sit her on the floor,
And give her so much of that (knock, knock, knock)
   she doesn't need any more. (twice)

The Virgin Sturgeon

Tune: *Reuben, Reuben*

D
Caviar comes from the virgin sturgeon,

Virgin sturgeon is a very good fish.
G   D
No good sturgeon wants to be a virgin,
        E7   A7   D
That's why caviar's a very rare dish.

I fed caviar to Louisa,
She's my honey tried and true.
Now Louisa needs no urgin',
I recommend caviar to you.

I fed caviar to my grandpa,
He was a man of ninety-three.
Screams and cries were heard from grandma,
Grandpa had her up a tree.

I put caviar in the soda,
That livened up the party, sure.
What am I doing stripped down naked?
Thought these girls were sweet and pure.

I fed caviar to my sweetheart,
She always did it cheerfully.
Now she does it with a vengeance,
Oh, my God, it's killing me.

Little Mary went sleigh riding,
And the sled turned up-side-down.
Little Mary started singing,
Massa's in the cold, cold ground.

The policeman came to visit one day,
Postman came and went away.
The baby came just nine months later,
Who fired the shot, the blue or the grey?

Keep My Skillet Good And Greasy

   G
I'm goin' downtown, gonna get me a sack of flour,

Gonna cook it every hour, keep my skillet good and greasy

All the time, time, time,
                                          C   G
Keep my skillet good and greasy all the time.

Well if you say so, I'll never work no more.
I'll lay around your shanty
All the time, time, time,
Lay around your shanty all the time.

Well I'm goin' down town, gonna get me
   a jug of brandy.
Gonna give it all to Nancy, keep
   her good and drunk and goozy
All the time, time, time,
Good and drunk and goozy all the time.

Gently Johnny, My Jingalo

F
I put my hand all in her own,
  C7   F
Fair maid is a lily, O!

She said "If you love me alone,

Refrain:

"Come to me quietly,
  Bb   C7
"Do not do me injury,
  F   C7   F
"Gently, Johnny, my Jingalo."

I said, "You know I love you, dear."
Fair maid is a lily, O!
She whispered softly in my ear—

I placed my arm around her waist.
Fair maid is a lily, O!
She laughed and turned away her face.

I kissed her lips like rubies red,
Fair maid is a lily, O!
She blushed; then tenderly she said—

I slipped a ring all in her hand,
Fair maid is a lily, O!
She said, "The parson's near at hand"—

I took her to the church next day;
Fair maid is a lily, O!
The birds did sing, and she did say—

Lavender Blue

D A7   D
Lavender blue, dilly dilly,
G A7   D
Lavender green,
G   A7 D
When I am king, dilly, dilly,
Em7 A7   D
You   shall be queen.

Lavender's green, dilly dilly,
Lavender's blue,
You must love me, dilly dilly,
'Cause I love you.

Down in the vale, dilly dilly,
Where flowers grow,
And the birds sing, dilly dilly,
All in a row.

A brisk young man, dilly dilly,
Met with a maid,
And laid her down, dilly dilly,
Under the shade.

There they did play, dilly dilly,
And kiss and court,
All the fine day, dilly dilly,
Making good sport.

I've heard them say, dilly dilly,
Since I came hither,
That you and I, dilly dilly,
Might lie together.

Therefore be kind, dilly dilly,
While here we lie,
And you will love, dilly dilly,
My dog and I.

For you and I, dilly dilly,
Now all are one,
And we will lie, dilly dilly,
No more alone.

Lavender's blue, dilly dilly,
Lavender's green,
Let me be king, dilly dilly,
You be the queen.

Lavender's green, dilly dilly,
Lavender's blue,
You must love me, dilly dilly,
'Cause I love you.

The Next Market Day

   Em   G   Bm   Em
A maid going to Comber, her markets to larn,
                       D   Em
To sell for her mammy three hanks of fine yarn,
                    D   Em
She met with a young man along the highway,
                G   Bm   Em
Which caused this young damsel to dally and stray.

Sit ye beside me, I mean you no harm,
Sit ye beside me, this new tune to larn,
Here is three guineas your mammy to pay,
And lay by your yarn till the next market day.

They sat down together, the grass it was green,
The day was the fairest that ever was seen;
O, the look in your eyes beats a morning in May,
I could sit by your side till the next market day.

This fair maid went home, and the words that he said
And the air that he played her still rang in her head,
She said, "I'll go seek him by land or by sea,
"Till he larns me that tune called the next market day."

Candy Man Blues

D
Well all you ladies gather 'round,

The good sweet candy man's in town,
     A   D
It's the candy man (candy man).

He's got a stick of candy nine-inch long,
He sells it as fast as a hog can chew corn,
It's the candy man, it's the candy man.

You all heard what Sister Jones has said,
Always takes a candy stick to bed,
It's the candy man, it's the candy man.

Don't stand close to the candy man,
He'll leave a candy stick in your hand,
It's the candy man, it's the candy man.

He sold some candy to Sister Bad,
The very next day, she took all he had,
It's the candy man, it's the candy man.

If you try his candy, good friend of mine,
You sure will want it for a long, long time,
It's the candy man, it's the candy man.

His stick candy don't melt away,
Just gets better so the ladies say,
It's the candy man, it's the candy man.

Roll In My Sweet Baby's Arms

A
Ain't gonna work on the railroad,
               E7
Ain't gonna work on the farm.
A   D
Lay 'round the shack till the mail train comes back,
     E7   A
Then I'll roll in my sweet baby's arms.

Roll in my sweet baby's arms,
Roll in my sweet baby's arms,
Lay around the shack 'til the mail train comes back,
Then I'll roll in my sweet baby's arms.

Can't see what's the matter with my own true love,
She done quit writing to me;
She must think I don't love her like I used to,
Ain't that a foolish idea.

Sometimes there's a change in the ocean;
Sometimes there's a change in the sea;
Sometimes there's a change in my own true love;
But there's never no change in me.

Mama's a ginger-cake baker;
Sister can weave and can spin;
Dad's got an interest in that old cotton mill,
Just watch that old money roll in.

They tell me that your parents do not like me;
They have drove me away from your door;
If I had all my time to do over,
I would never go there any more.

Now where was you last Friday night,
While I was locked up in jail;
Walking the streets with another man.
Wouldn't even go my bail.

The Foggy, Foggy Dew

        G   C
When I was a bachelor, I lived all alone,
    D7   G
I worked at the weaver's trade;
                    C
And the only only thing I did that was wrong
    D7   G
Was to woo a fair young maid.
D7   G
I wooed her in the wintertime,
D7   G
Part of the summer too;
                   C
And the only only thing I did that was wrong
    D7   G
Was to keep her from the foggy, foggy dew.

One night she knelt close by my side,
When I was fast asleep.
She threw her arms around my neck,
And then began to weep.
She wept, she cried, she tore her hair—
Ah me, what could I do?
So all night long I held her in my arms,
Just to keep her from the foggy, foggy dew.

Again I am a bachelor, I live with my son,
We work at the weaver's trade;
And every single time I look into his eyes
He reminds me of the fair young maid.
He reminds me of the wintertime
And of the summer too;
And the many, many times that I held her in my arms,
Just to keep her from the foggy, foggy dew.

Tom Cat Blues

C
I got an old tom cat;
    G7
When he steps out
C   F
All the pussy cats in the neighborhood
G7 C
They begin to shout.

"Here comes Ring-Tail Tom
      G7
"He's boss around the town
 C   F
"And if you got your heat turned up,
 G7   C
"You better turn your damper down."

Ring-Tail Tom on a fence,
The old pussy cat on the ground,
Ring-Tail Tom came off that fence
And they went 'round and 'round.
Lord, he's quick on the trigger,
He's a natural born crack shot,
He got a new target every night,
And he sure does practice a lot.

He makes them roustabout,
He makes them roll their eyes,
They just can't resist my Ring-Tail Tom
No matter how hard they tries;
You better watch old Ring-Tail Tom,
He's running around the town,
He won't have no pussy cats,
Come a-tomcattin' around.

Ring-Tail Tom is the stuff,
He's always running around,
All the pussy cats in the neighborhood
Can't get old Ring-Tail Tom down;
He's always running around,
Just can't be satisfied,
He goes out every night
With a new one by his side.

Green Grow The Rashes, O

Robert Burns

   C   Am
There's naught but care on ev'ry han'
 Dm F Dm
In ev'ry hour that passes O;
  F   C
What signifies that life o' man,
  Dm E7 Am
An' 'twere not for the lasses O?

Chorus:

C
Green grow the rashes O.
Dm
Green grow the rashes O;
  Am   C
The sweetest hours that e'er I spend,
 Dm E7 Am
Are spent among the lasses, O.

The war'ly race may riches chase,
An' riches still may fly them, O;
An' tho' at last they catch them fast,
Their hearts can ne'er enjoy them, O.

But gie me a cannie hour at e'en,
My arms about my dearie, O,
An' warily cares an' war'ly men
May a' gae tapsalteerie, O!

Two Maids Went A-Milking One Day

  D   A7   D
Two maids went a-milking one day.
     A7   D
Two maids went a-milking one day.
       Bm
And the wind it did blow high,
  Em E7 A
And the wind it did blow low,
A7 D   Em7 A7 D
And it tossed their pails to and fro, la la la,
     Em7 A7 D
And it tossed their pails to and fro.

They met with a man they did know,
They met with a man they did know,
And they said, "Have you the will?"
And they said, "Have you the skill
For to catch us a small bird or two?" (twice)

Here's a health to the blackbird in the bush.
Likewise to the merry, merry doe.
If you will come along with me
Under yonder flowering tree,
I might catch you a small bird or two, (twice)

So they went and they sat 'neath a tree.
They went and they sat 'neath two.
And the birds flew 'round about,
Pretty birds flew in and out,
And he caught them by one and by two, (twice)

Now my boys, let us drink down the sun,
My boys, let us drink down the moon.
Take your lady to the wood,
If you really think you should,
You might catch her a small bird or two, (twice)

The Trooper And The Maid
Child Ballad 299

Em   Bm
A trooper lad cam' here ae nicht,
    D   Em
And oh, but he was weary;
    D   Em
A trooper lad came here ae nicht,
     B7   Em
When the moon was shining cleary.

Chorus:

          Bm
Bonnie lassie, will ye lie near me?
    D   Em
Bonnie lassie, will ye lie near me?
    D   Em
An' I'll har a' your ribbons reel
    B7   Em
In the morn ere I leave ye.

She's ta'en the horse by the halter right,
And led it to the stable;
She's gi'en him oats and hay to eat,
As muckle as he was able.

She's ta'en the sodger by the lily-white hand,
And led him to her chamber;
She's gi'en him a stoup o'wine to drink,
His love it fleered like aimber.

She's made her bed baith lang and wide,
She's made it like a lady;
She's ta'en her wee coatie ower her heid,
Said, "Sodger, are ye ready?"

And he's ta'en aff his belted coat,
Likewise his hat and feather,
And leaned his sword against the door,
And noo he's doon aside her.

They hadna been but an hour in bed,
An hour but and a quarter,
When the drum cam' soundin' up the street,
And ilka beat was shorter.

"It's up, up, up, and our colonel cries,
It's up, up, up and away then;
I maun sheathe my sword in its scabbard case,
For tomorrow's our battle day then."

"And when will ye come back again,
My ain dear sodger laddie?
When will ye come back again,
And be your bairn's daddie?"

"O, haud your tongue, my bonnie wee lass,
Dinna let this pairtin' grieve ye;
When heather cowes grow ousen bows,
Bonnie lassie, I'll come and see ye."

She's ta'en her wee coatie ower her heid,
And followed him up to Stirlin',
She's grown sae fu'that she couldna boo,
And he's left her in Dunfermline.

It's breid and cheese for carles and dames,
And oats and hay for horses;
A cup of tea for auld maids,
And bonnie lads for lasses.

---

ae = one	aimber = amber
gar = make	ower = over
gien = given	ilka = every
muckle = much	cowes = bushes, twigs
stoup = jug	ousen bows = oxen yokes
fleered = flared	

THEY'LL LOVE YOU AND LEAVE YOU

*Songs of those who loved not wisely
but all too well. . . .*

Rue

Dm   F
Come all you fair and tender maids,
    Dm
That flourish in your prime, prime,
    F   C   Dm
Beware, beware, make your garden fair,
        C   Dm   C
Let no man steal your thyme, thyme,
    Dm   Am C Dm
Let no man steal your thyme.

And when your thyme is past and gone,
He'll care no more for you, you,
And every day that your garden is waste,
Will spread all over with rue, rue,
Will spread all over with rue.

A woman is a branching tree,
And man a singing wynde, wynde,
And from her branches carelessly,
He'll take what he can find, find,
He'll take what he can find.

The Water Is Wide

    G   C   G
The water is wide, I cannot get over,
              C   D7
And neither have I wings to fly.
          Bm   Em
Give me a boat that can carry two,
C   D7   G
And both shall row, my love and I.

A ship there is and she sails the sea,
She's loaded deep as deep can be.
But not so deep as the love I'm in,
And I know not how I sink or swim.

I leaned my back up against some young oak,
Thinking he was a trusty tree.
But first he bended, and then he broke,
And thus did my false love to me.

I put my hand into some soft bush,
Thinking the sweetest flower to find.
I pricked my finger to the bone,
And left the sweetest flower alone.

Oh, love is handsome and love is fine,
Gay as a jewel when first it is new,
But love grows old, and waxes cold,
And fades away like summer dew

Bucking Bronco

        F   E   Am
My love is a rider, wild broncos he breaks,
              F   E   Am
Though he's promised to quit it all, just for my sake.
    G   Am   C
He ties up one foot and the saddle puts on,
        Am   F   E   Am
With a swing and a jump he is mounted and gone.

The first time I met him, 'twas early one spring
Riding a bronco a high headed thing
He tipped me a wink as he gaily did go
For he wished me to look at his bucking bronco.

The next time I saw him, 'twas late in the fall
Swinging the girls at Tomlinson's ball
He laughed and he talked, as we danced to and fro
Promised never to ride on another bronco.

He made me some presents, among them a ring
The return that I made him was a far better thing
'Twas a young maiden's heart, I'd have you all know
He'd won it by riding his bucking bronco.

Now all you young maidens, where'er you reside
Beware of the cowboy who swings the rawhide
He'll court you and pet you and leave you and go
In the spring up the trail on his bucking bronco.

Careless Love

E   B7   E
Love, oh, love, oh careless love,
                       B7
Love, oh, love, oh careless love,
E   E7   A
Love, oh, love, oh careless love,
        E   B7   E
You see what love has done to me.

I love my mama and papa too, (3 times)
I'd leave them both to go with you.

What, oh what, will mama say, (3 times)
When she learns I've gone astray.

Once I wore my apron low, (3 times)
I couldn't scarcely keep you from my door.

Now my apron strings don't pin, (3 times)
You pass my door and you don't come in.

Dear Companion

Dm
Once I did have a dear companion

Indeed I thought his love my own,
C   Dm
Until a black-eyed girl betrayed me,
         Gm   F   Dm
And now he cares no more for me.

Just go and leave me if you wish to,
It will never trouble me,
For in your heart you love another,
And in my grave I'd rather die.

Last night you lay in some sweet slumber,
Dreaming of some sweet repose,
While me, poor girl, all broken hearted,
A-listnin' to the wind that blows.

When I see your baby laughin',
It makes me think of your sweet face,
But when I hear your baby crying,
It makes me think of your disgrace.

False True Love

     F   C   F   C
Come in, come in, you old true love,
     F   C   F
And chat for awhile with me,
      C   F
For it's been three quarters of a long year or more,
      C   F   G
Since I spoke one word to thee.

I shan't come in, I shan't set down,
I ain't got a moment's time,
And since you are engaged with another true love,
Then your heart is no longer mine.

When you were mine, my old true love,
Then your head lay on my breast,
You could make me believe by the falling of your arm,
That the sun rose up in the west.

There is many the star shall jingle in the west,
There is many the leaf below,
There is many the damn that shall light upon a man,
For treating a poor girl so.

I wish to the Lord I'd never been born,
Or had died when I was young,
Then I never would have mourned for my old true love,
Nor have courted no other one.

Come All You Fair And Tender Ladies

A   Bm E7   A
Come all ye fair and tender ladies,
           Bm   E7   F#m
Take warning how you court young men.
        E7   A   E7   A
They're like the stars of a summer's morning;
            D   C#m E
They'll first appear and then they're gone.

If I'd ha' known before I courted,
I never would have courted none.
I'd have locked my heart in a box of golden
And fastened it up with a silver pin.

I wish I were a little swallow,
And I had wings and I could fly.
I would fly away to my false-true lover
And when he would speak I would deny.

But I am not a little swallow,
I have no wings neither can I fly.
So I'll sit down here to weep in sorrow
And try to pass my troubles by.

Oh don't you remember our days of courting,
When your head lay upon my breast?
You could make me believe by the falling of your arm,
That the sun rose in the west.

The Cuckoo

    Gm   Dm   Gm F C Dm
The cuckoo is a funny bird, she sings as she flies.
      Gm   Dm   Gm F C Dm
She'll bring you glad tidings, she'll tell you no lies.
      Bb   F   Am   C Dm C   Dm
She sips from the pretty flowers to make her voice clear,
        Gm   Dm   Gm F C Dm
And she'll never sing cuckoo till the spring of the year.

A-walking and a-talking, and a-wandering go I,
A-waiting for my true love; he'll come by and by.
I'll meet him in the morning for he's all my delight.
I could walk with my true love from morning to night.

Come all you fair maidens, take warning from me,
Don't place your affections on a young man too free;
For leaves they do wither, and roots they do die,
And your love he will leave you and he'll never say why.

But if he will leave me, I'll not be forlorn,
And if he'll forswear me, I'll not be forsworn;
I'll get myself up in my best finery,
And I'll walk as proud by him as he walks by me.

The Girl On The Greenbriar Shore

A
'Twas in the year of '92,
　　D　　　　　A
In the merry month of June,

I left my mother and a home so dear
　　　　　　　E7　　　　　　　A
For the girl I loved on the greenbriar shore.

My mother dear, she came to me
And said "Oh son, don't go,"
"Don't leave your mother and a home so dear
To trust a girl on the greenbriar shore."

But I was young and reckless too,
And I craved a reckless life;
I left my mother with a broken heart,
And I choosed that girl to be my wife.

Her hair was dark and curly too,
And her loving eyes were blue;
Her cheeks were like the red red rose,
The girl I loved on the greenbriar shore.

The years rolled on and the months rolled by,
She left me all alone;
Now I remember what mother said,
Never trust a girl on the greenbriar shore.

Green Grow The Lilacs

Chorus:

G
Green grow the lilacs all sparkling with dew,
　　　　　　　　　　　　　D
I'm lonely, my darling, since parting with you.
　G　　　　　　G7　C
But by our next meeting I hope to prove true.
　G　　　　　　　　　　D7　　　　G
And change the green lilacs to the red, white and blue.

I used to have a sweetheart, but now I have none,
Since she's gone and left me, I care not for one.
Since she's gone and left me, contented I'll be,
For she loves another one better than me.

I passed my love's window, both early and late,
The look that she gave me, it made my heart ache.
Oh, the look that she gave me was painful to see,
For she loves another one better than me.

I wrote my love letters in rosy red lines,
She sent me an answer all twisted in twines,
Saying, "Keep your love letters and I will keep mine,
"Just you write to your love and I'll write to mine."

On Top Of Old Smoky

　　C　　　　F
On top of old Smoky
　　　　　　　C
All covered with snow,
　　　　　　G7
I lost my true lover,
　　　　　　　　　C
From courting too slow
　　　　　　　　F
Now courting is pleasure
　　　　　　　C
And parting is grief,
　　　　　　　　　　G7
And a false hearted lover,
　　　　　　　　　C
Is worse than a thief.

Say a thief will just rob you
And take what you have
But a false hearted lover
Will lead you to the grave.
And the grave will decay you
And turn you to dust
Not one boy in a hundred
A poor girl can trust.

They'll hug you and kiss you
And tell you more lies
Than the cross-ties on the railroad
Or the stars in the skies.
So come all you young maidens
And listen to me
Never place your affection
On a green willow tree.

For the leaves they will wither
And the roots they will die'
You'll all be forsaken
And never know why.
On top of Old Smoky
All covered with snow
I lost my true lover
From courting too slow.

Bell-Bottomed Trousers

G   D7
Once I was a lady's maid way down in Drury Lane,
           G
My master was so kind to me, my mistress was the same.
       D7
Along came a sailor as happy as can be,
        G
And he was the cause of all my misery.

Chorus:

          D7
Singing, "Bell-bottomed trousers, coats of navy blue,
         G
"He'll climb the rigging like his daddy used to do."

He asked me for a kerchief to tie around his head,
He asked me for a candle to light his way to bed,
And I like a silly maid, thinking it no harm,
Jumped right in beside him to keep the sailor warm.

Early in the morning before the break of day,
A one-pound note he gave me, and this to me did say:
"Maybe you'll have a daughter, maybe you'll have a son;
"Take this, oh, my darling, for the damage I have done.

"And if you have a daughter, bounce her on your knee;
"But if you have a son, send the rascal off to sea."
The moral of the story is as plain as plain can be:
Never trust a sailor an inch above your knee.

One Morning In May (The Nightingale)

 Dm   Gm Dm
One morning, one morning, one morning in May,
 F Am Dm Gm F Am Dm Am
I spied a fair couple a-winding their way.
  Bb Gm7 DmAm F   C   A
The one was a maiden and a fair one was she,
 Dm   Am   Dm
The other was a soldier and a brave one was he.

"Oh, where are you going, my pretty fair maid?
Oh, where are you going, sweet lady?" he said.
"I'm going," said she, "to the banks of the stream,
To see the waters gliding, hear the nightingales sing."

They had not been there but an hour or two,
Till out of his satchel a fiddle he drew.
He played her a love-song that made the valleys to ring,
"Hark, hark!" says the lady, "hear the nightingales sing!"

"Oh now," says the soldier, " 'tis time to give o'er."
"Oh, no," says the lady, "just play one tune more;
I'd rather hear you fiddle at the top of one string,
Than to see the waters gliding,
  hear the nightingale sing."

"Oh, now," says the lady, "it's won't you marry me?"
"Oh, no," says the soldier, "that never can be!
I've a wife back in Ireland with children twice three;
And two wives and the army's too many for me!

"I'll go home to Ireland and stay there one year.
In place of pure water, I'll drink wine and beer.
And if ever I return, 'twill be in the spring,
When the waters are gliding and the nightingales sing."

Come all ye fair damsels, take warning from me.
Never place your affections on a green willow tree;
For the leaves they will wither
  like flowers in the spring,
While the waters are a-gliding
  and the nightingales sing.

Come all ye fair damsels, take warning from me,
Never place your affections on a soldier so free.
For he'll love you and leave you without any ring
To rock your young baby, hear the nightingales sing!

Wildwood Flower

   C   G7   C
I will twine and will mingle, my waving black hair,
         G7 C
With the roses so red and the lily so fair.
         F   C
The myrtle so green of an emerald hue,
        G   C
The pale emanita, and eyes look like blue.

Oh he promised to love me, he promised to love,
To cherish me always, all others above.
I woke from my dream and my idol was clay,
My passion for loving had vanished away.

Oh, he taught me to love him, he called me his flower,
A blossom to cheer him through life's weary hour.
But now he has gone and left me alone,
The wild flowers to weep, and the wild birds to moan.

I'll dance and I'll sing, and my life shall be gay,
I'll charm every heart in the crowd I survey;
Though my heart now is breaking, he never shall know
How his name makes me tremble, my pale cheeks to glow.

I'll dance and I'll sing, and my heart will be gay,
I'll banish this weeping, drive troubles away;
I'll live yet to see him, regret this dark hour,
When he won and neglected, this frail wildwood flower.

Beware, Oh, Take Care

    C
Young men, they say, are bold and free,
  G7   C
Beware, oh, take care,

They say they're true, but they're liars you see,
  G7   C
Beware, oh, take care.

Chorus:

   F   C
Beware young ladies, they're fooling you,
G7   C
Trust them not, they're fooling you,
   F   C
Beware young ladies, they're fooling you,
  G7   C
Beware, oh, take care.

Around their neck they wear a guard,
Beware, oh, take care,
And in their pocket is a deck of cards,
Beware, oh, take care.

They wear fine clothes, they wear fine shoes,
Beware, oh, take care,
And in their pocket is a bottle of booze,
Beware, oh, take care.

They hold their hands up to their heart,
They sigh, oh they sigh,
They say they love no one but you,
They lie, oh they lie.

I'm Sad And I'm Lonely

    G
I'm sad and I'm lonely,
    A#dim
My heart it will break,
    G
For my sweetheart loves another;

Oh I wish I was dead.

Young ladies take warning,
Take warning from me,
Don't waste your affections
On a young man so free.

Because he'll hug you and he'll kiss you
And he'll tell you more lies
Than the cross-ties on the railroad
Or the stars in the sky.

My cheeks once were red
Like the red, red rose;
But now they are white
As the lily that grows.

I'll build me a cabin
On the mountain so high,
Where the blackbirds can't find me
Or hear my sad cry.

I'm troubled, yes, I'm troubled,
I'm troubled in my mind,
If this trouble don't kill me,
I'll live a long time.

DON'T MARRY A MAN BEFORE YOU TRY HIM

Songs of marriage, courtship and the vicissitudes of matrimony....

Cod Liver Oil

Em   B7   Em
I'm a young married man that is tired of life,
            Am   Em
Ten years I've been wed to a sickly wife.
G   D
She does nothing all day but sit down and cry,
Em   B7   Em
A praying to God she'd get better or die.

Chorus:

           B7   Em
Oh Doctor, dear Doctor, Oh Doctor dear John,
           Am Em
Your Cod liver oil is so pure and so strong,
G   D
I'm afraid of me life, I'd go down to the still,
Em   B7   Em
If me wife don't stop drinking your Cod liver oil.
Em
Cod liver oil, Cod liver oil.

Now, an old friend of mine came to see me one day,
He said that my wife, she was pinin' away.
He afterwards told me that she would get strong,
If I got her a bottle from Doctor, dear, John.

Well, I got her a bottle, 'twas just for to try,
And the way that she drank it, you'd think she was dry;
I got her another, it vanished the same,
And now she's got Cod liver oil on the brain.

Now, my house it resembles a big doctor's shop,
'Tis filled up with bottles from bottom to top,
And when in the mornin', the kettle does boil,
You'd swear it was singin' out: "Cod liver oil!"

Now, come all you young fellows, where e'er you may be,
I hope you will heed this fair warnin' from me,
From sickely women, I pray you recoil,
Or you'll end up a-swimmin' in Cod liver oil!

The Bold Soldier

C
Soldier, oh soldier, a-coming from the plain,
G7   C   G7
He courted the maiden through honor and through fame.
C
Her beauty shone so bright that it never could be told,
G7   C   G7   C
She always loved the soldier because he was so bold.

Chorus:

    G7
Fa-la-la-la, fa-la-la-la-la,
C   G7   C
Fa-la-la-la, fa-la-la-la.

"Soldier, oh soldier, it's I would be your bride,
But for fear of my father some danger might betide."
Then he pulled out sword and pistol,
    and he hung them by his side,
Swore he would be married no matter what betide.

Then he took her to the parson, and of course, home again,
There they met her father and seven arm-ed men.
"Let us fly," said the lady, "I fear we shall be slain."
"Hold your hand," said the soldier, "Never fear again."

Then he pulled out sword and pistol
    and he caus-ed them to rattle;
The lady held the horse while the soldier fought in battle.
"Hold your hand," said the old man, "Do not be so bold.
You shall have my daughter
    and a thousand pounds of gold."

"Fight on," said the lady, "The portion is too small."
"Hold your hand," said the old man,
    "And you shall have it all."
Then he took them right straight home,
    and he called them son and dear,
Not because he loved them, but only through fear.

When The Iceworms Nest Again
Robert W. Service

                  C   F
There's a dusky, husky maiden in the Arctic,
          G7   C
And she waits for me but it is not in vain;
G7   C   F
For some day I'll put my mukloks on and ask her
          G7   C
If she'll wed me when the iceworms nest again.

Chorus:

C
In the land of the pale blue snow,
           F
    where it's ninety-nine below,
        G7   C
And the polar bears are roaming o'er the plain;
G7   C   F
In the shadow of the pole, I will clasp her to my soul,
         G7   C
We'll be married when the iceworms nest again.

For our wedding feast we'll have seal oil and blubber;
In our kayak we will roam the bounding main;
All the walruses will look at us and rubber;
We'll be married when the iceworms nest again.

When some night at half-past two I return to my igloo,
After sittin' with a friend who was in pain,
She'll be waitin' for me there with hambone of a bear,
And she'll beat me till the iceworms nest again.

Bobby Shafto

F   Bb F
Bobby Shafto's gone to sea,
           C
Silver buckles on his knee,
F   Bb F
He'll come back and marry me,
C7   F
Bonnie Bobby Shafto.

Chorus:

F
Bobby Shafto's bright and fair,
C7
Combing down his yellow hair,
F
He's my ain for evermair,
C7   F
Bonnie Bobby Shafto.

Bobby Shafto's been to sea,
Silver buckles on his knee,
He's come back and married me,
Bonnie Bobby Shafto.

Bobby Shafto's tall and slim,
Always dressed so neat and trim,
Lassies they all keek at him,
Bonnie Bobby Shafto.

Bobby Shafto's getting a bairn,
For to dangle on his airm,
On his airm and on his knee,
Bonnie Bobby Shafto.

The Johnson Boys

F
Johnson boys were raised in the ashes,
                  C7
Didn't know how to court a maid;
F
Turn their backs and hide their faces,
Bb   C7
Sight of a pretty girl makes 'em afraid.
F
Sight of a pretty girl makes 'em afraid,

Sight of a pretty girl makes 'em afraid.

Johnson boys they went a-huntin',
Took two dogs and went astray;
Tore their clothes and scratched their faces,
Didn't come home till break of day. (3 times)

Johnson boys they went a-courtin',
Coon Creek girls so pretty and sweet,
They couldn't make no conversation,
They didn't know where to put their feet. (3 times)

Johnson boys, they went to the city
Ridin' in a Chevrolet,
They come back broke and hungry,
They had no money for to pay their way. (3 times)

Johnson boys'll never get married,
They'll stay single all their life;
They're too scared to pop the question,
Ain't no woman that'll be their wife. (twice)
Shame, shame, the Johnson boys.

Everyday Dirt

      A
Now John come home all in a wonder,
    D7
He rattled at the door just like thunder.
   G7
"Who is that?" Mister Henley cried.
             C
"'Tis my husband! You must hide!"

She held the door till old man Henley,
Jumping and a-jerking went up the chimney,
John come in, looking all around,
But not a soul could be found.

Then John sat down by the fireside a-weepin'
An' up that chimney he got to peepin'.
There he saw that poor old soul,
Settin' up a-straddle of the pot-rack pole.

Then John built on a rousing fire
Just to suit his own desire.
His wife got out with a free good will,
"Don't do that, for the man you'll kill!"

Then John renched up and down he fetched him
Like a coon when a dog had ketched him.
He blacked his eyes and then did better:
He kicked him out right on his setter.

Then his wife she crawled in under the bed,
And he pulled her out by the hair of the head.
"And when I'm gone, remember then!"
He kicked her where the chinches had been.

Now, the law went down and John went up.
He didn't have the chance of a yaller pup.
They sent him down to the old chain gang
For beatin' his wife, the dear little thing.

Well, John didn't worry, John didn't cry,
But when he got back home, he socked her in the eye.
They took him right back to the old town jail,
But his wife got lonesome and she paid his bail.

Then the judge sent him back, made him work so hard
He longed to be home in his own front yard.
They kept him there and wouldn't turn him loose.
I could tell you more about him, but there ain't no use.

Risselty-Rosselty

G   C   G
I married me a wife in the month of June,
  D7   G
Risselty-rosselty now, now, now!
           C   G
I carried her home in a silver spoon,

Risselty-rosselty, hey bom-bosselty,

Knicklety, knacklety, rustical quality,
D7   G
Willaby-wallaby now, now, now!

She swept the floor but once a year,
Risselty-rosselty now, now, now!
She swore her brooms were all too dear,
Risselty-rosselty, etc.

She combed her hair but once a year, etc.
At every rake she shed a tear, etc.

She churned the butter in dad's old boot, etc.
And for a dash she used her foot, etc.

The butter came out a grisly grey, etc.
The cheese took legs and ran away, etc.

The butter and cheese are on the shelf, etc.
If you want any more, you can sing it yourself, etc.

The Wagoner's Lad

   G
Oh, I am a poor girl, my fortune is sad,
     D   G   D
I have always been courted by the wagoner's lad;
      G   D
He courted me daily, by night and by day,
     G   C   G
And now he is loaded and going away.

Your parents don't like me because I am poor,
They say I'm not worthy of entering your door;
I work for my living, my money's my own,
And if they don't like me they can leave me alone.

Your horses are hungry, go feed them some hay,
Come sit down beside me as long as you stay.
My horses ain't hungry, they won't eat your hay,
So fare you well darling, I'll be on my way.

Your wagon needs greasing, your whip is to mend,
Come sit down here by me as long as you can.
My wagon is greasy, my whip's in my hand,
So fare you well darling, no longer to stand.

The Husband With No Courage In Him

  Gm   Am   Dm
As I walked out one summer's day
  Gm   Am
To view the fields and the lizards springing,
  Gm   Am   Dm
I saw two maidens standin' by,
    Gm   Am   Dm
And one of them her hands were wringin';
    Bb   Am   Dm
And all of her conversation was,
    Gm   Am
"My husband's got no courage in him,
  Dm   Gm
"Oh, dear no, oh dear no,
              Am   Dm
"My husband's got no courage in him,

"Oh, dear no."

"All sorts of meat I do preserve,
"All sorts of drink that's fittin' for him,
"Both oyster pies and rhubarb too,
"But nothing will put courage in him.
"Oh dear no, oh dear no,
"Nothing will put courage in him,
"Oh dear no."

"It's seven long years I've made his bed,
"And six of them I've lain agin him,
"And this morn I rose with my maidenhead,
"Now that shows he's got no courage in him.
"Oh dear no, oh dear no,
"That shows he's got no courage in him,
"Oh dear no."

"Come all pretty maids wherever you be,
"Don't marry a man before you try him,
"Lest you should sing a song like me,
"Now, my husband's got no courage in him.
"Oh dear no, oh dear no,
"Me husband's got no courage in him,
"Oh dear no."

"I wish to the Lord that he were dead,
"And in his grave I'd quickly laid him;
"Then I would try another one
"That had a little courage in him.
"Oh dear yes, oh dear yes,
"That had a little courage in him,
"Oh dear yes."

Reilly's Daughter

G
As I was sitting by the fire,
C
Talking to old Reilly's daughter,
G
Suddenly a thought came into my head,
C
I'd like to marry old Reilly's daughter.

Chorus:

G
Giddy-i-ae, giddy-i-ae,
C
Giddy-i-ae for the one-eyed Reilly,
G   (no chords)
Giddy-i-ae, (*bang, bang, bang*)
G   D7   G
Try it on your own big drum.

Reilly played on the big bass drum,
Reilly had a mind for murder and slaughter,
Reilly had a bright red, glittering eye,
And he kept that eye on his lovely daughter.

Her hair was black and her eyes were blue,
The colonel, and the major and the captain sought her,
The sergeant, and the private and the drummer boy, too,
But they never had a chance with Reilly's daughter.

I got me a ring and a parson, too,
Got me a scratch in a married quarter,
Settled me down to a peaceful life,
Happy as a king with Reilly's daughter.

Suddenly a footstep on the stairs,
Who should it be but Reilly out for slaughter,
With two pistols in his hands,
Looking for the man who had married his daughter.

I caught old Reilly by the hair,
Rammed his head on a pail of water,
Fired his pistols into the air,
A damned sight quicker than I married his daughter.

I Wish I Was Single Again

C
I wish I was single again,
                    G7
I wish I was single again,
      C   F
For when I was single my pockets did jingle,
    G7   C
I wish I was single again.

I married a wife, oh then; (twice)
I married a wife, she's the curse of my life,
I wish I was single again.

My wife, she died, oh then, (twice)
My wife, she died, and I laughed till I cried,
To think I was single again.

I went to the funeral, etc., and danced Yankee Doodle,
To think I was single again.

I married another, etc., the devil's grandmother,
I wish I was single again.

She beat me, she banged me, etc.,
    she said she would hang me,
I wish I was single again.

She went for the rope, etc., when she got it, 'twas broke,
I wish I was single again.

Now listen, all you young men, (twice)
Be good to the first, for the next will be worse,
I wish I was single again.

Common Bill

      C
I will tell you of a fellow,
      G7   C
Of a fellow I have seen.
      F   C
He is neither white nor yellow
      G7   C
But is altogether green.

His name is nothing charming,
It is only Common Bill,
He wishes me to wed him,
But I hardly think I will.

One night he came to see me,
And he made so long a stay,
I began to think that blockhead
Never meant to go away.

And the tears that creature wasted
Was enough to turn a mill,
He wishes me to wed him,
But I hardly think I will.

He said if I refuse him
He would not live one minute,
Now you know I wouldn't choose him
But the very deuce is in it.

Now you know the blessed Bible
Plainly says we mustn't kill,
So I thought the matter over
And I rather think I will.

Eggs And Marrowbone

       G
There was an old woman in our town,
  D7   G
In our town did dwell;
  G7
She loved her husband dearly
      Em   G   Em
But another man twice as well.

She went down to the doctor
To see what she could find,
To see what she could find, sir,
To make her old man blind.

Eggs, eggs and marrowbone,
Feed them to him all;
That will make him so gol-dern blind,
That he can't see you at all.

She fed him eggs and marrowbone,
Fed them to him all;
That did make him so gol-derned blind
That he couldn't see her at all.

"Now that I am old and blind,
"And tired of my life,
"I will go and drown myself,
"And that will end my strife."

"To drown yourself, to drown yourself,
"Now that would be a sin,
"So I will go with you to the water's edge
"And kindly push you in."

The old woman took a running jump
For to push the old man in;
The old man he stepped to one side
And the old woman she fell in.

She cried for help, screamed for help,
Loudly she did bawl.
The old man said, "I'm so gol-derned blind,
"I can't see you at all."

She swam along, she swam along,
Till she came to the river's brim.
The old man got a great, long pole,
And pushed her further in.

Now the old woman is dead and gone,
And the Devil's got her soul,
Wasn't she a blamed old fool
That she did not grab that pole?

Eggs, eggs and marrowbone
Won't make your old man blind,
So if you want to do him in,
You must sneak up behind.

Kansas Boys

C   G   C
Come along girls and listen to my noise,
                    G   C
Don'tcha never marry no Kansas boys;
            F   G
If you do your portion it'll be,
C   G   C
Hoecakes, hominy, sassafrass tea.

They'll take you out on a blackjack hill,
Leave you there against your will,
Leave you there to starve on the plains,
For that is the way with the Kansas range.

When they milk they milk in a gourd,
Throw it in a corner and cover it with a board;
Some gets little and some gets none,
That is the way with the Kansas run.

When they go a-courtin', the clothes that they wear,
Old brown coat, all picked and bare,
Old straw hat, more brim than crown,
And dirty cotton socks they wore the year around.

So come along girls and listen to my noise,
Don'tcha never marry no Kansas boys;
If you do your portion it'll be,
Hoecakes, hominy, sassafrass tea.

Sally My Dear

     Am   C
Oh, Sally, my dear, I wish I could wed you,
     Am   C
Oh, Sally, my dear, I wish I could wed you.
      F   C   E7   Am
She laughed and replied why you silly blockhead, you,
                       G   Am
Singing whack fall dingy di-do whack fall di day.

Oh, Sally my dear it's you I'd be kissin', (twice)
She laughed and replied,
   said you don't know what you're missin',
Singing, falla dingy-di-do, whack fall de-day.

If the girls were all blackbirds,
   the girls were all thrushes, (twice)
We'd see all of the boys go to beating the bushes.

If the girls were all panthers and
   raced round the mountain, (twice)
How many of the men would take guns to go huntin'?

Oh, Sally, my dear, I wish I could wed you, (twice)
Oh, sir, if you did, you'd say I misled you.

If all of the girls were like fish in the ocean, (twice)
And if I were a wave I'd raise a commotion.

My Horses Ain't Hungry

```
G                              C            G
My horses ain't hungry, they won't eat your hay.
                           C    G
So fare you well Polly, I'm going away.
                       Em     G      Em
Your parents don't like me, they say I'm too poor.
G                        C        G
They say I'm not worthy to enter your door.
```

My parents don't like you, you're poor I am told,
But it's your love I'm wanting, not silver or gold.
Then come with me Polly, we'll ride till we come
To some little cabin, we'll call it our home.

Sparking is pleasure, but parting is grief,
And a false hearted lover is worse than a thief.
A thief will just rob you and take what you have,
But a false hearted lover will lead you to the grave.

Johnny Todd

```
G            C    G
Johnny Todd he went a sailing
Em        Am   D7
For to cross the ocean wide
G        C        D7
But he left his true love behind him
G      D7         G
Walking by the Liverpool Tide.
```

For a week she wept full sorely,
Tore her hair and wrung her hands,
Till she met with another sailor
Walking on the Liverpool sands.

Oh fair maid, why are you weeping
For your Johnny gone to sea?
If you'll wed with me tomorrow
I will kind and constant be.

I will buy you sheets and blankets,
I'll buy you a wedding ring;
You shall have a silver cradle
For to rock the baby in.

Johnny Todd came home from sailing,
Sailing o'er the ocean wide;
But he found that his fair and false one
Was another sailor's bride.

Now young men who go a-sailing,
For to fight the foreign foe;
Do not leave your love like Johnny,
Marry her before you go.

The Wee Cooper Of Fife

```
         G              C    G
There was a wee cooper who lived in Fife,
                     D7
Nickety, nackety, noo, noo, noo;
     G          C    G
And he had gotten a gentle wife,
         D7        G
Hey, willy wallacky, hey, John Dougal,
             C       G
Alane, quo rushety, roo, roo, roo.
```

She would na bake nor would she brew, Nickety, etc.
For spilin' o' her comely hue. Hey, willy, etc.

She would na caird nor would she spin,
For shamin' o' her gentle kin,

The cooper has gone to his woo' pack,
And he's laid a sheep's skin on his wife's back.

"I'll no be shamin' your gentle kin,
But I will skelp my ain sheepskin."

"O I will bake and I will brew,
And think nae mair o' my comely hue."

"O I will wash and I will spin,
And think nae mair o' my gentle kin."

A' ye what hae gotten a gentle wife,
Send ye for the wee cooper o' Fife.

I Had A Wife

Tune: *What Shall We Do With A Drunken Sailor*

```
Dm
I had a wife and got no good of her,
C
Tell ye how I easy got rid of her,
Dm
Took her out and chopped the head of her,
     C    Dm
Early in the morning.
```

Seeing as how there was no evidence,
For the sheriff or his reverence,
They had to call it an act of providence,
Early in the morning.

So if you've a wife and get no good of her,
Here is how to easy get rid of her,
Take her out and chop the head of her,
Early in the morning.

Sally Ann

       C   Am
Did you ever see a muskrat, Sally Ann?
C   G
Pickin' a banjo, Sally Ann,
C
Draggin' his slick tail through the sand?
G   C
I'm gonna marry you, Sally Ann.

Chorus:

C
I'm gonna marry you, Sal, Sal,
G   C
I'm gonna marry you, Sally Ann.

Going to the wedding, Sally Ann (twice)
Sift that meal and save your bran,
I'm going home with Sally Ann.

Shake that little foot, Sally Ann, (twice)
Great big wedding up, Sally Ann,
I'm going home with Sally Ann.

Pass me the brandy, Sally Ann, (twice)
I'm going 'way with Sally Ann,
Great big wedding up, Sally Ann.

Wait For The Wagon
R. Bishop Buckley

        C
Will you come with me, my Phillis dear,
  G7   C
To yon blue mountain free?

Where the blossoms smell the sweetest,
     F   G7   C
Come rove along with me.

It's every Sunday morning,
    G7   C
When I am by your side,

We'll jump into the wagon
  F G7 C
And all take a ride.

Chorus:

C
Wait for the wagon,
     E7   F
Wait for the wagon,
C
Wait for the wagon,
       F G7   C
And we'll all take a ride.

Where the river runs like silver
And the birds they sing so sweet,
I have a cabin, Phillis,
And something good to eat;
Come listen to my story,
It will relieve my heart;
So jump into the wagon,
And off we will start.

Do you believe, my Phillis, dear,
Old Mike, with all this wealth,
Can make you half so happy
As I, with youth and health?
We'll have a little farm,
A horse, a pig and a cow;
And you will mind the dairy,
While I do guide the plough.

Your lips are red as poppies,
Your hair so slick and neat,
All braided up with dahlias,
And hollyhocks so sweet.
It's ev'ry Sunday morning,
When I am by your side,
We'll jump into the wagon,
And all take a ride.

Together, on life's journey,
We'll travel till we stop,
And if we have no trouble,
We'll reach the happy top;
Then come with me, sweet Phillis,
My dear, my lovely bride,
We'll jump into the wagon,
And all take a ride.

Red Apple Juice

       F   Dm
Well I ain't got no use for your red apple juice,
       F   Dm
Ain't got no honey baby now;

Ain't got no honey baby now.

Ain't got no use for your red rocking chair,
Ain't got no honey baby there. (twice)

It's who'll rock the cradle and who'll sing a song,
And it's who'll be your honey when I'm gone? (twice)

Done all I could do to try and live with you,
Send you back to your mama some old day. (twice)

DIED FOR LOVE

*Songs of broken hearts, untimely
deaths and lonesome graves....*

Frankie And Johnny

C
Frankie and Johnny were lovers
                                  C7
Oh Lordy how they could love.
   F
They swore to be true to each other,
                 C
True as the stars above,
      G7   C
He was her man, but he was doing her wrong.

Frankie she was a good woman
As everybody knows,
Spent a hundred dollars
Just to buy her man some clothes.
He was her man, but he was doing her wrong.

Frankie went down to the corner
Just for a bucket of beer,
Said: "Mr. bartender
Has my loving Johnny been here?
"He was my man, but he's a-doing me wrong."

"Now I don't want to tell you no stories
And I don't want to tell you no lies
I saw your man about and hour ago
With a gal named Nellie Bligh
He was your man, but he's a-doing you wrong."

Frankie she went down to the hotel
Didn't go there for fun,
Underneath her kimona
She carried a forty-four gun.
He was her man, but he was doing her wrong.

Frankie looked over the transom
To see what she could spy,
There sat Johnny on the sofa
Just loving up Nellie Bligh.
He was her man, but he was doing her wrong.

Frankie got down from that high stool
She didn't want to see no more;
Rooty-toot-toot three times she shot
Right through that hardwood door.
He was her man, but he was doing her wrong.

Now the first time that Frankie shot Johnny
He let out an awful yell,
Second time she shot him
There was a new man's face in hell.
He was her man, but he was doing her wrong.

"Oh roll me over easy
Roll me over slow
Roll me over on the right side
For the left side hurts me so."
He was her man, but he was doing her wrong.

Sixteen rubber-tired carriages
Sixteen rubber-tired hacks
They take poor Johnny to the graveyard
They ain't gonna bring him back.
He was her man, but he was doing her wrong.

Frankie looked out of the jailhouse
To see what she could see,
All she could hear was a two-string bow
Crying nearer my God to thee.
He was her man, but he was doing her wrong.

Frankie she said to the sheriff
"What do you reckon they'll do?"
Sheriff he said "Frankie,
"It's the electric chair for you."
He was her man, but he was doing her wrong.

This story has no moral
This story has no end
This story only goes to show
That there ain't no good in men!
He was her man, but he was doing her wrong.

Delia's Gone

D
Tony shot his Delia,
                        D7
'Twas on one Christmas night;
G   Em7
First thing she did
   A7   D
Was hang her head and die.

Chorus:

      Em7   A7
Delia's gone, one more round,
    D[maj7]   D(6)
Delia's gone, one more round,
      Em7   A7
Delia's gone, one more round,
    D[maj7]   D(6)
Delia's gone, one more round.

Sent for the doctor,
The doctor come too late.
Sent for the minister
To lay out Delia straight.

Delia, oh Delia,
Where you been so long?
Everybody's talkin' about
Poor Delia's dead and gone.

Lord Lovel

Child Ballad 75

```
        D              A7   D
Lord Lovel he stood at his castle gate,

A-combing his milk white steed,
        G                      D
When along came Lady Nancy Bell,
                             A7   D
A-wishing her lover good speed, speed, speed,
  A7             D
A-wishing her lover good speed.
```

"Oh, where are you going, Lord Lovel?" she said,
"Oh, where are you going?" said she.
"I'm going my dear Lady Nancy Bell,
Strange countries to see, see, see,
Strange countries to see."

"Oh, when will you be back?" she said,
"When will you be back?" said she.
"In a year or two, or three, three, three,
Then I'll come back to thee, thee, thee,
Then I'll come back to thee.

He had not been gone but a year and a day,
Strange countries for to see,
When ravishing thoughts came into his head.
His lady he wanted to see, see, see,
His lady he wanted to see.

He rode and he rode on his milk-white steed,
Till he came to London town;
And then he heard Saint Varnie's bell,
And the people all mourning around, round, round, round,
And the people all mourning around.

"Is somebody dead?" Lord Lovel he said,
"Is somebody dead?" said he.
"A lady is dead," the people all said,
"They call her the lady Nancy, cy, cy,
They call her the lady Nancy."

He ordered the grave to be opened forthwith,
And the shroud to be folded down;
And then he kissed her clay-cold lips,
Till the tears came trickling down, down, down,
Till the tears came trickling down.

Lady Nancy she died as it might be today,
Lord Lovel he died on the morrow;
And out of her bosom there grew a red rose,
And out of Lord Lovel's a briar-riar-riar,
And out of Lord Lovel's a briar.

They grew and they grew till they reached the church top,
And they could not grow any higher.
And there they entwined in a true lover's knot,
Which true lovers always admire-mire-mire,
Which true lovers always admire.

The Butcher's Boy

```
Dm
She went upstairs to make her bed,
           F              Dm
And not a word to her mother said.
```

Her mother she went upstairs too, saying,
                            F   Dm
"Daughter, oh, daughter what troubles you?"

"Oh mother, oh mother I cannot tell,
That butcher's boy I love so well,
He courted me my life away
And now at home he will not stay."

"There is a place in London town,
Where that butcher's boy goes and sits down.
He takes that strange girl on his knee
And tells to her what he won't tell me!"

Her father he came up from work,
Saying where is daughter, she seems so hurt.
He went upstairs to give her hope
And found her hanging from a rope.

He took his knife and cut her down,
And in her bosom these words he found:
Go dig my grave both wide and deep
Place a marble slab at my head and feet.

And over my coffin place a snow-white dove
To warn the world I died of love.

Bury Me Beneath The Willow

Chorus:

```
G            C
Bury me beneath the willow.
G                       D7
Neath the weeping willow tree
G               C
When he hears his love is sleeping
G      D7              G
Maybe then he'll think of me.
```

My heart is sad and I am lonely
Thinking of the one I love
When will I see him — oh, no never
Unless we meet in Heaven above.

She told me that she dearly loved me
How could I believe her untrue
Until the day some neighbors told me
She has proven untrue to you.

Tomorrow was to be our wedding
I pray, Oh Lord where can he be
He's gone, he's gone, to love another
He no longer cares for me.

The Dowie Dens of Yarrow
Child Ballad 214

<pre>
      Am   G   Am
There was a lady in the north,
   F   Am   C
I ne'er could find her marrow;
</pre>

She was courted by nine gentlemen,
<pre>
      Am   Em   Am
And a ploughboy lad frae Yarrow.
</pre>

These nine sat drinking at the wine,
As oft they'd done afore, O;
They hae made a vow amang themselves
Tae fecht wi' him on Yarrow.

She's washed his face and kaimed his hair,
As oft they'd done afore, O,
She's made him like a knight sae bright,
Tae fecht wi' her on Yarrow.

As he walked up yon high, high hill,
And doon by the holms o' Yarrow,
There he saw nine armed men,
Come to fecht wi' him on Yarrow.

"There's nine o' you, there's one o' me,
It's an unequal marrow,
But I'll fecht you a' one by one,
On the dowie dens o' Yarrow."

And there he flew and there he slew
And there he wounded sorely,
Till her brother John came in beyond,
And pierced his heart most foully.

"O, father, dear, I dreamed a dream,
A dream o' dule and sorrow;
I dreamed I was pu'in' the heather bell
On the dowie dens o' Yarrow."

As she walked up yon high, high hill,
And doon by the holms o' Yarrow,
There she saw her Willie dear,
Lying pale and dead on Yarrow.

Her hair it being three quarters lang,
The colour it was yellow;
She wrappit it round his middle sae sma',
And bore him down to Yarrow.

"O, faither dear, you've seiven sons,
You may wed them a' tomorrow,
For the fairest flooer among them a',
Was the lad I lo'ed on Yarrow."

This fair maid being big with child,
A fact which did cause her sorrow,
She lay deid in her lover's airms,
Between that day and morrow.

Barbara Allen
Child Ballad 84

<pre>
     E
In Scarlet Town where I was born,
        B7
There was a fair maid dwelling,
   E
Made many a youth cry well a day,
              B   E
Her name was Barbara Allen.
</pre>

It was in the merry month of May
When green buds they were swelling;
Sweet William came from the west country
And he courted Barbara Allen.

He sent his servant unto her
To the place where she was dwelling;
Said my master's sick, bids me call for you
If your name be Barbara Allen.

Well, slowly, slowly got she up
And slowly went she nigh him;
But all she said as she passed his bed
Young man I think you're dying.

Then lightly tripped she down the stairs
She heard those church bells tolling;
And each bell seemed to say as it tolled
Hard-hearted Barbara Allen.

O, mother, mother go make my bed
And make it long and narrow;
Sweet William died for me today
I'll die for him tomorrow.

They buried Barbara in the old church yard
They buried Sweet William beside her;
Out of his grave grew a red, red rose
And out of hers a briar.

They grew and grew up the old church wall
Till they could grow no higher;
And at the top twined in a lovers' knot
The red rose and the briar.

Banks Of The Ohio

```
D              A7        D
I asked my love to go with me,
         A7        D
To take a walk a little way.
                   D7      G
And as we walked, and as we talked
       D   A7      D
About our golden wedding day.
```

Chorus:
Then only say that you'll be mine,
In no other arms entwine.
Down beside where the waters flow,
On the banks of the Ohio.

I asked your mother for you, dear,
And she said you were too young;
Only say that you'll be mine —
Happiness in my home you'll find.

I held a knife against her breast,
And gently in my arms she pressed,
Crying: Willie, oh Willie, don't murder me,
For I'm unprepared for eternity.

I took her by her lily white hand,
Led her down where the waters stand.
I picked her up and I pitched her in,
Watched her as she floated down.

I started back home twixt twelve and one,
Crying, My God, what have I done?
I've murdered the only woman I love,
Because she would not be my bride.

Every Night When The Sun Goes In

```
C   Am Dm7 G7      C Am
Ev'ry night when the sun goes in,
C   Em G7   C7     C
Ev'ry night when the sun goes in,
C7  F7        G7 E7  Am
Ev'ry night when the sun goes in,
  C         Em Am Dm7 G7      C
I hang down my head      and     mournful cry.
```

Chorus:

```
C           Am Dm7 G7     C   Am
True love, don't weep, true  love, don't mourn,
C           Em  G7 C7      C
True love, don't weep, true love, don't mourn,
  C7    F7       G7   E7 Am
True love, don't weep nor mourn for me,
  C    Em Am Dm7G7 C
I'm going away to   Marble  town.
```

I wish to the Lord that train would come, (3 times)
To take me back to where I come from.

It's once my apron hung down low, (3 times)
He'd follow me through sleet and snow.

It's now my apron's to my chin, (3 times)
He'll face my door and won't come in.

I wish to the Lord my babe was born,
A-sitting on his papa's knee,
And me, poor girl, was dead and gone,
And the green grass growing over me.

There Is A Tavern In The Town

```
              C
There is a tavern in the town, in the town,
                              G7
And there my true love sits him down, sits him down
         C          C7 F
And drinks his wine as merry as can be,
    G7                 C
And never, never thinks of me.
```

Chorus:

```
         G7
Fare thee well, for I must leave thee,
        C
Do not let this parting grieve thee,
    G7                             C
And remember that the best of friends must part,
   F  G7 C
   must part.
```

Adieu, adieu, kind friends adieu, yes adieu,
```
                              G7
I can no longer stay with you, stay with you;
    C          C7 F
I'll hang my heart on a weeping willow tree,
  G7                    C
And may the world go well with thee.
```

He left me for a damsel dark, damsel dark,
Each Friday night they used to spark, used to spark,
And now my love who once was true to me,
Takes this dark damsel on his knee.

And now I see him nevermore, nevermore;
He never knocks upon my door, on my door;
Oh, woe is me; he pinned a little note,
And these were all the words he wrote:

Oh, dig my grave both wide and deep, wide and deep;
Put tombstones at my head and feet, head and feet,
And on my breast you may carve a turtle dove,
To signify I died for love.

I Never Will Marry

<pre>
    D   A7   D   G
One day as I rambled, down by the seashore,
            D   A7   D
The wind it did whistle, and the waters did roar
    D   A7   D   G
I spied a fair damsel, make a pitiful cry
              D   A7   D
It sounded so lonesome, in the waters nearby.
</pre>

Chorus:

<pre>
    D   A7   D   G
I never will marry, I'll be no man's wife,
              D   A7   D
I expect to live single all the days of my life.
      D   A7   D   G
The shells in the ocean will be my deathbed,
            D   A7   D
The fish in deep water, swim over my head.
</pre>

My love's gone and left me, he's the one I adore,
He's gone where I never shall see him any more.
She plunged her dear body, in the water so deep,
She closed her pretty blue eyes, in the waters to sleep.

Sailor On The Deep Blue Sea

<pre>
      A   D
It was on one summer's evening,
      A   E7
Just about the hour of three,
        A   D
When my darling started to leave me,
      A   E7   A
For to sail upon the deep blue sea.
</pre>

Oh, he promised to write me a letter,
He said he'd write to me;
But I've not heard from my darling
Who is sailing on the deep blue sea.

Oh, my mother's dead and buried,
My pa's forsaken me,
And I have no one for to love me
But the sailor on the deep blue sea.

Oh captain, can you tell me
Where can my sailor be;
Oh yes, my little maiden,
He is drownded in the deep blue sea.

Farewell to friends and relations,
It's the last you'll see of me;
For I'm going to end my troubles
By drowning in the deep blue sea.

Molly Brannigan

<pre>
Gm   Dm   A7   Dm
Ma'am dear, did ye never hear of pretty Molly Brannigan,
  F   Gm A7 Dm
In throth, then, she's left me and I'll never be a man again,
Gm   Dm   A7   Dm
Not a spot on my hide will a summer's sun e'er tan again,
   F   C7   F
Since Molly's gone and left me here alone for to die.
                                    Bb   F
The place where my heart was you'd aisy rowl a turnip in,
     Gm   Dm
'Tis as large as all Dublin,
         Gm   Dm
   and from Dublin to the Divil's glen;
       Gm   F
If she wish'd to take another,
         Gm   A7   Dm
   sure she might have left mine back again,
     F   C7   F
And not have gone and left me here alone for to die.
</pre>

Ma'am dear, I remember
   when the milking time was past and gone,
We strolled thro' the meadow,
   and she swore I was the only one
That ever she could love, but oh! the base and cruel one,
For all that she's left me here alone for to die.
Ma'am dear, I remember
   when coming home the rain began,
I wrapt my frieze-coat round her
   and ne'er a waistcoat had I on;
And my shirt was rather fine-drawn,
   but oh! the false and cruel one,
For all that she's left me here alone for to die.

The left side of my carcase
   is as weak as water gruel, ma'am,
There's not a pick upon my bones,
   since Molly's proved so cruel, ma'am;
Oh! if I had a blunder gun, I'd go and fight a duel, ma'am,
For sure I'd better shoot myself than live here to die.
I'm cool and determined as any salamander, ma'am,
Won't you come to my wake
   when I go the long meander, ma'am?
I'll think myself as valiant
   as the famous Alexander, ma'am,
When I hear ye cryin' o'er me, "Arrah! why did ye die?"

Rosewood Casket

      C   G7   C
There's a little rosewood casket
      F   G7 C
Lying on a marble stand
         F   C
And a packet of love letters
      G7   C
Written by my true love's hand.

Come and sit beside me, brother,
Come and sit upon my bed
Come and lay your head upon my pillow,
For my aching heart falls dead.

Last Sunday I saw him walking
With a lady by his side
And I thought I heard him tell her
She could never be his bride.

When I'm dead and in my coffin
And my shroud's around me bound
And my narrow grave is ready
In some lonesome churchyard ground,

Take his letters and his locket,
Place together o'er my heart
But the golden ring he gave me
From my finger never part.

Down By The Sally Gardens

William Butler Yeats

      C   G F C
It was down by the Sally Gardens,
   F   C G7 C
My love and I did meet.
           G   F   C
She passed the Sally Gardens
   F C G7   C
On little snow white feet.
   Am Em F   Am B7 Em
She bid me take love easy,
      F   Em Dm7 G7 C
As the leaves grow upon the tree.
   C7 F   Em D C
But I was young and foolish
      F   C G7 C
And with her did not agree.

In a field by the river
My love and I did stand.
And on my leaning shoulder
She placed her snow-white hand.

She bid me take life easy,
As the grass grows on the weirs,
But I was young and foolish
And now am full of tears.

Unfortunate Miss Bailey

   G
A captain bold from Halifax
      D7
   who dwelt in country quarters,
   G
Seduced a maid who hanged herself
      D7
   one morning in her garters.
    G
His wicked conscience smited him,
      C   Am
   he lost his stomach daily,
    D7
He took to drinking turpentine
        G
   and thought upon Miss Bailey.
               C   G
Oh, Miss Bailey! Unfortunate Miss Bailey.

One night betimes he went to rest,
   for he had caught a fever,
Says he, "I am a handsome man, but I'm a gay deceiver."
His candle just at twelve o'clock
   began to burn quite palely,
A ghost stepped up to his bed side and said,
   "Behold Miss Bailey!"
Oh, Miss Bailey! Unfortunate Miss Bailey.

"Avaunt, Miss Bailey!" then he cried,
   "Your face looks white and mealy,"
"Dear Captain Smith," the ghost replied,
   "You've used me ungenteely;
The Coroner's quest goes hard with me
   because I've acted frailly,
And Parson Biggs won't bury me,
   though I'm a dead Miss Bailey."
Oh, Miss Bailey! Unfortunate Miss Bailey.

"Dear Ma'am," said he,
   "since you and I accounts must once for all close,
I have a one-pound note in my regimental small clothes.
'Twill bribe the Sexton for your grave."
   The ghost then vanished gaily,
Crying, "Bless you wicked Captain Smith,
   remember poor Miss Bailey."
Oh, Miss Bailey! Unfortunate Miss Bailey.

HARD IS THE FORTUNE
OF ALL WOMANKIND

Housewives, betrayed lovers and
hard-working women....

Oh, Babe, It Ain't No Lie

Elizabeth Cotton

C   F
One old woman, Lord, in this town
   C G7 C
Keeps a-telling lies on me.
C   F
Wish to my soul that she would die, Lord,
   C G7 C
She's telling lies on me.

Chorus:

C F#dim G7   C
Oh, babe, it ain't no lie.
E7   F
Oh, babe, it ain't no lie.
       C
Oh, babe, it ain't no lie,
      G7 C
This life I'm livin' is very hard.

Been all around this whole round world,
Lord, and I just got back today.
Work all the week, honey and I give it all to you,
Honey baby, what more can I do?

The Housewife's Lament

  G   C
One day I was walking, I heard a complaining,
  D7   G
And saw an old woman the picture of gloom.
        C
She gazed at the mud on her doorstep ('twas raining),
  D7   G
And this was her song as she wielded her broom:

Chorus:

       B7
Oh, life is a toil, and love is a trouble,
Em   D7
Beauty will fade and riches will flee.
G   C
Pleasures they dwindle and prices they double,
  D7   G
And nothing is as I would wish it to be.

There's too much of worriment goes to a bonnet,
There's too much of ironing goes to a shirt.
There's nothing that pays for the time you waste on it,
There's nothing that lasts us but trouble and dirt.

In March it is mud, it is slush in December,
The midsummer breezes are loaded with dust.
In fall the leaves litter, in muddy September
The wallpaper rots and the candlesticks rust.

There are worms on the cherries and slugs on the roses,
And ants in the sugar and mice in the pies.
The rubbish of spiders no mortal supposes
And ravaging roaches and damaging flies.

It's sweeping at six and it's dusting at seven,
It's victuals at eight and it's dishes at nine.
It's potting and panning from ten to eleven
We scarce break our fast till we plan how to dine.

With grease and with grime from corner to center,
Forever at war and forever alert.
No rest for a day lest the enemy enter,
I spend my whole life in struggle with dirt.

Last night in my dreams I was stationed forever
On a far little rock in the midst of the sea.
My one chance of life was a ceaseless endeavor,
To sweep off the waves as they swept over me.

Alas! Twas no dream; ahead I behold it,
I see I am helpless my fate to avert.
She lay down her broom, her apron she folded,
She lay down and died and was buried in dirt.

House Of The Rising Sun

    Em   B7   Em
There is a house in New Orleans,
        D Em
They call the Rising Sun.
   A   Em7 Em6
Has been the ruin of many poor girls,
  Em B7   Em
And me, oh Lord, I'm one.

My mother she's a tailor,
She sews those new blue jeans,
My husband he's a gambling man,
Drinks down in New Orleans.

My husband he's a gambler,
He goes from town to town,
The only time he's satisfied is when
He drinks his liquor down.

Go tell my baby sister,
Never do like I have done,
Shun that house in New Orleans,
They call the Rising Sun.

One foot on the platform,
The other's on the train,
I'm going down to New Orleans,
To wear that ball and chain.

Going back to New Orleans,
My race is almost run,
I'm going to spend the rest of my life,
Beneath that Rising Sun.

Single Girl

D   A
Single girl, oh, single girl,
                      D
She's gone anywhere she please,
A   D
Oh, gone anywhere she please;
                    A
Married girl, oh, married girl,
             D
Got a baby on her knees,
A   D
Oh, got a baby on her knees.

Single girl, oh, single girl,
She's going dressed up so fine,
Oh, going dressed up so fine;
Married girl, oh, married girl,
She wears any kind,
Oh, she wears any kind.

Single girl, oh, single girl,
She goes to the store and buys,
Oh, goes to the store and buys;
Married girl, oh, married girl,
She rocks the cradle and cries,
Oh, rocks the cradle and cries.

Single girl, oh, single girl,
She lays in bed 'til one,
Oh, lays in bed 'til one;
Married girl, oh, married girl,
She's up before the sun,
Oh, up before the sun.

Single girl, oh, single girl,
She's looking for a man,
Oh, looking for a man;
Married girl, oh, married girl,
She's got her wedding band,
Oh, got her wedding band.

Early One Morning

D   G   A7
Early one morning, just as the sun was rising,
 D   A7   D
I heard a maiden singing in the valley below.
A7   D   A7   D
Oh, don't deceive me, Oh never leave me.
              G   A7   D
How can you use a poor maiden so?

Remember the vows that you made to me truly,
Remember how tenderly you nestled close to me.
Gay is the garland, fresh are the roses
I've culled from the garden, to bind over thee.

Here I now wander alone as I wonder
Why did you leave me to sigh and complain.
I ask of the roses, why should I be forsaken,
Why must I here in sorrow remain?

Through yonder grove by the spring that is running,
There you and I have so merrily played,
Kissing and courting and gently sporting,
Oh, my innocent heart you've betrayed.

How could you slight so pretty a girl who loves you,
A pretty girl who loves you so dearly and warm?
Though love's folly is surely but a fancy,
Still it should prove to me sweeter than your scorn.

Soon you will meet with another pretty maiden,
Some pretty maiden, you'll court her for a while;
Thus ever ranging, turning and changing,
Always seeking for a girl that is new.

Hard, Ain't It Hard

D   G
First time I seen my true love
D   A7
He was walkin' by my door
     D
The last time I saw
    G
His false hearted smile
A7   D
Dead on his coolin' board.

Chorus:

                          G
It's hard and it's hard ain't it hard
        D   A7
To love one that never did love you
D   G
Hard and it's hard ain't it hard, great God,
  A7   D
To love one that never will be true.

There is a house in this old town,
That's where my true love lays around.
Takes other women right down on his knee
Tells them a tale that he won't tell me.

Don't go to drinkin' and to gamblin',
Don't go there your sorrows to drown.
This hard-liquor place is a low-down disgrace,
The meanest damn place in this town.

Hard Is The Fortune Of All Womankind

G
Oh, hard is the fortune of all womankind,
    D   G   D
We're always controlled and we're always confined,
          G   D
And when we get married to end all our strife,
     G   C   G
We're slaves to our husbands for the rest of our lives.

All young girls, take warning, take warning from me,
Never place your affections on a young man so free,
They will hug you and kiss you and tell you more lies,
Than the cross-ties on the railroad or the stars in the sky.

Of meeting is a pleasure and parting is a grief,
And a false-hearted lover is worse than a thief,
For a thief will just rob you and take what you have,
But a false-hearted lover will make you his slave.

He'll call you his darling, he'll call you his pearl,
And go behind you with some other girl;
You'll cook just to please him and scrub all his floors,
And if you won't love him, he'll call you a whore.

Dink's Song

D
If I had wings like Noah's dove,
            Bm   G
I'd fly 'cross the river to the one I love.
    D   F♯m   A7 D
Fare thee well, oh, honey, fare thee well.

That man I love, he's long and tall.
He moves his body like a cannonball.
Fare thee well, etc.

One of these days, and it won't be long,
You call my name, and I'll be gone.
Fare thee well, etc.

When I wore my apron low,
Couldn't keep you from my door.
Fare thee well, etc.

Now I wear my apron high,
Scarcely ever see you passing by.
Fare thee well, etc.

One of these night, was a drizzling rain,
All around my heart was an aching pain.
Fare thee well, etc.

If I had wings, like Noah's dove,
I'd fly up the river, to the one I love.
Fare thee well, etc.

Old Maid's Song

Chorus:

A7   D   A7
Come a landsman, a pinsman, a tinker or a tailor,
D   Bm   A7
Fiddler or a dancer, a ploughboy or a sailor,
D   Bm   A7
Gentleman, a poor man, a fool or a witty,
       Bm   F♯m   G   A7
Don't you let me die an old maid, but take me out of pity.

Oh, I had a sister Sally, was younger than I am,
She had so many sweethearts, she had to deny them;
As for my own part I never had many,
If you all knew my heart, I'd be thankful for any.

Oh, I had a sister Susan, was ugly and misshapen,
Before she was sixteen years old she was taken,
Before she was eighteen, a son and a daughter,
Here am I six and forty and nary an offer.

Oh, I never will be scolding, I never will be jealous,
My husband shall have money to go to the alehouse,
While he's there a-spending, well I'll be home a-saving,
And I'll leave it to the world if I am worth having.

When I Was Single

C   G7   C
When I was single, I wore a plaid shawl,
              Am   G
Now that I'm married I've nothing at all.

Chorus:

     F   C   G7   C
Oh but still I love him, I'll forgive him,
F   C   G7   C
I'll go with him wherever he goes.

He came up our alley and he whistled me out,
But the tail of his shirt, from the trousers hung out.

He bought me a handkerchief, red, white and blue,
But before I could wear it, he tore it in two.

He brought me to an ale house,
   and he bought me some stout,
But before I could drink it he ordered me out.

He borrowed some money to buy me a ring,
Then he and the jeweler went off on a fling.

There's cakes in the oven, there's cheese on the shelf,
If you want any more, you can sing it yourself.

I KNOW WHERE I'M GOING

Songs of women who know what they want....

Lady Isabel And The Elf Knight

Child Ballad 4

    C Dm   C   Dm
There was a Lord in London town,
   F   G7 C
He courted a lady gay,
    F   G7   C Am
And all that he courted this lady for
     Dm   C   Dm
Was to take her sweet life away.

Come give to me of your father's gold,
Likewise your mother's fee,
And two of the best horses in your father's stable,
For there stand thirty and three.

She mounted on her milk-white steed,
And he the fast-traveling grey,
They rode till he came to the seashore side,
Three hours before it was day.

Alight, alight, my pretty Polly,
Alight, alight, said he,
For six pretty maids I have drownded here,
And you the seventh shall be.

Now take off your silken dress,
Likewise your golden stay,
For I think your clothing too rich and too gay
To rot all in the salt sea.

Yes, I'll take off my silken dress,
Likewise my golden stay,
But before I do so, you false young man,
You must face yon willow tree.

Then he turned his back around
And faced yon willow tree,
She caught him around the middle so small
And throwed him into the sea.

And as he rose and as he sank,
And as he rose, said he,
Oh, give me your hand, my pretty Polly,
My bride forever you'll be.

Lie there, lie there, you false young man,
Lie there instead of me,
For six pretty maids you've drownded here,
And the seventh one has drownded thee.

She lighted on her milk-white steed
And led the fast-traveling grey,
And rode till she came to her father's house
One hour before it was day.

The parrot in the garret so high
And unto pretty Polly did say,
What's the matter, my pretty Polly,
You're driving before it is day?

No tales, no tales, my pretty Polly,
No tales, no tales, said she.
Your cage will be made of the glittering gold,
And yours of ivory.

No tales, no tales, my pretty Polly,
No tales, no tales, said she.
Your cage will be made of the glittering gold,
And hung on yon willow tree.

Little Phoebe

D7   G
Equinoxial swore by the green leaves on the trees, trees,
        C   G
That he could do more work in a day

   than Phoebe could in three, three,
        C   G
That he could do more work in a day
       C   D7   G
   than Phoebe could in three.

Little Phoebe standing there and this is what she said:
"It's you may do the work in the house
   and I'll go follow the plow, plow,
"You may do the work in the house
   and I'll go follow the plow."

"It's you must milk the brindle cow
   that stands in yonder stall,
"And you must feed that little pig
   that stands in yonder sty." (twice)

"And you must churn that crock of cream
   that I left in the frame,
"And you must watch the fat in the pot,
   or it'll all go in a flame." (twice)

"And you must wind that hank of yarn
   that I spun yesterday,
"And you must watch that speckled hen
   before she runs astray." (twice)

Little Phoebe took the whip and went to follow the plow,
And Equinoxial took the pail and went to milk the cow.
   (twice)

The brindle cow she turned around
   and sniffled up her nose,
And give him a dip upon the lip,
   and the blood run to his toes. (twice)

Aimee McPherson

B7
Oh have you heard the story 'bout Aimee McPherson?
Em
Aimee McPherson that wonderful person.
B7
She weighed a hundred-eighty and her hair was red;
Em
She preached a wicked sermon so the papers all said.

Refrain:
A hi-dee hi-dee hi-dee hi ho-dee ho-dee ho-dee ho!

Now Aimee built herself a radio station
To broadcast her preaching to the nation.
She found a man named Armistad who knew enough
To run the radio while Aimee did her stuff.

Now they had a camp meeting down at Ocean Park
Preached from early morning till after dark
Said the benediction and folded up the tents
Then nobody knew where Aimee went.

Now Aimee McPherson got back from her journey
She told her story to the District Attorney
She said she had been kidnapped on a lonely trail
And in spite of a lot of questions she stuck to her tale.

Well the grand jury started an investigation
Uncovered a lot of spicy information
Found out about a love nest down at Carmel-by-the-sea.
Where the liquor is expensive and the loving is free.

Oh they found a little cottage with a breakfast nook
A folding bed with a worn-out look,
The slats was busted and the springs was loose
And the dents in the mattress fitted Aimee's caboose.

Well they took poor Aimee and they threw her in jail
Last I heard she was out on bail.
They'll send her up for a stretch I guess,
She worked herself up into an awful mess.

Radio Ray is a goin' hound
A-goin' yet and he ain't been found
They got his description but they got it too late
'Cause since they got it he's lost a lot of weight.

I'll end my story in the usual way
About a lady preacher's holiday;
If you don't get the moral then you're the gal for me,
'Cause there's still a lot of cottages
    down at Carmel-by-the-sea.

Old Man In The Wood

G   C   G
There was an old man that lived in a wood,
        D   G
As you can plainly see,
D   G   C   G
Who said that he could do more work in a day,
            D7 G
Than his wife could do in three.
            D7
"If that be so," the old woman said,
G   D
"Why this you must allow:
    G   C   G
"That you shall do my work for a day,
        D   G
"While I go drive the plough".

"But you must milk the Tiny cow,
"For fear she should go dry;
"And you must feed the little pigs
"That are within the sty,
"And you must watch the bracket hen
"Lest she should lay astray;
"And you must wind the reel of yarn
"That I spun yesterday."

The old woman took the staff in her hand
And went to drive the plough,
The old man took the pail in his hand,
And went to milk the cow.
But Tiny hinched and Tiny flinched,
And Tiny cocked her nose,
And Tiny hit the old man such a kick,
That the blood ran down his nose.

'Twas, "Hey, my good cow,"
And, "Ho, my good cow,"
And, "Now my good cow, stand still.
"If I ever milk this cow again,
'Twill be against my will."
And when he'd milked the Tiny cow,
For fear she should go dry,
Why then he fed the little pigs
That were within the sty.

And then he watched the bracket hen
Lest she should lay astray;
But he forgot the reel of yarn
His wife spun yesterday;
He swore by all the leaves on the tree,
And all the stars in Heaven,
That his wife could do more work in a day
Than he could do in seven.

189

Sweet Betsy From Pike

```
      C          G7          C
Oh don't you remember sweet Betsy from Pike,
                    D7          G
Who crossed the big mountains with her lover Ike,
      F       C    G7       C
With two yoke of cattle, a large yellow dog,
   Am      Dm      G7      C
A tall Shanghai rooster and a one-spotted hog.
```

Chorus:

```
            Em     G7     C
(Singin') Tooral lal looral lal looral lal la,
Em      G7     C
Tooral lal looral lal looral lal la.
```

One evening quite early they camped on the Platte,
'Twas near by the road on a green shady flat,
Where Betsy, sore-footed, lay down to repose,
With wonder Ike gazed on that Pike County rose.

Their wagons broke down with a terrible crash,
And out on the prairie rolled all kinds of trash;
A few little baby clothes done up with care,
'Twas rather suspicious, though all on the *square.*

The Shanghai ran off and their cattle all died,
That morning the last piece of bacon was fried;
Poor Ike was discouraged and Betsy got mad,
The dog drooped his tail and looked wondrously sad.

They stopped at Salt Lake to inquire the way,
When Brigham declared that sweet Betsy should stay;
But Betsy got frightened and ran like a deer,
While Brigham stood pawing the ground like a steer.

They soon reached the desert, where Betsy gave out,
And down in the sand she lay rolling about;
While Ike, half distracted, looked on with surprise,
Saying, "Betsy, get up, you'll get sand in your eyes."

Sweet Betsy got up in a great deal of pain,
Declared she'd go back to Pike County again;
But Ike gave a sigh, and they fondly embraced,
And they traveled along with his arm 'round her waist.

They suddenly stopped on a very high hill,
With wonder looked down upon old Placerville;
Ike sighed when he said, and he cast his eyes down,
"Sweet Betsy, my darling, we've got to Hangtown."

Long Ike and sweet Betsy attended a dance;
Ike wore a pair of his Pike County pants;
Sweet Betsy was covered with ribbons and rings;
Says Ike, "You're an angel, but where are your wings?"

A miner said, "Betsy, will you dance with me?"
"I will that, old hoss, if you don't make too free;
"But don't dance me hard, do you want to know why?
"Dog on you; I'm chock full of strong alkali!"

This Pike County couple got married of course,
But Ike became jealous, obtained a divorce;
Sweet Betsy, well satisfied, said with a great shout,
"Good-by, you big lummox, I'm glad you've backed out!"

Blow Away The Morning Dew

```
      G                 D          G
There was a farmer's son, kept sheep upon a hill,
                      D
And he went out one May morning
         Em        C
to see what he could kill,
```

Chorus:

```
D      G      C      G
Singing, blow away the morning dew,
              C
the dew and the dew,
G         Em     C
Blow away the morning dew,
          G      D      G
how sweet the winds do blow.
```

He looked high he looked low, he cast an under look,
And there he saw a fair pretty maid, a-bathing in the brook.

"Cast over me my mantle fair and pin it o'er my gown,
And if you will, take hold my hand
    and I will be your own."

"If you will come to my father's house,
    which is walled all around,
Then you shall have your will of me,
    and twenty thousand pound."

He mounted on a milk white steed,
    and she upon another,
And thus they rode along the way
    like sister and like brother.

But when they came to her father's gate,
    so quickly she popped in,
And said "There stands a fool without,
    and here's a maid within."

"There is a flower in our garden, we call it marigold,
And he who will not when he may,
    he shall not when he wold!"

And so this farmer's son went back upon the hill,
And raised his pipes up to his lips,
    and sadly he did trill.

Who's Gonna Shoe Your Pretty Little Foot?

C
Who's gonna shoe your pretty little foot?
F   C
Who's gonna glove your hand?
F   C
Who's gonna kiss your red ruby lips?
        G7   C
Who's gonna be your man?

Papa will shoe my pretty little foot,
Mama will glove my hand,
Sister's gonna kiss my red ruby lips,
I don't need no man.

I don't need no man, poor boy,
I don't need no man.
Sister's gonna kiss my red ruby lips
I don't need no man.

Longest train I ever did see,
Was sixteen coaches long.
The only girl I ever did love,
Was on that train and gone.

Devilish Mary

   D
I once dressed up and went to town
              Bm
To court a fair young lady.
D
I inquired about her name,
  A7   D
Her name was Devilish Mary.

Chorus:

        Bm
Come a-fa-la-ling,

Come a-ling, come l-ling,
     D
Come a-fa-la-ling,
    A7 D   A7 D
Come a dairy, come a dairy.

Me and Mary began to spark
She got all in a hurry,
She made it up all in her mind
She'd marry the very next Thursday.

We had not been married for about two weeks
Before we ought to been parted;
I hadn't said but a single word
She kicked up her heels and started.

She washed my clothes in old soap suds
She filled my bath with switches
She let me know right at the start
She was going to wear my britches.

Now if I ever marry again
It'll be for love not riches,
Marry a little girl 'bout two feet high
So she can't wear my britches.

The Rebel Girl
Joe Hill

G   C   G
There are women of many descriptions
G7 C   Cm   G
In this queer world as every one knows
            C   G
Some are living in beautiful mansions
    A7   D
And are wearing the finest of clothes.
D7   G   C   G
There are blue-blooded queens and princesses
G7   C   B
Who have charms made of diamonds and pearls.
G   E7   Am
But the only and Thorough-bred Lady
      A7 D7 G
Is the Rebel   Girl.

Chorus:

                      C
That's the Rebel Girl, that's the Rebel Girl,
    D   D7   G
To the working class she's a precious pearl.
                D7
She brings Courage, Pride and Joy
            G
To the fighting Rebel Boy
                 C
We've had girls before, but we need some more
        D C   B
In the Industrial Workers of the World
       E7   Am
For it's great to fight for Freedom
C   G D7 G
With a Rebel   Girl.

Yes, her hands may be hardened from labor
And her dress may not be very fine.
But a heart in her bosom is beating
Warm and true to her class and her kind.
And the grafters in terror are trembling
When her spite and defiance she'll hurl.
For the only and Thorough-bred Lady
Is the Rebel Girl.

The Handsome Cabin Boy

D   Am
'Tis of a handsome female
D
as you may understand.
                   C
Her mind being bent in rambling
  G   F   D
unto some foreign land,
                 C
She dressed herself in sailor's clothes,
  G   F   D
or so it does appear,
                Am
And hired with our captain
           D
to serve him for a year.

The captain's wife she being on board,
    she seem-ed in great joy,
To see her husband had engaged such a
    handsome cabin boy,
And now and then she'd slip in a kiss
    and she would have liked to toy
But it was the captain found out the
    secret of the handsome cabin boy.

Her cheeks were red and rosy and her
    hair hung in its curls,
The sailors often smiled and said he
    looks just like a girl.
But eating the captain's biscuits, their
    color didn't destroy,
And the waist did swell on pretty Nell,
    the handsome cabin boy.

'Twas in the Bay of Biscay our gallant
    ship did plow,
One night among the sailors was a
    fearful scurrying row,
They tumbled from their hammocks for
    their sleep it did destroy,
And swore about the groaning of the
    handsome cabin boy.

Oh, doctor, dear doctor, the cabin
    boy did cry,
My time has come, I am undone and I
    must surely die.
The doctor come a-running and smiled
    at the fun,
To think a sailor lad should have a
    daughter or a son.

The sailors when they heard the joke,
    they all did stand and stare
The child belonged to none of them
    they solemnly did swear.
The captain's wife she looked at him
    and said "I wish you joy,
For it's either you or I betrayed the
    handsome cabin boy."

Then each man took his tot of rum,
    and drunk success to trade,
And likewise to the cabin boy who was
    neither man nor maid.
Here's hopin' the wars don't rise again,
    our sailors to destroy,
And here's hoping for a jolly lot more
    like the handsome cabin boy.

Hangtown Girls
Tune: *Buffalo Girls*

C   F   C
Hangtown gals are plump and rosy,
G7   C
Hair in ringlets mighty cosy;

Painted cheeks and gassy bonnets;
G7   C
Touch them and they'll sting like hornets.

Chorus:

C
Oh, Hangtown gals are lovely creatures,
Gm7   C
Think they'll marry Mormon preachers;
F   Am
Heads thrown back to show their features—
G7   C
Ha, ha, ha! Hangtown gals.

They're dreadful shy of forty-niners,
Turn their noses up at miners;
Shocked to hear them say, "gol durn it!"
Try to blush, but cannot come it.

They'll catch a neighbor's cat and beat it,
Cut a bean in halves to eat it;
Promenade in silk and satin,
Cannot talk, but murder Latin.

On the streets they're always grinning,
Modestly they lift their linen;
Petticoats all trimmed with laces,
Matching well their painted faces.

To church they very seldom venture,
Hoops so large they cannot enter;
Go it, gals, you're young and tender,
Shun the pick-and-shovel gender.

Little Maggie

    D   C
Well yonder stands little Maggie,
    D   C   D
With a dram glass in her hand,
                  C
And she's drinkin' down her troubles,
     D   C   D
And she's foolin' some other man.

Tell me how can I ever stand it,
Just to see those two blue eyes.
They're shining like a diamond,
Like a diamond in the sky.

Sometimes I have a nickel,
Sometimes I have a dime.
And it's sometimes I have ten dollars,
Just to buy Little Maggie some wine.

Now she's marching down to the station,
Got a suitcase in her hand.
She's going for to leave me,
She is bound for some distant land.

Pretty flowers were made for blooming,
Pretty stars were meant to shine.
Pretty girls were made for boys to love,
And Little Maggie was made for mine.

Well the first time I seen Little Maggie,
She was sitting by the banks of the sea.
Had a forty-five strapped around her shoulder,
And a banjo on her knee.

Darlin' Corey

    A
Wake up, wake up, darlin' Corey,
What makes you sleep so sound?
The revenue officers are comin'
Gonna tear your still-house down.

Go 'way, go 'way darlin' Corey,
Quit hangin' around my bed,
Pretty women run me distracted,
Corn liquor's killed me most dead.

Oh yes, oh yes my darlin',
I'll do the best I can,
But I'll never give my pleasure,
To another gamblin' man.

The first time I saw darlin' Corey,
She was standing on the banks of the sea,
She had a pistol strapped around her body,
And a banjo on her knee.

The last time I saw darlin' Corey,
She had a dram glass in her hand,
She was drinkin' down her troubles,
With a low down gamblin' man.

Dig a hole, dig a hole in the meadow,
Dig a hole in the cold, cold ground,
Go and dig me a hole in the meadow,
Just to lay darlin' Corey down.

Don't you hear them blue-birds singing?
Don't you hear that mournful sound?
They're preachin' Corey's funeral,
In the lonesome graveyard ground.

Don't Sing Love Songs

           E7   A
Don't sing love songs, you'll wake my mother
        E7   F♯m
She's sleepin' close by my side.
            Bm
And in her right hand she holds a dagger
     F♯m   E7
And says that I can't be your bride.

All men are false, says my mother,
They'll tell you wicked, lovely lies,
And the very next evening, court another
Leaving you alone to pine and sigh.

My father is a handsome devil,
He's got a chain that's five miles long,
And every link a heart does dangle
Of some poor maid he's loved and wronged.

Wish that I was some little sparrow,
Yes, one of those that flies so high,
I'd fly away to my false true lover,
And when he'd speak I would deny.

On his breast, I'd light and flutter
With my little tender wings,
I'd ask him who he meant to flatter,
Or who he meant to deceive.

Go court some other tender lady,
And I hope that she will be your wife,
'Cause I've been warned and I've decided
To sleep alone all of my life.

Gypsy Davey

From Child Ballad 120

   D
It was late last night

When the boss come home,

Asking about his lady

And the only answer he received,
   A7   D
She's gone with the Gypsy Davey,
   A7   D
She's gone with the Gypsy Dave.

Go saddle for me my buckskin horse,
And my hundred dollar saddle,
Point out to me their wagon tracks,
And after them I'll travel,
Well, after them I'll ride.

Well, he had not rode to the midnight moon,
When he saw their campfire gleaming.
He heard the notes of the big guitar
And the voice of the gypsy singing
That song of the Gypsy Dave.

Take off, take off your kidskin gloves,
And your boots of Spanish leather,
And give to me your lily white hands,
We'll go back home together;
We'll ride back home again.

No, I won't take off my kidskin gloves,
Nor my boots of Spanish leather,
I'll go my way from day to day,
And sing with the Gypsy Davey,
I'll go with the Gypsy Dave.

Have you forsaken your house and home?
Have you forsaken your baby?
Have you forsaken your husband dear,
To go with the Gypsy Davey?
And sing with the Gypsy Dave?

Yes, I've forsaken my house and home,
To go with the Gypsy Davey,
And I've forsaken my husband dear,
But not my blue-eyed baby,
My pretty little blue-eyed babe.

Katy Cruel

Dm   Am
When I first came to town,
     Dm   Am
They called me a roving jewel,
Dm
Now they've changed their tune,
    F   Am
They call me Katy Cruel.
   Dm
Oh, diddle lilley day,
            Am Dm
Oh, de liddle-i-o   day.

Chorus:

Dm   Am Dm   Am
Oh that I was where I would be,
Dm   Am Dm   Am
Then I should be   where I am not,
       Dm   F
Here I am where I must be,
Am
Where I would be I cannot,
   Dm
Oh, diddle lilley day,
            Am Dm
Oh, de liddle-i-o   day.

When I first came to town,
They brought me bottles plenty,
Now they've changed their tune,
They bring me bottles empty, etc.

Through the woods I'll go,
And through the boggy mire,
Straight-way down the road,
Till I come to my heart's desire, etc.

Eyes as bright as fire,
Lips as red as a cherry,
And is her desire,
To make the young folks marry, etc.

I know where I'm going,
And I know who's going with me,
I know who I love,
But who knows who I'll marry, etc.

HEROES AND HELL-RAISERS

Sam Bass

```
        E                            B7              E
Sam Bass was born in Indiana, it was his native home,
        A        E        A              E
And at the age of seventeen, young Sam began to roam,
        B7           E      A6        B6
Sam first came out to Texas, a cowboy for to be—
     E      A    E     B7        E
A kinder-hearted fellow you seldom ever see.
```

Sam used to deal in race stock, one called the Denton mare;
He matched her in scrub races and took her to the fair.
Sam used to coin the money, and spent it just as free;
He always drank good whiskey wherever he might be.

Sam left the Collins ranch, in the merry month of May,
With a herd of Texas cattle the Black Hills for to see;
Sold out in Custer City, and then got on a spree—
A harder set of cowboys you seldom ever see.

On their way back to Texas they robbed the U.P. train,
And then split up in couples and started out again;
Joe Collins and his partner were overtaken soon,
With all their hard-earned money they had
    to meet their doom.

Sam made it back to Texas, all right up with care,
Rode into the town of Denton with all his friends to share.
Sam's life was short in Texas, three robberies did he do;
He robbed all the passenger mail and express cars too.

Sam had four companions, four bold and daring lads,
They were Richardson, Jackson, Joe Collins and Old Dad;
Four more bold and daring cowboys
    the Rangers never knew,
They whipped the Texas Rangers and ran the boys in blue.

Sam and another companion, called "Arkansas" for short,
Was shot by a Texas Ranger by the name of Thomas Floyd;
Oh, Tom is a big six-footer and thinks he's mighty fly,
But I can tell you his racket—he's a deadbeat on the sly.

Jim Murphy was arrested and then released on bail;
He jumped his bond at Tyler and then took the train
    for Terrell;
But Mayor Jones had posted Jim and that was all a stall,
'Twas only a plan to capture Sam before the coming fall.

Sam met his fate at Round Rock, July the twenty-first,
They pierced poor Sam with rifle balls
    and emptied out his purse.
Poor Sam he is a corpse and six foot under clay,
And Jackson in the bushes trying to get away.

Jim had borrowed Sam's good gold and didn't want to pay,
The only shot he saw was to give poor Sam away.
He sold out Sam and Barnes and left their friends
    to mourn—
Oh, what a scorching Jim will get when Gabriel
    blows his horn.

And so he sold out Sam and Barnes
    and left their friends to mourn—
Oh what a scorching Jim will get when Gabriel
    blows his horn.
Perhaps he's got to heaven, there's none of us can say,
But if I am right in my surmise, he's gone the other way.

The Man Who Broke The Bank At Monte Carlo
Fred Gilbert

```
       F              Gm
I've just got here, thro' Paris,
        C        F
    from the sunny southern shore.
D7 Gm         C          F
I to Monte Carlo went, just to raise my winter's rent.
C7   F       Dm    Gm   C    F
Dame Fortune smiled upon me as she'd never done before,
                  Dm7  G7   C
And I've now such lots of money, I'm a gent.
                  Dm   G7   C
Yes, I've now such lots of money, I'm a gent.
```

Chorus:

```
     C7
As I walk along the Bois Boolong
          F
    with an independent air,
         C7
You can hear the girls declare,
         F
    "He must be a millionaire."
D7    Gm              C7
You can hear them sigh, and wish to die,
        F     A7        D7
    you can see them wink the other eye
     G7           C7             F
At the man who broke the bank at Monte Carlo.
```

I stay indoors till after lunch, and then my daily walk
To the great Triumphal Arch is one great
    triumphal march.
Observed by each observer with the keenness of a hawk,
I'm a mass of money, linen, silk, and starch.
I'm a mass of money, linen, silk, and starch.

I patronized the tables at the Monte Carlo hell
Till they hadn't got a sou for a Christian or a Jew,
So I quickly went to Paris for the charms
    of mad'moiselle,
Who's the loadstone of my heart what can I do,
When with the twenty tongues she swears
    that she'll be true?
```
```

The Bastard King Of England

      C
Oh, the minstrels sing of an English king

of many long years ago,
     G7
Who ruled his land with an iron hand
        C
· though his morals were weak and low.

His only outer garment was a dirty undershirt
     G7
That managed to hide the royal pride
     C
    but never hid the dirt.

Chorus:

      F
He was wild and woolly and full of fleas
     C   G7
And he had his women by twos and threes.
C   Am   Em   Am   D7G7C
God bless the Bastard king of England.

Oh, the Queen of Spain was an amorous Jane,
    a lascivious wench was she,
Who loved to play in a royal way
    with the King across the sea.
She often sent a message by royal messenger,
To ask the king to come and spend a night or two with her.

Now, the King he had a rival bold
    whose name was Philip of France,
Who swore he'd stop this carrying on
    by the seat of his royal pants.
So off he sent straightway to Spain to steal the Queen away;
And foil the King with a royal ring
    and all on a summer's day.

When the news of this foul deed was heard
    within the royal halls,
The King he swore by the shirt he wore,
    he'd have his rival's neck.
So he sent for the Duke of Zippity-Zap,
    who had a dose of the clippety-clap,
To pass it on to Philip of France
    and all on a summer's day.

So, the Queen grew very wary when she next saw
    Philip of France.
She decided that the Frenchman had gone
    and lost his chance.
So then she straightway called our King
    and offered him her hand,
And the sound of wedding bells was heard
    throughout the land.

They had a royal wedding—all his subjects
    wish him well.
And the dancers danced without their pants,
    and so did the king as well.
His only outer garment was a dirty yellow shirt,
With which he tried to hide his hide
    but he couldn't hide the dirt.

John Hardy

D   G   D
John Hardy was a desperate little man,
   G   D
He carried two guns every day,
   G   D
He killed a man on the West Virginia line,

You ought to see John Hardy gettin' away,
                    G   D
You ought to see John Hardy gettin' away.

Well, John Hardy run for that old state line,
It was there he thought he'd go free,
But a man walked up and took him by the arm,
Saying "Johnny walk along with me,
Johnny walk along with me."

Well the first one to visit John Hardy in his cell,
Was a little girl dressed in blue,
She came down to that old jail cell,
Singing "Johnny, I've been true to you, Lord knows,
Johnny I've been true to you."

Then the next one to visit John Hardy in his cell,
A little girl dressed in red,
She came down to that old jail cell,
Singing "Johnny, I had rather see you dead,
God knows, Johnny I had rather see you dead."

John Hardy stood in his old jail cell,
The tears running down from his eyes,
He said "I've been the death of many poor boy,
But my six-shooter never told a lie,
No my six shooter never told a lie."

John Hardy was a desperate little man,
He carried two guns every day,
Well, he blowed down a man on the West Virginia line,
You ought to seen John Hardy getting away,
You ought to seen John Hardy getting away.

Bold Jack Donahue

D   G   D
In Dublin town I was brought up, a city of great fame,
                              A7
My honest friends and parents will tell to you the same,
D
It was for the sake of five hundred pounds
    G   D
  I was sent across the main,
G   A7
For seven long years in New South Wales
          D
  to wear a convict's chain.

Refrain:

D   G   D
So come all my hearties, we'll roam the mountains high,
                        A7
Together we will plunder, together we will die,
D
We'll wander through the valleys
    G   D
  and gallop o'er the plains,
G   A7   D
And scorn to live in slavery bound down by iron chains.

I'd scarce been there twelve months or more
    upon the Australian shore,
When I took to the highway, as I'd oftimes done before,
There was me and Jackie Underwood,
    and Webber and Webster too,
These were the true associates of bold Jack Donahue.

Now Donahue was taken, all for a notorious crime,
And sentenced to be hanged upon the gallows tree so high,
But when they came to Sydney gaol, he left them in a stew,
And when they came to call the roll,
    they missed bold Donahue.

As Donahue made his escape,
    to the bush he went straightway,
The people they were all afraid to travel night or day,
For every week in the newspapers
    there was published something new,
Of this brave and dauntless hero, that bold Jack Donahue.

As Donahue was cruising one summer's afternoon,
Little was his notion his death would be so soon,
When a sergeant discharged his carbine,
And called aloud for Donahue to fight or to resign.

"Resign to you? You cowardly dogs!
    Such a thing I'd never do!
"For I'll fight this night with all my might,"
    cried bold Jack Donahue,
"I'd rather roam these hills and dales
    like a wolf or kangaroo,
"Than work one hour for government,"
    said bold Jack Donahue.

He fought six rounds with the horse police
    until that fatal ball,
Which pierced his heart and made him start,
    caused Donahue to fall,
And as he closed his mournful eyes,
    he bade this world adieu,
Saying, "Convicts all, pray for the soul
    of bold Jack Donahue."

Stagolee

E
Stagolee was a bad man,
        E7
Ev'rybody knows.
A
Spent one hundred dollars
                  E
Just to buy him a suit of clothes.
      B7
He was a bad man,
                E
That mean old Stagolee

Stagolee shot Billy de Lyons
What do you think about that,
Shot him down in cold blood
Because he stole his Stetson hat;
He was a bad man,
That mean old Stagolee.

Billy de Lyons said, Stagolee
Please don't take my life,
I've got two little babes
And a darling, loving wife;
You are a bad man,
You mean old Stagolee.

What do I care about your two little babes,
Your darling loving wife,
You done stole my Stetson hat
I'm bound to take your life;
He was a bad man,
That mean old Stagolee.

The judge said, Stagolee,
What you doing in here,
You done shot Mr. Billy de Lyons,
You going to die in the electric chair;
He was a bad man,
That mean old Stagolee.

Twelve o'clock they killed him
Head reached up high,
Last thing that poor boy said
My six-shooter never lied.
He was a bad man,
That mean old Stagolee.

Roll On The Ground

Chorus:

C
Roll on the ground, boys,
F   C
Roll on the ground.
F   C
Eat soda crackers,
G7   C
Roll on the ground.

Verses:
Workin' on the railroad,
Dollar a day,
Eat soda crackers
And the wind blow 'em away.

Big Ball's in Nashville,
Big Ball's in town,
Big Ball's in Nashville,
We'll dance around.

Get on your big shoes,
Get on your gown,
Shake off those sad blues,
Big Ball's in town.

I'll stay in Asheville,
I'll stick around,
I'll stay in Asheville
When Big Ball's in town.

My love's in jail, boys,
My love's in jail,
My love's in jail, boys,
Who'll go her bail?

Get drunk in Asheville,
Dance 'round the town,
Board up your windows,
Big Ball's in town.

Let's have a party,
Let's have a time,
Let's have a party,
I've only a dime.

You shake it here, babe,
You shake it there,
You come with me, babe,
We'll go upstairs.

Barnyards Of Delgaty

   G   C   G
As I came in by Turra market,
           C   D
Turra market for to fee,
G   C   G
I fell in with a farmer child,
   D   G
The barnyards of Delgaty.

Chorus:

G   C   G
Linten addie toorin addie,
         C   D
Linten addie toorin ee;
G   C   G
Linten, lowrin, lowrin, lowrin,
   D   G
The barnyards of Delgaty.

He promised me the ae best pair
That ever I set my e'en upon,
When I gaed to the barnyards,
There was naething there but skin and bone.

The auld black horse sat on its rump,
The auld white mare lay on her wime,
And for a' that I could "Hup!" and crack,
They wouldna rise at yokin' time.

When I gae to the kirk on Sunday,
Mony's the bonnie lass I see,
Sitting by her father's side,
And winkin' owre the pews at me.

I can drink and no' be drunk,
I can fecht and no' be slain,
I can lie wi' anither man's lass,
And aye be welcome to my ain.

Noo my cannle is burnt oot,
My snotter's fairly on the wane,
Sae fare ye weel, ye barnyards,
Ye'll never catch me here again!

Captain Kidd

    E
Oh, my name is Captain Kidd,
      B7
As I sailed, as I sailed,
    E
My name is Captain Kidd,
A
As I sailed.
B7 E
My name is Captain Kidd,
    A   B7
God's laws I did forbid,
    A
And most wickedly I did,
    B7   E
As I sailed, as I sailed.

My parents taught me well
As I sailed, as I sailed,
My parents taught me well
As I sailed.
My parents taught me well
To shun the gates of hell,
But against them I rebelled,
As I sailed, as I sailed.

I murdered William Moore, etc.
And left him in his gore
Forty leagues from the shore, etc.

And being cruel still, etc.
My gunner I did kill
And his precious blood did spill, etc.

And being nigh to death, etc.
I vowed with every breath
To walk in wisdom's way, etc.

My repentance lasted not, etc.
My vows I soon forgot
Damnation was my lot, etc.

Now, to execution dock
I must go, I must go,
To execution dock,
I must go.
To execution dock,
Lay my head upon the block,
No more the laws I'll mock,
As I sailed, as I sailed.

Ballad Of Sam Hall

      D   A7   D
Oh, my name it is Sam Hall, it is Sam Hall
                    A7   D
Oh, my name it is Sam Hall, it is Sam Hall;

Oh, my name it is Sam Hall,
    G
And I hate you one and all,
      A7
You're a bunch of muckers all,
      D
God damn your eyes!

Oh, I killed a man, 'tis said, so 'tis said,
Yes, I killed a man, 'tis said, so 'tis said;
Oh, I killed a man 'tis said,
And I left him there for dead
I split his bloody head,
God damn his eyes!

So they put me in the quod, in the quod,
Oh, they put me in the quod, in the quod;
Yes, they put me in the quod,
And they said, "You'll hang, by God"
All right, I'll hang,
God damn their eyes!

Oh, the parson he did come, he did come,
Oh, the parson he did come, he did come;
Oh, the parson he did come,
And he looked so God damn glum,
He can kiss my ruddy bum,
God damn his eyes.

And the sheriff he came too, he came too,
Oh, the sheriff he came too, he came too;
Oh, the sheriff he came too,
With his little boys in blue
Lord, what a bloody crew,
God damn their eyes!

So, it's up the rope I go, up I go,
Yes, it's up the rope I go, up I go;
Yes, it's up the rope I go,
And the crowd all down below,
They'll say, "Sam, we told you so!"
God damn their eyes!

I saw Mollie in the crowd, in the crowd,
I saw Mollie in the crowd, in the crowd;
I saw Mollie in the crowd,
And I hollered right out loud
Say, Mollie, ain't you proud!
God damn their eyes!

The Wild Colonial Boy

D   G   D
'Tis of a wild colonial boy, Jack Dulan was his name,
            A7
Born of honest parents in the town of Castle-maine,
D   G
He was his father's only hope, his mother's pride and joy,
 A7   D
And dearly did his parents love their wild colonial boy.

He was just sixteen years of age when he
  left his fathers home,
And through Australia's sunny clime,
  a bushranger did roam,
He robbed the wealthy squatters, their stock he did destroy,
And a terror to Australia was the wild colonial boy.

Chorus:

G   D
So come all my hearties, we'll roam the mountains high,
G   D   A7
Together we will plunder, together we will die,
   D   G
We'll wander through the valleys and gallop

  o'er the plains,
  A7   D
And scorn to live in slavery, bound with iron chains.

In '61 this daring youth commenced his wild career;
With a heart that knew no danger, no foeman did he fear.
He stuck up the Beechworth mailcoach and robbed
  Judge McEvoy,
Who trembling cold gave up his gold
  to the wild colonial boy.

He bade the judge good morning and told him to beware;
He'd never rob a hearty chap that acted on the square,
But a man who'd rob a mother of her son and only joy,
He could expect no mercy from the wild colonial boy.

One day as he was riding the mountainside along,
Listening to the kookaburra's pleasant laughing song,
Three mounted troopers rode along, Kelly,
  Davis, and Fitzroy,
With a warrant for the capture of the wild colonial boy.

"Surrender now, Jack Dulan, you see it's three to one;
Surrender now, Jack Dulan, you daring highwayman!"
He drew a pistol from his belt and he fired the wicked toy,
"I'll fight but I won't surrender!"
  said the wild colonial boy.

He fired at Trooper Kelly and brought him to the ground,
And in return from Davis, received his mortal wound;
All shattered through the jaws he lay, still firing at Fitzroy,
And that's the way they captured him,
  the wild colonial boy.

Whiskey In The Jar

D   Bm
As I was a-goin' over Gilgary Mountain,
G   D   Bm
I met Colonel Pepper and his money he was countin'.
G   D   Bm
I drew forth my pistol and I rattled out my sabre saying:
G   D   Bm
"Stand and deliver for I am a bold deceiver."

Chorus:

  A7
Mush-a-rig-gum dur-um dye.
D
Whack fol di dad-dy-o,
G
Whack fol di dad-dy-o,
    D A7 D
There's whiskey in the jar.

Those gold and silver coins they sure did look inviting;
So I picked up the money and I took it home to Molly.
She promised and she swore that she never
  would deceive me;
But the Devil's in the women and they never can be easy.

When I awoke, 'twas between six and seven,
The guards they were around me, in numbers
  odd and even.
I sprang for my pistols, but alas I was mistaken;
For Molly took my pistols and prisoner I was taken.

They threw me in jail, without a judge or writin',
For robbin' Colonel Pepper on that damn
  Gilgary Mountain.
But they didn't take my fists, so I knocked
  the sentry down,
And bid a fond farewell to that jail in Salem town.

Now, some take delight in fishing and in bowling,
Others take delight in the carriages a-rolling.
But I take delight in the juice of the barley,
And courtin' pretty maidens in the morning,
  bright and early.

Jesse James

G   C   G
Jesse James was a lad that killed many a man,
               D
He robbed the Glendale train,
G   C   G
He stole from the rich and he gave to the poor,
             D   G
He'd a hand and a heart and a brain.

Chorus:

G7 C   G
Poor Jesse had a wife to mourn for his life,
                Dm
Three children they were brave,
G   C   G
But the dirty little coward that shot Mr. Howard,
         Dm   G
Has laid Jesse James in his grave.

It was Robert Ford, that dirty little coward,
I wonder how he does feel,
For he ate of Jesse's bread and he slept in Jesse's bed,
Then he laid poor Jesse in his grave.

Jesse James was a man, a friend to the poor,
He'd never see a man suffer pain;
And with his brother Frank, he robbed the Chicago bank,
And stopped the Glendale train.

It was on a Wednesday night and the moon
   was shining bright,
They robbed the Glendale train,
And the people they did say for many miles away,
It was robbed by Frank and Jesse James.

It was his brother Frank that robbed the Gallatin bank,
And carried the money from the town;
It was in this very place that they had a little race,
For they shot Captain Sheets to the ground.

They went to the crossing not very far from there,
And there they did the same;
With the agent on his knees, he delivered up the keys
To the outlaws, Frank and Jesse James.

It was on a Saturday night and Jesse was at home
Talking with his family brave,
Robert Ford came along like a thief in the night
And laid poor Jesse in his grave.

The people held their breath when they heard
   of Jesse's death,
And wondered how he ever came to die.
It was one of the gang called little Robert Ford,
He shot poor Jesse on the sly.

Jesse went to his rest with his hand on his breast,
The devil will be upon his knee.
He was born one day in the county of Clay,
And came from a solitary race.

This song was made by Billy Gashade
As soon as the news did arrive;
He said there was no man with the law in his hand
Who could take Jesse James when alive.

Old Rosin The Beau

D   G   D   G
I live for the good of my nation,
         D   Gm   Em   A7
And my sons are all growing low;
        D   G   D
But I hope the next generation
G   D   A7   D
Will resemble old Rosin the Beau.
             A   Bm   G
Resemble old Rosin the Beau,
    D   Bm   Em   A7
Resemble old Rosin the Beau,
    D   G   D
I hope that the next generation
G   D   A7   D
Will resemble old Rosin the Beau.

I've traveled this country over
And now to the next I will go,
For I know that good quarters await me
To welcome Old Rosin, the Beau.
To welcome Old Rosin, the Beau, etc.

In the gay round of pleasures I've traveled.
Nor will I leave behind a foe.
And when my companions are jovial
They will drink to Old Rosin, the Beau.

But my life is now drawn to a closing,
As all will at last be so.
So we'll take a full bumper at parting
To the name of Old Rosin, the Beau.

When I'm dead and laid out on the counter,
The people all making a show,
Just sprinkle plain whiskey and water
On the corpse of Old Rosin, the Beau.

Then pick me out six trusty fellows
And let them stand all in a row,
And dig a big hole in the meadow
And in it toss Rosin, the Beau.

Then bring out two little brown jugs:
Place one at my head and my toe;
And do not forget to scratch on them
The name of old Rosin, the Beau.

Didn't He Ramble

Will Handy

```
     G                               D7        G
Old Beebe had three full grown sons, Buster, Bill and Bee,

And Buster was the black sheep of the Beebe family;

They tried their best to break him of his rough
          D7    G
     and rowdy ways,

At last they had to get a judge to give him ninety days.
```

Chorus:

```
G
Oh! didn't he ramble, ramble?
          D7   G       D7
He rambled all around, in and out of town,
     G
Oh! didn't he ramble, ramble,
               C    D7   G
He rambled 'til the butchers cut him down.
```

This black sheep was a terror, oh! and such a ram was he,
That every "copper" knew by heart his rambling pedigree.
And when he took his ladder out to go and paint the town,
They had to take their megaphones to call
     the rambler down.

He rambled in a swell hotel, his appetite was stout,
When he refused to pay his bill the landlord
     kicked him out.
He reached to strike him with a brick but when he
     went to stoop,
The landlord kicked him in the pants and made him
     loop the loop.

He rambled in a gambling house, to gamble on the green,
But there they showed the ram a trick that
     he had never seen.
He lost his roll and jewelry and nearly lost his life,
He lost the car that took him home, and then he lost
     his wife.

He rambled to an Irish wake on one St. Patrick's night,
They asked him what he'd like to drink, they meant
     to treat him right.
But like the old Kilkenny cats, their backs began to arch,
When he called for orange phosphate, on the
     seventeenth of March.

He rambled to the races, to make a gallery bet,
He backed a horse named Hydrant, and Hydrant's
     running yet.
He would have had to walk back home, his friends
     all from him hid,
By luck he met old George Sedam, it's a damn good thing
     he did.

He rambled through the tunnel once on board
     a moving train,
Another train came rumbling in, and rammed him
     out again.
It rammed him just a block, and then, they caught him
     on the fly.
And with a ton of dynamite they rammed him to the sky.

Lincolnshire Poacher

```
          G                          D7      G
When I was bound apprentice in famous Lincolnshire,
                                     A7         D7
Full well I served my master for more than seven year,
          G                A7          D7
Till I took up to poaching, as you shall quickly hear.
          G
Oh, 'tis my delight on a shining night in the season
     D7
     of the year.
```

As me and my companions were setting of a snare,
'Twas then we spied the gamekeeper, for him
     we did not care,
For we can wrestle and fight, my boys,
     and jump out anywhere.
Oh, 'tis my delight on a shining night
     in the season of the year.

As me and my companions were setting four or five,
And taking on 'em up again, we caught a hare alive.
We took a hare alive, my boys,
     and through the woods did steer,
Oh, 'tis my delight on a shining night
     in the season of the year.

I threw him on my shoulder and then we trudged home,
We took him to a neighbor's house
     and sold him for a crown.
We sold him for a crown, my boys,
     but I did not tell you where.
Oh, 'tis my delight on a shining night
     in the season of the year.

Success to ev'ry gentleman that lives in Lincolnshire,
Success to ev'ry poacher that wants to sell a hare,
Bad luck to ev'ry gamekeeper that will not sell his deer.
Oh, 'tis my delight on a shining night
     in the season of the year.

Cole Younger

   C   G   F   C
I am a highway bandit man, Cole Younger is my name,
                         Bb   F   G
Though many a depredation has brought me to shame.
 Gm   Gm   Bb
A-robbing of the Northfield bank was a shame
                G
 I'll never deny;
  C   G   F   C
I'm doomed a poor prisoner, in the Stillwater Jail I lie.

'Tis one of the high, bold robberies
   the truth to you I'll tell,
A Californee miner whose fate to us befell,
Saying, "Hand your money over and make no long delay,"
A trick that I'll be sorry of until my dying day.

Then we left good old Texas,
   that good old Lone Star State,
Out on Nebraskee prairies the James Boys we did meet.
With knives and guns, and revolvers
   we all sat down to play
A good old game of poker to pass the time away.

Out on Nebraskee prairies the Denver came along,
Says I to Bob, "Let's rob her as she goes rolling on."
Killed the engineer and fireman, conductor 'scaped alive;
Their bodies now lie moulding beneath Nebraska's skies.

We saddled up our horses and northward we did go
To the God forsaken country called Minnesot-ee-oh.
I had my eye on the Northfield bank
   when brother Bob did say,
"Cole, if you undertake this job,
   you'll always curse the day."

We stationed out our pickets and up to the bank did go,
It was there upon the counter I struck my fatal blow,
Saying, "Hand your money over and make no long delay
For we're the noted Younger boys,
   and 'low no time to stay."

The cashier, being a true Westfield,
   refused our noble band;
It was Jesse James that pulled the trigger
   that killed that faithful man.
In vain we searched for the money drawers
   while the battle raged outside,
Until we saw our safety was a quick and desperate ride.

It was Charlie pitched off by his post,
   Doc Wheeler drew his gun;
He shot poor Charlie through the heart,
   who cried, "My God, I'm done."
Again Doc Wheeler drew his gun,
   results of which you'll see,
Well, Miller he fell from his horse in mortal agony.

"Come boys, and ride for life and death;
   there's hundreds on our trail!"
The Younger boys were doomed to fate
   and landed right in jail,
They've taken us to the Stillwater Jail
   to worry our lives away,
The James boys they can tell the tale
   of that eventful day.

Billy Barlow

C
Let's go hunting, says Risky Rob,
                        G7
Let's go hunting, says Robin to Bob,
C   F
Let's go hunting, says Dan'l to Joe,
G7   C
Let's go hunting, says Billy Barlow.

What shall I hunt? says Risky Rob,
What shall I hunt? says Robin to Bob,
What shall I hunt? says Dan'l to Joe,
Hunt for a rat, says Billy Barlow.

How shall I get him? says Risky Rob, etc.
Go borrow a gun, says Billy Barlow.

How shall I haul him? etc.
Go borrow a wagon, says Billy Barlow.

How shall we divide him? etc.
How shall we divide him? says Billy Barlow.

I'll take shoulder, says Risky Rob,
I'll take side, says Robin to Bob,
I'll take ham, says Dan'l to Joe,
Tail bone mine, says Billy Barlow.

How shall we cook him? etc.
How shall we cook him? says Billy Barlow.

I'll broil shoulder, says Risky Rob,
I'll fry side, says Robin to Bob,
I'll boil ham, says Dan'l to Joe,
Tail bone raw, says Billy Barlow.

Rothesay, O

```
        C       Dm  C
One Hogmany, at Glesca Fair,
                          B
There was me, my-sel' and sev'ral mair,
        C
We a went off to hae a tear
              G7         C
And spend the night in Rothesay, O.
              C7      F     C
We wandered thro' the Broom-i-law,
        G7                      C
Thro' wind and rain and sleet and snow.
    F   C7  F   C
And forty minutes after twa,
      Dm   G7      C
We got the length o' Rothesay, O.
```

Chorus:

```
                  B    C
A dir-rum a doo a dum a day,
                  B
A dir-rum a doo a daddy, O,
    C        B   C
A dir-rum a doo a dum a day,
                  G7      C
The day we went to Rothesay, O.
```

A sodger lad named Rutherglen Will,
Wha's regiment's lyin' at Barn Hill,
Went off wi' a tanner to get a jill
In a public hoose in Rothesay, O.
Said he, "By Christ, I'd like to sing."
Said I, "Ye'll no' dae sic a thing."
He said, "Clear the room and I'll mak' a ring
And I'll fecht them all in Rothesay, O."

I' search of lodgins we did slide,
To find a place where we could bide;
There was eichty-twa o' us inside
In a single room in Rothesay, O.
We a' lay doon to tak' our ease,
When somebody happened for to sneeze,
And he wakened half a million fleas
In that single room in Rothesay, O.

There were several different kinds of bugs,
Some had feet like dyers' clogs,
And they sat on the bed and they cockit their lugs
And cried, "Hurrah for Rothesay, O!"
I said, "I think we should elope!"
So we went and joined the Band O' Hope,
But the polis wouldna let us stop
Another nicht in Rothesay, O.

MacPherson's Farewell

```
        C      Em    Am     D7
Fareweel ye dungeons dark and strong,
        G      G7    C
Fareweel, Fareweel to thee.
D7 G        Em     Am   D7
MacPherson's time will no be long
        G    C    D7
On yonder gallows tree.
```

Chorus:

```
        G          D7
Sae rantin'ly, sae wantonly
                    C
Sae dauntin'ly, gaed he;
        G                D7
He played a tune and he danced it roon'
      Em    C     D
About the gallows tree.
```

It was by a woman's treacherous hand
That I was condemned to dee.
Below a ledge at a window she stood,
And a blanket she threw o'er me.

The Laird o' Grant, that Highland sant,
That first laid hands on me.
He played the cause on Peter Broon
To let MacPherson dee.

Untie these bands from off my hands
And gie to me my sword,
An' there's no' a man in all Scotland
But I'll brave him at a word.

There's some come here to see me hanged,
And some to buy my fiddle,
But before that I do part wi' her
I'll brak her thro' the middle.

He took the fiddle into both o' his hands
And he broke it o'er a stone.
Says, There's nae ither hand sall play on thee
When I am dead and gone.

O little did my mother think
When first she cradled me,
That I would turn a rovin boy
And die on the gallows tree.

The reprieve was comin' o'er the brig o' Banff
To let MacPherson free;
But they pit the clock a quarter afore
And hanged him to the tree.

Old Joe Clark

E
Old Joe Clark's a fine old man,

Tell you the reason why,

He keeps good likker 'round his house,
      D   E
Good old Rock and Rye.

Chorus:

E
Fare ye well, Old Joe Clark,

Fare ye well, I say

Fare ye well, Old Joe Clark,
      D E
I'm a-goin' away.

Old Joe Clark, the preacher's son,
Preached all over the plain,
The only text he ever knew
Was "High, low, jack and the game."

Old Joe Clark had a mule,
His name was Morgan Brown,
And every tooth in that mule's head
Was sixteen inches around.

Old Joe Clark had a yellow cat,
She would neither sing or pray,
She stuck her head in the buttermilk jar
And washed her sins away.

Old Joe Clark had a house
Fifteen stories high,
And every story in that house
Was filled with chicken pie.

I went down to old Joe's house,
He invited me to supper,
I stumped my toe on the table leg
And stuck my nose in the butter.

Now I wouldn't marry a widder,
Tell you the reason why,
She'd have so many children
They'd make those biscuits fly.

Sixteen horses in my team,
The leaders they are blind,
And every time the sun goes down
There's a pretty girl on my mind.

Eighteen miles of mountain road
And fifteen miles of sand,
If I ever travel this road again,
I'll be a married man.

Steamboat Bill

Tune: *In the style of Casey Jones*

A
Down the Mississippi steamed the *Whippoorwill,*
                  E   A
Commanded by the pilot, Mister Steamboat Bill.

The owners gave him orders on the strict Q.T.
                  E   A
To try to beat the record of the *Robert E. Lee.*

Just speed up your fire, let the old smoke roll,
Burn up all your cargo if you run out of coal.
"If we don't beat that record," Billy told the mate,
"Then the *Maiden Care*'ll beat us to the Golden Gate."

First Chorus:

     A
Oh, Steamboat Bill, steamin' down the Mississippi,
                    E
Steamboat Bill, a mighty man was he.
     A
Oh, Steamboat Bill, steamin' down the Mississippi,
           D   E A
Gonna beat the record of the *Robert E. Lee.*

Up then stepped a gambling man from Louisville,
Who tried to get a bet against the *Whippoorwill.*
Billy clasped the roll and surely was some bear,
The boiler it exploded, blew them up in the air.

The gambler said to Billy as they left the wreck,
"I don't know where we're going but we're neck and neck."
Said Billy to the gambler, "Tell you what I'll do:
I'll bet another thousand I'll go higher than you!"

Second Chorus:
Oh, Steamboat Bill, he tore up the Mississippi,
Oh, Steamboat Bill, the pilot made him swear.
Oh, Steamboat Bill, he tore up the Mississippi,
An explosion of the boiler put him up in the air!

The river's all in mourning now for Steamboat Bill,
No more you'll hear the popping of the *Whippoorwill,*
There's crepe on every steamboat that plows the stream,
From Memphis right to Natchez, down to New Orleans.

The wife of Mister William was at home in bed
When she got the telegram that Steamboat's dead.
Said she to the children, "Blessed honey lambs,
The next papa that you have'll be a railroad man!"

Third Chorus:
Oh, Steamboat Bill, missing 'long the Mississippi,
Oh, Steamboat Bill is with an angel band.
Oh, Steamboat Bill, missing 'long the Mississippi,
He's a fireman on a ferry in the Promised Land!

Joe Bowers

```
Dm              C  Am Dm            C
My name it is Joe Bowers, I've got a brother Ike;
   F          Gm6  A         Dm
I come from old Missouri, yes, all the way from Pike;
C  F         Gm6   A7         Bb
I'll tell you why I left there and how I came to roam,
   G7    C      F       G7        Dm
And leave my poor old mammy so far away from home.
```

I used to love a gal there, they called her Sally Black,
I axed her for to marry me, she said it was a whack;
Says she to me, "Joe Bowers, before we hitch for life,
You'd orter have a little home to keep your little wife."

Says I, "My dearest Sally, oh Sally, for your sake,
I'll go to Californy, and try to raise a stake."
Says she to me, "Joe Bowers, oh you're the chap to win.
Give me a buss to seal the bargain,"
      and she threw a dozen in.

I shall ne'er forgit my feelin's when I bid adieu to all;
Sally cotched me round the neck, then I began to bawl;
When I sot in, they all commenced—
      you ne'er did hear the like,
How they all took on and cried, the day I left old Pike.

When I got to this 'ere country, I hadn't nary a red,
I had such wolfish feelin's I wished myself most dead;
But the thoughts of my dear Sally
      soon made them feelin's git,
And whispered hopes to Bowers—
      Lord, I wish I had 'em yit!

It said my Sal was fickle, that her love for me had fled;
That she'd married with a butcher
      whose hair was awful red!
It told me more than that—
      oh! it's enough to make one swear,
It said Sally had a baby, and the baby had red hair!

Now, I've told you all I could tell, about this sad affair,
'Bout Sally marryin' the butcher,
      and the butcher had red hair.
Whether 'twas a boy or gal child, the letter never said,
It only said its cussed hair was inclined to be red!

At length I went to mining, put in my biggest licks,
Come down upon the boulders just like a thousand bricks;
I worked both late and early, in rain and sun and snow,
But I was working for my Sally,
      so 'twas all the same to Joe.

I made a very lucky strike, as the gold itself did tell,
And saved it for Sally, the gal I loved so well;
I saved it for my Sally, that I might pour it at her feet,
That she might kiss and hug me,
      and call me something sweet.

But one day I got a letter from my dear, kind brother, Ike,
It came from old Missouri, sent all the way from Pike;
It brought me the gol-darn'dest news as ever you did hear—
My heart is almost bustin', so pray, excuse this tear.

Hallelujah, I'm A Bum

```
F
Why don't you work like other men do?
                                    C7
How the hell can I work when there's no work to do?
```

Chorus:

```
     F
Hallelujah, I'm a bum
              C7
Hallelujah, bum again!
     F
Hallelujah, give us a handout
     C7      F
To revive us again.
```

Oh, I love my boss, and my boss loves me,
And that is the reason that I'm so hungry.

Oh, springtime has come, and I'm just out of jail,
Without any money, and without any bail.

I went to a house, and I knocked on the door,
The lady said, "Run, bum, you've been here before."

I went to a house, and I asked for some bread;
A lady came out, said, "The baker is dead."

When springtime does come, oh, won't we have fun,
We'll throw up our jobs and we'll go on the bum.

If I was to work, and save all I earn,
I could buy me a bar and have money to burn.

I passed by a saloon, and heard someone snore,
And I found the bartender asleep on the floor.

I stayed there and drank till a copper came in,
And he put me asleep with a slap on the chin.

Next morning in court I was still in a haze
When the judge looked at me, he said, "Thirty days."

Billy The Kid

    D   A
I'll sing you a true song of Billy the Kid,
    D   (Bm)   Em   A
I'll sing of the desperate deeds that he did;
A7 D   D7   G
'Way out in New Mexico long, long ago,
        D   (F♯m)   A7   D
When a man's only chance was his old forty-four.

When Billy the Kid was a very young lad,
In old Silver City, he went to the bad;
Way out in the West with a gun in his hand,
At the age of twelve years he killed his first man.

Fair Mexican maidens play guitars and sing,
A song about Billy, their boy bandit king;
How, ere his young manhood had reached its sad end,
Had a notch on his pistol for twenty-one men.

'Twas on the same night that poor Billy died,
He said to his friends, "I'm not satisfied;
"There are twenty-one men I've put bullets through,
"And Sheriff Pat Garrett must make twenty-two."

Now this is how Billy the Kid met his fate,
The bright moon was shining, the hour was late;
Shot down by Pat Garret who once was his friend,
The young outlaw's life had come to its end.

There's many a man with face fine and fair,
Who starts out in life with a chance to be square;
But just like poor Billy, he wanders astray,
And loses his life the very same way.

John Peel

           C
Do ye ken John Peel with his coat so gray?
        G7
Do ye ken John Peel at the break of day?
        C   F   G7   C
Do ye ken John Peel when he's far, far away,
          F   C   G7 C
With his hounds and his horn in the morning?

Chorus:

C
'Twas the sound of his horn brought me from my bed,
      G7
And the cry of his hounds which he ofttimes led,
    C   F   C
For Peel's "View hallo!" would wake the dead
      Dm   G7 C
Or the fox from his lair in the morning.

D'ye ken that bitch whose tongue is death?
D'ye ken her sons of peerless faith?
D'ye ken that a fox with his last breath
Cursed them all as he died in the morning?

Yes, I ken John Peel and Ruby too,
Ranter and Royal and Bellman as true;
From the drag to the chase, from the chase to a view,
From a view to a death in the morning.

And I've followed John Peel both often and far
O'er the rasper-fence and the gate and the bar,
From Low Denton Holme up to Scratchmere Scar
When we vied for the brush in the morning.

Then here's to John Peel with my heart and soul,
Come fill—fill to him another strong bowl:
And we'll follow John Peel through fair and through foul,
While we're waked by his horn in the morning.

DOWN, DERRY, DERRY DOWN

Traditional ballads from England,
Scotland and the U.S....

Young Charlotte

      D
Young Charlotte lived on the mountain side
   G   D
In a lonesome dreary spot;
   G   D
No neighbors lived for miles around
            A7   D
Near her father's lonely cot.

'Twas on those cold and wintry nights
Young swains would gather there.
Her father kept a social place
And Charlotte was very fair.

Her father liked to see her dressed
Like any city belle;
She was the only child he had,
And he loved his daughter well.

On a New Year's Eve when the sun went down,
She watched with wishful eye,
Out through the frosty windowpane
As the merry sleighs went by.

In a village fifteen miles away
There was a ball that night;
And though the air was piercing cold
Her heart was warm and light.

How brightly gleamed her loving eyes
As a well-known voice she heard;
And dashing up to her cottage door
Young Charlie's sleigh appeared.

"Oh, Charlotte, dear," her mother said,
"This blanket round you fold;
It is a dreadful night, you know,
You'll catch your death of cold."

"Oh, no, oh, no," young Charlotte said,
And she laughed like a gypsy queen,
"To ride in blankets muffled up,
I never would be seen."

"My silken cloak is quite enough,
It is lined, you know, throughout;
Besides I have my silken scarf
To tie my head about."

Her bonnet and her gloves put on,
She leaped into the sleigh,
And away they went o'er the mountain top
And the hills so far away.

There was music in the sound of bells
As o'er the hills they'd go.
What a crackling noise the runners made
As they bit the frozen snow.

With faces muffled silently,
For five long miles they rode,
Until at length with a few frozen words,
Young Charles the silence broke.

"Such a dreadful night I never saw,
The reins I scarce can hold."
Young Charlotte faintly then replied,
"I am exceedingly cold."

He cracked his whip; he urged his steed,
Much faster than before;
And thus five other weary miles
In silence were passed o'er.

Said Charles: "How fast the shivering ice
Is gathering on my brow."
And Charlotte then more faintly cried,
"I'm growing warmer now."

Thus on they rode through frosty air
And the glittering cold starlight,
Until at last the village lamps
And the ballroom came in sight.

They reached the door and Charles sprang out;
He reached his hand to her.
"Why sit you there like a monument
That has no power to stir?"

He called her once; he called her twice;
She answered not a word.
He asked her for her hand again,
But still she never stirred.

He took her hand all in his own;
It was cold and hard as stone;
He tore the mantle from her face,
And the cold stars on her shone.

Then quickly to the lighted hall
Her lifeless form he bore.
Young Charlotte's eyes had closed for all;
Her voice was heard no more.

He threw himself down on his knees
And the bitter tears did flow.
He said, "My young, intended bride,
No more with me you'll go."

He threw himself down by her side,
And he kissed her marble brow,
And his thoughts ran back to the place she said,
"I'm growing warmer now."

The Gypsy Rover

Child Ballad 120

```
    G   D7    G    D7
The gypsy rover come over the hill,
G            D7      G  D7
Bound through the valley so shady;
    G           D7      Bm      Em
He whistled and he sang till the green woods rang,
    Bm      Am7    GCG  D7
And he won the heart of a lady.
```

Chorus:

```
G   D7    G    D7
Ha di do, ah dido da day,
G    D7     G   D7
Ah di do, ah di day dee;
    G           D7      Bm      Em
He whistled and he sang till the green woods rang,
    Bm      Am     GCG
And he won the heart of a lady.
```

She left her father's castle gate,
She left her own true lover;
She left her servants and her estate,
To follow the gypsy rover.

Her father saddled his fastest steed,
Roamed the valley all over;
Sought his daughter at great speed,
And the whistling gypsy rover.

He came at last to a mansion fine,
Down by the river Clayde;
And there was music, and there was wine,
For the gypsy and his lady.

He's no gypsy, my father, said she,
My lord of freelands all over;
And I will stay till my dying day,
With my whistling gypsy rover.

The Gallows Pole

Derived from Child Ballad 95

```
Am
Hangman, hangman slack your rope,

Slack it for a while.
A7          D7
Think I see my father comin',
F7          Am
Ridin' many a mile.
```

Papa, did you bring me silver?
Papa, did you bring me gold?
Did you come to see me hangin'
By the gallows pole?

Well, I couldn't bring no silver,
I didn't bring no gold.
I come to see you hangin'
By the gallows pole.

Hangman, hangman, slack your rope,
Slack it for a while,
Think I see my mother comin',
Ridin' many a mile, etc.

Hangman, hangman, slack your rope,
Slack it for a while,
Think I see my sweetheart comin',
Ridin' many a mile.

Honey, did you bring me silver?
Honey, did you bring me gold?
Did you come to see me hangin'
By the gallows pole?

I brought you silver,
Brought you a little gold,
Didn't come to see you hangin'
By the gallows pole.

The Four Maries

```
    D                G  D
Last night there were four Maries,
               A
This night there'll be but three;
              D   G    D  Bm
There were Mary Beaton and Mary Seaton
    G    A7    D
And Mary Carmichael and me.
```

Oh often have I dressed my queen
And put on her braw silk gown,
But all the thanks I've got tonight,
Is to be hanged in Edinburgh town.

Full often have I dressed my queen,
Put gold upon her hair,
But I have got for my reward
The gallows to be my share.

Oh little did my mother know
The day she cradled me,
The land I was to travel in,
The death I was to dee.

Oh happy happy is the maid
That's born of beauty free;
Oh it was my rosy dimpled cheeks
That's been the devil to me.

They'll tie a kerchief around my eyes
That I may not see to dee,
And they'll never tell my father or mother
But that I'm across the sea.

Queen Jane
Child Ballad 170

      C   F   C
Queen Jane lay in labour for six weeks and some more;
      Bb   C   G7   C
Her women grew weary and the midwife give o'er.

O, women, kind women, as I know you to be;
Pray cut my side open and save my baby.

O, no, said the women, that never might be!
We'll send for King Henry in the hour of your need.

King Henry was sent for by horseback and speed,
King Henry he come there in the hour of her need.

King Henry he come in and stood by her bed:
What ails my pretty flower, her eyes look so red?

O, Henry, kind Henry, pray listen to me,
Pray cut my side open and save my baby.

O, no, said King Henry, that never might be!
I'd lose my pretty flower to save my baby.

Queen Jane she turned over and fell in a swound,
They cut her side open, her baby was found.

How black was the mourning, how yellow her bed;
How white the bright shroud Queen Jane was laid in.

Six followed after, six bore her along.
King Henry come after, his head hanging down.

King Henry he wept 'til his hands were wrung sore,
Says, the flower of England is blooming no more.

That baby was christened the very next day;
His mother's poor body lay mouldering away.

Lord Bateman
Child Ballad 53

D
There was a man that lived in England,
                A7
He sailed along the Turkish shore,
      D
Until he was taken and put in prison,
      A7   D
Where he could never be released any more.

This Turkey had one only daughter,
And she was of some high degree,
She stole the key to her father's prison,
And declared Lord Bateman she'd set free.

Let's make a vow, let's make a promise,
Let's make a vow, let's make it stand,
You vow you'll marry no other woman,
I'll vow I'll marry no other man.

They made that vow, they made that promise,
They made that vow, they made it stand,
He vowed he'd marry no other woman,
She vowed she'd marry no other man.

But seven long years had rolled around her,
It seemed as though they were twenty-nine.
She wrapped up her clothes in a great big bundle,
And declared Lord Bateman she'd go find.

She rode till she came to Lord Bateman's castle,
She jingled so loud, but she couldn't come in,
Saying, "Is this Lord Bateman's castle,
Or is it that he's brought his new bride in?"

Lord Bateman stood on the chamber floor,
He busted that table into pieces three,
Saying, "I'll forsake all my lands and my dwelling,
For that Turkish lady that set me free."

The Bonnie Earl Of Murray
Child Ballad 181

      E
Ye highlands and ye lowlands
B7
Where ha' ye been,
      E
They have slain the Duke of Murray,
      A   E
And they laid him on the green.

"Now wae be to thee, Huntly,
And wherefore did you sae?
I bade you bring him wi' ye,
But forbade you him to slay."

He was a braw gallant,
And he rid at the ring,
And the bonnie Earl of Murray,
He might have been a king.

He was a braw gallant,
And he play'd at the ba',
And the bonnie Earl of Murray,
Was the flower of them a'.

He was a braw gallant,
And he play'd at the glove,
And the bonnie Earl of Murray,
He was the Queen's own love.

Oh, lang will his lady,
Look o'er the castle down,
E'er she see the Earl of Murray,
Come sounding through the town.

The Golden Vanity
Child Ballad 286

```
C        F   C    G7        C
There was a lofty ship, and she put out to sea,
                                  F
And the name of the ship was the Golden Vanity,
    C          Em    Am       C
As she sailed upon the low and lonesome low,
                      G7      C
As she sailed upon the lonesome sea.
```

She had not been out but two weeks or three
When she was overtaken by a Turkish Revelee
As she sailed upon the low and lonesome low
As she sailed upon the lonesome sea.

Then up spake our little cabin boy
Saying "What will you give me if I will then destroy
If I sink them in the low and lonesome low
If I sink them in the lonesome sea?"

"Oh, the man that them destroys," our captain
    then replied,
"Five thousand pounds and my daughter for his bride
If he sinks them in the low and lonesome low
If he sinks them in the lonesome sea."

Then the boy smote his breast and down jumped he
He swum till he came to the Turkish Revelee
As she sailed upon the low and lonesome low
As she sailed upon the lonesome sea.

He had a little tool that was made for the use
He bored nine holes in her hull all at once
And he sunk her in the low and lonesome low
He sunk her in the lonesome sea.

He swum back to his ship and he beat upon the side
Cried, "Captain pick me up for I'm wearied with the tide
I am sinking in the low and lonesome low
I am sinking in the lonesome sea."

"No! I will not pick you up" the captain then replied
"I will shoot you I will drown you I will sink you
    in the tide
I will sink you in the low and lonesome low
I will sink you in the lonesome sea."

"If it was not for the love that I bear for your men
I would do unto you as I did unto 'them'
I would sink you in the low and lonesome low
I would sink you in the lonesome sea."

Then the boy bowed his head and down sunk he
Farewell, farewell to the Golden Vanity
As she sails upon the low and lonesome low
As she sails upon the lonesome sea.

The Wraggle-Taggle Gypsies
from Child Ballad 120

```
    Am             E7       Am
There were three Gypsies a-come to my door,
    F            Em
And downstairs ran this a lady-o,
C       Am      C    Dm
One sang high and the other sang low,
        Am     Em      Am Dm Am
And the other sang bonny, bonny Biscay-O!
```

Then she pulled off her silk-finished gown,
And put on hose of leather-o!
The ragged, ragged rags about our door,
And she's gone with the wraggle, taggle Gypsies O!

It was late last night when my Lord came home,
Inquiring for his a-lady, O!
The servants said on ev'ry hand:
She's gone with the wraggle-taggle Gypsies O!

O saddle to me my milk-white steed,
And go fetch me my pony, O!
That I may ride and seek my bride,
Who is gone with the wraggle-taggle Gypsies O!

O he rode high, and he rode low,
He rode through wood and copses too,
Until he came to a wide open field,
And there he espied his a-lady, O!

What makes you leave your house and land?
What makes you leave your money O!
What makes you leave your new-wedded Lord?
I'm off with the wraggle-taggle Gypsies O!

What care I for my house and land?
What care I for my money, O!
What care I for my new-wedded Lord?
I'm off with the wraggle-taggle Gypsies O!

Last night you slept on a goose-feather bed,
With the sheet turned down so bravely-O!
Tonight you'll sleep in a cold, open field,
Along with the wraggle-taggle Gypsies O!

What care I for a goose-feather bed,
With the sheet turned down so bravely-O!
For tonight I shall sleep in a cold, open field,
Along with the wraggle-taggle Gypsies O!

The Lass Of Roch Royal

Child Ballad 76

```
Am          G        Am
Who will shoe my pretty little foot?
G               Am
Who will glove my hand?
              G    Am
Who will kiss my ruby lips
         G        E7    Am
When you're in the foreign land?
```

Your papa can shoe your pretty little foot,
Your mama can glove your hand:
I will kiss your ruby lips
When I come back again.

O, if I had a sailing boat
And men to sail with me;
I'd go this night to my true love
For he will not come to me.

Her father gave her a sailing boat
And sent her to the strand;
She set her baby in her lap
And turned her back on land.

O, she wasn't sailing about three months,
I'm sure it was not four,
Till she had landed her sailing boat
Right at her lover's door.

She took her baby in her arms
And to his door she's gone,
She knocked and cried and knocked again,
But answer got she none.

The night was dark and the wind was cold,
Her true love was asleep;
And the baby in poor Annie's arms
Began to cry and weep.

Come, open the door, my own true love,
Come, open the door, I pray,
For your young child that's in my arms
Will be dead before it is day.

Go away, you wild woman,
For here you cannot stay.
Go drown you in the salt, salt sea
Or hang on the gallows tree.

O, don't you mind, my own true love,
When we were at the wine?
We changed the rings from our fingers
And the best of them was mine.

O, don't you mind, my own true love,
The vows you swore to me?
You made an oath and it bound us both
For the years that are to be.

Go away, you wild woman,
For here you cannot stay;
Go drown you in the salt, salt sea
Or hang on the gallows tree.

The cock did crow and the sun did rise
And through the window peep;
Then up he rose, her own true love
And sorely did he weep.

O mother, I dreamed of my true love,
She lives across the sea;
I dreamed she came to my front door
A-weeping loud for me.

There was a lady here last night
With a baby in her arms;
I did not let her in to you
For fear she'd do you harm.

He ran, he ran to the salt sea shore,
And looked out on the foam;
And there he saw his Annie's boat
A-tossing towards her home.

He called, he cried, he waved his hand,
He begged her sore to stay;
But the more he called and the more he cried,
The louder roared the sea.

The wind did blow and the sea did rise
It tossed her boat on shore;
It laid his true love at his feet,
But he saw his son no more.

The first he kissed her rosy cheek,
Then he kissed her chin;
And last he kissed her ruby lips,
There was no breath within.

Henry Martin
Child Ballad 250

     Dm   A7   Dm
There were three brothers in merry Scotland,
                        G   Dm
In Scotland there lived brothers three.
A7 Dm   G
And they did cast lots which of them should go,
        G   Dm
    should go should go
Bb   F   C   Dm
For to turn robber all on the salt sea.

The lot it fell upon Henry Martin
The youngest of all the three,
That he should turn robber all on the salt sea,
    salt sea, salt sea.
For to maintain his two brothers and he.

He had not been sailing but a long winter's night,
And part of a short winter's day,
When he espi-ed a lofty stout ship, stout ship, stout ship,
Come a-bibing down on him straightway.

"Hello, hello" cried Henry Martin,
"What makes you sail so high?"
"I'm a rich merchant ship bound for fair London Town,
    London Town, London Town,
Will you please for to let me pass by?"

"O no, O no," cried Henry Martin,
"That thing it never can be,
For I have turned robber all on the salt sea,
    salt sea, salt sea,
For to maintain my two brothers and me."

"So lower your topsail and brail up your mizzen,
Bow yourselves under my lee,
Or I shall give you a fast flowing ball,
    flowing ball, flowing ball,
And your dear bodies down in the salt sea."

With broadside and broadside and at it they went
For fully two hours or three,
Till Henry Martin gave to her the death shot,
    the death shot, the death shot,
Heavily listing to starboard went she.

The rich merchant vessel was wounded full sore,
Straight to the bottom went she,
And Henry Martin sailed away on the sea,
    salt sea, salt sea,
For to maintain his two brothers and he.

Bad news, bad news, to old England came,
Bad news to fair London Town,
There was a rich vessel and she's cast away,
    cast away, cast away,
And all of her merry men drowned.

The Three Ravens
Child Ballad 26

       Em   Am
There were three rav'ns sat on a tree,
Em   B
Down-a-down, hey down-a-down.
       Em   D   G
There were three ravens sat on a tree with a down,
B   G   D
There were three ravens sat on a tree,
         E   B
They were as black as they might be,
       G   B   Em
With a-down, derry, derry, derry down, down.

Then one of them said to his mate,
Down-a-down, hey down-a-down,
Then one of them said to his mate with a down,
Then one of them said to his mate,
"Where shall we our breakfast take?"
With a-down, derry, derry, derry down, down.

"Down in yonder greene field, etc.
There lies a knight slain under his shield." etc.

"His hounds they lie down at his feet,
So well they can their master keep."

"His hawks they fly so eagerly,
There's no fowle dare come him nigh."

Down there comes a fallow doe,
As great with young as she might go.

She lift up his bloody head,
And kissed his wound that were so red.

She got him up upon her back,
And carried him to an earthen lake.

She buried him before the prime,
She was dead herself ere evensong time.

God send every gentleman
Such hawks, such hounds and such a leman.

Earl Brand

Child Ballad 7

```
C        Am   G7      C
Rise up, rise up, you seven sleepers,
              G        Am
And do take a warning of me,
C                   F
Do watch after your eldest sister,
    G7                    C
The youngest is going with me.
```

Rise up, rise up, my seven bold sons,
And bring your sister down;
It'll never be said that a steward's son
Had carried her out of town.

I thank you kindly, sir, said he,
But I am no steward's son;
My father is a regis king
And my mother a Quaker queen.

He mounted her on the bonny, bonny black,
Himself on the ample grey,
And he threw his bugle all round her neck
And they went singing away.

Rise up, rise up, my seven bold sons,
Put on your arms so bright,
It'll never be said that a daughter of mine
Did sleep with a lord all night.

They were not three miles out of town
When he looked back again,
And he saw her father and seven brethren
Come a-trippling o'er the plain.

Light down, light down, Lady Margit, he said,
And hold my horse for awhile,
While I fight your seven bretheren
And your father a-walking so nigh.

And she held, and she held so still,
Nor never did speak a word,
Not even when she seen her seven brethren
Go a-tumbling in their blood.

And she held, and she bitter, bitter, held,
Nor never a word did speak.
Until she seen her father's head
Come a-tumbling by her feet.

O, hold your hand, love William, she said,
For your stroke is now full score;
It's many the true love I might have
But a father I have no more.

If you ain't pleased, Lady Margit, he said,
If you ain't pleased, said he;
You oughta stayed in your father's house
And me in a chambery.

But you must choose, Lady Margit, he said,
Will you go with me, he cried,
I'll go with, love William, she said,
For you left me without a guide.

Then wind you east and wind you west,
I'll wind along with thee,
So he hung his bugle all round her neck
And he went bleeding away.

They rode till they come to his mother's gate,
And he tingled at the pin;
Mother, mother, asleep or awake,
Arise and let us in.

Sister, sister, go make my bed,
For my wound is now full sore;
Mother, mother, bind up my head,
For me you'll bind no more.

Father, father, go dig my grave;
Dig it wide and deep;
And place Lady Margit in my arms,
Together that we may sleep.

Love William died as 'twas midnight;
Lady Margit just at day;
And I hope every couple that ever do love
May see more pleasure than they.

Springfield Mountain

```
G                                    D7
On Springfield Mountain there did dwell
                           G
A lovely youth, I knew him well.
```

Chorus:

```
                      D7
Tooroodi noo, Tooroodi nay
                 G
Tooroodi noo, Tooroodi nay.
```

He scarce had mowed half round the field
When an ug-lye serpent bit his heel.

They took him home to Mol-lye dear
Which made her feel so ve-rye queer.

Now Mol-lye had two ruby lips
With which the pizen she did sip.

Now Mol-lye had a rotten tooth
And so the pizen killed them both.

Old Bangum
Child Ballad 18

F   C7
Old Bangum, will you hunt and ride?
F   C7
Dillum down dillum.
   F   C7
Old Bangum, will you hunt and ride?
F   C7
Dillum down.

Old Bangum, will you hunt and ride,
Bb   C7
Sword and pistol by your side?
F   Bb   C7   F
Cubikee, cuddledum, kili quo quam.

There is a wild boar in these woods,
Dillum down dillum.
There is a wild boar in these woods,
Dillum down.
There is a wild boar in these woods,
Eats men's bones and drink their blood.
Cubikee, cuddledum, kili quo quam.

Old Bangum drew his wooden knife, etc.
And swore he'd take the wild boar's life, etc.

Old Bangum went to the wild boar's den, etc.
And fought the bones of a thousand men, etc.

They fought four hours in that day, etc.
The wild boar fled and slunk away, etc.

Old Bangum, did you win or lose?, etc.
He swore, by Jove, he'd won his shoes, etc.

Daily Growing

    Em   Am   Em Am   Em
The trees they are tall and the leaves they are green,
Bm   Em
Many a time my true love I've seen,
    Am   Em   Bm
Many an hour I have passed all alone,
   G   Am   Em
My bonnie lad's a long time a-growing.

Oh father, dear father, you've done me great wrong,
You've married me to a boy that's too young,
I am twice twelve and he is but fourteen,
He's young but he's daily growing.

Oh, daughter, dear daughter, I've done you no wrong,
I've married you to a rich lord's son,
He will make a lord for you to wait upon,
He's young but he's daily growing.

Oh, father, dear father, and if you see fit,
We'll send him to college for one year yet,
I'll bind a blue ribbon all about his hat,
To let the maids know that he's married.

One day as I looked o'er my father's castle wall,
There were all the boys, a-playing with their ball,
My own true love was the flower of them all,
He's young but he's daily growing.

I made him a shirt of the finest of lawn,
I sewed it all with my own lovely hand,
And with every stitch, the tears came flowing down,
He's young but he's daily growing.

So early in the morning at the dawning of the day
They went out in the hayfield to have some sport and play,
And what they did there, she never would declare,
But she never more complained of his growing.

At the age of fourteen he was a married man,
At the age of fifteen, the father of a son,
At the age of sixteen, his grave it was green,
And death put an end to his growing.

Young Man Cut Down In His Prime
(St. James Hospital)

    Em   Bm
As I was a-walking by Saint James Hospital,
Em   Am   Em
I was a-walking down by there one day;
            Am
What should I spy but one of my comrades,
    Em   D   Em
All wrapped up in flannel, though warm was the day.

I asked him what ailed him I asked him what failed him
I asked the cause of his complaint.
"It's all on account of some handsome young woman,
'Tis she that has caused me to weep and lament."
"And had she but told me before she disordered me,
Had she but told me of it in time
I might have got pills and salts of white mercury
But now I'm cut down in the height of my prime."

"Get six young soldiers to carry my coffin
Six young girls to sing me a song,
And each of them carry a bunch of green laurel
So they don't smell me as they bear me along."

"Don't muffle your drums and play your fifes merrily
Play a quick march as you carry me along
Fire your bright muskets all over my coffin
Saying, 'There goes an unfortunate lad to his home.' "

The House Carpenter's Wife

Child Ballad 243

```
      D      A      D G D
"Well met, well met, my own true love,
              C    G    A
Well met, well met," cried he;
      D    A        D G D
"I've just returned from the salt, salt sea,
                      A7   D
And it's all for the sake of thee."
```

"O I could have married the king's daughter dear,
And she would have married me;
But I have refused the crown of gold,
And it's all for the sake of thee."

"If you could have married the king's daughter dear,
I'm sure you are to blame;
For I am married to the house carpenter,
And he is a fine young man."

"If you'll forsake your house carpenter,
And fly away with me,
I'll take you to where the grass grows green,
On the banks of the Sweet Willie."

"If I forsake my house carpenter,
And fly away with thee,
What have you got to maintain me upon,
And keep me from slavery?"

"I've six ships sailing on the salt, salt sea,
A-sailing from dry land,
And a hundred and twenty jolly young men
Shall be at thy command."

She picked up her poor little babe,
Her kisses were one, two, three;
And as she trod upon her way,
She shone like glittering gold.

They had not been at sea two weeks,
I'm sure it was not three,
When this poor maid began to weep,
And she wept most bitterly.

"O do you weep for your gold?" he said,
"Your houses, your land, or your store?
Or do you weep for your house carpenter,
That you never shall see anymore?"

"I do not weep for my gold," she said,
"My houses, my land, or my store;
But I do weep for my poor little babe,
That I never shall see anymore."

They had not been at sea three weeks,
I'm sure it was not four,
When in the ship there sprang a leak,
And she sank, to rise no more.

Farewell, farewell," cried she;
"Farewell, farewell," cried she;
"O I have deserted my house carpenter,
For a grave in the depths of the sea."

The Unquiet Grave

Child Ballad 78

```
C    F           C
Cold blows the wind to my true love,
     G
And gently drops the rain;
   C    F    C    G7
I never had but one true love
C    F    G7    C
And in greenwood she lies slain,
     F      G7    C
And in greenwood she lies slain.
```

I'll do as much for my true love
As any young man may;
I'll sit and mourn all on her grave,
For a twelve-month and a day. (twice)

When the twelve-month and one day was past,
The ghost began to speak:
"Why sittest here all on my grave,
And will not let me sleep?" (twice)

My breast it is cold as clay,
My breath is earthly strong;
And if you kiss my cold clay lips
Your days they won't be long. (twice)

O down in yonder grave, sweetheart,
Where we were wont to walk;
The first flower that ever I saw,
Is withered to a stalk. (twice)

The stalk is withered and dead, sweetheart,
And the flower will never return;
And since I lost my own true love
What can I do but mourn? (twice)

When shall we meet again, sweetheart,
When shall we meet again?
When the oaken leaves that fall from the trees,
Are green and spring up again. (twice)

Bailiff's Daughter Of Islington
Child Ballad 105

<pre>
    D A7 D   A7 D   A7   D
There was a   youth and a well-beloved youth,
A7   D   G   D
And he was an esquire's son;
    G   D
He loved the bailiff's daughter dear
     A7   DA7 D
That lived in Islington.
</pre>

She was coy, and she would not believe
That he did love her so,
No, nor at any time she would
Any countenance to him show.

But when his friends did understand
His fond and foolish mind,
They sent him up to fair London,
An apprentice for to bind.

And when he had been seven long years,
And his love he had not seen,
"Many a tear have I shed for her sake
"When she little thought of me."

All the maids of Islington
Went forth to sport and play,
All but the bailiff's daughter,
She secretly stole away.

She put off her gown of gray,
And put on her puggish attire.
She's up to fair London gone
Her true love to require.

As she went along the road,
The weather being hot and dry,
There was she aware of her true love,
At length came riding by.

She stepped to him as red as any rose,
And took him by the bridle ring:
"I pray you, kind sir, give me one penny,
To ease my weary limb."

"I prithee, sweet heart, canst thou tell me
Whether thou dost know
The bailiff's daughter of Islington?"
"She's dead, sir, long ago."

"Then I will sell my goodly steed,
My saddle and my bow;
I will unto some far countree
Where no man doth me know."

"O stay, O stay, thou goodly youth,
She's alive, she is not dead;
Here she standeth by thy side,
And is ready to be thy bride."

"O farewell grief, and welcome joy,
Ten thousand times and more,
For now I have seen my own true love
That I tho't I should have seen no more."

The Great Silkie
Based upon Child Ballad 113

<pre>
   G   F   G
An earthly nouris sits and sings,
   Em   Am   D   Bm
And aye she sings "ba lily wean."
C   Bm Am   Em
Little Ken I my bairnis father,
   Am   Em   F   G
Far less the land that he saps in.
</pre>

Then in steps he to her bed fit,
And a grumley guest I'm sure was he,
Saying, here I am, thy bairny's father,
Although I be not comely.

I am a man upon the land,
And I am a silky in the sea,
And when I'm far and far from land,
My home it is in Sule Skerry.

It was na weel, quo the maiden fair,
It was na weel, indeed quo she.
That the great silky from Sule Skerry
Should hae come and aught a bairn ta me.

Then he has taken a purse of gold,
And he has pat it upon her knee,
Saying, gie to me my little young son,
And take thee up thy nourris fee.

It shall come to pass on a summer's day,
When the sun shines hot on every stone,
That I shall take my little young son
And teach him for to swim the foam.

And thou shall marry a proud gunner,
And a proud gunner I'm sure he'll be,
And the very first shot that ever he'll shoot
He'll kill both my young son and me.

Alas, alas, the maiden cried,
This weary fate's been laid for me;
And then she said and then she said,
I'll bury me in Sule Skerry.

Geordie

Child Ballad 209

```
      Em    D      C      G
As I walked out of a London bridge,
Em                    D
One misty morning early,
Em            D        Bm
I overhead a fair pretty maid
C     G      B7     Em
Was lamenting for her Geordie.
```

Ah my Geordie will be hanged in a golden chain
'Tis not the chain of many
He was born of King's royal breed
And lost to a virtuous lady.

Go bridle me my milk white steed
Go bridle me my pony
I will ride to London's court
To plead for the life of Geordie.

Ah my Geordie never stole nor cow nor calf
He never hurted any
Stole sixteen of the King's royal deer
And he sold them in Gilhooley.

Two pretty babies have I born
The third lies in my body
I'd freely part with them everyone
If you'd spare the life of Geordie.

The judge looked over his left shoulder
He said, "Fair maid, I'm sorry."
Said, "Fair maid, you must be gone
For I cannot pardon Geordie."

Ah my Geordie will be hanged in a golden chain
'Tis not the chain of many
Stole sixteen of the King's royal deer
And he sold them in Gilhooley.

Lady Margaret

Child Ballad 74

```
      Em
Lady Margaret sittin' in her high hall door,
                         D
Combing her long yellow hair.
    G                        D
She saw sweet William and his new made bride,
Bm                    Em
Ridin' from the Church so near.
```

Well she throwed down her ivory comb,
Throwed back her long yellow hair,
Said, I'll go down to bid him farewell,
And never more go there.

It was all lately in the night
When they were fast asleep,
Little Margaret appeared all dressed in white,
Standin' at their bed feet.

How do you like your pillow, says she,
How do you like your sheet?
And how do you like that gay young bride,
Lyin' in your arms asleep?

Very well do I like my pillow, says he,
Very well do I like my sheet.
Better do I like that fair young lady
Standin' at my bed feet.

Well once he kissed her lily white hand;
Twice he kissed her cheek,
Three times he kissed her cold corpsey lips,
And fell in her arms asleep.

Is little Margaret in her room,
Or is she in the hall?
No, Little Margaret's in her cold black coffin
With her pale face to the wall.

MURDER MOST CRUEL

Songs of cruel mothers, jealous lovers, quarreling brothers and other bloody ballads....

Fair Ellender

Child Ballad 295

```
    D        G        C      G
Oh, father, oh, father, come riddle to me,
 D    G          D
Come riddle it all as one;
    G              C        G
And tell me whether to marry fair Ellen,
              C       G
Or bring the Brown girl home.
```

"The Brown Girl, she has house and land,
Fair Ellender, she has none;
And there I charge you with a blessing
To bring the Brown Girl home."

He got on his horse and he rode and he rode,
He rode till he come to her home;
An no one so ready as Fair Ellen herself,
To rise and welcome him in.

"What news have you brought unto me, Lord Thomas,
What news have you brought unto me?"
"I've come to ask you to my wedding,
A sorrowful wedding to be."

"Oh, mother, oh, mother, would you go or stay?"
"Fair child, do as you please,
But I'm afraid if you go you'll never return,
To see your dear mother any more."

She turned around all dressed in white,
Her sisters dressed in green;
And every town that they rode through,
They took her to be some queen.

They rode and they rode till they come to the hall,
She pulled on the bell and it rang;
And no one so ready as Lord Thomas himself,
To rise and bid her in.

Then taking her by her lily-white hand,
And leading her through the hall;
Saying, "Fifty gay ladies are here today,
But here is the flower of all."

The Brown Girl, she was standing by,
With knives ground keen and sharp;
Between the long ribs and the short,
She pierced Fair Ellender's heart.

Lord Thomas, he was standing by,
With knife ground keen and sharp;
Between the long ribs and the short,
He pierced his own bride's heart.

Then placing the handle against the wall,
The point against his breast;
Saying, "This is the ending of three true lovers,
God sends them all to rest."

"Oh father, oh father, go dig my grave,
Go dig it wide and deep;
And place Fair Ellender in my arms,
And the Brown Girl at my feet."

The Cruel Mother

Child Ballad 20

```
G         D          G
There was a lady, lived in York,
       D7          G
All alone and aloney,
                          D      C
She fell in love with her father's clerk,
Dm                  G
Down by the greenwood sidey.
```

She loved him up, she loved him down,
All alone and aloney
She loved him till he filled her arms
Down by the greenwood sidey.

She leaned her back against an oak, All alone, etc.
First it bent and then it broke. Down, etc.

She leaned her back against a thorn,
And there she had two fine babies born.

She pulled down her yellow hair,
She bound it around their feet and hands.

She pulled out a wee penknife,
Stabbed those two babes to the heart.

She laid them under a marble stone,
Then she turned as a fair maid home.

One day she was sitting in her father's hall,
She saw two babes come playing at ball.

Babes, oh babes, if you was mine,
I'd dress you up in scarlet fine.

Mother, oh, mother, it's we was yours,
Scarlet fine was our own heart's blood.

You wiped your penknife on your shoe,
The more you wiped, more red it grew.

You laid us under a marble stone,
Now you sit as a fair maid home.

Babes, oh, babes, it's Heaven for you,
Mother, oh, mother, it's Hell for you.

Johnson

```
C                                      G7
Johnson, he was riding out as fast as he could ride,
        C                      G7
When he thought he heard a woman,
        C      G7    C
   he heard a woman cry.
```

Johnson getting off his horse
   and proceeding to look around,
When he came upon a woman
   with her hair pinned to the ground.

"Woman, dearest woman, who brought you here in spite?
Who brought you here this morning
   with your hair pinned to the ground?"

"It were three bold and struggling men
   with swords keen in hand,
That brought me here this morning
   and pinned me to the ground."

Johnson being a man of his word and being a man so bold,
He took off his overcoat to cover her from the cold.

Johnson getting on his horse, she's getting on behind,
Down that long and lonesome highway
   their fortunes for to find.

Out sprang three bold and struggling men
   with swords keen in hand,
And they commanded Johnson, commanded him to stand.

"I'll stand, then," says Johnson, "I'll stand, then," says he,
"For I never was in my life afraid of any a three."

Johnson killing two of them,
   not watching the woman behind,
While he was upon the other one,
   she stabbed him from behind.

The day was clear and a market day
   and the people all passing by,
Who did see this awful murder
   and watch poor Johnson die?

Edward

Child Ballad 13

```
     Dm
What makes that blood on the point of your knife?
```

My son, now tell to me.
```
F              Dm
It is the blood of my old gray mare
              Gm     Dm   Gm
Who plowed the fields for me, me, me,
     Dm      Gm      Dm
Who plowed the fields for me.
```

It is too red for your old gray mare,
My son, now tell to me.
It is the blood of my old coon dog
Who chased the fox for me, me, me,
Who chased the fox for me.

It is too red for your old coon dog, etc.
It is the blood of my brother John,
Who hoed the corn for me, me, me, etc.

What did you fall out about, my own dear son, etc.
Because he cut yon holly bush
Which might have been a tree, tree, tree, etc.

What will you say when your father comes home? etc.
I'll set my foot in yonder boat,
And I'll sail the ocean round, round, round, etc.

When will you come back, my own dear son? etc.
When the sun it sets in yonder sycamore tree,
And that will never be, be, be,
And that will never be.

Down In The Willow Garden

```
          E           A
Down in the willow garden
          E       E      C♯m
Where me and my true love did meet,
          E           A
'Twas there we sat a-courting,
     E        B7   E
My love dropped off to sleep.
     A    G♯m          A
I had a bottle of burgundy wine
          E           C♯m
Which my true love did not know.
          E                    C♯m
And there I poisoned that dear little girl
     E      A    E
Down under the bank below.
```

I stabbed her with my dagger,
Which was a bloody knife;
I threw her in the river,
Which was a dreadful sight.
My father often told me
That money would set me free,
If I would murder that dear little girl
Whose name was Rose Connelly.

And now he sits in his cottage door,
A-wiping his weeping eye.
And now he waits for his own dear son,
Upon the scaffold high.
My race is run beneath the sun,
Cruel Hell's now waiting for me,
For I have murdered my own true love,
Whose name was Rose Connelly.

Knoxville Girl

D   D7
I met a little girl in Knoxville,
  G   D
A town you all know well,

And every Sunday evening
      E7   A7
Out in her home I'd dwell;
   D   D7
We went to take an evening walk
  G   D
About a mile from town,

I picked a stick up off of the ground
     A7   D
And knocked that fair girl down.

She fell down on her bended knees,
For mercy she did cry;
Oh, Willy dear, don't kill me here,
I'm unprepared to die;
She never spoke one other word;
I only beat her more,
Until the ground around me
Within her blood did flow.

I taken her by her golden curls,
I drug her 'round and 'round,
Throwing her into the river
That flows through Knoxville town;
Go there, go there, you Knoxville girl,
Got dark and rolling eyes,
Go there, go there, you Knoxville girl,
You can never be my bride.

Starting back to Knoxville,
Got there about midnight,
My mother she was worried
And woke up in a fright,
Saying, son, oh son, what have you done
To bloody your clothes so?
I told my anxious mother,
Been bleeding at my nose.

Called for me a candle
To light myself to bed,
Called for me a handkerchief
To bind my aching head,
Rolled and tumbled the whole night through
As troubles were for me
Like flames of Hell around my bed
And in my eyes could see.

They carried me down to Knoxville,
They put me in a cell,
My friends all tried to get me out,
But none could go my bail;
I'm here to waste my life away
Down in this dirty old jail,
Because I murdered that Knoxville girl,
The girl I loved so well.

The Two Sisters
Child Ballad 10

D   G   D
There was an old woman lived on the seashore,
G   D   Bm
Bow and balance to me,
      G   D
There was an old woman lived on the seashore,
      G   A7
Her number of daughters one, two, three, four,
    D A7 D   G   D A7   D
And I'll be true to my love, if my love will be true to me.

There was a young man came courtin' them then,
Bow and balance to me,
There was a young man came courtin' them then,
And the oldest one got struck on him,
And I'll be true to my love, if my love will be true to me.

He bought the youngest a beaver hat, . . . etc.
And the oldest one thought hard of that . . . etc.

"O sister, O sister, let's walk the seashore,
And see the ships as they sail o'er."

While these two sisters were walking the shore,
The oldest pushed the youngest o'er.

"O sister, O sister, please lend me your hand,
And you may have Willie and all of his land."

"I never, I never will lend you my hand,
But I'll have Willie and all of his land."

Sometimes she sank and sometimes she swam,
Until she came to the old mill dam.

The miller, he got his fishing hook
And fished the maiden out of the brook.

"O miller, O miller, here's five gold rings,
To push the maiden in again.

The miller received those five gold rings
And pushed the maiden in again.

The sister was hung on the gallows high,
And the miller was burned at the stake nearby.

Tom Dooley

G
Hang down your head Tom Dooley,

Hang down your head and cry,
          D
Killed poor Laura Foster,
          G
You know you're bound to die.

You took her on the hillside
As God almighty knows,
You took her on the hillside
And there you hid her clothes.

You took her by the roadside
Where you begged to be excused,
You took her by the roadside
Where there you hid her shoes.

You took her on the hillside
To make her your wife,
You took her on the hillside
Where there you took her life.

Take down my old violin
And play it all you please,
At this time tomorrow
It'll be no use to me.

I dug a grave four feet long,
I dug it three feet deep,
And throwed the cold clay o'er her
And tramped it with my feet.

This world and one more then
Where do you reckon I'd be,
If it hadn't been for Grayson
I'd-a-been in Tennessee.

Omie Wise

      D   G
I'll tell you a story about Omie Wise,
      A7   D
And how she was deluded by John Lewis' lies.

He promised to meet her at Adamses' Springs,
Some money he'd bring her and other fine things.

He gave her no money, but flattered the case,
Saying, "We will get married, 'twill be no disgrace."

She got up behind him, away they did go,
Down to the river where the fast waters flow.

"John Lewis, John Lewis, please tell me your mind,
Do you mean to marry me or leave me behind?"

"Little Omie, Little Omie, I'll tell you my mind,
My mind is to drown you and leave you behind."

He beat her and he banged her 'til she could hardly go,
Then he threw her in the river where the fast waters flow.

Two little boys went fishing just at the break of dawn,
They saw little Omie come floating along.

They arrested John Lewis, they arrested him today,
They buried little Omie down in the cold clay.

"My name it is John Lewis, my name I'll never deny,
I murdered little Omie, now I'm condemned to die."

"Go hang me, go kill me, for I am the man,
Who murdered little Omie down by the mill dam."

Lily Of The West

     Am   C   G
When first I came to Louisville,
              F   Am
  some pleasure there to find.
  C   G   F   C   Am
A damsel there from Lexington was pleasing to my mind.
   F   G   Am
Her rosy cheeks, her ruby lips like arrows pierced my breast
                       C   G   F   Am
And the name she bore was Flora the Lily of the West.

I courted lovely Flora some pleasure there to find
But she turned unto another man
    which sore distressed my mind
She robbed me of my liberty, deprived me of my rest
Then go my lovely Flora, the Lily of the West.

Way down in yonder shady grove, a man of high degree,
Conversing with my Flora there,
    it seemed so strange to me
And the answer that she gave to him it sore did me oppress
I was betrayed by Flora, the Lily of the West.

I stepped up to my rival, my dagger in my hand
I siezed him by the collar and I boldly bade him stand
Being mad to desperation I pierced him in the breast
Then go my lovely Flora, the Lily of the West.

I had to stand my trial, I had to make my plea
They placed me in a criminal box and
    then commenced on me,
Although she swore my life away, deprived me of my rest,
Still I love my faithless Flora, the Lily of the West.

Matty Groves

Child Ballad 81

    G
One high, one high, one high holiday,
                       D7
On the very first day of the year,
    G
When little Matty Groves to the church did go,
    C   G
Some holy words to hear.

The first to come in was the lily white,
The next was the pink and the blue;
The next to come was Lord Arnold's wife,
The flower amongst the few.

She stepped up to Matty Groves,
Her eyes so low cast down,
Saying, "Pray come spend the night with me
As you pass through the town."

"I dare not come, I cannot come,
I dare not for my life,
For I see by the ring that you wear on your finger
That you are Lord Arnold's wife."

"So what if I am Lord Arnold's wife,
Lord Arnold ain't at home;
He's off in some foreign country,
A-learning the tailors' trade."

She looked at him, he looked at her,
The like had never been done.
Lord Arnold's foot-page swore to tell
Before the rising sun.

He run till he come to the broad river bank,
He bowed his breast and he swum,
He swum till he come to the other side,
Then he buckled on his shoes and he run.

He run till he came to Lord Arnold's castle,
And he tingled at the ring,
And nobody there but Arnold himself,
To rise and bid him come in.

"What news, what news, my little page,
What news have you to tell?
Have any of my castle walls burned down
Or any of my works undone?"

"No, none of your castle walls burned down,
None of your works undone.
But little Matty Groves in the North Scotland
A-bed with the gaily one."

He run till he come to the broad river bank,
He bowed his breast and he swum.
He swum till he come to the other side,
Then he buckled on his shoes and he run.

It's there they lay a-huggin' and a-kissin',
And it's there they fell asleep;
And when they woke on the next day's morn,
Lord Arnold stood at their bed feet.

Saying, "How do you like my clean white pillow,
And how do you like my sheets?
And how do you like my fair young bride
That lies in your arms asleep?"

"Pretty well do I like your clean white pillow,
Pretty well do I like your sheets.
Much better do I like your fair young bride,
Which lies in my arms asleep."

"Rise up, rise up, now, Matty Groves,
Put on your clothes just as quick as you can;
Never let it be said in the North Scotland,
I slew a naked man."

"I can not rise, I dare not rise,
I dare not for my life;
For you have got two bitter swords,
And I have nary a knife."

"Yes, I have got two bitter swords,
They cost me deep in the purse;
And you shall have the very best one,
And I will take the worst."

"And you will strike the first blow,
Strike it like a man,
And I will strike the next blow,
And I'll kill you if I can."

The first blow Little Matty struck,
It hurt Lord Arnold sore,
Lord Arnold struck the next blow,
Little Matty struck no more.

He took his wife by her lily-white hand,
And put her on his knee;
Saying, "Who do you like the best now,
Little Matty Groves or me?"

She lifted Matty's dying face,
And kissed from cheek to chin;
Said, "I love Matty Groves and his gour of blood,
More than Arnold and all of his kin."

So he took his wife by her lily-white hand,
And led her out in the hall;
And with his sword he cut off her head
And he kicked it against the wall.

Pretty Polly

Em
I courted pretty Polly the live long night,
 G
I courted pretty Polly the live long night,
  Em   Am   Em
And left her next morning before it was light.

"Pretty Polly, pretty Polly, come go along with me, (twice)
Before we get married some pleasures to see."

She jumped on behind him and away they did go, (twice)
Over the hills and the valley below.

Then went a little farther and what did they spy, (twice)
But a new dug grave with a spade lying by.

"Oh Willie, oh Willie, I'm afraid of your ways, (twice)
I'm afraid you will lead my poor body astray."

"Pretty Polly, pretty Polly,
   you've guessed about right, (twice)
I dug on your grave for the most of last night."

He throwed her on the ground
   and she broke into tears, (twice)
She throwed her arms around him and trembled with fear.

"There's no time to talk now,
   there's no time to stand," (twice)
He drew out his knife all in his right hand.

He stabbed her in the heart
   and the blood it did flow, (twice)
And into the grave pretty Polly did go.

He threw on some dirt and he started for home, (twice)
Leaving none back behind but the wild birds to moan.

Now a debt to the devil, Willie must pay, (twice)
For killing pretty Polly and running away.

Deep Water

E   A
You promised to meet me down by the spring,
  B7   E
Some money you'd bring me or some other fine thing,
                                      A
No money, no money, to flatter the case,
  B7   E
We'll have to be married so there'll be no disgrace.

He said, "Jump up beside me and away we will ride,
To yonder fair country and I'll make you my bride."
She jumped up beside him and away they did go,
Till they came to the deep water
    where the Doss River flows.

"Now get you down, Romy, while I tell you my mind,
My mind is to drown you and leave you behind."
"Have pity, have pity, and spare me my life,
And I will deny you and not be your wife."

But he kicked her and cuffed her to the worst understand,
And he threw her in the deep water
    that flows through the land,
And he jumped on his stallion, rode away with great speed,
Saying, "Fare you well, Romy,
    from your bondage I'm freed."

Then Romy was missin', no more to be found,
The people to seek her were all gathered 'round,
Then up spoke her mother, in her words was a sting,
No one but George Lewis could have done such a thing.

They trailed him up to Elk River to Dutch Charley's Bend,
They found him in prison for killing a man,
Go hang him, go hang him, was the judge's command,
And throw him in the deep water
    that flows through the land.

JUG OF PUNCH

Songs of the joys and perils of drink....

Landlord Fill The Flowing Bowl

```
G                        D7        G
Landlord fill the flowing bowl, until it doth run over.
                         D7        G
Landlord fill the flowing bowl, until it doth run over.
                  C
For tonight we'll merry, merry be,
D7        G
For tonight we'll merry, merry be.
                  C
For tonight we'll merry, merry be,
      D7        G
      tomorrow we'll be sober.
```

The man who drinks cold water pure,
   and goes to bed quite sober, (twice)
Falls as the leaves do fall, (twice)
Falls as the leaves do fall, so early in October.

The man who drinks good whiskey clear
   and goes to bed right mellow, (twice)
Lives as he ought to live, (twice)
Lives as he ought to live, and dies a jolly good fellow.

But he who drinks just what he likes,
   and getteth half seas over, (twice)
Lives until he dies, (twice)
Lives until he dies, and then lies down in clover.

The little girl who gets a kiss,
   and runs and tells her mother, (twice)
Does a very foolish thing, (twice)
Does a very foolish thing, and seldom gets another.

Moonshiner

```
      G                    C
I've been a moonshiner for seventeen years,
      D7                             G
I've spent all my money on whiskey and beer,
                          C
I'll go up some holler, I'll put up my still,
      D7                         G
I'll make you one gallon for a two-dollar bill.
```

Chorus:

```
      G                         C
I'm a rambler, I'm a gambler, I'm a long ways from home,
      D7                      G
And if you don't like me, well leave me alone.
                          C
I'll eat when I'm hungry, I'll drink when I'm dry
      D7                              G
And if moonshine don't kill me, I'll live till I die.
```

I'll go to some grocery and drink with my friends,
No women to follow to see what I spend,
God bless those pretty women, I wish they were mine,
Their breath smells as sweet as the dew on the vine.

I'll eat when I'm hungry, I'll drink when I'm dry,
If moonshine don't kill me, I'll live till I die,
God bless those moonshiners, I wish they were mine,
Their breath smells as sweet as the good old moonshine.

For work I'm too lazy, beginnin's too slow,
Train robbin's too dangerous so to campin' I'll go,
Life is a bottle and I'm but a dram,
When a bottle is empty it ain't worth a damn.

It's grub when you're hungry and booze when you're dry,
Pretty women when you're lonely
   and religion when you die,
Life is a bottle and I'm but a dram,
When the bottle is empty it ain't worth a damn.

Real Old Mountain Dew

```
      E              A
Let grass grow, and waters flow,
      E              B7
In a free and easy way,
      E                        A
But give me enough of the fine old stuff
      E        B7      E
That's made near Galway Bay.
```

```
Oh, peelers all, from Dongegal.
                       C#m
Galway and E-Trim too—
B7    E                          A
We'll give them the slip and we'll take a sip
      E          B7   E
Of the real old Mountain Dew.
```

At the foot of the hill there's a neat little still
Where the smoke curls up to the sky.
By the smoke and the smell you can plainly tell
That there's whiskey brewing nearby.
For it fills the air with odor rare,
And betwixt both me and you,
When home you roll you can take a bowl
Or a bucket of the mountain dew.

Now learned men who use the pen
Who've wrote your praises high,
This sweet 'pocheen' (potion) from Ireland's green
Distilled from wheat and rye.
Throw away your pills—it'll cure all ills
Of pagan or Christian, Jew.
Take off your coat and free your throat
With the real old Mountain Dew.

The Jug Of Punch

```
        D
As I was sitting with a jug and spoon,
      A7          D
On one fine morn in the month of June.
                Em
A birdie sang on an ivy bunch,
        D    G      A7   D
And the song he sang was "The Jug Of Punch."
```

First Chorus:

```
A7    D
Too ra loo ra loo too ra loo ra loo,
       A7           D
Too ra loo ra loo too ra loo ra loo.
                Em
A birdie sang on an ivy bunch,
        D    G          A
And the song he sang was "The Jug Of Punch."
```

What more diversion can a man desire?
Than to court a girl by a neat turf fire?
A Kerry pipen and the crack and crunch,
And on the table a jug of punch.

Second chorus:
Too ra loo ra loo too ra loo ra loo, (twice)
A Kerry pipin and the crack and crunch,
And on the table a jug of punch.

All ye mortal lords drink your nectar wine,
And the quality folks drink their claret fine.
I'll give them all the grapes in the bunch,
For a jolly pull at the jug of punch.
Too ra loo, etc.

Oh! But when I'm dead and in my grave,
No costly tombstone I will crave.
Just lay me down in my native peat,
With a jug of punch at my head and feet.
Too ra loo, etc.

The learned doctors with all their art,
Cannot cure a depression once it's on the heart.
Even a cripple forgets his hunch,
When he's safe outside of a jug of punch.
Too ra loo, etc.

If I drink too much, well my money's my own,
And them as don't like me can leave me alone.
But I'll tune my fiddle and I'll rosin my bow,
And I'll be welcome wherever I go.
Too ra loo, etc.

Kentucky Bootlegger

```
    G                          D       G
Come all you booze buyers, if you want to hear,
                              C      G
About the kind of booze they sell around here;
        C              G
Made way back in the swamps and hills,
                      D      G
Where there's plenty of moonshine stills.
```

Some moonshiners make pretty good stuff.
Bootleggers use it to mix it up;
He'll make one gallon, well he'll make two,
If you don't mind boys, he'll get the best of you.

One drop will make a rabbit whip a fool dog.
And a taste will make a rabbit whip a wild hog;
It'll make a toad spit in a black snake's face,
Make a hard shell preacher fall from grace.

A lamb will lay down with a lion
After drinking that old moonshine,
So throw back your head and take a little drink,
And for a week you won't be able to think.

The moonshiners are getting mighty thick,
And the bootleggers are getting mighty slick;
If they keep on bagging, they better beware,
They'll be selling each other I do declare.

Beautiful Brown Eyes

Chorus:

```
C                 F
Beautiful, beautiful brown eyes,
C                   G7
Beautiful, beautiful brown eyes,
C                 F
Beautiful, beautiful brown eyes,
   G7            C
I'll never see blue eyes again.
```

Willie, my darling, I love you,
Love you with all of my heart;
Tomorrow we were to be married,
But liquor has kept us apart.

I staggered into the barroom,
I fell down on the floor,
And the very last words that I uttered,
"I'll never get drunk any more."

Seven long years I've been married,
I wish I was single again,
A woman don't know half her troubles
Until she has married a man.

Johnson's Ale

G
Five jolly rogues of a feather,
D7   G
Walked o'er the hill together
     D
And who could be so bold
A7   D   A7 D   D7
As to join our jovial crew?
         G
And they called for their pots of beer and their sherry
     D
To help them o'er the hills so merry,
    C   G
To help them o'er the hills so merry.

Chorus:

     D7   G
When Johnson's ale was new, my boys,
         D7   G
When Johnson's ale was new.

Now the first to come in was the dyer,
And he sat down by the fire.
And who could be so bold
As to join our jovial crew?
And the landlady told him straight to his face,
That the chimney corner was his own place,
And there he could sit and dye his old face.

The next to come in was the hatter,
And no man could be fatter.
And who could be so bold
As to join our jovial crew?
And he threw his big hat down on the ground;
He swore all men should stand a-crowned,
For that would pay for the drinks all around.

The next to come in was the mason;
His hammer it needed a facing
And who could be so bold
As to join our jovial crew?
And he threw his hammer against the wall,
He swore all cellars and chimneys should fall,
For that would give work to the masons all.

The next to come in was the sailor,
With his marlin spike and his heaver.
And who could be so bold
As to join our jovial crew?
And he told the landlord straight to his face,
He thought it was time to splice the main brace,
With his tarpaulin hat he was a hard case.

Now the last to come in was the soldier,
With his flintlock on his shoulder.
And who could be so bold
As to join our jovial crew?
And the landlady's daughter she came in,
And he kissed her o'er from cheek to chin,
Then the pots of beer come a rolling in.

Brandy Leave Me Alone

        F
Oh, Brandy leave me alone.
               Gm
Oh, Brandy leave me alone.
               C7
Oh, Brandy leave me alone
               F
Remember I must go home.

Oh Brandy you broke my heart (twice)
Oh Brandy leave me alone
Remember I must go home.

Whiskey Johnny

Dm   Am Dm Am
Whiskey is the life of man,
Dm Am Dm Am
Whiskey, Johnny,
     Dm   Am   Dm   Am
Oh, I'll drink whiskey while I can,
     Dm   Am
Whiskey for my Johnny.

Oh whiskey straight and whiskey strong,
Give me some whiskey and I'll sing you a song.

Oh, whiskey makes me wear old clothes,
Whiskey gave me a broken nose.

Whiskey killed my poor old dad,
Whiskey drove my mother mad.

If whiskey comes too near my nose,
I tip it up and down she goes.

I had a gal and her name was Lize,
She puts whiskey in her pies.

My wife and I cannot agree,
She puts whiskey in her tea.

Here comes the cook with a whiskey can,
A glass of grog for every man.

A glass of grog for every man,
And a bottle full for the shantyman.

I drink it hot and I drink it cold,
I drink it new and I drink it old.

Finnegan's Wake

Am
Tim Finnegan lived in Walkin' Street
    G7
A gentle Irishman mighty odd,
 Am
He'd a beautiful brogue so rich and sweet
       F G7 C
And to rise in the world he carried a hod.
         Am
You see he'd a sort of the tipplin' way,
  C   Am
With a love for the liquor poor Tim was born,
  C   Am
To help him on with his work each day,
   F   G7 C
He'd a "drop o' the cray-thur" ev'ry morn.

Chorus:

Am   Em
Whack fol the da now, dance to your partner
Am   G7
Welt the floor your trotters shake
Am   Em
Wasn't it the truth I told you,
Am   F G7 C
Lots of fun at Finnegan's Wake.

One mornin' Tim was rather full,
His head felt heavy which made him shake,
He fell from a ladder, and he broke his skull,
And they carried him home his corpse to wake.
They rolled him up in a nice clean ship,
And laid him out upon the bed,
A gallon of whisky at his feet,
And a barrel of porter at his head.

His friends assembled at the Wake,
And Mrs. Finnegan called for lunch,
First they brought in tay, and cake,
Then pipes, tobacco, and whisky punch.
Biddy O'Brien began to cry,
Such a nice clean corpse did you ever see?
Tim Mavourneen why did you die?
Arrah hold your gob said Paddy McGhee.

Then Maggie O'Connor took up the job,
Oh Biddy says she, you're wrong I'm sure,
Biddy gave her a belt in the gob,
And left her sprawling on the floor.
Then the war did soon engage,
'Twas woman to woman, and man to man,
Shelelaigh law was all the rage,
And a row, and a ruction soon began.

Then Mickey Maloney raised his head,
When a noggin of whisky flew at him,
It missed and falling on the bed,
The liquor scattered over Tim.
Tim revives see how he rises,
Timothy rising from the bed,
Said, "Whirl your whisky around like blazes,
Thanum an dial do you think I'm dead?"

Tom Brown

  C
The King will take the Queen,
  G7   C
But the Queen will take the Knave,

And since we're in good company,
  F   G7
More liquor let us have.

Chorus:

     C   G7   C
Here's to you, Tom Brown, and to you me jolly soul,
G7   C
And to you with all me heart,
  G7   C
 and with you I'll take a quart,
   F   C   G7
With you I'll drink a drop or two before that we do part,
  C G7   F G7 C
Here's to you, Tom Brown, Here's to you, Tom Brown.

The Knave will take the ten,
But the ten will take the nine,
And since we're in good company,
Come let us have more wine.

The nine will take the eight,
But the eight will take the seven,
And since we're in good company,
We'll drink to past eleven.

The seven will take the six,
But the six will take the five,
And since we're in good company,
As sure as I'm alive.

The five will take the four,
But the four will take the trey,
And since we're in good company,
We'll drink to break of day.

The trey will take the deuce,
But the ace will take them all,
And since we're in good company,
We won't go home at all.

Four Nights Drunk

E
I came home the other night as drunk as I could be,
  A   E   B7   E
I saw a horse in the stable where my horse ought to be.

So I said to my wife, my pretty little wife,

   "Won't you tell me please,
A   E
What's this horse a-doin' here
      B7   E
  where my horse ought to be?"
         A   E
She said, "You darn fool, you drunken fool,
  B7   E
  can't you never see?
    A   E   B7   E
It's nothin' but a milk cow that your mother gave to me."

Well, I've travelled this wide world over,

   some crazy things I've saw,
    A   E   B7   E
But a saddle on a milk cow I never seen before.

I came home, etc.
I saw a hat on the table, etc.
So I said, etc.
What's this hat, etc.
But a bedpan marked size 7¾ I never seen before.

I saw a pair of pants in the closet, etc.
It's nothing but a tablecloth, etc.
But a tablecloth with a zipper I never seen before.

I saw a head on the pillow, etc.
It's nothing but a cabbage head, etc.
But a moustache on a cabbagehead I never seen before.

Rye Whiskey

   D
Rye whiskey, rye whiskey, rye whiskey I cry,
            G   D
If I don't get rye whiskey, I surely will die.

Way up on Clinch Mountain I wander alone,
I'm drunk as the devil, just leave me alone.

I'll eat when I'm hungry, I'll drink when I'm dry,
If a tree don't fall on me, I'll live till I die.

It's whiskey, rye whiskey, you're no friend to me,
You killed my poor daddy, Goddam you try me.

It's whiskey, you villain, you've been my downfall,
You've kicked me, you've cuffed me, but I love you for all.

Oh baby, oh baby, I've told you before,
To make me a pallet, I'll lay on the floor.

Your parents don't like me, they say I'm too poor,
They say I'm not worthy to enter your door.

They say I drink whiskey, but my money's my own,
And if they don't like me, they can leave me alone.

It's beefsteak when I'm hungry, rye whiskey when I'm dry,
Greenbacks when I'm hard-up, and heaven when I die.

If the ocean was whiskey, and I was a duck,
I would dive to the bottom to get one sweet sup.

But the ocean ain't whiskey, and I ain't no duck,
So I'll play Jack Of Diamonds and try to change my luck.

Jack Of Diamonds, Jack Of Diamonds, I know you of old,
You've robbed my poor pockets of silver and gold.

Away With Rum

        E   B7   E
We're coming, we're coming, our brave little band.
                       B7   E
On the right side of temp'rance we now take our stand.
   B7   E   B7   E
We don't use tobacco because we do think,
                 B7   E
That the people who use it are likely to drink!

Chorus:

E
Away, away with rum, by gum,
   B7   E
With rum by gum with rum, by gum.

Away, away with rum by gum;
   B7   E
The song of the Salvation Army.

We never eat cookies because they have yeast,
And one little bite makes a man like a beast.
Oh, can you imagine a sadder disgrace
Than a man in the gutter with crumbs on his face.

We never eat fruitcake because it has rum,
And one little slice puts a man on the bum.
Oh can you imagine a sorrier sight
Than a man eating fruitcake until he gets tight.

The Intoxicated Rat

      D
Well, the other night when I came home

As drunk as I could be,

I got tangled up in the old doormat,
  A7   D
Fell flat as I could be.

Well I had me a little old bottle of rum,
And I didn't have any more,
And the cap flew off when I went down,
And I spilled it on the floor.

Then the rat came out of his hiding place,
And he got that whiskey scent,
And he ran right up and he got a little shot,
Then back to his hole he went.

Well back to his hole he went,
Right back to his hole he went,
He ran right up and he got a little shot,
Then back to his hole he went.

Then the rat came out of his hole once more,
Sidled up to the rum on the floor;
He was a little bit shy, but he winked one eye
Then he got him a little bit more.

And he didn't go back to his hole that time,
But he stayed by the puddle of gin,
And he said, doggone my pop-eyed soul,
I'm gonna get drunk again.

Well, he washed his face with his front feet
And on his hind legs sat,
And with a twisted smile and a half closed eye
Said, "Where's that doggone cat."

And he didn't go back to his hole,
He said, "Doggone my soul,
I'm only a rat but a doggone cat
Can't run me back to my hole."

Well, his little old eyes begin to shine
As he lapped up more and more,
And it made me glad that I had stumbled
And spilled it on the floor.

And soon the puddle of rum was gone
And I didn't have any more gin,
And the little old rat was a-having a time
When the old tom-cat walked in.

Well the cat made a pass, and the rat made a dash,
His boldness faded thin;
Well the cat jumped over and the rat got sober,
Ran back to his hole again.

Ran back to his hole again,
Ran back to his hole again,
Well the cat jumped over and the rat got sober,
Ran back to his hole again.

The Calton Weaver

F   Dm   B♭   C7
I'm a weaver, a Calton weaver,
Dm Am   B♭   C
I'm a rash and a roving blade;
B♭   Dm
I've got siller in my pouches,
          B♭   C7
I'll gang and follow the roving trade.

Chorus:

  F   Dm   B♭   C7
O whisky, whisky, Nancy Whisky,
Dm   Am   C7   F
Whisky, whisky, Nancy, O.

As I came in by Glesca city,
Nancy Whisky I chanced to smell,
I gaed in, sat doon beside her,
Seven lang years I lo'ed her well.

The mair I kissed her the mair I lo'ed her,
The mair I kissed her the mair she smiled,
And I forgot my mither's teaching,
Nancy soon had me beguiled.

I woke early in the morning,
To slake my drouth it was my need;
I tried to rise but I wasna able,
Nancy had me by the heid.

"C'wa, landlady, whit's the lawin'?
Tell me whit there is to pay."
"Fifteen shillings is the reckoning,
Pay me quickly and go away."

As I went oot by Glesca city,
Nancy Whisky I chanced to smell;
I gaed in, drank four and sixpence,
A't was left was a crooked scale.

I'll gang back to the Calton weaving,
I'll surely mak' the shuttles fly;
I'll mak mair at the Calton weaving
Than ever I did in a roving way.

Come all ye weavers, Calton weavers,
A'ye weavers where e'er ye be;
Beware of Whisky, Nancy Whisky,
She'll ruin you as she ruined me.

Sweet Thing

F
What you gonna do when the liquor gives out,

   sweet thing?
F7
What you gonna do when the liquor gives out,
      F
  sweet thing?
F7
What you gonna do when the liquor gives out,
F
Stand around the corner with your mouth in a pout,
          C7   F
Sweet thing, sweet thing, sweet thing.

What you gonna do when your shoes give out,
  sweet thing? (twice)
When my shoes give out, I'm gonna quit the street,
Take a chair and put a fan at my feet,
Sweet thing, sweet thing, sweet thing.

What you gonna do when your chair gives out,
  sweet thing? (twice)
When I got no liquor, no chair, no shoes,
I'll lay 'cross the bed, with my head in the blues,
Sweet thing, sweet thing, sweet thing.

Slats on the bed go blamety-blam, in the mornin', (twice)
Slats on the bed go blamety-blam,
But I'll keep on a-sleepin' like I don't give a damn,
Sweet thing, sweet thing, sweet thing.

Drunk Last Night

G   D7
Drunk last night, drunk the night before,
                   G
Gonna get drunk tonight like I've never been drunk before,
  C   G
For when I'm drunk I'm as happy as can be,
  A7   D7
For I am a member of the Souse family.
    G
Singin' glorious, glorious,
D7   G
One keg of beer for the four of us;
   C   G
Sing glory be to God that there are no more of us,
  A7   D7   G
For one of us could drink it all alone.
    D7   G
All alone (damn near), all alone (damn near),
C   G
Glory be to God that there are no more of us,
  A7   D7   G
For one of us could drink it all alone.

Vive La Compagnie (Vive l'Amour)

    G
Let every good fellow now fill up his glass
      D7   G
Vive la compagnie
                 Am7
And drink to the health of our glorious class
    D7   G
Vive la compagnie.

Chorus:

G
Vive la, vive la, vive l'amour,
D   G
Vive la, vive la, vive l'amour,
Em   Am   D7   G
Vive l'amour, Vive l'amour, vive la compagnie.

Now let every married man drink to his wife,
Vive, etc.
The joy of his bosom and plague of his life.
Vive, etc.

Come fill up your glasses, I'll give you a toast,
A health to our dear friend, our kind worthy host.

Since all with good humor I've toasted so free,
I hope it will please you to drink now with me.

Let every good fellow now join in a song,
Success to each other and pass it along.

Take A Drink On Me

A
Now, what did you do with the gun in your hand,
  D
You give it to a rounder and he shot a good man,
  E7   A
Oh, Lord, honey, take a drink on me.

Chorus:

A
Take a drink on me, take a drink on me,
D
All you rounders, take a drink on me,
E7   A
Oh, Lord, honey, take a drink on me.

If you keep on stalling, you'll make me think
Your daddy was a monkey and mama was an ape,
Oh, Lord, honey, take a drink on me.

You see that gal with a hobble on,
She's good looking just as sure as you're born.
Oh, Lord, honey, take a drink on me.

Little Brown Jug

Joseph E. Winner

```
      G            G
My wife and I live all alone,
    D7             G
In a little brown hut we call our own;
                C
She loves gin and I love rum,
    D7                G
Oh, don't you know that we have fun?
```

Chorus:

```
          C
Ha, ha, ha, you and me,
D7              G
Little brown jug don't I love thee?
          C
Ha, ha, ha, you and me,
D7              G
Little brown jug don't I love thee?
```

'Tis you who makes my friends, my foes,
'Tis you who makes me wear old clothes,
But here you are so near my nose,
So tip her up and down she goes.

When I go toiling on my farm,
Little brown jug under my arm,
Place her under a shady tree,
Little brown jug, don't I love thee?

I lay in the shade of a tree,
Little brown jug in the shade of me,
I raise her up and give a pull,
Little brown jug's about half full.

Crossed the creek on a hollow log,
Me and the wife and the little brown dog;
The wife and the dog fell in kerplunk,
But I held on to the little brown jug.

One day when I went out to my barn,
Little brown jug under my arm,
Tripped me toe and down I fell,
Broke that little jug all to hell.

If I had a cow that gave such milk,
I'd dress her in the finest silk,
Feed her on the choicest hay,
And milk her forty times a day.

I bought a cow from farmer Jones,
And she was nothing but skin and bones;
I fed her up as fine as silk,
She jumped the fence and strained her milk.

When I die, don't bury me at all,
Just pickle my bones in alcohol;
Put a bottle o' booze at my head and feet,
And then I know that I will keep!

If all the folks in Adam's race
Were gathered together in one place
Then I'd prepare to shed a tear
Before I'd part with you, my dear.

The rose is red, my nose is too,
The violet's blue, and so are you.
And I guess, before I stop,
I'd better take another drop!

Mountain Dew

```
        G
There's a big hollow tree down the road here from me,
            C               G
Where you lay down a dollar or two.
```

You stroll 'round the bend and you come back again.
```
                    D7        G
There's a jug full of good old mountain dew.
```

Chorus:

```
                         G7
They call it that old mountain dew,
        C               G
And them that refuse it are few.
```

You may go 'round the bend,

```
But you'll come back again
                D7        G
For that good old mountain dew.
```

My uncle Nort, he's sawed-off and short,
He measures about four-foot two,
But he thinks he's a giant when you give him a pint
Of that good old mountain dew.

Well, my old aunt June bought some brand-new perfume,
It had such a sweet smellin' pew.
But to her surprise when she had it analyzed
It was nothin' but good old mountain dew.

Well, the preacher rode by with his head histed high,
Said his wife had been down with the flu.
And he thought that I ort just to seel him a quart
Of that good old mountain dew.

Well, my brother Bill's got a still on the hill
Where he runs off a gallon or two.
The buzzards in the sky get so drunk they can't fly
From smellin' that good old mountain dew.

Chevaliers De La Table Ronde
(Let Us Drink Knights Of The Round Table)

French

     F
Chevaliers de la table ronde,
    C7   F
Goutons voir si le vin est bon.

Chevaliers de la table ronde,
    C7   F
Goutons voir si le vin est bon.
    B♭
Goutons voir, oui, oui, oui,
    F
Goutons voir, non, non, non,
    C7   F
Goutons voir si le vin est bon.
    B♭
Goutons voir, oui, oui, oui,
    F
Goutons voir, non, non, non,
    C7   F
Goutons voir si le vin est bon.

S'il est bon, s'il est agréable,
J'en boirai jusqu'à mon plaisir.   (twice)
J'en boirai, oui, oui, oui,
J'en boirai, non, non, non,   (twice)
J'en boirai jusqu'a mon plaisir.

J'en boirai cinq ou six bouteilles,
Une femme sur les genoux, etc.
Une femme, oui, etc.

Toc, toc, toc, on frappe à la porte,
Je crois bien que c'est son mari, etc.
Je crois bien, oui, etc.

Si c'est lui, que le diable l'emporte,
Car il vient troubler mon plaisir, etc.
Car il vient, oui, etc.

Si je meurs, je veux qu'on m'enterre,
Dans la cave où i ly a du bon vin, etc.
Dans la cave, oui, etc.

Et les quatre plus grands ivrognes,
Porteront les quat' coins du drap, etc.
Porteront, oui, etc.

Les deux pieds contre la muraille,
Et la tête sous le robinet, etc.
Et la tête, oui, etc.

Sur ma tombe je veux qu'on inscrive,
"Içi git le roi des bouveurs." etc.
Içi git, oui, etc.

La morale de cette histoire,
C'est à boire avant de mourir, etc.
C'est à boire, oui, etc.

Singable Translation:

Let us drink knights of the round table,
Let us see if the wine is good, etc.

If it's good and if it is pleasant,
I will drink it for pleasure sweet, etc.

I will drink down five or six bottles,
With a girl sitting on my knee, etc.

Rap, rap, rap, on the door a-tapping,
I suspect that it is her spouse, etc.

If it is, then the devil sent him,
To disturb me in pleasure sweet, etc.

When I die let me then be buried,
In a cave that is full of wine, etc.

Let the world's four biggest drunkards,
Transport me in my black shroud, etc.

My two feet up on a partition,
And my head right beneath the tap, etc.

On my tombstone I would have written,
"Here asleep lies the king of drunks." etc.

Now the moral of this long story,
Is to drink while you're still alive, etc.

THERE AIN'T NO BUGS ON ME!

Fun and games and fancy nonsense....

Dunderbeck

G
Oh, Dunderbeck, oh Dunderbeck,
 D7   G
How could you be so mean,

To ever have invented
 A7   D
The sausage meat machine?
 C   G
Now long-tailed rats and pussy-cats
 Am   D7
Will never more be seen,
 G
They'll all be ground to sausage meat
 D7   G
In Dunderbeck's machine.

One day a little fat boy came
Walking in the store,
He bought a pound of sausages
And laid them on the floor.
Then he began to whistle,
He whistled up a tune,
The sausages, they jumped, they barked,
They danced 'round the room. Bang!

One day the thing got busted,
The darn thing wouldn't go,
And Dunderbeck he crawled inside
To see what made it so.
His wife came walking in just then,
From shopping in the street,
She brushed against the starting rod
And Dunderbeck was meat! Bang!

Sipping Cider Through A Straw

         C
The prettiest girl (the prettiest girl),
 G7
I ever saw (I ever saw),

Was sippin' ci- (was sippin' ci-)
         C
Der through a straw (der through a straw).
         C7 F
The prettiest girl I ever saw
 G7   C
Was sipping cider through a straw.

I told that gal (I told that gal),
I didn't see how (I didn't see how),
She sipped that ci- (she sipped that ci-)
Der through a straw (der through a straw),
I told that gal I didn't see how,
She sipped that cider through a straw.

Then cheek to cheek,
And jaw to jaw,
We sipped that ci-
Der through a straw.

And now and then
The straw would slip,
And I'd sip some ci-
Der from her lip.

And now I've got
A mother-in-law
From sipping ci-
Der through a straw.

Chewing Gum

F   C7
Mama sent me to the spring,
         F
She told me not to stay,
         C7
Fell in love with a pretty little girl,
         F
Could not get away.

Chorus:

F   C7   F
Chawing chewing gum, chewing chawing gum,
         C7   F
Chawing chewing gum, chewing chawing gum.

First she gave me peaches nice,
Then she gave me pears,
Next she gave me 50 cents,
She kissed me on the stairs.

I wouldn't have a lawyer,
Now here's the reason why,
Every time he opens his mouth,
He tells a great big lie.

I wouldn't have a doctor,
Now here's the reason why,
He rides all over the country,
A-making the people die.

I took my girl to the church last night,
And what do you reckon she done,
She walked right up to the preacher's face
And chawed her chewing gum.

Mama don't 'low me to whistle,
Poppa don't 'low me to sing,
They don't want me to marry,
I'll marry just the same.

Once There Were Three Fishermen

```
F                    C7
Once there were three fishermen,
                         F
Once there were three fishermen.
```

Fisher, fisher, men, men, men,

Fisher, fisher, men, men, men,
```
                           C7  F
Once there were three fishermen.
```

The first one's name was Abraham,
The first one's name was Abraham,
Abra, Abra, ham, ham, ham,
Abra, Abra, ham, ham, ham,
The first one's name was Abraham.

The second one's name was Isaac.
Isey, Isey, ack, ack, ack.

The third one's name was Jacob.
Jakey, Jakey, cub, cub, cub.

They all sailed up to Jericho.
Jerry, Jerry, cho, cho, cho.

Instead of going to Amsterdam.
Amster, Amster, sh, sh, sh.

Oh, do not say that naughty word.
Naughty, naughty, word, word, word.

I think I'll say it anyhow.
Any, any, how, how, how.

Instead of going to Amsterdam.
Amster, amster, dam, dam, dam.

(Some evil-hearted souls sing):
They walked along a precipice, etc.
This is how we finish it, etc.

John Jacob Jingleheimer Schmidt

```
F           Bb
John Jacob Jingleheimer Schmidt
C7                    F
His name is my name, too.
```

Whenever we go out,
```
     Bb
The people always shout:
C7                    F
"John Jacob Jingleheimer Schmidt!"
G7
Dah, dah, dah, dah, dah, dah, dah.
```


Old Dan Tucker

Dan Emmett

```
     G
Now old Dan Tucker's a fine old man,
                    D7
Washed his face in a fryin' pan,
G
Combed his head with a wagon wheel,
                            D7
And died with a toothache in his heel.
```

Chorus:
```
G              C
Get out the way, old Dan Tucker,
D7             G
You're too late to get your supper.
                  C
Get out the way old Dan Tucker,
D7             G
You're too late to get your supper.
```

Now old Dan Tucker is come to town,
Riding a billy goat—leading a hound,
Hound dog bark and the billy goat jump,
Landed Dan Tucker on top of the stump.

Now old Dan Tucker he got drunk,
Fell in the fire and kicked up a chunk,
Red hot coal got in his shoe,
And oh my lawd how the ashes flew.

Now old Dan Tucker is come to town,
Swinging the ladies round and round,
First to the right and then to the left,
Then to the girl that he loves best.

Polly Wolly Doodle

```
     G
Oh I went down South for to see my Sal,
                             D7
Sing polly wolly doodle all the day,
```

My Sal she is a spunky gal,
```
                          G
Sing polly wolly doodle all the day.
```

Chorus:
```
G
Fare thee well, fare thee well,
                        D7
Fare thee well my fairy fay,
```

For I'm goin' to Lou'siana for to see my Susianna,
```
                              G
Singing polly wolly doodle all the day.
```

Oh my Sal she is a maiden fair, etc.
With curly eyes and laughing hair, etc.

Peter Gray

```
     Dm
Once on a time there lived a man,
     F      A7  Dm
His name was Peter Gray;
```

He lived way down in that there town
```
               A        Dm
Called Penn-syl-va-ni-a.
```

Chorus:
```
Dm
Blow ye winds of morning,
F                    A
Blow ye winds heigh-o,
Dm
Blow ye winds of morning,
A     A7   Dm
Blow, blow, blow.
```

Now Peter fell in love all with
A nice young girl,
The first two letters of her name
Were Lucy, Annie, Pearl.

Just as they were gwine to wed
Her father did say no;
And quin-ci-cont-ly she was sent
Beyond the Oh-i-o.

When Peter heard his love was lost,
He knew not what to say,
He'd half a mind to jump into
The Susquehan-i-a.

But he went traveling to the west
For furs and other skins;
Till he was caught and scal-pi-ed
By blood-i In-ji-ins.

When Lucy-Annie heard the news,
She straightway took to bed,
And never did get up again
Until she di-i-ed.

You fathers all a warning take,
Each one as has a girl;
And think upon poor Peter Gray
And Lucy, Annie, Pearl.

Father's Whiskers

G
We have a dear old daddy
A7
For whom we daily pray,
D7
He's got a set of whiskers,
G
They're always in the way.

Chorus:

G
Oh, they're always in the way,
A7
The cows eat them for hay,
D7
They hide the dirt on father's shirt,
G
They're always in the way.

Father had a strong back,
Now it's all caved in,
He stepped upon his whiskers
And walked up to his chin.

We have a dear old mother,
With him at night she sleeps,
She wakes up in the morning
Eating shredded wheat.

We have a dear old brother,
He has a Ford machine,
He uses father's whiskers
To strain the gasoline.

We have a dear old sister,
It really is a laugh,
She sprinkle's father's whiskers
As bath salts in her bath.

Father has a daughter,
Her name is Ella Mae,
She climbs up father's whiskers
And braids them all the way.

Around the supper table
We make a merry group,
Until dear father's whiskers
Get tangled in the soup.

Father fought in Flanders,
He wasn't killed, you see,
His whiskers looked like bushes
And fooled the enemy.

When father goes in swimming,
No bathing suit for him,
He ties his whiskers 'round his waist
And gaily plunges in.

Father in a tavern,
He likes his lager beer,
He pins a pretzel on his nose
To keep his whiskers clear.

A Horse Named Bill

Tune: *Dixie*

C
I had a horse, his name was Bill,
F   G7
And when he ran he couldn't stand still,
C
He ran away one day,
G7   C
And also I ran with him.

He ran so hard he couldn't stop.
He ran into a barber shop.
He fell exhausted with his teeth
In the barber's left shoulder.

O, I went out into the woods last year
To hunt for beer and not for deer
I am I ain't
A great sharpshooter.

At shooting birds I am a beaut.
There is no bird I cannot shoot
In the eye in the ear
In the finger.

In Frisco Bay there lives a whale
And she eats pork chops by the bale
By the hatbox, by the pillbox
By the hogshead, and schooner.

Her name in Lena, she is a peach
But don't leave food within her reach
Or babies or nursemaids
Or chocolate ice cream sodas.

She loves to laugh and when she smiles
You just see teeth for miles and miles
And tonsils and spareribs
And things too fierce to mention.

She knows no games so when she plays
She rolls her eyes for days and days
She vibrates and yodels
And breaks the Ten Commandments.

O, what can you do in a case like that
O, what can you do but stamp on your hat
Or on an eggshell or a toothbrush
Or anything that's helpless.

Clementine

E
In a cavern, in a canyon,
B7
Excavating for a mine,
E
Lived a miner, forty niner,
B7   E
And his daughter, Clementine.

Chorus:

E
Oh, my darling, Oh, my darling,
B7
Oh, my darling, Clementine,
E
You are lost and gone forever,
B7   E
Dreadful sorry, Clementine.

Light she was and, like a fairy,
And her shoes were number nine,
Herring boxes, without topses,
Sandals were for Clementine.

Drove she ducklings to the water,
Every morning just at nine,
Stubbed her toe upon a splinter,
Fell into the foaming brine.

Ruby lips above the water,
Blowing bubbles soft and fine,
But alas I was no swimmer,
So I lost my Clementine.

There's a churchyard, on the hillside,
Where the flowers grow and twine,
There grow roses, 'mongst the posies,
Fertilized by Clementine.

Around The Corner

          F   C7
Around the corner behind the tree
                        F
A sergeant major he said to me:

"Oh, how'd you like to marry me?
G7
"I would like to know,
        C7
"For every time I look in your eyes,
                    F
"I feel I'd like to go:

"Around the corner . . ."

There Was An Old Soldier

Tune: *Turkey In The Straw*

D   A7   D
There was an old soldier and he had a wooden leg,
                       E7   A7
He had no tobacco, no tobacco could he beg,
D   D7   G   Em
Another old soldier as sly as a fox,
D   A7
He always kept tobacco in his old tobacco box;
D   A7   D
He always kept tobacco in his old tobacco box.

Said the one old soldier, "Won't you give me a chew?"
Said the other old soldier, "I'll be hanged if I do,
Just save up your money and put away your rocks,
And you'll always have tobacco
     in your old tobacco box." (twice)

Well, the one old soldier he was feeling mighty bad,
He said, "I'll get even, I will, begad!"
He goes to a corner, takes a rifle from the peg,
And stabs the other soldier
     with a splinter from his leg. (twice)

Now there was an old hen and she had a wooden foot,
And she made her nest by the mulberry root,
She laid more eggs than any hen on the farm,
And another wooden leg
     wouldn't do her any harm. (twice)

The Hearse Song

    G
Did you ever think as a hearse rolls by,
               D7
That sooner or later you're going to die,
    G
With your boots a-swingin' from the back of a roan,
               D7   G
And the undertaker inscribin' your stone?

They'll take you out and lower you down,
And men with shovels will stand around;
They'll shovel in dirt and they'll throw in rocks,
And they won't give a damn if they break the box.

Oh, the worms crawl in, the worms crawl out,
They do right dress and they turn about;
Then each one takes a bite or two
Of what Washington used to call you.

Oh, your eyes drop out, and your teeth fall in,
And the worms crawl over your mouth and chin;
They bring all their friends, and their friends' friends, too,
And you're chewed all to hell
     when they're through with you.

Michael Finnigan

    G   D7   G
There was an old man named Michael Finnigan,
D7
He grew whiskers on his chin-i-gin,
    G   D7
The wind came up and blew them in a-gin,
D7   G
Poor old Michael Finnigan, begin a-g'in.

There was an old man named Michael Finnigan,
He got drunk through drinking ginigin,
That's how he wasted all his tinnigin,
Poor old Michael Finnigan, begin ag'in.

There was an old man named Michael Finnigan,
He grew fat and then grew thin ag'in,
Then he died, and had to begin ag'in,
Poor old Michael, please don't begin ag'in.

Whoa Back, Buck

D
Tom done buck and Bill won't pull,
               G
Papa gonna cut that other little bull.
D
Whoa back, Buck, an' gee, by the Lamb!
D7   A7   D
Who made the back-band? Whoa, goddam!

Chorus:

D   A7
Whoa, Buck, an' gee by the Lamb!
D7   A7   D
Who made the back-band? Whoa, goddam!

Eighteen, nineteen, twenty years ago,
I taken Sal to the party-o, (twice)
Wouldn't let her dance but a set or so.

Me an' my gal come walkin' down the road,
Wind from her feet knockin' "Sugar in the Gourd."
Sugar in the gourd and the gourd on the ground,
Want to get the sugar gotta roll the gourd around.

Chicken in the bread-tray, mighty good stuff,
Mama cook him chicken an' he never get enough,
Jawbone eat an'-a jawbone talk,
Jawbone eat with a knife an' fawk.

A Capital Ship

```
     C
A capital ship for an ocean trip
         G7            C
Was the Walloping Window Blind.
     D7           G
No wind that blew dismayed her crew,
   D7              G
Or troubled the captain's mind.
G7 C
The man at the wheel was made to feel
     G7
Contempt for the wildest blow-ow-ow,
        C
Tho it oft appeared when the gale had cleared,
        G7           C
He had been in his bunk below.
```

Chorus:

```
G7 C                    F        C
Oh, blow ye winds, heigh-ho, a-roving I will go,

I'll stay no more on England's shore,
   G7
So let the music play-ay-ay.
   C                    F        C
I'm off for the morning train, I'll cross the raging main,

I'm off for my love with a boxing glove,
       G7        C
Ten thousand miles away.
```

The bo'sun's mate was very sedate,
Yet fond of amusement, too.
He played hop-scotch with the starboard watch,
While the captain tickled the crew.
The gunner we had was apparently mad,
For he sat on the after ra-ai-ail,
And fired salutes with the captain's boots
In the teeth of a booming gale.

The captain sat on the commodore's hat,
And dined in a royal way
Off pickles and figs, and little roast pigs,
And gunnery bread each day.
The cook was Dutch and behaved as such,
For the diet he served the crew-ew-ew,
Was a couple of tons of hot-cross buns
Served up with sugar and glue.

Then we all fell ill as mariners will
On a diet that's rough and crude;
And we shivered and shook as we dipped the cook
In a tub of his gluesome food.
All nautical pride we cast aside,
And we ran the vessel asho-o-ore
On the Gulliby Isles, where the poopoo smiles,
And the rubbily ubdugs roar.

Composed of sand was that favored land,
And trimmed with cinnamon straws,
And pink and blue was the pleasing hue
Of the tickle-toe-teaser's claws.
We sat on the edge of a sandy ledge,
And shot at the whistling bee-ee-ee,
While the ring-tailed bats wore waterproof hats
As they dipped in the shining sea.

On rugbug bark from dawn till dark
We dined till we all had grown
Uncommonly shrunk, when a Chinese junk
Came up from the Torrible Zone.
She was chubby and square, but we didn't much care,
So we cheerily put to sea-ee-ea,
And we left all the crew of the junk to chew
On the bark of the rugbug tree.

Cape Ann

```
      Bb
We hunted and we halloed
              Cm          F7
   and the first thing that we found
         Bb              Cm      F7
Was a barn in the meadow, and that we left behind.

Look ye there!
D      Gm  D           Gm  D
One said it was a barn, but the other said nay,
C    F  C    F
He said it was a meeting-house
            C7            F
   with the steeple blown away,
F7    Bb
Look ye there!
```

So we hunted and we halloed
    and the next thing we did find,
Was a frog in the mill pond, and that we left behind.
Look ye there!
One said it was a frog, but the other said nay;
He said it was a canary bird with its feathers washed away.
Look ye there!

The moon in the element, etc.
He said it was a Yankee cheese with one half cut away, etc.

The lighthouse in Cape Ann, etc.
He said it was a sugar loaf with the paper blown away, etc.

The owl in the olive bush, etc.
He said it was the Evil One, and we all three ran away, etc.

Oh, Susanna

```
    D                                     A7
I come from Alabama with a banjo on my knee,
    D                              A7    D
I'm goin' to Lou'siana, my true love for to see.
    D                                          A7
It rained all night the day I left, the weather it was dry,
        D                              A7      D
The sun so hot I froze to death, Susanna don't you cry.
```

Chorus:

```
G               D          A7
Oh, Susanna, Oh, don't you cry for me.
    D                              A7    D
I come from Alabama with a banjo on my knee.
```

I had a dream the other night,
When everything was still
I dreamed I saw Susanna
A-coming down the hill.

A red red rose was in her cheek,
A tear was in her eye
I said to her, Susanna girl,
Susanna don't you cry.

There Ain't No Bugs On Me

Tune: *It Ain't Gonna Rain*

```
E
Well, the night was dark and drizzly
                            B7
And the air was full of sleet,

The old man joined the Ku Klux
                      E
And ma she lost her sheet.
```

Chorus:

```
E
Oh, there ain't no bugs on me,
                         B7
There ain't no bugs on me,

There may be bugs on some of you mugs,
                                      E
But there ain't no bugs on me.
```

Well, the Juney bug comes in the month of June,
And the lightning bug in May,
Bed bug comes just any old time,
But they're not going to stay.

Billy Sunday is a preacher,
His church is always full,
The neighbors gather from miles around
To hear him shoot the bull.

Well, the monkey swings by the end of his tail,
And jumps from tree to tree,
There may be monkey in some of you guys,
But there ain't no monkey in me!

Alternate chorus:
Well, there ain't no flies on me,
There ain't no flies on me,
There may be flies on some of you guys,
But there ain't no flies on me.

Talking Nothin'

```
            G                       C
I looked from the hall to the top of the stair,
        D7                  G
Didn't see a man who wasn't there,
G7              C
Nothin', nothin', nothin' at all,
        D7    G
Nothin' at all all over the wall.
    C         D7  G C   D7  G
A predominance of vacancy.
```

There's a man on the corner standin' 'round,
Spreading nothin' all over the ground.
Heard some passin' people say
All that nothin' gets in the way.
Oughta be a law.

Went to the cupboard, cupboard was bare,
Nothin', nothin', nothin' was there.
Turned around scratched my face.
So damn much nothin' all over the place.
On the floor and in the chairs.

Well, I thought I'd better lay in a supply,
So I went to the store some nothin' to buy.
In the window, a big display,
We got plenty o' nothin' today.
All vacuum packed.

Clerk come 'round, said "What'll it be?"
"Nothin', nothin', nothin' for me."
"How do you want it, large or small,
Fat or skinny, short or tall?"
I'll take some with bows on. Wrap it up nice—for a gift.

Well this song was written with nothin' in mind,
Nothin' at all of any kind.
Nothin' at all of any degree,
And there's nothin' in it as you can see.
Nothin', nothin', nothin'.
We was aided by a poverty of intellect.

IN THE EVENING BY THE MOONLIGHT

Old Favorites . . . of home, hearth and living room piano

The Band Played On

John E. Palmer

    Ab
Matt Casey formed a social club
    B b m
  that beat the town for style,
  Eb   Ab
And hired for a meeting place a hall

When pay day came around each week
    B b m
  they greased the floor with wax.
  Eb   Ab
And danced with noise and vigor at the ball,
  Fm   B b m
Each Saturday you'd see them
      Cm7   Fm
  dressed up in Sunday clothes,
  Bb   Eb
Each lad would have his sweetheart by his side.
  Ab
When Casey led the first grand march
    B b m
  they all would fall in line,
  E b 7   Ab
Behind the man who was their joy and pride.

Chorus:

    Ab
For—Casey would waltz with a strawberry blonde,
  E b 7
And the Band played on,

He'd glide cross the floor with the girl he adored,
    Ab
And the Band played on.
          E b 7 A b 7   Db
But his brain was so loaded it nearly exploded,

The poor girl would shake with alarm.
  B b m   Ddim   Ab   Fm
He'd ne'er leave the girl with the strawberry curls,
  B b 7 E b 7 Ab
And the Band played on.

Such kissing in the corner
    and such whisp'ring in the hall,
And telling tales of love behind the stairs
As Casey was the favorite and he that ran the ball.
Of kissing and love making did his share,
At twelve o'clock exactly they all would fall in line
Then march down to the dining hall and eat.
But Casey would not join them
    although ev'rything was fine,
But he stay'd upstairs and exercised his feet.

Now when the dance was over
    and the band played Home Sweet Home,
They played a tune at Casey's own request.
He thanked them very kindly for
    the favors they had shown,
Then he'd waltz once with the girl that he loved best.
Most all the friends are married that Casey used to know,
And Casey too has taken him a wife.
The blonde he used to waltz and glide with
    on the ballroom floor,
Is happy Misses Casey now for life.

My Old Kentucky Home

Stephen Foster

  D   D7 G   D
The sun shines bright on my old Kentucky home,
   Bm   E7   A A7
'Tis summer, the folks there are gay.
  D   D7 G   D
The corn top's ripe and the meadow's in the bloom,
E7   D   A7   D
While the birds make music all the day.
  D   D7 G   D
The young folks roll on the little cabin floor,
  Bm   E7   A   A7
All merry, all happy and bright.
   D   D7 G   D
By 'n by hard times comes a-knocking at the door,
E7   D   A7   D
Then my old Kentucky home, good night.

Chorus:
D   G   D
Weep no more, my lady,
F # 7G   D
Oh, weep no more today.
  A7 D   D7 G   D
We will sing one song for the old Kentucky home,
E7   D   A7   D
For the old Kentucky home far away.

They hunt no more for the 'possum and the coon,
On meadow, the hill and the shore,
They sing no more by the glimmer of the moon,
On the bench by that old cabin door.
The day goes by like a shadow o'er the heart,
With sorrow where all was delight.
The time has come when the darkies have to part,
Then my old Kentucky home, good night.

The head must bow and the back will have to bend,
Wherever the poor folks may go.
A few more days and the trouble will end,
In the field where sugar-canes may grow.
A few more days for to tote the weary load,
No matter, 'twill never be light.
A few more days till we totter on the road,
Then my old Kentucky home, good night.

My Wild Irish Rose

Chauncey Olcott

```
        C      C5#    F      C
If you listen, I'll sing you a sweet little song
                   D          G7
Of a flower that's now drooped and dead,
        C      C5#    F      C
Yet dearer to me, yes than all of its mates,
        C         Fm          C
Tho' each holds aloft its proud head.
        G7           C
'Twas given to me by a girl that I know;
                Am         D7       G7
Since we've met, faith, I've known no repose,
        C      C5#        F
She is dearer by far than the world's brightest star,
        C         F      C
And I call her my wild Irish rose.
```

Chorus:

```
    C   Fm  C     F              C
My wild Irish rose, the sweetest flow'r that grows,
        G7        C   C#dim G7        C
You may search ev'rywhere, but none can compare
   Am    D   D7  G7
   with my wild Irish rose.
    C   Fm  C     F              C
My wild Irish rose, the dearest flow'r that grows,
C#dim       G7          C    C#dim G7       C
And some day for my sake, she may let me take
        F      C  D7  G7  C
        the bloom from my wild Irish rose.
```

They may sing of their roses which by other names,
Would smell just as sweetly, they say,
But I know that my Rose would never consent
To have that sweet name taken away.
Her glances are shy when e'er I pass by
The bower where my true love grows.
And my one wish has been that some day I may win
The heart of my wild Irish rose.

A Bicycle Built For Two (Daisy Bell)

Harry Dacre

```
F              C7        Gm7  C7  F
There is a flower within my heart, Daisy, Daisy!
                   C7
Planted one day by a glancing dart,
F       C  C7 F
Planted by Daisy Bell!
Dm        A7        Dm
Whether she loves me or loves me not,
Gm            Bb7    A7
Sometimes it's hard to    tell;
Dm    A7   Dm          G7        C
Yet I am longing to share the lot of beautiful Daisy Bell!
```

Chorus:

```
F           Bb                F
Daisy, Daisy, give me your answer, do!
C7      F    G7           C7
I'm half crazy, all for the love of you!
D Gm    C   C7 F
It won't be a stylish marriage,
C F    Bb       F
I can't afford a carriage
C7 F      C7  F   C
But you'll look sweet on the seat
        F    Gm7 C7 F
Of a bicycle built for two
```

We will go "tandem" as man and wife, Daisy, Daisy!
"Peddling" away down the road of life,
I and my Daisy Bell!
When the road's dark we can both despise
P'licemen and "lamps" as well;
There are "bright lights" in the dazzling eyes
   of beautiful Daisy Bell!

I will stand by you in "wheel" or woe, Daisy, Daisy!
You'll be the bell(e) which I'll ring, you know!
Sweet little Daisy Bell!
You'll take the "lead" in each "trip" we take,
Then, if I don't do well,
I will permit you to use the brake, my beautiful Daisy Bell!

Sweet and Low

Alfred Tennyson and Joseph Barnby

```
C        D#dim C   F   C
Sweet and low, sweet and low, wind of the
    G     D7   G7
    western sea;
C    D#dim C   D7   G
Low, low, breathe and blow, wind of the
    C    D7   G7
    western sea;
                  C      G7             C
Over the rolling waters go, come from the dying moon,
 D#dim C
 and blow,
Am                 F Fm C   G7
Blow him again to me, while my little one,
    C     G7    C      Fm
    while my pretty one sleeps.
```

Sleep and rest, sleep and rest,
   Father will come to thee soon;
Rest, rest on Mother's breast,
   Father will come to thee soon;
Father will come to his babe in the nest,
   silver sails all out of the west,
Under the silver moon, sleep, my little one,
   sleep my pretty one, sleep.

When You And I Were Young, Maggie
George W. Johnson and James Austin Butterfield

F   Bb
I wander'd today to the hill, Maggie,
  F   C7
To watch the scene below;
   F   F7 Ab
The creek and the old rusty mill, Maggie,
       F   C7   F
Where we sat in the long, long ago.
  Bb   F
The green grove is gone from the hill, Maggie,
   C   G7   C
Where first the daisies sprung;
  F   F7 Bb
The creaking old mill is still, Maggie,
   F   C7   F
Since you and I were young.

Chorus:

  Bb   F
And now we are aged and gray, Maggie,
   C   G7   C
And the trials of life nearly done;
  F   F7   Bb
But to me you're as fair as you were, Maggie,
   F   C7   F
When you and I were young.

A city so silent and lone, Maggie,
Where the young and the gay and the best,
In polished white mansions of stone, Maggie,
Have each found a place of rest,
Is built where the birds used to play, Maggie,
And join in the songs that were sung;
For we sang as gay as they, Maggie,
When you and I were young.

School Days
Will Cobb and Gus Edwards

Bb   Db dim F7
School days, school days, dear old Golden Rule days,

Reading and writing and 'rithmatic,
Bb   Bb6
Taught to the tune of a hick'ry stick,
Bb   G7   C7
You were my queen in calico,
        Bb
I was your bashful barefoot beau,
   Eb   Edim Bb   D7
And you wrote on my slate "I love you, Joe,"
Gm C7   F7 Bb
When we were a couple of kids.

When You Were Sweet Sixteen
George Cooper and James Thornton

       C   E7   F A7 Dm
When first I saw the lovelight in your eye,
               G7   C
I dreamt the world held naught but joy for me.
            E7   F A7 Dm
And even though we drifted far apart,
  D7   G7
I never dream but what I dream of thee.

Chorus:

  C   E7   F A7 Dm
I love you as I never loved before,
           G7   C   G7
Since first I met you on the village green.
   C   E7   F A7 Dm
Come to me or my dream of love is o'er,
  F   C   D9
I love you as I loved you, when you were sweet
       Dm7 G7C
When you were sweet sixteen.

Last night I dreamt I held your hand in mine,
And once again you were my happy bride.
I kissed you as I did in Auld Lang Syne
As to the church we wandered side by side.

While Strolling Through The Park One Day
Ed Haley

     A   D
While strolling through the park one day, (one day,)
  B7   E7
All in the merry month of May, (month of May)
    A   D   B7
I was taken by surprise, by a pair of roguish eyes,
  E7   A
In a moment my poor heart was stole a way.
  C#   F#m G#7 F#m
A smile was all she gave to   me,
     B   E B7 E
Of course we were as happy as can be.
   A   D
I immediately raised my hat, (my hat)
  B7   E7
And finally she remarked, (she remarked)
  A   D   B7
I never shall forget that lovely afternoon,
  E7   A
I met her at the fountain in the park.

Jeanie With The Light Brown Hair
Stephen Foster

  F
I dream of Jeanie with the light brown hair,
Dm   FBb F   G7   C7
Borne, like a vapor, on the summer's air;
  F
I see her tripping where the bright streams play,
G7   C Dm   C   G7   C
Happy as the daisies that dance on her way.
C7   F
Many were the wild notes her merry voice would pour,
Bb   F   F7 Am   C7
Many were the blithe birds that warbled them o'er;
  F
Ah! I dream of Jeanie with the light brown hair,
Gm6Dm Bb   F   Ab   G C7   F
Floating   like a vapor on the soft summer air.

I long for Jeanie with the day-dawn smile,
Radiant in gladness, warm with winning guile;
I hear her melodies, like joys gone by,
Sighing round my heart o'er the fond hopes that die;
Sighing like the night wind and sobbing like the rain,
Waiting for the lost one that comes not again;
Ah! I long for Jeanie and my heart bows low,
Never more to find her where the bright waters flow.

Juanita
Caroline Norton

D   A7   D
Soft o'er the fountain, ling-'ring falls the southern moon,
        A7   D
Far o'er the mountain, breaks the day too soon.
            G
In thy dark eyes' splendor,
  A7   D
   where the warm light loves to dwell,
          G   A7   D
Weary looks, yet tender, speak their fond farewell.
     A7   D
Nita, Juanita, ask thy soul if we should part!
     A7   D
Nita, Juanita, lean thou on my heart.

When in thy dreaming, moons like these shall shine again,
And daylight beaming, prove thy dreams are vain;
Wilt thou not relenting, for thine absent lover sigh?
In thy heart consenting to a prayer gone by?
Nita! Juanita! Let me linger by thy side!
Nita! Juanita! Be my own fair bride.

Listen To The Mockingbird
Alice Hawthorne

  C7   F
I'm dreaming now of Hallie,
    C7   F
Sweet Hallie, sweet Hallie,
    C7   F
I'm dreaming now of Hallie,
F7   Bb   C7   F
For the thought of her is one that never dies.
     C7   F
She's sleeping in the valley,
     C7   F
The valley, the valley,
     C7   F
She's sleeping in the valley,
F7   Bb   C7   F
And the mockingbird is singing where she lies.

Chorus:

F   C7
Listen to the mockingbird,
           F
Listen to the mockingbird,
      C   C7   F
The mockingbird is singing o'er her grave;
          C7
Listen to the mockingbird,
           F
Listen to the mockingbird,
D Gmin   C7   F
Still singing where the weeping willows wave.

Ah well I yet can remember, I remember, I remember
Ah well I yet can remember
When we gathered in the cotton side by side
'Twas in the mild mid-September, in September,
  in September
'Twas in the mild mid-September
And the mocking bird was singing far and wide

When charms of spring are awaken, are awaken,
  are awaken
When charms of spring are awaken
And the mocking bird is singing on the bough
I feel like one so forsaken, so forsaken, so forsaken
I feel like one so forsaken
Since my Hallie is no longer with me now

In The Evening By The Moonlight

James A. Bland

    F
In the evening by the moonlight,
       Bb   F
  you can hear the young folks singin';

In the evening by the moonlight,
       G7   C7
  you can hear those banjoes ringin'.
     F   F7
How the old folks would enjoy it,
       Bb   Bbm   F
  they would sit all night and listen,
       Bb F G7   C7   F
As we sang in   the evening by the moonlight,

  rah da doo day,
     F
In the evening, rah da doo day,

    by the moonlight, rah da doo day,
     Bb   F
You can hear those young folks singin', rah da doo day;

In the evening, rah da doo day,

    by the moonlight, rah da doo day,
       G7   C7
You can hear those banjoes ringin', rah da doo day.
      F   F7
How the old folks would enjoy it,
       Bb   Bbm   F
  they would sit all night and listen,
       Bb F G7   C7   F
As we sang in   the evening by the moonlight,
  rah da doo day.

For He's A Jolly Good Fellow

     F   BbF
For he's a jolly good fellow,
     C7   F
For he's a jolly good fellow,
             BbBdim
For he's a jolly good fellow,
     F   C7 F
Which nobody can deny!

We won't go home until morning, (3 times)
Till daylight doth appear!

The bear went over the mountain, (3 times)
To see what he could see!
(Yell) And all that he could see was

The other side of the mountain, (3 times)
Was all that he could see!

Golden Slippers

James A. Bland

      G
Oh, my golden slippers are laid away,
                        D7
'Cause I don't 'spect to wear 'em till my wedding day,

And my long tail coat that I love so well,
                    G
I will wear up in the chariot in the morn.

And my long white robe that I bought last June,
                D7
I'm gonna get changed 'cause it fits too soon,

And the old grey horse that I used to drive,
                  G
I will hitch him to the chariot in the morn.

Chorus:

G
Oh, them golden slippers,
C
Oh, them golden slippers,
D7
Golden slippers I'm gonna wear,
  G
Because they look so neat.

Oh, them golden slippers,
C
Oh, them golden slippers,
D7
Golden slippers I'm a-gonna wear
        G
To walk the golden street.

Oh, my ol' banjo hangs on the wall,
'Cause it ain't been tuned since 'way last fall,
But the folks all say we'll have a good time,
When we ride up in the chariot in the morn.
There's old Brother Ben an' his sister Luce,
They will telegraph the news to Uncle Bacco Juice,
What a great camp meetin' there will be that day,
When we ride up in the chariot in the morn.

So, it's good-bye, children, I will have to go,
Where the rain don't fall and the wind don't blow,
And your ulster coats, why, you will not need,
When you ride up in the chariot in the morn;
But your golden slippers must be nice and clean,
And your age must be just sweet sixteen,
And your white kid gloves you will have to wear,
When you ride up in the chariot in the morn.

Bonny Eloise
C. W. Elliot and J. R. Thomas

    D   G   D
O, sweet is the vale where the Mohawk gently glides
                 E7   A7
On its clear winding way to the sea,
    D   G   D
And dearer than all storied streams on earth besides,
              A7   D
Is this bright rolling river to me;

Refrain:
    G   D
But sweeter, dearer, yes, dearer far than these,
   A7   D
Who charms where others all fail,
    G   D
Is blue-eyed, Bonny, Bonny Eloise,
G D   A7   D
The Belle of the Mohawk Vale.

O, sweet are the moments when dreaming I roam,
Thro' my loved haunts now mossy and grey,
And dearer than all is my childhood's hallow'd home,
That is crumbling now slowly away;

Darling Nelly Gray
B. R. Hanby

       C   F
There's a low green valley by the old Kentucky shore,
     C   D7   G
Where we've whiled many happy hours away,
G7C   C7   F
A-sitting and a-singing by the little cottage door,
   C   G7   C
Where lived my darling Nelly Gray.

Chorus:
   G7   C
Oh my poor Nelly Gray, they have taken you away,
               D7 G
And I'll never see my darling any more.
   C   C7   F   F#min7
I'm a-sitting by the river and I'm weeping all the day,
    C   G7   C
For you're gone from the old Kentucky shore.

One night I went to see her but "she's gone"
   the neighbors say,
The white man bound her with his chain,
They have taken her to Georgia to wear her life away,
As she toils in the cotton and the cane.

Grandfather's Clock
Henry Clay Work

   G   D7   G   C
My grandfather's clock was too large for the shelf,
  G   D7   G
So it stood ninety years on the floor;
          D7   G   C
It was taller by half than the old man himself,
       G   D7   G
Though it weighed not a pennyweight more.
                   D7   G
It was bought on the morn of the day that he was born,
        A7   D7
And was always his treasure and pride;
   G   D7 G   C
But it stopped short never to go again
     G D7 G
When the old man died.

Chorus:

   G
Ninety years without slumbering,

Tick tock, tick tock,

His life seconds numbering,

Tick tock, tick tock,
        D7 G   C
It stopped short never to go again
     G D7 G
When the old man died.

In watching its pendulum swing to and fro,
Many hours had he spent while a boy;
And in childhood and manhood the clock seemed to know,
And to share both his grief and his joy.
For it struck twenty-four when he entered at the door,
With a blooming and beautiful bride, etc.

My grandfather said that of those he could hire,
Not a servant so faithful he found;
For it wasted no time, and had but one desire,
At the close of each week to be wound.
And it kept in its place, not a frown upon its face,
And its hands never hung by its side, etc.

It rang an alarm in the dead of the night,
An alarm that for years had been dumb;
And we knew that his spirit was pluming its flight,
That his hour of departure had come.
Still the clock kept the time, with a soft and muffled chime,
As we silently stood by his side, etc.

Believe Me, If All Those Endearing Young Charms
Thomas Moore

C   F
Believe me if all those endearing young charms
      C   G   C
Which I gaze on so fondly today,
G7   C   F
Were to change by tomorrow and fleet in my arms
      C   G   C
Like the fairy gifts fading away.

Thou wouldst still be adored
     F
As this moment thou art,
    C   G   C
Let thy loveliness fade as it will,
G7 C
And around the dear ruin
  F   A°
Each wish of my heart
      C   G   C
Would entwine itself verdantly still.

It is not that while beauty and youth are thine own
And thy cheeks unprofaned by a tear,
That the fervor and faith of a soul can be known
To which time will but make thee more dear.
No, the heart that has truly loved never forgets,
But as truly lives on to the close,
As the sunflower turns on her God when he sets,
The same look which she turned when he rose.

The Rose Of Tralee
Mordaunt Spencer and Charles W. Glover

E7 A   D   E7 A E7
The pale moon was rising above the green mountain,
    A   B7   E7
The sun was declining beneath the blue sea,
    A   D   E7 A
When I strayed with my love to the pure crystal fountain
    E7   A D   D
That stands in the beautiful vale of Tralee.

Chorus:

A   F♯m   Bm7   C♯
She was lovely and fair as the rose of the summer,
  F♯m Bm F♯m   C♯ F♯m
Yet 'twas not her beauty alone that won me.
E7 A E7   A7   D   A
Oh, no, 'twas the truth in her eyes ever dawning
    E7   A   D A D7 E7 A
That made me love Mary, the Rose of Tralee.

The cool shades of evening their mantle were spreading,
And Mary, all smiling, was list'ning to me;
The moon thro' the valley her pale rays was shedding,
When I won the heart of the Rose of Tralee.

Ben Bolt
Dr. Thomas Dunn and Nelson Kneass

D   A7
Oh don't you remember sweet Alice, Ben Bolt,
                    D
Sweet Alice whose hair was so brown,
            D7   G   Em7
Who wept with delight when you gave her a smile,
  D   A7   D
And trembled with fear at your frown?
E7   A   E7   A   E7 A
In the old church yard, in the valley, Ben Bolt,
   Bm7 E7   A
In a corner obscure and alone
A7   D   D7 G   Em7
They have fitted a slab of granite so gray
         D   A7   F♯7
And sweet Alice lies under the stone.
A7   D   D7 G   Em7
They have fitted a slab of granite so gray
         D   A7   D
And sweet Alice lies under the stone.

Under the hickory tree, Ben Bolt,
Which stood at the end of the hill,
Together we've lain in the noonday shade
And listen'd to Appleton's mill.
The mill wheel has fallen to pieces, Ben Bolt,
The rafters have tumbled in,
And a quiet that crawls 'round the walls as you gaze,
Has followed the olden din.

And don't you remember the school, Ben Bolt,
With the master so cruel and grim,
And the shaded nook by the running brook,
Where the children went to swim?
Grass grows on the master's grave, Ben Bolt,
The spring of the brook is dry,
And of all the boys who were schoolmates then,
There are only you and I.

The Last Rose Of Summer
Thomas Moore

D   Bm G D   G D   A7D
'Tis the Last Rose of Summer, left blooming alone;
G A7 D Bm Em D Bm G D   A7 D
All her lovely companions, are faded and gone;
  Bm G A7 D   Bm C♯m Bm F♯Bm
No flow'r of her kindred, no rose   bud is nigh
Gm D   Em D   G D Em7 A7 D
To reflect back her blushes, or give sigh for sigh.

So soon may I follow when friendships decay;
And from Love's shining circle the gems drop away!
When true hearts lie withered, and fond ones are flow'n,
Oh! who would inhabit this bleak world alone.

Flow Gently Sweet Afton
Robert Burns and James Spilman

```
F                    Bb              F
Flow gently sweet Afton, among thy green braes,
         C  F              G7 C
Flow gently, I'll sing thee a song in thy praise.
       F              Bb              F
My Mary's asleep by thy murmuring stream,
       C   F      BbF    C7 F
Flow gently sweet Afton, disturb not her dream.
       C                G7                C
Thou stock-dove whose echo resounds from the glen,
                      G7            C
Ye wild whistling blackbirds in yon thorny den,
C9   F                       Bb              F
Thou green-crested lapwing, thy screaming forbear,
       C  F      BbF    C7 F
I charge you disturb not my slumbering fair.
```

How lofty sweet Afton, thy neighboring hills,
Far marked with the courses of clear winding rills.
There daily I wander as morn rises high,
My flocks and my Mary's sweet cot in my eye.
How pleasant thy banks and green valleys below,
Where wild in the woodlands the primroses blow.
There oft as mild evening creeps over the lea,
The sweet-scented birk shades my Mary and me.

Thy crystal stream Afton, how lovely it glides,
And winds by the cot where my Mary resides.
How wanton thy waters her snowy feet lave,
As gath'ring sweet flow'rets, she stems thy clear wave.
Flow gently sweet Afton, among thy green braes,
Flow gently sweet river, the theme of my lays.
My Mary's asleep by the murmuring stream,
Flow gently sweet Afton, disturb not her dream.

Bill Bailey
Hughie Cannon

```
D
Won't you come home Bill Bailey,

Won't you come home?
             D#o  A7
She cried the whole night long.

I'll do the dishes, honey, I'll pay the rent.
                 D
I know I done you wrong.
```

'Member that rainy evening I drove you out
```
         D7          G   B7   Em
With nothin' but a fine tooth comb?
 G    E7        D        B7
I know I'm to blame, Well ain't that a shame,
   Em7         A7         D
Bill Bailey won't you please come home.
```

Kathleen Mavourneen
Mrs. A. B. Crawford and F. Nicholls Crouch

```
D                    G        D
Kathleen Mavourneen! The gray dawn is breaking,
    D   B7   Em     A7         D
The horn of the hunter is heard on the hill;
                              G    F#7 G
The lark from her light wing the bright dew is shaking,
D                    A7        D
Kathleen Mavourneen! What, slumbering still?
F#7  G        F#7      Bm         F#7
Oh, hast thou forgotten how soon we must sever?
     G        Em    G+G7 E7      G—
Oh, hast thou forgotten this day we must part?
```

Chorus:

```
A7  D              G
It may be for years and it may be forever,
     D       G A7      Em       E
Oh, why art thou silent, thou voice of my heart?
A7  Em      D—       D  G A7 D
It may be for years and it may be forever;
      Em       E7   A7          D
Then why art thou silent, Kathleen Mavourneen?
```

Kathleen Mavourneen! Awake from the slumbers,
The blue mountains glow in the sun's golden light;
Ah! Where is the spell that once hung on my numbers?
Arise in thy beauty, thou star of my night.
Mavourneen, Mavourneen, my sad tears are falling,
To think that from Erin and thee I must part.

Woodman, Spare That Tree
George Morris and Henry Russell

```
F        C7      F       C7 F   C7
Woodman, spare that tree; Touch not a single bough;
   F      A7    Dm    F   C7  F
In youth it sheltered me, and I'll protect it now.
     C    G7     C      G7          C7
'Twas my forefather's hand, that placed it near his cot;
       F            Bb       F    C7  F
There, woodman, let it stand, thy axe shall harm it not!
```

That old familiar tree, its glory and renown
Are spread o'er land and sea,
    and woulds't thou hack it down?
Woodman, forbear thy stroke, cut not its earthbound ties,
Oh, spare that aged oak, now tow'ring to the skies.

When but an idle boy, I sought its grateful shade,
In all their gushing joy, here, too, my sisters played;
My mother kissed me here, my father pressed my hand,
Forgive this foolish tear, but let that old oak stand!

Wait Till The Sun Shines Nellie
Andrew Sterling and Harry Von Tilzer

C7
On a Sunday morn sat a maid forlorn
   F   E7 F
With her sweetheart by her side,
   C7
Through the window pane, she looked at the rain,
 F   Bb F
"We must stay home, Joe," she cried.
   C7
"There's a picnic, too, at the old Point View,
  F   Bb
It's a shame it rained today."
      D F D7
Then the boy drew near, kissed away each tear,
  G7   C7
And she heard him softly say:

Chorus:

 F   F7 Bb   F
"Wait till the sun shines, Nellie,
C7 C C7   F D F
When the clouds go drifting by,
Bb D F   Dm
We will be happy, Nellie,
  G7 C7
Don't you sigh.
F   Bb   F
Down Lover's Lane we'll wander,
C7   A
Sweethearts you and I.
D D7 Gm
Wait till the sun shines, Nellie,
Am C7 F
Bye and bye."

"How I long," she sighed, "for a trolley ride
Just to show my brand new gown."
Then she gazed on high with a gladsome cry
For the sun came shining down.
And she looked so sweet on the big front seat
As the car sped on its way,
And she whispered low, "Say you're all right, Joe,
You just won my heart today."

Home, Sweet Home
John Howard Payne and Henry Rowley Bishop

D G   D Em A7 D
'Mid pleasures and palaces though I may roam,
  G D   Em7 A7   D
Be it ever so humble, there's no place like home;
 F#7   Bm   A7   Bm
A charm from the sky seems to hallow us there,
   A7   D   B7 Em A7   D
Which, seek thro' the world, is never met with elsewhere.

Chorus:

   Em7 Bm A   D
Home! Home! Sweet, sweet home!
     G   D
There's no place like home,
B7 Em7 A7   D
There's no place like home.

An exile from home, splendor dazzles in vain,
Oh, give me my lowly thatched cottage again;
The birds singing gaily, that come at my call;
Give me them, with that peace of mind, dearer than all.

To thee, I'll return, overburdened with care,
The heart's dearest solace will smile on me there.
No more from that cottage again will I roam,
Be it ever so humble, there's no place like home.

Seeing Nellie Home (Aunt Dinah's Quilting Party)
Francis Kyle and James Fletcher

      C
In the sky the bright stars glittered,
    F   C
On the bank the pale moon shone;
           F
And 'twas from Aunt Dinah's quilting party,
  G7   C
I was seeing Nellie home.

Chorus:

   C
I was seeing Nellie home,
  F   C
I was seeing Nellie home;
           F
And 'twas from Aunt Dinah's quilting party,
  G7   C
I was seeing Nellie home.

On my arm a soft hand rested,
Rested light as ocean foam;
And 'twas from Aunt Dinah's quilting party,
I was seeing Nellie home.

On my lips a whisper trembled,
Trembled till it dared to come;
And 'twas from Aunt Dinah's quilting party,
I was seeing Nellie home.

On my life new hopes were dawning,
And those hopes have liv'd and grown;
And 'twas from Aunt Dinah's quilting party,
I was seeing Nellie home.

Lorena

H. D. L. Webster and J. P. Webster

```
       G            G7   C
The years creep slowly by, Lorena
       D7               G
The snow is on the grass again;
                       G7   C
The sun's low down the sky, Lorena,
       D7                       G
The frost gleams where the flow'rs have been.
       Em                Am
But the heart throbs on as warmly now,
B7                       Em
As when the summer days were nigh;
D7   G          G7   C
Oh! the sun can never dip so low,
       D7               G
A-down affection's cloudless sky.
```

A hundred months have passed, Lorena,
Since last I held that hand in mine,
And felt the pulse beat fast, Lorena,
Though mine beat faster far than thine.
A hundred months, 'twas flowery May,
When up the hilly slope we climbed,
To watch the dying of the day,
And hear the distant church bells chime.

We loved each other then, Lorena,
More than we ever dared to tell;
And what we might have been, Lorena,
Had but our lovings prospered well—
But then, 'tis part, the years are gone,
I'll not call up their shadowy forms;
I'll say to them, "Lost years, sleep on!
Sleep on! nor heed life's pelting storms.

The story of that past, Lorena,
Alas! I care not to repeat,
The hopes that could not last, Lorena,
They lived, but only lived to cheat.
I would not cause e'en one regret
To rankle in your bosom now;
For "if we try, we may forget,"
Were words of thine long years ago.

Yes, these were words of thine, Lorena,
They burn within my memory, yet;
They touched some tender chords, Lorena,
Which thrill and tremble with regret.
'Twas not thy woman's heart that spoke;
Thy heart was always true to me;
A duty, stern and pressing, broke
The tie which linked my soul with thee.

It matters little now, Lorena,
The past is in the eternal past;
Our heads will soon lie low, Lorena,
Life's tide is ebbing out so fast.
There is a Future! O, thank God!
Of life this is so small a part!
'Tis dust to dust beneath the sod;
But then, up there, 'tis heart to heart.

Meet Me In St. Louis, Louis

Andrew B. Sterling and Kerry Mills

```
       Bb
When Louis came home to the flat
                       F7
He hung up his coat and his hat,
                       Bb      Edim7Bb
He gazed all around, but no wifey he      found,
   Edim7 F            C7          F7
So he      said "Where can Flossie be at?"
   Bb
A note on the table he spied,
                       Bbaug.  Eb
He read it just once, then he          cried,
G7 Cm        C7        Edim7Bb       Edim7Bb
It  ran "Louis dear, it's too     slow for me      here,
Bbm+6F              C7        F7
So      I think I will go for a ride."
```

Chorus:

```
Bb
Meet me in St. Louis, Louis,
Eb          Bb
Meet me at the fair,

Don't tell me the lights are shining
C7          F7
Any place but there.
       Eb7 D7              G7
We will  dance the Hoochee Koochee,
       C7              F7
I will be your tootsie wootsie
          Bb
If you will meet me in St. Louis, Louis,
C7      F7    Bb
Meet me at the fair."
```

The dresses that hung in the hall
Were gone, she had taken them all.
She took all his rings and the rest of his things;
The picture he missed from the wall.
"What! moving?" the janitor said,
"Your rent is paid three months ahead."
"What good is the flat?" said poor Louis, "read that."
And the janitor smiled as he read:

The Old Oaken Bucket

Samuel Woodworth and George Kiallmark

```
        G              D7        G
How dear to the heart are the scenes of my childhood,
      C       G          D7          G
When fond recollection presents them to view!
                         D7         G
The orchard, the meadow, the deep tangled wildwood,
      C       G            D7       G
And ev'ry loved spot which my infancy knew:
     D7        G            D7          G
The wide spreading pond, and the mill that stood by it,
     D7       G             D    A7  D
The bridge and the rock where the cataract fell;
D7 G     G           D7             G
The cot of my father, the dairy house nigh it,
G7  C          G          D7        G
And e'en the rude bucket that hung in the well.
```

That moss covered bucket I hailed as a treasure,
For often at noon, when return'd from the field,
I found it the source of an exquisite pleasure,
The purest and sweetest that nature can yield.
How ardent I seized it, with hands that were glowing,
And quick to the white pebbled bottom it fell
Then soon, with the emblem of turth overflowing,
And dripping with coolness, it rose from the well.

How sweet from the green, mossy brim to receive it,
As, poised on the curb, it inclined to my lips!
Not a full blishing goblet could tempt me to leave it,
Tho' filled with the nectar that Jupiter sips.
And now, far removed from the loved habitation,
The tear of regret will intrusively swell,
As fancy reverts to my father's plantation,
And sighs for the bucket that hung in the well.

Long, Long Ago

Thomas H. Bayly

```
G          Em   G
Tell me the tales that to me were so dear,
D7                 G
Long, long ago, long, long ago,
          Em   G      Em
Sing me the songs I delighted to hear,
D7              G
Long, long ago, long ago.
D7              C    D7
Now you are come all my grief is remov'd,
D7            C   D7    G
Let me forget that so long you have rov'd,
                    C    Em
Let me believe that you love as you lov'd,
            D7   G
Long, long ago, long ago.
```

Do you remember the path where we met,
Long, long ago, long, long ago,
Ah, yes, you told me you ne'er would forget,
Long, long ago, long ago,
Then, to all others my smile you preferr'd,
Love when you spoke gave a charm to each word,
Still my heart treasures the praises I heard,
Long, long ago, long ago.

Tho' by your kindness my fond hopes were rais'd,
Long, long ago, long, long ago,
You by more eloquent lips have been prais'd,
Long, long ago, long ago.
But by long absence your truth has been tried,
Still to your accents I listen with pride,
Blest as I was when I sat by your side,
Long, long ago, long ago.

Hello! My Baby

Joseph Howard and Ida Emerson

```
      F        Dm    F
I've got a little baby, but she's out of sight,
  Dm              C7
I talk to her across the telephone;
     C7
I've never seen my honey, but she's mine all right;
                             F
So take my tip and leave this gal alone.
         Dm      F
Ev'ry single morning you will hear me yell,
     D7                       Gm
"Hey Central! fix me up along the line."
               G#dim          D7
He connects me with my honey, then I ring the bell,
     G7                      C
And this is what I say to baby mine:
```

Chorus:

```
F            D7          G7
Hello! my baby, hello! my honey, hello! my ragtime girl;
C7           F             C7
Send me a kiss by wire; baby, my heart's on fire!
F            D7
If you refuse me, honey, you'll lose me,
G7
Then you'll be left alone; oh, baby,
C7       Cdim C7         F
Telephone and   tell me I'm your own.
```

This morning through the phone
    she said her name was Bess,
And now I kind of know where I am at;
I'm satisfied because I've got my babe's address,
Here pasted in the lining of my hat.
I am mighty scared 'cause if the wires got crossed,
'Twill separate me from my baby mine,
Then some other guy will win her and my game is lost,
So I shout each day along the line:

In The Good Old Summertime

Ren Shields and George Evans

```
        G
There's a time in each year that we always hold dear,
C           G
Good old summertime.
                                        D7 G
With the birds and the treeses and sweet scented breezes,
D      A7    D7
Good old summertime.
        G
When your day's work is over then you are in clover,
   C          G
And life is one beautiful rhyme,
  C     G       Edim   G
No trouble annoying, each one is enjoying
Gm6  D    A7     D7
The good old summertime.
```

Chorus:

```
      G
In the good old summertime,
G7   C        G
In the good old summertime,
                   Em   A7        D7
Strolling through the shady lanes with that baby mine.
   G
You hold her hand and she holds yours,
    C          G
And that's a very good sign,
                       B7
That she's your tootsey-wootsey
Em   A7     Am7 D7 G
In the good old summertime.
```

Oh to swim in the pool you'd play hooky from school
Good old summer time
You would play "ring-a-rosie" with Jim, Kate and Josie
Good old summer time
Those are days full of pleasure we now fondly treasure
When we never thought it a crime
To go stealing cherries with face brown as berries
In good old summer time

Sweet Evelina

```
  Bb
Way down in the meadow where the lily first blows,
     F7                               Bb
Where the wind from the mountains ne'er ruffles the rose
                          Eb Bb
Lives fond Evelina, the sweet little dove,
   F7                          Bb
The pride of the valley the girl that I love.
```

Chorus:

```
Bb
Dear Evelina, Sweet Evelina,
F7                  Bb
My love for thee shall never die

Dear Evelina, Sweet Evelina,
F7                  Bb
My love for thee shall never, never die.
```

She's fair like a rose, like a lamb she is meek,
And she never was known to put paint on her cheek;
In the most graceful curls hangs her raven black hair,
And she never requires perfumery there.

Evelina and I one fine evening in June
Took a walk all alone by the light of the moon;
The planets all shone for the heavens were clear,
And I felt round the heart tremendously queer.

Three years have gone by and I've not got a dollar,
Evelina still lives in that green grassy holler;
Although I am fated to marry her never,
I've sworn that I'll love her forever and ever.

Loch Lomond

Lady Scott

```
   G                  C
By yon bonnie banks and by yon bonnie braes,
D7    G      C  G7    C G
Where the sun shines bright on Loch Lomond,
        Em     G          C
Where me and my true love were ever wont to go,
D7   G       C   G     D7 G
On the bonnie, bonnie banks of Loch Lomond.
```

Chorus:

```
D7 G           B7        Em C     G  D7
Oh, you'll take the high road and I'll take the low road,
  Em C  G       C  G
And I'll be in Scotland afore ye,
      Em     G        C
But me and my true love will never meet again
D7   G       C   G     D7 G
On the bonnie, bonnie banks of Loch Lomond.
```

'Twas then that we parted in yon shady glen,
On the steep, steep side of Ben Lomond,
Where in purple hue the Highland hills we view
And the moon coming out in the gloaming.

The wee birdies sing and the wild flowers spring,
And in sunshine the waters are sleeping,
But the broken heart it kens nae second spring again
Though the woeful may cease from their greeting.

Goodnight Ladies

A
Goodnight ladies,
      E7
Goodnight ladies,
A   D
Goodnight ladies,
    A   E7   A
We're going to leave you now.

Merrily we roll along,
E7   A
Roll along, roll along,

Merrily we roll along,
  E7   A
Over the deep blue sea.

Farewell ladies,
Farewell ladies,
Farewell ladies,
We're going to leave you now.

Sweet dreams, ladies,
Sweet dreams, ladies,
Sweet dreams, ladies,
We're going to leave you now.

Sally In Our Alley
Henry Carey

Bb   Cm7 Bb Cm Bb
Of all the girls that are so smart,
    Eb   F7   Bb
There's none like pretty Sally;
    Cm7 BbCm Bb
She is the darling of my heart,
  Eb   F7   Bb
And lives in our alley;
    Bb   Bb7 Eb
There's ne'er a lady in the land
G7 Cm G7 Cm C7 F
Is half so sweet as Sally;
F7   Gm Cm Bb
She is the darling of my heart,
  Eb Cm F7 Bb
And lives in our alley.

Of all the days within the week
I dearly love but one day,
And that's the day that comes betwixt
A Saturday and Monday:
O, then I'm dressed all in my best
To walk a-broad with Sally;
She is the darling of my heart,
And lives in our alley.

When Christmas comes about again,
O, then I shall have money;
I'll save it up, and box and all
I'll give unto my honey;
And when my sev'n long years are out,
O, then I'll marry Sally,
And then how happily we'll live!
But not in our alley.

Old Folks At Home
Stephen Foster

C   F
Way down upon the Swanee River,
C   G7
Far, far away,
C   F
There's where my heart is turning ever,
C   G7   C
There's where the old folks stay.
C   F
All up and down the whole creation,
C   G7
Sadly I roam,
C   F
Still longing for the old plantation,
C   G7   C
And for the old folks at home.

Chorus:

G7   C
All the world is sad and dreary
F   G7
Everywhere I roam;
C   F
Oh, brothers, how my heart grows weary,
C   G7   C
Far from the old folks at home.

All roun' the little farm I wandered,
When I was young;
Then many happy days I squandered,
Many the songs I sung.
When I was playing with my brother,
Happy was I;
Oh! take me to my kind old mother,
There let me live and die.

One little hut among the bushes,
One that I love,
Still sadly to my mem'ry rushes,
No matter where I rove.
When will I see the bees a-humming
All roun' the comb?
When will I hear the banjo strumming,
Down in my good old home?

A Life On The Ocean Wave
Epes Sargent and Henry Russell

  G
A life on the ocean wave,
           D7
A home on the rolling deep,

Where the scattered waters rave,
           G
And the winds their revels keep.
  C   B7
Like an eagle caged I pine
  C   B7
On this dull unchanging shore,
          Em
Oh give me the flashing brine,
  G dim   D7
The spray and the tempest roar!

Once more on the deck I stand
Of my own swift-gliding craft,
Set sail! Farewell to the land,
The gale follows far abaft.
We shoot through the sparkling foam
Like an ocean bird set free,
Like the ocean bird, our home
We'll find far out on the sea.

The land is no longer in view,
The clouds have begun to frown,
But with a stout vessel and crew
We'll say, "Let the storm come down!"
And the song of our heart shall be,
While the winds and the waters rave,
A life on the heaving sea,
A home on the bounding wave!

Sweet Genevieve

George Cooper and Henry Tucker

```
    G          D7
Oh Genevieve, I'd give the world
         G
To live again the lovely past!
          G7   C
The rose of youth was dew impearl'd
Gm G        D7   G
But now it withers in the blast.
   G7    C    G
I see thy face in ev'ry dream;
    G7     C       G
My waking thoughts are full of thee.
                  B7   Em
Thy glance is in the starry beam
    G6   A7     F#7   B7
That falls along the summer sea.
```

Chorus:
```
D7 G             D7
Oh, Genevieve, Sweet Genevieve,
                  G
The days may come, the days may go,
          G7         C
But still the hands of mem'ry weave
Cm G          D7  G
The blissful dreams of long ago.
```

Fair Genevieve, my early love
The years but make thee dearer far.
My heart shall never, never rove,
Thou art my only guiding star.
For me the past has no regret;
Whate'er the years may bring to me,
I bless the hour when first we met,
The hour that gave me love and thee.

What A Friend We Have In Mother

Charles E. Roat /
Tune: *What A Friend We Have In Jesus*

```
Bb                     Eb
What a friend we have in mother,
F                 Bb
When our lives are young and gay;
              Eb
What a friend we have in mother,
F                 Bb
When with age we're turning gray.
F              Bb
If misfortunes 'round us gather,
Bb
And our hearts feel deep despair;

What a friend we have in mother,

With her tender love and care.
```

What a friend we have in mother,
Ev'ry smile and tear to share;
What a friend we have in mother,
As she kneels in evening prayer.
All the world may turn against us,
Clouds of darkness ev'rywhere;
What a friend we have in mother,
Love is always waiting there.

I'll Take You Home Again, Kathleen

Thomas Westendorf

```
    D       A7        C# D
I'll take you home again, Kathleen,
  A7    A°A7        D
Across the ocean wild and wide,
             A7      C# D
To where your heart has ever been
    A    E7    D E7 A
Since first you were my bonny bride.
    A7          C#  D
The roses all have left your cheek,
    A7                    D
I've watched them fade away and die;
F#7 Bm            Em    F# B7
Your voice is sad when e'er you speak
    E7      D  E7  D E7 A
And tears be-dim your loving eyes.
```

Chorus:
```
    D     A7        C# D
Oh, I will take you back, Kathleen,
    A7      A°  A7       D
To where your heart will feel no pain;
            D7            G
And when the fields are fresh and green,
D°D     A7        D
I'll take you to your home again.
```

I know you love me, Kathleen dear,
Your heart was ever fond and true,
I always feel when you are near,
That life holds nothing, dear, but you.
The smiles that once you gave to me,
I scarcely ever see them now;
Though many times I see
A dark'ning shadow on your brow.

To that dear home beyond the sea,
My Kathleen shall again return,
And when thy old friends welcome thee,
Thy loving heart will cease to yearn.
Where laughs the little silver stream,
Beside your mother's humble cot,
And brightest rays of sunshine gleam,
There all your grief will be forgot.

Silver Threads Among The Gold

Eben E. Rexford and Hart Pease Danks

```
G C G   D7   G
Darling, I am growing old,
D7              G
Silver threads among the gold
     C G   D7   G
Shine upon my brow today,
D7              G
Life is fading fast away.
D7                    G
But, my darling, you will be, will be,
D    A7          D
Always young and fair to me,
G   C G   D7   G
Yes, my darling, you will be,
D7              G
Always young and fair to me.
```

Chorus:
```
D7               G
Darling, I am growing old,
D    A7          D
Silver threads among the gold.
G   C G   D7   G
Shine upon my brow today,
D               G
Life is fading fast away.
```

When your hair is silver white,
And your cheeks no longer bright,
With the roses of the May,
I will kiss your lips and say:
Oh! my darling, mine alone, alone,
You have never older grown,
Yes, my darling, mine alone,
You have never older grown.

Love can never more grow old.
Locks may lose their brown and gold,
Cheeks may fade and hollow grow,
But the hearts that love will know
Never, never, winter's frost and chill,
Summer warmth is in them still;
Never winter's frost and chill,
Summer warmth is in them still.

Love is always young and fair.
What to us is silver hair,
Faded cheeks or steps grown slow,
To the heart that beats below?
Since I kissed you, mine alone, alone,
You have never older grown;
Since I kissed you, mine alone,
You have never older grown.

Drink To Me Only With Thine Eyes

Ben Jonson

```
C        G7  C         Dm
Drink to me only with thine eyes,
   C G7  C      G7  C
And I   will pledge with mine;
        G7      C    Dm
Or leave a kiss within the cup,
   C  G7  C  G7 C
And I'll not ask for wine.
```

```
The thirst that from the soul doth rise,
        F   C          G
Doth ask a drink divine,
C        G7      C    Dm
But might I of Jove's nectar sip,
  C   G7  C     G7  C
I would not change for thine.
```

I sent thee late a rosy wreath,
Not so much hon'ring thee,
As giving it a hope that there
It could not withered be;
But thou thereon dids't only breathe,
And send'st it back to me,
Since when it grows and smells, I swear,
Not of itself, but thee.

In The Gloaming

Meta Orred and Annie F. Harrison

```
F            C7   C#dimDm
In the gloaming, oh my darling!
Gm     F     C7    F
When the lights are dim and low,
            C7     C#dimDm
And the quiet shadows falling
Gm   C7          F
Softly come and softly go,
F7   Bb       F7    Bb
When the winds are sobbing faintly
G7    F    BbF   C7
With a gentle, unknown woe,
F            C7   C#dim Dm
Will you think of me and love      me
Gm   C7          F
As you did once long ago?
```

In the gloaming, oh my darling!
Think not bitterly of me!
Though I passed away in silence,
Left you lonely, set you free,
For my heart was crushed with longing;
What had been could never be.
It was best to leave you thus, dear,
Best for you and best for me.

Summer Is A-Coming In

```
D      A  D    A D    A7    D
Summer is a-coming in, loudly sing, cuckoo.
      A      D
Groweth seed and bloweth mead,
            G    D      G D
And springs the wood anew, Sing, cuckoo.
     A7    D   A7
Ewe now bleateth after lamb,
     D    A7    D
Low'th after calf the cow,
Bm     Em   D      A7   D    A   D
Bullock starteth, buck now verteth Merry sing, cuckoo.
  G  D  A7 D       A7        D
Cuckoo, cuckoo, We'll sing'st thou, cuckoo
A7  D       A7  D
Nor cease thou never now.
```

Sweet Adeline

Richard H. Gerard and Harry Armstrong

```
   G          C        G
In the evening when I sit alone a-dreaming
    E7      A7     D7   G
Of days gone by, love, to me so dear,
D7     G         C       G
There's a picture that in fancy oft' appearing,
    E7      A7         D7     G
Brings back the time, love, when you were near.
     G7     C     Cm    G
It is then I wonder where you are, my darling,
    A7                 D7
And if your heart to me is still the same.
     G          C        G
For the sighing wind and nightingale a-singing
    E7      A7     D7     G
Are breathing only your own sweet name.
```

Chorus:

```
G   A7 D7G    B7 C
Sweet Adeline, My Adeline,
A7          D7          G
At night, dear heart, for you I pine.
D7     G         B7      C
In all my dreams, your fair face beams.
C#dim7 G   E7   A7       D7 G
You're the flower of my heart, Sweet Adeline.
```

I can see your smiling face as when we wandered
Down by the brookside, just you and I.
And it seems so real at times till I awaken,
To find all vanished, a dream gone by.
If we meet sometime in after years, my darling,
I trust that I will find your love still mine.
Tho' my heart is sad and clouds above are hov'ring
The sun again, love, for me would shine.

Beautiful Dreamer

Stephen Foster

```
C                    Dm
Beautiful dreamer, wake unto me,
G7                               C
Starlight and dewdrops are waiting for thee.
                         Dm
Sounds of the ruse world heard in the day,
G7                             C
Lulled by the moonlight have all passed away.
G7            C
Beautiful dreamer, queen of my song,
Am         D7     G7
List while I woo thee with soft melody.
C                    Dm
Gone are the cares of life's busy throng,
G7                        C   E7  Am
Beautiful dreamer, awake unto me,
F     C     G7      C
Beautiful dreamer, awake unto me.
```

Beautiful dreamer, out on the sea
Mermaids are chanting the wild Lorelei,
Over the streamlet vapors are borne
Waiting to fade at the bright coming morn.
Beautiful dreamer, beam on my heart
E'en as the morn on the streamlet and sea,
Then will all clouds of sorrow depart.
Beautiful dreamer, awake unto me,
Beautiful dreamer, awake unto me.

PICTURES FROM LIFE'S OTHER SIDE

Tear-jerkers, tragedies and sentimental songs

Father, Dear Father, Come Home With Me Now

Henry Clay Work

```
Ab        Ab7     Db
Father, dear father, come home with me now!
Ab                  Eb7
The clock in the steeple strikes one;
    Ab       Ab7     Db
You said you were coming right home from the shop,
    Ab       Eb7       Ab
As soon as your day's work was done.
    Eb7           Ab        Ab7
Our fire has gone out, our house is all dark,
    Db      Bb7          Eb7
And mother's been watching for you;
    Ab         Ab7    Db
With poor brother Benny so sick in her arms,
    Ab        Eb7       Ab
Without you, oh, what can she do?
    Eb7       Ab      Db
Come home! Come home! Come home!
    Ab        Eb7     Ab
Please, father, dear father, come home.
```

Chorus:

```
Eb7                       Ab
Hear the sweet voice of your own little child,
    Fm      Bb7     Eb7
As she tearfully begs you to come!
    Ab        Ab7     Db
Oh, who could resist this most pitiful pray'r,
    Ab       Eb7      Ab
"Please, father, dear father, come home!
```

Father, dear father, come home with me now!
The clock in the steeple strikes two;
The night has grown colder and Benny is worse,
But he has been calling for you.
Indeed, he is worse, Ma says he will die,
Perhaps before morning shall dawn;
And this is the message she sent me to bring,
"Come quickly, or he will be gone."
Come home! Come home! Come home!
Please, father, dear father, come home.

Father, dear father, come home with me now!
The clock in the steeple strikes three;
The house is so lonely, the hours are long,
For poor weeping mother and me.
Yes, we are alone, poor Benny is dead,
And gone with the Angels of light;
And these were the very last words that he said,
"I want to kiss Papa good night."
Come home! Come home! Come home!
Please, father, dear father, come home.

When The Work's All Done This Fall

```
    G                            C
A group of jolly cowboys discussin' plans at ease,
    D
Says one, "I'll tell you somethin' boys,
                        G
    if you will listen please.
                                   C
I am an old cow-puncher and here I'm dressed in rags,
    D                                          G
But I used to be a wild one and to go on great big jags
                          C
Now I have a home boys, a good one, you all know,
D                                     G
Though I have not seen it since long, long ago,

I'm goin' home to see my mother,
        C
    once more to see them all,
    D
I'm a-goin' to see my mother, boys,
                               G
    when the work's done this fall."
```

Refrain:
"After the round-up's over, after the shipping's done,
I am going right straight home, boys,
    ere all my money's gone.
I have changed my ways, boys, no more will I fall;
And I am going home boys,
    when the work's all done this fall."

That very night this cowboy
    went out to stand his guard,
Well, the night was dark and stormy
    and rainin' very hard,
Them cattle got excited, they rushed in wild stampede,
And the cowboy tried to head them,
    runnin' at full speed.
Ridin' through the darkness so loudly did he shout,
Doin' his best to head them and turn the herd about,
His saddle horse did stumble and down on him did fall,
And he won't see his mother
    when the work's all done this fall.

His body was so mangled, we boys all thought him dead,
Till he opened wide his blue eyes
    and this is what he said:
Said, "Cisco, take my saddle,"
    he said, "Moe, you take my gun,
Jack, you take my horses after I am done,
Send mother my wages, the wages I have earned,
For I am afraid, boys, my last steer I have turned.
I'm going to a new range, I hear my master call,
And carve upon my tombstone, I won't be home this fall."

A Picture From Life's Other Side

D
In the world's mighty gall'ry of pictures

Hang scenes that are painted from life;
G   D
There's pictures of joy and of sorrow,
E7   A7
There's pictures of peace and of strife,
D
There's pictures of youth and of beauty,

Old age and the blushing young bride.
G   D   B7
All hang on the wall, but the saddest of all,
G   A7   D
Is a picture from life's other side.

Refrain:

D
It's a picture from life's other side,

Someone who fell by the way;
G   D
A life has gone out with the tide
E7   A7
That may have been happy one day;
D
Some poor old mother at home

Is watching and waiting alone,
G   D   B7
Just longing to hear from her loved ones so dear,
G   A7   D
It's a picture from life's other side.

The first scene is that of a gambler,
Who lost all his money at play,
Draws his dead mother's ring from his finger
That she wore on her wedding day.
His last earthly treasure, he stakes it,
Bows his head that his shame he might hide,
When they lifted his head, they found he was dead,
It's a picture from life's other side.

The next scene is that of two brothers
Whose paths in life different ways led,
The one was a-livin' in luxury
While t'other one begged for his bread;
One dark night they met on a highway,
"Your money or life," the thief cried;
Then he took with his knife, his dear brother's life,
It's a picture from life's other side.

The next scene is down by the river,
A heart-broken mother and child,
The old harbor lights stand and shiver,
On an outcast that no one will save;
Perhaps she was once a good woman,
Somebody's darlin' and pride,
God help her, she leaps, there is no one to weep,
It's a picture from life's other side.

One Fish Ball

        C   G7
A man went walking up and down,
                 C
To find a place where he could dine in town.
          G7
A man went walking up and down
                 C
To find a place where he could dine in town.

He found himself an expensive place, } (twice)
And entered in with modest face.

He took his purse his pocket hence, } (twice)
But all he had was fifteen cents.

He looked the menu through and through, } (twice)
To see what fifteen cents would do.

The cheapest item of them all, } (twice)
Was thirty cents for two fish balls.

The waiter, he, on him did call, } (twice)
He softly whispered, "One fish ball."

The waiter bellowed down the hall, } (twice)
"This creep here wants just one fish ball!"

The guests, they turned, both one and all, } (twice)
To see who wanted one fish ball.

The man then said, quite ill at ease, } (twice)
"And a piece of bread, Sir, if you please."

The waiter bellowed down the hall, } (twice)
"You get no bread with one fish ball!"

There is a moral to this all. } (twice)
You get no bread with one fish ball.

Who would have bread with his fish ball, } (twice)
Must get it first, or not at all.

Who would fish balls with fixin's eat, } (twice)
Must get some friend to stand a treat.

Little Joe The Wrangler

N. Howard Thorp / Tune: *Little Old Log Cabin*
In The Lane

```
        E                            A          E
It was Little Joe, the wrangler, he'll wrangle never more,
                       B7
His days with the cavvy they are done.
        E                            A          E
Twas a year ago last summer, he rode up to the herd,
           B7             E
Just a little Texas stray and all alone.
           A
Well it's long late in the evening
              E
   when he rode up to the herd
                           B7
On a little brown pony he called Chaw.
        E                            A          E
With his broken shoes and overalls, a tougher lookin' kid,
              B7             E
Well, I never in my life had seen before.
```

His saddle was a Southern kack built many years ago
And an O.K. spur from one foot idly hung,
While the hot roll in the cotton sack
    was loosely tied behind
And a canteen from the saddle horn was slung.

He left his home in Texas, his ma had married twice,
And his old man beat him every day or two,
So he saddled up old Chaw one night
    and lit a chuck this way,
Thought he'd try and paddle now his own canoe.

Well, he was looking for a job
But he didn't know straight up about no cow,
But the boss kind of liked the kid and
    cuts him out a mount,
'Cause he sort-a liked that little stray somehow.

Taught him how to herd the horses
    and to know them all by name
And to get 'em in by daylight if he could,
And to load the chuck wagon
    and to always hitch the team
And to help the old cookie rustle wood.

We was camped down in Red River
    and the weather she was fine,
We was settin' on the south side in a bend,
When a norther commenced blowin'
    and we all doubles up our guard
'Cause it took all hands to hold them cattle then.

Well, little Joe the wrangler
    was called out with the rest
And hardly had that kid got to that herd
When them devils they stampeded
    like a hail storm long they flew
And all of us was ridin' for the lead.

'Tween the streak of lightnin'
    we could see that horse there out ahead,
It was little Joe the wrangler in the lead,
He was ridin' old Blue Rocket
    with his slicker for a blind,
A-tryin' to check them lead cows in their speed.

Well, he got them kind a-millin'
    and sort-a quieted down
And the extra guard back to the camp did go,
But one of them was missin' and we all saw at a glance
'Twas our little lost horse herder, wrangler Joe.

Next mornin' just at sun-up we found where Rocket fell,
Down in a washout forty feet below,
Beneath his horse smashed to a pulp,
    his spurs had rung the knell
For our little lost horse herder, wrangler Joe.

The Drunkard's Doom

```
     Eb      Ab         Eb
At dawn today I saw a man
                    Bb7
Come out of a saloon;
Eb7 Ab              Abm Eb Ebm F7
His   eyes were sunk, his   lips were   parched,
      Bb7             Eb
Oh, that's the drunkard's doom.
```

His little son stood by his side,
And to his father said,
"Father, mother lies sick at home
And sister cries for bread."

He rose and staggered to the bar
As oft he'd done before,
And to the landlord smilingly said,
"Just fill me one glass more."

The cup was filled at his command,
He drank of the poisoned bowl,
He drank, while wife and children starved,
And ruined his won soul.

A year had passed, I went that way,
A hearse stood at the door;
I paused to ask, and one replied,
"The drunkard is no more."

I saw the hearse move slowly on,
No wife nor child was there;
They too had flown to heaven's bright home
And left a world of care.

Now all young men, a warning take,
And shun the poisoned bowl;
'Twill lead you down to hell's dark gate,
And ruin your own soul.

A Bird In A Gilded Cage

Arthur J. Lamb and Harry Von Tilzer

G   Am
The ballroom was filled with fashion's throng,
D7   G
It shone with a thousand lights;
Am A7 G AD7
And there was a woman who passed along,
G A7   D7
The fairest of all the sights.
 G   Am
A girl to her lover then softly sighed,
  D7   C7 B
"There's riches at her command."
  Am Edim7 G E7
"But she married for wealth, not for love," he cried,
    A7   D7
"Though she lives in a mansion grand."

Chorus:

  G   Am
"She's only a bird in a gilded cage,
  D7   G
A beautiful sight to see.
    Am   A7 G Adim7
You may think she's happy and free from care,
Em A7   D7
She's not, though she seems to be.
  G   C6 Am
'Tis sad when you think of her wasted life,
  D7   G
For youth cannot mate with age;
  Am A7 G E7
And her beauty was sold for an old man's gold,
  A7 D7 G
She's a bird in a gilded cage."

I stood in a churchyard just at eve,
When sunset adorned the West;
And looked at the people who'd come to grieve
For loved ones now laid at rest.
A tall marble monument marked the grave
Of one who'd been fashion's queen;
And I thought "She is happier here at rest,
Than to have people say when seen:"

Villikins And His Dinah

Tune: *Sweet Betsy from Pike*

  C G7   C
'Tis of a rich merchant who in London did dwell,
     F   C7
He had but one daughter, an uncommon nice girl.
  F   C   F   C
Her name it was Dinah, scarce sixteen years old,
      G7   C
With a very large fortune in silver and gold.

Refrain:

    C G7 C
Singing tu la lol la rol lal to rol lal la.

As Dinah was a-walking her garden one day,
Her papa he came to her, and thus he did say—
"Go dress yourself, Dinah, in gorgeous array,
And get you a husband both gallant and gay!"

"Oh, papa, oh, papa, I've not made up my mind,
And to marry just yet, why I don't feel inclined;
To you my large fortune I'll gladly give o'er,
If you'll let me live single a year or two more."

"Go, go, boldest daughter," the parent replied;
"If you won't consent to be this here young man's bride,
I'll give your large fortune to the nearest of kin,
And you shan't reap the benefit of one single pin."

As Villikins was walking the garden around,
He spied his dear Dinah lying dead on the ground;
And a cup of cold pizen it lay by her side,
With a *billet-doux* stating 'twas by pizen she died.

He kissed her cold corpus a thousand times oer,
And called her his Dinah though she was no more,
Then swallowed the pizen like a lover so brave,
And Villikins and his Dinah lie both in one grave.

Moral:
Now all you young maidens take warning by her,
Never not by no means disobey your governor,
And all you young fellows mind who you clap eyes on,
Think of Villikins and Dinah and the cup of cold pizen.

She Is More To Be Pitied Than Censured

William B. Gray

```
      F                 G7
At the old concert hall on the Bowery,
      C7              F
'Round a table were seated one night,
                         G7
A crowd of young fellows carousing,
A    C7                     F
With them life seemed cheerful and bright.
      C    G7       C
At the very next table was seated
   G7              C
A girl who had fallen to shame,
      F                    G7
All the young fellows jeered at her weakness,
      C7             F
Till they heard an old woman explain:
```

Chorus:

```
      F         C7       F
She is more to be pitied than censured,
   D7                  G7
For a moment just stop and consider,
   Bb      Bbm        F
She is more to be helped than despised,
      C7              F
That a man was the cause of it all.
            C7      F
She is only a lassie who ventured,
   G7              C7
On life's stormy path, ill-advised,
      F          C7          F  F7
Do not scorn her with words fierce and bitter,
   Bb         Bbm        A7
Do not laugh at her shame and downfall.
```

There's an old-fashioned church 'round the corner,
Where the neighbors all gathered one day,
While the parson was preaching a sermon,
O'er a soul that had just passed away,
'Twas this same wayward girl from the Bow'ry,
Who a life of adventure had led,
Did the clergyman jeer at her downfall?
No, he asked for God's Mercy and said—

They're Moving Father's Grave

```
      D
They're moving father's grave to build a sewer.
      A7               D
They're moving it regardless of expense.
      G            D
They're shifting his remains to put in nine inch drains,
            A7           D
To irrigate some plush bloke's residence.
```

Now what's the use in having a religion,
And thinking when you're dead your troubles cease,
If some rich city chap wants a pipeline to his—tank.
And they'll never let a workman sleep in peace.

Now father in his life was never a quitter,
And I don't suppose he'll be a quitter now.
'Cause when the job's complete,
    he'll haunt that sewer sweet,
And they'll only turn the tap when he'll allow.

And won't there be some bleeding consternation,
And won't them city toffs begin to rave.
Which is more than they deserve
    for they had the bleeding nerve
To muck about a British workman's grave.

The Letter Edged In Black

```
      D                          A7
I was standing by the window yesterday morning,
                          D
Without a thought of worry or of care,
                              E7
When I saw the postman coming up the pathway
   A7                 D
With such a happy look and jolly air.
```

Oh, he rang the bell and whistled while he waited,
And then he said, "Good morning to you, Jack."
But he little knew the sorrow that he brought me
When he handed me a letter edged in black.

With trembling hand I took the letter from him,
I broke the seal and this is what it said:
"Come home, my boy, your dear old father wants you!
Come home, my boy, your dear old mother's dead!"

"The last words that your mother ever uttered—
'Tell my boy I want him to come back,'
My eyes were blurred, my poor old heart is breaking,
As I'm writing you this letter edged in black."

I bow my head in sorrow and in silence,
The sunshine of my life it all has fled,
Since the postman brought that letter yesterday morning
Saying, "Come home, my boy,
    your poor old mother's dead!"

"Those angry words, I wish I'd never spoken,
You know I never meant them, don't you, Jack?
May the angels bear me witness, I am asking
Your forgiveness in this letter edged in black."

I could hear the postman whistling yesterday morning,
Coming down the pathway with his pack,
But he little knew the sorrow that he brought me
When he handed me that letter edged in black.

After The Ball Is Over

Charles K. Harris

```
F                               C7
A little maiden climbed on an old man's knee,
                                F
Begged for a story, "Do, uncle, please,
               D7       Gm
Why are you single, why live alone?
Bb        F D7  G7  C7    Bb
Have you no babies, have you no home?"
 Dm   A7        Bb   C7 Bb F
"I had a sweetheart, years, years ago;
Bb        F    Dm G7        Bb
Where she is now, pet, you soon will know,
F          D7      Gm
List to the story, I'll tell it all,
Bb        F     D7   G7 C7    F
I believed her faithless—after the ball."
```

Chorus:

```
       Bb   F                   C7
After the ball is over, after the break of morn,
Gm   D7       Gm C7         F
After the dancers leaving, after the stars are gone,
    Bb   F    D7              G7
Many a heart is aching, if you could read them all,
C7             F  D7   G7 C7   F
Many the hopes that have vanished, after the ball.
```

Bright lights were flashing in the grand ballroom,
Softly the music, playing sweet tunes,
There came my sweetheart, my love, my own,
I wish some water, leave me alone!
When I returned, dear, there stood a man,
Kissing my sweetheart as lovers can,
Down fell the glass, pet, broken, that's all,
Just as my heart was, after the ball.

Long years have passed, child, I've never wed,
True to my last love, though she is dead,
She tried to tell me, tried to explain,
I would not listen, pleadings were vain.
One day a letter came from that man,
He was her brother, the letter ran,
That's why I'm lonely, no home at all,
I broke her heart, pet, after the ball.

The Ship That Never Returned

Henry Clay Work

```
     C                F
On a summer's day when the wave was rippled
     C             G7
By the softest, gentlest breeze,
     C              F
Did a ship set sail with a cargo laden
     C     G7    C
For a port beyond the seas;
          C                      F
There were sweet farewells, there were loving signals,
        C            G7
While a form was yet discerned,
            C             F
Though they knew it not, 'twas a solemn parting
       C        G7   C
For the ship—she never returned.
```

Chorus:

```
        C                F
Did she ever return? No, she never returned.
   C           G7
Her fate is still unlearned;
           C                      F
Though for years and years there were fond ones watching,
     C     G7   C
Yet the ship, she never returned.
```

Said a feeble lad to his anxious mother,
"I must cross the wide, wide sea;
For they say, perchance, in a foreign climate,
There is health and strength for me."
'Twas a gleam of hope in a maze of danger,
And her heart for her youngest yearned;
Yet she sent him forth with a smile and blessing
On the ship that never returned.

"Only one more trip," said a gallant seaman,
As he kissed his weeping wife;
"Only one more bag of the golden treasure,
And 'twill last us all through life.
Then I'll spend my days in my cozy cottage,
And enjoy the rest I've earned";
But alas! poor man! for he sailed commander
Of the ship that never returned.

Little Rosewood Casket

     E   B7   E
There's a little rosewood casket
         B7   E
Sitting on a marble stand,
            A   E
There's a package of love letters
     B7   E
Written by my true lover's hand.

"Will you go and get them, sister?
And read them o'er tonight,
For I woke and tried, but could not,
For the tears would blind my sight.

"Please go trace the lines so slowly,
Then I'll not miss even one,
For the precious hand that wrote this,
Its last work for me is done.

"You have got them now, dear sister,
Come sit down upon my bed,
And press gently to your bosom
This poor throbbing, aching head.

"Tell him that I never blamed him,
Not an unkind word was said. (spoke?)
Tell, oh tell him, sister, tell him
That my heart in coldness broke.

"Tell him that I never blamed him,
Though to me he proved untrue;
Tell him that I'll never forget him,
Till I bid this world adieu.

"When I'm dead and in my coffin,
And my shroud's around me bound,
And my little bed is ready
In the cold and silent ground,

"Place his letters and his locket
Close together o'er my heart;
Let the little ring he gave me,
From my finger never part.

"You have finished now, dear sister.
If you read them o'er again,
While I listen to you read them,
I will lose all sense of pain.

"While I listen to you read them,
I will gently fall asleep,
For it's sweet to wake with Jesus.
Oh, dear sister, do not weep."

The Vacant Chair

Henry F. Washburn and George F. Root
Civil War Song

       A
We shall meet but we shall miss him,
     E7
There will be one vacant chair;
     A   D
We shall linger to caress him,
    E7   A
While we breathe our ev'ning pray'r;
    E   B7   E
When a year ago we gathered,
     B7   E
Joy was in his mild blue eye,
     B7   E
But a golden chord is severed,
     B7   E
And our hopes in ruin lie.

Chorus:

E7   A
We shall meet but we shall miss him,
     E7
There will be one vacant chair,
     A   D
We shall linger to caress him,
    E7   A
While we breathe our ev'ning pray'r.

At our fireside, sad and lonely,
Often will the bosom swell
At remembrance of the story,
How our noble Willie fell;
How he strove to bear our banner
Through the thickest of the fight,
And uphold our country's honor,
In the strength of manhood's night.

True, they tell us wreaths of glory
Ever more will deck his brow,
But this soothes the anguish only,
Sweeping o'er our heartstrings now.
Sleep today, Oh early fallen,
In thy green and narrow bed,
Dirges from the pine and cypress
Mingle with the tears we shed.

The Man On The Flying Trapeze

G   C
Oh, once I was happy, but now I'm forlorn,
D7   G
Like an old coat that is tatter'd and torn.
         C
I'm left in this wide world to fret and to mourn,
 D7   G
Betrayed by a maid in her teens.
    Em   B7
Now this girl that I loved, she was handsome and swell,
   Em   B7
And I tried all I knew her to please;
   Em   B7
But I never could please her one quarter so well,
   E7   A7
As that man on the flying trapeze.

Chorus:

  G   C
Oh, he flies thro' the air with the greatest of ease,
  D7   G
The daring young man on the flying trapeze.
         C
His movements are graceful; all girls he does please,
  D7   G
And my love he has purloinéd away.

Now the young man by name was Señor Boni Slang,
Tall, big and handsome, as well made as Chang.
Where'er he appeared, how the hall loudly rang,
With ovations from all people there.
He'd smile from the bar on the people below
And one night he smiled on my love,
She winked back at him, and she shouted "Bravo!"
As he hung by his nose from above.

Her father and mother were both on my side
And tried very hard to make her my bride.
Her father, he sighed, and her mother, she cried
To see her throw herself away.
'Twas all no avail, she went there ev'ry night
And threw her bouquets on the stage,
Which caused him to meet her—how he ran me down,
To tell it would take a whole page.

One night I as usual went to her dear home,
And found there her mother and father alone.
I asked for my love, and soon 'twas made known,
To my horror, that she'd run away.
She packed up her boxes and eloped in the night,
With him with the greatest of ease.
From two stories high he had lowered her down
To the ground on his flying trapeze.

Some months after that I went into a hall;
To my surprise I found there on the wall
A bill in red letters which did my heart gall,
That she was appearing with him.
He'd taught her gymnastics, and dressed her in tights
To help him live at ease.
He'd made her assume a masculine name,
And now she goes on the trapeze.

Final Chorus:
She floats through the air with the greatest of ease;
You'd think her a man on the flying trapeze.
She does all the work while he takes his ease,
And that's what's become of my love.

Where Is My Wandering Boy Tonight?
Robert Lowry

G   C   D7 G
Where is my wand'ring boy tonight?
    Em   C   C
The boy of my tenderest care,
  G   C   D7 G
The boy that was once my joy and light,
  D7   G
The child of my love and prayer?

Chorus:

  C   Cm6 G
O where is my boy tonight?
  D7   A7 D7
O where is my boy tonight?
  G   D7 G7 C
My heart o'erflows, for I love him, he knows,
Cm G   D7   G
O where is my boy tonight?

Once he was pure as morning dew,
As he knelt at his mother's knee;
No face was so bright, no heart more true,
And none was so sweet as he.

O could I see you now my boy
As fair as in olden time,
When prattle and smile made home a joy,
And life was a merry chime!

Go for my wand'ring boy tonight;
Go search for him where you will;
But bring him to me with all his blight,
And tell him I love him still.

WITH YOUR GUNS AND DRUMS

Songs of soldiers, war and peace....

The Cruel War Is Raging

```
      G              C           D7
The cruel war is raging and Johnny has to fight,
    G          C          D7      G
I want to be with him from morning till night.
    G                C          D7
I want to be with him, it grieves my heart so,
    G         C         D7       G
Oh, let me go with you; no, my love, no.
```

I'd go to your captain, get down upon my knees,
Ten thousand gold guineas I would give for your release;
Ten thousand gold guineas, it grieves my heart so,
Won't you let me go with you?—no, my love, no.

Tomorrow is Sunday and Monday is the day
Your captain calls for you and you must obey;
Your captain calls for you, it grieves my heart so,
Won't you let me go with you?—no, my love, no.

Your waist is too slender, your fingers are too small,
Your cheeks are too rosy to face the cannon ball;
Your cheeks are too rosy, it grieves my heart so,
Won't you let me go with you?—no, my love, no.

Johnny, oh Johnny, I think you are unkind,
I love you far better than all other mankind;
I love you far better than tongue can express,
Won't you let me go with you?—yes, my love, yes.

I'll roach back my hair, men's clothing I'll put on,
I'll pass for your comrade as we march along;
I'll pass for your comrade and none can ever guess,
Won't you let me go with you?—yes, my love, yes.

Bobby Campbell

```
    D             C
The cry of the raven rang over the moor,
    D              C
The pipes were calling the clans to war,
    C     D        C      D
A lad, Bobby Campbell, he wept for the dead,
    C                    D
And he remembered the words that his father had said.
```

Remember, my son, who you are,
Never dishonor the clan,
For your fathers before you, have died in the field,
They have died for our green pasture land.

They rolled out the cannons and assembled the men,
The women were prayin' that they'd come home again,
Goodby to my Mary, I'm going to war,
To fight for the honor of the son that you bore.

Now the pipes they are still and the victory's at hand,
But now for his Mary, no peace in the land,
And young Bobby Campbell lies dead in the field,
His gun still clutched in his hand.

The Quartermaster Store

```
        F
Oh, it's beer, beer, that makes you feel so queer,
    C7        F
In the store, in the store,
```

It's beer, beer, that makes you feel so queer,
    C7   F
In the quartermaster store.

Refrain:

```
                    Bb
Mine eyes are dim, I cannot see,
    Gm            C7
I have not brought my specs with me,
    F        C7           F
I—have—not—brought—my specs with me.
```

Oh, it's cheese, cheese,
    that brings you to your knees, etc.

Oh, it's tea, tea, but not for you and me, etc.

Oh, it's beans, beans, that make you fill your jeans, etc.

The Yellow Rose Of Texas

```
        A
There's a yellow rose in Texas that I am going to see,
        E7
No other soldier knows her, no soldier, only me;
    A
She cried so when I left her, it like to broke my heart,
    E7     A        E7      A
And if I ever find her, we never more will part.
```

Chorus:

```
A
She's the sweetest rose of color this soldier ever knew,
        E7
Her eyes are bright as diamonds, they sparkle like the dew;
        A
You may talk about your dearest May and sing of Rosa Lee,
    E7          B7
But the Yellow Rose of Texas
        A     E7    A
    beat the belles of Tennessee.
```

When the Rio Grande is flowing
    and the starry skies are bright,
She walks along the river in the quiet summer night;
She thinks if I remember, when we parted long ago,
I promised to come back again and not to leave her so.

Oh, now I'm going to find her, for my heart is full of woe,
And we'll sing the song together, that we sung so long ago;
We'll play the banjo gaily, and we'll sing the songs of yore,
And the Yellow Rose of Texas shall be mine forevermore.

I Come And Stand At Every Door

Nazim Hikmet / Tune: The Great Silkie

```
  G       F         G
I come and stand at ev'ry door,
    Em      Am    D    Bm
But none can hear my silent tread,
C        Bm  Am    Em
I knock and yet remain unseen,
   Am  Em    F    G
For I am dead, for I am dead.
```

I'm only seven, although I died
In Hiroshima long ago,
I'm seven now as I was then—
When children die, they do not grow.

My hair was scorched by swirling flame,
My eyes grew dim and then grew blind;
Death came and turned my bones to dust,
And that was scattered by the wind.

I need no fruit, I need no rice,
I need no sweets or even bread;
I ask for nothing for myself,
For I am dead, for I am dead.

All that I ask is that for peace,
You fight today, you fight today,
So that the children of the world
May live and grow and laugh and play.

I Just Wanna Stay Home

New words by Irwin Silber

```
G
I don't wanna march in the infantry,
D              G
Ride in the cavalry, shoot with artillery,
```

```
I don't wanna fly over Germany,
D           G
I just wanna stay home.
```

Chorus:
```
G    C       G
I just wanna stay home,
     C       G
I just wanna stay home,
```

```
I just wanna be real neighborly,
D7             G
Raise a family, have two kids or three,
```

```
I just wanna live in peace you see,
D           G
I just wanna stay home.
```

I don't wanna make the battle news,
Wear those army shoes, nothing I can use,
I don't wanna sing the G.I. Blues,
I just wanna stay home.

I don't want those army ration kits,
Capture Austerlitz, insurance benefits,
I don't wanna get those G.I.—fits,
I just wanna stay home.

I don't wanna make the G.I. change,
Shoot on the rifle range, go to a land that's strange,
I don't wanna die for the Stock Exchange,
I just wanna stay home.

I ain't gonna fall for phony lies,
Save free enterprise, for some other guys,
I'm sure gonna go out and organize,
'Cause I just wanna stay home.

I've Got To Know

Woody Guthrie / Tune: Farther Along

```
D                  G        D
Why do your warships sail on my waters?
                        E7          A
Why do your bombs drop down from my sky?
D                G         D
Why do you burn my towns and my cities?
                A7      D
I want to know, friend, I want to know.
```

Chorus:

```
D              G       D
I've got to know, friend, I've got to know,
                    E7    A
Hungry lips ask me wherever I go.
D                  G     D
Comrades and friends all falling around me,
                  A7      D
I've got to know friend, I've got to know.
```

Why do these boats haul death to my people?
Nitro explosives, cannons and guns?
Where is my food, my soap, and my warm clothes?
I've got to know, friend, I've got to know.

You keep me in jail and you lock me in prison,
Your hospital's jammed and your asylum is full.
What made your cop kill my trade union worker?
I've got to know, friend, I've got to know.

Why do these warships sail on my ocean?
Why do these bombs drop down from my sky?
Why doesn't your ship bring
    some food and some clothing?
I've got to know, friend, I've got to know.

The Kerry Recruit

G   D7   G
At the age of nineteen I was diggin' the land,
      A7   D
With me brogues on me feet and me spade in me hand,
    G   Bm
"Oh," says I to meself, "What a pity to see,
    Em   D
Such a fine Kerry lad diggin' spuds in Tralee."

Chorus:

      G   Em
With me kerry-ay-ay, fa la de ral lay,
D   G
Kerry ay-ay, fa la de ral lay.

So I buttered me brogues and shook hands with me spade,
And went off to the fair like a dashing young blade,
A sergeant comes up and says, "Will ye enlist?"
"Sure, sergeant," says I, "slip the bob in me fist!"

Then up steps the captain, a man of great fame,
And straightway he asks me my country and name.
"I've told ye before, and I tell ye again,
Me father and mother were two Kerry men."

The first thing they gave me, it was a red coat,
With a lump of black leather to tie round me throat.
The next thing they gave me, says I, "What is that?"
"Sure man, a cockade for to stick in yer hat."

The next thing they gave me they called it a gun,
And under the trigger I settled me thumb,
The gun it belched fire and vomited smoke,
And gave me poor shoulder the devil's own stroke.

The next thing they gave me they called it a horse,
With a saddle and bridle me two legs across.
So I gave it the bit and I gave it the steel,
And, Holy Mother! she went like an eel!

Now the first place they took us was down to the sea,
Aboard a great ship bound for the Crimee.
With three sticks in the middle all hung with white sheets,
She walked on the water without any feet.

We reached the Balaclave all safe and sound,
And hungry and weary we lay on the ground,
Next morning at daybreak a bugle did call,
And served us a breakfast of powder and ball.

We licked them at Alma and then Innerman,
But the Russians they foiled us at the Redan,
While scaling the ramparts meself lost an eye,
And a great Russian bullet ran away with me thigh,

All bleeding and dying I lay on the ground,
With arms, legs and feet all scattered around,
Says I to meself, "If me father were nigh,
He'd have buried me now just in case I should die."

But a surgeon comes by and he soon stops the blood,
And he gave me an iligant leg made of wood,
And they made me a pension of ten pence a day,
And contented with shellocks I live on half pay.

Texas Rangers

      D   A E7   A
Come all you Texas Rangers, wherever you may be,
    D   A   D A
I'll tell you of some troubles that happened unto me,
                     D
My name is nothing extra so that I will not tell,
   A   D E7   A
And here's to all you Rangers, I'm sure I wish you well.

'Twas at the age of seventeen, I joined the jolly band,
We marched from San Antonio down to the Rio Grande,
Our captain he informed us,
    perhaps he thought it right,
Before we reach the station, boys,
    you'll surely have to fight.

And when the bugle sounded, our captain gave commands,
"To arms, to arms," he shouted,
    "And by your horses stand,"
I saw the smoke ascending, it seemed to reach the sky,
And then the thought it struck me,
    my time had come to die.

I saw the Indians coming, I heard them give a yell,
My feelings at that moment no tongue can ever tell,
I saw the glittering lances,
    their arrows round me flew,
And all my strength had left me,
    and all my courage too.

We fought for nine hours fully
    before the strife was o'er,
The likes of dead and wounded I never saw before,
And when the sun had risen
    and the Indians they had fled,
We loaded up our rifles and counted up our dead.

And all of us were wounded, our noble captain slain,
The sun was shining sadly across the bloody plain,
Sixteen as brave a Rangers as ever rode the West,
Were buried by their comrades
    with arrows in their breasts.

And now my song is ended, I guess I've sung enough,
The life of any Ranger you see is very tough,
And if you have a mother that don't want you to roam,
I advise you by experience, you'd better stay at home.

That Crazy War

C
Now over there across the sea they've got another war,
  F
But oh, I wonder if they know
          C
   just what they're fighting for,
  G7   C
In that war, that crazy war.

In 1917, you know, we helped them win their fight,
But all we got was a lesson
   in what Sherman said was right,
In that war, that crazy war.

I was a simple country lad; I lived down on the farm,
I'd never even killed a gnat nor done a body harm,
Until that war, that crazy war.

One day the sheriff caught me, said "Come along, my son,
Your Uncle Sam is needing you to help him tote a gun,
In that war, that crazy war."

They took me down to the courthouse,
   my head was in a whirl,
And when the doctors passed on me,
   I wished I'd been a girl,
In that war, that crazy war.

They took me out to the rifle range
   to hear the bullets sing,
I shot and shot that whole day long and never hit a thing,
In that war, that crazy war.

The captain said to fire at will and I said who is he,
The old fool got so raving mad he fired his gun at me,
In that war, that crazy war.

When first we got to sunny France,
   I looked around with glee,
But rain and kil-o-meters was all that I could see,
In that war, that crazy war.

A cannonball flew overhead, I started home right then,
The corporal he was after me but the general beat us in,
In that war, that crazy war.

And now we're back at home again
   from over there in France,
The enemy lost the battle and we lost all our pants,
In that war, that crazy war.

I run all over Europe a-trying to save my life,
There will come another war, I'll send my darling wife,
In that war, that crazy war.

Well, wars may come and wars may go,
   but get this on your mind,
There will come another war, I'll be hard to find,
In that war, that crazy war.

Mrs. McGrath

     G   D7
"Oh, Mrs. McGrath," the sergeant said,
         G
"Would you like to make a soldier out of your son Ted?
      D7   G   D7
With a scarlet coat and a big cocked hat;
   G   D7   G
Now Mrs. McGrath, wouldn't you like that?"

Chorus:

G   Em G
Wid yer too-ri-aa, fol-the-did-dle-aa
Em   D   G
Too-ri-oo-ri-oo-ri-aa.
         Em   G
Wid yer too-ri-aa, fol-the-did-dle-aa.
Em   D   G
Too-ri-oo-ri-oo-ri-aa.

So Mrs. McGrath lived on the seashore
For the space of seven long years or more
Till she saw a big ship sailing into the bay,
"Hullaloo, bubaloo, and I think it is he!"

"Oh, Captain dear, where have ye been?
Have you been sailing on the Mediterreen?
Or have you any tidings of my son Ted?
Is the poor boy living or is he dead?"

Then up comes Ted without any legs,
And in their place two wooden pegs.
She kissed him a dozen times or two,
Saying, "Holy Moses, 'tisn't you."

"Oh then were ye drunk or were ye blind
That ye left yer two fine legs behind?
Or was it walking up the sea
Wore yer two fine legs from the knees away?"

"Oh I wasn't drunk and I wasn't blind,
But I left my two fine legs behind;
For a cannon ball on the fifth of May
Took my two fine legs from the knees away."

"Oh, then, Teddy me boy," the widow cried,
"Yer two fine legs were yer mama's pride.
Them stumps of a tree wouldn't do at all,
Why didn't ye run from the big cannon ball?

"All foreign wars I do proclaim
Between Don John and the King of Spain.
And by herrins I'll make them rue the time
That they swept the legs from a child of mine.

"Oh then, if I had ye back again,
I'd never let ye go to fight the King of Spain.
For I'd rather my Ted as he used to be
Than the King of France and his whole Navee."

Weeping Sad And Lonely (When This Cruel War Is Over)

Charles C. Sawyer and Henry Tucker

```
G              C      G     A7    D7
Dearest love, do you remember when we last did meet,
G                 C       G     D7   G
How you told me that you loved me, kneeling at my feet?
D7                   G     C    A7    D7
Oh! how proud you stood before me in your suit of blue,
B7                   Em   G  D7  G
When you vowed to me and country ever to be true.
```

Chorus:

```
C         G      A7          D7
Weeping sad and lonely, hopes and fears how vain!
             G      G7       C
(Yet praying) When this cruel war is over,
G    D7       G
Praying that we meet again.
```

When the summer breeze is sighing mournfully along,
Or when autumn leaves are falling,
    sadly breathes the song.
Oft in dreams I see thee lying on the battle plain,
Lonely, wounded, even dying, calling but in vain.

If amid the din of battle, nobly you should fall,
Far away from those who love you, none to hear you call,
Who would whisper words of comfort,
    who would soothe your pain?
Ah, the many cruel fancies ever in my brain.

But our country called you, darling,
    angels cheer your way;
While our nation's sons are fighting, we can only pray.
Nobly strike for God and liberty, let all nations see,
How we love the starry banner, emblem of the free.

Goober Peas

```
C              F        C
Sitting by the roadside on a summer's day,
                    Dm       D7G
Chatting with my messmates, passing time away,
C              F         C
Lying in the shadow, underneath the trees,
            F    C   G7    C
Goodness how delicious, eating Goober Peas!
```

Chorus:

```
         F
Peas! Peas! Peas! Peas!
G7        C
Eating Goober Peas!
         F    C   G7    C
Goodness how delicious, eating Goober Peas!
```

When a horseman passes, the soldiers have a rule,
To cry out at their loudest, "Mister, here's your mule!"
But another pleasure enchantinger than these,
Is wearing out your grinders, eating goober peas!

Just before the battle the Gen'ral hears a row,
He says, "The Yanks are coming, I hear their rifles now."
He turns around in wonder,
    and what do you think he sees?
The Georgia Militia—eating goober peas!

I think my song has lasted almost long enough,
The subject's interesting, but rhymes are mighty rough,
I wish this war was over, when free from rags and fleas,
We'd kiss our wives and sweethearts
    and gobble goober peas!

Gee, But I Want To Go Home

```
   G
The coffee that they give us,
    D7
They say is mighty fine,

It's good for cuts and bruises
       G
And tastes like iodine.
```

Chorus:

```
C                    G
I don't want no more of army life,
               D7    G    D7      G
Gee, but I want to go, Gee, but I want to go home.
```

The biscuits that they give us,
They say are mighty fine,
One fell off a table
And killed a pal of mine.

The clothes that they give us,
They say are mighty fine,
Me and my buddy,
Can both fit into mine.

They treat us all like monkeys
And make us stand in line,
They give you fifty dollars a week
And take back forty-nine.

The girls at the service club
They say are mighty fine,
Most are over eighty
And the rest are under nine.

Mademoiselle From Armentieres

```
F                          C7
Mademoiselle from Armentieres, parlez-vous,
                           F
Mademoiselle from Armentieres, parlez-vous,
                 C7
Mademoiselle from Armentieres,
        F            C7
She hasn't been kissed* in forty years,
F          C7 F
Hinky dinky parlez-vous.
```

She might have been old for all we knew, etc.
When Napoleon flopped at Waterloo, etc.

You might forget the gas and the shell,
But you'll never forget the mademoiselle.

Oh, madam, have you a daughter fair?
To wash a soldier's underwear?

She got the palms and the Croix-de-Guerre
For washing soldiers' underwear.

The General got the Croix-de-Guerre,
The son-of-a-bitch was never there.

The officers get all the steak,
And all we get is the belly-ache.

The MPs say they won the war,
Standing on guard at the cafe door.

I didn't care what became of me,
So I went and joined the infantry.

They say they mechanized the war,
So what the hell are we marching for?

---

* an obvious euphemism

Old Soldiers Never Die

```
C                        G7      C
There is an old cook house not far away,
                         G7          C
Where we get sweet damn all three times a day.
F              C
Ham and eggs we never see, damn all sugar in our tea,
F        C     G7     C
As we are gradually fading away.
```

Chorus:

```
C                    G7       C
Old soldiers never die, never die, never die,
```

Old soldiers never die,
```
G7            C
They just fade away.
```

(An alternate chorus left over from the
    Eisenhower administration)
Old golfers never die, never die, never die,
Old golfers never die—
They just lose their balls.

Bring 'Em Home

Barbara Dane and active duty GI's adapted from
Pete Seeger's If You Love Your Uncle Sam

```
        C
Seventy thousand* dead and gone,
            Am
Bring 'em home, bring 'em home,
        F          C
Uncle Sam is in the wrong,
F      C     G7
Bring 'em home, bring 'em home.
```

Wash the blood off of our hands,
Bring 'em home, bring 'em home,
Stop the war in Vietnam!
Bring 'em home, bring 'em home.

We wanna end this war right now,
Don't take a genius to figure out how.

Let 'em fly or let 'em float,
Pack 'em all up in a big-ass boat.

GIs fight and GIs die,
Some people get rich while Nixon lies.

They said it was a freedom fight,
Don't you know that's about half-past right.

I'm gonna let Vietnam alone,
Fight for my own rights here at home.

In Chicago and Vietnam,
They want to get us to be "the man."

Buddy, I got news for you,
I got better things to do.

We've been marching a long, long time,
But now we're marching with our minds.

If they tell us that's not the way,
We'll give 'em one big FTA!**

---

* Total U.S. casualties in Southeast Asia
** "Free" (or some other word) The Army!

Old King Cole

```
G        D7       G        C
Old King Cole was a merry old soul,
    G        D7       G
And a merry old soul was he.
               D7
He called for his pipe and he called for his bowl,
    G        D7       G
And he called for his privates three.
```

Chorus:

```
G    C    G
Beer, beer, beer said the privates,
    D7       G
Merry men are we.
           D7   G7   C
There's none so fair as can compare
        A7   D7   G
With the fighting infantry.
        G    C    G
(Hut two, hut two, hut said the corp'rals
G    D7   G
Merry men are we.)
```

Old King Cole was a merry old soul,
And a merry old soul was he.
He called for his pipe and he called for his bowl
And he called for the corporals three.
"Hut two, hut two, hut," said the corporals,
"Beer, beer, beer" said the privates,
"Merry men are we,
There's none so fair as can compare
With the fighting infantry."

(The chorus is cumulative, adding in
the following order:)
"Right by squads, squads right," said the sergeants.
"We do all the work," said the shavetails.
"We want a ten day leave," said the captains.
"The Army's shot to Hell," said the chaplains.
"Da, what's my next command," said the colonels.

Old King Cole was a merry old soul,
And a merry old soul was he,
He called for his pipe and he called for his bowl
And he called for the generals three.
"Beer, beer, beer," said the generals.
"Beer, beer, beer," said the colonels.
"Beer, beer, beer," said the chaplains.
"Beer, beer, beer," said the captains.
"We're too young to drink," said the shavetails.
"Beer, beer, beer," said the corporals.
"Beer, beer, beer," said the privates,
"Merry men are we,
There's none so fair as can compare
With the fighting infantry."

Marching Through Georgia

Henry Clay Work

```
A                              D        A
Bring the good old bugle, boys, we'll sing another song;
                        B7       E7
Sing it with a spirit that will start the world along,
A        D        A
Sing it as we used to sing it, fifty thousand strong,
E                        A
While we were marching through Georgia.
```

Chorus:

```
                  D        A
Hurrah! Hurrah! We bring the jubilee!
                  E
Hurrah! Hurrah! The flag that makes you free!
A        D        A        C#
So we sang the chorus from Atlanta to the sea,
D    B7   E    E7        A
While we were marching through Georgia.
```

How the people shouted when they heard the joyful sound!
How the turkeys gobbled which our commissary found!
How the sweet potatoes even started from the ground,
While we were marching through Georgia.

Yes, and there were Union men
    who wept with joyful tears,
When they saw the honored flag
    they had not seen for years;
Hardly could they be restrained
    from breaking forth in cheers,
While we were marching through Georgia.

"Sherman's dashing Yankee boys
    will never reach the coast!"
So the saucy Rebels said, and 'twas a handsome boast;
Had they not forgot, alas! to reckon with the host,
While we were marching through Georgia.

So we made a thoroughfare for Freedom and her train,
Sixty miles in latitude, three hundred to the main;
Treason fled before us, for resistance was in vain,
While we were marching through Georgia.

Johnny I Hardly Knew You

```
        Gm
With your guns and drums and drums and guns,
    Dm
Hurroo, hurroo.
        Gm
With your guns and drums and drums and guns,
    Bb       D7
Hurroo, hurroo.
```

```
         Gm                Cm
With your guns and drums and drums and guns,
       Gm         D7
The enemy nearly slew you.
         Gm   Cm   Gm   D7
Oh, my darling dear you look so queer,
         Gm   Cm   Gm
Oh, Johnny I hardly knew you.
```

Where are your eyes that were so mild, etc.,
When my heart you so beguiled?
Why did you run from me and the child?
Oh, Johnny I hardly knew you.

Where are your legs that used to run, etc.,
When you went for to carry a gun,
Indeed your dancin' days are done,
Oh, Johnny I hardly knew you.

I'm happy for to see you home, etc.,
Oh my darlin' so pale and wan,
So low in flesh, so high in bone—
Oh, Johnny I hardly knew you.

They're rolling out the guns again, etc.,
But they never will take our sons again,
No, they never will take our sons again,
Johnny, I'm swearin' to you.

The British Grenadiers

```
      F    C  F C  F        Bb6 C7 F
Some talk of Alexander and some of Hercules,
         C F  C   F           Bb   C7 F
Of Hector and Lysander and such great names as   these.
```

```
But of all the world's brave heroes,
    F7   Bb              FC
   there's none that can compare
C7   F          C   F   C
With a tow, row, row, row, row, row,
    F      Dm Bb6 C7 F
   to the British  Grenadier.
```

Whene'er we are commanded to storm the palisades,
Our leaders march with fuses and we with hand grenades.
We throw them from the glacis about the enemy's ears,
With a tow, row, row, etc.

And when the siege is over, we to the town repair,
The townsmen cry, "Hurrah, boys, here comes a Grenadier;
Here come the Grenadiers, my boys,
   who know no doubts or fears!"
With a tow, row, row, etc.

Then let us fill a bumper and drink a health to those
Who carry caps and pouches, and wear the louped clothes,
May they and their commanders live happy all their years,
With a tow, row, row, etc.

The Minstrel Boy

Thomas Moore

```
(A)  D                   (A)  D
The  minstrel boy to the war is    gone,
     G     D        Em(7)  D
In the ranks of death you'll find    him,
(A)    D                   (A)  D
His  father's sword he has girded    on
        G              Em(7)  D
And  his  wild  harp  slung  behind   him.
Bm   F#7 Bm            A   E7   A
"Land  of  song,"  said  the warrior  bard,
F#     Bm         F#  Bm
"Though  all  the  world  betrays  thee,
G     D                  A7   D
One  sword at least thy rights shall guard,
F#7 G   D              Em7  A D
One  faithful harp  shall  praise  thee.
```

The minstrel fell but the foeman's chain
Could not bring his proud soul under,
The harp he loved ne'er spoke again,
For he tore its chords asunder.
And said, "No chains shall sully thee,
Thou soul of love and bravery!
Thy songs were made for the pure and free,
They shall never sound in slavery!"

High Germany

```
A7  Dm      C  DmF    Gm          Dm
O   Polly dear, O Polly, the rout has now begun,
       F            Bb    F     C     F
And we must march away at the beginning of the drum.
                  Bb    Am  Bb        Gm
Go dress yourself all in your best and come along with me,
Bb F   Bb    C   F       Am  Gm        Dm
I'll take you to the cruel wars in   High Germany.
```

I'll buy a horse, my love, and on it you shall ride,
And all of my delight shall be riding by your side;
We'll call at every ale house, and drink when we are dry,
So quickly on the road, my love, we'll marry by and by.

O Harry, dear Harry, you mind what I do say,
My feet they are so tender I cannot march away,
And besides, my dearest Harry,
   though I'm in love with thee,
I am not fit for cruel wars in High Germany.

O cursed were the cruel wars that ever they should rise,
And out of merry England press many a lad likewise!
They pressed young Harry from me,
   likewise my brothers three,
And sent them to the cruel wars in High Germany.

Just Before The Battle, Mother

George F. Root

A   D
Just before the battle, mother,
E7   A
I am thinking most of you,
           D
While upon the field we're watching,
E7   A
With the enemy in view.
           D
Comrades brave are 'round me lying,
B7   E7
Filled with thought of home and God;
    A   D
For well they know that on the morrow,
E7   A
Some will sleep beneath the sod.

Chorus:

A   D
Farewell, mother, you may never
B7   E7
Press me to your breast again;
   A   D
But, oh, you'll not forget me, mother,
E7   A
If I'm numbered with the slain.

Oh, I long to see you, mother,
And the loving ones at home,
But I'll never leave the banner,
Till in honor I can come.
Tell the traitors all around you
That cruel words we know,
In every battle kill our soldiers
By the help they give the foe.

Hark! I hear the bugles sounding,
'Tis the signal for the fight,
Now may God protect us, mother,
As He ever does the right.
Hear the "Battle Cry of Freedom,"
How it swells upon the air,
Oh, yes, we'll rally 'round the standard,
Oh we'll perish nobly there.

Buttermilk Hill

Am   Em   Am
Here I sit on Buttermilk Hill,
C   Am
Who can blame me, cry my fill,
    C   Am   F
And every tear will turn a mill,
Am   E   Am
Johnny has gone for a soldier.

I'll sell my rod, I'll sell my reel,
Likewise I'll sell my spinning wheel,
And buy my love a sword of steel,
Johnny has gone for a soldier.

Me, oh my, I love him so,
Broke my heart to see him go,
And only time can heal my woe,
Johnny has gone for a soldier.

The Riflemen At Bennington

    G   D7   G
Why come ye hither, Redcoats,
           D7   G
Your minds what madness fills?
     D7   G
In our valleys there is danger
         D7   G
And there's danger in our hills.
       C
Oh, hear ye not the singing
       G
Of the bugle wild and free?

Full soon you'll know the ringing
         D7   G
Of the rifle from the tree.

Chorus:

     C
Oh, the rifle *(clap——)*
     G
Oh, the rifle *(clap——)*

In our hands
    D7   G
Will prove no trifle.

Ye ride a goodly steed,
Ye may know another master
Ye forward come with speed,
But you'll learn to back much faster
When you meet our mountain boys
And their leader Johnny Stark
Lads who make but little noise,
But who always hit the mark.

Have ye no graves at home,
Across the briny water?
That hither you must come
Like the bullocks to the slaughter,
If we the work must do
Why the sooner 'tis begun,
If flint and trigger hold but true,
The sooner 'twill be done.

The Blue Bells Of Scotland

Annie McVicar and Dorothy Jordan

      C   F   C   F
Oh where, please tell me where
         C   G7   C
Is your highland laddie gone?
      C   F   C   F
Oh where, please tell me where
         C   G7   C
Is your highland laddie gone?
                Am
He's gone with streaming banners
        G   D7   G7
Where the noble deeds are done,
        C   F   C   F
And my sad heart will tremble
        C   G7   C
Until he comes safely home.

Oh, where, please tell me where   } *(twice)*
Does your highland laddie dwell?
He dwells in merry Scotland
At the sign of the blue bell
And my blessing went with him
On the day he went away.

Oh what, please tell me what   } *(twice)*
Does your highland laddie wear?
A bonnet with a proud plume,
'Tis the gallant badge of war
And a plaid 'cross his bold breast
That will one day wear a star.

Suppose, oh supposing that   } *(twice)*
Your highland lad should die?
The bagpipes shall play o'er him
And I'd lay me down and cry
But it's oh! in my heart that
I do wish he may not die.

Hey Betty Martin

G
Hey Betty Martin, tip toe, tip toe,
               D7   G
Hey Betty Martin, tip toe fine.

Johnny get your gun and sword and pistol,
Johnny get your gun and come with me.

Johnny get your hair cut, hair cut, hair cut,
Johnny get your hair cut, hair cut short.

Dumbarton's Drums

from the singing of Bob Beers

Chorus:

        D   A
Dumbarton's drums they sound so bonnie.
                    D
When they remind me of my Johnnie;
       G   D
What fond delight can steal upon me,
        A   D
When Johnnie kneels and kisses me.

Across the fields of bounding heather,
Dumbarton tolls the hour of pleasure;
A song of love that has no measure,
When Johnnie kneels and sings to me.

'Tis he alone that can delight me,
His graceful eye, it doth invite me;
And when his tender arms enfold me,
The blackest night doth turn and dee.

My love he is a handsome laddie,
And though he is Dumbarton's caddie,
Some day I'll be a captain's lady,
When Johnnie tends his vow to me.

The Campbells Are Comin'

Chorus:

  C
The Campbells are comin',

O-ho, O-ho!
G7 C
The Campbells are comin',
 G7
O-ho, O-ho!
C
The Campbells are comin'

From bonnie Loch Lomond,
    F   F♯dim C
The Campbells are   comin',

O-ho, O-ho!

Verses:

   C
The great Argyle, he goes before,
               F
He makes the guns and cannons roar,
G7 C
With sound of trumpet, pipe and drum,
C7 F F♯dim C
And banners   waving in the sun.

With bonnet blue, auld Scotties pride,
And broad claymore hung at their side,
With plumes all nodding in the wind,
They have not left a man behind.

Hark! hark! the Pibroch's sound I hear,
Now bonnie lassie, dinna fear;
'Tis honor calls, I must away,
Argyle's the word and ours the day.

Study War No More

       G
I'm gonna lay down my sword and shield,

Down by the river side,
D7
Down by the river side,
G
Down by the river side,

I'm gonna lay down my sword and shield,

Down by the river side,
         D7   G
Gonna study war no more.

Chorus:

        C
I ain't gonna study war no more,
        G
I ain't gonna study war no more,
         D7   G G7
I ain't gonna study war no more,
        C
I ain't gonna study war no more,
        G
I ain't gonna study war no more,
         D7   G
I ain't gonna study war no more.

I'm gonna walk with the Prince of Peace,
Down by the riverside, (3 times)
I'm gonna walk with the Prince of Peace,
Down by the riverside,
And study war no more.

Yes, I'm a'gonna shake hands around the world,
Down by the riverside, (3 times)
I'm gonna shake hands around the world,
Down by the riverside,
And study war no more.

The Girl I Left Behind Me

Samuel Lover

    D   G
I'm lonesome since I crossed the hill,
    D   F♯m
And o'er the moor and valley,
    Bm   G
Such heavy thoughts my heart do fill,
    A7   D
Since parting with my Sally.

I seek no more the fine and gay,
              Bm F♯
For each but doth remind me
    G   E7
How swift the hours did pass away

With the girl I left behind me.

Oh, ne'er shall I forget the night,
The stars were bright above me,
And gently lent their silv'ry light,
When first she vowed she loved me.
But now I'm bound to Brighton camp,
Kind heaven, may favor find me,
And send me safely back again
To the girl I left behind me.

The bee shall honey taste no more,
The dove become a ranger,
The dashing waves shall cease to roar,
Ere she's to me a stranger.
The vows we registered above
Shall ever cheer and bind me,
In constancy to her I love,
The girl I left behind me.

My mind her form shall still retain,
In sleeping or in waking,
Until I see my love again
For whom my heart is breaking.
If ever I should see the day
When Mars shall have resigned me,
For evermore I'll glady stay
With the girl I left behind me.

The D-Day Dodgers

Hamish Henderson / Tune: *Lili Marlene*

```
C                              G7
We're the D-Day Dodgers, way off in Italy
                                C
Always on the vino, always on the spree.
F                 C
Eighth Army scroungers and their tanks,
   G7          C
We live in Rome, among the Yanks.
G7        C        G7    C
We are the D-Day Dodgers, way out in Italy;
G7        C        G7    C
We are the D-Day Dodgers, way out in Italy.
```

We landed in Salerno, a holiday with pay,
The Jerries brought the bands out to greet us on the way,
Showed us the sights and gave us tea,
We all sang songs, the beer was free,
To welcome D-Day Dodgers to sunny Italy. (twice)

Naples and Casino were taken in our stride,
We didn't go to fight there, we went just for the ride.
Anzio and Sangro were just names,
We only went to look for dames,
The artful D-Day Dodgers way out in Italy. (twice)

Dear Lady Astor, you think you're mighty hot,
Standing on the platform talking tommyrot,
You're England's sweetheart and her pride,
We think your mouth's too bleeding wide,
We are the D-Day Dodgers in sunny Italy. (twice)

Look around the mountains in the mud and rain,
You'll find the scattered crosses,
    the sum that have no name,
Heartbreak and toil and suffering gone,
The boys beneath them slumber on,
They are the D-Day Dodgers who stay in Italy. (twice)

When Johnny Comes Marching Home

```
     Em
When Johnny comes marching home again,
   G
Hurrah, hurrah!
     Em
We'll give him a hearty welcome then,
   G     B7
Hurrah, hurrah!
     Em            Am
The men will cheer, the boys will shout,
     Em           B7
The ladies they will all turn out,
        Em D  Em B7
And we'll all  feel gay when
Em        B7       Em
Johnny comes marching home.
```

The old church bell will peal with joy, etc.
To welcome home our darling boy, etc.
The village lads and lassies say,
With roses they will strew the way,
And we'll all feel gay when Johnny comes marching home.

Get ready for the Jubilee, etc.
We'll give the hero three times three, etc.
The laurel wreath is ready now
To place upon his loyal brow,
And we'll all feel gay when Johnny comes marching home.

Let love and friendship on that day, etc.
Their choicest treasures then display, etc.
And let each one perform some part,
To fill with joy the warrior's heart,
And we'll all feel gay when Johnny comes marching home.

Peggy-O

```
    D         Bm   F♯m G D
As we marched down to Fernario
                    F♯m    Bm D A
As we marched down to Fernario,
    G         D
Our captain fell in love
              Bm
With a lady like a dove,
        D       Bm      F♯m G     D
And the name she was called was pretty Peggy-O.
```

"Come go along with me, pretty Peggy-o (twice)
In coaches you shall ride
With your true love by your side,
Just as grand as any lady in the areo."

"What would your mother think, pretty Peggy-o? (twice)
What would your mother think
For to hear the guineas clink,
And the soldiers all are marching before ye-o?"

"You're the man that I adore, handsome Willy-o, (twice)
You're the man that I adore,
But your fortune is too low,
I'm afraid my mother would be angry O."

"Come a-trippin' down the stair, pretty Peggy-o (twice)
Come a-trippin' down the stair
And tie up your yellow hair,
Bid a last farewell to handsome Willy-o."

"If ever I return, pretty Peggy-o (twice)
If ever I return
The city I will burn,
And destroy all the ladies in the areo!"

"Our captain, he is dead, pretty Peggy-o, (twice)
Our captain he is dead
And he died for a maid,
And he's buried in the Louisiana Country-o."

YANKEE DOODLES

Songs from American history....

Fair And Free Elections

Tune: *Yankee Doodle*

      G   D7
While some on rights and some on wrongs,
   G   D7
Prefer their own reflections,
   G   C
The people's rights demand our song,
   D7   G
The rights of free elections.

Chorus:

C
Law and order be the stake,
   G
With freedom and protection,
  C
Let all stand by the ballot box,
   G   D7 G
For fair and free elections.

For government and order's sake
And law's important sections,
Let all stand by the ballot box
For freedom of elections.

Each town and county's wealth and peace,
Its trade and all connections.
With science, arts must all increase
By fair and free elections.

Then thwart the schemes of fighting lands
And traitor disaffections.
Stand up with willing hearts and hands
For fair and free elections.

Should enemies beset us round
Of foreign fierce complexions.
Undaunted we can stand our ground
Upheld by free elections.

Elections are to make us laws,
For trade, peace and protection.
Who fails to vote forsakes the cause
Of fair and free elections.

Free America

Dr. Joseph Warren / Tune: *British Grenadier*
American Revolution

     F   B♭6 F   C   F
Born from a world of tyrants beneath the western sky,
                       B♭6 F   C F
We'll form a new dominion, a land of liberty.

The world shall own we're masters here,
    B♭   F   C
Then hasten on the day,
   F   B♭6 F   C F
Oppose, oppose, oppose, oppose for North Americay.

Lift up your heads, ye heroes,
   and swear with proud disdain,
That wretch that would ensnare you
   shall lay his snares in vain,
Should Europe empty all her force, we'll meet her in array,
And fight and shout and shout and fight
   for North Americay!

The Days Of Forty-Nine

```
    Dm          C
Oh, here you see old Tom Moore,
   Dm    C    Dm
A relic of former days,
                    AM
And a bummer, too, they call me now—
   G           Dm
But what care I for praise?
      D7              Gm
For my heart is filled with the days of yore,
   Dm        Am
And oft do I repine,
C7    F           C
For the days of old, the days of gold,
     B♭maj7   G    Dm
And the days      of Forty-nine.
```

I'd comrades then who loved me well,
A jovial, saucy crew;
There were some hard cases, I must confess,
But still they were brave and true;
Who'd never flinch, whate'er the pinch,
Would never fret or whine,
But like good old bricks, they stood the kicks,
In the days of Forty-nine.

There was Kentuck' Bill, I knew him well,
A fellow so full of tricks,
At a poker game he was always thar,
And as heavy too, as bricks.
He'd play you draw, he'd ante a slug,
And go a hatful blind,
But in a game with Death, Bill lost his breath,
In the days of Forty-nine.

There was Monte Pete, I'll ne'er forget,
For the luck that he always had,
He'd deal for you both night and day,
Or as long as you had a sace.
One night a pistol laid him out,
'Twas his last lay-out in fine,
It caught Pete sure, right in the door,
In the days of Forty-nine.

There was New York Jake, a butcher boy,
So fond of getting tight;
And whenever Jake got on a spree,
He was sp'iling for a fight.
One day he ran agin' a knife,
In the hands of old Bob Cline,
So over Jake we held a wake,
In the days of Forty-nine.

There was Rackensack Jim who could outroar
A buffalo bull, you bet;
He roared all day, he roared all night,
And I believe he's roaring yet.
One night he fell in a prospect hole,
'Twas a roaring bad design,
For in that hole Jim roared out his soul,
In the days of Forty-nine.

There was poor lame Jess, a hard old case,
Who never would repent;
Jess never missed a single meal,
Nor ever paid a cent.
But poor old Jess like all the rest,
Did to death at last resign,
For in his bloom, he went up the flume,
In the days of Forty-nine.

Of all the comrades I had then,
Not one remains to toast;
They have left me in my misery,
Like some poor wandering ghost.
And as I go from place to place,
Folks call me a traveling sign:
Saying, "Here's Tom Moore, a bummer sure,
Of the days of Forty-nine."

The Battle Cry Of Freedom

George F. Root

```
         G          Em         C  G   C
Oh, we'll rally 'round the flag, boys, we'll rally once again,
G                 D7 G
Shouting the battle cry of freedom;
```

We will rally from the hillside,
```
        C
    we'll gather from the plain,
G                 D7 G
Shouting the battle cry of freedom.
```

Chorus:

```
G
The Union forever, hurrah, boys, hurrah!
                      A7       D
Down with the traitor, up with the star;
D7   G  B7   Em     C  G   C
While we rally 'round the flag, boys, rally once again,
G                 D7 G
Shouting the battle cry of freedom.
```

We are springing to the call of our brothers gone before,
Shouting the battle cry of freedom,
And we'll fill the vacant ranks
    with a million freemen more,
Shouting the battle cry of freedom.

We will welcome to our numbers the loyal, true, and brave,
Shouting the battle cry of freedom,
And although they may be poor not a man shall be a slave,
Shouting the battle cry of freedom.

So we're springing to the call
    from the East and from the West,
Shouting the battle cry of freedom,
And we'll hurl the rebel crew
    from the land we love the best,
Shouting the battle cry of freedom.

The Battle Hymn Of The Republic

*Julia Ward Howe/*Tune: *John Brown's Body*

G
Mine eyes have seen the glory of the coming of the Lord;
    C
He is trampling out the vintage
       G
   where the grapes of wrath are stored;

He hath loosed the fateful lightning
     G B7   Em
  of His terrible swift sword,
   Am   G   D7 G
His truth is marching on.

Chorus:

G
Glory, Glory Hallelujah,
C   G
Glory, Glory Hallelujah,
         GEm
Glory, Glory Hallelujah
   Am   G   D7 G
His truth is marching on.

I have seen him in the watch fires
   of a hundred circling camps;
They have builded him an altar
   in the evening dews and damps;
I can read his righteous sentence
   by the dim and flaring lamps,
His day is marching on.

I have read a fiery gospel writ in burnished rows of steel:
"As ye deal with My contemners,
   so with you My Grace shall deal;
Let the Hero, born of woman,
   crush the serpent with his heel,
Since God is marching on.

He has sounded for the trumphet
   that shall never call retreat;
He is sifting out the hearts of men
   before His Judgement Seat;
Oh! Be swift, my soul, to answer Him,
   be jubilant, my feet!
Our God is marching on.

In the beauties of the lilies Christ was born across the sea,
With a glory in his bosom that transfigures you and me;
As He died to make men holy, let us die to make men free,
While God is marching on.

The Constitution And Guerriere

  F
It oft-times has been told, that the British seamen bold
                        C7
Could flog the tars of France so neat and handy, O;
         F
But they never met their match
     Bb
   till the Yankees did them catch,
  C7   F
O the Yankee boys for fighting are the dandy, O!
Bb C7   F
O the Yankee boys for fighting are the dandy, O!

The *Guerriere,* a frigate bold, on the foaming ocean rolled,
Commanded by Dacres the grandee, O;
With as proud a British crew as a rammer ever drew,
They could flog the tars of France
   so neat and handy, O! (twice)

Then Dacres loudly cries,
   "Make this Yankee ship your prize,
You can do it in thirty minutes so neat and handy, O;
Twenty-five's enough, I'm sure,
   and if you'll do it in a score,
I'll treat you to a double tot of brandy, O!" (twice)

The British shot flew hot, which the Yankees answered not,
'Til they got within a space they thought was handy, O;
"Now," Hull says to his crew,
   "Boys, let's see what you can do,
If we take this boasting Briton
   we're the dandy, O!" (twice)

The first broadside we poured
   swept their mainmast overboard,
Which made this lofty frigate look abandoned, O;
Then Dacres he did sigh, and to his officers did cry,
"I did not think these Yankees were so handy, O!" (twice)

Our second told so well, that their fore and mizzen fell,
Which doused the royal ensign so neat and handy, O;
"By George!" says he, "We're done!"
   and they fired a lee gun,
And the Yankees struck up
   Yankee Doodle Dandy, O! (twice)

Now fill your glasses full,
   let's drink a toast to Captain Hull,
So merrily we'll push around the brandy, O;
For John Bull may drink his fill,
   and the world say what it will,
The Yankee tars for fighting are the dandy, O! (twice)

Franklin D. Roosevelt's Back Again

```
C                        F         C
Just hand me my old Martin, for soon I will be startin',
                    G7
Back to dear old Charleston far away;
          C                      F           C
Since Roosevelt's been re-elected, we'll not be neglected,
          G7                         C
We've got Franklin D. Roosevelt back again.
```

First Chorus:

```
                        F
Back again (back again), back again (back again),
          C                      G7
We've got Franklin D. Roosevelt back again.
          C
Since Roosevelt's been elected
          F              C
   moonshine liquor's been corrected,
          G7                         C
We've got legal wine, whiskey, beer and gin.
```

I'll take a drink of brandy and let myself be handy,
Good old times are coming back again;
You can laugh and tell a joke,
   you can dance and drink and smoke,
We've got Franklin D. Roosevelt back again.

Second Chorus:
Back again (back again), back again (back again),
We've got Franklin D. Roosevelt back again;
We'll have money in our jeans,
   we can travel with the queen,
We've got Franklin D. Roosevelt back again.

No more breadlines we're glad to say,
   the donkey won election day,
No more standing in the blowing, snowing rain;
He's got things in full sway,
   we're all working and getting our pay,
We've got Franklin D. Roosevelt
   back again. (First Chorus)

Old Abe Lincoln Came Out Of The Wilderness
Tune: *The Old Gray Mare*

```
G          D     G
Old Abe Lincoln came out of the wilderness,
D7
Out of the wilderness,
G
Out of the wilderness,
              D    G
Old Abe Lincoln came out of the wilderness,
A7        D     G
Many long years a go.
```

Chorus:

```
          C   G
Many long years ago,
          D7  G
Many long years ago,
              D   G
Old Abe Lincoln came out of the wilderness,
A7        D7   G
Many long years ago.
```

Old Jeff Davis tore down the government, etc.

But old Abe Lincoln built up a better one, etc.

White House Blues

```
    E                  E7
McKinley hollered, McKinley squalled,
    A7                    E
The Doc said, McKinley, I can't find the cause.
                      B7      E
You're bound to die—bound to die.
```

Oh it's look here you rascal see what you done
You shot my husband and I got your gun
I'm takin' you back to Washington.

Oh the doc come a-running took off his specs
Said Mr. McKinley better cash in your checks
You're bound to die, bound to die.

Oh Roosevelt in the White House doin' his best
McKinley in the graveyard takin' a rest
He's gone, long gone.

The engine she whistled all down the line
Blowin' at every station, "McKinley is dyin'."
From Buffalo to Washington.

Roosevelt in the White House, drinkin' out a silver cup,
McKinley in the graveyard, he'll never wake up,
He's gone a long, old time.

Battleship Of Maine

```
        C
McKinley called for volunteers,

Then I got my gun,
        F
First Spaniard I saw coming
                    C
I dropped my gun and run,
        G7                  C
It was all about that Battleship of Maine.
```

Chorus:

```
C
At war with that great nation Spain,

When I get back to Spain I want to honor my name,
        G7                  C
It was all about that Battleship of Maine.
```

Why are you running,
Are you afraid to die,
The reason that I'm running
Is because I cannot fly,
It was all about that Battleship of Maine.

The blood was a-running
And I was running too,
I give my feet good exercise,
I had nothing else to do,
It was all about that Battleship of Maine.

When they were a-chasing me,
I fell down on my knees,
First thing I cast my eyes upon
Was a great big pot of peas,
It was all about that Battleship of Maine.

The peas they were greasy,
The meat it was fat,
The boys was fighting Spaniards
While I was fighting that,
It was all about that Battleship of Maine.

Hunters Of Kentucky

Samuel Woodworth / Tune: *Unfortunate Miss Bailey*

```
        F
Ye gentlemen and ladies fair
        C7
Who grace this famous city,
        F
Just listen if you've time to spare,
        C7
While I rehearse this ditty;
        F
And for the opportunity,
        Bb              C7
Conceive yourselves quite lucky,

For 'tis not often that you see
                F
A hunter of Kentucky.
```

Chorus:

```
        Bb
Oh, Kentucky,
                    C7
The hunters of Kentucky!

Oh, Kentucky,
                    F
The hunters of Kentucky!
```

We are a hardy, free-born race,
Each man to fear a stranger;
Whate'er the game we join in chase,
Despoiling time and danger;
And if a daring foe annoys,
Whate'er his strength and forces,
We'll show him that Kentucky boys
Are alligator horses.

I s'pose you've read it in the prints,
How Packenham attempted
To make Old Hickory Jackson wince,
But soon his scheme repented;
For we, with rifles ready cock'd,
Thought such occasion lucky,
And soon around the gen'ral flocked
The hunters of Kentucky.

Tenting On The Old Camp Ground

Walter Kittredge

```
         A                    D        A
We're tenting tonight on the old camp ground,
         E7      A
Give us a song to cheer
              D        A
Our weary hearts, a song of home
       E7            A
And friends we love so dear.
```

Chorus:

```
                          D
Many are the hearts that are weary tonight,
A        D       A      E
Wishing for the war to cease;
C#7           F#m        D          A
Many  are  the  hearts  that  are  looking  for  the  right
       B7    E7     A
To see the dawn of peace.
              D
Tenting tonight, tenting tonight,
E7                    A
Tenting on the old camp ground.
```

```
We've been tenting tonight on the old camp ground,
Thinking of days gone by,
Of the loved ones at home that gave us the hand,
And the tear that said, "Goodbye!"
```

```
We are tired of war on the old camp ground,
Many are dead and gone,
Of the brave and true who've left their homes,
Others been wounded long.
```

```
We've been fighting today on the old camp ground,
Many are lying near;
Some are dead and some are dying,
Many are in tears.
```

Final Chorus:
```
Many are the hearts that are weary tonight,
Wishing for the war to cease;
Many are the hearts that are looking for the right
To see the dawn of peace.
Dying tonight, dying tonight,
Dying on the old camp ground.
```

Beans, Bacon And Gravy

```
             E
I was born long ago,
     A
In eighteen ninety-four.
      B7                  E
I've seen many a panic, I will own,
```

```
I've been hungry, I've been cold,
        A
And now I'm growing old.
       B7                        E
But the worst I've seen is nineteen thirty-one.
```

Chorus:

```
               A
Oh, those beans, bacon and gravy,
       E
They almost drive me crazy,
                             B7
I eat them I see them in my dreams.
        E
When I wake up each morning
         A
And another day is dawning,
     B7                        E
I know I'll have another mess of beans.
```

```
We congregate each morning
At the county barn at dawning,
And everyone is happy, so it seems.
But when our work is done
We file in one by one,
And thank the Lord for one more mess of beans.
```

```
We have Hooverized on butter,
For milk we've only water,
And I haven't seen a steak in many a day.
For cakes and pies and jellies
We substitute sow bellies,
For which we work the county road each day.
```

```
If there ever comes a time
When I have more than a dime,
They will have to put me under lock and key.
For I've been broke so long
I can only sing this song
Of the workers and their misery.
```

Brigham Young

<pre>
        A
Brigham Young was a Mormon bold,
        E   A
And a leader of the roaring ram,
                              D
And the shepherd of a flock of fine tub sheep
        A   E   A
And a passel of pretty little lambs;
        E   A
And he lived with his five and forty wives
        E   A
In the city of the Great Salt Lake,
                                  D
Where they breed and swarm like hens on a farm
        A   E   A
And cackle like ducks to a drake.
</pre>

Chorus:

<pre>
A
Brigham Young, Brigham Young,
        E   A
It's a miracle he survived,
                                  D
With his roaring rams, and his pretty little lambs,
        A   E   A
And his five and forty wives.
</pre>

Number forty-five's about sixteen,
Number one is sixty and three,
And among such a riot how he ever keeps 'em quiet
Is a downright mystery to me,
For they cackle and claw and they jaw, jaw, jaw,
Each one has a different desire,
It would aid the renown of the best shop in town
To supply them with half they require.

Brigham Young was a stout man once,
But now he is thin and old,
And I'm sorry to relate, there's no hair upon his pate,
Where he once wore a covering of gold.
For his oldest wife won't wear white wool,
The young ones won't take red,
And in tearing it out and taking turn about,
They have torn all the wool from his head.

The Good Old Rebel

Tune: *Joe Bowers*

<pre>
C   G7   C
O I'm a good old rebel, now that's just what I am;
                                  Am
For this "fair land of freedom" I do not care a damn.
        C   Am
I'm glad I fit against it, I only wish we'd won,
        C   AmG7   C
And I don't want any pardon for anything I done.
</pre>

I hates the Constitution, this great republic, too.
I hates the Freedmen's Bureau in uniforms of blue.
I hates the nasty eagle, with all his brag and fuss,
But the lyin', thievin' Yankees, I hates 'em wuss and wuss.

I hates the Yankee nation and everything they do;
I hates the Declaration of Independence, too.
I hates the glorious Union, 'tis dripping with our blood;
And I hates the striped banner and I fit it all I could.

I followed Old Marse Robert for four year, near about,
Got wounded in three places, and starved at Point Lookout.
I cotch the rheumatism a-campin' in the snow,
But I killed a chance of Yankees—
        and I'd like to kill some mo'.

Three hundred thousand Yankees is stiff in Southern dust;
We got three hundred thousand befo' they conquered us;
They died of Southern fever, and Southern steel and shot,
And I wish it was three million instead of what we got.

I can't take up my musket and fight 'em now no mo';
But I ain't a-goin' to love 'em, now that is sartin sho;
And I don't want no pardon for what I was and am,
And I won't be reconstructed, and I do not give a damn.

Charles Guiteau

<pre>
E   B7
Come all you Christian people, wherever you may be,
                                          E
And likewise pay attention to these few lines from me,
                              B7
On the thirtieth day of June, I am condemned to die,

For the murder of James A. Garfield,
                E
        upon the scaffold high.
</pre>

Chorus:

<pre>
E   B7
My name is Charles Guiteau, my name I'll never deny,
                                  E
To leave my aged parents in sorrow for to die,
                                      B7
But little did I think, while in my youthful bloom,
                                      E
I'd be carried to the scaffold to meet my fatal doom.
</pre>

I tried to play off insane, but found it would not do,
The people all against me, it proved to make no show.
Judge Cox passed the sentence, the clerk he wrote it down,
On the thirtieth day of June to die I was condemned.

And now I'm at the scaffold to bid you all adieu,
The hangman now is waiting, it's a quarter after two;
The black cap is on my face, no longer can I see,
But when I'm dead and buried, dear Lord, remember me.

Wake Nicodemus

Henry Clay Work
Abolitionist Song

C7 F B♭   F
Nicodemus, the slave, was of African birth,
C7   F   B♭   F
And was bought for a bagful of gold;
C7   F   B♭ F
He was reckon'd as part of the salt of the earth,
C7   F   B♭   F
But he died years ago, very old.
          C   B♭ Am Dm
'Twas his last sad request, so we laid him away
F   C   Am B♭   C
In the trunk of an old hollow tree.
C7   F   B♭   F
"Wake me up!" was his charge, "at the first break of day—
C7   F   B♭   F
Wake me up for the great Jubilee!"

Chorus:

    F   Dm   C F   C F
The "Good Time Coming" is almost here!
C   F   B♭ F B♭   C
It was long, long, long on the way!
    F   C   Dm   F
Now run and tell Elijah to hurry up Pomp,
  Gm7   C7   F   C7
And meet us at the gum-tree down in the swamp,
    F   B♭   F
To wake Nicodemus today.

He was known as a prophet—at least was as wise—
For he told of the battles to come;
And he trembled with dread when he rolled up his eyes,
And we heeded the shake of the thumb.
Though he clothed us with fear, yet the garments he wore
Were in patches at elbow and knee;
And he still wears the suit, that he used to of yore,
And he sleeps in the old hollow tree!

Nicodemus was never the sport of the lash,
Though the bullet has oft cross'd his path;
There were none of his masters so brave or so rash,
As to face such a man in his wrath.
Yet his great heart with kindness was filled to the brim—
He obeyed who was born to command;
But he long'd for the morning which then was so dim—
For the morning which is now at hand.

'Twas a long weary night—we were almost in fear
That the future was more than he knew;
'Twas a long weary night—but the morning is near,
And the words of our prophet are true.
There are signs in the sky that the darkness is gone—
There are tokens in endless array;
While the storm which had seemingly banished the dawn,
Only hastens the advent of day.

Johnny Bull, My Jo, John

Tune: *John Anderson, My Jo, John*
War of 1812

    Dm   C Dm   Am Dm
O, Johnny Bull, my jo, John, I wonder what you mean;

Are you on foreign conquest bent,
    F   Am
  or what ambitious scheme?
    F
Now list to brother Jonathan,
    Dm   Am
  your fruitless plans forego,
Dm   C   Dm   Am
Remain on your fast-anchored isle,
    Dm   Am Dm
  O Johnny Bull, my jo.

O Johnny Bull, my jo, John, don't come across the main;
Our fathers bled and suffered, John,
  our freedom to maintain,
And him who in the cradle, John, repelled the ruthless foe,
Provoke not when to manhood grown,
  O Johnny Bull, my jo.

O Johnny Bull, my jo, John, on Erie's distant shores,
See how the battle rages, and loud the cannon roars;
But Perry taught our seamen to crush the assailing foe,
He met and made them ours, O Johnny Bull, my jo.

What though at Washington a base marauding band,
Our monuments of art, John,
  destroyed with ruthless hand?
It was a savage warfare, beneath a generous foe,
And brings the more disgrace on you,
  O Johnny Bull my jo.

O Johnny Bull, my jo, John,
  when all your schemes have failed,
To wipe away the stigmas, John,
  for New Orleans you sailed;
Far heavier woes await thee, John,
  for Jackson meets the foe,
Whose name and fame's immortal, O Johnny Bull, my jo.

Your schemes to gather laurels here
  I guess were badly planned;
We have whipped you on the ocean, jo,
  we have bothered you on land:
Then hie to old England, John, thy fruitless plans forego,
And haste to thy fast-anchored isle,
  O Johnny Bull, my jo.

Yankee Doodle

G   D7
Yankee Doodle went to town,
  G   D7
A-riding on a pony;
G   C
Stuck a feather in his hat
    D7   G
And called it macaroni.

Chorus:
C
Yankee Doodle keep it up,
G
Yankee Doodle dandy,
C
Mind the music and the step
       G   D7   G
And with the girls be handy.

Father and I went down to camp
Along with Captain Gooding;
And there we saw the men and boys,
As thick as hasty pudding.

There was Captain Washington,
Upon a slapping stallion,
A-giving orders to his men,
I guess there was a million.

And there we saw a thousand men,
As rich as 'Squire David;
And what they wasted every day,
I wish it could be sa-ved.

And there I saw a pumpkin shell,
As big as mother's basin,
And every time they touched it off,
They scamper'd like the nation.

Jefferson And Liberty

   Em
The gloomy night before us flies,
  D
The Reign of terror now is o'er;
  Em
It's gags, inquisitors and spies,
       B7   Em
It's herds of harpies are no more.

Chorus:
  Em   G
Rejoice, Columbia's sons, rejoice;
     D
To tyrants never bend the knee,
    Em   D6   Em   Am6
But join with heart and soul and voice
  Em   B7   Em
For Jefferson and Liberty.

No lordling here, with gorging jaws,
Shall wring from industry the food;
Nor fiery bigot's holy laws
Lay waste our fields and streets in blood!

Here strangers from a thousand shores,
Compelled by tyranny to roam
Shall find, amidst abundant stores,
A nobler and a happier home.

Lincoln And Liberty

Jesse Hutchinson/Tune: *Rosin The Beau*

      E   A
Hurrah for the choice of the nation,
      E   C♯m B7
Our chieftain so brave and so true,
      E
We'll go for the great reformation,
A E   B7   E
For Lincoln and Liberty, too!
                  A
We'll go for the son of Kentucky
   E   C♯m B7
The hero of Hoosierdom through,
      E
The pride of the "Suckers" so lucky,
A E   B7   E
For Lincoln and Liberty, too!

They'll find what by felling and mauling,
Our railmaker statesman can do;
For the people are everywhere calling
For Lincoln and Liberty too.
Then up with the banner so glorious,
The star-spangled red, white, and blue,
We'll fight till our banner's victorious,
For Lincoln and Liberty, too.

Our David's good sling is unerring,
The Slavocrat's giant he slew,
Then shout for the freedom preferring,
For Lincoln and Liberty, too.
We'll go for the son of Kentucky,
The hero of Hoosierdom through,
The pride of the "Suckers" so lucky,
For Lincoln and Liberty, too.

No Irish Need Apply

      C
I'm a decent boy just landed
      F   G7
From the town of Balyfad,
   C   F
I want a situation
          C   G7
And I want it very bad.
        C
I have seen employment advertised,
     F   G7
'Tis just the thing, says I,
      C   F
But the dirty spalpeen ended with,
    C G7 C
"No Irish need apply."
            F
"Whoo!" says I "but that's an insult,
         C
Tho to get the place I'll try,"
  D7
So I went to see this black guard
         G   D7   G
With his "No Irish need apply."

Refrain:
        C
Some do count it a misfortune
     F   G7
To be christened Pat or Dan,
      C   F
But to me it is an honor
     C   G7 C
To be born an Irishman.

I started out to find the house,
I got it mighty soon,
There I found the old chap seated,
He was reading the Tribune.
I told him what I came for,
When he in a rage did fly,
"No," he says, "You are a Paddy,
And no Irish need apply."
Then I gets my dander rising
And I'd like to black his eye,
To tell an Irish gentleman,
"No Irish need apply."

I couldn't stand it longer—
So a-hold of him I took,
And gave him such a welting
As he'd get at Donnybrook.
He hollered, "Millia Murther,"
And to get away did try,
And swore he'd never write again,
"No Irish need apply."
Well, he made a big apology,
I bid him then good-bye,
Saying, "When next you want a beating,
Write 'No Irish need apply.' "

WE SHALL OVERCOME

Songs of struggle and liberation. . . .

The Kent State Massacre

Jack Warshaw and Barbara Dane
Tune: *The Death Of Harry Simms*

Cm
Sisters, listen to my story,
     Fm   Cm
Brothers, listen to my song;

I'll sing of four young people
     Gm   Cm
Who now are dead and gone.

Well, two of them were twenty,
     Gm   Cm
And two were just nineteen,
    Fm   Cm
Just coming out to meet the world,
    Fm   Cm
Like so many you have seen.

It was in Kent State, Ohio,
On a Monday afternoon,
The air was full of springtime,
The flowers were in bloom.
It was a scene of terror
That none will soon forget;
Young students stood with empty hands
To face the bayonets.

Alli Krause and Sandy Scheuer
Marched and sang a peaceful song,
Like Bill Schroeder and Jeff Miller,
They did not think it wrong.
They laughed and joked with troopers,
And some to them did say:
"We march to bring the GIs home,
"And we are not afraid!"

No warning were they given,
No mercy and no chance.
The air was filled with teargas,
The troopers did advance.
Then suddenly they knelt and fired,
The students turned and fled,
Fifteen fell at that moment,
And four of them were dead.

On the campus they were murdered
In the springtime of their lives.
As angry sorrow swept the land,
Their friends and parents cried.
They'd hardly learned to struggle,
But witness they will be.
They died for those in Vietnam,
Also for you and me.

But while we march and mourn today,
There's much more we must do;
We must teach ourselves to organize
And see the struggle through.
Blood flowed upon the 4th of May,
And we'll know it's color well,
Till we sink this murdering system
In the darkest pits of hell!

Viva La Quince Brigada

Adapted by Bart Van der Schelling
Spanish Civil War

Am
Viva la Quince Brigada,
E
Rhumbala, rhumbala, rhumbala.
Am
Viva la Quince Brigada,
E
Rhumbala, rhumbala, rhumbala.
Am   G
Que se ha cubierta de gloria,
        F   E
Ay Manuela, Ay Manuela.
Am   G
Que se ha cubierta de gloria,
        F   E
Ay Manuela, Ay Manuela.

Luchamos contra los Morros,
Rhumbala, . . . etc.
Luchamos contra los Morros,
Rhumbala, . . . etc.
Mercenarios y fascistas, } twice
Ay Manuela, Ay Manuela.

Solo es nuestro deseo . . .
Acabar con el fascismo . . .

En el frente de Jarama . . .
No tenemos ni aviones,
Ni tankes, ni cañones, Ay Manuela . . .

Ya salimos de España . . .
Por luchar en otras frentes . . .

Go Down Moses

     Em   Am Em
When Israel was in Egypt land,
B7   Em
Let my people go,
         Am   Em
Oppressed so hard, she could not stand,
B7   Em
Let my people go.

Chorus:

        A
"Go down, Moses,
G   B7 Em
Way down in Egypt land,

Tell old Pharoah
C7 B7   Em
To let my people go."

Thus saith the Lord, bold Moses said,
Let my people go,
If not, I'll smite your first-born dead,
Let my people go.

No more shall they in bondage toil,
Let them come out with Egypt's spoil.

The Lord told Moses what to do,
To lead the Hebrew children through.

O come along Moses, you'll not get lost,
Stretch out your rod and come across.

As Israel stood by the waterside,
At God's command it did divide.

When they reached the other shore,
They sang a song of triumph o'er.

Pharaoh said he'd go across,
But Pharaoh and his host were lost.

Jordan shall stand up like a wall,
And the walls of Jericho shall fall.

Your foes shall not before you stand,
And you'll possess fair Canaan's Land.

O let us all from bondage flee,
And let us all in Christ be free.

We need not always weep and mourn,
And wear these slavery chains forlorn.

Venga Jaleo
(El Quinto Regimiento)

Spanish Civil War

```
      B7          Em
El diez y ocho de julio;
      D   C     B
En el patio de un convento;
       C    B
El pueblo madrileño;
         C        C   B
Fundó el quinto regimiento.
```

Refrain:

```
B
Venga jaleo, jaleo,
Em          C       D
Sueño de unaametralladora;
C      B
Y Franco se va paseo;
Em D  C    D   C B
Y  Franco se va  paseo.
```

```
Con el quinto, quinto, quinto,
Con el quinto regimiento,
Tengo que marchar al frente
Porque quiero entrar en fuego.
```

```
Con los cuatro batallones
Que estan Madrid defendiendo,
Va toda la flor de Espana,
La flor mas roja del pueblo.
```

```
Madre, madre, madre,
Vaya usted mirando,
Nuestro Regimiento
Se aleja cantando.
```

Oh Freedom

```
G  C  G     D G
Oh freedom, oh freedom,
Bm C  G     D7
Oh  freedom over me,
   G7
And before I'll be a slave,
   C7      G
I'll be buried in my grave,
              D7
And go home to my Lord
   G
And be free.
```

No more weeping, etc.

No more shooting, etc.

There'll be singing, etc.

Los Cuatro Generales
(The Four Insurgent Generals)

Spanish Civil War

```
F       Bb F
Los cuatro generales,
        Bb  F
Los cuatro generales,
Gm       C    F    Bb  F
Los cuatro generales, mamita mia,
   C7   F        C7     F
Qué se han alzado, qué se han alzado.
```

```
Para la Nochebuena (3 times)
Mamita mia
Serán ahorcados. . .
```

```
Madrid, qué bien resistes (3 times)
Mamita mia,
Los bombarderos. . .
```

```
De las bombas se rien (3 times)
Mamita mia,
Los Madrileños. . .
```

```
Puente de los Franceses (3 times)
Mamita mia,
Nadie te pasa. . .
```

```
Porque tus milicianos (3 times)
Mamita mia,
Que bien te guardan. . .
```

Singable Translation:

```
The four insurgent generals (3 times)
Mamita mia,
They tried to betray us. . .
```

```
One Christmas Holy evening (3 times)
Mamita mia,
They'll all be hanging . . .
```

```
Madrid, you wondrous city (3 times)
Mamita mia,
They wanted to take you. . .
```

```
But your courageous children (3 times)
Mamita mia,
They did not disgrace you. . .
```

Shtil Di Nacht
(Silent Is The Night)

Hirsh Glik

Yiddish; Song of the Warsaw Ghetto

```
Em    Am      B7   Em
Shtil, di nacht iz oysgeshternt,
G     C      D7    G
Un der frost hot shtark gebrent.
B7  C       Am   Em   B7 Em
Tsi gedenkstu vi ich hob dich gelernt
Bm            Em
Haltn a shpayer in di hent?
```

```
A moyd, a peltsl un a beret,
Un halt in hant fest a nagan.
A moyd mit a sametenem ponim,
Hit op dem soyne's karavan.
```

```
Getsilt, geshosn un getrofn!
Hot ir kleyninker pistoyl.
An oto, a fulinkn mit vofn
Farhaltn hot zi mit eyn kol!
```

```
Fartog, fun vald aroysgekrochn,
Mit shney girlandn oyf di hor.
Gemutikt fun kleyninkn nitsochn
Far undzer nayem, frayen dor!
```

Singable Translation:

```
Silence, and a starry night,
Frost crackling, fine as sand,
Remember how I taught you
To hold a gun in your hand?
```

```
In fur jacket and beret,
Clutching a hand grenade,
A girl whose skin is velvet
Ambushes a cavalcade.
```

```
Aim, fire, shoot—and hit!
She, with her pistol small,
Halts an autoful,
Arms and all!
```

```
Morning, emerging from the wood,
In her hair, a snow carnation.
Proud of her small victory
For the new, free generation!
```

Hans Beimler

Ernst Busch

German language, Spanish Civil War

G
Vor Madrid im Schutzengraben,

In der Stunde der Gefahr,

Mit den eisernen Brigaden,
D
Sein Herz voll Hass geladen,
G   D   G
Stand Hans, der Kommissar,
D   G   D7   G
Stand Hans, der Kommissar.

Seine Heimat musst er lassen,
Weil er Freiheitskampfer war.
Auf Spaniens blut'gen Strassen,
Fur das Recht der armen Klassen.
    Starb Hans, der Kommissar. (twice)

Eine Kugel kam geflogen
Aus der "heimat" fur ihn her.
Der Schuss war gut erwogen,
Der lauf war gut gezogen—
    Ein deutsches Schiessgewehr. (twice)

Kann dir die Hand draug geben
Derweil ich eben lad'—
Du bleibst in unserm Leben,
Dem feind wird nicht vergeben,
    Hans Beimler, Kamerad. (twice)

Singable Translation:

In Madrid's outlying trenches,
In the hour of danger grim,
With the International Shock brigades,
His heart with hatred all ablaze,
Stood Hans, the Commissar,

Because he fought for freedom,
He was forced to leave his home.
Near the blood-stained Manzanares,
Where he led the fight to hold Madrid,
Died Hans, the Commissar,

A bullet came a-flying
From his Fascist "Fatherland."
The shot struck home, the aim was true,
The rifle barrel well made, too,
A German Army gun,

With heart and hand I pledge you,
While I load my gun again,
You will never be forgotten,
Nor the enemy forgiven,
    Hans Beimler, our Comrade.

We Shall Overcome

C   F   C
We shall overcome,
    F   C
We shall overcome,
    F G7 Am D   G
We shall overcome some day.
F G C   F   C
Oh, deep in my heart (I know that)
F G G7 Am
I do believe,
C   F   C   G7 C
We shall overcome someday.

We'll walk hand in hand, (twice)
We'll walk hand in hand someday,
Oh, deep in my heart
I do believe,
We shall overcome someday.

We shall live in peace, etc.

We shall all be free, etc.

We shall end Jim Crow, etc.

We are not afraid, etc.

The Lord will see us through, etc.

We are not alone, etc.

The whole wide world around, etc.

We shall overcome, etc.

Many Thousand Gone

D   G   D
No more auction block for me,
Em D   Em7 A
No more, no   more;
D   G   D   Bm
No more auction block for me,
Em A   D
Many thousand gone.

No more peck of corn for me,
No more, no more;
No more peck of corn for me,
Many thousand gone.

No more driver's lash for me.

No more pint o' salt for me.

No more hundred lash for me.

No more mistress' call for me.

Bella Ciao

Italian Partisan Song, World War II

Em
Esta mattina mi sono alzato,
                    B7
Oh, Bella ciao, bella ciao, bella ciao, ciao, ciao,
    Am   Em
Esta mattina mi sono alzato
    B7   Em
E ko trovato l'invasor.

Partigiano portami via,
Bella ciao, etc.
Partigiano portami via,
Che mi sento di morir.

E se morio la partigiano,
Bella ciao, etc.
E se morio la partigiano,
Tu mi devi seppellir.

Seppellire lasul montagna,
Bella ciao, etc.
Seppellire lasul montagna,
Sotto l'ombra di un bel fior.

E le genti che passeranno,
Bella ciao, etc.
E le genti che passeranno,
Grideranno che bel fior.

Il piú bel fior del partigiano,
Bella ciao, etc.
Il piú bel fior del partigiano,
Morto per la libertá.

Literal Translation:

This morning when I awoke,
I found the enemy had invaded.

Partisan, take me away,
I feel I am going to die.

If I die as a Partisan,
You have to bury me.

Bury me up in the mountains
Under the shadow of a beautiful flower.

And the people who will pass by
Will say to me: "What a beautiful flower!"

This is the most beautiful flower
Of the Partisans who died for freedom.

A Man's A Man For A' That

Robert Burns

    G   Em   Bm   Em
Is there for honest poverty, that hangs his head and a' that,
   G   Em
The coward slave, we pass him by,
     Bm   D7 G
   we dare be poor for a' that;
    Bm   F♯   Bm   D7
For a' that and a' that, our toils obscure and a' that,
  G   G7   C
The rank is but the Guinea stamp,
    D   D7   G
   the man's the gowd for a' that.

What tho' on homely fare we dine,
   wear hodden gray and a' that,
Give fools their silk and knaves their wine,
   a man's a man for a' that;
For a' that and a' that, their tinsel show and a' that,
The honest man tho' e'er sae poor is king o' men for a' that.

Ye son yon birkie called a lord,
   who struts and stares and a' that,
Tho' hundreds worship at his word,
   he's but a fool for a' that;
For a' that and a' that, his ribband star and a' that,
The man of independent mind,
   he looks and laughs at a' that.

A prince can make a belted knight,
   a marquis, duke and a' that,
But an honest man's above his might,
   good faith he keeps for a' that.
For a' that and a' that, their dignities and a' that,
The pith o' sense and pride o' worth
   are higher rank than a' that.

Then let us pray that come it may,
   as come it will for a' that,
That sense and worth o'er a' the earth
   shall win the fight for a' that.
For a' that and a' that, it's comin' yet for a' that,
That man to man the world o'er,
   shall brothers be for a' that.

The Internationale

Eugene Potter and Pierre Degeyter

  C   F Dm
Arise, you pris'ners of starvation,
  G7   C
Arise you wretched of the earth;
                  F Dm
For justice thunders condemnation,
  G7   C
A better world's in birth.
   G   D   G7
No more tradition's chains shall bind us,

       D   G
Arise, you slaves, no more in thrall,
  G7   C Am7
The earth shall rise on new foundations,
           D   G7
We have been naught, we shall be all.

Refrain:

           C F Dm   G7   C
'Tis the final conflict, let each stand in his place,
         CG C Am   D7   G7
The Internationale shall be the human race,
         C F   Dm7 G7   C
'Tis the final conflict, let each stand in his place,
     A7   DmD   C   G   C
The Internationale shall be the human race.

Keep Your Eyes On The Prize

Tune: *Hold On*

Freedom Riders' Song; SNCC

       Am
Paul and Silas bound in jail,
                E7   Am
Had no money for to go their bail,
                 E7   Am
Keep your eyes on the prize, hold on.

Chorus:

    Em   Am
Hold on, hold on,

Keep your eyes on the prize,
E7   Am
Hold on.

Paul and Silas began to shout,
Jail door opened and they walked out, etc.

Freedom's name is mighty sweet,
Soon one day we're gonna meet.

Got my hand on the gospel plow,
Wouldn't take nothing for my journey now.

The only chain that a man can stand,
Is that chain of hand in hand.

The only thing that we did wrong,
Stayed in the wilderness a day too long.

But the one thing that we did right,
Was the day we started to fight.

We're gonna board that big Greyhound,
Carryin' love from town to town.

We're gonna ride for civil rights,
We're gonna ride for both black and white.

Freedom Is A Constant Struggle

      Dm
They say that freedom is a constant struggle,
      Gm   Dm
They say that freedom is a constant struggle,

They say that freedom is a constant struggle,
           Gm
Oh Lord, we've struggled so long,
Dm   A   Dm
We must be free, we must be free.

They say that freedom is a constant crying, (3 times)
Oh, Lord, we've cried so long,
We must be free, we must be free.

They say that freedom is a constant sorrow, (3 times)
Oh Lord, we've sorrowed so long,
We must be free, we must be free.

They say that freedom is a constant moaning, (3 times)
Oh Lord, we've moaned so long,
We must be free, we must be free.

They say that freedom is a constant dying, (3 times)
Oh Lord, we've died so long,
We must be free, we must be free.

Whirlwinds Of Danger

Polish Revolution of 1848

Dm
Whirlwinds of danger are raging around us,
A   Dm Bb   A
O'erwhelming forces of darkness assail,
Dm
Still in the fight see advancing before us
A   Dm A7   Dm
Red flag of liberty that yet shall prevail.

Chorus:

C7 F   C
Then forward, you workers, freedom awaits you,
C7   F   A7
O'er all the world on land and the sea.
Dm
On with the fight for the cause of humanity,
A   Dm A7   Dm
March, march you toilers, the world will be free.

Women and children in hunger are calling,
Shall we be silent to their sorrow and woe?
While in the fight see our brothers are falling,
Up, then, united, and conquer the foe.

Off with the crown of the tyrants of favor,
Down in the dust with the prince and the peer!
Strike off your chains all you brave sons of labor,
Wake all humanity for victory is near.

The Red Flag

James Connell/Tune: *O Tannenbaum*

C   F   C F
The workers' flag is deepest red,
  Gm   C C7   F
It shrouded oft our martyred dead.
C   E   C F
And 'ere their limbs grew stiff and cold,
  Gm   C C7   F
Their heart's blood dyed its every fold.

Chorus:

   F   Bb F   C7
Then raise the scarlet standard high!
         C7   F
Within its shade we'll live or die.
C   F   C F   D7
Though cowards flinch and traitors sneer,
  Gm D7 Gm C7   F
We'll keep the red flag flying here.

It waved above our infant might
When all ahead seemed dark as night;
It witnessed many a deed and vow:
We must not change its color now.

It well recalls the triumphs past;
It gives the hope of peace at last—
The banner bright, the symbol plain
Of human right and human gain.

With heads uncovered swear we all
To bear it onward till we fall.
Come dungeon dark or gallows grim,
This song shall be our parting hymn.

Slavery Chain Done Broke At Last

Tune: *Joshua Fit The Battle of Jericho*

Em
Slavery chain done broke at last,
Am   B7
Broke at last, broke at last,
Em
Slavery chain done broke at last,
       B7   Em
Gonna praise God till I die.

Chorus:

Em   B7
Way up in that valley,
Em   B7
Prayin' on my knees,
Em
Tellin' God about my troubles,
       B7   Em
And to help me if He please.

I did tell Him how I suffer,
In the dungeon and the chain;
And the days I went with head bowed down,
An' my broken flesh and pain.

I did know my Jesus heard me,
'Cause the spirit spoke to me,
An' said, "Rise my child, your children
An' you too shall be free."

I done p'int one mighty captain
For to marshall all my hosts;
An' to bring my bleeding ones to me,
An' not one shall be lost.

Now no more weary trav'lin',
'Cause my Jesus set me free,
And there's no more auction block for me
Since He gave me liberty.

Raise A Ruckus Tonight

E
My old master promised me,
A   B7   E
Raise a ruckus tonight,
                  C#m
That when he died, he'd set me free,
A   B7   E
Raise a ruckus tonight.

He lived so long that his head got bald,
A   B7   E
Raise a ruckus tonight,
                  C#m
And he got out the notion of dying at all,
A   B7   E
Raise a ruckus tonight.

Chorus:

      E   A   E
Oh, come along, little children, come along,
                             F#m
Come while the moon is shining bright.
B7   A   E
Get on board, little children, get on board,
A#dim   E   B7   E
We're gonna raise a ruckus tonight.

My old mistress promised me, Raise etc.
Sara, I'm gonna set you free, Raise, etc.
She lived till her head got slick and bald,
And the Lord couldn't kill her with a big green maul.

Yes, they both done promised me,
But their papers didn't set me free,
A dose of pizin helped them along,
May the devil preach their funeral song.

Scots Wha Ha'e Wi' Wallace Bled
Robert Burns

G
Scots, wha ha'e wi' Wallace bled!
C
Scots, wham Bruce has aften led!
G   B7   Em Bm
Welcome to your gory bed,
C   G   D7
Or to victory!
G
Now's the day and now's the hour;
D7
See the front of battle lour!
G   B7   Em   Bm
See approach proud Edward's pow'r,
C   G
Chains and slavery!

Wha would be a traitor knave?
Wha will fill a coward's grave?
Wha sae base as be a slave?
Let him turn an' flee!
Wha, for Scotland's king an' law,
Freedom's sword would strongly draw,
Freeman stand, and freeman fa',
Let him on wi' me!

By oppression's woes an' pains,
By your sons in servile chains,
We will drain our dearest veins,
But they shall be free.
Lay the proud usurpers low!
Tyrants fall in every foe!
Liberty's in every blow!
Let us do or dee!

The Star Spangled Banner

Francis Scott Key/Tune: To Anacreon In Heaven

Ab   Fm C7   Fm   Bb 7 Eb
Oh say, can you see, by the dawn's early light,
     Ab   Eb
What so proudly we hailed,
  Eb7 Ab
  at the twilight's last gleaming?
                 Fm
Whose broad stripes and bright stars,
  C7   Fm Bb7 Eb
  thru the perilous fight,
    Ab   Eb
O'er the ramparts we watched,
  Eb7   A
  were so gallantly streaming?
                 Eb7
And the rockets' red glare, the bombs bursting in air,
  Ab   Eb   E7   Ab   Bb7 Eb
Gave proof thru the night, that our flag was still there,
  Ab Bbm7 Ab Db   F7 Bb7   Ab
Oh, say, does   that Star Spangled Banner yet wave,
Eb   Ab   Fm   Bb7 Ab Eb7 Ab
O'er the land of the free and the home of the   brave.

On the shore, dimly seen thro' the mists of the deep,
Where the foe's haughty host in dread silence reposes,
What is that which the breeze, o'er the towering steep,
As it fitfully blows, half conceals half discloses?
Now it catches the gleam of the morning's first beam
In full glory reflected now shines on the stream;
'Tis the Star Spangled Banner, Oh, long may it wave
O'er the land of the free and the home of the brave.

Oh, thus be it ever when free men shall stand
Between their lov'd homes and the war's desolation!
Blest with vict'ry and peace,
   may the heav'n rescued land
Praise the Pow'r that hath made
   and preserved us a nation!
Then conquer we must, when our cause it is just,
And this be our motto: "In God is our trust!"
And the Star Spangled Banner in triumph shall wave
O'er the land of the free and the home of the brave.

Woke Up This Morning With My Mind On Freedom

Southern Civil Rights Song

G
Woke up this morning with my mind stayed on freedom,
C7   G
Woke up this morning with my mind stayed on freedom,
                      B7   Em C
Woke up this morning with my mind stayed on freedom,
  G   Em A7 D7   C G
Hallelu, hallelu, hallelu, hallelu, hallelujah!

Ain't no harm to keep your mind stayed on freedom, etc.

Walkin' and talkin' with my mind stayed on freedom, etc.

Singin' and prayin' with my mind stayed on freedom, etc.

Doin' the twist with my mind stayed on freedom, etc.

Lift Every Voice And Sing

James Weldon Johnson and J. Rosamond Johnson

D   G   B7 Em   G D#dim Em
Lift ev'ry voice and sing, till earth and heaven ring,
   F#dim Em AmB7C   G C#dimD
Ring with   the harmonies of liberty;
       G B7 E   G#dim AmB7 C
Let our rejoicing rise, high as   the list'ning skies,
C#dim G   D#dim Em D7   G
Let it resound loud as   the rolling sea.
G   Em
Sing a song full of the faith
                  G
  that the dark pas has taught us;
        E   Cm
Sing a song full of the hope
          G   G#dim
  that the present has brought us.
     G B7 E G#dim   Am B7C
Facing the rising sun of our new day begun,
G#dim   G   D#dimEmD7G
Let us march on till victory is won.

Stony the road we trod, bitter the chastening rod
Felt in the days when hope unborn had died;
Yet with a steady beat, have not our weary feet
Come to the place for which our fathers sighed?
We have come over a way that with tears has been watered;
We have come, treading our path
   through the blood of the slaughtered;
Out from the gloomy past, 'til now we stand at last
Where the white gleam of our bright star is cast.

God of our weary years, God of our silent tears,
Thou who hast brought us thus far on the way;
Thou who hast by Thy might led us into the light,
Keep us forever in the path, we pray.
Lest our feet stray from the place, our God,
   where we meet Thee,
Lest our hearts, drunk with the wine of the world,
   we forget Thee;
Shadowed beneath Thy hand, may we forever stand,
True to our God, true to our native land.

Ballad Of Ho Chi Minh

Ewan MacColl

   Dm
Far away across the ocean,
           Am
Far beyond the sea's eastern rim,
 Dm
Lives a man who is father of the Indo-Chinese people,
    Bb A7 Dm
And his name it is Ho Chi Minh.

Refrain:

   A7 Dm
Ho, Ho, Ho Chi Minh.
   A7 Dm
Ho, Ho, Ho Chi Minh.

From Viet back to the Saigon Delta
From the mountains and plains below
Young and old workers, peasants
  and the toiling tenant farmers
Fight for freedom with Uncle Ho.
Ho, Ho, Ho Chi Minh, etc.

Now Ho Chi Minh was a deep sea sailor
He served his time out on the seven seas
Work and hardship were part of his early education
Exploitation his ABC.

Now Ho Chi Minh came home from sailing
And he looked out on his native land
Saw the want and the hunger
  of the Indo-Chinese people
Foreign soldiers on every hand.

Now Ho Chi Minh went to the mountains
And he trained a determined band
Heroes all, sworn to liberate the Indo-Chinese people
Drive invaders from the land.

Fourteen men became a hundred
A hundred thousand and Ho Chi Minh
Forged and tempered the army
  of the Indo-Chinese people
Freedom's Army of Viet Minh.

Every soldier is a farmer
Comes the evening and he grabs his hoe
Comes the morning he swings his rifle on his shoulder
This the army of Uncle Ho.

From the mountains and the jungles
From the ricelands and the Plain of Reeds
March the men and the women of the Indo-Chinese Army
Planting freedom with vict'ry seeds.

From Viet back to the Saigon Delta
Marched the armies of Viet Minh
And the wind stirs the banners
  of the Indo-Chinese people
Peace and freedom and Ho Chi Minh.

Chee Lai!

(Arise!)

National Anthem of The People's Republic of China

G   Gdim G D7   G Gdim
Chee-lai! boo yuan tzo noo lee dee run men,
G C   G Gdim G
Bah women dee shueh ro tzo chen women sin dee
  D (susG)
  chang chung.
Em D Am Em Bm   Em
Joong hwa ming joo dow liow tzuay way shien dee
    Bm
  shur hoe;
G   Em6 G Am
May guh ren bay po jo fah choo tzuay hoe dee hoe shun:
D7 G Gdim G C G
Chee lai! Chee lai! Chee lai!
Gdim G   C G   Gdim   G
Women wan joong ee sing, Mow jo dee run dee pow ho,
  Gdim G
  Chien jing!
G   Gdim G   Gdim G Gdim G
Mow jo dee run dee pow ho, Chien jing! Chien jing!
  Gdim G
  Chien jing! Jing!

Singable Translation:

 G Gdim G D7   G Gdim
Arise! you who refuse to be bond-slaves,
G C   G Gdim G   D(susG)
Let's stand up and fight for liberty and true democracy.
Em D Am Em Bm   Em   Bm
All our world is facing the chains of the tyrant;
G   Em6 G Am
Ev'ry one who works for freedom now is crying:
D7 G Gdim G C G
Arise! Arise! Arise!
Gdim G   C G   Gdim G
All of us with one heart, with the torch of freedom,
  Gdim G
  March on!
G Gdim G   Gdim G Gdim G
With the torch of freedom, March on! March on!
  Gdim G
  March on and on!

Si Me Quieres Escribir
(If You Want To Write Me)
Spanish Civil War

```
        Dm        A  A7      Dm   A
Si me quieres escribir, ya sabes mi paradero,
        Dm        A  A7      Dm   A
Si me quieres escribir, ya sabes mi paradero,
            C   Dm      C  Bb   A
En el frente de Gandesa primera linea de fuego.
Dm             C  Bb            A
En el frente de Gandesa primera linea de fuego.
```

Si tu quieres comer bien, } (twice)
Barato y de buena forma. }
En el frente de Gandesa, } (twice)
Alli tienen una fonda. }

En la entrada de la fonda,
Hay un moro Mojama. . . .
Que te dice, "Pasa, pasa
Que quieres para comer. . . ."

El primer plato que dan,
Son grenadas rompedoras. . . .
El segundo de matralla
Para recordar memorias. . . .

Singable Translation:

If you want to write me a letter,
You already know my whereabouts.
I'm on the Gandesa Front,
In the first line of the fighting.

If you want to eat your fill,
Good food and not too many pesos,
On that bloody battlefield
Stands an inn where you are welcome.

At the entrance of this inn there
Waits a Moor by name Mohammed,
Who warmly greets you, "Hurry, hurry,
"Rare and spicy food awaits you."

The first dish which they serve
Is hot grenades in quick succession,
Followed by a burst of shrapnel,
Makes a meal you'll all remember.

I'm On My Way

```
        G              D7
I'm on my way to Freedom land
                       G
I'm on my way to Freedom land
        G7             C
I'm on my way to Freedom land
        G       D7        G
I'm on my way, great God, I'm on my way.
```

I asked my brother to come with me, (3 times)
I'm on my way, great God, I'm on my way.
I asked my sister to come with me, etc.

I asked my boss to let me go.
If he says no, I'll go anyhow.
If you won't go, let your children go.
If you won't go, let your mother go.

I'm on my way, and I won't turn back.

La Marseillaise
Rouget de Lisle
French National Anthem

```
        G      D D7 G
Allons, enfants de la Patrie!
        C   Am D7 G
Le jour de gloire est arrivé!
        G      D7  G  D
Contre nous de la tyrannie,
D7              G
L'étendard sanglant est levé!
                        D
L'étendard sanglant est levé!
            D7   G
Entendez-vous dans les campagnes
  G7 C     A7   D
Mugir ces féroces soldats?
  Gm              D
Ils viennent jusque dans nos bras;
D7+ Gm              D
Egorger nos fils, nos compagnes.
     G      D
Aux armes, citoyens!
     G      D
Formez vos bataillons!
     G   D   G   C    G   C#dim D
Marchons! Marchons! Qu'un sang impur,
D9 G D7   G
Abreuve nos sillons!
```

Singable Translation:

Arise, ye sons of France, to glory!
Your day of freedom bids you rise!
Your children, wives and grandsires hoary,
Behold their tears and hear their cries,
Behold their tears and hear their cries!
Shall hateful tyrants mischief breeding,
With hireling hosts, a ruffian band,
Affright and desolate this land
While peace and liberty lie bleeding?

To arms, you sons of France!
To arms, your ranks advance!
March on! March on!
All hearts resolved.
On liberty or death!

Ain't Gonna Let Nobody Turn Me Round

Civil Rights Song

Em
Ain't gonna let nobody, Lordy,
    Am   B7
Turn me round, turn me round, turn me round,
    Em
Ain't gonna let nobody, Lordy,

Turn me round,
    Am
I'm gonna keep on a-walkin', keep on a-talkin',
  B7   Em
Lord, marching up to freedom land.

Ain't gonna let Nervous Nelly turn me round, etc.

Ain't gonna let Chief Pritchett, etc.

Ain't gonna let segregation, etc.

Ain't gonna let no jailhouse, etc.

Joshua Fought The Battle Of Jericho

Chorus:

Dm
Joshua fought the battle of Jericho,
A7 Dm
Jericho, Jericho—

Joshua fought the battle of Jericho,
    A7
And the walls came tumbling down.
Dm   A7
You may talk about your kings of Gideon,
  Dm   A7
You may talk about your men of Saul,
    Dm
But there's none like good old Josh-u-ay
  A7   Dm
At the battle of Jericho (that morning.)

Up to the walls of Jericho
He marched with spear in hand,
"Go blow those ram-horns," Joshua cried,
"Cause the battle is in my hands."

Then the lamb ram sheephorns began to blow,
The trumpets began to sound.
Joshua commanded the children to shout,
And the walls come a tumbling down.

There's no man like Joshua
No man like Saul
No man like Joshua
At the battle of Jericho.

Lilli Burlero

D   A
Ho brother Teague, dost hear the decree?
D   G D A   D
Lilli burlero, bullen a la;
D   A
That we shall have a new deputy,
D   G D A   D
Lilli burlero, bullen a la.

Chorus:

D
Lero, lero, lilli burlero,
A   D   A
Lilli burlero, bullen a la
G   D G D7
Lero, lero, lero lero,
G   A   D
Lilli burlero, bullen a la.

Ho, by my soul, it is a Talbot;
  Lilli burlero, etc.
And he will cut all the English throat,
  Lilli burlero, etc.

Though, by my soul, the English do prate, etc.
The law's on their side and the devil knows what. etc.

But if Dispense do come from the Pope,
We'll hang Magna Carta and themselves on a rope.

And the good Talbot is now made a Lord,
And with his brave lads he's coming aboard.

Who all in France have taken a swear,
That they will have no Protestant heir.

O but why does he stay behind?
Ho, by my soul, 'tis a Protestant wind.

Now that Tyrconnel is come ashore,
And we shall have Commissions galore.

And he that will not go to the Mass,
Shall be turned out and look like an ass.

Now, now the hereticks all will go down,
By Christ and St. Patrick's the nation's our own.

There was an old prophecy found in a bog,
That our land would be ruled by an ass and a dog.

So now this old prophecy's coming to pass,
For James is the dog and Tyrconnel's the ass.

Hallelujah, I'm A-Travelin'

Harry Raymond / Tune: Hallelujah, I'm A Bum

     D
Stand up and rejoice! a great day is here!
                  A7
We are fighting Jim Crow and the vict'ry is near.

Chorus:

    D
Hallelujah, I'm a-travelin',
            A7
Hallelujah, ain't it fine?
          G
Hallelujah, I'm a travelin'
 A7   D
Down Freedom's main line.

I read in the news, the Supreme Court has said,
"Listen here, mister Jim Crow, it's time you was dead."

The judges declared in Washington town,
"You white folks must take that old Jim Crow sign down."

I'm paying my fare on the Greyhound Bus line,
I'm riding the front seat to Nashville this time.

Columbia's the gem of the ocean, they say,
We're fighting Jim Crow in Columbia today.

I hate Jim Crow and Jim Crow hates me,
And that's why I'm fighting for my liberty.

Jarama Valley

Tune: *Red River Valley*

       G   C
There's a valley in Spain called Jarama,
       G   D7
It's a place that we all know so well.
       G   C
It was there that we gave of our manhood,
       G   D7   G
Where so many of our brave comrades fell!

We are proud of the Lincoln Battalion
And the fight for Madrid that it made,
There we fought like true sons of the people
As part of the Fifteenth Brigade.

Now we're far from that valley of sorrow,
But its mem'ry we'll never forget,
In the midst of the struggles around us,
Let's remember our glorious dead.

Freiheit
(Freedom)

Karl Ernst and Peter Daniel
Spanish Civil War

       F   C7   F
Spaniens Himmel breitet seine Sterne
       F   C7   F
Uber unsre Schutzengraben aus;
         C7   F
Und der Morgen grusst schon aus der Ferne,
       C   G7   C
Bald geht es zum neuen Kampf himaus.

Chorus:

       F   Bb F
Die Heimat ist weit,
        C   F
Doch wir sind Bereit,
F7 Bb   F
Wir kampfen und siegen fur dich,
C7 F
Freiheit!

Dem Faschisten werden wir nicht weichen,
Schickt er auch die Kugeln hageldicht.
Mit uns stehn Kameraden ohne gleichen
Und ein Rückwärts gibt es fur uns nicht.

Rührt die Trommel. Fällt die Bajonette.
Vorwarts marsch. Der Sieg ist unser Lohn.
Mit der roten Fahne brecht die Kette.
Auf zum Kampf das Thälmann Bataillon.

Singable Translation:

Spanish heavens spread their brilliant starlight
High above our trenches in the plain;
From the distance morning comes to greet us,
Calling us to battle once again.

Far off is our land,
Yet ready we stand,
We're fighting and winning for you—
Freiheit!

We'll not yield a foot to Franco's fascists,
Even though the bullets fall like sleet,
With us stand those peerless men, our comrades,
And for us there can be no retreat.

Beat the drums. Ready the bayonets. (charge)
Forward, march. Victory our reward.
With our scarlet banner. Smash their column.
Thaelmann Battalion. Ready, forward march.

We're Gonna Move When The Spirit Says Move!

Civil Rights Movement Song

        C
We're gonna move when the spirit says move!
                 C7
We're gonna move when the spirit says move!
    F
'Cause when the spirit says move
    G7   C
Then you move with the spirit,
               G7   C
We're gonna move when the spirit says move.

We're gonna sing, etc.

We're gonna march, etc.

We're gonna talk, etc.

John Brown's Body

G
John Brown's body lies a-mouldering in the grave,
           C   G
John Brown's body lies a-mouldering in the grave,
               G B7   Em
John Brown's body lies a-mouldering in the grave,
   Am   G D7 G
But his soul goes marching on.

Chorus:

G
Glory, glory, hallelujah,
C   G
Glory, glory, hallelujah,
             GEm
Glory, glory, hallelujah,
   Am   G D7 G
His soul goes marching on.

He's gone to be a soldier in the Army of the Lord,
   (3 times)
His soul goes marching on.

John Brown's knapsack is strapped upon his back,
   (3 times)
His soul goes marching on.

John Brown died that the slaves might be free, (3 times)
But his soul goes marching on.

The stars above in Heaven now are looking kindly down,
   (3 times)
On the grave of old John Brown.

Zog Nit Keynmol
(Tell Us No More)

Yiddish: Song of the Warsaw Ghetto

Em   B7   Em
Zog nit keynmol az du geyst dem letstn veg,
               D7   G
Chotsh himlen blayene farshtein bloye teg;
           E7   Am
Vail kumen vet noch undzer oysgebenktte sho,
     B7   Em
Es vet a poyk ton undzer trot: mir zenen do!
    E7   Am   E7   Am
Vail kumen vet noch undzer oysgebenktte sho,
    B7   Em
Es vet a poyk ton undzer trot: mir zenen do.

Fun grinem palmen-land biz vaytn land fun shney,
Mir kumen on mit undzer payn, mit undzer vey;
Un vu gefaln iz a shprits fund undzer blut,   } (twice)
Shprotsn vet fort undzer g'vure, undzer mut.

S'vet di morgn-zun bagildn unz dem haynt,
Undzer nechtn vet farshvindn mitn faynt;
Nor oyb farzamen vet di zun un der kayor,   } (twice)
Vi a parol zol geyn dos lid fun dor tsu for!

Dos lid geshribn iz mit blut un nit mit blay,
S'iz nit kayn lidl fun a foygl oyf der fray;
Dos hot a folk ts'vishn falndike vent   } (twice)
Dos lid gezungen mit nagenes in di hent!

Singable Translation:

Never say that there is only death for you,
Though leaden skies may be concealing days of blue,
Because the hour we have hungered for is near;
Beneath our tread the earth shall tremble, } (twice)
   we are here!

From land of palm-tree to the far-off land of snow,
We shall be coming with our torment and our woe,
And everywhere our blood has sunk into
   the earth,   } (twice)
Shall our bravery, our vigor blossom forth.

We'll have the morning sun to set our day a-glow,
And all our yesterdays shall vanish with the foe,
And if the time is long before the sun appears
Then let this song go   } (twice)
   like a signal through the years.

This song was written with our blood and not with lead;
It's not a song that summer birds sing overhead,
It was a people among toppling barricades,
That sang this song of ours   } (twice)
   with pistols and grenades.

The 1913 Massacre

Woody Guthrie

      C
Take a trip with me in nineteen thirteen,
  F   G7   C
To Calumet, Michigan in the copper country,
               F   C
I'll take you to a place called "Italian Hall,"
              G7   C
Where miners are having their big Christmas ball.

I will take you in a door and up a high stairs,
Singing and dancing is heard everywhere,
I will let you shake hands with the people you see,
And watch the kids dance 'round the big Christmas tree.

You ask about work and you ask about pay,
They'll tell you they make less than a dollar a day,
Working the copper claims, risking their lives,
So it's fun to spend Christmas with children and wives.

There's talking and laughing and songs in the air,
And the spirit of Christmas is there everywhere,
Before you know it you're friends with us all,
And you're dancing around and around in the hall.

Well a little girl sits down
   by the Christmas tree lights,
To play the piano, so you gotta keep quiet,
To hear all this fun you would not realize,
That the copper boss thug-men are milling outside.

The copper boss thugs stuck their heads in the door,
One of them yelled and screamed, "There's a fire!"
A lady, she hollered, "There's no such a thing,
Keep on with your party, there's no such a thing."

A few people rushed, and it was only a few,
"It's just the thugs and the scabs fooling you."
A man grabbed his daughter and carried her down,
But the thugs held the door and he could not get out.

And then others followed, a hundred or more,
But most everybody remained on the floor,
The gun-thugs they laughed at their murderous joke,
While the children were smothered
   on the stairs by the door.

Such a terrible sight I never did see,
We carried our children back up to their tree,
The scabs outside still laughed at their spree,
And the children that died there were seventy-three.

The piano played a slow funeral tune,
The town was lit up by a cold Christmas moon,
The parents they cried and the miners they moaned,
"See what your greed for money has done."

The Preacher And The Slave

Joe Hill/Tune: *In The Sweet Bye and Bye*

              G   C   G
Long-haired preachers come out every night,
                                    D
Try to tell you what's wrong and what's right;
       G   C   G
But when asked about something to eat,
          Em   D D7   G
They will answer with voices so sweet:
     Gm
(Oh so sweet):

Chorus:

G   D
You will eat, by and by,
      C   D7   G
In that glorious land above the sky,

(Way up high),

Work and pray,
  C
Live on hay,
          G   D D7   G
You'll get pie in the sky when you die,
        E♭ G
(That's a lie!)

And the salvation army they play,
And they sing and they clap and they pray,
Till they get all your coin on the drum,
Then they'll tell you when you're on the bum:

Holy Rollers and jumpers come out,
And they holler, they jump and they shout.
"Give your money to Jesus," they say,
"He will cure all diseases today."

If you fight hard for children and wife,
Try to get something good in this life,
You're a sinner and bad man, they tell,
When you die you will sure go to hell.

Workingmen of all countries unite,
Side by side we for freedom will fight!
When the world and its wealth we have gained,
To the gafters we'll sing this refrain:

Final Chorus:
You will eat, by and by,
When you've learned how to cook and to fry,
Chop some wood,
'Twill do you good,
And you'll eat in the sweet by and by.
(That's no lie!)

United Front

Bertolt Brecht and Hans Eisler

Em   Am6
And just because he's human,
B7   Bm7 D♯dim Em
A man would like a little bite   to eat;
   G   G♯dim Am
He won't get full on a lot of talk
        F♯7   B+   Em
That won't give him bread and meat.

Chorus:

Am Em7   Am7 D♯dim
So left, two, three, so   left, two, three,
Em G   G♯dim   Am
To the work that we must do,
    C7   Am E   Em
March on in the worker's united front,
   Am   B7   Em
For you are a worker too.

And just because he's human,
He doesn't like a pistol to his head,
He wants no servants under him
And no boss over his head.

And just because he's a worker,
The job is all his own,
The liberation of the working class,
Is the job of the workers alone.

Peat Bog Soldiers

German Concentration Camp Song

Em
Far and wide as the eye can wander
AmG   Em   B7   Em
Heath and bog are ev'ry where.
G
Not a bird sings out to cheer us,
Am6   Em   B7   Em
Oaks are standing gaunt and bare.

Chorus:

D7 G   D
We are the peat bog soldiers;
D7   Em   Am6 B7 Em
We're marching with our spades to the bog.

Up and down the guards are pacing,
No one, no one can go through.
Flight would mean a sure death facing;
Guns and barbed wire greet our view.

But for us there is no complaining,
Winter will in time be past;
One day we shall cry rejoicing,
Homeland dear, you're mine at last.

Final chorus:
Then will the peat bog soldiers
March no more with the spades to the bog.

DING DONG DOLLAR, EVERYBODY HOLLER!

*A handful of topical songs of
yesterday and today....*

Doctor Freud

David Lazar

```
         D                          G
Oh it happen'd in Vienna not so very long ago
         D                          A7
When not enough folks were getting sick,

That a starving young physician
              G
    tried to better his position
         D              A7
By discovering what made his patients tick.
```

Chorus:

```
          G              D
Oh, Doctor Freud, oh, Doctor Freud,
                                  A7
How I wish you had been otherwise employed,
         D
For that set of circumstances
              G
    sure enhances the finances
    D        A7         D
Of the followers of Doctor Sigmund Freud.
```

He forgot about sclerosis, but invented the psychosis,
And a hundred ways that sex could be enjoyed.
He adopted as his credo: "Down Repression—Up Libido!"
And that was the start of Doctor Sigmund Freud.

Then he analyzed the dreams of the teens and libertines,
And he substituted monologues for pills.
He drew crowds just like Wells-Sadler,
    when along come Jung and Adler,
Who said, "By God, there's gold in them thar ills."

They encountered no resistance
    when they served as Freud's assistants,
As with Ego and with Id they deftly toyed.
And instead of toting bed pans,
    they bore analytic dead pans—
Those ambitious doctors Adler, Jung and Freud.

Now, the Big Three have departed,
    but not so the cult they started—
It's been carried on by many a goodly band.
And to trauma, shock and war-shock,
    someone went and added Rorshach,
Now the thing has got completely out of hand.

Now old men with double chinseys
    and a million would-be Kinseys
Will discuss it at the drop of a repression.
Now, I wouldn't be complaining,
    but for all the dough I'm paying,
To lie down on someone's couch and say confession.

Ding Dong Dollar

Hamish Henderson
Tune: *She'll Be Coming 'Round The Mountain*
Scottish Anti-Polaris Song

Chorus:

```
            G
Oh you canna spend a dollar when you're dead,
                                         D7
Oh you canna spend a dollar when you're dead,
        G
Singing ding dong dollar,
C
Everybody holler,
        G           D7           G
Oh, you canna spend a dollar when you're dead.
```

Oh, the Yanks have just dropped anchor in Dunoon,
And they've had their civic welcome from the toon,
As they marched the measured mile,
Bonnie Mary of Argyle
Was a-wearin' spangled drawers below her gown.

And the publicans will all be doin' swell,
For it's just the thing that's sure to ring the bell,
Oh, the dollars they will jingle,
There'll be no lassie single,
Even though they maybe blow us all to hell.

But the Glasgow Moderator doesn't mind,
In fact, he thinks the Yanks are awfully kind
For it's heaven that you're goin',
It's a quicker way than rowin',
And there's sure to be nobody left behind.

Oh, we'll all go together when it comes (twice)
Yes, we'll all go together,
However nice the weather,
Yes, we'll all go together when it comes.

It'll all be accidental when it comes (twice)
It'll all be accidental,
Just that some poor guy went mental,
It'll all be accidental when it comes.

It'll be too late to stop it when it comes (twice)
It'll be too late to stop it
When we're just about to cop it,
It'll be too late to stop it when it comes.

So, let's stop it now before it comes (twice)
Yes, let's stop it now,
Make a devil of a row,
Let's stop it now before it comes.

Shootin' With Rasputin

Em   Am   Am6
An intimate friend of the Czar was I,
  Em   Am   B7
A personal friend of the great Nikolai.
  Em   Am   Am6
We practic'ly slept in the same double bed,
    Em   Am   B7
It was I at the foot and he at the head.

Chorus:

  Em,   D♯   Em7   Em6
But all that seems distant, and all that seems far,
C   B7 Em   Am   Em   F♯7
From those glorious days at the palace of the Czar,
B7   Em
When I went shootin' with Rasputin,

   ate farina with Czarina,
B7   Em   Am B7
Blintzes with the princess and the Czar, hey, hey, hey.
Em
We were sharing tea and herring,

   dipped banana in smetana,
B7   Em
Borscht and wurst around the samovar.

A friend of the Czar was I all his gracious life,
But friendlier still was I with his young wife.
We practically slept in the same double bed,
Till the Czar kicked me out and slept there instead.

But one awful day revolution broke out,
I failed to see what the fuss was about.
But after a while I bid Russia goodbye—
It was simply a case of Lenin or I.

The Reds took my dough, kicked me out in the cold,
All I had left were some diamonds and gold.
The Bolsheviks gave me the gate without pity—
But I get my revenge by working for
   the Un-American Committee.

Hallelujah I'm A Bum

Barbara Dane and Irwin Silber
© 1970.

  D
I read in the news, the President said,
                      A7
He's declaring that "bum" is the new word for red.

Chorus:

  D
Hallelujah, I'm a bum,
          A7
Hallelujah, who are you?
          G
Hallelujah, speak your mind out—
    A7   D
You can be a bum, too!

When he first called us bums, didn't see what he meant,
But the Guard has defined it on the campus at Kent.

Old Spiro's no bum, you all know that is true,
But he sits up nights wond'ring what Kim's gonna do.

Well, power corrupts, we know that by heart,
But you gotta admit Nixon had a head start!

Some say his name is Slippery Dick,
Well, we know he's no bum,
   but he sure is some P — resident!

They can blindfold their eyes
   with their red, white and blue,
But we'll show 'em what millions of us bums can do

Well Mexico's hot and Canada's cold,
So I'll stay here and fight if I never get old.

They may not know now, but they'll know before long,
That Kent was Cambodia and we are the Cong!

Put My Name Down

Irwin Silber / Tune: *Hard Travelin'*

G
I had a brother in the infantry,

I thought you know'd.

I had a brother in the infantry,
D7
Way down the road.
G
He's got a home and wife and baby,
   C
He don't like war

And he don't mean maybe,
    D7   G
And he's gonna put his name down.

Chorus:

G
Put my name down, brother, where do I sign?
                  D7
I'm gonna join the fight for peace right down the line.
G
Ashes to ashes and dust to dust
    C
If you don't sign up the world goes bust,
  D7   G
So I'm gonna put my name down.

I've got a sister in Portland, Maine,
I thought you know'd.
I've got a sister in Portland, Maine,
Way down the road.
She lost a son at Anzio,
And now she wants the world to know,
That she's gonna put her name down.

I've got a brother in Birmingham,
I thought you know'd.
I've got a brother in Birmingham,
Way down the road.
He don't want an ocean trip,
In a Jim Crow Navy, on a Jim Crow ship,
And he's gonna put his name down.

I've got a brother in Leningrad,
I thought you know'd.
I've got a brother in Leningrad,
Way down the road.
On lots of things we don't agree,
But he wants peace, just like me,
So, he's gonna put his name down.

I've got brothers throughout this land,
I thought you know'd.
I've got brothers throughout this land,
Way down the road.
From the Golden Gate to Baltimore,
We all say we don't want war,
And I'm gonna put my name down.

Soup Song

Maurice Sugar / Tune: *My Bonnie Lies Over The Ocean*

     E   A   E
I'm spending my nights in the flop house,
                    B7
I'm spending my days on the street,
     E   A   E
I'm looking for work but I find none,
  A   B7   E
I wish I had something to eat.

Chorus:

       A   B7   E
So-up, so-up, they gave me a bowl of soup, soup, soup,
       A   B7   E
So-up, so-up, they gave me a bowl of soup.

I spent twenty years in the factory,
I did everything I was told.
They said I was loyal and faithful,
Now even before I am old.

I saved fifteen bucks with my banker,
To buy me a car and a yacht.
I went down to draw out my money
And this is the answer I·got.

I thought that my country would help me,
I went out to bleed and to die,
I fought in the war for my country,
But this was my country's reply:

What Have They Done To The Rain

Malvina Reynolds

C   Dm   G
Just a little rain falling all around,
                     Dm   G
The grass lifts its head to the heavenly sound,
Am   Em
Just a little rain, just a little rain,
F   G
What have they done to the rain?
C   Dm   G
Just a little boy standing in the rain,
   Em   Dm   C
The gentle rain that falls for years.
    Am   Em
And the grass is gone, the boy disappears,
   F   C
And rain keeps falling like helpless tears,
  Dm   G
And what have they done to the rain?

Just a little breeze out of the sky,
The leaves pat their hands as the breeze blows by,
Just a little breeze with some smoke in its eye,
What have they done to the rain?

Venezuela

```
B7 Em       B7   Em  B7   Em   B7
I   met him in Venezue. . . . .la,
        Em  B7    Em....B7
Down from the U.S.A.,
        Em      D    C      B7
And why he was there he would not say,
        Em       B7     Em   B7
But he sure wasn't there to pass away,
        Em  Am    Em    B7   Em    .....B7
To pass away the time in Venezue.....la,
Em  Am     Em      B7    Em  B7  Em
Pass away the time in Venezue. . . . .la.
```

He paid ready cash for the army of Venezue. . . . .la,
For the Police and Cabinet too;
I saw him do what he'd come to do,
With all the tricks I knew he knew,
To get all the oil out of Venezue. . . . .la,
To get Standard Oil the oil of Venezue. . . . .la.

And when the tankers were sailing out so sea,
Were sailing out to sea,
And he was taking leave of me,
I said, "Watch out, there'll always be
Venezuelans in Venezue. . . . .la,
Who thinks that the oil belongs to Venezue. . . . .la."

They dumped the chump in a sump in Venezue.....la,
That free-enterprising Yank,
He sputtered and spattered and splashed as he sank,
And their laugh will outlast the Chase National Bank;
He's still stuck down there in Venezue.....la,
Unless he's drunk all the oil in Venezue.....la.

Plastic Jesus

```
C
Well, I don't care if it rains or freezes,
F
Long as I have my plastic Jesus,
C                           G7
Riding on the dashboard of my car;
C
Through all trials and tribulations,
F
We will travel every nation,
C          G7       C
With my plastic Jesus I'll go far.
      F          C
Plastic Jesus, Plastic Jesus,
                           G7
Riding on the dashboard of my car,
C
Through all trials and tribulations,
F
We will travel every nation,
C          G7       C
With my plastic Jesus I'll go far.
```

I don't care if it's dark or scary,
Long as I have magnetic Mary,
Ridin' on the dashboard of my car,
I feel I'm protected amply,
I've got the whole damn Holy Family,
Riding on the dashboard of my car.
No, I don't care if it rains or freezes,
Long as I have my plastic Jesus,
Riding on the dashboard of my car,
But I think he'll have to go,
His magnet ruins my radio,
And if we have a wreck he'll leave a scar.

Riding down a thoroughfare,
With His nose up in the air,
A wreck may be ahead, but He don't mind,
Trouble coming He don't see,
He just keeps His eye on me,
And any other thing that lies behind.
Plastic Jesus, Plastic Jesus,
Riding on the dashboard of my car:
Though the sunshine on His back,
Makes Him peel, chip and crack,
A little patching keeps Him up to par.

When pedestrians try to cross,
I let them know who's boss,
I never blow the horn or give them warning;
I ride all over town,
Trying to run them down,
And it's seldom that they live to see the morning.
Plastic Jesus, Plastic Jesus,
Riding on the dashboard of my car:
His halo fits just right
And I use it for a sight,
And they'll scatter or they'll splatter near and far.

When I'm in a traffic jam,
He don't care if I say "damn",
I can let all sorts of curses roll,
Plastic Jesus doesn't hear,
For He has a plastic ear—
The man who invented plastic saved my soul.
Plastic Jesus, Plastic Jesus,
Riding on the dashboard of my car:
Once His robe was snowy white,
Now it isn't quite so bright,
Stained by the smoke of my cigar.

If I weave around at night,
And the police think I'm tight,
They'll never find my bottle, though they ask;
Plastic Jesus shelters me,
For His head comes off, you see—
He's hollow, and I use Him for a flask.
Plastic Jesus, Plastic Jesus,
Riding on the dashboard of my car:
Ride with me and have a dram,
Of the blood of the Lamb,
Plastic Jesus is a holy bar.

Go Down You Murderers

Ewan MacColl

    Am
Tim Evans was a prisoner,
  G
Fast in his prison cell.
    Am
And those who read about his crimes
    Em   D
They damned his soul to Hell.

Refrain:

Em   Am   G   Am
Saying, "Go down, you murderer, go down."

For the murder of his own true wife
And the killing of his own child,
The jury found him guilty
And the hanging judge he smiled.

Now Evans pleaded innocent
And swore by Him on high,
That he never killed his own dear wife
Nor caused his child to die.

They moved him out at nine o'clock
To his final flowery-dell,
And day and night two screws were there
And never left his cell.

Sometimes they played draughts with him,
And solo and pontoon,
To stop him brooding on the rope
That was to be his doom.

They brought his grub in on a tray,
There was eggs and meat and ham,
And all the snout that he could smoke
Was there at his command.

I Don't Want Your Millions Mister

Jim Garland

Chorus:

    C
I don't want your millions, mister,
    F   C
I don't want your diamond ring,
    F   C
All I want is the right to live, mister,
    G7   C
Give me back my job again.

Verses:
I don't want your Rolls-Royce, mister,
I don't want your pleasure yacht,
All I want is food for my babies,
Give to me my old job back.

We worked to build this country, mister,
While you enjoyed a life of ease,
You've stolen all that we built, mister,
Now our children starve and freeze.

Think me dumb if you wish, mister,
Call me green or blue or red,
This one thing I sure know, mister,
My hungry babies must be fed.

Take the two old parties, mister,
No difference in them I can see,
But with a Farmer-Labor Party,
We could set the people free.

Money Is King

The Tiger

Calypso

        A7   Dm
Now if a man has money today,
A7   Dm
People run to shake his hand right away.
       A7   Dm
Yes if a man has money today,
A7   Dm
People run to shake his hand right away.
         D7   Gm
He can commit murder and get off free,
         C7   F
And live in the governor's company;
         D7   Gm
But if you're poor, why God help you,
       Dm A7   Dm
Even a dog is better than you.

Now a man with money can go to the store,
The boss will run to shake his hand at the door.
Call ten clerks to write down everything—
Suits, hats, whisky, and diamond rings!
They will take it to your home on a motor bike,
You can pay for it whenever you like;
Not a soul will ask you a thing,
They know very well that Money is King!

Even a dog can run around and pick up bones,
Salt fish, codfish, meat and pone;
If it's a good breed and not too wild,
People will take it and mind it like a child.
But a hungry man goes out to beg,
They will set the bulldog behind his leg.
So most of you will agree, it is true —
Even a dog is better than you.

The Vicar Of Bray

```
         C            G7    C
In good King Charles' golden time,
       F    G7   C
When loyalty no harm meant.
       C        G7           C
A zealous high churchman was I,
       F      G7C
And so I gained preferment.
     Am     G    Am   Em
To teach my flock I never missed,
     Am    G    D7   G
Kings are by God appointed,
       C           G7        C
And damned are those who dare resist,
       F      G7   C
Or touch the Lord's annointed.
```

Chorus:

```
     Am  G   Am       Em
And this is law, that I'll maintain,
     Am  G   D7  G
Until my dying day, sir,
       C        G7   C
That whatsoever king may reign,
       F      G7   C
Still I'll be the Vicar of Bray, sir!
```

When Royal James possessed the crown,
And popery came in fashion,
The Penal Laws I hooted down,
And read the Declaration.
The Church of Rome I found did fit
Full well my constitution
And I had been a Jesuit,
But for the Revolution.

When William was our King declared,
To ease the nation's grievance,
With this new wind about I steered
And swore to him allegiance.
Old principles I did revoke,
Set conscience at a distance,
Passive obedience was a joke,
A jest was non-resistance.

When Royal Anne became our queen,
The Church of England's Glory,
Another face of things was seen,
And I became a Tory.
Occasional conformists base,
I blamed their moderation,
And thought the Church in danger was
By such prevarication.

When George in pudding time came o'er,
And moderate men looked big, Sir,
My principles I changed once more,
And so became a Whig, sir.
And thus preferment I procured
From our new faith's defender,
And almost every day abjured
The Pope and the Pretender.

The illustrious house of Hanover
And Protestant succession,
To thee I do allegiance swear,
While they can keep possession.
For in my faith and loyalty
I never more will falter,
And George my lawful king shall be
Until the times do alter.

Little Boxes
Malvina Reynolds

Copyright © 1962 by Schroder Music Co.
All Rights Reserved. Used by Permission.

```
       D
Little boxes on the hillside,
     G           D
Little boxes made of ticky-tacky,
                 A7
Little boxes on the hillside,
     D           A7
Little boxes all the same.
         D
There's a green one and a pink one
     G           D
And a blue one and a yellow one,
                   A7
And they're all made out of ticky-tacky
       D      A7    D
And they all look just the same.
```

And the people in the houses
All went to the university,
Where they were put in boxes
And they came out all the same,
And there's doctors and lawyers,
And business executives,
And they're all made out of ticky-tacky
And they all look just the same.

And they all play on the golf course
And drink their martinis dry,
And they all have pretty children
And the children go to school,
And the children go to summer camp
And then to the university,
Where they are put in boxes
And they come out all the same.

And the boys go into business
And marry and raise a family
In boxes made of ticky tacky
And they all look just the same.
There's a green one and a pink one,
And a blue one and a yellow one,
And they're all made out of ticky tacky
And they all look just the same.

Round And Round Hitler's Grave
Almanac Singers / Tune: *Old Joe Clark*

```
     F
I wish I had a nickel,

I wish I had a peck,

I wish I had a rope to tie
              C7    F
Around old Hitler's neck
```

Chorus:

```
Hey! Round and round, Hitler's grave,
                       C7
Round and round we'll go.
F
Gonna lay that poor boy down.
         C7    F
He won't get up no more.
```

Mussolini won't last long,
Tell you the reason why:
We're a-gonna salt his beef
And hang it up to dry.

I'm a-going to Berlin,
To Mister Hitler's Town,
I'm gonna take my forty-four
And blow his playhouse down.

The German Army general staff,
I guessed they missed connections.
They went a hundred miles a day,
But in the wrong direction.

Hitler went to Russia,
In search of Russian oil,
But the only oil he'll find there's in
A pot in which he'll boil.

Mister Hitler's traveling mighty fast,
But he's on a single track.
He started down that Moscow road,
But now he's coming back.

Is This Land Your Land?

Tune: *This Land Is Your Land*

Indian version:

```
G              C
This land is your land,
              G
It once was my land,
              D7              G
Before we sold you Manhattan Island,
              C
You pushed our nations
              G
To the reservations
D7                      G
This land was stole by you from me.
```

Ecology version:

I've roamed and rambled
And followed the beer cans,
From the toxic cities
To the flooded canyons.
And all around me
Were the billboards reading:
This land was made for you and me!

As I was walking
That ribbon of highway,
I heard the buzzing
Of a hundred chain saws,
And the redwoods falling,
And the loggers calling—
This land was made for you and me.

GI Vietnam version:

This land is your land,
But it isn't my land,
From the Mekong Delta
To the Pleiku Highland,
When we get shot at
The ARVN flee,
This land was meant for the V.C.!

Rebel version:

This land is their land,
It isn't our land,
From the Wall Street office
To the Cadillac car-land;
From the plush apartments
To the Hollywood starland,
This land is not for you and me.

If this is our land,
You'd never know it,
So take your bullshit
And kindly stow it,
Let's get together
And overthrow it,
Then this land will be for you and me.

The Asteroid Light

Tune: *The Keeper of the Eddystone Light*

   C
My father was the keeper of the Asteroid Light,
F   G7   C
He slept with a Martian one fine night.

Out of this match came children three.
F   G7   C
Two were mutants and the other was me.

Chorus:

D7   G
Yo, ho, ho, the jets run free;
G7   C
Oh, for the life at the speed of c!

When I was but a space cadet,
They put me in charge of a proton jet;
I cleaned the tubes and filled them with fuel,
And picked my teeth with an old slide rule.

One night as I was heading for the Moon
And singing a well known spaceman's tune,
I heard a voice cry out of the void,
And there sat my mother on her asteroid.

"Oh, what has become of my children three?"
My mother then she asked me.
"One is on exhibit in a zoo on Venus,
And the other keeps a telepathic link between us."

The deuterons flashed in her hydrogen hair;
I looked again, and my mother wasn't there.
But she telepathed angrily out of the night,
"Then to hell with the keeper of the Asteroid Light!"

Pity The Down-Trodden Landlord

B. Woolf and Arnold Clayton, adapted from
She's More To Be Pitied Than Censured

      F   Bb   F
Please open your hearts and your purses
F7 Bb   Bbm   F
To a man who is misunderstood,
    A   A7   Dm
He gets all the kicks and the curses,
            G   G7   C7
Though he wishes you nothing but good.
    F   Bb   F
He wistfully begs you to show him
F7 Bb   Bbm   F
You think he's a friend not a louse;
              F#dim   C
So remember the debt that you owe him,
C#dim   Dm7   G7   C7
The   landlord who lends you his house.

Chorus:

    F   Bb   F
So pity the down-trodden landlord,
    F7 Bb   Bb   F
And his back that is burdened and bent.
F#dim   Gm   C7   F
Respect his gray hairs, don't ask for repairs,
    Gm   C7   F
And don't be behind with the rent.

When thunder clouds gather and darken,
You can sleep undisturbed in your bed;
But the landlord must sit up and hearken,
And shiver, and wonder, and dread;
If you're killed, then you die in a hurry,
And you never will know your bad luck,
But the landlord is shaking with worry—
"Has one of my houses been struck?"

When a landlord resorts to eviction,
Don't think that he does it for spite;
He is acting from deepest conviction,
And what's right, after all, is what's right.
But I see that your hearts are all hardened,
And I fear I'm appealing in vain;
Yet I hope my last plea will be pardoned,
If I beg on my knees once again.

ERIN GO BRAUGH!

*Songs of croppy boys and bold Fenian men,
of Easter rebels and the Shan Van Vogt....*

The Old Orange Flute

```
        C                     G7         C
In the County Tyrone near the town of Dungannon,
                      F         G7
Where many the ructions meself had a hand in,
        C        Em     F       C
Bob Williamson lived, a weaver by trade,
                    F          G7        C
And all of us thought him a stout Orange blade.
        C                 F
On the twelfth of July as it yearly did come,
        C                         G7
Bob played with his flute to the sound of a drum.
        F        Em     F    C
You may talk of your harp, your piano or lute,
                         F      G7       C
But there's none can compare with the old orange flute.
```

Now Bob, the deceiver, he took us all in,
He married a Papist named Bridget McGinn,
Turned Papish himself, and forsook the old cause,
That gave us our freedom, religion, and laws.
Now the boys of the place made some comment upon it,
And Bob had to fly to the province of Connaught,
He fled with his wife and his fixings to boot,
And along with the latter, his old Orange flute.

At the chapel on Sunday to atone for past deeds,
Said paters and aves and counted his beads,
'Till after some time at the priest's own desire,
He went with the old flute to play in the choir.
He went with the old flute for to play for the mass,
But the instrument shivered, and sighed, oh, alas,
And try though he would, though it made a great noise,
The flute would play only "The Protestant Boys."

Bob jumped and he started and got in a flutter,
And threw the old flute in the blessed holy water,
He thought that this charm would bring some other sound,
When he tried it again, it played "Croppies Lie Down."
Now for all he could whistle and finger and blow,
To play Papish music he found it no go,
"Kick the Pope," and "Boil Water" it freely would sound,
But one Papish squeak in it couldn't be found.

At the council of priests that was held the next day,
They decided to banish the old flute away,
They couldn't knock heresy out of its head,
So they bought Bob a new one to play in its stead.
Now the old flute was doomed, and its fate was pathetic,
'Twas fastened and burned at the stake as heretic,
As the flames soared around it, they heard a strange noise,
'Twas the old flute still whistling "The Protestant Boys."
Toora lu, toora lay, oh, it's six miles
    from Bangor to Donnahadee.

The Croppy Boy

```
    G  C
It was early in the spring,
    D7              G
The birds did whistle and sweetly sing.
                        Am  D7 Em
Changing their notes from tree to tree,
    Am          D7      G
And the song they sang was Old Ireland free.
```

It was early, early in the night,
The yeoman cavalry gave me a fright;
The yeoman cavalry was my downfall
And I was taken by Lord Cornwall.

'Twas in the guardhouse where I was laid
And in a parlor where I was tried;
My sentence passed and my courage low
When to Dungannon I was forced to go.

As I was passing my father's door,
My brother William stood at the door;
My aged father stood at the door,
And my tender mother her hair she tore.

As I was going up Wexford Street,
My own first cousin I chanced to meet;
My own first cousin did me betray,
And for one bare guinea swore my life away.

As I was walking up Wexford Hill,
Who could blame me to cry my fill?
I looked behind and I looked before,
But my aged mother I shall ne'er see more.

As I was mounted on the platform high
My aged father was standing by;
My aged father did me deny,
And the name he gave me was the Croppy Boy.

It was in Dungannon this young man died
And in Dungannon his body lies;
And you good people that do pass by
Oh, shed a tear for the Croppy Boy.

Ballymurphy

Tune: *She'll Be Coming 'Round the Mountain*

From the recording by The Men of No Property, Paredon Records, © 1972 by Paredon Records.

       F
If you hate the British Army, clap your hands,
                            C7
If you hate the British Army, clap your hands.
       F   F7
If you hate the British Army,
    Bb
If you hate the British Army,
      F   C7   F
If you hate the British Army, clap your hands.

They come down from Ballymurphy when they come,
   (twice)
Sure the children won the day,
When they all ran away,
They were only little childer, every one.

We don't want the British Army here to stay, (twice)
We don't want to be defended
By an army that surrendered
When the kids of Ballymurphy came to play.

Oh, the general he has fainted, is he dead? (twice)
For if the women join the fight,
We'll wipe the Army out tonight,
For them women are all Ballymurphy bred.

A coded message came from nowhere, it did say,
At the peril of your lives, ah if you stay,
Oh now men don't be surprised,
But Turf Lodge has organized,
And a doubledecker bus is on its way.

The British Army they will never be the same, (twice)
The bravest of them fighting men,
They were beat by kids of ten,
Aye, Ballymurphy put the army all to shame.

If you hate the R.U.C.*, clap your hands,
If you hate the R.U.C., then clap your hands,
If you hate the R.U.C., if you hate the R.U.C.,
If you hate the R.U.C., clap your hands.

---

* Royal Ulster Constabulary

O'Donnell Aboo

M. J. McCann

C
Proudly the note of the trumpet is sounding,
G7   C
Loudly the war cries arise on the gale,

Fleetly the steed by Lough Swilly is bounding,
  G7   C   F   C
To join the thick squadrons in Saimears green vale.
              F   C F   C
On every mountaineer strangers to flight and fear!
G7   C   D7   G7
Rush to the standards of dauntless Red Hugh!
C
Bonnaught and gallow glass throng

   from each mountain pass;
G7   C   F C
On for old Erin, "O'Donnell Aboo!"

Princely O'Neill to our aid is advancing
With many a chieftain and warrior clan,
A thousand proud steeds in his vanguard are prancing
'Neath the borderers brave from the banks of the Bann;
Many a heart shall quail, under its coal of mail;
Deeply the merciless foreman shall rue,
When on his ear shall ring, borne on the breezes' wing,
Tir Connell's dread war-cry, "O'Donnell Aboo!"

Wildly o'er Desmond the war-wolf is howling,
Fearless the eagle sweeps over the plain,
The fox in the streets of the city is prowling;
All, all who would scare them are banished or slain.
Grasp every stalwart hand hackbut and battle brand,
Pay them all back the debt so long due;
Norris and Clifford well can of Tir Connell tell;
Onward to glory, "O'Donnell Aboo!"

Sacred the cause of Clan Connaill's defending,
The altars we kneel at, the homes of our sires;
Ruthless the ruin the foe is extending,
Midnight is red with the plunderers' fires.
On with O'Donnell, then, fight the old fight again,
Sons of Tir Connell, all valiant and true.
Make the false Saxon feel Erin's avenging steel!
Strike for your country, "O'Donnell Aboo!"

Johnson's Motor Car

    C
'Twas down by Brannigan's Corner,
        G7
  one morning I did stray.
                     F   C
I met a fellow rebel, and to me he did say,
                         F   C
"We've orders from the captain to assemble at Dunbar,
                             G7 C
But how are we to get there, without a motor car?"

"Oh Barney dear, be of good cheer,
  I'll tell you what we'll do.
The specials they are plentiful, the I.R.A. are few,
We'll send a wire to Johnson to meet us at Stranlar
And we'll give the boys a bloody good ride
  in Johnson's Motor Car."

When Dr. Johnson heard the news he soon put on his shoes
He says this is an urgent case, there is no time to lose,
He then put on his castor hat and on his breast a star
You could hear the din all through Glenfin
  of Johnson's Motor Car.

But when he got to the railway bridge,
  some rebels he saw there
Old Johnson knew the game was up,
  for at him they did stare
He said "I have a permit, to travel near and far."
"To hell with your English permit,
  we want your motor car."

"What will my loyal brethren think,
  when they hear the news,
My car it has been commandeered,
  by the rebels at Dunluce."
"We'll give you a receipt for it, all signed by Captain Barr.
And when Ireland gets her freedom, boy,
  you'll get your motor car."

Well we put that car in motion and filled it to the brim,
With guns and bayonets shining
  which made old Johnson grim,
And Barney hoisted a Sinn Fein flag,
  and it fluttered like a star,
And we gave three cheers for the I.R.A.
  and Johnson's Motor Car.

The Bard Of Armagh

This tune is better known in the U.S.A. as
Streets Of Laredo

      F   C7   Dm   C7
Oh! List to the tale of a poor Irish harper,
      F   C7   Dm   Gm
And scorn not the strings in his old withered hand;
C7 F   C7   Dm   Am
But remember those fingers could once move more sharper,
C7 Dm   C7   B♭ C7 F
To waken the echoes of his dear native land.

How I long for to muse on the days of my boyhood,
Though four score and three years have fled by since then;
Still it gives sweet reflections, as every young joy should,
That merry-hearted boys make the best of old men.

At wake or at fair I would twirl my shillelah,
And trip through the jig in my brogues bound with straw;
And all the pretty maidens from the village and the valley,
Loved the bold Phelim Brady, the Bard of Armagh.

And when Sergeant Death in his cold arms
  shall embrace me,
O lull me to sleep with sweet Erin go bragh;
By the side of my Kathleen, my own love, then place me,
And forget Phelim Brady, the Bard of Armagh.

The Harp That Once Thro' Tara's Halls

Thomas Moore

      D   D7 G
The harp that once thro' Tara's halls
      D   A7   D
The soul of music shed;
              E7   A7
Now hangs as mute on Tara's walls
      D   A7
As tho' that soul were fled.
      D   E7   A7
So sleeps the pride of former days,
      D   A7 D G
So glory's thrill is o'er,
      D   G   D G   A7 G
And hearts that once beat high for praise
      D   A7   D
Now feel that pulse no more.

No more to chiefs and ladies bright
The harp of Tara swells;
The chord alone that breaks at night
Its tail of ruin tells.
Thus Freedom now so seldom wakes;
The only throb she gives
Is when some heart, indignant, breaks,
To show that she still lives.

Erin Go Braugh!

```
Am          Em    Am
I'll tell you a story of a row in the town,
                    G
When the green flag went up
       C           Am
   and the Crown rag came down,
              G         Am     G
T'was the neatest and sweetest thing ever you saw,
           Am       G         Am
And they played the best games played in Erin Go Braugh.
```

One of our comrades was down at Ring's end,
For the honor of Ireland to hold and defend,
He had no veteran soldiers but volunteers raw,
Playing sweet Mauser music for Erin Go Braugh.

Now here's to Tom Pearce and our comrades who died,
Tom Clark, McDunna, McDurmott, McBryde,
And here's to Jan Connelly who gave one hurrah,
And placed the machine guns for Erin Go Braugh.

One brave English captain was ranting that day,
Saying, "Give me one hour and I'll blow you away,"
But a big Mauser bullet got stuck in his craw,
And he died of lead poisoning in Erin Go Braugh.

Old Kent and his comrades like lions at bay,
From the South Dublin Union poured death and dismay,
And what was their horror when the Englishmen saw,
All the dead khaki soldiers in Erin Go Braugh.

Now here's to old Dublin, and here's her renown,
In the long generation her fame will go down,
And our children will tell how their forefathers saw,
The red blaze of freedom in Erin Go Braugh.

Bendemeer's Stream

Thomas Moore

```
          F         C7       F
There's a bower of roses by Bendemeer's stream,
       C7                          F
And the nightingale sings 'round it all the day long.
       F              C7        F
In the time of my childhood 'twas like a sweet dream,
   C7                           F
To sit in the roses and hear the bird's song,
       C7   Gm  Cm7  C7        F
That bow'r and its   music I'll never forget,
                         G7        C7
But oft when alone in the bloom of the year,
   F              C7        F
I think, "Is the nightingale singing there yet?
       C7                        F
Are the roses still bright by the calm Bendemeer?"
```

The Patriot Game

```
C                F C   G7        C
Come all you young rebels and list while I sing,
   G7        C
For love of one's land is a terrible thing.
   G7       C
It banishes fear with the speed of a flame.
               F   C G7   C
And makes us all part of the patriot game.
```

My name is O'Hanlon, I'm just gone sixteen
My home is in Monaghan, there I was weaned
I was taught all my life cruel England to blame
And so I'm a part of the patriot game.

'Tis barely two years since I wandered away
With the local battalion of the bold IRA;
I read of our heroes and wanted the same,
To play up my part in the patriot game.

They told me how Connolly was shot in a chair,
His wounds from the battle all bleeding and bare,
His fine body twisted, all battered and lame,
They soon made him part of the patriot game.

I joined a battalion from dear Bally Bay,
And gave up my boyhood so happy and gay,
For now as a soldier I'd drill and I'd train
To play my full part in the patriot game.

This Ireland of mine has for long been half free,
Six counties are under John Bull's tyranny.
And still De Valera is greatly to blame
For shirking his part in the patriot game.

I don't mind a bit if I shoot down police,
They're lackeys for war never guardians of peace
But yet at deserters I'll never let aim
Those rebels who sold out the patriot game.

And now as I lie with my body all holes,
I think of those traitors who bargained and sold.
I'm sorry my rifle has not done the same,
For the quisling who sold out the patriot game.

The Rising Of The Moon

        C
"Oh! then tell me, Sean O'Farrell,
      G7
Tell me why you hurry so."
       F   C
"Hush, ma bouchal, hush and listen,"
      F   C
And his cheeks were all aglow.

"I bear orders from the captain,
      G7
Get you ready, quick and soon,
      F   C
For the pikes must be together
      F   C
At the rising of the moon."

Chorus:

       C
By the rising of the moon,
      G7
By the rising of the moon,
      F   C
For the pikes must be together
      F   C
By the rising of the moon.

Oh then tell me Sean O'Farrell,
Where the gathering is to be;
In the old spot by the river
Right well known to you and me.
One more word for signal token,
Whistle up the marching tune,
With your pike upon your shoulder
By The Rising Of The Moon.

By the rising of the moon, (twice)
With your pike upon your shoulder,
By the rising of the moon.

Out of many a mud wall cabin,
Eyes were watching thru the night,
Many a manly heart was throbbing
For the coming morning light.
Murmers ran along the valley,
Like the banshees lonely croon,
And a thousand pikes were flashing
By The Rising Of The Moon.

By the rising of the moon, (twice)
And a thousand pikes were flashing
By the rising of the moon.

There beside the singing river
That dark mass of men were seen,
Far above their shining weapons hung
Their own beloved green;
Death to every foe and traitor,
Forward strike the marching tune,
And hurrah me boys for freedom,
Tis The Rising Of The Moon.

Tis the rising of the moon, (twice)
And hurrah me boys for freedom,
Tis the rising of the moon.

Shan Van Voght

C7   F   Gm Dm   Gm   C
Oh, The French are on the sea, says the Shan Van Voght,
          F   Gm Dm   B♭   F
Oh! The French are on the sea, says the Shan Van Voght.
      C   Dm
Oh, the French are in the bay,
           Am B♭   C
they'll be here at break of day,
          F   Gm Dm   B♭   C
And the Orange will decay, says the Shan Van Voght.
          F   Gm Dm   B♭   F
And the Orange will decay, says the Shan Van Voght.

And where will they have their camp?
  says the Shan Van Voght. (twice)
On the Curragh of Kildare and the boys will all be there
With their pikes in good repair
  says the Shan Van Voght. (twice)

And what will the yeoman do?
  says the Shan Van Voght. (twice)
What will the yeoman do but throw off the red and blue
And swear they will be true
  to the Shan Van Voght. (twice)

Then what color will be seen?
  says the Shan Van Voght. (twice)
What color should be seen
  where our fathers' homes have been
But our own immortal green?
  says the Shan Van Voght. (twice)

Will old Ireland then be free?
  says the Shan Van Voght. (twice)
Old Ireland will be free from the centre to the sea
Then, hurrah for liberty!
  says the Shan Van Voght. (twice)

Wearing Of The Green

D
Oh! Paddy dear and did you hear
      E7   A
the news that's going round?
G   D   G   D
The shamrock is forbid by law to grow on Irish ground.
D
Saint Patrick's day no more we'll keep,
     E7   A
his color can't be seen,
G   D   G
For there's a cruel law agin' the wearing of the green.
      D
I met with Napper Tandy, and he took me by the hand,
G   D
And he said how's poor ould Ireland,
     E   A
and how does she stand?
      D   G E7   A
She's the most distressful country that ever you have seen;
G   D
They're hanging men and women there
    G   D
    for wearin' of the green.

Then if the color we must wear is England's cruel red,
Sure Ireland's sons shall ne'er forget
    the blood that they have shed.
You may take the shamrock from your hat
    and cast it on the sod,
But 'twill take root and flourish there,
    though underfoot 'tis trod.
When laws can stop the blades of grass
    from growin' as they grow,
And when the leaves in summertime,
    their verdure dare not show,
Then I will change the color that I wear in my caubeen —
But till that day, please God,
    I'll stick to wearin' of the green.

Danny Boy

        C   F
Oh Danny boy, the pipes, the pipes are calling,
        C   Dm7
From glen to glen and down the mountain side,
        C   C7   F
The summer's gone and all the flowers are dying,
        C
'Tis you, 'tis you must go and I must bide.

But come you back when Summer's in the meadow,
Or when the valley's hushed and white with snow,
'Tis I'll be there in sunshine or in shadow,
Oh Danny boy, oh Danny boy, I love you so.

And if you come when all the flowers are dying,
And I am dead, as dead I well may be,
You'll come and find the place where I am lying,
And kneel and say an 'Ave' there for me.

And I shall hear, tho' soft you tread above me,
And all my dreams will warm and sweeter be,
If you will not fail to tell me that you love me,
Then I simply sleep in peace, until you come to me.

The Bold Fenian Men

F   Dm   Gm   C7
See who comes over the red blossomed heather,
    F   C7   F Gm F C7   F
Their green banners kissing the pure mountain air.
C7   F   Dm   Gm   C7
Heads erect, eyes to front, stepping proudly together,
   F C7   F   Gm F C7 F
Sure freedom sits throned on each proud spirit there.
                    Bb   C7
Down the hill twining, their blessed steel shining,
   F   G7   C7
Like rivers of beauty that flow from each glen.
      F   Dm   Gm   C7
From mountain and valleys 'tis liberty's rally;
F   C7   F   C7 F   C7   F
Out and make way for the bold Fenian Men.

Our prayers and our tears they have scoffed and derided,
They've shut out the sunlight from spirit and mind.
Our foes were united and we were divided,
We met and they scattered our ranks to the wind.
But once more returning, within our veins burning
The fires that illumined dark Aherlow Glen;
We raise the old cry anew, slogan of Conn and Hugh;
Out and make way for the bold Fenian Men!

We're men from the Nore, from the Suir and the Shannon,
Let tyrants come forth, we'll bring force against force.
Our pen is the sword and our voice is the cannon,
Rifle for rifle and horse against horse.
We've made the false Saxon yield many a red battlefield:
God on our side, we will triumph again;
Pay them back woe for woe,
    give them back blow for blow—
Out and make way for the bold Fenian Men!

Side by side for the cause have our forefathers battled,
Our hills never echoed the tread of a slave.
In many a field where the leaden hail rattled,
Through the red gap of glory they marched to the grave.
And those who inherit their name and their spirit,
Will march 'neath the banners of Liberty then;
All who love foreign law—Native or Sassanach—
Must out and make way for the bold Fenian Men!

Roddy M'Corley

G
Ho! See the fleet foot hosts of men,
C   G
Who speed with faces wan
                   C   G
From farmstead and from fisher's cot
  C   Am   D7
Upon the banks of Bann
      G   C   G
They come with vengeance in their eyes,
   Em   Am   D7
Too late, too late are they
        G
For young Roddy M'Corley goes to die
     C   Cm G
On the Bridge of Toome today.

Up the narrow street he stepped,
Smiling and proud and young;
About the hemp-rope on his neck
The golden ringlets clung.
There's never a tear in his blue eyes,
Both glad and bright are they—
As young Roddy M'Corley goes to die
On the Bridge of Toome today.

When he last stepped up that street
His shining pike in hand,
Behind him marched in grim array
A stalwart earnest band!
For Antrim town! for Antrim town!
He led them to the fray—
And young Roddy M'Corley goes to die
On the bridge of Toome today.

There is never a one of all your dead
More bravely fell in fray,
Then he who marches to his fate
On the Bridge of Toome today.
True to the last, true to the last,
He treads the upward way—
And young Roddy M'Corley goes to die
On the Bridge of Toome today.

Kevin Barry

C
Early on a Sunday morning,
                    F
High upon the gallows tree,
    G7   C
Kevin Barry gave his young life
     G7   C
For the cause of liberty.

Only a lad of eighteen summers,
                    F
Yet there's no one can deny,
   G7   C
As he walked to death that morning,
     G7   C
He nobly held his head up high.

Chorus:
Shoot me like an Irish soldier,
Do not hang me like a dog,
For I fought for Ireland's freedom
On that bright September morn.
All around that little bakery
Where we fought them hand to hand,
Shoot me like an Irish soldier,
For I fought to free Ireland.

Just before he faced the hangman
In his lonely prison cell,
British soldiers tortured Barry
Just because he would not tell
Them the names of his brave companions
And other things they wished to know—
"Turn informer and we'll free you,"
Proudly Barry answered, "No!"

Another martyr for old Ireland,
Another murder for the crown!
Brutal laws to crush the Irish
Cannot keep their spirit down.
Lads like Barry are no cowards,
From their foes they do not fly,
For their bravery always has been
Ireland's cause to live or die.

Brennan On The Moor

A
'Tis of brave young highwayman

This story I will tell,

His name was Willie Brennan

And in Ireland he did dwell,

It was on the Kilwood mountain

He commenced his wild career,
    D
And many a wealthy nobleman
  A
Before him shook with fear.

Chorus:

E7   A
It was Brennan on the Moor,

Brennan on the Moor,
     D   A
Bold, brave and undaunted
           D   A
Was young Brennan on the Moor.

One day upon the highway
As Willie he went down,
He met the Mayor of Cashiell
A mile outside the town.
The mayor he knew his features,
And he said, "Young man," said he,
"Your name is Willie Brennan,
You must come along with me."
And it's Brennan, etc.

Now Brennan's wife had gone to town,
Provisions for to buy,
And when she saw her Willie,
She commenced to weep and cry;
Said, "Hand to me that tenpenny."
As soon as Willie spoke,
She handed him a blunderbuss
From underneath her cloak.
And it's Brennan, etc.

Now with this loaded blunderbuss—
The truth I will unfold—
He made the mayor to tremble
And he robbed him of his gold.
One hundred pounds was offered
For his apprehension there,
So he, with horse and saddle,
To the mountains did repair.
Did young Brennan, etc.

Now Brennan being an outlaw
Upon the mountains high,
With cavalry and infantry
To take him they did try.
He laughed at them with scorn
Until at last, 'twas said,
By a false-hearted woman
He was cruelly betrayed.
Was young Brennan, etc.

ALL OVER THIS WORLD

Ah! Si Mon Moine Voulait Danser
Quebec

```
G            D7   G
Ah! Si mon moine voulait danser!
             D7   G
Ah! Si mon moine voulait danser!
             D7   G
Un capuchon je lui donnerais!
             D7   G
Un capuchon je lui donnerais!
```

Chorus:

```
Danse, mon moin', danse!

Tu n'entends pas la danse!
                        D7   G
Tu n'entends pas mon moulin, lon la!
                        D7    G
Tu n'entends pas mon moulin marcher!
```

Ah! Si mon moine voulais danser! (twice)
Un ceinturon je lui donnerais! (twice)

Ah! Si mon moine voulait danser! (twice)
Un chapelet je lui donnerais! (twice)

S'il n'avait fait voue de pauverte! (twice)
Bien d'autres chos' je lui donnerais! (twice)

Cielito Lindo
Mexico

```
A     E7   A
De la Sierra Morena,
  E7   A           E7
Cielito Lindo vienen bajando.

Un par de ojitos negros,
                    A
Cielito Lindo, los contrabando.
```

Chorus:

```
      D    Bm
Ay, ay, ay, ay
  E7    A
Canta y no llores,
                  Bm
Porque cantando se a legran,
  E7           A
Cielito Lindo los corazones.
```

Una flecha en el aire,
Cielito Lindo, lanzó Cupido
Y como fué jugando,
Cielito Lindo, yo fuí el herido.

Ragupati Ragava Rajah Ram
India; Hindu hymn

Refrain:

```
E
Ragupati ragava rajah Ram

Puhtita bhavana si ta ram.
```

Verses:

```
Em
Si ta ram je si ta ram,

Puhtita bhavana si ta ram.

Ishere Allah tere nam
Tubko sunmutti de bhagawan.
```

Literal Translation:

Oh God! Please give good counsel
To us who may call you Ishere
And to us who may call you Allah
And lead us properly.

Du, Du Liegst Mir Im Herzen
Germany

```
C               G7
Du, du liegst mir im Herzen,
                C
Du, du liegst mir im Sinn;
                   G7
Du, du machst mir viel Schmerzen,
                   C
Weisst nicht wie gut ich dir bin;
F   C  G7 C
Ja, Ja, ja,  ja
G7                        C
Weisst nicht wie gut ich dir bin.
```

So, so wie ich dich liebe,
So, so liebe auch mich!
Die, die zärtlichsten Triebe
Fühl ich allein nur für dich.
Ja, ja, ja, ja,
Fühl ich allein, etc.

Doch, doch darf ich dir trauen,
Dir, dir mit leichtem Sinn?
Du, du darfst auf mich bauen,
Weisst ja, wie gut ich dir bin!. . . .

Und, und wenn in der Ferne,
Dir, dir mein Bild erscheint,
Dann, dann wünscht ich so gerne,
Dass uns die Liebe vereint!. . . .

Walking At Night

Czechoslovakia

G   C
Walking at night along the meadow way,
D7   G
Home from the dance beside my maiden gay;
                      C
Walking at night along the meadow way,
G   D7   G
Home from the dance beside my maiden gay.

Chorus:

    G
Hey! Stodole, stodole, stodole pumpa,
D7   G
Stodole pumpa, stodole pumpa,

Stodole, stodole, stodole pumpa,
D7   G
Stodole pumpa, pum, pum, pum.

Nearing the wood, we heard the nightingale, } (twice)
Sweetly it helped me tell my begging tale. }

Many the stars that brightly shone above, } (twice)
But none so bright as her one word of love. }

Suliram

Indonesia

    C   G7
Suliram, suliram, ram, ram,
    C   F   C   F   C   G7   C
Suliram yang manis Aduhai indung suher rang
        G7   C
Bidjalka sana di pandang manis
   Am G C   G7
La suliram, suliram, ram, ram,
    C   F   C   F   C   G7   C
Suliram yang manis Aduhai indung suher rang
        G7   C
Bidjalka sana di pandang manis.

      C   G   C
Tingi la tingi, si mata hari.
Am G C   F   C
Suliram. Anakla koorbau mati toor-tam-bat.
Am G C   F   C G7   C
Suliram. Sudala lama saiya menchari.
     G7   C
Baruse klarung saiya mendabat.
   Am G C
La suliram, etc.

Santa Lucia

Italy

C   G7   C
Now 'neath the silver moon ocean, is glowing,
               G7   C
O'er the calm billows, soft winds are blowing.
C   G7   C
Here balmy breezes blow, pure joys invite us,
              G7   C
And as we gently row, all things delight us.

Chorus:

                  F   C
Hark, how the sailor's cry joyously echoes night:
          G7   C
Santa Lucia, Santa Lucia!
                  F   C
Home of fair poesy, realm of pure harmony,
          G7   C
Santa Lucia, Santa Lucia!

When o'er the waters light winds are playing,
Thy spell can soothe us, all care allaying.
To thee sweet Napoli, what charms are given,
Where smiles creation, toil blest by heaven.

A New Jerusalem

William Blake and Sir C. Hubert Parry
England

C   G   Am   F   C
And did those feet in ancient time
F   C   Am   F
Walk upon England's mountains green?
    C   Am   Em   Am
And was the holy Lamb of God
      Em   Am   Em D C   G
On England's pleasant pastures seen?
    Dm A7 Dm   Gm   Dm
And did the countenance divine
      G7   F   C7   F
Shine forth upon our clouded hills?
        C Dm G G7   C
And was Jerusalem builded here
G Am F   C   F G7 C
Among these dark, satanic mills?

Bring me my bow of burning gold,
Bring me my arrows of desire.
Bring me my spear, oh, clouds unfold!
Bring me my chariot of fire.
I will not cease from mental fight,
Nor shall my sword sleep in my hand,
Till we have built Jerusalem
In England's green and pleasant land.

Auprès De Ma Blonde

France

Refrain:

```
G  D7      G
Auprès de ma blonde,
D7              G
Qu'il fait bon, fait bon, fait bon!
   D7       G
Auprès de ma blonde,
D7          G
Qu'il fait bon rester.
```

Verse:

```
       D7    G
Au jardin de mon père
         C      G
Les lauriers sont fleuris,
       D7    G
Au jardin de mon père
         C      G
Les lauriers sont fleuris,
      E7          Am
Tous les oiseaux du monde
     D7           G
S'en vont y fair' leurs nids.
```

La caill', la tourterelle,
Et la jolie perdrix,
La caill', la tourterelle,
Et la jolie perdrix,
Et ma jolie colombe
Qui chante jour et nuit.

Qui chante pour les filles
Qui n'ont pas de mari,
Qui chante pour les filles
Qui n'ont pas de mari.
Pour moi, ne chante guère,
Car j'en ai un joli,

Dites-nous donc, la belle,
Où donc est vot' mari?
Dites-nous donc, la belle,
Où donc est vot' mari?
Il est dans la Hollande,
Les Hollandais l'ont pris,

Que donneriez-vous, belle,
Pour avoir votre ami?
Que donneriez-vous, belle,
Pour avoir votre ami?
Je donnerais Versailles,
Paris et Saint-Denis,

Je donnerais Versailles,
Paris et Saint-Denis,
Je donnerais Versailles,
Paris et Saint-Denis,
Les tours de Notre-Dame,
Et l'clocher d'mon pays;

Marching To Pretoria

South Africa

```
C
I'm with you and you're with me and

So we are all together,
G7
So we are all together,
C
So we are all together.

Sing with me, I'll sing with you and

So we will sing together
G7          C
As we march along.
```

Chorus:

```
        F          C
We are marching to Pretoria,
   G7        C
Pretoria, Pretoria,
        F          C
We are marching to Pretoria,
   G7        C
Pretoria, Hurrah.
```

We have food, the food is good, and
So let us eat together, (3 times)
When we eat, it is a treat, and
So we will sing together,
As we march along.

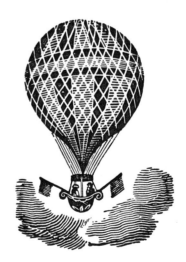

Stenka Razin

Russia

```
          F              C7
From beyond the wooded island,
                          F
To the river wide and free,
         Bb            F
Proudly sailed the arrow-breasted
         C7           F
Ships of Cossack yeomanry.
```

On the first is Stenka Razin,
With his princess by his side,
Drunken holds in marriage revels
With his beauteous young bride.

From behind there comes a murmur,
"He has left his sword to woo;
One short night and Stenka Razin
Has become a woman too."

Stenka Razin hears the murmur
Of his discontented band,
And his lovely Persian princess
He has circled with his hand.

His dark brows are drawn together
As the waves of anger rise,
And the blood comes rushing swiftly
To his piercing jet black eyes.

I will give you all you ask for,
Head and heart and life and hand,
And his voice rolls out like thunder,
Out across the distant land.

Volga, Volga, Mother Volga,
Wide and deep beneath the sun,
You have never such a present
From the Cossacks of the Don.

So that peace may reign forever
In this band so free and brave,
Volga, Volga, Mother Volga,
Make this lovely girl a grave.

Now, with one swift mighty motion,
He has raised his bride on high,
And has cast her where the waters
Of the Volga roll and sigh.

Now a silence like the grave sinks
To all who stand to see,
And the battle-hardened Cossacks
Sink to weep on bended knees.

"Dance you fools and let's be merry,
What is this that's in your eyes?
Let us thunder out a chantey,
To the place where beauty lies."

From beyond the wooded island
To the river wide and free,
Proudly sailed the arrow-breasted
Ships of Cossack yeomanry.

Salute To Life

Dmitri Shostakovitch

U.S.S.R.

The melody of this song was subsequently used for the *United Nations Hymn*.

```
F            C7   F
The voice of the city is sleepless,
              C7         F
The factories thunder and beat.
              C7         F
How bitter the wind and relentless,
Gm  C7        F
That echoes our shuffling feet.
```

Chorus:

```
   Gm    C7    F       Bb  F
You hear the whistle calling to ev'ry hand,
   Bb          F        Gm C7  F
And radiant as the morning is our fair land.
```

The morning greets us with coolness,
The river greets us with light;
The summer in radiant fullness
Awakens from the darkness of night.

For the wind has a breath of the morning;
They meet it with banners unfurled.
Let joy be your clarion, comrade,
We'll march in the dawn of the world.

Salute to the soldiers of freedom,
To comrades whose burden we share.
Divide with them sorrow and gladness,
Our labor, our plans and our care.

The universe envies us, comrades,
Our hearts are made strong in the strife.
Salute to the struggle for freedom!
Salute to the morning of life!

Vive La Canadienne

Quebec

D
Vive la Canadienne!
               Em A7
Vole, mon coeur, vole!
D   Bm
Vive la Canadienne!
  Em A7   D
Et ses jolis yeux doux!
           D   G   D7
Et ses jolis yeux doux, doux, doux,
         G   D
Et ses jolis yeux doux!
           D   G   D7
Et ses jolis yeux doux, doux, doux,
         G   A7
Et ses jolis yeux doux!

Nous la menons aux noces!
Vole, mon coeur, vole! Vive la Canadienne!
Nous la menons aux noces
Dans tous ses beaux atours,
Dans tous ses beaux atours—tours—tours, } (twice)
Dans tous ses beaux atours!

Nous faisons bonne chere! etc.
Et nous avons bon gout! etc.

On danse avec nos blondes! etc.
Nous changeons tour à tour! etc.

Ainsi le temps se passe! etc.
Il est vraiment bien doux! etc.

Singable Translation:

Here's to "La Canadienne"!
Fly, my heart, Oh fly away!
Here's to "La Canadienne"!
And her sweet eyes so gay!
And her sweet eyes so gay, gay, gay, } (twice)
And her sweet eyes so gay!

Off to the wedding take her!
Fly my heart, oh fly away!
Here's to "La Canadienne"!
In all her fine array! etc.

Oh, we have fun and laughter! etc.
And everyone is gay! etc.

Then with the girls we dance around, etc.
In the old fashioned way! etc.

And so the time soon passes, etc.
Until it's almost day! etc.

Que Bonita Bandera

(How Beautiful Is The Flag)

Puerto Rico

Chorus:

Cm   G7
Que bonita bandera,
              Cm
Que bonita bandera,
              Fm
Que bonita bandera,
       Cm G7   Cm
Es la bandera Puertoriqueña.

Verses:

          G7   Cm
Azul blanca y colorada,
       G7   Cm
Y en el medio tiene un estrella;
G7   Cm
Bonita señores es
F   Cm G7   Cm
La bandera Puertoriqueña.

Todo buen Puertoriqueña,
Es bueno que la defienda,
Bonita señores, es la bandera Puertoriqueña.

Bonita señora es,
Que bonita es ella,
Que bonita es la bandera Puertoriqueña.

Singable Translation:

How beautiful is the flag, (3 times)
It is the flag of Puerto Rico.

Blue, white and red,
And in the center, one star.
It is beautiful,
The flag of Puerto Rico.

All good Puerto Ricans,
It is good that they defend it,
Beautiful is the Puerto Rican flag.

Guantanamera

By Jose Marti
Adapted by Pete Seeger and Hector Angulo

Cuba

Chorus:

```
E      A    B7    E       A
Guantanamera guajira Guantanamera
E      A  B7     E        A    B7
Guantanamera guajira Guantanamera.
```

```
B7      E         A
Yo soy un hombre sincero
B7      E         A
De donde crece la palma
B7      E         A
Yo soy un hombre sincero
B7      E  A    B7
De donde crece la palma
           E      A    B7
Y antes de morrir me quiero,
           E      AB7
Echar mis versos del alma.
```

Mi verso es de un verde claro ⎫
Y de un carmin encendido   ⎬ (twice)
Mi verso es un cierro herido ⎭
Que busca en el monte amparo

Con los pobres de la tierra ⎫
Quiero yo mi suerte echar   ⎬ (twice)
El arroyo de las sierra   ⎭
Me complace mas que el mar.

Literal Translation:

A truthful man, that's me;
From where the palm trees grow,
Before dying, I should like to pour forth
The poems of my soul.

My verses are of soft green,
But also a flowing red.
My verse is a wounded fawn
Seeking refuge in the woods.

With the humble of the earth,
My fate I want to share,
For the gentle stream of a mountain
Pleases me more than the sea.

Au Clair De La Lune

Charles Fonteyn Manney and J. B. Lully
France

```
D           A7 D  A7    D
Au claire de la lune mon ami Pierrot;
            A7 D    A7    D
Prête-moi ta plume pour écrire un mot.
G                            A7
Ma chandelle est morte, Je n'ai plus de feu,
D           A7 D    A7      D
Ouvre-moi ta porte pour l'amour de Dieu.
```

Au clair de la lune Pierrot répondit,
"Je n'ai pas de plume, je suis dans mon lit.
Va chez la voisine, je crois qu'elle y est.
Car dans sa cuisine on bat le briquet."

Au clair de la lune s'en fût Arlequin,
Frapper chez la brune, ell' répond soudain:
"Qui frapp' de la sorte?" Il dit à son tour:
"Ouvrez votre porte, pour le dieu d'amour!"

Au clair de la lune, on n'y voit qu'un peu.
On chercha la plume, on chercha du feu.
En cherchant d'la sorte, je n'sais c'qu'on trouva;
Mais je sais qu'la porte sur eux se ferma.

Singable Translation:

"At thy door I'm knocking, by the pale moonlight,
Lend a pen, I pray thee, I've a word to write;
Guttered is my candle, my fire burns no more;
For the love of heaven, open up the door!"

Pierrot cried in answer by the pale moonlight,
"In my bed I'm lying, late and chill the night;
Yonder at my neighbor's, someone is astir;
Fire is freshly kindled, get a light from her."

To the neighbor's house then, by the pale moonlight,
Goes our gentle Lubin to beg a pen to write;
"Who knocks there so softly?" calls a voice above.
"Open wide your door now for the God of Love!"

Seek they pen and candle by the pale moonlight,
They can see so little since dark is now the night;
What they find while seeking, that is not revealed;
All behind her door is carefully concealed.

A La Claire Fontaine
(By Yonder Flowing Fountain)

English text: Arthur Kevess

France

```
F          C7
A la claire fontaine
F          C7      F
M'en allant promener,
           Dm
J'ai trouvé l'eau si belle
F        G7    C7
Que je m'y suis baigné.
```

Refrain:

```
F        Dm        F
Lui ya long temps que je t'aime
G7       C7        F
Jamais je ne t'oublierai.
```

J'ai trouvé l'eau si belle
Que je m'y suis baigné;
Sous les feuille d'un chêne
Je me suis fait sécher.

Sous les feuilles d'un chêne
Je me suis fait sécher,
Sur la plus haute branche
Le rossignol chantait.

Sur la plus haute branche
Le rossignol chantait.
Chante, rossignol, chante,
Toi qui as le coeur gai.

Chante, rossignol, chante,
Toi qui as le coeur gai,
Tu as le coeur a rire,
Moi je l'ai-t-a pleurer.

Tu as le coeur à rire,
Moi je l'ai-t-a pleurer;
J'ai perdu ma maîtresse
Sans l'avoir mérité.

J'ai perdu ma maitresse
Sans l'avoir merite,
Pour un bouquet de roses
Que je lui refusai.

Pour un bouquet de roses
Que je lui refusai.
Je voudrais que la rose
Fût encore au rosier.

Je voudrais que la rose
Fût encore au rosier,
Et moi et ma maîtresse
Dans les mêm's amitiés.

Singable Translation:

By yonder flowing fountain
I went my lonely way,
That fountain was so lovely
I lingered in the spray.

Long, long the time I've loved you,
Always will I think of you.

Then underneath an oak tree
I passed the hours away,
High in the tree above me
Birds sang the livelong day.

They sing a song of rapture,
My heart it cries all day,
I lost my darling mistress
In such a foolish way.

I lost my darling mistress
In such a foolish way,
Due to some red red roses
For which I would not pay.

If she would but forgive me
I'd buy her that bouquet,
And we would walk together
Lovers the same old way.

Hava Nagila

Israel

```
E                      Am        E
Hava nagila, hava nagila, hava nagila V' nism'cha.
                       Am        E
Hava nagila, hava nagila, hava nagila V' nism'cha.
                  Dm
Hava n' ran'na, hava n' ran'na,
                  E
  hava n' ran'na, v' nism'cha.
                  Dm
Hava n' ran'na, hava n' ran'na,
                  E
  hava n' ran'na, v' nism'cha.
Am                            Dm
Uru, uru achim, uru a chim b'lev sameach, uru a chim

  b'lev sameach,
E            E7      Am
Uru a chim uru a chim b'lev sameach.
```

Mi Caballo Blanco
(My White Horse)
Chile

```
Em              Am              Em
Es mi caballo blanco como un amanecer,
Am              Em B7           Em
Siempre juntitos vamos, es mi amigo más fiel.
```

Chorus:

```
Am      Em      B7      Em
Mi caballo, mi caballo galopando va.
Am      Em      B7      Em
Mi caballo, mi caballo, se va y se va.
```

Ah

En alas de una dicha, mi caballo corrió,
En alas de una pena, el también me llevó.

Al taita Dios le pido, y Él lo sabe muy bien,
Si a su lado me llama en mi baballo iré.

Singable Translation:

It is my white horse, just like the dawn,
We always go together, he is my most faithful friend.

My horse, my horse is galloping,
My horse, my horse goes on and on.

My horse runs on wings of joy,
He runs on wings of sorrow, he also carries me.

I pray to God, and He knows it well.
If He calls me to His side, I will go on my horse.

Everybody Loves Saturday Night

```
G       D7          G
Ev'rybody loves Saturday night.
        D7          G
Ev'rybody loves Saturday night.
G       C       G       D7
Ev'rybody, ev'rybody, ev'rybody, ev'rybody,
G       D7          G
Ev'rybody loves Saturday night.
```

Nigeria:
Bobo waro fero Satodeh,
Bobo waro fero Satodeh,
Bobowaro, bobowaro, bobowaro, bobowaro,
Bobowaro fero Satodeh.

France:
Tout le monde aime Samedi soir.

China:
Ren ren si huan li pai lu.

Russia:
Vsiem nravitsa sabbota vietcheram.

Czechoslovakia:
Kazhdi ma rad sabotu vietcher.

Spanish:
A todos les gusta la noche del Sabádo.

Yiddish:
Jeder eyne hot lieb Shabas ba nacht.

Van Dieman's Land
Australia

```
        C           Gm      Dm
Come all you gallant poachers,
    Bb      C       F
That ramble void of care,
C7  F       Dm C7 Bb
That walk out on a moonlight night
        C7      F       C
With dog and gun and snare.
        F       Dm C7      Bb
By the keepers of the land, my boys,
        C7      F       C
One night we were trepanned,
                        Gm      Dm
And for fourteen years transported
    Bb      C       F
Unto Van Dieman's land.
```

The first day that we landed
Upon that fateful shore,
The planters came round us,
They might be twenty score.
They ranked us off like horses
And sold us out of hand,
And yoked us to the plough, brave boys,
To plough Van Dieman's Land.

God bless our wives and families,
Likewise that happy shore,
That isle of sweet contentment
Which we shall see no more;
As for the wretched females,
See them we seldom can,
There are fourteen men to every woman
In Van Dieman's Land.

Oh, if I had a thousand pounds
All laid out in my hand,
I'd give it all for liberty
If that I could command;
Again to England I'd return
And be a happy man,
And bid adieu to poaching
And to Van Dieman's Land.

Adelita

Mexico

```
G        D7    G
Adelita se llama la ingrata,
         C              D7
La qu'era dueña de todo mi placer.
                          G
Nunca piensas que llegue a olvidarla
         D7      G
Ní cambiarla por otra mujer.
```

Si Adelita quisiera ser mi esposa,
Si Adelita fuera mi mujer,
Le compraía un vestido de seda
Y la llevara a pasear el cuartel.

Ya me llama el clarín de campaña
Como soldado valiente a pelear.
Correrrá por los calles la sangre
Pero olvidare jamás me verá.

Si acaso yo muero en campaña
Y mi cadaver en la tierra va a quedar,
Adelita, por Dos te la ruego
Que por mí muerte tu vayas a llorar.

Adelita es una fronteriza
Con ojos verdes, color de la mar,
Que trae locos a todos los hombres
Y a todos les hace llorar.

Si Adelita se fuere con otro
La seguiría la huella sin cesar,
En aeroplanos y buques de guerra
Y por tierra hast' en tren militar.

Singable Translation:

Adelita's the name of the lady
Who was the mistress of all my pleasures here.
Never think I can come to forget her,
Not to change her for any other dear.

If Adelita would take me for a husband,
If Adelita would only be my wife,
I would buy her a costume of satin
And I'd give her a taste of barracks life.

Now the trumpet to battle does call me
To fight as every valiant soldier should.
In the streets then the blood will be running,
But 'twill never see me forget thee.

If perhaps I should die in the battle,
And my poor corpse be left upon the field,
Adelita, for God's sake I pray thee
For my death thou wilt shed but one tear.

Adelita's a desperate coquette
With deep green eyes, the color of the sea,
Who drives all the men to distraction
And makes them all weep bitterly.

Should Adelita run off with another,
I'd trail her always, forever, near and far,
Both in airplanes and ships of the navy,
And on land in a military train.

Linstead Market

Calypso style, Trinidad

```
    D
He promised to meet me at Linstead Market,
A7          D
Take me out to a show.
```

He promised to meet me at Linstead Market,
A7   D
Take me out to a show.

Chorus:

```
                    A7          D
I tell you, Oh what a night, what a night
     A7          D
Oh what a Saturday night.
                    A7          D
I tell you oh what a night, what a night,
G       A7      D
Oh what a Saturday night.
```

I waited and waited at Linstead Market } (twice)
Not a sign of my Joe.

Everybody coming to Linstead Market, } (twice)
Everybody but Joe.

Then I got a letter to Linstead Market, } (twice)
Explaining everything then.

Sorry can't meet you at Linstead Market, } (twice)
I just got married today.

But I'll meet you tomorrow at Linstead Market, } (twice)
And take you out to the show.

Coplas

Mexico

Am   E
Chile verde me perdiste,
F   C
Chile verde te dare.
Am   G
Vamanos pa la la huerta
F   E
Que allate lo cortare.

Chorus:

Am   G
Ay la la la lai la la la
F   E
Lai la la la la
Am   G
Ay la la la lai la la la
F   E
Lai la la la la.

Dicen que los de tu casa
Ninguno me puede ver,
Diles que no batan l'agua,
Que al cabo lo han de beber.

La mujer que quiere a dos
Los quiere como hermanitos.
Al uno le pone cuernos
Y al otro lo pitoncitos.

La mula que yo monte
La monta hoy mi compadre,
Eso a mi no me importa
Pues yo la monte primero.

La noche que me casa,
No pude dormirme un rato.
Por estrar toda la noche
Corriendo detra de un gato.

Me dijiste que fue un gato
El que entro por tu balcon,
Yo no he visto gato prieto
Con sombrero y pantalon.

Literal Translation:

You asked for green pepper,
I'll give you green pepper.
Let's go to the garden
And I'll pick it for you.

They say your family
Can't stand to see me.
Tell them not to muddy the water;
In the end they'll have to drink it.

The woman who loves two men
Loves them like brothers.
She puts big horns on one
And budding horns on the other.

The mule I used to ride
Is now ridden by my friend;
I don't care
Because I broke her in.

The night I got married
I couldn't sleep all night.
I spent the whole night
Chasing a black cat.

You said it was a black cat
That came in through your balcony.
I've never seen a black cat before
Wearing a hat and trousers.

The Ash Grove

Wales

    G   Em   Am   D
The ash grove, how graceful, how plainly 'tis speaking.
    Em   C   D7   G
The harp thro' it playing has language for me.
          Em   Am   D
Whenever the light through its branches is breaking,
    Em   C   D7   G
A host of kind faces is gazing on me.
    G   Am   D   G
The friends of my childhood again are before me;
    B7   Em   A7   D
Each step wakes a mem'ry as freely I roam;
    G   Em   Am   D
With soft whispers laden, its leaves rustle o'er me,
    Em   C   D7   G
The ash grove, the ash grove alone is my home.

My laughter is over, my step loses lightness,
Old countryside measures steal soft on my ears;
I only remember the past and its brightness,
The dear ones I mourn for again gather here.
From out of the shadows their loving looks greet me,
And wistfully searching the leafy green dome,
I find other faces fond bending to greet me,
The ash grove, the ash grove alone is my home.

Muss I Denn
(Must I Then)
Germany

```
         D          G      A7       D
Muss i denn, muss i denn zum städtle hinaus,
A7       D       A7              D
Städtle hinaus, und du, mein Schatz, bleibst hier.
      D          G          A7       D
Wenn i komm, wenn i komm, wenn i wieder um komm,
A7        D       A7               D
Wieder um komm, kehr i ein, mein Schatz, bei dir.
```

Chorus:

```
      A7              D
Kann i gleich net all-weil bei dir sein
    G              D
Han i doch mein Freud an dir.
                          A7       D
Wenn i komm, wenn i komm, wenn i wieder um komm,
A7        D       A7               D
Wieder um komm, kehr i ein, mein Schatz, bei dir.
```

Wie du weinst, wie du weinst, dass i wandere muss,
Wandere muss, wie wenn d'Lieb jetzt war vorbei.
Sind au drauss, sind au drauss der Mädele viel,
Mädele viel, lieber Schatz, i bleib dir treu.
Denk du net, wenn i andre seh,
So sei mein Lieb vorbei.
Sind au drauss, sind au drauss der Mädele viel,
Mädele viel, lieber Schatz, i bleib dir treu.

Ubers Jahr, ubers jahr, wenn mi Träubele schneid't,
Träubele schneid't, stell i hier mi wiedrum ein;
Bin i dann, bin i dann dein Schätzele noch,
Schätzele noch, so soll die Hochzeit sein,
Ubers Jahr, da ist mein Zeit vorbei,
Da g'hör i mein und dein,
Bin i dann, bin i dann dein Schätzele noch,
Schätzele noch, so soll die Hoghzeit sein.

Singable Translation:

Must I then, must I then leave the village today,
    village today,
While you, my love, stay there?
When I come, when I come, when I come back again,
    come back again,
I'll return, my love, to you.
May I always come to you, my dear,
For I know no joy but with you.
When I come, when I come, when I come back again,
    come back again,
I'll return, my love, to you.

Moscow Nights
M. Matusovskii and V. Solovyov-Sedoi
U.S.R.R.

```
Am         D    Dm   E7     Am
Stillness in the grove, not a rustling sound;
C              G7          C
Softly shines the moon clear and bright.
B7  E7 Am                  Dm
Dear, if you could know how I treasure so
          Am     Dm E7 Am
This most beautiful Moscow night.
B7  E7 Am                  Dm
Dear if you could know how I treasure so
          Am     Dm E7 Am
This most beautiful Moscow night.
```

Lazily the brook, like a silv'ry stream
Ripples gently in the moonlight;
And a song afar fades as in a dream ⎫
In the spell of this summer night.   ⎬ (twice)

Dearest, why so sad, why the downcast eyes,
And your lovely head bent so low?
Oh, it's hard to speak—and yet not to speak ⎫
Of the longing my heart does know.   ⎬ (twice)

Promise me, my love, as the dawn appears
And the darkness turns into light,
That you'll cherish, dear,   ⎫
    through the passing years   ⎬ (twice)
This most beautiful Moscow night.   ⎭

Ach Du Lieber Augustin
Germany

```
G
Ach, du lieber Augustin,
D7        G
Augustin, Augustin.
```

```
Ach, du lieber Augustin,
D7        G
Alles ist hin.
D7          G
Geld ist weg, Gut ist Weg,
D7        G
Augustin liegt im Dreck,
```

```
Ach, du lieber Augustin,
D7        G
Alles ist hin.
```

The Keeper

England

```
       D        G    D
The keeper did a hunting go,
                   G      D
And under his coat he carried a bow,

All for to shoot at a merry little doe,
                        A7
Among the leaves so green, O.
```

Chorus:

```
D
O. Jackie boy! (Master) Sing ye well? (Very well)
                              A7
Hey down (Ho down) Derry, derry down.
     D            A7    D
Among the leaves so green, O.
            D
To my hey down, down! (To my ho down, down!)
                         A7
Hey down (Ho down)! Derry, derry down.
     D            A7    D
Among the leaves so green, O.
```

The first doe she did cross the plain:
The keeper fetched her back again,
Where she is now she may remain,
Among the leaves so green, O.

The second doe she cross'd the brook:
The keeper fetched her back with his hook
Where she is now you may go and look,
Among the leaves so green, O.

Hymn For Nations

Tune: *Ode To Joy From Beethoven's Ninth Symphony*

```
D    Em7 D    A7 D A
Brother shout your country's anthem,
D      A7   D     A
Sing your land's undying fame,
D      Em7 D7  G    D A7
Light the wondrous tale of nations
D       A7 D  A    D
With your people's golden name;
A      D    A    D
Tell your father's noble story,
A7     F 7   Bm E7  A
Raise on high your country's sign.
D     Em D  G   D Em
Join then in   the final glory,
D     A7 D  A7    D
Brother lift your flag with mine.
```

Hail the sun of peace, now rising.
Hold the war clouds ever furled;
Blend your banners, O my brother,
In the rainbow of the world!
Red as blood and blue as heaven,
Wise as age and proud as youth,
Melt your colors, wonder woven,
In the great white light of truth.

Build the road of peace before us,
Build it wide and deep and long;
Speed the slow, remind the eager,
Help the weak and guide the strong.
None shall push aside another,
None shall let another fall,
Work beside me, O my brother,
All for one and one for all!

Meadowland

Red Army Song, U.S.S.R.

```
Am        Em
Meadowland, meadowland,
Am                 Em
Meadows green and fields in blossom,
Dm              E
Merrily greet the plucky heroes,
Dm
Yes, the heroes of the great Red Army.
```

Maidens fair, why d'you cry?
Blushing maids are sad and weary,
Having to part from handsome lovers,
As the boys are off to join the army.

Oh, maidens dear, never fear,
Staunch and faithful are your lovers.
Wish us good speed for we are leaving
To defend our happy land of Soviets.

Oh, Steppe land, so vast and free,
Tilled by flourishing Kolkhozes,
Everywhere factories and houses
Newly built, the fruits of Revolution.

Oh, working folks, peasant folks,
Keep on building, keep on tilling.
Staunchly we hold our constant vigil,
We, the peoples of the land of Soviets.

Waltzing Matilda

Australia

Words: A. B. Paterson
Music: Marie Cowan

Eb   Bb7   Cm   Fm Fm7
Once a jolly swagman camped by a billabong
Eb   Gm   Bb7 Eb Bb7
Under the shade of a coolibah tree,
      Eb   Bb7   Cm   Fm Fm7
And he sang as he watched and waited till his billy boiled,
  Eb   Bbdim C7   Fm7 Bb7   Eb
"You'll come a-waltzing Matil-   da with me!"

Chorus:

Eb   Eb7 Ab   Fm7   Ebdim
Waltzing Matilda, Waltzing Matilda,
Eb   Fm7 Eb   Fm7   Bb7
You'll come a-waltzing Matilda with me.
      Eb   Bb7   Fdim Cm   Fm Fm7
And he sang as he watched and waited till his billy boiled.
               stowed that jump-buck in his tucker bag
  Eb   C7   Fm7 Bb7   Eb
"You'll come a-waltzing Matil-   da with me!"

Down came a jumbuck to drink at the billabong,
Up jumped the swagman and grabbed him with glee,
And he sang as he stowed that jumbuck in his tucker bag,
"You'll come a-waltzing Matilda with me!"

Up rode the squatter, mounted on his thoroughbred,
Down came the troopers, one, two three:
"Where's that jolly jumbuck
   You've got in your tucker bag?"
"You'll come a-waltzing Matilda with me!"

Up jumped the swagman, sprang into the billabong.
"You'll never catch me alive," said he.
And his ghost may be heard as you pass by that billabong,
"You'll come a-waltzing Matil-da with me!"

Salangadou

French Creole

     Fm C7 Fm   C7
Salangadou,   Salangadou,
Fm   C7 Fm   C7 Fm
Salangadou,   Salangadou,
Bb min   C
Coté piti fille la yé,
Fm   C7   Fm   C7 Fm
Salangadou-ou-ou, Salangadou-ou-ou?

Singable Translation:

Salangadou, Salangadou,
Salangadou, Salangadou,
Oh, where is my little girl gone,
Salangadou-ou-ou, Salangadou-ou-ou?

Un Canadien Errant
(An Exiled Canadien)

Quebec

F   C
Un Canadien errant, banni de ses foyers,
F   C
Un Canadien errant, banni de ses foyers,
                      C7 F
Parcourait en pleurant des pays étrangers,
          Bb   F   Gm   C7 F
Parcourait en pleurant des pays étrangers.

Un jour, triste et pensif, assis au bord des flots, (twice)
Au courant fugitif il adressa ces mots: (twice)

"Si tu vois mon pays, mon pays malheureux, (twice)
Va, dis a mes amis que je me souviens d'eux." (twice)

"O jours si pleins d'appas vous êtes disparus (twice)
Et ma patrie, hélas! Je ne la verrai plus!" (twice)

"Non, mais en expirant, O mon cher Canada! (twice)
Mon regard languissant vers toi se portera." (twice)

Singable Translation:

Once, a young "Canadien,"
   banished from his dear home, (twice)
All thru' a foreign land, tearfully he did roam, (twice)

Down by a riverside, watching how swift it fled, (twice)
He sat him down and cried,
   and these sad words he said: (twice)

"If you should chance to see
   my poor unhappy land, (twice)
Tell all my friends for me that
   I remember them." (twice)

"Happy days that have passed
   never again shall be, (twice)
And my dear land, alas, never again I'll see." (twice)

"Oh Canada, I cry, my land you'll always be, (twice)
And till the day I die, my thoughts
   will be of thee." (twice)

O Canada!

Words: Adolphe Routhier, Music: Calixa Lavilee
English Text: Stanley Weir
Quebec

```
D A7 Bm A7 D          A7
O Canada! Terre de nos aieux,
D    E7      A   Bm A   E7  A
Ton front est ceint de fleurons glorieux!
       A7            D
Car ton bras sait porter l'épée,
  G        E7 A
Il sait porter la croix!
       A7          D E b dim
Ton histoire est une épopée.
    A    E7    A
Des plus brillants exploits.
D   A7   Bm Em        A
Et ta valeur, de foi trempee,
D Daug G        Bm Em  F
Protêgera nos foyers et nos droits,
D Daug G      D A7 D
Protêgera nos foyers et nos droits.
```

Sous l'oeil de Dieu, près du fleuve géant,
Le Canadien grandit en espérant,
Il est né d'une race fière,
Bèni fut son berceau.
Le ciel a marque sa carrière,
Dans ce monde nouveau.
Toujours guidé pras sa lumiére,
Il garders l'honneur de son drapeau. (twice)

De son patron, précurseur du vrai Dieu,
Il porte au front l'auréole de feu.
Ennemi de la tyrannie,
Mais plein de loyauté,
Il veut garder dans l'harmonie
Sa fière liberté;
Et par l'effort de son génie,
Sur notre sol asseoir la verité. (twice)

Amour sacré du trône de l'autel,
Remplis nos coeurs de ton souffle immortel!
Parmi les races étrangères,
Notre guide est la loi:
Sachons être un peiple de freres
Sous le joug de la foi.
Et répétons, comme nos pères,
Le cri vainqueur "Pour le Christ et le Roi! (twice)

Singable Translation:

O Canada! Our home and native land,
True patriot love in all thy sons command.
With glowing hearts we see thee rise,
The true North strong and free;
And stand on guard, O Canada,
We stand on guard for thee.
O Canada! glorious and free!
O Canada! We stand on guard for thee!

O Canada! Where pines and maples grow,
Great prairies spread and lordly rivers flow.
How dear to us thy vast domain,
From East to Western sea,
Thou land of hope for all who toil,
Thou true North, strong and free!

O Canada! Beneath thy shining skies
May stalwart sons and gentle maidens rise;
To keep thee steadfast through the years
From East to Western sea,
Our Fatherland, our Motherland!
Our true North strong and free!

Ruler Supreme, Who hearest humble pray'r,
Hold our dominions all Thy loving care.
Help us to find, O God, in Thee,
A lasting, rich reward,
As waiting for the better day
We ever stand on guard.

Zum Gali Gali

Israel

```
Em
Zum gali gali gali, zum gali gali, zum gali gali
Hechalutz le'man avodah
Zum gali gali, Zum gali gali gali, zum gali gali
Avodah le man hecahlutz.
Zum gali gali gali, zum gali gali.
```

World Youth Song

Cm   G7
One great vision unites us,

                                Cm
Though remote be the lands of our birth.
E♭   B♭7
Foes may threaten and smite us,

                        E♭
Still we live to bring peace to the earth.
Cm   Fm
Ev'ry country and nation,
B7   E♭
Stirs with youth's inspiration;
A♭   E♭   Fm   Cm
Young folks are singing, happiness bringing,
Fm6   G
Friendship to all the world.

Chorus:

G7 C
Ev'rywhere the youth is singing freedom's song,
          G7   C
Freedom's song, freedom's song.

We rejoice to show the world that we are strong,
          G7   C
We are strong, we are strong.
G C   G   Am   Dm   C Dm
We are the youth and the world acclaims
   F   dim G   D7 G
   our   song of truth.
G7 C   G7
Everywhere the youth is singing freedom's song,
                     C
Freedom's song, freedom's song.

We remember the battle,
And the heroes who fell on the field,
Sacred blood running crimson,
Our invincible friendship has sealed.
All who cherish the vision
Make the final decision,
Struggle for justice, peace and goodwill
For peoples throughout the world.

Solemnly our young voices
Take the vow to be true to our cause.
We are proud of our choices,
We are serving humanity's cause.
Still the forces of evil
Lead the world to upheaval;
Down with their lying! End useless dying!
Fight for a happy world!

FOLK DIALOGUES

concerning marriage, murder, money
and most anything else

Whistle, Daughter, Whistle

```
Dm      A7      Dm      A7 Dm   A7 Dm
```
Mother, I would marry, yes I would be a bride,
```
A7          A7      Dm          A7 Dm C   F
```
And I would have a young man for ever at my side.
```
A7 Dm A7   Dm          D7   Gm   D7   Gm
```
For if I had a young man, oh how happy I would be,
```
A7 Dm A7   Dm      A7          Dm A7 Dm
```
For I am tired and oh, so weary of my singularity.

Whistle, daughter, whistle, and you shall have a cow.
I cannot whistle, mother, I guess I don't know how.
But if I had a young man, oh, how happy I would be,
For I am tired and so weary of my propriety.

Whistle, daughter, whistle, and you shall have a sheep.
I cannot whistle mother, I can only weep.
But if I had a young man, oh, how happy I would be,
For I am tired and oh, so weary of my virginity.

Whistle, daughter, whistle, and you shall have a man.
I cannot whistle, mother, . . . (whistles)
You impudent little daughter,
    what makes you whistle now?
I'd rather whistle for a man than for a sheep or cow.

Daughters Will You Marry?

Daughters will you marry?
```
G    D7   G
```
Yea, father, yea.

Will you marry a farmer?
```
G    D7   G
```
Nay, father, nay.
```
                    C
```
A farmer's wife I will not be,
```
        D7          G
```
Cleaning out stables is not for me,
```
        D7   G
```
Nay, father, nay.

Daughters will you marry?
Yea, father, yea.
Will you marry a doctor?
Nay, father, nay.
A doctor's wife I will not be,
Torturing people is not for me,
Nay, father, nay.

Will you marry a teacher?
A teacher's wife I will not be,
Punishing children is not for me,

Will you marry a lawyer?
A lawyer's wife I will not be,
Cheating people is not for me,

Will you marry a fisherman?
A fisherman's wife I will not be,
Digging up worms is not for me,

Daughters will you marry?
Yea, father, yea.
Will you marry a fiddler?
Yea, father, yea.
I'd like to be a fiddler's wife,
Singing and dancing all of my life,
Yea, father, yea.

Tumbalalaika

Yiddish

```
Am              E7
```
Shtayt a bocher un er tracht
```
                        Am
```
Tracht un tracht die gantze nacht.

Vemen tzu nemen un nit farshemen,
```
Dm      E7          Am
```
Vemen tzu nemen un nit farshemen.

Chorus:

```
Am              E7
```
Tumbala, tumbala, tumbala-lai-ka.
```
                        Am
```
Tumbala tumbala, tumbala-lai-ka
```
                Dm      Am
```
Tumbala lai-ka, shpiel balalaika,
```
Dm      E7          Am
```
Tumbala-lai-ka, fraylach zol zain.

Maydl, maydl, 'chvel bai dir fregn,
Vos ken vaksn, vaksn on regn,
Vos ken brenen un nit oifhern,
Vos ken benken, vaynen on trern.

Narishe bocher, vos darfst du fregn,
A shtayn ken vaksn, vaksn on regn,
A liebe ken brenen un nit oifhern,
A hartz ken benken, vaynen on trern.

Literal Translation:

A youth worries all night long about whether he can
overcome his shyness enough to find himself a girl.

(The youth speaks:) "Maiden, I would ask you:
What can grow without rain; what can burn without
burning itself out; and what can cry without tears?"

(The maiden replies:) "Foolish boy, how can you be
so stupid? A stone (implying nothing) can grow
without rain; love can burn without burning itself
out; and a heart can cry without tears."

Soldier, Soldier, Won't You Marry Me?

F
"Soldier, soldier, won't you marry me?

With your musket, fife and drum?"
Dm
"Oh, how can I marry such a pretty girl as you,
      F
When I have no coat to put on,
    Dm   F
When I have no coat to put on?"

So off to the tailor's she did go,
As fast as she could run,
And she bought him a coat of the very, very best,
And the soldier put it on. (twice)

"Soldier, soldier, won't you marry me, now,
With your musket, fife and drum?"
"Oh, how can I marry such a pretty girl as you,
When I have no hat to put on?" (twice)

So off to the hat-maker's she did go, etc.

"Soldier, soldier, won't you marry me, now,
With your musket, fife and drum?"
"Oh how can I marry such a pretty girl as you,
With a wife and two babies at home,
With a wife and two babies at home?"

Where Are You Going, My Good Old Man?

    G
Oh, where are you going, my good old man?
                           D7
Where are you going, my honey-lovey lamb?
G
Where are you going, my good old man?
         D7   G
The best old man in the world?

(*Spoken*): Goin' to the saloon where I always go.

Oh, why are you going there, my good old man? etc.
(*Spoken*): To get drunk like I always do.

Won't you go after supper, my good old man? etc.
(*Spoken*): All right, if you'll quit jawin' and fix it.

Oh, what'll you have for supper my good old man? etc.
(*Spoken*): A bushelful of eggs, like I always have.

Ain't you afraid they'll kill you, my good old man? etc.
(*Spoken*): I don't care if they do.

Where shall I bury you, my good old man? etc.
(*Spoken*): In the chimney corner.

Ain't you afraid of sniffin' ashes, my good old man? etc.
(*Spoken*): I don't care if I do.

Why do you want to be buried there,
    my good old man? etc.
(*Spoken*): So I can haunt you!

But a haunt can't haunt a haunt, my good old man,
A haunt can't haunt a haunt, my honey-lovey lamb.
A haunt can't haunt a haunt, my good old man,
Meanest old devil in the world.

Lolly-Too-Dum

     C
As I went out one morning to take the pleasant air,
                    G7   C
Lolly-too-dum, too-dum, lolly-too-dum day
                              F
As I went out one morning to take the pleasant air,
 C
I overheard a mother a-scoldin' her daughter fair,
                    G7   C
Lolly-too-dum, too-dum, lolly-too-dum day.

"You better go wash them dishes,
    and hush that clattering tongue,
Lolly, etc.
I know you want to get married
    and that you are too young."
Lolly, etc.

"Oh, pity my condition as you would your own,
For seventeen long years I've been sleeping all alone."

"Yes, I'm seventeen and over, and that you will allow—
I must and I will get married for I'm in the notion now."

"Supposin' I was willin', where would you get your man?"
"Why, Lordy mercy, Mammy, I'd marry handsome Sam."

"Supposin' he should slight you
    like you done him before?"
"Why, Lordy mercy, Mammy, I could marry forty more."

"There's peddlers and there's tinkers
    and boys from the plow,
Oh Lordy mercy, Mammy, I'm gettin' that feeling now!"

"Now my daughter's married and well fer to do,
Gather 'round young fellers, I'm on the market too."

"Lordy mercy, Mammy, and who would marry you?
Ain't no man alive wants a wife as old as you."

"There's doctors and there's lawyers
    and men of high degree,
And some of them will marry and one will marry me."

"Now we both are married and well fer to be.
Ha ha ha, you pretty young girls,
    that feeling's off of me."

No John

```
    F     C7    F     G7
On yonder hill there stands a creature,
    F        C7
Who she is I do not know,
    F                    C7
I'll go and court her for her beauty,
    F        B     C7
She must answer yes or no.
```

Chorus:

```
  F   C7    F    C7    F
Oh, no John, no John, no John, no.
```

My father was a Spanish captain,
Went to sea a month ago;
First he kissed me, then he left me;
Told me always answer no.

Oh, madam, in your face is beauty,
On your lips red roses' glow,
Will you take me for your lover?
Madam, answer yes or no.

Oh, madam, I will give you jewels,
I will make you rich and free,
I will give you silken dresses;
Madam, will you marry me?

Oh, madam, since you are so cruel,
And since you do scorn me so,
If I may not be your lover,
Madam, will you let me go?

Then I will stay with you forever,
If you will not be unkind,
Madam, I have vowed to love you,
Would you have me change my mind?

Oh, hark, I hear the church bells ringing,
Will you come and be my wife?
Or, dear madam, have you settled
To live single all your life?

Buffalo Boy

```
D                      A7
When are we gonna get married
D
Married, married?
```

```
When are we gonna get married,
A7           D
Dear old buffalo boy?
```

I guess we'll marry in a week,
A week, a week,
I guess we'll marry in a week,
That is, if the weather be good.

How're you gonna come to the wedding,
The wedding, the wedding?
How're you gonna come to the wedding
Dear old buffalo boy?

I guess I'll come in my ox-cart, etc.
That is, if the weather be good.

Why don't you come in your buggy, etc.
Dear old buffalo boy?

My ox won't fit in the buggy, etc.
Not even if the weather be good.

Who you gonna bring to the wedding, etc.
Dear old buffalo boy.

I guess I'll bring my children, etc.
That is, if the weather be good.

I didn't know you had no children, etc.
Dear old buffalo boy.

Oh, yes, I have five children, etc.
Six if the weather be good.

There ain't gonna be no wedding, etc.
Not even if the weather be good.

Reuben, Reuben

```
D
Reuben, Reuben, I've been thinking
```

```
What a fine world this would be,
Bm  D      G     D
If the men were all transported
Bm E7   D      E7  A7  D
Far beyond the northern sea.
```

Oh, my goodness, gracious Rachel,
What a queer world this would be,
If the men were all transported
Far beyond the northern sea.

Reuben, Reuben, I've been thinking,
What a gay life girls would lead,
If they had no men about them,
None to tease them, none to heed.

Reuben, Reuben, stop your teasing,
If you've any love for me,
I was only just a-fooling,
As I thought, of course, you'd see.

Rachel, if you'll not transport us,
I will take you for my wife,
And I'll split with you my money
Every pay-day of my life.

Paper Of Pins

```
   G         D7
I'll give to you a paper of pins,
                      G
And that's the way my love begins,
   C                  G
If you will marry me, me, me,
   D7         G
If you will marry me.
```

I'll not accept your paper of pins,
If that's the way your love begins,
And I'll not marry you, you, you,
For I'll not marry you.

I'll give to you a dress of red
All bound round with golden thread,
If you will marry me, etc.

I'll not accept your dress of red, etc.

I'll give to you the key to my heart,
To show that we will never part, etc.

No, I'll not accept the key to your heart, etc.

I'll give to you the keys to my chest,
That you may have gold at your request, etc.

I will accept the keys to your chest,
That you may have gold at your request, etc.
And I will marry you, you, you,
And I will marry you.

Oh, you love coffee and you love tea,
You love my gold, but you don't love me,
And I'll not marry you, you, you,
And I'll not marry you.

I'd rather be a lonely old maid,
Take my stool and sit in the shade,
For I won't marry you, you, you,
For I won't marry you.

Lord Randall
Child Ballad 12

```
   D                       A
Oh, where have you been, Lord Randall, my son?
D                         A
Where have you been, oh my pretty one?
   Dm             A
I've been to my sweetheart, mother,
   Dm             A
I've been to my sweetheart, mother.
D                 Gm      D
Make my bed soon for I'm sick to my heart
   A7         D
And I fain would lie down.
```

Oh, what did you have for your supper, my son?
What did you have, oh my pretty one?
A cup of cold poison, mother. (twice)
Make my bed soon for I'm sick to my heart
And I would fain lie down.

Oh, what will you leave your father, my son?
My wagon and oxen, mother.

Oh, what will you leave your mother, my son?
My house and my lands.

Oh, what will you leave your brother, my son?
My horn and my hounds.

Oh, what will you leave your sister, my son?
The rings on my fingers.

Oh, what will you leave your sweetheart, my son?
A rope that will hang her.

Jenny Jenkins

```
   C                          G7
Oh, will you wear white, oh my dear, oh my dear?
   C                          G7
Oh, will you wear white, Jenny Jenkins?
     C                     F
No, I won't wear white, the color's too bright.
```

Chorus:

```
   C
I'll buy me a foldy roldy, tildy toldy
```

Seek a double use a cause a roll to find me.
```
       G7      C
Roll, Jenny Jenkins, roll.
```

Oh will you wear brown, oh my dear, oh my dear?
Oh will you wear brown, Jenny Jenkins?
No I won't wear brown, it's all around town.

Oh will you wear black, etc.
No . . . it's the color of a sack.

Oh, will you wear purple, etc.
No . . . it's the color of a turtle.

Oh, will you wear red, etc.
No . . . it's the color of my head.

Oh, will you wear green, etc.
No . . . it's a shame to be seen.

Then what will you wear, etc.
Oh, what do you care if I just go bare.

Yomi, Yomi*

Yiddish

Em
Yomi, Yomi, zing mir a lidele,
     B7   Em
Vos dos meydele vil?

Dos meydele vil a por shichelech hobn,

Darf men geyn dem shusterl zogn.

Chorus:

    B7   Em
Neyn, mamenyu, neyn,
        B7   Em
Du kenst mich nit farshteyn.
      B7   Em
Du veyst nit vos ich meyn.

Yomi, Yomi, zing mir a lidele,
Vos dos meydele vil?
Dos meydele vil a kleydele hobn,
Darf men geyn dem shnayderl zogn.

Yomi, Yomi, zing mir a lidele,
Vos dos meydele vil?
Dos meydele vil a chosendl hobn,
Darf men geyn dem shadchendl zogn.

Last Chorus:
Ya, mamenyu, ya,
Du veyst shoyn vos ich meyn,
Di kenst mich shoyn farshteyn!

Literal Translation:

Yomi, Yomi, sing me a ditty,
What does my little girl want?
The maiden wants a pair of shoes,
Let us go to the cobbler's then.

No, mother, no,
You do not understand me,
You don't know what I mean.

Yomi, Yomi, sing me a ditty,
What does my little girl want?
The maiden wants a little dress,
Let us go to the tailor's then.

Yomi, Yomi, sing me a ditty,
What does my little girl want?
The maiden wants a husband,
Let us go to the match-maker's then.

Yes mother, oh yes,
You know now what I mean,
You now understand me!

Yomi means the sea.

The Cutty Wren

     D   C   D   C
Oh, where are you going? said Milder to Malder,
     D   C   D   Am
Oh we may not tell you, said Festle to Fose.
        D   Am   D   C
We're off to the woods, said John the Red Nose;
      D   C   D   C D
We're off to the woods, said John the Red Nose.

What will you do there? said Milder to Malder,
Oh, we may not tell you, said Festle to Fose.
We'll shoot the Cutty Wren,
   said John the Red Nose. (twice)

How will you shoot her? said Milder to Malder,
Oh, we may not tell you, said Festle to Fose.
With bows and with arrows,
   said John the Red Nose. (twice)

That will not do, said Milder to Malder,
Oh, what will do then? said Festle to Fose.
Big guns and big cannons, said John the Red Nose. (twice)

How will you bring her home? said Milder to Malder,
Oh, we may not tell you, said Festle to Fose.
On four strong men's shoulders,
   said John the Red Nose. (twice)

That will not do, said Milder to Malder,
Oh, what will do then? said Festle to Fose.
Big carts and big wagons, said John the Red Nose. (twice)

How will you cut her up? said Milder to Malder,
Oh, we may not tell you, said Festle to Fose.
With knives and with forks,
   said John the Red Nose. (twice)

That will not do, said Milder to Malder,
Oh, what will do then, said Festle to Fose.
Big hatchets and cleavers, said John the Red Nose. (twice)

Who'll get the spare ribs? said Milder to Malder,
Oh, we may not tell you, said Festle to Fose.
We'll give it all to the poor,
   said John the Red Nose. (twice)

GIVE ME THAT OLD TIME RELIGION

348

Great Getting Up Morning

C
I'm a-goin' to tell you 'bout the comin' of a new day,
F
Fare you well, fare you well,
C   Em   Am
I'm a-goin' to tell you 'bout the comin' of a new day,
    C G7
Fare you well, fare you well.
C
There's a better day a-comin',
         F   C
Fare you well, fare you well,
  Em   Fm
Oh preachers fold your bibles,
     C G7   C
Fare you well, fare you well.

Chorus:

C
In that great getting up morning,
       F   C
Fare you well, fare you well,
      F   C
In that great getting up morning,
        G7   C
Fare you well, fare you well.

God's gonna up and speak to Gabriel, fare, etc.
Run and look behind the altar, fare, etc.
Now pick up your silver trumpet, fare, etc.
Blow your trumpet, Gabriel, fare, etc.

"Lord, how loud should I blow it?"
"Blow it so my people will know it",
"Blow one blast right calm and easy",
"To wake my children, that are sleeping"

Twelve Gates To The City

Chorus:

C
Oh, what a beautiful city;
G   C
Oh, what a beautiful city;

Oh, what a beautiful city,
C7   F   C G7 C   G7
Twelve gates to the city, hallelujah!
C
Three gates in the East;

Three gates in the West;

Three gates in the North;

Three gates in the South;

C7   F   C G7   C
There's twelve gates to the city, hallelujah!

Verses:

C
Who are those children there dressed in red?
     C7   F   C G7   C
There's twelve gates to the city, hallelujah!

It must be the children that Moses led,
         C7   F   C G7 C
There's twelve gates to the city, hallelujah!

My God done just what He said, etc.
He healed the sick and He raised the dead, etc.

When I get to heaven, going to sing and shout, etc.
Ain't nobody there going to put me out, etc.

It's G-L-O-R-Y To Know I'm S-A-V-E-D

     C   G7
Some folks jump up and down all night and d-a-n-c-e,
                                           C
While others go to church to show their brand new h-a-t,
                                   F
And on their face they put great gobs of p-a-i-n-t,
 G7   C
And then they'll have the brass to say they're s-a-v-e-d.

Chorus:
It's g-l-o-r-y to know I'm s-a-v-e-d,
I'm h-a-p-p-y because I'm f-r-double-e,
I once was b-o-u-n-d in the chains of s-i-n,
But it's v-i-c-t-o-r-y to know I've Christ within.

I've seen some girls in our town who are so n-i-c-e,
They do their hair in the latest style that's b-o-b-e-d,
They go to parties every night, drink w-i-n-e,
And then they'll have the nerve to say they're s-a-v-e-d.

I've seen some boys lean back and puff their s-m-o-k-e,
While others chew and spit out all their j-u-i-c-e,
They play their cards and shoot their guns
    and drink their p-o-p.
And then they'll have the brass to say they're s-a-v-e-d.

I know a man, I think his name is G-r-o-w-n,
He prays for prohibition, and then he votes for gin,
He helps to put the poison in his neighbor's c-u-p,
And then he'll have the brass to say he's s-a-v-e-d!

Wondrous Love

Tune: *Captain Kidd*

```
        E                                B7
What wondrous love is this, oh my soul, oh my soul,
        E                          A
What wondrous love is this, oh my soul,
B7  E                          A        B7
What wondrous love is this that caused the Lord of bliss
      A                    B7        E
To bear the dreadful curse for my soul, for my soul,
      A                    B7
To bear the dreadful curse for my soul.
```

When I was sinking down, sinking down, sinking down,
When I was sinking down, sinking down,
When I was sinking down beneath God's righteous frown
Christ laid aside his crown for my soul, for my soul,
Christ laid aside his crown for my soul.

To God and to the Lamb I will sing, I will sing, etc.
To God and to the Lamb, who is the great I AM
While millions join the theme, I will sing,
    I will sing, etc.

And when from death I'm free, I'll sing on,
    I'll sing on, etc.
And when from death I'm free, I'll sing and joyful be,
And through eternity I'll sing on, I'll sing on, etc.

It's Me, Oh Lord

Chorus:

```
E
It's me, it's me, it's me, oh Lord,
          B7    E
Standing in the need of prayer.
```

```
It's me, it's me, it's me, oh Lord,
          B7    E
Standing in the need of prayer.
```

Verses:

```
E
'Tain't my mother or my father,
```

```
But it's me, oh Lord,
          B7    E
Standing in the need of prayer.
```

'Tain't my mother or my father,

```
But it's me, oh Lord,
          B7    E
Standing in the need of prayer.
```

'Tain't my brother or my sister, etc.

'Tain't my deacon or my leader, etc.

Dig My Grave

```
      C  F   C   G7 C      G
Gonna dig my grave both long and narrow,
C      F          C
Make my coffin neat and strong.
              G
Two, two to my head,
C        G
Two, two to my feet,
C  C7  F          C   G7 C
Two, two to carry me, Lord, when I  die.
          C
My soul's gonna shine like a star,
```

Like a star, oh Lord, like a star,

```
My soul's gonna shine like a star,
            G7        C
I'm bound to go to heaven when I die.
```

Don't You Weep After Me

```
E
When I'm dead and buried,
            B7
Don't you weep after me.
```

```
When I'm dead and buried,
       E
Don't you weep after me.
            E7
When I'm dead and buried,
          A    E
Don't you weep after me.
                B7       E
Oh, I don't want you to weep after me.
```

On the good ship of Zion }
Don't you weep after me   } (3 times)
O I don't want you to weep after me.

King Peter is my captain, etc.

Jordan is my river, etc.

Oh, look-a Mary, etc.

She's a-looking over Jordan, etc.

Bright angels are the sailors, etc.

Sailing on the ocean, etc.

When I do cross over, etc.

I Couldn't Hear Nobody Pray

Chorus:

   C
Oh, I couldn't hear nobody pray,
  F   C
Oh, couldn't hear nobody pray,
        Am
Oh, way down yonder by myself,
  C   F C
And I couldn't hear nobody pray.

(Oh, Lord) Couldn't hear nobody pray,
  F   C
Oh, couldn't hear nobody pray,
        Am
Oh, way down yonder by myself,
  C   F C
And I couldn't hear nobody pray.

Verses:

       C   F C
In the valley (couldn't hear nobody pray)
         F C
On my knees (Couldn't hear nobody pray)
          F   C
With my burden (Couldn't hear nobody pray)
          F   C
And my Savior (Couldn't hear nobody pray).

Chilly waters! (Couldn't hear nobody pray)
In the Jordan! (Couldn't hear nobody pray)
Crossing over! (Couldn't hear nobody pray)
Into Canaan! (Couldn't hear nobody pray)

Hallelujah! (Couldn't hear nobody pray)
Troubles over! (Couldn't hear nobody pray)
In Heaven! (Couldn't hear nobody pray)
With my Jesus! (Couldn't hear nobody pray)

You Can Dig My Grave

    C
You can dig my grave with a silver spade,
  G7   C C7
You can dig my grave with a silver spade,
     F   C
You can dig my grave with a silver spade,
  G7   C
'Cause I ain't gonna stay here any longer.

There's a long white robe up in Heaven for me. (3 times)
'Cause I ain't gonna stay here any longer.

There's a starry crown up in Heaven for me., etc.

There's a golden harp up in Heaven for me., etc.

When you pluck one string all of Heaven rings., etc.

The Old Gospel Ship

  C
I have good news to bring and that is why I sing.
        G7
All my joys with you I will share,
C
I'm gonna take a trip on that old gospel ship,
     G7   C
And go sailin' through the air.

Chorus:

  C
I'm gonna take a trip on that old gospel ship,
        G7
I'm goin' far beyond the sky,
C
I'm gonna shout and sing, until the bells do ring,
      G7   C
When I'm sailing through the sky.

If you are ashamed of me, you ought not to be,
And you better have a care,
If too much fault you find, you'll sure be left behind,
When I'm sailing through the air.

I can hardly wait, I know I won't be late,
I'll spend all my time in prayer,
And when my ship come in, I'll leave this world of sin,
And go sailin' through the air.

Bringing In The Sheaves
Knowles Shaw and George A. Minor

Sowing in the morning, sowing seeds of kindness,
Sowing in the noontide and dewy eves;
Waiting for the harvest, and the time of reaping,
We shall come, rejoicing, bringing in the sheaves.

Chorus:
Bringing in the sheaves, bringing in the sheaves,
We shall come, rejoicing, bringing in the sheaves;
Bringing in the sheaves, bringing in the sheaves,
We shall come, rejoicing, bringing in the sheaves.

Sowing in the sunshine, sowing in the shadows,
Fearing neither clouds nor winter's chilling breeze;
By and by the harvest, and the labor ended,
We shall come, rejoicing, bringing in the sheaves.

Going forth with weeping, sowing for the Master,
Tho' the loss sustained our spirit often grieves;
When our weeping's over, He will bid us welcome,
We shall come, rejoicing, bringing in the sheaves.

Wayfaring Stranger

```
Em              B7    Em
I'm just a poor wayfaring stranger,
          Am              B
A-traveling through this world of woe;
       Em      B7    Em
But there's no sickness no toil nor danger,
          A    Am Bm    Em
In that bright world to which I go.
                       Am
I'm going there to see my father,
     Em   C   D   G
I'm going there no more to roam,
          B7   Em
I'm just a-going over Jordan,
      A Am Bm Em
I'm just a-going over home.
```

I know dark clouds will gather 'round me,
I know my way is steep and rough,
But beauteous fields lie just beyond me,
Where souls redeemed their vigil keep.
I'm going there to meet my mother,
She said she'd meet me when I come;
I'm only going over Jordan,
I'm only going over home.

I want to wear a crown of glory,
When I get home to that bright land;
I want to shout Salvation's story,
In concert with that bloodwashed band.
I'm going there to meet my Saviour,
To sing His praises for evermore;
I'm only going over Jordan,
I'm only going over home.

Onward Christian Soldiers

Sabine Baring-Gould and Sir Arthur Sullivan

```
C           G    G7         C
Onward Christian soldiers, marching as to war,
           G   D7    G
With the cross of Jesus going on before.
G7          C                   F
Christ, the royal Master, leads against the foe;
                              G7
Forward into battle see His banners go.
```

Chorus:

```
C           G7               C
Onward Christian soldiers, marching as to war,
     G7    C   F D7 G7  C
With the cross of Jesus going on before.
```

Like a mighty army, moves the Church of God,
Brothers, we are treading where the Saints have trod;
We are not divided, all one body we,
One in hope and doctrine, one in charity.

Crowns and thrones may perish, kingdoms rise and wane,
But the Church of Jesus constant will remain;
Gates of Hell can never 'gainst that Church prevail,
We have Christ's own promise, and that can never fail.

Onward, then, ye people, join our happy throng,
Blend with our your voices in the triumph song;
Glory, laud and honor unto Christ the King,
This through countless ages, men and angels sing.

This Little Light Of Mine

Chorus:

```
G                            G7
This little light of mine, I'm going to let it shine.
C
This little light of mine, I'm going to let it shine.
G              B7               Em
This little light of mine, I'm going to let it shine,
     G    E b7  G     A7
Ev'ry day, ev'ry day, ev'ry day, ev'ry day,
     G   D7    G
Gonna let my little light shine.
```

Verses:

```
G                            G7
On Monday, He gave me the gift of love;
     C           B b dim
On Tuesday, peace came from above.
     G
On Wednesday, told me to have more faith;
     A7          D7
On Thursday, gave me a little more grace.
     G              G7
On Friday, told me to watch and pray;
     C               Bdim
On Saturday, told me just what to say,
     G       Em
On Sunday, gave power divine
          A7  D   G   D7
Just to let my little light shine. (Oh)
```

Now some say you got to run and hide,
But we say there's no place to hide.
And some say let others decide,
But we say let the people decide.
Some say the time's not right,
But we say the time's just right.
If there's a dark corner in our land,
You got to let your little light shine. (Oh)

How Can I Keep From Singing?

```
      E        A
My life flows on in endless song,
      E            B7
Above earth's lamentation.
      E            A
I hear the real, though far off hymn,
      E        B7 E
That hails a new creation.
```

No storm can shake my inmost calm

```
While to that rock I'm clinging.
             A        E
It sounds an echo in my soul.
             B7       E
How can I keep from singing?
```

What though the tempest round me roars,
I know the truth, it liveth,
What though the darkness round me close,
Songs in the night it giveth.
No storm can shake my inmost calm
While to that rock I'm clinging.
Since love is lord of Heaven and earth,
How can I keep from singing?

When tyrants tremble, sick with fear
And hear their death knells ringing;
When friends rejoice both far and near,
How can I keep from singing?
In prison cell and dungeon vile
Our thoughts to them are winging.
When friends by shame are undefiled,
How can I keep from singing?

I Am A Pilgrim

```
      D7              G
I am a pilgrim, and a stranger,
          C            G
Traveling through this wearisome land;
  D7  G   G7        C
I got a home in that yonder city, oh Lord,
          G  D7        G
And it's not made, not made by hand.
```

I got a mother, a sister, and a brother,
Who have gone to that sweet land.
I'm determined to go and see them, good Lord,
All over on that distant shore.

As I go down to that river of Jordan,
Just to bathe my weary soul,
If I could touch but the hem of His garment, good Lord,
Well, I believe it would make me whole.

Nearer My God To Thee

Lowell Mason

```
G          C        G      D
Nearer, my God, to Thee, nearer to Thee;
G          C      G  D7  G
E'en though it be a cross that raiseth me;
G   C    G
Still all my song shall be
Bm  Em    Bm      D7
Nearer, my God, to Thee,
G          C        G  D7  G
Nearer, my God, to Thee, nearer to Thee.
```

Though, like the wanderer, the sun gone down,
Darkness be over me, my rest a stone,
Yet in my dreams I'd be
Nearer, my God, to Thee,
Nearer, my God, to Thee, nearer to Thee.

There let the way appear steps unto heaven;
All that Thou sendest me in mercy given;
Angels to beckon me
Nearer, my God, to Thee,
Nearer, my God, to Thee, nearer to Thee.

Swing Low, Sweet Chariot

Chorus:

```
      E
Swing low, sweet chariot,

Coming for to carry me home,
             A  E
Swing low, sweet chariot,
             B7       E
Coming for to carry me home,
```

Verses:

```
                         A       E
I looked over Jordan and what did I see?
                    B7
Coming for to carry me home.
  C#m         A          E
A band of angels coming after me,
C#m         A6  B7 E
Coming for to carry me home.
```

If you get there, before I do, etc.
Tell all my friends, I'm coming too., etc.

Lonesome Valley

A
You got to walk that lonesome valley,
        E7   A
You got to go there by yourself,
      D   A
Ain't nobody here can go there for you,
   B7 A   E7   A
You got to go there by yourself.

If you cannot preach like Peter,
If you cannot pray like Paul,
You can tell the love of Jesus,
You can say He died for all.

Your mother's got to walk that lonesome valley,
She's got to go there by herself,
Ain't nobody else can go there for her,
She's got to go there by herself.

Your father's got to walk that lonesome valley, etc.

Your brother's got to walk that lonesome valley, etc.

Meeting At The Building

G   D7
Meeting at the building will soon be over with,
G
Soon be over with, soon be over with,

Meeting at the building will soon be over with,
D7   G
All over this world.
C
All over this world, my Lord,
G
All over this world,
C
All over this world, my Lord,
G (D7)   G
All over this world.

Preaching at the building, etc.

Shouting at the building, etc.

Praying at the building, etc.

Singing at the building, etc.

Oh, Mary Don't You Weep

G   D7
If I could I surely would,
                    G
Stand on the rock where Moses stood.
C   G
Pharoah's army got drownded,
      D7   G
Oh, Mary don't you weep.

Chorus:

G   D7
Oh, Mary don't you weep don't you mourn,
               G
Oh, Mary don't you weep don't you mourn,
C   G
Pharoah's army got drownded,
      D7   G
Oh, Mary don't you weep.

Mary wore three links of chain,
Every link was Jesus name.
Pharoah's army got drownded
Oh, Mary don't you weep.

Mary wore three links of chain,
Every link was Freedom's name, etc.

One of these nights about twelve o'clock,
This old world is gonna reel and rock.

Moses stood on the Red Sea shore,
Smotin' the water with a two-by-four.

God gave Noah the rainbow sign,
No more water but fire next time.

The Lord told Moses what to do,
To lead those Hebrew children through.

Streets Of Glory

E   E7
I'm gonna walk the Streets of Glory,
A
I'm gonna walk the Streets of Glory,

One of these days, hallelujah,
E
I'm gonna walk the Streets of Glory,
B7   E
Walk the Streets of Glory one of these days.

I'm gonna tell God how you treat me, (twice)
One of these days, hallelujah.
I'm gonna tell God how you treat me,
Tell God how you treat me one of these days.

I'm gonna walk and talk with Jesus, etc.

Home In That Rock

```
          F    Bb7    F    Bb    F
I've got a home in-a that Rock, don't you see?
    Bb        F
    Don't you see?
              C        F           C
I've got a home in-a that Rock, don't you see?
C7   F       F7        F
Up between the earth and sky,
              Bb       Bb 7 Bb
Thought I heard my Savior cry:
              F    Bb 7  F    Bb     F
"You've got a Home in-a that Rock, don't you see?
    Bb        F
    Don't you see?"
```

Poor man Lazarus, poor as I, don't you see?
   Don't you see? (twice)
Poor man Lazarus, poor as I,
When he died he found a Home on High,
He had a Home in that Rock, don't you see?

Rich man Dives lived so well, don't you see?
   Don't you see? (twice)
Rich man Dives lived so well,
When he died he found a Home in Hell,
Had no Home in-a that Rock, don't you see?

God gave Noah the rainbow sign, don't you see?
   Don't you see? (twice)
God gave Noah the rainbow sign,
No more water—but fire next time,
Noah had a Home in that Rock, don't you see?

I Can't Feel At Home In This World Anymore

```
      E                     A        E
This world is not my home, I'm just a-passing through,
                F#7              B7
My treasures and my hopes are all beyond the blue,
      E                    A         E
Where many Christian children have gone on before,
                      B7  E
And I can't feel at home in this world anymore.
```

Over in glory land there is no dying there,
The saints are shouting Vict'ry and singing everywhere,
I hear the voice of Nell that I have heard before,
And I can't feel at home in this world anymore.

Oh, Lord, you know I have no friend like You,
If Heaven's not my home, Oh Lord what would I do?
Angels have taken me to Heaven's open door,
And I can't feel at home in this world anymore.

I Don't Want To Get Adjusted

```
C    F     C
In this world of toil and trouble,
            Ab7    G7       C
Sometimes lonesome, sometimes blue;
        F       C
Yet the hope of life eternal,
          D9   G7    C
Brighten all our hopes a-new.
          F            C                    G
I don't want to get adjusted to this world, to this world.
          F
I got a home that's so much better,
              C
I want to go to sooner or later;
              G7          C
I don't want to get adjusted to this world.
```

In The Sweet Bye And Bye
S. Fillmore Bennett and Joseph P. Webster

```
           F        Bb+6     F
There's a land that is fairer than day,
                              C
And by faith we can see it afar;
           F         Bb      F
For the Father waits over the way
B b min F         C7           F
To  prepare  us  a  dwelling  place   there.
```

Chorus:

```
        F           Bb+6
In the sweet bye and bye,
         Gmin7    C7      F
We shall meet on that beautiful shore,
        F   F7      Bb
In the sweet bye and bye
         F        C7     F
We shall meet on that beautiful shore.
```

We shall sing on that beautiful shore
The melodious songs of the blessed,
And our spirits shall sorrow no more,
Not a sigh for the blessing of rest.

To our bountiful father above,
We will offer our tribute of praise,
For the glorious gift of His love
And the blessings that hallow our days.

Chorus:

Em
Wade in the water,
B7   Em
Wade in the water children,
      Am
Wade in the water,
Am   B7   Em
God's a-gonna trouble the water.

Verses:

      G   Am   Em
Jordan's water is chilly and cold,
Am   B7Em
God's a-gonna trouble the water,
      G   Am   Em
It chills the body but lifts up the soul,
Am   B7Em
God's a-gonna trouble the water.

If you get there before I do,
God's a-gonna trouble the water,
Tell all of my friends I'm coming too,
God's a-gonna trouble the water.

Walk In Jerusalem, Just Like John

Chorus:

E
I want to be ready,
A   E
I want to be ready,
     B7 E
I want to be ready,
   E   A   E A E
To walk in Jerusalem just like John.

Verses:

E
John said the city was just four square,
     A   E A E
Walk in Jerusalem, just like John,

And he declared he'd meet me there,
     F♯m A B7 E
Walk in Jerusalem just like john.

Oh, John, Oh, John, what do you say? Walk, etc.
That I'll be there in the coming day, Walk, etc.

When Peter was preaching at Pentacost,
He was endowed with the Holy Ghost,

D   G   D
Tempted and tried, we're oft made to wonder
          E7   A
Why it should be thus all the day long.
D   G   D
While there are others living about us,
         A7   D
Never molested, though in the wrong.

Chorus:

D   G   D
Farther along we'll know all about it;
         E7   A
Farther along we'll understand why.
D   G   D
Cheer up my brothers, live in the sunshine,
         A7   D
We'll understand it all by and by.

When death has come and taken our loved ones,
Leaving our homes so lonely and drear;
Then do we wonder why others prosper,
Living as sinners year after year.

Often I wonder why I must journey
Over a road so rugged and steep;
While there are others living in comfort,
While with the lost I labour and weep.

We Need A Whole Lot More Of Jesus

     A
You can read it in the morning paper,
    D7
You can hear it on the radio,
    A
How crime is sweeping the nation,
    E
This old world's about to go.

Refrain:
We need a brand new case of salvation,
To keep the love of God in our soul,
We need a whole lot more of Jesus,
And a lot less rock 'n roll.

We need more old time camp meetings,
And a lot more prayers of faith,
Prayers that'll move the mountain,
Save our soul from the burnin' wave.

We need more old-fashioned preachers,
Pouring out their hearts in prayer,
When you're in their presence,
You know that the Lord is there.

Just A Closer Walk With Thee

C   G7
Just a closer walk with Thee,
                     C
Grant it Jesus if you please;
C7   F
Daily walkin' close to Thee,
    C   G   C
Let it be, dear Lord, let it be.

Through the days of toil that's near,
If I fall, dear Lord, who cares?
Who with me my burden share,
None but Thee, dear Lord, none but Thee.

When my feeble life is o'er,
Time for me will be no more;
Guide me gently, safely on,
To Thy shore, dear Lord, to Thy shore.

Ezekiel Saw The Wheel

Chorus:

F
Ezekiel saw the wheel, 'way in the middle of the air,
                                C7   F
Ezekiel saw the wheel, 'way in the middle of the air;

And the little wheel run by faith,

And the big wheel run by the grace of God,

A wheel in a wheel, (wheel in a wheel),
           C7   F
Way in the middle of the air.

Verses:

F
Some go to church for to sing and shout,
           C7   F
 'way in the middle of the air,

Before six months they's shouted out,
           C7   F
 'way in the middle of the air.

Let me tell you what a hypocrite'll do, etc.
He'll talk about me and he'll talk about you, etc.

Don't pray for things that you don't need, etc.
The Lord don't like no sin and greed, etc.

There's one thing sure that you can't do, etc.
You can't serve God and Satan, too, etc.

One of these days about twelve o'clock, etc.
This old world's gonna reel and rock, etc.

Rock-A My Soul

    F   C7
Oh, rock-a my soul in the bosom of Abraham,

Rock-a my soul in the bosom of Abraham,
F   C7
Rock-a my soul in the bosom of Abraham,
           F
Oh, rock-a my soul.

Verses:

                              C7
When I went down in the valley to pray,

Oh, rock-a my soul.
      F   C7
My soul got happy and I stayed all day,
         F
Oh, rock-a my soul.

When I was a mourner just like you,
Oh, rock-a my soul,
I mourned and mourned till I come through,
Oh, rock-a my soul.

Rock Of Ages
Augustus M. Toplady and Thomas Hastings

Rock of Ages, cleft for me,
Let me hide myself in Thee;
Let the water and the blood,
From Thy wounded side which flowed,
Be of sin the double cure,
Save from guilt and make me pure.

Not the labor of my hands
Can fulfil Thy law's demands;
Could my zeal no respite know,
Could my tears forever flow,
All for sin could not atone,
Thou must save, and Thou alone.

While I draw this fleeting breath,
While my eyes shall close in death,
When I soar to worlds unknown,
See Thee on The judgement throne,
Rock of Ages cleft for me,
Let me hide myself in Thee.

Jacob's Ladder

D
We are climbing Jacob's ladder,
A7   D
We are climbing Jacob's ladder,
          G   D
We are climbing Jacob's ladder,
      A7   D
Soldiers of the Cross.

Every rung goes higher, higher, (3 times)
Soldiers of the Cross.

Sinner, do you love your Jesus?, etc.

If you love Him, why not serve Him?, etc.

Do you think I'd make a soldier?, etc.

We are climbing higher and higher, etc.

Ninety And Nine

Elizabeth C. Clephane and Ira D. Sankey

F
There were ninety and nine that safely lay
    Bb   F
In the shelter of the fold,
    Bb   F
But one was out on the hills away,
    C
Far off from the gates of gold.
     F
Away on the mountains wild and bare,
 Bb   F
Away from the tender Shepherd's care,
    C7   F
Away from the tender Shepherd's care.

"Lord, Thou hast here Thy ninety and nine;
Are they not enough for Thee?"
But the Shepherd made an answer: "This of nine
Has wandered away from me,
And although the road be rough and steep,
I go to the desert to find my sheep." (twice)

But all through the mountains thunder-riven,
And up from the rocky steep,
There rose a glad cry to the gate of heaven,
"Rejoice, I have found my sheep!"
And the angels echoed around the throne,
"Rejoice, for the Lord brings back his own!" (twice)

Nobody Knows The Trouble I've Seen

Chorus:

F   Bb   F
Nobody knows the trouble I've seen,
     Bb   F
Nobody knows but Jesus,
     Bb   F
Nobody knows the trouble I've seen,
    C7 F
Glory hallelujah!

Verses:

F   C7
Sometimes I'm up, sometimes I'm down, Oh, yes, Lord!
   F   C7 F
Sometimes I'm almost to the ground, oh, yes, Lord!

Now, you may think that I don't know, etc.
But I've had my troubles here below, etc.

One day when I was walkin' along,
The sky opened up and love came down.

What make old Satan hate me so?
He had me once and had to let me go.

I never shall forget that day,
When Jesus washed my sins away.

By And By

C
By and by, by and by

Star shines down on number one

Number two, number three,

Number four,
          G7   C G7   C
Good Lord, by and by, by and by
          G7   C
Good Lord, by and by.

By and by, by and by
Star shines down on number five,
Number six, number seven,
Number eight,
Good Lord, by and by, by and by
Good Lord, by and by.

We Shall Walk Through The Valley

      E   B7
We shall walk through the valley in the shadows of death,
      E   B7
We shall walk through the valley in peace,
      E   E7   A
And if Jesus himself shall be our leader,
B7   E
We shall walk through the valley in peace.

We will meet our Father over there, (twice)
If Jesus Himself shall be our Leader,
We shall meet our Father over there.

Green Grow The Rushes

Bb   F   Bb
I'll sing you one-o, green grow the rushes-o.

What is your one-o?
           Gm   Cm F   Bb
One is one and all alone and evermore shall be
                         F   Bb
So, I'll sing you two-o, green grow the rushes-o.

What is your two-o?
         Eb   Cm   F
Two, two the little boys, clothed all in green-o,
Bb   Eb   F7   Bb
One is one and all alone and evermore shall be.
                     F   Bb
I'll sing you three-o, green grow the rushes-o.

What is your three-o?
      F   GmDm
Three, three, the rivals,
Bb   Eb   C7   F   F7
Two, two the little boys, clothed all in green-o,
Bb   Eb Cm
One is one and all alone and evermore shall be.

Four for the Gospel makers, etc.

Five for the symbols at your door, etc.

Six for the six proud walkers, etc.

Seven for the seven stars in the sky, etc.

Eight for the April rainers, etc.

Nine for the nine bright shiners, etc.

Ten for the Ten Commandments, etc.

Eleven for the eleven went up to heaven, etc.

Twelve for the twelve Apostles, etc.

All God's Children Got Shoes

G
I got a shoe, you got a shoe,

All God's children got shoes;
                           D7
When I get to heaven gonna put on my shoes,
      G   D7   G   D7   G
I'm gonna tromp all over God's heaven, heaven, heaven,
                         D7
Everybody talkin' 'bout heaven ain't a goin' there,
G   D7   G   D7   G
Heaven, heaven, gonna tromp all over God's heaven.

I got a robe, you got a robe, etc.
Gonna shout all over God's heaven, etc.

I got a harp, you got a harp,
Gonna play all over God's heaven.

I got a song, you got a song,
Gonna sing all over God's heaven.

I got wings, you got wings,
Gonna fly all over God's heaven.

All My Trials

D   F
If religion was a thing that money could buy,
         D   F#m   Em7
The rich would live and the poor would die.
F#m Em7   A7   D
All my trials, Lord, soon be over.
                                  D7 Gm
Too late my brothers, too late, but never mind,
F#m Em7   A7   D
All my trials, Lord, soon be over.

Hush little baby, don't you cry
You know your daddy was born to die
All my trials, Lord, etc.

I had a little book, 'twas given to me,
And every page spelled "Victory."
All my trials, Lord, etc.

Balm In Gilead

Chorus:

```
G               Em      G       C    G D7
There is a balm in Gilead, to make the wounded whole
G                          D7   G D7
There is a balm in Gilead, to heal the sin-sick soul.
G               Em      G       C    G D7
There is a balm in Gilead, to make the wounded whole
G                          D7   G
There is a balm in Gilead, to heal the sin-sick soul.
```

Verses:

```
     G          C  Bm
Sometimes I feel discouraged,
C    G    C   D    G D7
And think my work's in vain,
     G          C    E7
But then the Holy Spirit
Am  G C  D6 D7 G
Revives my soul again.
```

If you can preach like Peter,
If you can pray like Paul,
Go home and tell your neighbor,
"He died to save us all."

My Lord, What A Mourning

Chorus:

```
G    D7   G
My Lord, what a mourning,
     E7   A7    D7
My Lord, what a mourning,
 E7  D7   C    A7
My Lord, what a mourning,
Eb 7  G   A7    D7  Cm G
When  the  stars  begin  to  fall.
```

Verses:

```
G
You'll hear the trumpet sound
```

To wake the nations underground,

Looking to my God's right hand,
```
C     G    D7 G
When the stars begin to fall.
```

You'll hear the sinner mourn,
To wake the nations underground,
Looking to my God's right hand,
When the stars begin to fall.

You'll hear the Christian shout,
To wake the nations underground,
Looking to my God's right hand,
When the stars begin to fall.

The Old Ark's A-Moverin'

Chorus:

```
           F            C7         F
The old ark's a-moverin', a-moverin', a-moverin'
                          C7        F
The old ark's a-moverin', by the spirit of God!
                          C7        F
The old ark's a-moverin', a-moverin', a-moverin'
                          C7   F
The old ark's a-movin' and I thank God.
```

Verses:

```
F
How many days did the water fall?
C7            F
Forty days and nights in all.
```

Old ark she reel. Old ark she rock,
```
             C7         F
Old ark she landed on a mountain top.
```

Ham, Shem, and Japheth was settin' one day,
Talkin' on the upper deck and lookin' at the bay,
While they was disputin' 'bout this and that,
The ark done bump on Ararat.

See that sister dressed so fine?
She ain't got religion on her mind.
See that brother dressed so gay?
Devil's gonna come and carry him away.

Every Time I Feel The Spirit

```
C
Up on the mountain my Lord spoke,
                      G7   C
Out of His mouth came fire and smoke.
                             Am
Looked all around me, it looked so fine,
                 G7 C
I asked the Lord could it be mine.
```

Chorus:

```
C7        F    F#dim C
Well every time I feel the spirit,
A7    D7         G  C
Moving in my heart, I will pray,
C7        F          C
Yes every time I feel the spirit
A7    D7        G7 C
Moving in my heart I will pray.
```

Oh, I have sorrows and I have woe,
And I have heart-ache here below;
But while God leads me, I'll never fear,
For I am sheltered by His care.

Little David

Chorus:

```
D                                          A7   D
Little David, play on your harp, Hallelu, Hallelu;
                                     A7      D
Little David, play on your harp, Hallelu.

Little David, play on your harp, Hallelu, Hallelu;
                                     A7      D
Little David, play on your harp, Hallelu.
```

Verses:

```
D           F♯m
David was a shepherd boy
   G     D      A7      D
He killed Goliath and shouted for joy.
D           F♯m
David was a shepherd boy
   G     D      A7       D
He killed Goliath and shouted for joy.
```

Old Joshua was the son of Nun,
He never would stop till his work was done. } (twice)

I've sung this song in rhythm and rhyme, } (twice)
Let's sing it again for the very last time.

Keep Your Lamp Trimmed And Burning

Chorus:

```
Em
Keep your lamp trimmed and a-burning,
D           Em
Keep your lamp trimmed and burning,

Keep your lamp trimmed and burning,
C       Em      B7   Em
For this old world it is almost gone.
```

Verses:

```
Em
Brother, don't you get a-worried,
B7      C7
Brother, don't get worried,
Em
Brother, don't get a-worried,
C       Em      B7   Em
For this old world it is almost gone.
```

Sister, don't stop prayin', etc.

Preacher, don't stop preachin', etc.

Auntie, don't stop praying, etc.

Alternate Chorus:
Got my lamp trimmed and burning.

Little Moses

```
   G       D7     G
A-way by the river so clear,
                  D7         G
The ladies were winding their way,
      D7
And Pharaoh's young daughter stepp'd down in the water,
   G       D7     G
To bathe in the cool of the day.
        D7    G      C
Before it was dark she opened the ark
   G           D7   G
And found the sweet infant there.
        D7    G      C
Before it was dark she opened the ark
   G           D7
And found the sweet infant there.
```

Away by the waters so blue,
The infant was lonely and sad,
She took him in pity and thought him so pretty,
And made Little Moses so glad.
She called him her own, her beautiful son, } (twice)
And sent for a nurse that was near.

Away by the river so clear,
They carried the beautiful child,
To his tender mother, his sister and brother,
And Moses looked happy and smiled.
His mother so good did all that she could } (twice)
To rear him and teach him with care.

Away by the sea that was red,
Little Moses the servant of God,
While in him confided, the sea was divided,
As upward he lifted his rod.
The Jews safely crossed
   while King Pharaoh's host } (twice)
Was drowned in the waters and lost.

Away on a mountain so high,
And the last one that ever might see.
While in him victorious, his hope was most glorious,
He'd soon over Jordan be free.
When his labor did cease,
   he left there in peace, } (twice)
And rested in Heaven above.

Get On Board, Little Children

Chorus:

G C
Get on board, little children,
 G
Get on board, little children,
 C
Get on board, little children,
 G D7 G
There's room for many a more.

Verses:

 G
The gospel train's a-comin',
    D7
I hear it just at hand,
 G   C
I hear the car wheels rumblin'
 G D7   G
And rollin' through the land.

I hear that train a-comin',
She's comin' 'round the curve,
She's loosened all her steam and brakes
And straining every nerve.

The fare is cheap and all can go,
The rich and poor are there,
No second class aboard this train,
No difference in the fare.

Give Me That Old Time Religion

   G
Give me that old time religion,
   D7
Give me that old time religion,
   G   C
Give me that old time religion,
 G   D7 G
It's good enough for me.

It was good for my father, etc.

It was good for my mother, etc.

It was good for the Hebrew children. . . .

It was good for Paul and Silas, etc.

He's Got The Whole World In His Hands

     F   B   F
He's got the whole world in His hands,
     C7   B F
He's got the whole world in His hands,
        B   F
He's got the whole world in His hands,
     C7   F
He's got the whole world in His hands.

He's got the little babies in His hands, (3 times)
He's got the whole world in His hands.

He's got you and me, brother, in His hands,
He's got you and me, sister, in His hands,
He's got you and me, brother, in His hands,
He's got the whole world in His hands.

He's got the gamblin' man in His hands, (3 times)
He's got the whole world in His hands.

He's got the whole world in His hands, (4 times)

Hold On

 Em
Mary wore three links of chain,
     Am7 Em
Every link was Jesus' name.
         B7 Em
Keep your hand on that plow, hold on.

Chorus:

B7   Em
Hold on, hold on,
         B7 Em
Keep your hand on that plow, hold on.

God gave Noah the rainbow sign,
No more water but fire next time, etc.

Paul and Silas bound in jail,
Had no money for to go their bail, etc.

The very moment I thought I was lost,
The dungeon shook and the chains fell off, etc.

Paul and Silas began to shout,
Jail doors opened and they walked out, etc.

Peter was so nice and neat,
Wouldn't let Jesus wash his feet, etc.

Got my hands on the gospel plow,
Wouldn't take nothin' for my journey now, etc.

Sowing On The Mountain

$\quad\quad\quad$ G
Sowing on the mountain, reaping in the valley;

Sowing on the mountain, reaping in the valley;
$\quad\quad\quad\quad\quad\quad\quad\quad\quad\quad\quad$ C
Sowing on the mountain, reaping in the valley,
$\quad\quad$ G$\quad$ D7$\quad\quad$ G
You're gonna reap just what you sow.

God gave Noah the rainbow sign (3 times)
It won't be water, but fire next time.

Won't be water, but fire next time (3 times)
God gave Noah the rainbow sign.

Hold The Fort

Philip Paul Bliss

C$\quad\quad\quad\quad\quad\quad$ F
Ho, my comrades, see the signal
C$\quad\quad\quad\quad\quad$ G
Waving in the sky;
C$\quad\quad\quad\quad\quad\quad$ F
Reinforcements now appearing,
D7$\quad\quad$ G7
Victory is nigh.

Chorus:

C$\quad\quad\quad$ F$\quad\quad$ C$\quad$ Em
Hold the fort, for I am coming,
F$\quad\quad\quad$ G7
Jesus signals still,
C$\quad\quad\quad\quad\quad\quad$ F
Wave the answer back to heaven,
$\quad$ G$\quad\quad\quad\quad$ C
"By Thy Grace, we will."

See the mighty host advancing,
Satan leading on,
Mighty men around us falling,
Courage almost gone.

See the glorious banner waving,
Hear the bugle blow,
In our Leader's name we'll triumph
Over every foe.

Fierce and long the battle rages,
But our Help is near,
Onward comes our great Commander,
Cheer, my comrades, cheer.

The Seven Blessings Of Mary

$\quad\quad$ D
The very first blessing that Mary had,
$\quad\quad\quad\quad\quad\quad\quad\quad\quad$ A7
It was the blessing of one,
$\quad$ D$\quad\quad\quad\quad\quad\quad$ A7
To know that her son, Jesus,
D$\quad\quad\quad\quad\quad\quad$ A7
Was God's only Son,
G$\quad\quad\quad\quad\quad$ D
Was God's only Son.

Chorus:

D
Come all ye to the wilderness,
A7$\quad\quad\quad\quad$ D
Glory, glory, be,
$\quad\quad\quad\quad\quad\quad\quad\quad$ G$\quad$ D
Father, Son and the Holy Ghost,
$\quad\quad$ A7$\quad\quad$ D
Through all eternity.

The second blessing that Mary had,
It was the blessing of two,
To know that her son, Jesus,
Could read the Bible through. (twice)

The very next blessing that Mary had,
It was the blessing of three,
To know that her son, Jesus,
Could make the blind to see. (twice)

The very next blessing that Mary had,
It was the blessing of four,
To know that her son, Jesus,
Would live to help the poor. (twice)

The very next blessing that Mary had,
It was the blessing of five,
To know that her son, Jesus,
Could bring the dead alive. (twice)

Mary counted her blessings,
She counted them one by one,
She found that her greatest blessing,
Was her Godly son. (twice)

The very last blessing that Mary had,
It was the blessing of seven,
To know that her son, Jesus,
Was safe at last in Heaven. (twice)

What A Friend We Have In Jesus

Joseph Scriven and Charles C. Converse

Bb   Eb
What a friend we have in Jesus,
F   Bb
All our sins and griefs to bear!
        Eb
What a privilege to carry
F   Bb
Ev'rything to God in prayer!
F   Bb
Oh what peace we often forfeit,
Eb
Oh what needless pain we bear,

All because we do not carry

Ev'rything to God in prayer!

Have we trials and temptations?
Is there trouble anywhere?
We should never be discouraged,
Take it to the Lord in prayer.
Can we find a friend so faithful
Who will all our sorrows share?
Jesus knows our ev'ry weakness,
Take it to the Lord in prayer.

Are we weak and heavy laden,
Cumbered with a load of care?
Precious Savior, still our refuge,
Take it to the Lord in prayer.
Do thy friends despise, forsake thee?
Take it to the Lord in prayer;
In His arms He'll take and shield thee,
Thou wilt find a solace there.

Life Is Like A Mountain Railroad

E   B7   E
Life is like a mountain railroad,
      A   E
With an engineer that's brave,
      A   E
You can make the run successful,
    B7
From the cradle to the grave,
       E   B7   E
Watch the hills, the curves and tunnels,
     A   E
Never falter, never fail.
      A   E
Keep your hands upon the throttle,
       B7   E
And your eyes upon the rail.

You will roll up grades of trial,
You will cross the ridge of strife,
See that Christ is your connection
On the lightning train of life,
Always mindful of obstruction,
Do your duty, never fail,
Keep your hand upon the throttle,
And your eyes upon the rail.

You will often find obstructions,
Look for storm of wind and rain,
On a fill or curve or trestle,
They will almost ditch your train,
Put your trust alone in Jesus,
Never falter, never fail,
Keep your hand upon the throttle,
And your eye upon the rail.

As you roll across the trestle
Spanning Jordan's swelling tide,
You behold the union depot
Into which your train will glide,
There you'll find the superintendent,
God the Father, God the Son,
With a hearty joyous plaudit,
Weary pilgrim, welcome home!

Let Me Fly

G   C   G   C   G   C   GC
Way down yonder in the middle of the field,
G CG   C   GCG   C
Angel workin' at the chariot wheel.
G   C   G C   G   C   G
Not so particular 'bout workin' at the wheel,
C   G   C   G C   G CG
But I just wanna see how the chariot feels.

Chorus:

C   G   Bm
Now let me fly, now let me fly.
      C D7 Em G   C D7 G
Now let me fly unto Mount Zion, Lord, Lord.

I got a mother in the Promised Land,
Ain't gonna stop till I shake her hand.
Not so particular 'bout shakin' her hand,
But I just wanna go up in the Promised Land.

Meet that hypocrite on the street,
First thing he'll do is to show his teeth.
Next thing he'll do is to tell a lie,
And the best thing to do is to pass him by.

Beulah Land

Edgar Page and John R. Sweeney

    E
I've reached the land of corn and wine,
  B7   E
And all its riches freely mine;
            B7 C♯m
Here shines undimmed one blissful day,
  A6   B7   E
For all my night has passed away.

Chorus:

    B   E
Oh, Beulah Land, sweet Beulah Land,
E7 A   B7   E
As on thy highest mount I stand,
  A6   C♯ F♯m
I look away across the sea,
B7   E
Where mansions are prepared for me,
E7 A   A7 E
And view the shining glory shore,
    A6   B7   E
My heav'n, my home forevermore.

The Saviour comes and walks with me,
And sweet communion here have we;
He gently leads me with His hand,
For this is heaven's borderland.

A sweet perfume upon the breeze
Is borne from ever vernal trees,
And flow'rs that never fading grow
Where streams of life forever flow.

The zephyrs seem to float to me,
Sweet sounds of heaven's melody,
As angels, with the white-robed throng,
Join in the sweet redemption song.

Let Us Break Bread Together

    F   Dm   Gm C7   F
Let us break bread together on our knees,
    Am F   Dm   G7   C
Let us break bread together on our knees.
     F Cm D7   Gm   Gm7 C7
When I fall on my knees with my face to the rising sun,
   F   F7 Dm Gm F
Oh, Lord, have mercy if you please.

Let us drink wine together, etc.

Let us praise God together, etc.

All The Way My Savior Leads Me

Fanny J. Crosby and Robert Lowry

     A
All the way my Saviour leads me;
    E7   A
What have I to ask beside?
  D   E
Can I doubt His tender mercy,
       B7   E
Who through life has been my Guide?
    A
Heav'nly peace, divinest comfort,
           E
Here by faith in Him to dwell!
    A   D
For I know, whate'er befall me,
    A   E   A
Jesus doeth all things well;
              D
For I know whate'er befall me,
   A   E   A
Jesus doeth all things well.

All the way my Saviour leads me;
Cheers each winding path I tread,
Gives me grace for ev'ry trial,
Feeds me with the living bread.
Though my weary steps may falter,
And my soul a-thirst may be,
Gushing from the rock before me, ⎫
Lo! a spring of joy I see.   ⎬ (twice)
                             ⎭

All the way my Saviour leads me;
Oh, the fullness of His love!
Perfect rest to me is promised
In my Father's house above.
When my spirit, clothed immortal,
Wings its flight to realms of day,
This my song thro' endless ages: ⎫
Jesus led me all the way.   ⎬ (twice)
                             ⎭

Sinner Man

Dm
Oh, sinner man, where you gonna run to?
C
Oh, sinner man, where you gonna run to?
Dm
Oh, sinner man, where you gonna run to?
    Am   Dm
All on that day?

Run to the rock,
The rock was a-melting (3 times)
All on that day.

Run to the sea,
The sea was a-boiling, etc.

Run to the moon,
The moon was a-bleeding, etc.

Run to the Lord,
Lord won't you hide me? etc.

Oh, sinner man,
You oughta been a-praying, etc.

Steal Away

Chorus:

F
Steal away, steal away,
        C7 F
Steal away to Jesus.

Steal away, steal away home,
            C7 F
I ain't got long to stay here.

Verses:

Dm   F
My Lord calls me,

He calls me by the thunder,

The trumpet sounds within-a my soul;
           C7 F
I ain't got long to stay here.

Green trees are bending,
Poor sinner stands a-trembling,
The trumpet sounds within-a my soul,
I ain't got long to stay here.

Tombstones are bursting,
Poor sinner stands a-trembling, etc.

My Lord calls me,
He calls me by the lightning, etc.

Old Hundred

G   D Em Bm Em   D
All people that on earth do dwell,
G   D7 Em C G D7
Sing to the Lord with cheerful voice;
G D7 G   D7 G C   D7 G
Him serve with fear, His praise forth tell,
       EmD7 Am G   D7G
Come ye before Him and rejoice.

The Lord, ye know, is God indeed;
Without our aid He did us make;
We are His flock, He doth us feed,
And for His sheep He doth us take.

O enter then His gates with praise,
Approach with joy His courts unto:
Praise, laud, and bless His name always,
For it is seemly so to do.

Praise God, from whom all blessings flow;
Praise Him all creatures here below;
Praise Him above, ye heav'nly host;
Praise Father, Son and Holy Ghost.

Old Ship Of Zion

       D   F#m   G   D
What ship is this that will take us all home?
   G   A7 DGD
O glory hallelujah!
A7 D   F#min G   D
And safely land us on Canaan's bright shores?
   G   A7 DGD
O glory hallelujah!

Chorus:

A   D   G
'Tis the old ship of Zion,
     F#m7 Bm7
Hallelu,   hallelu,
      D7   G
'Tis the old ship of Zion,
A7 DGD
Hallelujah!

The winds may blow and the billows may foam, etc.
But she is able to land us all home. etc.

She's landed all who've gone before, etc.
And yet she's able to land still more. etc.

If I get there before you do, etc.
I'll tell them that you're coming too. etc.

Revive Us Again

William Porter Mackay and
John J. Husband

F   Bb   F
We praise Thee, Oh God!
      Bb   F
For the Son of Thy love,
      Bb
For Jesus who died
F   C7
And is now gone above.

Refrain:

    F   C7   F
Hallelujah! Thine the glory,
        C7
Hallelujah, amen!
    F   A7   Dm
Hallelujah! Thine the glory,
F Bb F C7F
Revive us again!

We praise Thee, Oh God!
For Thy Spirit of light,
Who has shown us our Savior
And scattered our night.

All glory and praise
To the Lamb that was slain,
Who has borne all our sins
And hath cleansed every stain.

Revive us again;
Fill each heart with Thy love;
May each soul be rekindled
With fire from above.

Were You There When They Crucified My Lord?

      F   Bb C7   Bb
Were you there when they crucified my Lord?
F   Am   Bb Am Bb C
Were you there when they crucified my Lord?
  Dm Am   Dm F7 Bb   F   Gm Am
O sometimes it causes me to tremble, tremble, tremble;
Dm BbmF   Bb Am C7 Bb
Were you there when they crucified my Lord?

Were you there when they nailed Him to the tree? (twice)
O sometimes it causes me to tremble, tremble, tremble;
Were you there when they nailed Him to the tree?

Were you there when they pierced Him in the side?, etc.

Were you there when the sun refused to shine?, etc.

Were you there when they laid Him in the tomb?, etc.

Set Down, Servant

Chorus:

  Am   C   Am7
"Set down, servant." "I can't set down."
  F   Am7   Em
"Set down, servant." "I can't set down."
  Dm   Am7
"Set down, servant." "I can't set down."
  G Am G F   Am
"My soul's so happy that I can't set down."

Verses:

F
"My Lord, you know

That you promise me,

Promise me a long white robe
Bb   F
An' a pair of shoes."
  Am   Am7
"Go yonder, angel,
F   Am
Fetch me a pair of shoes,
Dm   Am
Place them on-a my servant's feet.
G   AmG F   Am
Now, servant, please set down."

"My Lord, you know
That you promise me,
Promise me a long white robe
An' a starry crown."
"Go yonder angel,
Fetch me a starry crown,
Place it on-a my servant's head . . .
Now servant, please set down."

"My Lord, you know
That you promise me.
Promise me a long white robe
An' a golden waistband."
"Go yonder angel,
Fetch me a golden waistband,
Place it 'round my servant's waist . . .
Now, servant, please set down."

Free At Last

Chorus:

```
E            A    E
Free at last! Free at last!
A          E        B
Thank God a'mighty, I'm free at last!
E            A    E
Free at last! Free at last!
                 B    E
Thank God a'mighty, I'm free at last!
```

Verses:

```
E    A   E               A
One of these mornings bright and fair,
B
Thank God a'mighty, I'm free at last!
              E
I'm gonna put on my wings and try the air,
A       E        B  E
Thank God a'mighty, I'm free at last!
```

Old Satan's mad because we're glad,
Thank God a'mighty, we're free at last!
He missed a crowd he thought he had,
Thank God a'mighty, we're free at last!

I wonder what old Satan's grumblin' 'bout,
Thank God a'mighty, we're free at last!
'Cause he's chained in hell, and can't get out,
Thank God a'mighty, we're free at last!

The Great Speckled Bird

```
        A    A7      D
What a beautiful thought I'm thinking,
E                        A
Concerning the great speckled bird,
A         A7      D
Remember his name is recorded,
         E                A
In the great Book of God's Holy Word.
```

The great speckled bird sits in splendor,
All surrounded and despised by the squab,
The great speckled bird is the Bible,
Representing the Great Church of God.

I am glad that I come to your meeting,
I'm proud that my name is of a bird,
For I want to be one never fearing,
In the arms of my Savior's true word.

When He comes, if He comes, I will greet Him,
On a cloud that is floating in the Word,
I will rise up my savior to greet Him,
On the wings of a great speckled bird.

Great Day

```
C
The chariot rode on the mountain top,
                  G    C
God's gonna build up Zion's walls.
```

```
My God spoke and the chariot stop,
                  G    C
God's gonna build up Zion's walls.
```

Chorus:

```
C
Great day! Great day the righteous marching,
                              G    C
Great day! God's gonna build up Zion's walls.
```

This is the year of Jubilee,
The Lord will set His people free.

We want no cowards in our band,
We call for valiant-hearted men.

Union Version

One of these mornings bright and fair,
We're gonna build our union strong.
Put on your wings and try the air,
We're gonna build our union strong.

Chorus:

Great day! Great day the Union's marching,
Great day! We're gonna build our union strong.

One of these mornings and it won't be long,
Look for the scabs and they'll be gone.

One of these mornings pretty damn soon,
The boss will sing a different tune.

Kum Ba Yah (Come By Here)

```
        C           F     C
Kum ba yah, my Lord, Kum ba yah!
        C           F     G
Kum ba yah, my Lord, Kum ba yah!
C                   F     C
Kum ba yah, my Lord, Kum ba yah!
F C    G7      C
O Lord, Kum ba yah.
```

Someone's crying, Lord, Kum ba yah!, etc.

Someone's singing, Lord, Kum ba yah!, etc.

Someone's praying, Lord, Kum ba yah!, etc.

When The Saints Go Marching In

         F
Oh, when the Saints go marching in,
              C7
Oh, when the Saints go marching in,
  F   F7   Bb
Lord, I want to be in that number,
       F   C7 F
When the Saints go marching in.

And when the revelation comes, etc.

Oh, when the new world is revealed, etc.

Oh, when they gather 'round the throne, etc.

And when they crown him King of Kings, etc.

And when the sun no more will shine, etc.

And when the moon has turned to blood, etc.

And on that hallelujah day, etc.

And when the earth has turned to fire, etc.

Oh, when the Saints go marching in, etc.

Amazing Grace

G   Bm C   G
Amazing grace, how sweet the sound,
             A7 D
That saved a wretch like me.
 G   C   G
I once was lost, but now am found
     Em   G   D7 G
Was blind, but now I see,

'Twas grace that taught my heart to fear,
And grace my fears relieved;
How precious did that grace appear
The hour I first believed.

Thro' many dangers, toils and snares,
I have already come;
'Tis grace hath bro't me safe thus far,
And grace will lead me home.

How sweet the name of Jesus sounds
In a believer's ear.
It soothes his sorrows, heals his wounds,
And drives away his fear.

Must Jesus bear the cross alone
And all the world go free?
No, there's a cross for ev'ry one
And there's a cross for me.

Roll, Jordan, Roll

  D
O, brothers, you oughta been there,
   G A
Yes, my Lord,
   D
A-sitting in the Kingdom
Bm D   A7   D
To   hear Jordan roll.

Chorus:

D
Roll, Jordan, roll,
C   D
Roll, Jordan, roll.
A7 D   Bm Am7   D
I   want to go to Heaven when I die
G D   A7   D
To hear Jordan roll.

O, sisters, you oughta been there, etc.

O, children, you oughta been there, etc.

O, seekers, you oughta been there, etc.

Scandalize My Name

  G
I met my preacher the other day,
          D7
I gave him my right hand,
  G
And just as soon as my back was turned,
  C   G
He scandalized my name.

Chorus:

     G
Do you call that religion? (No, no.)
             D7
Do you call that religion? (No, no.)
     G   Em
Do you call that religion? (No, no.)
     G   C   G
He was scandalizin' my name.

I met my sister the other day
I gave her my right hand, etc.
Do you call that a sister? etc.

I met my brother the other day
I gave him my right hand, etc.
Do you call that a brother? etc.

Deep River

Chorus:

```
C    F    G7          Em C7
Deep river, my home is over Jordan,
      F       Dm           G7 C
Deep river, Lord, I want to cross over into camp ground.
```

Verses:

```
A          Em      Am    E
Oh, don't you want to go to that gospel feast,
      Am     E         Am  E
That promised land where all is peace.
```

I'll go up to Heaven and take my seat,
And cast my crown at Jesus' feet.

When I go up to Heaven I'll walk about,
There's nobody there to turn me out.

Didn't My Lord Deliver Daniel?

Chorus:

```
         Am
Didn't my Lord deliver Daniel,
      E7          Am
Deliver Daniel, deliver Daniel,
```

```
Didn't my Lord deliver Daniel,
      Dm    E7  Am
Then why not every man?
```

Verses:

```
      Dm
He delivered Daniel from the lion's den,
Am
Jonah from the belly of the whale,
         Dm              Am
And the Hebrew children from the fiery furnace,
      Dm   E7  Am
Then why not every man?
```

The moon run down in a purple stream,
The sun forbear to shine;
And every star will disappear,
King Jesus shall be mine.

I set my foot on the Gospel ship,
And the ship began for to sail,
It landed me over on Canaan's shore,
And I'll never come back no more.

Good News

Chorus:

```
     D
Good news, chariot's a-comin',
      A7   D
Good news, chariot's a-comin',
      D
Good news, chariot's a-comin',
      D        A7       D
And I don't want it to leave me behind.
```

Verse:

```
D
There's a long white robe in Heaven I know,
```

There's a long white robe in Heaven I know,

There's a long white robe in Heaven I know,
```
                     A7        D
And I don't want it to leave me behind.
```

There's a better land in this world I know, etc.

There's a pair of wings in Heaven I know, etc.

There's a starry crown in Heaven I know, etc.

There's a golden harp in Heaven I know, etc.

No Hiding Place

```
       C
There's no hiding place down here;
                          B7
There's no hiding place down here.
     E
Oh, I ran to the rock to hide my face,
              A      E     B7
The rock cried out, "no hiding place,"
E        B7       E
No hiding place down here.
```

The rock cried out, "I'm burning too." (twice)
Oh, the rock cried out, "I'm burning too,
I want to go to Heaven the same as you,"
There's no hiding place down here.

Sinner man he stumbled and he fell. (twice)
Oh, the sinner man stumbled and he fell,
Wanted to go to Heaven but he had to go to ---- Well,
There's no hiding place down here.

Can The Circle Be Unbroken?

E
I was standing by the window
     A   E
On one cold and cloudy day;

And I saw the hearse come rolling
         B7
For to carry my mother away.

Chorus:

E
O, can the circle be unbroken?
    A   E
Bye and bye, Lord, bye and bye.

There's a better home a-waiting
        B7   E
In the sky, Lord, in the sky.

Lord, I told the undertaker,
"Undertaker, please drive slow;
For this body you are hauling,
Lord, I hate to see her go."

I followed close behind her,
Tried to hold up and be brave;
But I could not hide my sorrow
When they laid her in the grave.

Went back home, Lord, my home was lonesome
Since my mother she was gone:
All my brothers, sisters crying,
What a home so sad and lone.

Come And Go With Me To That Land

E
Come and go with me to that land,
      A   E
Come and go with me to that land;
              B7
Go with me to that land where I'm bound.
         E   E7
Come and go with me to that land,
      A   E
Come and go with me to that land,
        B7   E
Go with me to that land where I'm bound.

There ain't no moanin' in that land, etc.

There ain't no bowin' in that land, etc.

There ain't no kneelin' in that land, etc.

There ain't no Jim Crow in that land, etc.

THE SEASON OF THE YEAR

Songs of Christmas, Chanuke and the New Year....

Rise Up, Shepherd, And Follow

    D
There's a star in the East on Christmas morn,
  F   D
Rise up shepherd and follow;
  G   D
It will lead to the place where the Saviour's born,
  G   D
Rise up shepherd and follow.
        G   D
Leave your sheep and leave your lambs,
  F   D
Rise up shepherd and follow;

Leave your ewes and leave your rams,
     G   D
Rise up shepherd and follow.

Chorus:

    F
Follow, follow,
D   D7   D
Rise up shepherd and follow.

Follow the star of Bethlehem,
     G   D
Rise up shepherd and follow.

If you take good heed to the angel's words, Rise up, etc.
You'll forget your flocks, you'll forget your herds, etc.
Leave your sheep and leave your lambs, etc.
Leave your ewes and leave your rams, etc.

It's Almost Day

F
Chickens crowing for midnight
  Bb
And it's almost day,
C7
Chickens crowing for midnight
     F
And it's almost day.

Santa Claus is coming } (twice)
And it's almost day, }

I think I heard my mother say } (twice)
It's almost day, }

Think I heard my papa say } (twice)
It's almost day, }

Christmas is a-coming } (twice)
And it's almost day, }

Children are all happy } (twice)
On Christmas Day, etc. }

Poor Little Jesus

Em
It was poor little Jesus, yes, yes,

He was born on Christmas, yes, yes,

And laid in a manger, yes, yes.

Refrain:

            B7 Em
Wasn't that a pity and a shame?
Am
Lord, Lord,
Em   B7 Em
Wasn't that a pity and a shame?

Poor little Jesus, yes, yes,
They took him from a manger, etc.
They took him from his mother, etc.

Poor little Jesus, yes, yes,
They bound him with a halter, etc.
And whipped him up the mountain, etc.

Poor little Jesus, yes, yes,
They nailed him to the cross, Lord, etc.
They hung him with a robber, etc.

Poor little Jesus, yes, yes,
He's risen from darkness, etc.
He's ascended into glory, etc.

He was poor little Jesus, yes, yes
Born on Friday, etc.
Born on Christmas, etc.

Away In A Manger

  F   Bb
Away in a manger, no crib for a bed,
    C7   F
The little Lord Jesus lay down his sweet head.
                  Bb   F
The stars in the sky looked down where he lay,
    C7   F   Bb   C7 F
The little Lord Jesus, asleep on the hay.

The cattle are lowing, the baby awakes,
But little Lord Jesus, no crying he makes.
I love thee, Lord Jesus, look down from the sky,
And stay by my cradle till morning is nigh.

Be near me, Lord Jesus, I ask thee to stay
Close by me forever, and love me, I pray.
Bless all the dear children in thy tender care,
And fit us for heaven to live with thee there.

No Room At The Inn

```
        F      Dm     Gm    C7  F
When Caesar Augustus had raised a taxation,
              Dm     Gm    C7  F
He assessed all the people that dwelt in the nation,
      C       F      G7         C
The Jews at that time being under Rome's way,
F  Bb                   Gm   C7 F
Appeared in the city their tribute to pay.
```

Then Joseph and Mary, who from David did spring,
Went up to the city of David their king,
And there, being entered, cold welcome they did find,
From the rich to the poor they are mostly unkind.

They sought entertainment, but none could they find,
Great numbers of strangers had filled up the inn.
They knocked and called all this at the door,
But found not a friend where in kind they had store.

Their kindred accounted they come were too soon,
"Too late," said the inn-keeper, "here is no room."
Amongst strangers and kinfolk cold welcome they find,
From the rich to the poor they are mostly unkind.

Good Joseph was troubled, but most for his dear,
For her blessed burden whose time now drew near;
His heart with true sorrow was sorely afflicted
That his virgin spouse was so rudely neglected.

He could get no house-room who houses did frame,
But Joseph and Mary must go as they came.
For little is the favor the poor man can find,
From the rich to the poor they are mostly unkind.

Whilst the great and the wealthy do frolic in hall,
Possess all the ground-rooms and chambers and all,
Poor Joseph and Mary are thrust in a stable
In Bethlehem city, ground inhospitable.

And with their mean lodging contented they be,
For the minds of the just with their fortunes agree;
They bear all affronts with their meekness of mind,
And be not offended though the rich be unkind.

Oh Bethlehem, Bethlehem, welcome this stranger
That was born in a stable and laid in a manger;
For he is a physician to heal all our smarts—
Come welcome, sweet Jesus, and lodge in our hearts.

Oh Tannenbaum
(Oh Christmas Tree)
Germany

```
   G          D  G
Oh Tannenbaum, Oh Tannenbaum,
      Am      D7    G
Wie treu sind deine Blätter!
   G              D7
Du grünst nicht nur zur Sommerzeit,
                  G
Nein, auch im Winter, wenn es schneit.
   G          D7 Dmin6  E7
Oh Tannenbaum, Oh Tannenbaum,
      Am      D7 D7  G
Wie treu sind deine Blätter!
```

Oh Tannenbaum, Oh Tannenbaum,
Du kannst mir sehr gefallen!
Wie oft hat mich zur Weihnachtszeit
Ein Braum von dir mich hoch erfreut!
Oh Tannenbaum, Oh Tannenbaum,
Du kannst mir sehr gefallen!

Oh Tannenbaum, Oh Tannenbaum,
Dein Kleid soll mich was lehren!
Die Hoffnung und Beständigkeit
Gibt trost und Kraft zu aller Zeit.
Oh Tannenbaum, Oh Tannenbaum,
Dein Kleid soll mich was lehren!

Singable Translation:

Oh Christmas tree, Oh Christmas tree,
With faithful leaves unchanging;
Not only green in summer's heat,
But also winter's snow and sleet,
Oh Christmas tree, Oh Christmas tree
With faithful leaves unchanging.

Oh Christmas tree, Oh Christmas tree,
Of all the trees most lovely;
Each year, you bring to me delight
Gleaming in the Christmas night.
Oh Christmas tree, Oh Christmas tree,
Of all the trees most lovely.

Oh Christmas tree, Oh Christmas tree,
Your leaves will teach me, also,
That hope and love and faithfulness
Are precious things I can possess.
Oh Christmas tree, Oh Christmas tree,
Your leaves will teach me, also.

Joy To The World

Isaac Watts / Tune: adapted from
Handel's Messiah by Lowell Mason

```
D  G   D   G D  A D
```
Joy to the world, the Lord is come;
```
   G    A7     D
```
Let Earth receive her King;
```
     G D       G  D
```
Let every heart prepare Him room,

And Heaven and nature sing,
```
    A7
```
And Heaven and nature sing,
```
    D   G  D   G  D A7 D
```
And Heaven and Heaven and nature sing!

Joy to the world! the Savior reigns.
Let men their songs employ,
While fields and floods,
Rocks, hills and plains
Repeat the sounding joy, (twice)
Repeat, repeat, the sounding joy.

He rules the world with truth and grace,
And makes the nations prove
The glories of
His righteousness,
And wonders of His love, (twice)
And wonders, wonders, of His love.

Mary Had A Baby

```
E
```
Mary had a baby, Oh Lord;
```
              A  B7
```
Mary had a baby, Oh my Lord;
```
E        A   E
```
Mary had a baby, Oh, Lord;
```
         C#m E    A  B7  E
```
The people keep a-coming and the train done gone.

What did she name Him? etc.

She called Him Jesus, etc.

Where was He born? etc.

Born in a stable, etc.

Where did they lay Him? etc.

Laid Him in a manger, etc.

Masters In This Hall

William Morris

```
Em    B7  Em B7        Em
```
Masters in this hall, hear ye news today;
```
          B7  Em Am B7      Em
```
Brought from oversea and now rejoice, I pray.

Chorus:

```
        B7      Em          B7    Em
```
No-well, No-well, No-well! No-well sing we clear!
```
E7    Am   B7   Em  C   B7       Em
```
Hol-pen are all folk on earth, gone is sorrowing and fear.
```
          B7      Em          B7     Em
```
No-well, No-well, No-well! No-well sing we loud!
```
E7   Am   B7    Em   C
```
For today are poor fold raised up
```
        B7          Em
```
   and cast a-down the proud.

Going o'er the hills, through the milk-white snow,
Heard I ewes a-bleating while the wind did blow.

Shepherds, many a one, sat among the sheep,
No man spake more word than had they been asleep.

Quoth I, "Fellows mind, why this guise sit ye?
Making but dull cheer, shepherds though ye be?"

"Shepherds should of right leap and dance and sing.
Thus to see ye sit is a right strange thing."

Quoth these fellows then, "To Bethl'em Town we go,
To see a mighty Lord lie in a manger low."

"How name ye this lord, Shepherds?" then said I,
"Very God," they said, "Come from Heaven high."

Then to Bethl'em Town, we went two and two,
And in a sorry place heard the oxen low.

Therein did we see a sweet and goodly may,
And a fair old man, upon the straw she lay.

And a little child, on her arm had she,
"Wot ye who this is?" said the hinds to me.

Ox and ass him know, kneeling on their knee,
Wondrous joy had I this little babe to see.

This is Christ the Lord, masters be ye glad!
Christmas is come in and no folk should be sad.

The First Noel

```
     D    AG  D   G D
The first Noel the angels did say
G     D    G   D G   AD     A7 D
Was to certain poor shepherds in fields as they lay;
A7 D        A   G   D    G D
In  fields where they lay keeping their sheep
G   D    G  D   GA  D  A7 D
On a cold winter's night    that was so  deep.
```

Chorus:

```
A7 Bm   A D G    D
No-el, No-el, No-el, No-el,
Bm  F♯m G D   G A7D A7D
Born is     the king  of Is-ra-el.
```

They looked up and saw a star
Shining in the East, beyond them far,
And to the earth it gave great light,
And so it continued, both day and night.

And by the light of that same star
Three wise men came from country far,
To seek for a King was their intent,
And to follow the star wherever it went.

This star drew night to the northwest;
O'er Bethlehem it took its rest.
And there it did both stop and stay,
Right over the place where Jesus lay.

Then they did know assuredly
Within that house, the King did lie
One entered in then for to see
And found the babe in poverty.

Then entered in those Wise Men three,
Full reverently, upon bended knee,
And offered there, in His presence,
Their gold and myrrh and frankincense.

If we in our time do will
We shall be free from death and hell
For God hath prepared for us all
A resting place in general.

Jingle Bells

J. S. Pierpont

```
G
Dashing through the snow
              C
In a one-horse open sleigh,
                D7
O'er the fields we go,
```

```
               G
Laughing all the way;
```

```
Bells on bob-tail ring,
              C
Making spirits bright;
            D7
What fun it is to ride and sing
                G
A sleighing song tonight!
```

Chorus:

```
G
Jingle bells! Jingle bells!
```

```
Jingle all the way!
C              G
Oh what fun it is to ride
     A7        D
In a one-horse open sleigh.
D7 G
Oh! Jingle bells! Jingle bells!
```

```
Jingle all the way!
C              G
Oh what fun it is to ride
    D7         G
In a one-horse open sleigh.
```

A day or two ago
I thought I'd take a ride,
And soon Miss Fannie Bright
Was seated by my side;
The horse was lean and lank,
Misfortune seem'd his lot,
He got into a drifted bank,
And then we got upsot!

We Wish You A Merry Christmas

```
        E           A
We wish you a Merry Christmas,
     F♯          B7
We wish you a Merry Christmas,
     C♯m          A
We wish you a Merry Christmas,
     B7          E
And a Happy New Year.
```

We want some figgy pudding, (3 times)
And a cup of good cheer!

We won't go until we get some, (3 times)
So bring it out here!

We wish you a Merry Christmas, (3 times)
And a Happy New Year!

Child Of God

   F
If anybody ask ye who I am,
Bb   C7
Who I am, who I am,
   F
If anybody ask ye who I am,
Bb   C7   F
Tell him I'm a child of God.

Peace on earth, Mary rock the cradle,
Mary rock the cradle, Mary rock the cradle,
Peace on earth, Mary rock the cradle,
The Christ child borned in glory.

The Christ child passing, singing softly,
Singing softly, singing softly,
The Christ child passing, singing softly,
The Christ child borned in glory.

If anybody ask you where I'm bound,
Where I'm bound, where I'm bound,
If anybody ask you where I'm bound
Tell him that I'm bound for glory.

Can't you hear the foot in the treetop,
Foot in the treetop, foot in the treetop,
Can't you hear the foot in the treetop,
Soft like the south wind blow?

If anybody ask ye who I am,
Who I am, who I am,
If anybody ask ye who I am,
Tell him I'm a child of God.

Comfort And Tidings Of Joy

    D A B7 A7 B7 G
Come all you worthy gentlemen
D7 G   B7 G A
That may be standing by,
D   A7   Em6 D
Christ our blessed   Saviour
A   G   A7 D   G A
Was born on Christmas day.
   G   D Em6 Am
The blessed Virgin Mary
D G F m Bm F m Em
Unto the   Lord did   say,
F m Em G6 D Em D   Bm E6 Em A7 D
O   we wish you the comfort and tidings of joy!

God bless the ruler of this house,
And long on may he reign,
Many happy Christmases
He live to see again!
God bless our generation
Who live both far and near,
And we wish them a happy, a happy New Year!

Chanuke, O Chanuke

Yiddish

Em
Chanuke, O Chanuke, a yontev a sheyner,

A lustiger, a freylicher, nite noch a zoyner!
             Am Em
Ale nacht in dreydl shpiln mir,
ı   Am Em
Zudigheyse latkes esn mir.

Chorus:

Em
Geshivinder, tsindt kinder,
          Am   Em
Di dininke lichtelech on.
      Am   Em   Am
Zogt "Alhanisim," loybt Got far di nisim,
    Em   Am Em
Un kumt gichertansn in kon!

Yehuda hot fartribn dem soyne, dem rotseyach,
Un hot in Beys-hamikdesh gezungen "Lamnatseyach",
Di shtot Yerusholayim hot vider oyfgelebt,
Un tsu a nayem lebn hot yederer geshtrebt.

Second Chorus:
Deriber, dem giber,
Yehuda Makabi loybt hoych!
Zol yeder bazunder, bazingen di vunder,
Un libn dos folk zolt ir oych!

Singable Translation:

Chanukah, O Chanukah, O holiday so fair,
So happy and so merry, there's none can compare.
We spin the dreydl-top every night,
Red-hot pancakes do we eat.

Come children, we'll light
The thin, little candles you see,
For the salvation of a grateful nation,
Thank God and dance merrily!

Maccabee defeated and cast out the cruel enemy,
And in the Holy Temple sang hymns of victory,
The city of Jerusalem revived and grew,
And everyone began to build his life anew.

Come children prepare for
A real tribute to the Maccabee.
Let us all sing of the victory
And a people so brave and so free.

God Rest You Merry Gentlemen

```
A7 Dm    A7   Dm
God rest you merry gentlemen,
F  Gm        A
Let nothing you dismay;
A7Dm    A7    Dm
Remember Christ our Saviour
F  Gm            A
Was born on Christmas Day;
   Bb          F
To save us all from Satan's power
      Dm        C
When we were gone astray.
```

Refrain:

```
    F      A7      Dm
Oh tidings of comfort and joy,
        C
Comfort and joy,
          A7      Dm
Oh tidings of comfort and joy.
```

'Twas in the town of Bethlehem
This blessed infant lay;
They found him in a manger
Where oxen feed on hay;
His mother Mary kneeling
Unto the Lord did pray.
Oh, tidings of comfort and joy,
Comfort and joy,
Oh,tidings of comfort and joy.

Now to the Lord sing praises,
All you within this place;
And with true love and brotherhood
Each other now embrace;
God bless your friends and kindred
That live both far and near,
And God send you a happy New Year!
Happy New Year!
And God send you a happy New Year!

Oh, Little Town Of Bethlehem
Philip Brooks and Lewis H. Redner

```
   G          Am
Oh little town of Bethlehem,
   G    D7    G
How still we see thee lie,
       E7      Am
Above thy deep and dreamless sleep
   G    D7    G
The silent stars go by;
      Adim7 A# dim7 B
Yet in thy dark   streets   shineth
   Em  C      B
The everlasting light,
```

```
G              Am
The hopes and fears of all the years,
   G    D7   G
Are met in thee tonight.
```

For Christ is born of Mary,
And gathered all above,
While mortals sleep, the angels keep
Their watch of wondering love.
Oh morning stars, together
Proclaim the holy birth,
And praises sing to God the King,
And peace to men on earth.

How silently, how silently
The wondrous gift is given!
So God imparts to human hearts
The blessings of His heaven.
No ear may hear His coming,
But in this world of sin,
Where meek souls will receive Him still,
The dear Christ enters in.

Oh holy Child of Bethlehem!
Descend to us, we pray;
Cast out the sin and enter in,
Be born in us today.
We hear the Christmas angels
The great glad tidings tell;
Oh come to us, abide with us,
Our Lord Immanuel!

Angels We Have Heard On High

```
F           C7      F
Angels we have heard on high,
   C F        C7 F
Sweetly singing o'er the plains;
      Dm  C    F C7 Dm
And the mountains in reply
F   C F      C7 F
Echoing their joyous strains.
```

Refrain:

```
Bb  C F  C F Bb  F C
Gloria in excelsis Deo,
Bb  C F  C F Bb  F C7 F
Gloria in excelsis Deo.
```

Shepherds, why this jubilee?
Why your joyous songs prolong?
What the gladsome tidings be
Which inspire your heav'nly song?

Come to Bethlehem and see
Him whose birth the angels sing;
Come adore on bended knee
Christ, the Lord, our new-born King.

I Saw Three Ships Come Sailing In

```
 G                        D
I saw three ships come sailing in
C G              D
On Christmas Day, on Christmas Day,
 G                    Bm   D
I saw three ships come sailing in
C G              D      G
On Christmas Day in the morning.
```

And what was in those ships all three
On Christmas Day, on Christmas Day?
And what was in those ships all three
On Christmas Day in the morning?

The mother Mary and her baby, etc.

Pray, whither sailed those ships all three, etc.

Oh, they sailed into Bethlehem, etc.

And all the bells on earth shall ring, etc.

And all the angels in Heaven shall sing, etc.

And all the souls on earth shall sing, etc.

Then let us all rejoice amain, etc.

What Child Is This?

William C. Dix / Tune: *Greensleeves*

```
   Em                    D
What Child is this, who laid to rest,
   Em    C    B7
On Mary's lap is sleeping?
    Em              D
Who angels greet with anthems sweet,
       Em     B7    Em
While shepherds watch are keeping?
```

Refrain:

```
G         D
This, this is Christ the King,
        Em      C    B7
Whom shepherds guard and angels sing;
G            D
Haste, haste to Bring Him laud,
     Em    B7    Em
The Babe, the Son of Mary.
```

Why lies He in such mean estate,
Where ox and ass are feeding?
Good Christian fear, for sinners here,
The silent word is pleading?

So bring Him incense, gold and myrrh,
Come peasant kind, to own Him.
The Kind of kings salvation brings,
Let loving hearts enthrone him.

Wassail Song

```
D   Em  F♯m  EmDEmF♯m
Here we  come  a-wassailing,
EmD     A7      D
Among the leaves so green;
G   A7 D     F♯m Em
Here we   come a-wandering,
D  G  A7  D
So fair to be seen:
```

Chorus:

```
        D       Bm D
Love and joy come to   you,
Bm Em D          Bm D
And to   you your wassail, too,
   G  D  Bm   Em D A D      G
And God bless you and send you a  happy New Year,
D   G   A  G  Bm EmD A    D
And God send you a  happy New Year.
```

Our wassail cup is made
Of the rosemary tree,
And so is your beer
Of the best barley.

We are not daily beggars
That beg from door to door,
But we are neighbors' children
Whom you have seen before.

Call up the butler of this house,
Put on his golden ring,
Let him bring us up a glass of beer,
And better we shall sing.

We have got a little purse
Of stretching leather skin;
We want a little of your money
To line it well within.

Bring us out a table,
And spread it with a cloth;
Bring us out mouldy cheese,
And some of your Christmas loaf.

God bless the master of this house,
Likewise the mistress, too;
And all the little children
That round the table go.

Good master and good mistress,
While you're sitting by the fire,
Pray think of us poor children
Who are wandering in the mire.

O, Come, All Ye Faithful

```
    G        D      G D G  C G D
O, come all ye faithful, joyful and triumphant,
Em      D A D     G D   A D
O, come ye, O, come ye to Bethlehem;
G    D7 G Am G   D   G Em  Am D
Come and behold him, born the king of    angels;
```

Chorus:

```
   G    D  G  D7 G
O, come, let us adore him
      D  G  D7 G  D
O, come, let us adore him
G D7   G  D7  A7 D G   Am
O, come, let us  adore him
G     D7 G
Christ, the Lord!
```

Sing chorus of angels, sing in exultation
O, sing all ye citizens of heaven above!
Glory to God, all glory in the highest;

Yea Lord, we greet thee, born this happy morning
Jesus, to thee be all glory giv'n:
Word of the father. Now in flesh appearing;

Latin:

Adeste, fideles,
Laeti triumphantes,
Venite, venite in Bethlehem.
Natum videte,
Regem angelorum,
Venite, adoremus,
Venite, adoremus,
Venite, adoremus Dominum.

Cherry Tree Carol

```
    D
When Joseph was an old man,
  F♯m      A
An old man was he,
   G        D
He courted Virgin Mary
   Bm        F♯m
The Queen of Galilee,
   G        Bm
He courted Virgin Mary,
   D    A7 D
The Queen of Galilee.
```

As Joseph and Mary
Were walking one day,
"Here are apples and cherries,"
Oh, Mary did say.
"Here are apples and cherries,"
Oh, Mary did say.

Then Mary said to Joseph
So meek and so mild,
"Joseph, gather me some cherries,   } (twice)
For I am with child."

Then Joseph flew in anger,
In anger flew he,
"Let the father of the Baby   } (twice)
Gather cherries for thee."

Then Jesus spoke a few words,
A few words spoke He,
"Give my mother some cherries,   } (twice)
Bow down you cherry tree!"

"Bow down, O cherry tree,
Bow down to the ground!"
Then Mary gathered cherries   } (twice)
And Joseph stood around.

Then Joseph took Mary
All on his right knee,
"What have I done, Lord,   } (twice)
Have mercy on me."

Mi Y'Malel
(Who Can Retell?)
Hebrew; Chanukah Song

```
E
Mi Y'malel g'vurot Yisrael,

Otan mi yimneh?

Hen bekhol dor yakum hagibor,
     C♯mE
Goel haam.
Bm B Em        F♯            Bm  B
Sh'ma! Bayamim hahem baz'mam hazzeh
Em   F♯      Bm  B
Makabi moshia ufodeh.
Em        F♯      B  Bm
Uv'yamenu kol am Yisrael.
G      F♯   Em
Yitahed, yakum veyigael.
```

Singable Translation:

Who can retell the things that befell us,
Who can count them?
In every age a hero or sage
Came to our aid.
Hark! At this time of year
In days of yore,
Maccabees the Temple did restore.
But now all Israel must as one rise,
Redeem itself through deed and sacrifice.

Go Tell It On The Mountain

```
G          Em7 Em
When I was a learner,
Am7      D         D7 G
I    sought   both night and day,
                    Em7 Em
I asked the Lord to help  me,
Am7     Am         D
And He showed me the way.
```

Chorus:

```
G
Go tell it on the mountain;
D                  D7
Over the hills and ev'ry where;
                      Em
Go tell it on the mountain,
Am7 G    D    D7 G
Our  Jesus Christ is  born.
```

While shepherds kept their watching;
O'er wand'ring flock by night;
Behold! From out the Heavens,
There shone a holy light.

He made me a watchman
Upon the city wall,
And if I am a Christian
I am the least of all.

And, lo, when they had seen it,
They all bowed down and prayed;
Then travelled on together,
To where the Babe was laid.

Auld Lang Syne
Robert Burns

```
      F              C7
Should auld acquaintance be forgot,
      F              Bb
And never brought to mind?
      F              C7
Should auld acquaintance be forgot,
      F          C7 F
And days of auld lang syne?
```

Chorus:

```
    F        C7
For auld lang syne, my dear
    F        Bb
For auld lang syne
    F              C7
We'll take a cup o' kindness yet,
    F    C7 F
For auld lang syne.
```

We twa ha'e ran aboot the braes
And pu'd the gowans fine,
We've wandered many a weary foot
Sin auld lang syne.

We twa ha'e sported i' the burn
Frae mornin' sun till dine,
But seas between us braid ha'e roared
Sin auld lang syne.

And here's a hand my trusty frien',
And gie's a hand o' thine;
We'll tak' a cup o' kindness yet
For auld lang syne.

Hark! The Herald Angels Sing
Charles Wesley and Felix Mendelssohn

```
G      D    G    D
Hark! the herald angels sing,
G    C    G  D7 G
Glory to the new-born King;
G         D   Emin A7
Peace on earth and mercy mild,
Bmin   D    G7A7D
God and sinners reconciled!
G              D
Joyful all ye nations rise,
G                   D
Join the triumph of the skies;
C             Amin E7 Amin
With angelic host    proclaim,
D7    G    G  D7G
Christ is born in Bethlehem.
```

Chorus:

```
C              E   Amin
Hark! the herald angels sing,
D7  G      D7 G
Glory to the new-born King.
```

Christ, by highest heav'n adored;
Christ, the everlasting Lord;
Late in time behold Him come,
Offspring of the Virgin's womb.
Veil'd in flesh the Godhead see;
Hail th' Incarnate Deity,
Pleased as Man with man to dwell,
Jesus, our Emmanuel!

Mild He lays His glory by,
Born that man no more may die,
Born to raise the sons of earth,
Born to give them second birth.
Ris'n with healing in His wings,
Light and life to all He brings,
Hail, the Sun of Righteousness!
Hail, the heav'n born Prince of Peace!

Deck The Halls

```
E        B     E
Deck the halls with boughs of holly,
A      E     B7  E
Fa la la la la, la la la  la.
E        B    E
'Tis the season to be jolly,
A      E     B7  E
Fa la la la la, la la la  la.
B            E       B
Don we now our gay apparel,
E      C#m   B F#7 B
Fa la la, la la la, la la     la.
E           B      E
Troll the ancient Yuletide carol,
A      E     B7  E
Fa la la la la, la la la  la.
```

See the blazing yule before us, Fa la, etc.
Strike the harp and join the chorus, Fa la, etc.
Follow me in merry measure, Fa la, etc.
While I tell of Christmas treasure, Fa la, etc.

Fast away the old year passes,
Hail the new, ye lads and lasses,
Sing we joyous all together,
Heedless of the wind and weather,

Down In Yon Forest

```
Em        Bm        Em      Bm
Down in yon forest there stands a hall:
   Em         Dsus       D
The bells of paradise, I heard them ring;
   Em       D     C      B
It's covered all over with purple and pall:
   A        Bm   C   G E
And I love my Lord Jesus above anything.
```

Down in that hall, there is a bed,
The bells of paradise, I heard them ring,
All scarlet the coverlet's over it spread,
And I love my Lord Jesus above anything.

Down under that bed there runs a flood,
The bells of paradise, I heard them ring,
The half it runs water, the half it runs blood,
And I love my Lord Jesus above anything.

Down at the bed feet there springs a thorn,
The bells of paradise, I heard them ring,
It bloomed its white blossoms the day He was born,
And I love my Lord Jesus above anything.

Over that place the moon shines bright,
The bells of paradise, I heard them ring,
To show that our Saviour was born this night,
And I love my Lord Jesus above anything.

Good King Wenceslas

```
G
Good King Wenceslas looked out
C  G C   D7 G
On the feast of  Stephen,
```

```
When the snow lay 'round about
C   G C   D7 G
Deep and crisp and even.
    C G    D7 G    D7 Em
Brightly shone the moon that night,
C    G C   D7 G
Though the frost was cruel,
    C   D7 Em      D
When a poor man came in sight,
G   D7 G  D7 Em C  G
Gath'ring winter fu  -  el.
```

"Hither page, and stand by me,
If thou know'st it, telling,
Yonder peasant who is he?
Where and what his dwelling?"
"Sire, he lives a good league hence,
Underneath the mountains;
Right against the forest fence,
By Saint Agnes' fountain."

"Bring me flesh and bring me wine,
Bring me pine logs hither.
Thou and I will see him dine
When we bear them thither."
Page and monarch, forth they went,
Forth they went together,
Through the rude winds wild lament,
And the bitter weather.

"Sire, the night is darker now,
And the wind blows stronger.
Fails my heart, I know not how
I can go no longer."
"Mark my footsteps, my good page,
Tread thou in them boldly;
Thou shalt find the winter's rage
Freeze thy blood less coldly."

In his master's steps he trod,
Where the snow lay dinted.
Heat was in the very sod
Which the saint had printed.
Therefore, Christian men, be sure,
Wealth or rank possessing,
Ye who now will bless the poor
Shall yourselves find blessing.

Children, Go Where I Send Thee

     E
Children, go where I send thee,

How shall I send thee?

I'm gonna send thee one by one,

One for the little bitty baby,
     A   E   B7 E
Was born, born, born in Bethlehem.

Children, go where I send thee,
How shall I send thee?
I'm gonna send thee two by two,
Two for Paul and Silas,
One for the little bitty baby,
Was born, born, born in Bethlehem.

Three for the Hebrew Children.

Four for the four who stood at the door.

Five for the gospel preachers.

Six for the six that never got fixed.

Seven for the seven that never got to heaven.

Eight for the eight who stood at the gate.

Nine for the nine who looked so fine.

Ten for the ten commandments.

Eleven for the eleven deriders.

Twelve for the twelve Apostles.

The Holly And The Ivy

   G   C G
The holly and the ivy,
          C   G
When they are both full grown,
  G   C G
Of all the trees that are in the wood,
     D7 G
The holly bears the crown.

Chorus:

      C G
The rising of the sun
        C G
And the running of the deer,
         C G
The playing of the merry organ,
     D7 G
Sweet singing in the choir.

The holly bears a blossom
As white as the lily flower,
And Mary bore sweet Jesus Christ
To be our sweet saviour.

The holly bears a berry
As red as any blood,
And Mary bore sweet Jesus Christ
To do poor sinners good.

The holly bears a prickle
As sharp as any thorn,
And Mary bore sweet Jesus Christ
On Christmas Day in the morn.

The holly bears a bark,
As bitter as any gall,
And Mary bore sweet Jesus Christ
For to redeem us all.

Duérmete, Niño Lindo
Spanish

    D   A7 D
Duérmete, niño lindo,
     Bm   F♯m
En los brazos del amor
     Bm   G7
Mientras que duerme y descansa
  D/A A7   D
La pena de mi dolor.

Chorus:

   G   D
A la ru, a la me,
    Em A7 D
A la ru, a la me,
D7 G   D
A la ru, a la me,
      A7   D
A la ru, a la ru, a la me.

No temas al rey Herodes
Que nada te ha de hacer;
En los brazos de tu madre
Y ahi nadie te ha de ofender.

Singable Translation:

Oh sleep, thou holy baby,
With thy head against my breast;
Meanwhile the pangs of my sorrow
Are soothed and put to rest.

Thou need'st not fear King Herod,
He will bring no harm to you;
So rest in the arms of your mother
Who sings you a la ru.

The Twelve Days Of Christmas

      F   Bb   C7   F
On the first day of Christmas my true love gave to me
  Bb   F C7 F
A partridge in a pear tree.
          F   Dm   C7   F
On the second day of Christmas my true love gave to me
C   F   Bb F C7 F
Two turtle doves and a partridge in a pear tree.
          F   C   Gm
On the third day . . . three French hens
          F   C   Gm
On the fourth day . . . four colly birds
          F   Dm G7 C7
On the fifth day . . . five golden rings.
F   Gm Bb Dm G   C
Four colly birds, three French hens, two turtle doves,
F   Bb   C7 F
And a partridge in a pear tree.
C7   Gm7
Six geese a-laying, etc.

Seven swans a-swimming, etc.

Eight maids a-milking, etc.

Nine ladies dancing, etc.

Ten lords a-leaping, etc.

Eleven pipers piping, etc.

Twelve drummers drumming, etc.

Virgin Mary Had One Son

   Am
The Virgin Mary had a-one son,
F   G
Oh, glory hallelujah,
C C   Am
Oh, pretty little baby,
C   E7   Am
Glory be to the new-born King.

Mary, what you gonna name that pretty little baby?
Oh, glory hallelujah,
Oh, pretty little baby,
Glory be to the new-born King.

Some call Him a-one thing, think I'll call Him Jesus, etc.

Some call Him a-one thing, think I'll call Him Manuel, etc.

Some call Him a-one thing,
   think I'll call Him Counselor, etc.

Mary, what you gonna name that pretty little baby? etc.

The Virgin Mary had a-one son, etc.

Silent Night

Joseph Mohr and Franz Gruber

C
Silent night, Holy night,
G7   C
All is calm, all is bright,
F   C
Round yon Virgin Mother and Child,
F   C
Holy Infant so tender and mild,
G7   Am
Sleep in heavenly peace,
C   G7   C
Sleep in heavenly peace.

Silent night, Holy night,
Shepherds quake at the sight;
Glories stream from heaven afar,
Heavenly hosts sing alleluia,
Christ, the Savior, is born! (twice)

Silent night, Holy night,
Son of God, love's pure light
Radiant beams from Thy holy face,
With the dawn of redeeming grace,
Jesus, Lord at Thy birth, (twice)

Tell Me What Month Was My Jesus Born In

       Em
Tell me what month was my Jesus born in?
Am B7   Em
Last month of the year.

Tell me what month was my Jesus born in?
Am B7   Em
Last month of the year.
                   Am   B7
Well, you got January, February, March, oh Lord.
             Em
You got April, May and June, Lord
         C   Em   C   Em
You got July, August, September, October and November,
                 Am
You got the twenty-fifth day of December,
B7   Em
Last month of the year.

He was born in an ox-stall manger, } (twice)
Last month in the year,

Oh, Lord, you got January, etc.

I'm talking about Mary's baby, } (twice)
Last month in the year.

Oh, Lord, you got January, etc.

HA, HA, THIS A-WAY

Playparties, singing games and children's songs....

Ha Ha This-A-Way

G
Ha ha this-a-way,
D
Ha ha that-a-way,
G
Ha ha this-a-way,
D   G
Then, Oh, then.
G   D   G
When I was a little boy, little boy, little boy,
              D7   G
When I was a little boy, twelve years old,
G   D   G
Papa went and left me, left me, left me,
              D7   G
Papa went and left me, save my soul.

Mama come and got me, got me, got me,
Mama come and got me to save my soul.
Mama didn't whip me, whip me, whip me,
Mama didn't whip me, so I was told.

I went to school, etc.
Teacher didn't whip me, etc.

Learned my lesson, etc.
Wasn't that a blessin', etc.

Liked my teacher, etc.
Prayed like a preacher, etc.

A Big Ship Sailing

        D   A
There's a big ship sailing on the il-li-al-lay oh,
  D
The il-li-ay-lay Oh,
  A
The il-li-ay-lay oh.
        D   A
There's a big ship sailing on the il-li-al-lay oh,
G   A D
Heigh-ho, il-li-al-lay oh.

There's a big ship sailing,
Rocking on the sea, (3 times)
There's a big ship sailing,
Rocking on the sea,
Heigh-ho, rocking on the sea.

There's a big ship sailing,
Back again, (3 times)
There's a big ship sailing,
Back again,
Heigh-ho, back again.

Who Did Swallow Jonah?

G
Who did, who did, who did, who did,

Who did swallow Jo-Jo-Jonah?
D7
Who did, who did, who did, who did,

Who did swallow Jo-Jo-Jonah?
G
Who did, who did, who did, who did,

Who did swallow Jo-Jo-Jonah?
D7
Who did swallow Jonah, who did swallow Jonah,
                    G
Who did swallow Jonah down?

The whale did, whale did, whale did,
   whale did,   } (3 times)
The whale did swallow Jo-Jo-Jonah
The whale did swallow Jonah,
   the whale did swallow Jonah
The whale did swallow Jonah—up!

Shadrack, Shadrack, Shadrack, Shadrack,
Shadrack, Meshak, Abindigo. (3 times)
Shadrack, Meshak, Abindi— (twice)
Shadrack, Meshak, Abindigo.

Noah, Noah, Noah, Noah, } (3 times)
Noah in the ark, ark, arky
Noah in the arky, Noah in the arky,
Noah in the arky—bailed!

Daniel, Daniel, Daniel, Daniel, } (3 times)
Daniel in the li-li-lion
Daniel in the lion, Daniel in the lion,
Daniel in the lion's den!

David, David, David, David, } (3 times)
David killed Goli-li-liath
David killed Goliath, David killed Goliath,
David killed Goliath—dead!

Roll Over

        G
There were ten in the bed
And the little one said,
"Roll over, roll over."
So they all rolled over
And one fell out.
There were nine in the bed
And the little one said. . . . etc.

One in the bed
And the little one said,
"Good night."

Here We Go Looby Loo

Chorus:

```
F              C
Here we go looby loo,
F              C
Here we go looby light,
F              Am
Here we go looby loo,
Bb     C      F
All on a Saturday night.
```

Verses:

```
F
I put my right hand in,

I put my right hand out,
           C7    F         Dm
I give my hand a shake, shake, shake
     F     C7   F
And turn myself about.
```

I put my left hand in, etc.

I put my right foot in, etc.

I put my left foot in, etc.

I put my whole self in, etc.

I Had A Rooster

(Cumulative Song)

```
C
I had a rooster and the rooster pleased me,
              G7
I fed my rooster on a greenberry tree.
     C              F
The little rooster went cock-a-doodle doo,
     C      F      G7         C
Dee doodle-dee, doodle-dee, doodle-dee doo.
```

```
C
I had a cat and the cat pleased me,
           G7
I fed my cat on a greenberry tree,
C
The little cat went "meow, meow,"
                         F
The little rooster went cock-a-doodle doo,
     C      F      G7         C
Dee doodle-dee, doodle-dee, doodle-dee doo.
```

I had a pig ("oink, oink")

I had a cow ("moo, moo")

I had a baby ("waagh, waagh")

I Sent My Brown Jug Downtown

```
Eb
I sent my brown jug downtown,
  Bb 7
I sent my brown jug downtown,
  Eb
I sent my brown jug downtown,
   Bb 7      Eb
So early in the morning.
```

```
It came back with a waltz around,
Bb 7
It came back with a waltz around,
Eb
It came back with a waltz around,
Bb 7        Eb
So early in the morning.
                              Bb 7
Railroad, steamboat, river and canoe,
                              Eb
Lost my true love, what shall I do?
```

```
Let her go, go, go,
    Bb 7
Let her go, go, go,
                         Eb
Let her go on that raging canal.
```

```
Now she's gone, gone, gone,
    Bb 7
Now she's gone, gone, gone,
                         Eb
Now she's gone on that raging canal.
```


Turn The Glasses Over

```
G
I've been to Haarlem, I've been to Dover,

I've traveled this wide world all over,
          C       G
Over, over, three times over,
                                  D7    G
Drink up all the brandy wine and turn the glasses over.
                                Em    A7D7
Sailing east, sailing west, sailing over the ocean,
                            C          G
Oh you better watch out when the boat begins to rock,
                    D7G
Or you'll lose your girl in the ocean.
```

Little Brass Wagon

C
Ride her up and down in your little brass wagon,
G
Ride her up and down in your little brass wagon,
C
Ride her up and down in your little brass wagon,
G   C
Fare you well, my darling.

Chorus:

C
Round and round in your little brass wagon,
G
Round and round in your little brass wagon,
C
Round and round in your little brass wagon,
G   C
Fare you well, my darling.

One wheel's off and the axle's dragging, (3 times)
Fare you well, my darling.

Two wheels off and the axle's dragging,
Sure is dragging, with two wheels off,
Two wheels off and the axle's dragging,
Fare you well, my darling.

Hush your mouth and stop your bragging, (3 times)
Fare you well, my darling.

'Cause you'll fall out of the little brass wagon,
You'll fall out of the little brass wagon, (2 times)
Look out, my darling.

Final Chorus:
Round and round in your little brass wagon,
Round the other way so you won't get dizzy,
Round and round in your little brass wagon,
Fare you well, my darling.

Shoo Fly, Don't Bother Me

F   C7
Shoo, fly, don't bother me!
             F
Shoo, fly, don't bother me!
             C7
Shoo, fly, don't bother me,
        F
I belong to somebody.

F   C7
I feel, I feel, I feel like a morning star,
                  F
I feel, I feel, I feel like a morning star.

Rise And Shine

C   F
Rise and shine and give God the glory, glory,
C   F
Rise and shine and give God the glory, glory,
C   F   C
Rise and shine and give God the glory, glory,
      G7   C
Children of the Lord.

God said to Noah, there's going to be a flood-y,
    flood-y, (twice)
Get your children out of the mud-y, mud-y,
Children of the Lord.

God said to Noah to build him an ark-y, ark-y, (twice)
Build it out of hickory bark-y, bark-y,
Children of the Lord.

The animals they came in, they came in by twos-y,
    twos-y, (twice)
Elephants and kangaroos-y, roos-y,
Children of the Lord.

It rained and rained for forty days-y, days-y, (twice)
Drove those counselors nearly crazy, crazy,
Children of the Lord.

Buckeye Jim

C
Way up yonder in the sky,
            Am
A bluebird lived in a jaybird's eye,

Refrain:

C   G7 C
Buckeye Jim, you can't go,
               Am
Go weave and spin, you can't go,
G7   C
Buckeye Jim.

Way up yonder in the moon,
A jaybird rests in a silver spoon,

Way down yonder in a hollow log,
A red bird danced with a green bullfrog,

Way down yonder in a wooden trough,
On old woman died of the whooping cough,

Way up yonder on a shootin' star,
A bullfrog jumped, but he jumped too far,

Bluebird, Bluebird, Fly Through My Window

E
Bluebird, bluebird, fly through my window,
B7   E
Bluebird, bluebird, fly through my window,

Bluebird, bluebird, fly through my window,
  B7   E
And buy molasses candy.
  B7   E   B7
Go through my window, my sugar lump,
           E
Go through my window, my sugar lump,
  B7   E
And buy molasses candy.

Little bird, little bird, go through my window, etc.
Fly through my window, my sugar lump, etc.

Skip To My Lou

D
Lost my partner what'll I do,
A7
Lost my partner what'll I do,
D
Lost my partner what'll I do,
A7   D
Skip to my Lou my darling.

Chorus:

D
Gone again, skip to my Lou,
A7
Gone again, skip to my Lou,
D
Gone again, skip to my Lou,
A7   D
Skip to my Lou my darling.

I'll get another one prettier than you (3 times)
Skip to my Lou my darling.

Little red wagon painted blue, etc.

Flies in the buttermilk two by two, etc.

Flies in the sugar bowl shoo shoo shoo, etc.

Going to Texas two by two, etc.

Cat's in the cream jar what'll I do?, etc.

Alouette
France

G   D7   G
Alouette, gentille Alouette
         D7   G
Alouette, je te plumerai.

Je te plumerai la tête,
D7   G
Je te plumerai la tête;
              D7
Et la tête, et la tête, Oh. . .

Et le bec (et le bec),
Et la tête (et la tête, Oh, etc.)

Le nez

Le dos

Les jambes

Les pieds

Les pattes

Le cou

Old MacDonald Had A Farm

F   Bb F
Old MacDonald had a farm,
G   C   F
E - I, E - I, Oh!
                 Bb   F
And on this farm he had some chicks,
G7 C7 F
E - I, E - I, Oh!

With a chick chick here

And a chick chick there,
Bb
Here a chick, there a chick,
F   Gm
Everywhere a chick chick,
F   Bb F
Old MacDonald had a farm,
G7 C7 F
E - I, E - I, Oh!

Ducks—quack, quack

Dogs—bow, wow

Cows—moo, moo

Pigs—oink, oink.

Etc.

Sur Le Pont D'Avignon
(On The Bridge At Avignon)
France

Refrain:

```
G        D7
Sur le pont d'Avignon,
G          D7
L'on y danse, l'on y danse,
G          D7
Sur le pont d'Avignon,
G        D7   G
L'on y danse tout en rond!

G                  D7   G
Les beaux messieurs font comm' çi,
        D7    G
Et puis encor' comm' ça.
```

Les belles dam's font comm' çi,
Et puis encor' comm' ça.

Les militair's font comm' çi,
Et puis encor' comm' ça.

Singable Translation:

On the bridge at Avignon,
See them dancing, see them dancing,
On the bridge at Avignon,
See them dancing round and round!

Gentlemen bow this way,
Then again bow that way.

Ladies all bow this way,
Then again bow that way.

Soldiers, they bow this way,
Then again bow that way.

The Noble Duke of York

```
D7    G
Oh, the noble duke of York,
   D
He had ten thousand men,
   G            C      Am7
He marched them up to the top of the hill,
      Bm      D7   G
And he marched them down again.
```

Oh, when you're up, you're up,
And when you're down, you're down,
But when you're only halfway up,
You're neither up nor down.

This Old Man

```
C
This old man, he played one,
F              G
He played knick-knack on my thumb,
      C
With a knick-knack, paddy wack,

Give the dog a bone,
G7              C
This old man came rolling home.
```

This old man, he played two,
He played knick-knack on my shoe, etc.

This old man, he played three,
He played knick-knack on my knee, etc.

This old man, he played four,
He played knick-knack on my door, etc.

This old man, he played five,
He played knick-knack on my hive, etc.

This old man, he played six,
He played knick-knack on my sticks, etc.

This old man, he played seven,
He played knick-knack up in heaven, etc.

This old man, he played eight,
He played knick-knack on my gate, etc.

This old man, he played nine,
He played knick-knack on my vine, etc.

This old man, he played ten,
He played knick-knack all over again, etc.

Bingo

```
   G        C    D
There was a farmer had a dog,
     G      D    G
And Bingo was his name, sir.
Em     Am
B - I - N - G - O,
D      G
B - I - N - G - O,
C      Am
B - I - N - G - O,
D7        C     G
Bingo was his name, sir.
```

That farmer's dog's at our back door,
Begging for a bone, sir.
B-I-N-G-O, B-I-N-G-O,
B-I-N-G-O,
Bingo was his name, sir.

The Green Grass Grew All Around

(Cumulative Song)

```
        G           D7
Oh, there was once a tree,
      G           D7
A pretty little tree,
        G           D7
The prettiest little tree
          G           D7
That you ever did see.
        G       D7      G       D7
Oh, the tree in a hole and the hole in the ground,
        G       D7      G
And the green grass grew all around, all around,
      D7              G
The green grass grew all around.
```

Now on this tree, there was a limb,
The prettiest little limb
That you ever did see.
The limb on the tree and the tree in a hole
And the hole in the ground,
And the green grass grew all around, all around,
And the green grass grew all around.

Now on this limb, there was a branch, etc.

On this branch there was a bough, etc.

On this bough there was a twig, etc.

On this twig there was a leaf, etc.

On this leaf there was a nest, etc.

In this nest there was a bird, etc.

On this bird there was a feather, etc.

On this feather there was a flea, etc.

Free Little Bird

```
      C
I'm as free a little bird as I can be,
                              G7
I'm as free a little bird as I can be,
      C               F
I'm as free at my age as a birdie in the cage,
      G7              C
I'm as free a little bird as I can be.
```

Carry me home, little birdie, carry me home (twice)
Carry me home to my wife, she's the joy of my life
Carry me home, little birdie, carry me home.

I'll never build my nest on the ground
Neither in the forks of a tree
I'll build my nest in the ruffle of her dress
Where the bad boys can never bother me.

Paw-Paw Patch

```
D
Where oh where is little Susie?
A7
Where oh where is little Susie?
D
Where oh where is little Susie?
A7              D
Way down yonder in the paw-paw patch.
```

Come on, boys, let's go find her, (3 times)
Way down yonder in the paw paw patch.

Picking up paw-paws, put 'em in your pocket, (3 times)
Way down yonder in the paw-paw patch.

Continue with other names

Going To Boston

```
D               G
Goodby girls, I'm goin' to Boston,
A7              D
Goodby girls, I'm goin' to Boston,
                G
Goodby girls, I'm goin' to Boston,
A7      D
Early in the morning.
```

Chorus:

```
Won't we look pretty in the ballroom?
C                       Am
Won't we look pretty in the ballroom?
D
Won't we look pretty in the ballroom?
A7      D
Early in the morning.
```

Saddle up, girls, and let's go with 'em, (3 times)
Early in the morning.

Out of the way, you'll get run over (3 times)
Early in the morning.

Rights and lefts will make it better, etc.

Swing your partner all the way to Boston, etc.

Johnny, Johnny, gonna tell your Pappy, etc.

Little Sally Walker

G
Little Sally Walker, sitting in a saucer,
                           C   G
Weeping and a-moaning like a turtle dove.

Rise, Sally, rise, wipe your weeping eyes,

Fly to the east, fly to the west,
                 D7
Fly to the one that you love the best.

Repeat, substituting names of other children.

Jane, Jane

Em
Hey, hey Jane, Jane,
My Lordy, Lord, Jane, Jane,
I'm a gonna buy, Jane, Jane,
Three mocking birds; Jane, Jane,
One a-for to whistle, Jane, Jane
One a-for to sing, Jane, Jane
One a-for to do, Jane, Jane
Most any little thing, Jane, Jane.

Hey, he-ey,
My Lordy, Lord,
I'm a-gonna buy,
Three hunting dogs,
One for to run,
One for to shout,
One to talk to,
When I go out.

Hey, he-ey,
My Lordy, Lord,
I'm a-gonna buy,
Three muley cows,
One a-for to milk,
One to plough my corn,
One for to pray,
On Christmas morn.

Hey, hey-ey,
My Lordy, Lord,
I'm a-gonna buy,
Three little blue birds,
One a-for to weep,
One for to mourn,
One for to grieve,
When I am gone.

One More River To Cross

     F
Old Noah he built himself an ark,
  C7   F
There's one more river to cross.

He built it out of hickory bark,
  C7   F
Oh, one more river to cross.

Chorus:

                        C7   F
There's one more river, and that's the river Jordan,
                   C7   F
There's one more river, just one more river to cross.

He anchored the ark to a great big rock,
There's one more river to cross,
And then he began to load his stock,
Oh, one more river to cross.

The animals went in one by one, etc.
The Elephant chewing a carroway bun, etc.

The animals went in two by two,
The Crocodile and the Kangaroo,

The animals went in three by three,
The tall Giraffe and the tiny Flea,

The animals went in four by four,
The Hippopotamus stuck in the door,

The animals went in five by five,
The Bees mistook the Bear for a hive,

The animals went in six by six,
The Monkey was up to his usual tricks,

The animals went in sev'n by sev'n,
Said the Ant to the Elephant: "Who're ye shovin'?"

The animals went in eight by eight,
Some were early and some were late,

The animals went in nine by nine,
They all formed fours and marched in line,

The animals went in ten by ten,
If you want any more I will sing it again,

ANIMAL FAIR

Songs of birds, beasts, bugs,
big and little fishes....

Mole In The Ground

A
I wish't I was a mole in the ground;
           E7
I wish't I was a mole in the ground;
 A
If I was a mole in the ground,

I would root that mountain down,
      E7   A
If I was a mole in the ground.

Well, I wish't I was a lizard in the tree; (twice)
If I was a lizard in that tree,
I would have you there with me;
I wish't I was a lizard in the tree.

Well, I wish't I was a turtle in that pond; (twice)
Well, if I was a turtle in that pond,
I would stay there all day long;
I wish't I was a turtle in that pond.

I wish't I was a mole in the ground; (twice)
If I was a mole in the ground,
I would root that mountain down;
If I was a mole in the ground.

Muskrat

G
Muskrat, oh, muskrat,

What makes you smell so bad?

I've been in the bottom all my life
      C   G
Till I'm mortified in my head, head,
      C   G
Till I'm mortified in my head.

Rattlesnake, oh, rattlesnake,
What makes your teeth so white?
I've been in the bottom all my life
And I ain't done nothin' but bite, bite, etc.

Groundhog, oh, groundhog,
What makes your back so brown?
It's a wonder I don't smotherfy,
Livin' down in the ground, ground, etc.

Rooster, oh, rooster,
What makes your claws so hard?
Been scratchin' this gravel all my days,
It's a wonder I ain't tired, etc.

Jaybird, oh, jaybird,
What makes you fly so high?
Been robbin' your cornpatch all my life,
It's a wonder I don't die, die, etc.

Little Brown Dog

  Dm   Am
I buyed me a little dog,
   Dm   C
Its color it was brown,
   Dm   Am
I learned him to whistle,
Dm   C
Sing, dance and run.
    C7   F
His legs they were fourteen yards long,
    C7   F
His ears they were broad.
    C7   F
Around the world in half a day,
        Dm   Am
And on him I could ride.
Dm Bb   C
Sing taddle-o-day.

I buyed me a little bull,
About four inches high,
Everybody feared him
That ever heard him cry,
When he begin to bellow,
It made such melodious sound,
Till all the walls from London
Came a-tumbling to the ground.
Sing taddle-o-day.

I buyed me a flock of sheep,
I thought they were all wethers,
Sometimes they yielded wool,
Sometimes they yielded feathers.
I think mine are the best of sheep
For yielding me increase,
For every full and change of the moon
They bring both lambs and geese.
Sing taddle-o-day.

I buyed me a little box
About four acres square,
I filled it with guinea
And silver so fair.
Oh, now I'm bound for Turkey,
I'll travel like an ox,
In my breeches pocket
I'll carry my little box.
Sing taddle-o-day.

I buyed me a little hen,
All speckled, gay and fair;
I sat her on an oyster shell,
She hatched me out a hair,
The hair it sprang a handsome horse,
Full fifteen hands-full high,
And him that tells a bigger tale
Would have to tell a lie.
Sing taddle-o-day.

Stewball

    E
Stewball was a good horse,
       A
And he held a high head,
      B7
And the mane on his fore-top
    E
Was fine as silk thread.

I rode him in England,
I rode him in Spain,
And I never did lose boys,
I always did gain.

So come all of you gamblers,
From near and from far,
Don't bet your gold dollar
On that little gray mare.

Most likely she'll stumble,
Most likely she'll fall,
But you never will lose
On my noble Stewball.

Sit tight in your saddle,
Let slack on your rein,
And you never will lose boys,
You always will gain.

As they were riding
'Bout half way 'round,
That gray mare she stumbled
And fell to the ground.

And away out yonder,
Ahead of them all,
Come dancing and prancing
My noble Stewball.

Stewball was a good horse,
And he held a high head,
And the mane on his foretop
Was fine as silk thread.

I rode him in England,
And I rode him in Spain,
And I never did lose boys,
I always did gain.

Old Rattler

C
Rattler was a good old dog,
        G7
As blind as he could be.

But every night at suppertime,
         C
I believe that dog could see.

Chorus:

C
Here, Rattler, here,
       G7
Here, Rattler, here,

Call old Rattler from the barn,
        C
Here, Rattler, here.

Rattler barked the other night,
I thought he treed a coon,
When I come to find him,
He's barkin' at the moon.

Rattler was a friendly dog,
Even though he was blind.
He wouldn't hurt a living thing,
He was so very kind.

One night I saw a big fat coon,
Climb into a tree.
I called Ol' Rattler right away,
To fetch him down for me.

But Rattler wouldn't fetch for me,
Because he liked that coon.
I saw them walkin' paw in paw,
Later by the light of the moon.

Grandpa had a muley cow,
Muley since she was born,
It took a jaybird forty years,
To fly from horn to horn.

Now old Rattler's dead and gone,
Like all the good dogs do.
Don't put on the dog yourself,
Or you'll be goin' there too.

Old Blue

       C
Well, I had an old dog and his name was Blue;
                    G7   C
I had an old dog and his name was Blue;

Well, I had an old dog and his name was Blue;
               G7   C
My old Blue was a good dog too.

Refrain:

                  G7   C
Singin' ya old Blue, you good dog you.

Well, old Blue's feet was big and round (3 times)
He never 'lowed a possum to touch ground.

I'll take my axe and I'll take my horn
And I'll get me a possum in the new round courn.
Well old Blue barked and I went to see
And Blue had a possum up in a tree.

Well the possum crawled out on a limb
Blue barked at the possum, possum growled at him.
Well he treed a possum in a hollow log
You could tell from that he was a good old dog.

Well Blue, what makes your eyes so red (3 times)
You run that possum 'til you're almost dead.

Well when old Blue died he died so hard
He shook the ground in my back yard
I dug his grave with a silver spade
And lowered him down with a golden chain.

Now every time I hear Blue bark (3 times)
He's treeing possums in Noah's ark

Well I'm gonna tell you so you know (3 times)
That old Blue's gone where the good dogs go.

Well there's only one thing that troubles my mind
Blue's gone to heaven left me behind.

The Old Cow Died

Refrain:

  Am
The old cow died, sail a-round,

The old cow died, sail a-round,

The old cow died, sail a-round,

The old cow died, sail a-round.

Verses:

           Em   Am   Em
"Did you give her hot water?" "Yes, ma'am."
                       Am   Em
"Did you give her any soda?" "Yes, ma'am."

"Did you send for the doctor?" "Yes, ma'am."
"Did the doctor come?" "Yes, ma'am."

"What'n the world's ailed her?" "Yes, ma'am."
"Did she die of the cholera?" "Yes, ma'am."

"Did the buzzards come?" "Yes, ma'am."
"Did the buzzards eat her?" "Yes, ma'am."

"Did they sail high?" "Yes, ma'am."
"Did they sail low?" "Yes, ma'am."

Old Dog Tray

Stephen Foster

        G   D7
The morn of life is past,
                       G
And evening comes at last,
              D7   G   D7
It brings me a dream of a once happy day,
     G D7
Of merry form 've seen
                 G·
Upon the village reen,
Am   G D7 G
Sporting with my old dog Tray.

Chorus:

D7   G
Old dog Tray's ever faithful,
D7   G
Grief cannot drive him away,
         D7
He's gentle, he is kind,
          G
I'll never never find
G7 C   G D7 G
A better friend than old dog Tray.

The forms I called my own
Have vanished one by one,
The loved ones, the dear ones,
Have all passed away.
Their happy smiles have flown,
Their gentle voices gone,
I've nothing left but old dog Tray.

When thoughts recall the past,
His eyes are on me cast;
I know that he feels what my breaking heart would say.
Although he cannot speak,
I'll vainly, vainly seek
A better friend than old dog Tray.

Hoosen Johnny

     G   C   G
The little black bull came down the meadow,
D7   G   D7   G
Hoosen Johnny, Hoosen Johnny;
            C   G
The little black bull came down the meadow,
  D7 G
Long time ago.
      C   G   C   G
Long time ago, long time ago,
            C   G
The little black bull came down the meadow,
  D7 G
Long time ago.

First he'd paw and then he'd bellow,
Hoosen Johnny, Hoosen Johnny,
First he'd paw and then he'd bellow,
Long time ago.
Long time ago, long time ago,
First he'd paw and then he'd bellow,
Long time ago.

He whet his horn on a white oak sapling, etc.

He shake his tail, he jar the river, etc.

He wink his eye at the little red heifer, etc.

He paw his dirt in the heifer's faces, etc.

Leatherwing Bat

Am   G
"Hi," said the little leatherwing bat,
Am   C
"I'll tell you the reason that,
             Am
The reason that I fly by night,
     E7   Am
I have lost my heart's delight."

Chorus:

Am   G
Li li low, and a diddle um-a-day,
Am   C
Li li low, and a diddle um-a-day,
            Am
Li li low, and a diddle um-a-day
   E7   Am
Hey lee lee, and lye li lo.

"Hi," said the little mourning dove,
"I'll tell you how to regain your love,
Court her night, court her day,
Never give her time to say you nay."

"Hi," said the owl with head so white,
"Another day and a lonesome night,
Thought I heard a pretty girl say
She'd court all night and sleep all day."

"Hey," said the redbird, sitting on a chair,
"Once I courted a lady fair,
She got saucy and then she fled,
Ever since then my head's been red."

"Hi," said the blackbird, sitting on a bench,
"Once I courted a handsome wench,
She got fickle and turned her back,
Ever since then I've dressed in black."

"Hi," said the bluebird as he flew,
"If I were a young man I would have two,
If one got saucy and wanted to go,
I'd have a new string to my bow."

"Hi," said the jaybird sitting in a tree,
"When I was a young man I had three,
Two got saucy and took to flight,
The one that's left don't treat me right."

Little Birdie

C   G
Little Birdie, Little Birdie,
              C
What makes you fly so high?
            G
It's because I am a true little bird
            C
And I do not fear to die.

Little birdie, little birdie,
What makes your wing so blue?
It's because I've been a-grievin',
Grievin' after you.

Little birdie, little birdie,
What makes your head so red?
Well, after all that I been through,
It's a wonder I ain't dead.

Little birdie, little birdie,
Come sing to me a song.
I've a short while to be here,
And a long time to be gone.

Tam Pierce

```
      G                D7          G
Tam Pierce, Tam Pierce, lend me your gray mare,
                 D7
All along down along out along lea.
G         D7          Em
Us wants to go to Widdecombe Fair,
```

Bill Brewer, Jan Stewer, Peter Gurney, Peter Davey,

```
Daniel Whiddon, Harry Hawk,
      D7
   Old Uncle Tom Cobbley and all,
     G      D7      G
Old Uncle Tom Cobbley and all.
```

When shall I see again my gray mare?
All along down along out along lea.
By Friday noon or Saturday soon,
With Bill Brewer, etc.

Then Friday came and Saturday soon, etc.
And Tam's old mare she ne'er did come home., etc.

So Tam he went to the top of the hill,
And seed his old mare a-making her will.

So Tam Pierce's old mare, she took sick and died,
And Tam he sat down on a stone and he cried.

When the wind whistles cold on the moors at night,
Tam's old gray mare doth appear ghastly white.

And all the night long be heard skirling and groans,
From Tam's old gray mare and her rattling bones.

The Old Gray Mare

```
          G          D G
Oh, the old gray mare, she ain't what she used to be,
D7                    G
Ain't what she used to be, ain't what she used to be,
                   D G
The old gray mare, she ain't what she used to be,
A7      D7    G
Many long years ago.
           C   G        D7  G
Many long years ago, many long years ago,
                 D  G
The old gray mare, she ain't what she used to be,
A7      D7    G
Many long years ago.
```

The old gray mare, she kicked on the whiffletree,
Kicked on the whiffletree, kicked on the whiffletree,
The old gray mare, she kicked on the whiffletree,
Many long years ago.
Many long years ago, many long years ago,
The old gray mare, she ain't what she used to be,
Many long years ago.

Raccoon's Got A Bushy Tail

```
E
Raccoon's got a bushy tail,

Possum tail goes bare,
E          A
Rabbit's got no tail at all,
      B7       E
Just a little old bunch of hair.
```

I met that raccoon in the road,
Raccoon, where you goin'?
Look out, man, don't bother me,
I'm huntin' muscadine.

I met that rabbit in the road,
Rabbit where you goin'?
Look out, man, don't bother me,
The old grey hound's behind.

Possum's in the gum stump,
Coonie's in the holler;
Rabbit's in the 'tater patch
As fat as he can wallow.

Raccoon and the possum
Racking cross the prairie,
Raccoon asked the possum,
Well, does she want to marry?

Miss Rabbit she's a gay young gal
Sitting under the moon,
Something bound to happen
If the preacher doesn't come soon.

There's a thousand verses to this song,
I hope I've sung 'em well,
Before I sing 'em all again
I'd see you all in hell.

The Boothbay Whale

    C
It was way up north in Boothbay Harbor
               G7
Where the water's always cold,

The fisher folk are a clever lot,
          C
Or so I have been told.

Chorus:

G7   C
Blow hi for his big black head,
      F   C
Blow low for his big black tail,

Now step right up and take a little swig
           G7   C
And you'll soon see a Boothbay whale.

They catch their pollack, cod and Cusk
By the mouth, the fin or the tail.
One day they got a heck of a jolt,
When into the bay swam a whale.

Says Captain Pete, "I've harpooned tuna,
And caught them with my rig,
But I can't gettin' near no eighty-foot whale,
That fish is too darned big!"

Well, Skipper Jake was a ready man,
Though he had a wooden leg.
Says he, "I think I'll catch that whale;
Let me have that old rum keg."

Well, he stood on the bow of the Nancy U.
And followed that whale for a ride,
And when that whale she surfaced and blowed,
He steered her to starboard side.

The whale blowed steam from his big spout hole
While Jake took a slug from his keg;
And before he could dive, Jake jumped on his back
Hangin' on with his one good leg.

Well, Jake took his keg and used it like a plug,
Pushed it tight in the old whale's spout.
He kicked it hard, then jumped on board,
Saying', "Boys, it will never come out."

Well, the whale he blew, he puffed, he heaved,
And the boys all gave a shout;
And the very next time he rose to blow
He blew his brains right out.

You bold seafarin' whalermen,
You've wasted all these years,
With race boats, harpoons, ropes and hooks,
And all that other gear.

All you need is a big old plug
Next time you see him spout,
Just kick it in, sit back and rest,
While he blows his brains right out.

If you ever meet a fisherman from Boothbay, Maine,
And you want to hear a dreadful tale,
Well, step right up and offer him a keg,
And learn how to catch a Boothbay whale.

The Bulldog on the Bank

           G   D7
Oh, the bulldog on the bank, and the bullfrog in the pool,
                                      G
The bulldog on the bank, and the bullfrog in the pool,
                                    C
Oh, the bulldog on the bank, and the bullfrog in the pool.
    G   D7   G
The bulldog called the bullfrog a green old water fool.

Chorus:

G
Singing tra la la la la la,
       D7   G
Singing tra la la la la la la,
                    C
Singing tra la la, singing tra la la,
G   D7   G
Tra la la la, tra la la la, tra la la la la.

Oh, the bulldog stopped to catch him,
    and the snapper caught his paw, (3 times)
The pollywog died a-laughing, to see him wag his jaw.

Says the monkey to the owl,
    "Oh, what'll you have to drink?" (3 times)
"Since you are so very kind, I'll take a bottle of ink."

Pharoh's daughter on the bank,
    little Moses in the pool; (3 times)
She fished him out with a ten-foot pole
    and sent him off to school.

The Cat Came Back

```
Em          D        C         B7
Old Mister Johnson had troubles of his own,
    Em        D          C        B7
He had a yellow cat which wouldn't leave its home;
   Em        D        C       B7
He tried and he tried to give the cat away,
    Em      D         C      B7
He gave it to a man going far, far away.
```

Chorus:

```
        Em     D      C       B7
But the cat came back the very next day,
        Em       D         C         B7
The cat came back, they thought he was a goner;
        Em       D      C        B7   Em
But the cat came back, it just couldn't stay away.
```

The man around the corner swore
    he'd kill the cat on sight,
He loaded up his shotgun with nails and dynamite;
He waited and he waited for the cat to come around,
Ninety-seven pieces of the man is all they found.

He gave it to a little boy with a dollar note,
Told him for to take it up the river in a boat;
They tied a rope around it's neck,
    it must have weighed a pound,
Now they drag the river for a little boy that's drowned.

He gave it to a man going up in a balloon,
He told him for to take it to the man in the moon;
The balloon came down about ninety miles away,
Where he is now, well, I dare not say.

He gave it to a man going way out west,
Told him for to take it to the one he loved the best;
First the train hit the curve, then it jumped the rail,
Not a soul was left behind to tell the gruesome tale.

The cat it had some company one night out in the yard,
Someone threw a boot-jack,
    and they threw it mighty hard;
It caught the cat behind the ear,
    she thought it rather slight,
When along came a brick-bat and
    knocked the cat out of sight.

Away across the ocean they did send the cat at last,
Vessel only out a day and making water fast;
People all began to pray, the boat began to toss,
A great big gust of wind came by and every soul was lost.

On a telegraph wire, sparrows sitting in a bunch,
The cat was feeling hungry,
    thought she'd like 'em for a lunch;
Climbing softly up the pole, and when she reached the top,
Put her foot upon the electric wire,
    which tied her in a knot.

The cat was a possessor of a family of its own,
With seven little kittens, till there came a cyclone;
Blew the houses all apart and tossed the cat around,
The air was full of kittens, and not a one was ever found.

The atom bomb fell just the other day,
The H-Bomb fell in the very same way;
Russia went, England went, and then the U.S.A.,
The human race was finished without a chance to pray.

The Chivalrous Shark

```
          G                  D7
The most chivalrous fish of the ocean
              G
To ladies forebearing and mild
          C
Though his record be dark
          G
Is the man-eating shark
          D7                 G
Who will eat neither woman nor child.
```

He dines upon seamen and skippers,
And tourists his hunger assuage,
And a fresh cabin boy
Will inspire him with joy
If he's past the maturity age.

A doctor, a lawyer, a preacher,
He'll gobble one any fine day
But the ladies, God bless 'em,
He'll only address 'em
Politely and go on his way.

I can readily cite you an instance
Where a lovely young lady of Breem,
Who was tender and sweet
And delicious to eat,
Fell into the bay with a scream.

She struggled and flounced in the water
And signaled in vain for her bark,
And she'd surely been drowned
If she hadn't been found
By a chivalrous man-eating shark.

He bowed in a manner most polished,
Thus soothing her impulses wild;
Don't be frightened," he said,
"I've been properly bred
And will eat neither woman nor child."

Then he proffered his fin and she took it—
Such a gallantry none can dispute—
While the passengers cheered as the
Vessel they neared
And a broadside was fired in salute.

And they stood alongside the vessel,
When a life-saving dinghy was lowered
With the pick of the crew,
And her relatives, too
And the mate and the skipper aboard.

So they took her aboard in a jiffy,
And the shark stood at attention the while,
Then he raised on his flipper
And ate up the skipper
And went on his way with a smile.

And this shows that the prince of the ocean,
To ladies forebearing and mild,
Though his record be dark,
He's the man-eating shark
Who will eat neither woman nor child.

The Squirrel

D
Squirrel he's a funny little thing,
   A7
Carries a bushy tail;
D
Steals away the farmer's corn
   G D
And he hides it on the rail,
   G A7
And he hides it on the rail.

Partridge she's a pretty little thing,
Carries a speckled breast;
Steals away the farmer's corn
And she carries it to her nest. (twice)

Possum he's a cunning little thing,
Travels after dark;
Ain't afraid of any old thing
Till he hears old rattler bark. (twice)

Raccoon's tail is ringed all around,
Possum's tail is bare,
Rabbit ain't got no tail at all,
Just a little wee bunch of hair. (twice)

The Fox

 D
The fox went out on a chilly night,
     A7
Prayed for the moon to give him light,
  D   G
For he'd many a mile to go that night,
 D A7   D
Before he reached the town-o
A7 D
Town-o, town-o
  G   D
He'd many a mile to go that night,
 A7   D
Before he reached the town-o.

He ran till he came to a great big bin
The ducks and the geese were put therein,
Said, a couple of you will grease my chin
Before I leave this town-o, etc.

He grabbed the grey goose by the neck
Slung the little one over his back,
He didn't mind their quack-quack-quack
And the legs all dangling down-o, etc.

Old mother pitter-patter jumped out of bed
Out of the window she cocked her head
Crying, John, John, the grey goose is gone
And the fox is on the town-o, etc.

John, he went to the top of the hill
Blew his horn both loud and shrill;
The fox, he said, I better flee with my kill
He'll soon be on my trail-o, etc.

He ran till he came to his cozy den
There were the little ones, eight, nine, ten,
They said daddy, you better go back again,
'Cause it must be a mighty fine town-o, etc.

Then the fox and his wife without any strife
Cut up the goose with fork and knife,
They never had such a supper in their life
And the little ones chewed on the bones-o, etc.

Groundhog

```
E          D      E
Whet up your axe and whistle up your dog,
         A        B7
Whet up your axe and whistle up your dog,
     E   B7    E      B7
We're off to the woods, to hunt ground hog,
```

Refrain:

```
E
Ground hog.
```
Old Joe Digger, Sam and Dave (twice)
Went a-hog hunting as hard as they could stave,
Groundhog.

Too many rocks, too many logs,
Too many rocks to hunt groundhogs.

He's in here, boys, the hole's wore slick,
Run here, Sam, with your forked stick.

Stand back, boys, let's be wise,
I think I see his beaded eyes.

Yonder comes Sam with a ten-foot pole,
To roust that groundhog out of his hole.

Grab him by the tail and pull him out,
Great God Almighty, ain't a groundhog stout?

Here he comes all in a whirl,
He's the biggest groundhog in this world.

Work, boys, work, hard as you can tear,
The meat'll do to eat and the hide'll do to tear.

Skin him out and tan his hide,
Best durn shoestrings ever I tried.

I love my groundhog stewed and fried,
Little plate of soup a-sittin' by the side.

The children screamed, the children cried,
They love that groundhog cooked and fried.

Up stepped Sal with a snigger and a grin,
Groundhog grease all over her chin.

Hello, Mamma, make Sam quit,
He's eatin' all the hog and don't leave me a bit.

Hello, boys, ain't it a sin,
Watch that gravy run down Sam's chin.

Watch him, boys, he's about to fall,
He's et 'til his pants won't button at all.

Grizzly Bear

```
       Dm
I'm gonna tell you a story 'bout grizzly bear,

Jack o'Diamonds wasn't nothin but grizzly bear,

Oh, the grizzly, grizzly grizzly bear,

Oh, the grizzly, grizzly, grizzly bear.
```

He had great long tushes like a, etc.
He made a track in the bottom like a, etc.
Well, that grizly, grizzly, etc.
Oh, that grizzly, grizzly, etc.
Tell me, who was the grizzly, etc.
Tell, a-who was the grizzly, etc.
Jack o'Diamonds was the grizzly, etc. (twice)
He made a noise in the bottom like a, etc. (twice)
Well, my mama was scared of that, etc. (twice)
Well, my papa went a-hunting for the, etc. (twice)
Well, my brother wasn't scared of that, etc. (twice)
Oh, the grizzly, grizzly, etc. (twice)
Well-a, I'm gonna kill that, etc. (twice)
Well, the grizzly, grizzly, etc.
Oh, that grizzly, grizzly, etc.
Well, I looked in Louisiana for the, etc. (twice)
Well, the grizzly, grizzly, etc.
Well, that grizzly, grizzly, etc.
I'm gonna tell you a story 'bout the, etc.
Jack o'Diamonds wasn't nothing but, etc.
He come a-huffing and a-blowing like, etc.
He had great long tushes like, etc.
He come a-wobbling and a-squabbling like, etc.
And Jack o'Diamonds was the great big, etc.
He was a great big grizzly, etc.
He was the great big grizzly, etc.
Everybody was scared of that, etc. (twice)
Oh, the grizzly, grizzly, etc.
Oh, the grizzly, the grizzly, etc.
Jack o'Diamonds was the great big, etc.
He come a-wobbling and a-squabbling like, etc.
He come a-huffing and a-blowing like, etc.
He come a-walking and a-talking like, etc.
He had great long tushes like, etc.
He had big blue eyes like, etc.
He had great long hair like, etc.
Oh, the grizzly, grizzly, etc. (twice)
I'm gonna tell you people 'bout, etc.
I'm gonna warn you and gonna tell you 'bout, etc.
You better watch that grizzly, etc.
You better watch that grizzly, etc.
Well, the bear's gonna get you now, etc.
Oh, the grizzly, grizzly, etc.
Oh, the great big grizzly, etc.

Froggie Went A-Courtin'

D
Froggie went a-courtin' and he did ride, a-huh, a-huh,
                                             G   D
Froggie went a-courtin' and he did ride,
              A7   D
Sword and pistol by his side, a-huh, a-huh.

Well, he rode down to Miss Mouse's door, a-huh, a-huh,
Well, he rode down to Miss Mouse's door,
Where he had often been before, a-huh, a-huh.

He took Miss Mousie on his knee, a-huh, a-huh,
He took Miss Mousie on his knee,
Said, "Miss Mousie will you marry me?" A-huh, a-huh.

"I'll have to ask my Uncle Rat, etc.
See what he will say to that.", etc.

"Without my Uncle Rat's consent,
I would not marry the President."

Well, Uncle Rat laughed and shook his fat sides,
To think his niece would be a bride.

Well, Uncle Rat rode off to town
To buy his niece a wedding gown.

"Where will the wedding supper be?"
"Way down yonder in a hollow tree."

"What will the wedding supper be?"
"A fried mosquito and a roasted flea."

First to come in were two little ants,
Fixing around to have a dance.

Next to come in was a bumble bee,
Bouncing a fiddle on his knee.

Next to come in was a fat sassy lad,
Thinks himself as big as his dad.

Thinks himself a man indeed,
Because he chews the tobacco weed.

And next to come in was a big tomcat,
He swallowed the frog and the mouse and the rat.

Next to come in was a big old snake,
He chased the party into the lake.

The Gray Goose

        D
Well last Monday morning,
A
Lord, Lord, Lord,

Well last Monday morning,
          D
Lord, Lord, Lord.

My daddy went a-huntin', Lord, Lord, Lord (twice)

Well along come a grey goose, Lord . . . etc.

Throwed the gun to his shoulder, etc.

Well, he pulled on the trigger, etc.

He was six weeks a-fallin', etc.

He was six weeks a-findin', etc.

And we put him on the wagon, etc.

And we took him to the farmhouse, etc.

He was six weeks a-pickin', etc.

And we put him on to parboil, etc.

He was six months a-parboil, etc.

And we put him on the table, etc.

Now the forks couldn't stick him, etc.

And the knife couldn't cut him, etc.

And we throwed him in the hogpen, etc.

And he broke the sow's jawbone, etc.

And we took him to the sawmill, etc.

And he broke the saw's teeth out, etc.

And the last time I seed him, etc.

He was flyin' 'cross the ocean, etc.

With a long string of goslin's, etc.

And he's goin', "Quank, quink-quank," etc.

Aunt Rhody

D
Go tell Aunt Rhody,
A7   D
Go tell Aunt Rhody,

Go tell Aunt Rhody,
      G   A7   D
That the old gray goose is dead.

The one she's been saving (3 times)
To make a feather bed.

Old gander's weeping (3 times)
Because his wife is dead.

And the goslings are mourning (3 times)
Because their mother's dead.

She died in the mill-pond (3 times)
Standing on her head.

Bill Groggin's Goat

G
There was a man (there was a man),
           C
Now please take note (now please take note),
    D7
There was a man (there was a man)
     G
Who had a goat (who had a goat).

He loved that goat (he loved that goat),
         C
Indeed he did (indeed he did),
      D7
He loved that goat (he loved that goat)
      G
Just like a kid (just like a kid).

One day the goat, etc.
Felt frisk and fine, etc.
Ate three red shirts, etc.
Right off the line., etc.
The man, he grabbed, etc.
Him by the back, etc.
And tied him to, etc.
A railroad track., etc.

Now when that train, etc.
Hove into sight, etc.
That goat grew pale, etc.
And green with fright., etc.
He heaved a sigh, etc.
As if in pain, etc.
Coughed up the shirts, etc.
And flagged the train., etc.

The Darby Ram

    D
As I was going to Darby
        A7   D
Upon a market day,
   G   A
I saw the biggest ram, sir,
     G   A   D
That ever was fed on hay,
     G   A7   D
That ever was fed on hay.

The ram was fat behind, sir,
The ram was fat before.
He measured ten yards round, sir,
I think it was no more. (twice)

And he who knocked this ram down
Was drowned in the blood,
And he who held the dish, sir,
Was carried away by the flood. (twice)

The wool grew on his back, sir,
It reached to the sky.
And there the eagles built their nests,
I heard the young ones cry. (twice)

And all the boys in Darby, sir,
Came begging for his eyes,
To kick about the street, sir,
As any good football flies. (twice)

The wool grew on his belly, sir,
It reached to the ground.
It was sold in Darby Town, sir,
For forty thousand pound. (twice)

The wool upon his tail, sir,
Filled more than fifty bags.
You'd better keep away, sir,
When that tail shakes and wags. (twice)

The horns upon his head, sir,
As high as a man could reach,
And there they built a pulpit, sir,
The Quakers for to preach. (twice)

And one of this ram's teeth, sir,
Was hollow as a horn;
And when they took its measure, sir
It held a bushel of corn. (twice)

The mutton that the ram made
Gave the whole Army meat,
And what was left, I'm told, sir,
Was served out to the fleet. (twice)

The man who owned this ram, sir,
Was considered mighty rich,
But the man who told this story, sir,
Was a lyin' son of a ————. (twice)

Red Bird

Chorus:

A
Red bird soon in the morning,
E7   A
Red bird soon in the morning, } (twice)

Red bird, red bird soon in the morning,
             E7
Red bird, red bird soon in the morning. } (twice)

Verses:

       A
What's the matter with the red bird soon in the morning,
                            E7
What's the matter with the red bird soon in the morning,

Cat got the red bird soon in the morning, (4 times)

Hog got the red bird soon in the morning, (4 times)

The Sow Took The Measles

D
How do you think I began in the world?
 A7   D
I got me a sow and sev'ral other things.
D   A7   D
The sow took the measles and she died in the spring.

D
What do you think I made of her hide?
 A7   D
The very best saddle that you ever did ride.
               D
Saddle or bridle or any such thing.
                    A7   D
The sow took the measles and she died in the spring.

What do you think I made of her nose?
The very best thimble that ever sewed clothes,
Thimble or thread or any such thing.
The sow took the measles and she died in the spring.

What do you think I made of her tail?
The very best whup that ever sought sail.
Whup or whup socket, any such thing.
The sow took the measles and she died in the spring.

What do you think I made of her feet?
The very best pickles you ever did eat.
Pickles or glue or any such thing.
The sow took the measles and she died in the spring.

Billy Magee Magaw

    Em
There were three crows sat on a tree,
  G   D
Oh, Billy Magee Magaw;
    Em
There were three crows sat on a tree,
  G   B7
Oh, Billy Magee Magaw;
    G   D
There were three crows sat on a tree,
    Em   B7
And they were black as crows could be.

Chorus:

     G D   Em   B7
And they all flapped their wings and cried:
Em Am Em   Am   Em
"Caw, caw, caw! Billy Magee Magaw!"
     G D   Em   B7
And they all flapped their wings and cried:
Em Am Em
"Billy Magee Magaw!"

Said one crow unto his mate, etc.
"What shall we do for grub to ate?"

"There lies a horse on yonder plain, etc.
Who's by some cruel butcher slain.

We'll perch ourselves on his backbone, etc.
And pick his eyes out one by one.

The meat we'll eat before it's stale, etc.
Till naught remains but bones and tail."

HUSH LITTLE BABY

*Lullabies . . . work songs for mothers,
fathers and baby-sitters*

All The Pretty Little Horses

```
Am    Am7 Dm7
Hushabye,  don't  you  cry,
C      E7        Am
Go to sleepy, little baby.
          Am7 Dm
When you wake, you shall have
C      E7        Am
All the pretty little horses.
C            F
Blacks and bays, dapples and grays,
C      E7        Am
Coach and six a little horses.
```

Way down yonder in the meadow
There's a poor little lambie;
The bees and the butterflies pickin' out his eyes,
The poor little thing cried "Mammy."

Oyfn Pripetshuk
(On The Hearth)

Mark Warshawsky
Yiddish

```
Em            Am    B7 Em
Oyfn pripetshok brent a fayerl,
G       .    D7 G
Un in shtub iz heys;
Am            Em
Un der rebe lerent kleyne kinderlech
B7       Em E7
Dem alef beys;
Am            Em
Un der rebe lerent kleyne kinderlech
B7       Em
Dem alef beys.
```

Refrain:

```
B7                  Em
Zetshe kinderlech, gedenkt zhe tayere,
D7        G   E7
Vos it lerent do;
Am            Em
Zogt-she noch amol un take noch amol:
B7       E
Komets alef O.
```

Lernt kinder, mit groys cheyshek,
Azoy zog ich aych on;
Ver s'vet gicher fun aych kenen "Ivre,"
Der bakumt a fon.

Lernt kinder, hot nit moyre,
Yeder onhoyb iz shver;
Gliklech iz der vos lernt Toyre,
Tsi darf der mentsh noch mer?

Ir vet, kinder, elter vern,
Vet ir aleyn farshteyn,
Vifil in di oysyes lign trern,
Un vifil geveyn.

Az ir vet, kinder dem goles shlepn,
Oysgemutshet zayn,
Zolt ir fun di oysyes koyech shepn,
Kukt in zey arayn!

Literal Translation:

On the hearth a little fire burns,
And it is hot in the house,
And the "rebe" is teaching the little children,
The a-b-c.

See now, little children, remember dear ones,
What you are learning here;
Say it over and over again:
"A" with a "komets" spells "O!"

Study children, with great interest,
That is what I tell you;
The one who will know his "ivre" first
Will get a banner (for a prize).

Study children, do not fear,
Every beginning is difficult;
Happy is the one who studies Torah,
Need a man more?

When you will grow older, children,
You will understand,
How many tears lie in these letters
And how much weeping.

When you children will be exiled,
And be tortured,
May you gain strength from these letters,
Study, look into them now.

Prettiest Little Baby In The County-O

```
E                      B7
What are we gonna do with the baby-o?
G♯m          A      B7
What are we gonna do with the baby-o?
E                      B7
What are we gonna do with the baby-o?
G♯m      C♯m B7
Whoop him up and let him go.
```

Prettiest little baby in the county-o, (3 times)
Mammy and pappy both say it's so.

What are we gonna do with the baby-o? (3 times)
Send him off to sleepy-o.

Shlof Mayn Kind, Shlof Keseyder
(Sleep My Child)
Yiddish

```
Em              B7
Shlof mayn kind, Shlof keseyder,
Em              Am
Zingen vel ich dir a lid.
  B7                 Em  B7 Em
Az du mayn kind, vest elter vern,
B7          Em
Vestu visn an unter shid.
```

Az du mayn kind, vest elter vern
Vestu vern mit laytn glaych.
Demolst vestu gevoyre vern
Vost heyst orim uns vos heyst raych.

Di tayerste palatsn, di shenste hayzer,
Dos alts macht der oriman.
Nor veystu ver es tut in zey voynen?
Gor nisht er, nor der raycher man.

Der oriman, er ligt in keler,
Der vilgotsh rint im fun di vent.
Derfun bakumt er a rematn-feler
In di fis un in di hent.

Singable translation:

Sleep my child, sleep,
I'll sing you a lullaby.
When my little baby's grown,
He'll know the difference—and why.

When my little baby's grown,
You'll soon see which is which.
Like the rest of us you'll know
The difference between poor and rich.

The largest mansions, finest homes,
The poor man builds them on the hill.
But do you know who'll live in them?
Why, of course, the rich man will!

The poor man lives in a cellar,
The walls are wet with damp.
He gets pains in his arms and legs
And a rheumatic cramp.

Rock-A-Bye, Baby

```
G
Rock-a-bye baby, in the tree top,

When the wind blows the cradle will rock;
                              C        Am
When the bough breaks the cradle will fall,
  D7              G
And down will come baby, cradle and all.
```

Riddle Song

```
  D
I gave my love a cherry that had no stone;
  A7        D            A7
I gave my love a chicken that had no bone;
              D            A7
I told my love a story that had no end;
  D        G          D
I gave my love a baby that's no cryin'.
```

How can there be a cherry that has no stone?
How can there be a chicken that has no bone?
How can there be a story that has no end?
How can there be a baby that's no crying?

A cherry when it's blooming, it has no stone,
A chicken when it's pippin' it has no bone;
The story that I love you, it has no end,
A baby when it's sleeping, it's no crying.

What'll We Do With The Baby-O?

```
D
What'll we do with the baby-o?

What'll we do with the baby-o?

What'll we do with the baby-o?
              A7   D
If he don't go to sleepy-o?
          G  D
Wrap him up in calico,
          A7 D
Wrap him up in calico,
          G  D
Wrap him up in calico,
              A7    D
Send him to his mammy-o.
```

What'll we do with the baby-o? etc.
Wrap him up in a table-cloth, (3 times)
Throw him up in the fodder-loft.

What'll we do with the baby-o? etc.
Tell your daddy when he comes home, (3 times)
And give Old Blue your chicken bone.

What'll we do with the baby-o? etc.
Dance him north, dance him south, (3 times)
Pour a little moonshine in his mouth.

What'll we do with the baby-o? etc.
Everytime the baby cries,
Stick my finger in the baby's eye!
That's what we'll do with the baby-o, (twice)

Dance To Your Daddy

```
Am              C
Dance to your daddy, my little laddie,
Am              E7      Am
Dance to your daddy, my little man.
                        C
Thou shalt have a fish and thou shalt have a fin,
Am              E7              Am
Thou shalt have a coddlin' when the boat comes in;
                        C
Thou shalt have a haddock boiled in a pan,
Am              E7              Am
Dance to your daddy, my little man.
```

Dance to your daddy, my little laddie,
Dance to your daddie, my little lamb.
When thou art a man and come to take a wife,
Thou shalt wed a lass and love her all your life,
She shall be your lass and thou shalt be her man,
Dance to your daddy, my little lamb.

Hush Little Baby

```
E
Hush little baby, don't say a word,
  B7                    E
Mama's gonna buy you a mocking bird.
```

If that mocking bird won't sing,
```
B7                      E
```
Mama's gonna buy you a diamond ring.

If that diamond ring turns glass,
Mama's gonna buy you a looking glass.

If that looking glass gets broke,
Mama's gonna buy you a billy goat.

If that billy goat won't pull,
Mama's gonna buy you a cart and bull.

If that cart and bull turn over,
Mama's gonna buy you a dog named Rover.

If that dog named Rover won't bark,
Mama's gonna buy you a horse and cart.

If that horse and cart fall down,
You'll be the sweetest little baby in town.

Vigndig A Fremd Kind
(Babysitter's Song)
Yiddish

```
Dm                  F
Zolst azoy lebn un zayn gezint
    C7      A7          Dm
Vi ich vel dir zitsn un vign s'kind.
```

Chorus:

```
Dm              F
Ay-lyu-lyu, Sha-sha-sha!
        C7          A7          Dm
Dayn mameshi z'gegangen in mark arayn.
                F
Ay-lyu-lyu, shlop mayn kind,
        C7          A7          Dm
Di mameshi vet kimen gich un geshvind.
```

Zolst azoy lebn, s'geyt mir derinen!
Dayn mameshi z'gegangen in mark arayn fardinen.

Andere meydelech tantsn un shpringen
Un ich muz n'kind vign un zingen!

Andere meydelech tsukerkelech nashn
Un ich muz n's'kind vindelech vashn!

Singable Translation:

May you live long and be well,
My lady, while I sit here and rock your baby.

Hush, your mother's gone to the marketplace,
Hush, mama will soon be back.

Long may you live for I wish it to be true.
Mama's gone to provide for you.

Other little girls can dance and swing,
But I must rock the baby and sing!

Other girls can buy goodies and candy,
But I must wash the baby's panties!

Cannily, Cannily

```
Em        D            Bm
Cannily, cannily, bonnie wee bairnikie,
Em        D            Bm
Don't you cry, now, my little pet,
Em              G        Em    D
Hush-a you bye, now, your daddy is sleeping,
   Em       Bm        Em
It's not time to waken him yet.
```

Soon he'll go through the shed for his engine,
Soon he'll be driving his train through the night,
Working for pennies, for you my little treasure,
So hold thy noise, honey, your daddy sleeps light.

When you are grown you shall have your own engine,
The biggest that ever was seen on the line,
And all of our neighbors will point to my Johnny,
And know he's the king of the North Eastern Line.

All Through The Night

Sir Harold Boulton

```
F       Bb  F  Gmin7 C
Sleep, my child and peace attend thee
Bb  C7          F
All through the night;
F       Bb  F  G7      C
Guardian angels God will send thee,
Bb  C7          F
All through the night.
C7                      F
Soft the drowsy hours are creeping,
Gmin7  D7  Gmin7 G7 F       C
Hill    and vale   in slumber  sleeping,
F    Bb  F  G7  C
I my loving vigil keeping,
Bb  C7          F
All through the night.
```

While the moon her watch is keeping,
All through the night;
While the weary world is sleeping,
All through the night.
O'er thy spirit gently stealing,
Visions of delight revealing,
Breathes a pure and holy feeling,
All through the night.

Rozhinkes Mit Mandlen

Yiddish

```
        Dm
In dem bays hamikdosh,
    Am  Dm
In a vinkl chayder,
Am    C        E       Am
Zitzt di almone bas Tziyom aleyn.
        F
Ir ben yochidl Yidele vigt si k'seyder.
                Dm   A   Dm
Un zingt im tzum shlofen a lidele sheyn.
        A Dm
Unter Yidele's vigele
            C F
Shteyt a klor veis tzigele.
    A               Dm
Dos tzigele is geforen handlen;
Gm              Dm
Dos vet zein dein beruf.
A           Dm
Rozhinkes mit mandlen.
A           Dm
Shlof-zhe, Yidele, shlof.
```


Hobo's Lullaby

Chorus:

```
E                   A
Go to sleep you weary hobo,
B7              E
Let the town drift slowly by,
                    A
Listen to the steel rails humming,
    B7          E
Well, that's the hobo's lullaby.
```

Do not think about tomorrow,
Let tomorrow come and go,
Tonight you have a nice warm boxcar,
Free from all the ice and snow.

I know the police cause you trouble,
They make trouble everywhere.
But when you die and go to heaven,
Well, you will find no police there.

Now, do not let your heart be troubled
If the world calls you a bum,
'Cause if your mother lives, she'll love you,
Well, you are still your mother's son.

ROUNDS

Music Alone Shall Live

All things shall perish from under the sky,
Music alone shall live, music alone shall live,
Music alone shall live, never to die.

Oh, Absalom, My Son

Oh, Absalom, my son, my son, (twice)
Would to God I had died for thee, my son, (twice)
Oh, Absalom, my son, my son. (twice)

Oh, How Lovely Is The Evening

G   C G C G
Oh, how lovely is the evening, is the evening.
        C G C G
When the bells are sweetly ringing, sweetly ringing.
     C G C G
Ding, dong, ding; ding, dong, ding.

Row, Row, Row Your Boat

C F   C
Row, Row, Row Your Boat,
     F   C
Gently down the stream,
    G   C Am
Merrily, merrily, merrily, merrily,
F   G   C
Life is but a dream.

Scotland's Burning

 D   G   D   G
Scotland's burning, Scotland's burning
D G D G
Look out, look out
D G D G
Fire, fire, fire, fire
D G   D   G
Pour on water, pour on water.

Ah, Poor Bird

Ah, poor bird,
Take your flight,
Far above the sorrows of
This sad night.

Frère Jacques
(Brother John)
French

F C7 F   C7 F
Frère Jacques, frère Jacques
 C7 F   C7 F
Dormez-vous, dormez-vous,
     C7 F   C7 F
Sonnez les matines, sonnez les matines,
  C7 F   C7 F
Din, din, don, din, din, don.

Singable Translation:

Are you sleeping, are you sleeping,
Brother John, Brother John?
Morning bells are ringing, morning bells are ringing,
Ding ding dong, ding ding dong.

Hava Na Shira
Hebrew

    A   E A D A E7 A
 I. Hava na Shira Shire Hallelujah.
    A   E A D A E7 A
 II. Hava na Shira Shire Hallelujah.
    A   E A D A E7 A
III. Hava na Shira Shire Hallelujah.

Hey, Ho, Nobody Home

Hey, ho, nobody home;
Meat nor drink nor money have I none,
Yet will I be mer-r-r-r-r-r-y.

Shalom Aleichem

Hebrew

Cm G7 Cm   G7   Cm
Havenu Shalom Aleichem!
C7   Fm
Havenu Shalom Aleichem!
G7 Cm G7   Cm
Havenu Shalom Aleichem!
   G7
Havenu Shalom! Shalom!
         Cm
Shalom Aleichem!

Shalom Chaverim

Hebrew

   Dm
Shalom chaverim, shalom chaverim,
Shalom, shalom,
L'hit ra-ot, l'hit ra-ot,
Shalom, shalom.

Singable Translation:

Glad tidings we bring of peace on earth,
Good will towards men,
Of peace on earth, of peace on earth,
Good will towards men.

Three Blind Mice

D   A7 D   A7 D
Three blind mice, three blind mice,
   A7   D   A7   D
See how they run, see how they run;
         A7   D
They all ran after the farmer's wife,
          A7   D
She cut off their tails with a carving knife,
          A7   D   A7
Did ever you see such a sight in your life,
  D   A7 D
As three blind mice?

Vine And Fig Tree

Shalom Altman

          Em   Am
And ev'ry man 'neath his vine and fig tree,
         B7   Em
Shall live in peace and unafraid.

                        Am
And ev'ry man 'neath his vine and fig tree
         B7   Em
Shall live in peace and unafraid.
               Am
And into plough-shares turn their swords,
B7   Em
Nations shall learn war no more.
               Am
And into plough-shares turn their swords,
B7   Em
Nations shall learn war no more.

What A Grand And Glorious Feeling

Bill Wolff/Tune: *Oh, How Lovely Is The Evening*

D   G D   G D
What a grand and glorious feeling, glorious feeling,
D   G D   G D
When the bells of peace are ringing, peace are ringing,
D   G D G D
Peace on earth, peace on earth, peace on earth.

Kookaburra

Kookaburra sits on an old gum tree,
Merry, merry king of the bush is he.
Laugh, kookaburra, laugh, kookaburra,
Gay your life must be.

Kookaburra sits on the old gum tree,
Eating all the gum drops he can see.
Stop! Kookaburra, stop! Kookaburra,
Leave some there for me.

BIBLIOGRAPHY

Obviously, no one collection would contain the tunes for all the songs in this book. However, certain readily available song books are almost indispensable tools for singers and musicians working with such materials. The following books are recommended as useful sources for the tunes to a majority of the songs in this collection and also as a source for historical and musical information on the background of these songs:

Oak Publications:

Asch, Moses, and Lomax, Alan:
The Leadbelly Songbook

Edwards, Jay, and Kelley, Robert:
The Coffee House Songbook

Guthrie, Woody, Lomax, Alan, and Seeger, Pete:
Hard Hitting Songs For Hard-Hit People

Hill, Waldemer:
The People's Song Book

900 Miles And Other Songs of Cisco Houston

The New Lost City Ramblers Songbook

Folksongs Of Peggy Seeger

Seeger, Pete:
American Favorite Ballads

Silber, Irwin:
Lift Every Voice

Silber, Irwin:
Reprints From The People's Songs Bulletins

Reprints From Sing Out! (11 volumes)

Other Publishers:

Guthrie, Woody:
The Nearly Complete Collection Of Woody Guthrie Folksongs (TRO)

Kolb, John and Sylvia:
A Treasury Of Folk Songs (Bantam)

Leisy, James:
The Folk Song ABCDEDARY (Hawthorn)

Lomax, Alan:
Folk Song U.S.A. (MacMillan)

Lomax, Alan:
Folk Songs Of North America (Doubleday)

Silber, Irwin:
The Great Atlantic And Pacific Songbook (Amsco)

Silber, Irwin:
The Hootenanny Songbook (Consolidated)

Silber, Irwin:
Songs America Voted By (Stackpole)

Silber, Irwin:
Songs Of The Civil War (Columbia University Press)

Silber, Irwin:
Songs Of The Great American West (MacMillan)

Silber, Irwin, and Dane, Barbara:
The Vietnam Songbook (Guardian)

GUITAR CHORDS

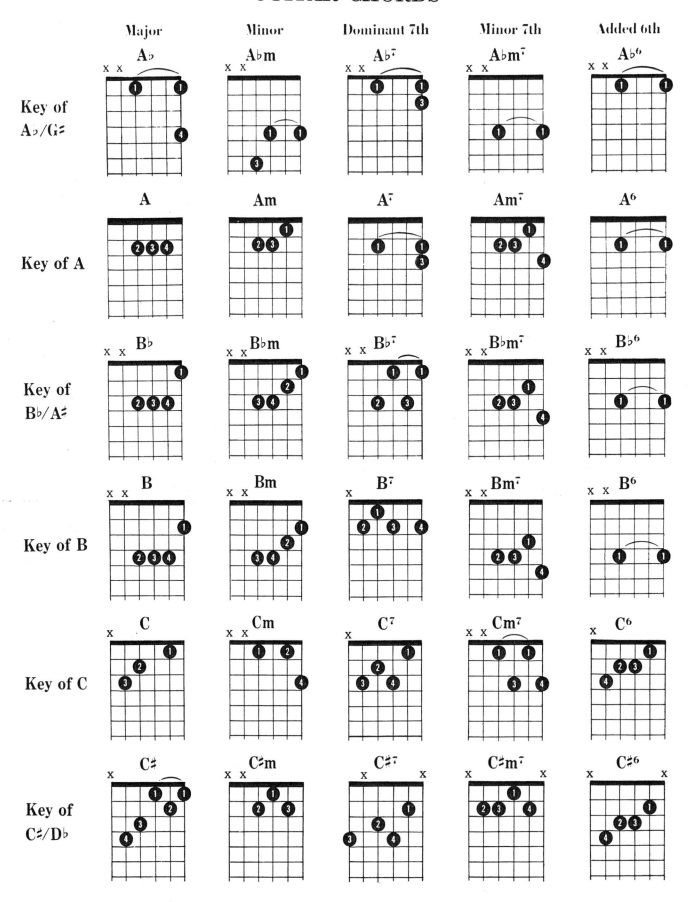

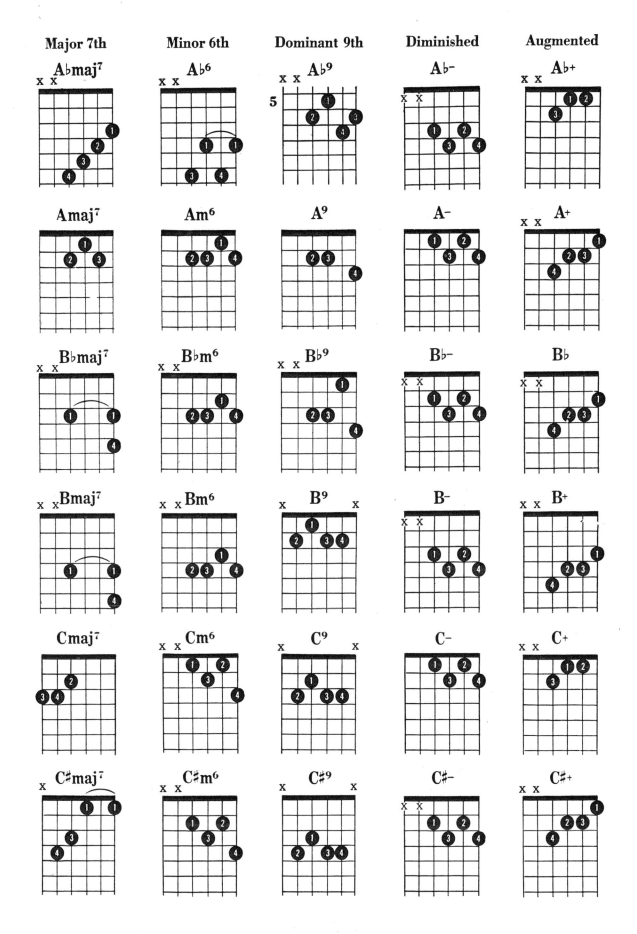

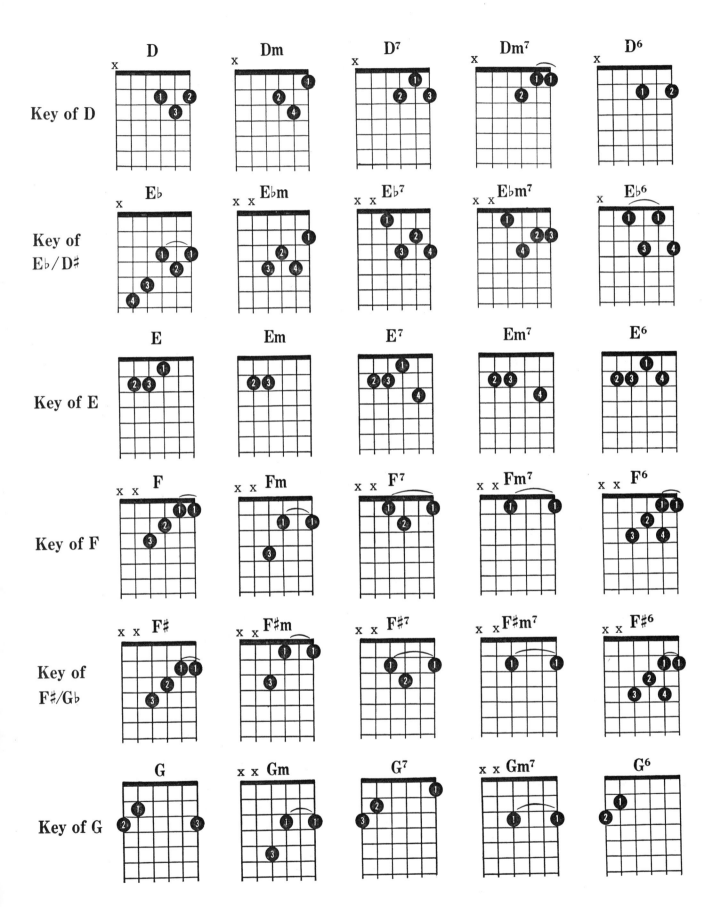

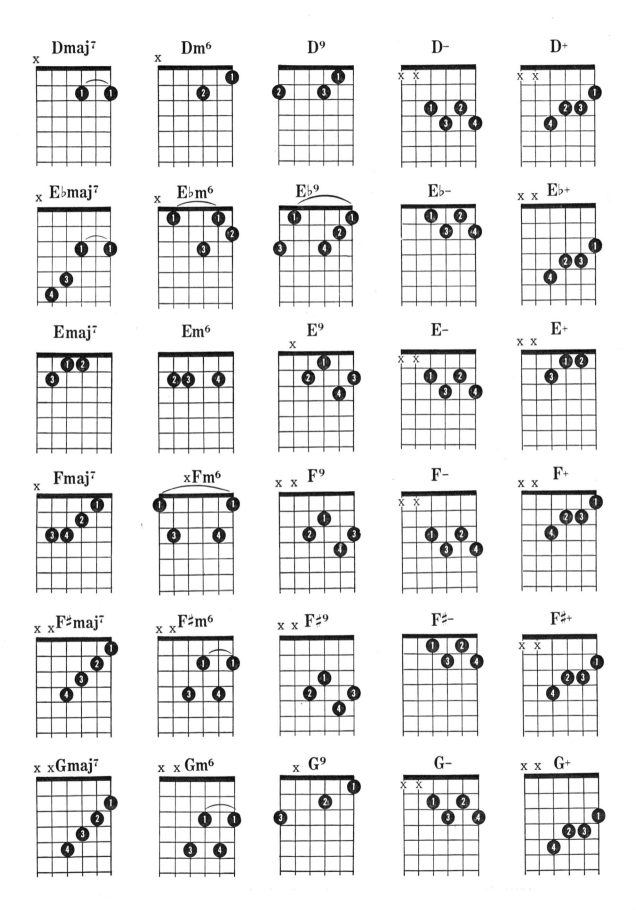

INDEX TO SONGS